Building Electronic Commerce
with Web Database Constructions

Anne Nelson
William H. M. Nelson III

Addison
Wesley

Boston San Francisco New York
London Toronto Sydney Tokyo Singapore Madrid
Mexico City Munich Paris Cape Town Hong Kong Montreal

Senior Acquisitions Editor	*Maite Suarez-Rivas*
Associate Managing Editor	*Pat Mahtani*
Assistant Editor	*Lisa Hogue*
Executive Marketing Manager	*Michael Hirsch*
Production Services	*Sandra Rigney*
Composition	*Gillian Hall, The Aardvark Group*
Copyeditor	*Linda Mehta*
Technical Illustrator	*George Nichols*
Proofreader	*Holly McLean-Aldis*
Indexer	*Alexandra Nickerson*
Interior Design	*Sandra Rigney*
Cover Design	*Gina Hagen Kolenda*
Cover Image	*PhotoDisc*
Prepress and Manufacturing	*Caroline Fell*

Access the latest information about Addison-Wesley titles from our World Wide Web site: http://www.aw.com/cs

Many of the designations used by manufacturers and sellers to distinguish their products are claimed as trademarks. Where those designations appear in this book, and Addison-Wesley was aware of a trademark claim, the designations have been printed in initial caps or all caps.

The programs and applications presented in this book have been included for their instructional value. They have been tested with care, but are not guaranteed for any particular purpose. The publisher does not offer any warranties or representations, nor does it accept any liabilities with respect to the programs or applications.

Library of Congress Cataloging-in-Publication Data

Nelson, Anne.
  Building electronic commerce with Web database constructions / by Anne Nelson and William Nelson.
      p. cm.
  Includes index.
   ISBN 0-201-74130-X (pbk.)
   1. Electronic commerce. 2. Web sites. I. Nelson, William. II. Title.

  HF5548.32 .N45 2002
  658.8'4--dc21

2001045800
CIP

12345678910-CRW-04030201

Foreword

Electronic commerce is a maturing industry, nearing what we might call its late adolescence. Its childhood was marked, as all childhoods are, by a mixture of optimism and mythology: Santa Claus would come every Christmas Day and bring all the good boys and girls just what they asked for. All children grow up, however, and are greeted by the harsh realities of their teenage years: the recent tech crash had less to do with inherent weaknesses in electronic commerce than with the fact that people simply did not want to buy dog food online. The world of electronic commerce discovered a real business environment out there that it would have to wrestle with, and solid business plans and practices would be required, as well as interesting technologies, in order to survive.

Electronic commerce has evolved into more than a marketing tool or storefront for traditional enterprises. Indeed, virtually every aspect of the contemporary enterprise has been affected by electronic commerce. Customized marketing, customer relationship management, customized manufacturing, and online communities compose the marketing elements spawned by electronic commerce. Web-based EDI, enterprise resource planning, extra/intranets, and decision support systems have profoundly affected how corporations manage their internal structures and strategic alliances; financial forecasting models, market trends, and risk analysis are now routinely assigned to new (and still newer) technologies. Moreover, the structure of the enterprise itself has radically changed: networked organizations, virtual organizations, and team-based distributed organizations are all predicated and depend exclusively on the technology tools that have been developed by electronic commerce. Where once business leaders turned to scientific management for their inspiration and management models, they now turn to new science and its array of nonlinear theories to describe the new corporation. Electronic commerce has changed the function and role of management, the relationships among the functions of the enterprise, and the relationship between the enterprise and its customer. This adolescent discipline is now meeting challenges of the "real world" with a new set of tools, ideas, practices, and theories unparalleled since the commercial revolution 500 years ago.

I first met the Nelsons in France while developing content for an École Supérieure de Commerce MBA program, which would be taught entirely online to managers and executives who needed better preparation for the New Economy than that offered by more traditional programs. Our courses, and subsequently our students, have benefited greatly by the contributions of Anne and Will and this book articulates much of their knowledge and expertise on the subject. The Nelsons not only provide the reader with the theories behind electronic commerce, but also offer a rare source that merges these theories with an examination of the tools and practices behind successful e-commerce implementations. It is a source of great pleasure for me as a teacher to know that their audience will be extended beyond the traditional classroom boundaries.

William Painter, Ph.D.
Directeur des Programmes d'Éducation à Distance
Groupe École Supérieure de Commerce
Pau, France

Preface

Today, the Web has become synonymous with the Internet. Web browsers are used to display, disseminate, and drive information within a business as well as to extend the functionality of the Web pages outside the traditional business boundaries. Electronic commerce Web constructions used for advertising products and taking sales orders are fueling an electronic commerce industry that exceeds $100 billion. These electronic commerce applications require developers to create dynamic Web front-ends that can easily and efficiently interact with back-end databases. *Building Electronic Commerce with Web Database Constructions* is the first in a series of books designed to give today's developers the electronic commerce theory, techniques, and tools needed to build successful Web sites.

The purpose of this book is to provide an overview of the topics that electronic commerce developers must understand in order to create successful Web database constructions. The book is aimed toward readers with knowledge of computer information systems, management information systems, or computer science, who have had some previous programming and database coursework or experience. In this book the reader will learn how to build the front-end, middleware, and back-end components that drive electronic commerce.

Pedagogical Approach

A series of chapters, following a lesson-oriented format, rapidly provides foundation material in electronic commerce theory, techniques, and tools. Because technology in this area is rapidly changing, the chapters begin with an explanation of electronic commerce theory and the architectures and approaches, rather than with specific tools. Thereafter, each chapter proceeds to a discussion of current tools and step-by-step techniques that implement the concepts. These step-by-step examples are carried throughout the chapters and provide the reader with the opportunity to create two business-specific Web database constructions, a kennel and a music publishing company. The specific software tools taught are provided on the companion Web site that accompanies the book. After working through the chapters, readers will be able to develop their own Web database constructions, put into practice the key concepts learned, and apply these concepts to other situations and practical applications. Appendix E suggests six different business scenarios as potential electronic commerce implementations.

In a recent survey, chief information officers from the nation's leading Fortune 500 companies were surveyed for skills they most desired in employees. Ranking in the first position, above technical skills, was a need for employees to possess strong communication skills. This book is the only book on the market to combine electronic commerce theory, tools, and techniques, but great care has also been taken to include opportunities for the reader to hone clean, clear, and concise writing skills. There is also an emphasis on the application of knowledge. Critical thinking exercises using the Web are included in each chapter to bridge the gap some readers may find between theory and practical application.

Book Overview

In **Chapter 1**, electronic commerce is defined and the basic terminology discussed. Traditional commerce is compared to the new commerce model in the new economy with an introduction to the electronic data interchange. The new electronic commerce strategies and techniques used by today's businesses are developed within the client/server architecture, and the relationship between electronic commerce and Web database constructions is introduced. **Chapter 2** details Web database constructions, and their three major components (front-end, middleware, and back-end) are introduced. The relationship of HTTP to client/server interaction is examined within the light of the integral nature of the Web server to the electronic commerce model. The different database processing architectures are analyzed for their benefits to and challenges within the Web construction. Client-side and server-side technologies are defined and introduced. A methodology for Web assessment and design is provided. In **Chapter 3**, the Web server software is introduced, and the reader is walked through the installation and setup process.

Chapter 4 provides a framework for understanding the most common types of electronic commerce business models used today. Differences between electronic commerce pull and push technology and necessary steps in planning an electronic commerce business are explored. Three specific electronic commerce models are demonstrated: the guestbook, the survey, and the job listing service. Metrics to measure the success of the electronic commerce business are provided. **Chapter 5** reviews database terms, types, and structures and examines the necessary steps to build a back-end database using Microsoft Access 2000 or XP version 2002. The creation of advanced queries and data analysis through the use of total queries and nested queries are detailed. Parameter-based queries, which are heavily used for designing the advanced electronic commerce constructions described in the book, are also taught.

Chapter 6 explains the client-side technologies of HTML forms, cascading style sheets (CSS), XHTML, and DHTML. The purpose of hypertext links and hypermedia in the canonical model is discussed, and the use of cookies for state management in hidden HTML form fields is introduced. Chapters 7 through 9 concentrate on Common Gateway Interface (CGI) technologies. **Chapter 7** details the workings of CGI. Readers are walked through the creation of CGI applications using Visual Basic. **Chapter 8** explains the benefits of using template files in the electronic commerce model. Readers are taught to design and test a CGI template file as well as how to send output, evaluate expressions, specify conditions, create loops, and include the contents of another file within a template file. In **Chapter 9**, using CGI and Visual Basic, the front-end of the electronic commerce model is connected to a back-end database. Table records are added through the front-end. Database error trapping is discussed. Queries and filters are used in the model for datamining and supporting management decision-making processes. In Chapters 10 through 12, the focus turns to the technology of ASP using VBScript. **Chapter 10** introduces ASP server-side technology, the ASP Object model, and the Five Intrinsics. Readers are stepped through the installation and set-up process of Chili!Soft ASP software. ASP applications are created, banner ads incorporated into the Web database construction, and an ASP guestbook with security features is demonstrated. **Chapter 11** teaches the connection of ASP to back-end databases. Queries and filters are used to support management decision-making processes. In **Chapter 12**, ASP template files are created. **Chapter 13** looks at browser programs and other server-side technologies. The basic components of JavaScript and Java Server Pages (JSP) are discussed, and readers are stepped through the creation of both technologies. ActiveX is also introduced, and compiled browser programs using ActiveX are created. **Chapter 14** teaches methods for enhancing the electronic commerce business model.

Features

Within the structure of each chapter, several pedagogical features are included. Each chapter includes an **outline** to step the reader through the arrangement of the chapter. **Timely quotes** on relevant issues are included near the beginning of each chapter. Thoroughout each chapter, succinct reference boxes, called **Web Breaks**, are used to extend the chapter learning to the World Wide Web. These Web Breaks reinforce the learning points in the chapter and introduce the reader to other electronic commerce tools and techniques used by today's businesses.

Each chapter also includes relevant and recent news articles with a focus on electronic commerce demonstrating the application theory and technique with specific tools. Current business uses of electronic commerce and the Web database construction are highlighted in each **Focus on Electronic Commerce** box and each contains critical thinking questions at the conclusion of the case. **Tutorial-based cases** teach the techniques and provide specific tools needed to implement the electronic commerce theory discussed in the chapter. The culmination of the book contains a complete electronic commerce design for the running case business, Kanthaka Farms.

End-of-chapter material includes **summaries**, **review questions**, **critical thinking exercises using the Web**, and a **continuing case study**. Each learning objective is summarized at the chapter's end to provide a succinct method of reviewing the chapter's main points. Chapter assessments are provided with review questions to reinforce the chapter's main learning concepts. Critical thinking scenarios using the Web are included in each chapter to extend the chapter theory by applying the theory to current real-world business scenarios. An end-of-chapter running case, Albatross Records, provides the reader with the opportunity to practice learned theory using the tools and the techniques to build electronic commerce Web database constructions discussed in the chapter. Where the Kanthaka Farms case walked the reader step-by-step through the process, Albatross Records allows the reader to practice application of the chapter's theory and provides an opportunity to demonstrate learning of chapter techniques.

Appendices include an **HTML primer** and **Front Page primer** and suggest six different **business case studies** to which students can refer in setting up their own electronic commerce Web database construc-

tions using WebSite server software to illustrate creation and administration principles and provide a test environment.

Software Accompanying the Book

Learning resources for this book include a companion Web site at
http://www.aw.com/nelson. Provided on the companion Web site are
links for software introduced in the book, including a 120-day trial version of **Deerfield's WebSite Professional 3**, a feature-rich Web server specifically designed for developing and deploying Web database
constructions. WebSite Professional 3 server software provides the
electronic commerce developer with an easy-to-use Web server configuration and administration; multiple and virtual domain support,
allowing electronic commerce developers to host multiple sites;
improved logging, utilizing cycling and archiving to speed performance;
and enhanced security support, ensuring a protected platform for the
electronic commerce application.

Also included on this book's companion Web site is a 31-day shareware evaluation copy **Style Master 2.0**, a specialized CSS integrated
development environment, featuring everything needed to develop, test,
and deploy sophisticated style sheets for electronic commerce Web
database constructions. The application comes with a collection of var-
ied samples and other CSS resources and is much easier to use than CSS
tools offered in many HTML editors. Style Master 2.0 supports both
CSS1 and CSS2, as well as the new CSS3 mobile profile, the complete
style sheets standards from the World Wide Web Consortium and is an
excellent add-on for the electronic commerce developer's toolkit.

First Page 2000 2.0 HTML Editor is available as a freeware copy
from the companion Web site. This application combines the power of
text editing with a user-friendly interface and provides hundreds of
tools and options for producing successful electronic commerce constructions, including 450 JavaScripts and a tool for creating Java
applets. First Page is scalable to the user's skill level and supports most
languages, including all versions of HTML, DHTML, CSS, ASP, Perl,
JavaScript, and VBScript.

The companion Web site also includes a 30-day full-version trial of
Sun Chili!Soft ASP for Windows 2000/NT server-side scripting and
runtime environment for the cross platform deployment of Active Server
Pages. Chili!Soft, a wholly-owned subsidiary of Sun Microsystems,
enables electronic commerce developers to build dynamic Web database constructions generated by popular design tools and deployed on

the most reliable and scalable platforms, removing the dependency of ASP on Microsoft Windows servers.

Another freeware software available from the companion Web site is the versatile browser/authoring tool, **Amaya XHTML Editor**, which allows the publishing of documents on the Web. Amaya supports HTML and XHTML pages, as well as cascading style sheets, MathML expressions, and SVG drawings.

A 30-day demo of **XML Spy**, the award-winning Integrated Development Environment for the Extensible Markup Language, is provided for users of this book on the companion Web site. The XML Spy application includes a validating XML editor that provides developers with five advanced document views: an Enhanced Grid View for structured editing, a Database/Table view that shows repeated elements in a tabular fashion, a Text View with syntax-coloring for low-level work, a graphical XML Schema design view, and an integrated Browser View that supports both CSS and XSL style sheets.

An evaluation copy of **JRun Server 3.0** J2EE application server and integrated development environment for building and deploying server-side Java applications is provided at the companion Web site. JRun delivers the full capabilities of the J2EE specifications JSP, servlets, and Enterprise Java Beans.

The companion Web site also includes the necessary data files for creating electronic commerce applications for Kanthaka Farms and Albatross Records, running cases in the book. The book also discusses Microsoft's Internet Information Server (IIS), a solution bundled with the Microsoft Operating Systems for no additional cost, which can be downloaded from the Microsoft Web site.

Teaching Tools

Building Electronic Commerce with Web Database Constructions includes teaching supplements when the book is used in the classroom. These are the following:

- *Complete Kanthaka Farms and Albatross Records sample case solutions.* The running case solutions include a complete electronic commerce Web database construction with front-end, middleware, and back-end as an example of what students can design and create from the case exercises.
- *Complete supplemental Case Scenarios sample solutions.* The six end-of-text case solutions include a complete electronic commerce Web

database construction with front-end, middleware, and back-end as examples of what students can design and create from the case exercises.

■ *Powerpoint slides for classroom use.*

For more information, contact your local sales representative, or go to http://www.aw.com/cssupport.

Acknowledgments

Without the encouragement and support of so many, this book would not be a reality. As with most projects, this book is an unbelievable team effort. We gratefully acknowledge all those at Addison-Wesley Publishing Company who were part of the project, with special appreciation to Maite Suarez-Rivas, Lisa Hogue, Pat Mahtani, Gina Hagen Kolenda, Susan Hartman, Michael Hirsch, Gillian Hall, Linda Mehta, Holly McLean-Aldis, George Nichols, Alexandra Nickerson, and Sandra Rigney. Their dedication, enthusiasm, wisdom, high standards, and unending patience fueled our spirits and determination.

Many thanks are extended to Dr. David Little and our colleagues in the CIS Department and to the students of High Point University. Thanks also to William Painter and Francine Maubourguet at L'École Supérieure de Commerce, Pau, France. Our reviewers added much to the project, especially David Zolzer, whose suggestions were always timely and on target. The reviewers include David Zolzer, Northwestern State University; Jack Brzezinski, Ph.D., DePaul University; Vicki L. Sauter, University of Missouri–St. Louis; Meg Kletka, Oklahoma State University; William T. Schiano, Bentley College; Rebecca Rutherfoord, Southern Polytechnic State; Kevin Treu, Furman University; Sharma Pillutla, Townson University; and Lakshmi Iyer, University of North Carolina–Greensboro.

We are grateful to Cleo Fulcher, Tricia and Roger Nolan, Al and Juanita Bolton, Charles Stout, Chuck West, Pranab Das, and Kate Fowkes for their hours of listening about the project, encouraging words, and insightful suggestions. Special gratitude also goes to Ted Dillon for the gift of flight when the manuscript reached fruition.

Finally, we dedicate this book to those family members and friends who are no longer with us, but live on in our hearts and memories.

Anne Nelson
William H. M. Nelson III
August 2001

About the Authors

Dr. Anne Nelson is an assistant professor in the Earl N. Phillips School of Business, Department of Computer Information Systems, at High Point University, a top-tier regional liberal arts university in High Point, North Carolina. She holds a Doctor of Business Administration in Management with a concentration in Information Systems and has completed post-doctoral studies in electronic commerce, Web site development, and telecommunications at Stanford University. She has also authored a number of distance education IT-based courses and has been a contributing author and reviewer of numerous Web technology titles.

William H. M. Nelson III is President of Nelson Management Associates, a management consulting firm specializing in management information systems and collaborative technologies. He is a member of the adjunct faculty of High Point University. Professor Nelson has completed doctoral work in Organization and Management with a specialization in Information Technology and holds an M.S. in the same discipline area and concentration. He brings a wealth of IT industry experience in systems and programming and is a former newspaper owner and publisher.

The Nelsons have worked as academic and collaborative technology consultants for Groupe École Supérieure de Commerce de Pau (ESC Pau), Pau, France and various colleges and universities in the United States. Their primary research focuses on the organizational impacts of electronic commerce, computer-supported collaborative work, and information resource dependency.

Brief Contents

Contents

XV

1

Introduction to Electronic Commerce

Learning Objectives

Upon completion of this chapter, you will be able to

- Define electronic commerce
- Define basic electronic commerce terms
- Compare traditional commerce with electronic commerce
- Compare electronic commerce with electronic data interchange
- Describe electronic commerce strategies and techniques used by businesses
- Discuss electronic commerce and client/server architecture
- Discuss the relationship between electronic commerce and Web database constructions

We are on the verge of a revolution that is just as profound as the change in the economy that came with the industrial revolution. Soon electronic networks will allow people to transcend the barriers of time and distance and take advantage of global markets and business opportunities not even imaginable today, opening up a new world of economic possibility and progress.

—Albert Gore Jr., U.S. Vice President from 1992 to 2000,
A Framework for Global Electronic Commerce, 1997

Kanthaka Farms

Kanthaka Farms is a continuing case study in this book that will illustrate the process of building electronic commerce with Web database constructions. In Chapter 1, you will get started by investigating the subject on the World Wide Web and creating a proposal for Kanthaka Farms. You will justify to Kanthaka Farms the decision to incorporate electronic commerce in their business—citing both the opportunities of electronic commerce as well as the challenges. As you continue through the text, you will complete different facets of electronic commerce Web database construction, resulting in a complete Web site for Kanthaka Farms.

Kanthaka Farms breeds Italian greyhounds. It also trains, shows, and sells these specialty dogs throughout the world. Founded in 1991, and located in Chapel Hill, North Carolina, Kanthaka Farms is owned and operated by Harris and Anicca Vita and family. The Vitas are dedicated to breeding stylish Italian greyhounds that excel in the breed's correct temperament and flawless movement. Kanthaka Farms has earned an international reputation for breeding dogs that have been raised with love and care and shown with pride.

The Italian greyhound is the only type of dog that Kanthaka Farms breeds, trains, and shows. The smallest in the greyhound family, it is a graceful breed said to have originated 2,000 years ago in Egypt. Measuring no higher than 15 inches at the shoulder, the breed is popular for its adaptability to small places. The Kanthaka Farms greyhounds have short, silky coats that come in a variety of colors and shades, including fawn, cream, blue, and black. The Vitas stress that their dogs make excellent house pets and loyal companions, well suited for the family.

Anicca Vita has begun to think of the World Wide Web as a viable delivery medium for both selling her Italian greyhounds as well as promoting the Farms' many awards and champion dogs. Her research of other breeders on the Web shows sites that provide interactive menus with links to the Italian Greyhound Club of America, the Italian Greyhound Rescue Organization, and the Carolina Pet Rescue, to name a few. Mostly, she is interested in sharing with others the benefits of the breed. She has determined that the following benefits of owning Italian greyhounds should be included on the site:

- Italian greyhounds are beautiful and clean without expensive and time-consuming grooming.
- They are small enough to fit into any living situation, and still large enough to be real dogs.
- Although they are small in size, they bark rather than yap.
- They have an extremely loving, devoted nature and a scintillating, sometimes unpredictable charm that never allows for a dull moment.
- They are sweet, gentle, affectionate, sprightly, and imaginative.
- They are one-person or one-family dogs that want to be physically close to their humans.
- They are a unique breed that has the ability to completely entrance its devotees, although a few of its more whimsical attributes might charm some and be a turnoff for others.

All electronic commerce constructions should begin with a sound understanding of the task at hand and thorough planning for the design *before* any code is written or database created. To begin the understanding and planning stages for your design, the first step is to research the Italian greyhound breed and other dog kennels on the Internet. Create a one- to two-page document that will state the basic factors or elements to include in your Web database construction as well as a preliminary sketch of your design. Keep in mind that your design will undergo considerable transformation as you continue to understand and plan for your electronic commerce construction for Kanthaka Farms. Your preliminary plan should include but not be limited to the items that follow. To get you started, the first has been completed for you. Now it's your turn. Complete the preliminary plan for Kanthaka Farms.

- List electronic commerce construction benefits to be gained by Kanthaka Farms and the value added from a Web presence.

The benefits of using Internet-based technologies for electronic commerce can be simply stated: Kanthaka Farms will expand their markets to increase revenues; they will reduce overall business costs; they will strengthen customer relationships; they will disseminate information on the Italian greyhound breed and their business' goods and services. Early kennel entrants like Kanthaka Farms to electronic commerce will have "first mover" advantages that late entrants will find almost impossible to overcome.

- Specific utilization of the Internet
- Estimated Web site audience
- Estimated Web site foot traffic
- Working Web site title
- Justification for design focus
- Content and goals of the site
- Design considerations
- Limiting technical or audience factors that could limit the design goals of the site

Figure 1-1

How Kanthaka Farms Will Utilize the Internet

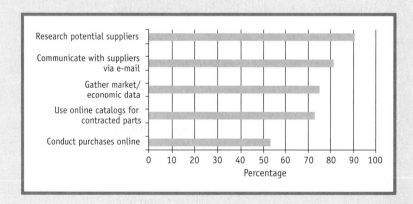

1.1 The Relationship Between Electronic Commerce and Business

The owners of Kanthaka Farms saw in electronic commerce a new way of conducting their business, utilizing the power of electronic networks and the Internet. Just what is electronic commerce? You can begin by thinking of it as the paperless exchange of business information that uses a variety of technologies to accomplish this task—from e-mail and electronic bulletin boards to electronic funds transfer and electronic data interchange. Electronic commerce seeks to automate business tasks, including the generation, processing, coordination, distribution, and reconciliation of business transactions, through the Internet and other electronic media.

Often the terminology associated with electronic commerce can be confusing. Whether you call it Internet commerce, or ecommerce, or ecom, or even ec, it's all the same technology. **Electronic commerce**, and all the other associated terms, means buying or selling goods or services of a business electronically. It allows businesses to exchange goods and services immediately while overcoming barriers of time or distance. Any time of the day or night, customers can go online and buy almost anything they want. Business can count on increased market share and market reach with electronic commerce.

Electronic commerce is one of the most important aspects to emerge from the Internet. But what is the *Internet*—also called the Net, the Information Superhighway, or Cyberspace? The Internet is all about **connectivity**. Basically, it is a network of computers that are connected to other computers for the purpose of resource and information sharing. One part of the Internet is the **World Wide Web**, usually just called the Web. This network connects electronic documents, referred to as Web pages, that contain information that may be in the form of basic text or intricate multimedia consisting of graphics, sound, video, or animation. Web pages contain hypertext links, or links, that when selected, connect the user to other Web pages of related information. Each Web page has an address or **Uniform Resource Locator (URL)**. The pages on the Web are stored in computers called **Web servers** that are connected to and make up the Internet. The term Web server also refers to the software these computers use to add functionality to a Web database construction in order to create electronic commerce.

Today, the Web is a powerful communication interface that brings businesses and customers closer together through technology. It is

Web Break

For an excellent Internet timeline, visit PBS television's Web site at http://www.pbs.org/opb/nerds2.0.1/timeline. Based on the Hobbes' Internet Timeline by Robert H. Zakon, the site traces the development of the Internet from the early days of ARPANET to today.

difficult for us to imagine that less than a decade ago the Web was just an idea in the minds of visionaries like Marc Andreesen, Jean-Francois Groff , and **Tim Berners-Lee**. Berners-Lee has been credited with inventing the World Wide Web in late 1990 while working at the Centre pour Européenne Recherche du Nucléaire (**CERN**), a European particle physics laboratory in Geneva, Switzerland. He defined the initial Web specifications and wrote the first Web client, a browser-editor, and created the first Web server. Berners-Lee is also credited with creating most of the communications software used by electronic commerce today, including **Hypertext Transfer Protocol (HTTP)**, and **Hypertext Markup Language (HTML)**. His Web client and server software technologies are still the current model used to create electronic commerce Web database constructions today.

Web Break

Visit Tim Berners-Lee on the Web at http://www.w3.org/People/Berners-Lee/. He writes that he has been working for a long time on a special, new idea that will revolutionize computing. He has already done it once. No doubt he can do it again!

Like the Internet, electronic commerce is all about connectivity. Think of electronic commerce as an enabler. It provides both the ways and the means for Internet access and Web presence for an unlimited number of businesses today. Many low-cost, start-up opportunities now exist for businesses because of electronic commerce. Small businesses as well as national-level or global firms recognize long-term opportunities through the strategic acquisition and aggressive marketing capabilities of electronic commerce. The emphasis of electronic commerce is on both investments being made in technology as well as supporting business processes. Electronic commerce is conducted through the electronic exchange of digitally encoded information. As all sectors of the economy share a common interest in and an increasing dependence on such information exchanges, electronic commerce may become the commerce of choice.

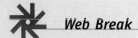 **Web Break**

Visit CERN on the Web at http://public.web.cern.ch/Public/Welcome.htm. They bill themselves as "the site where the Web was born."

Business has moved at a rapid pace from an agricultural-based industrial era to a postindustrial or information era. It is clear that in today's world, the success of a business lies more in its intellectual assets than in its physical assets or natural resources. Electronic commerce enables the maximization of intellectual assets through connectivity and exchange of digital information between the organizational stakeholders, who may be customers, employees, shareholders, vendors, suppliers, third parties, or even competitors. Technology is no longer only connecting electronic commerce constituents, but it is also the foundation on which virtual communities are built. Today's **New Economy** constitutes a revolution in the rules of business and is being driven by this connectivity of electronic commerce. Businesses can now process information more effectively and efficiently than they can move their physical products. Increasingly, the value of a company is measured by intangibles—people, procedures, processes, ideas, and the strategic aggregation of key information-driven assets—rather than by its tangible assets. In the New Economy, people are more and more being considered assets. In the industrial era, employees were often considered drains on the financial strength of the business. In the 1980s, when short-term profits were mandated and downsizing was the buzzword of the decade, human capital was exchanged for quick increases in profit margins. A prime factor driving the New Economy is the recognition of employees as assets. More than ever in history, huge value is being leveraged from the capture of employees' experience and knowledge. Electronic commerce is becoming invaluable as a method for capturing the product of human capital—knowledge—and is transforming the methods of recruiting and managing employees.

 Web Break

Find out more about the New Economy that is powered by electronic commerce. Visit Wired's Encyclopedia of the New Economy on the Web at http://hotwired.lycos.com/special/ene/.

Before the Internet and technologies of the Web, information systems were primarily used by businesses to maximize shareholder wealth and increase profitability through the elimination of extraneous costs and reducing expenses. Today, electronic commerce technologies and their information systems also help businesses reach their mission through increased revenue and customer service. The old IBM acronym **IR AC IS**—pronounced *ear-ack-iss* and standing for *Increase Revenue, Avoid Costs, Improve Service*—can be applied to electronic commerce construction objectives. Electronic commerce is a modern business methodology that addresses the need felt by both businesses and customers alike to cut costs while at the same time improving the quality of goods and services and increasing the speed of service delivery.

Electronic commerce can also be an invaluable aid in helping a company increase perceived value. Market share and value rise together. For products that help establish a platform or a standard, the effect of electronic commerce is even more pronounced. Electronic commerce also adds value through the production and capture of managerial decision support information. Therefore, the term electronic commerce also applies to whenever computer networks are used to search and retrieve information in support of human and corporate decision making. The business processes and activities that are being supported by electronic commerce are usually in the form of business transactions that fall into several broad categories:

- Business and customer

  Example: Electronic commerce supports the transactions between businesses and customers over public networks for the purpose of online shopping or online banking using encryption for security and electronic cash, credit, or debit tokens for payment.

- Trading partners using electronic data interchange

  Example: EDI does not work without trading partners. Virtually all public and private sectors of industry use EDI. Even an increasing number of smaller companies are being pushed into implementing EDI in order to maintain relationships with larger trading partners or to remain competitive and expand business opportunities.

- Information gathering

  Example: Electronic commerce supports market research using bar code scanners, information processing for managerial decision making, or organizational problem solving. It can also be used for information manipulation for operations management such as supply chain management.

- Information distribution with prospective customers

  Example: Electronic commerce supports information sharing with customers using interactive advertising, sales, and marketing.

One of the early challenges of electronic commerce was the issue of connectivity. Today, connectivity is not the enabler of electronic commerce it once was, but it is increasingly being used to create relationships and manage these new relationships. Internet-enhanced word of mouth can dramatically boost the adoption of a product or service through **virual marketing**—the leveraged network of Internet affiliates—advertising that propagates itself through an electronic commerce site. An example of virual marketing is placing an advertisement at the end of an e-mail message each time a user sends an e-mail using a free Web-based account. Probably the best known virual marketing success story is the *Blair Witch Project*. Without its skillfully focused Web page, the movie would never have been the financial success it was.

Product awareness is no longer the challenge it once was in the New Economy's networked communication. With the growth opportunity afforded businesses in the New Economy, first-mover advantages are greater than ever. Enabled by electronic commerce, once a

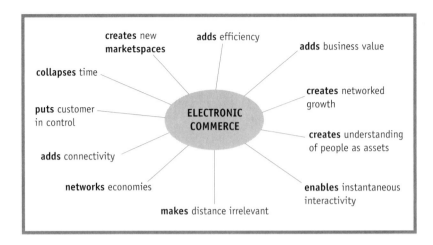

Figure 1-2
The Many Benefits of Electronic Commerce

company reaches critical mass, it can experience increasing returns leading to explosive growth. As depicted in Figure 1-2, Internet connectivity is a major benefit of electronic commerce. The Internet already connects at least 20 million users in more than 130 countries. At current growth rates, it will link 50 million users by 2005.

Geography has always played a key role in determining who competed with whom. Today, the Internet has eliminated such restrictions. Businesses now have to be prepared to market their wares instantly to a global electronic marketplace, or **marketspace**. Barriers to entry are lowered and businesses are now exposed to worldwide competitors.

In the New Economy, businesses must face the challenge of instantaneous interactivity where time is critical. In such a world, there is a huge premium on instant response and the ability to learn from and adapt to the marketspace in real time. This real-time interactivity is also breeding rapid change. Successful companies in the New Economy accept a culture of constant change and are willing to embrace reengineering—a business process in which they constantly break down and reconstruct their products and processes, even the most successful ones.

The Internet provides connectivity between far more points than any alternative, and does so at very low cost. Anything less is a competitive disadvantage.

1.2 Comparing Electronic Commerce with Traditional Commerce

The exponential growth of the Internet can be largely attributed to its business users. Though there have been many dot.com failures recently, Internet and intranet-related applications are the fastest growing segment of business today. Businesses using electronic commerce are experiencing dramatic changes in the way they conduct business. Face-to-face interaction, printed and written documents, telephone communication, and postal mail are all examples of media used in **traditional commerce**. Most of us are familiar with a traditional commerce scenario. Imagine that a customer wants to buy a hat. In the traditional commerce model, the customer goes to a store and requests the item. The request, which may be in the form of an informal verbal appeal, will contain specific information, such as hat size, color, material, cost parameters, delivery instructions, and credit card information. The customer may want to wear the hat out of the store or may want to send it to a favorite aunt as a gift. The sales associate ascertains all this information and then moves the customer's request through the traditional commerce model. The hat is found, the customer's credit is approved, inventory is checked, the delivery of the hat made. Assuming that the customer wants delivery of the hat then and there, she walks out of the store wearing the hat.

Now consider how the hat might have been purchased using the electronic commerce model. The customer visits the Web site of Hats R Us. The selection of the appropriate hat is made matching the needs discussed above—color, size, cost— with the data found in an online catalog. The customer uses an electronic form to send a digital request for the hat to the store for approval. The purchasing department verifies the customer's credit, puts the necessary information into the store's order database, and sends an electronic order to the supplier, via electronic data interchange or another electronic form if the hat is not in the store's inventory. When the supplier receives the order, it is electronically inserted into a database of pending orders. The inventory is checked, the company's credit is checked, and the item is pulled from inventory and marked for delivery. A shipping order may be submitted electronically to the shipping agent. Once the hat is shipped, the customer's credit card is debited by the accounts payable department at the credit card company and instructs the bank, via e-mail, to transfer the appropriate funds. A graphical representation of the traditional commerce model can be seen in Figure 1-3.

Compare the two versions of commerce. Many of the steps are the same, but the way in which the information is obtained and transferred throughout the process is different. Many of the media used in the traditional commerce model—for example, the magazines, flyers, and printed catalogs used by traditional commerce to promulgate product information—have been supplanted by the Web pages of the electronic commerce process. Requests for items in traditional commerce were made on printed forms or in letters; in electronic commerce the process uses e-mail. The printed catalogs that buyers once used to check prices and select products in traditional commerce are now replaced with online catalogs. Online databases are used in the electronic commerce model to prioritize orders, check inventory at the warehouse, schedule delivery, generate invoices, and even schedule payments. Printed forms and postal mail in traditional commerce were used for checking inventory, scheduling delivery, generating an invoice, confirming a receipt, scheduling a payment from a buyer, and receiving payment from a customer. In electronic commerce these steps are now accomplished by e-mail and electronic data interchange. The electronic commerce model is shown in Figure 1-4.

Businesses are relying more and more on technology. In order to gain and maintain competitive advantage, speed is essential in

Figure 1-3

The Traditional Commerce Model

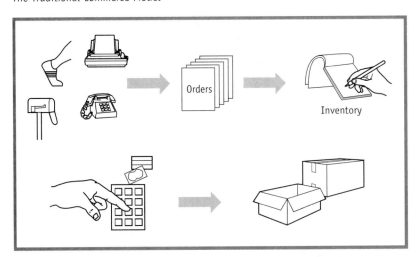

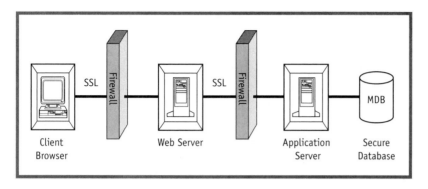

Figure 1-4
The Electronic Commerce Model

today's business environment—from speed to market, and speed to product development, to speed in management decision making. Electronic commerce and its technologies are helping businesses reach this goal. Voice mail, cellular phones, collaborative software, video conferencing, and e-mail all contribute to reducing the time as well as distance factors of conducting business today.

Companies concerned with speed have utilized electronic commerce and created Web database constructions to reach the marketplace as a whole—customers, suppliers, vendors, and employees. The more speed is incorporated into the marketplace, the more important speed is to the success of a business. Think about the convenience of using a single medium for all steps in the commerce process. That's the promise of electronic commerce.

1.3 Comparing Electronic Commerce with Electronic Data Interchange

Electronic data interchange (EDI), a technology that has been used by businesses since the 1960s, emerged when industry groups such as railroads, airlines, motor carriers, and shipping companies realized that processing the large volume of paper documentation accompanying the shipment of goods resulted in significant delays in settlement and product deliveries. Early electronic interchanges used proprietary formats agreed upon between two trading partners (commercial entities that conduct business with each other electronically). While this was a step in the right direction, the result was that organizations needed to maintain a different set of standards for each of their trading partners. This additional effort mitigated some of the benefits gained by conducting business electronically, and it led to an agreement to jointly develop standards for EDI messages.

EDI refers to the computer-to-computer transmission of business information from one business computer to another in standard data formats. It is used mostly by large corporations and their satellite suppliers working together over a private network called a **value-added network (VAN)**. The Data Interchange Standards Association (DISA) estimates that more than 15,000 companies around the world currently conduct business using EDI. The list of industries includes shipping, retail, grocery, apparel manufacturing and textiles, warehousing, aerospace, chemicals, construction, automotive, financial, electrical and electronics, utilities, health care, petroleum, pharmaceutical, metals, paper, entertainment, and higher education. The security offered by these VANs set the benchmark for early electronic commerce on the Internet. VANs offer reliability and security that was difficult to duplicate on business transactions on the public lines of the Internet in the early days of electronic commerce. EDI exchange of business documents can be in the form of purchase orders, invoices, or application forms. EDI is based on a set of standard formats that define transaction sets, or messages, that can be used to send basic business data from one computer to another. These transaction sets replace paper documents such as purchase orders, invoices, and bills of lading.

An EDI service provider will maintain a VAN, with messaging boxes for each business associated with the service. The provider will store and forward the EDI messages between partners. Each business using EDI agrees on the standardization of the formats prior to conducting business. Businesses that change partners often are not well suited to the EDI model. In today's business environment, rapid change in strategic business alliances and partners is more and more the norm, giving rise to business looking for alternatives to EDI. Setting up partnership agreements and terminating them is both expensive and slow to implement, especially by today's standards, where speed is paramount to success.

EDI service providers are now offering public line Internet access as a component of their service. Not only does this attenuate some of the change factors in partnering relationships, but it also minimizes the need for businesses to maintain the costly VAN-associated hardware and software needed to maintain format standards. Using the Internet, forms can be completed using a Web page. Businesses can also use EDI to automate the transfer of information within as well as between businesses. For example, EDI-based data can be exchanged among the accounting, production, and shipping function areas of a business. Electronic commerce automates the purchase and payment processes and increases the speed of move-

FOCUS ON ELECTRONIC COMMERCE

Understanding and Planning Before Building: Creative Good and BestBuy.com

Creative Good, a strategic consulting firm, observed that many electronic commerce Web database constructions were not meeting the strategic needs of the businesses—they just weren't making the sales. They estimated online customers were not completing their Web orders more than 40 percent of the time. Creative Good hypothesized that correcting a small set of problems in the Web database design could yield significant gains for any electronic commerce site. To test their hypothesis, they looked at several sites without the knowledge or participation of the business. One of these test sites was BestBuy.com. Creative Good spent a great deal of time in preparation during the summer in 2000. To better understand where customers had difficulty on the BestBuy.com site, they surveyed customers and tested the site. From their understanding of the problem at hand, Creative Good was guided by four factors: (1) customer objectives, as observed in their initial tests; (2) BestBuy's business objectives, based on research on the company and basic assumptions about the objectives of any electronic commerce site; (3) best practices of online retailing, based on past research and client work; and (4) an informal competitive analysis of five other electronic commerce sites selling electronics.

After a thorough review, Creative Good came up with a new version of the BestBuy site. Although it was only a prototype, it addressed the areas of the site that confused customers in the first set of tests. Creative Good tested only a few pages from the site with their prototype, but results were dramatic. They found that the prototype significantly improved the BestBuy customer experience and increased completed sales as well, even though only a relatively small amount of time and effort had been invested into the project. Their conclusion: many electronic commerce sites could also be significantly improved with a small investment in the customer experience.

What benefits did BestBuy.com gain from Creative Good's understanding and planning for electronic commerce improvements before creating the prototype?

Source: Aamir Rehman, "BestBuy.com Case Study: Even Better Than the Real Thing," *ZDNet E-Commerce, Best Practices Evaluation,* 2000.

ment from one part of the process to another. EDI often is associated with the banking industry because of its high need for security and reliability of transmission and data. Financial Electronic Data Interchange, or **Financial EDI**, is defined as the electronic transmission of funds and related data through the banking system, using standard formats. It is also called Electronic Funds Transfer, or EFT, by the Federal Reserve System. Because the cost of operations on the public lines of the Internet is lower than using the private lines of a VAN, many businesses and financial institutions have experimented with EDI over the Internet.

1.4 Electronic Commerce Strategies and Techniques

The modern business methodology of electronic commerce addresses the need felt by business to cut costs while at the same time improving the quality of goods and services and increasing the speed of time to market. But electronic commerce also applies to decision support. Whenever computer networks are used to search and retrieve information to support decision making, that too is electronic commerce. As shown in Figure 1-5, there are five broad information-processing strategies and techniques that are utilized in the electronic commerce model: (1) business-to-business, (2) business-

Figure 1-5

The Five Categories of Electronic Commerce

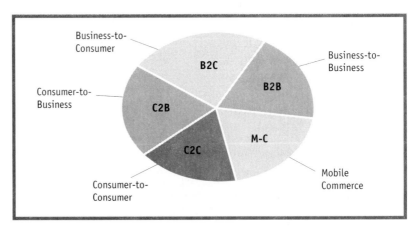

to-consumer, (3) consumer-to-business, (4) consumer-to-consumer, and, (5) mobile commerce.

Business-to-Business Electronic Commerce

Business-to-business electronic commerce (B2B) refers to the relationship between two or more businesses using the Internet for the relationship channel. Most electronic commerce today is B2B. The Aberdeen Group has reported that the volume of money involved in B2B transactions has already surpassed individual consumer transactions by 10 to 1. And the potential growth is impressive. The Yankee Group predicts American B2B commerce will grow 41 percent annually over the next five years. GartnerGroup has estimated that the B2B industry will be a $7.29 trillion worldwide industry by 2004 and that electronic markets will account for 37 percent of the B2B market by the same year.

There are two B2B models: (1) the vertical model, which provides specialized goods or services across many different types of industries, and (2) the horizontal model, which provides goods or services for one particular industry. The reason for the growth in the B2B market is purely economics, whether it follows the vertical or the horizontal model. B2B provides infrastructure for supply chains and trading sites that help corporations streamline the way they do business with customers and suppliers. With B2B, businesses are able to consolidate suppliers and harness the buying power of the conglomerate. A good example of B2B is Covisint, the Internet auto parts supply exchange formed by General Motors Corporation, Ford Motor Company, and DaimlerChrysler. This exchange, an Internet portal that links an online supply chain, is now the world's largest Internet company. Covisint's B2B is also a key step in the application of Internet technology to traditional industry.

 Web Break

Visit Covisint on the Web at http://www.covisint.com/ and investigate its plans to harness the power of electronic commerce to enhance the supply chain and reinforce competitiveness.

Business-to-Consumer Electronic Commerce

Another example of electronic commerce is **business-to-consumer (B2C)**—a popular form of e-commerce today, in which a business sells directly to a consumer. One of the world's largest B2C examples is Amazon.com, the U.S. book retailer. B2C actually refers to the retailing relationship between a business and the end consumer. With B2C, the retailing part of the commerce is accomplished via the Internet. In this electronic commerce model, businesses market toward consumers rather than other businesses. Businesses advertise and distribute their own products or services to customers via the Internet-based electronic store utilizing Web database constructions without intervention of any intermediaries. Traditional distributors and agents are seriously threatened by a networked economy in which buyers can deal directly with sellers. This process removes the middleman and is termed **disintermediation**. The term describes the new model of electronic commerce where businesses using the Web and other Internet-based technologies sell directly to their customers rather than going through their traditional relationship channels. One advantage of disintermediation is that by eliminating the middleman, businesses can sell their products or services cheaper and faster. Disintermediation is the driving force behind the idea that electronic commerce will revolutionize the way products are bought and sold.

As electronic commerce has eliminated the traditional mediaries, it has led to the emergence of new **infomediaries** in their place. Infomediaries are needed to turn the massive amounts of "dumb" data into usable information. They offer aggregated services such as intelligent customer assistance, powerful technology-based buying aids, and even attractive, community-based buying environments.

B2C is similar to the traditional commerce relationship of business to customer, except for the fact that the Internet itself becomes the relationship channel. The idea of using different channels for commerce is not new. In 1886, a jeweler unhappy with a shipment of watches refused to accept them. Being an opportunist, a local telegraph operator bought the entire shipment and used the telegraph as the commerce channel to sell all the watches to fellow operators and railroad employees. In only a few months this young entrepreneur was so successful that he had quit his job and started his own store, naming it after himself: Sears.

With electronic commerce and the B2C business model, **customer relationship management (CRM)** has undergone radical changes.

Customer centricity is on the rapid rise. Leading-edge businesses the world over are recognizing that intimate, one-to-one relationships with their customers are critical to survival in an increasingly global and competitive marketplace. What used to be a typical customer service setup—a call center with customer service representative that had access to a customer and product database—is now based on the B2C model, a complex, multifaceted undertaking. **Electronic CRM (eCRM)** is rapidly becoming the business standard—embracing customer service and support features, data collection and analysis, and marketing campaign and sales applications. eCRM is a tool for the B2C virtual marketspace. It completely integrates the contact center of a business, where their representatives answer customer e-mails and phone calls. eCRM allows synchronous interaction between the customer and the business through live chat interaction while representatives access a fully integrated customer database connected to a supply chain.

Consumer-to-Business Electronic Commerce

Consumer-to-Business (C2B) is where the consumer takes the initiative in the buying and selling relationship to contact the business. C2B involves consumers naming their price for various products or services offered by businesses and is the smallest and least-developed sector of electronic commerce. The most visible example of C2B is the faltering Priceline.com, a company that allows consumers to name a price at which they would be willing to buy a specific product or service. Priceline.com acts as the broker to find a supplier that is willing to sell a product at that price. In this electronic commerce model, the business has become reactive rather than taking the traditional proactive approach. This type of electronic commerce includes customers who may sell their products or services to businesses as well as customers who seek out sellers, interact with them, and complete the commerce relationship.

Consumer-to-Consumer Electronic Commerce

Internet auctions have given rise to another category of electronic commerce, **consumer-to-consumer (C2C)**—the process whereby consumers sell to other consumers. Consumers are easily able to set up their operations and develop an online presence with support of a third-party provider. Leading third-party suppliers in the U.S. are eBay.com and Yahoo auctions. In this electronic commerce model, the consumer initiates the selling to another consumer using electronic commerce as an intermediary.

Mobile Electronic Commerce

With the advent of today's more powerful mobile phones, the ability to browse, search, and buy over the Internet has created **mobile electronic commerce**, or **M-commerce**, a fast-emerging specialized class of electronic commerce that brings with it the promise of true comparison shopping whether in a store or listening to the car radio. Wireless data services are increasingly being used in the B2B, B2C, and C2C relationship channels. With the coming of wireless access to the Internet through handheld devices, retailers are eager to make it convenient for the consumer to shop anywhere, anytime. M-commerce eliminates the need for retailing to be restricted to a set location. As long as consumers have wireless Internet access, with M-commerce, they can shop even when they are mobile.

With M-commerce comes the emergence of **person-to-person commerce (P2P)**, a business model that refers to any transaction that transfers money from one individual to another. M-commerce enables such P2P transactions as the transfer of money from one handheld personal digital assistant (PDA), like a Palm Pilot, to another. One example of a business capitalizing on the potential of M-commerce is X.com. X.com has a service called PayPal that will handle money transfers to pay someone without waiting for a check to clear. Individuals who auction items on X.com use this service. It also allows them to accept credit card payments.

With so many individuals wanting to pay each other by e-mail, there is expected to be much growth of small transactions using P2P and M-commerce. Businesses are also investigating payment opportunities using the electronic commerce models of P2P and M-commerce.

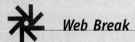

Web Break

Visit M-Commerce World to read the latest articles on M-Commerce. Global M-commerce conferences are also listed on their Web site at http://www.m-commercesource.com/convention.htm.

Western Union, Bank One, eCount, and ProPay.com are already utilizing the power of this medium. These companies are now focused on auction transactions, but they see the potential of expanding P2P and M-commerce into the broader spectrum of small payments.

1.5 Electronic Commerce and Client/Server Architecture

Electronic commerce is based on **client/server architecture**, an arrangement that involves client processes requesting service from server processes. The term client/server was first used in the 1980s in reference to personal computers on a network. By the late 1980s, the actual client/server model started gaining acceptance because of its versatility and message-based modular infrastructure. Today, the model improves electronic commerce usability, flexibility, interoperability, and scalability.

In the electronic commerce model, a client is defined as the requestor of a service and a server is the provider of service. For example, the user of a Web browser is the client, making requests for pages from servers all over the Web. The browser itself is a client in the relationship as well as the customer. The computer handling the request and sending back the HTML files is the server. The server in the client/server model can also be a computer program that provides services to other computer programs. Generally, in the client/server programming model, a server is a program that waits for and fills client program requests. A given program in a computer may function both as a client sending requests for services and as a server of requests.

Specific to the electronic commerce model, a Web server is the computer program that serves requested HTML pages, or files. A Web server is a program that, using the client/server model and the Web's Hypertext Transfer Protocol (HTTP), serves the files that form Web pages to the Web client. Every computer on the Internet that contains a Web site must have a Web server program. Two of the most popular Web servers for the Microsoft Windows environment are Deerfield's **WebSite** and Microsoft's **Internet Information Server (IIS)**, which comes packaged with the Windows NT server and Windows 2000 Server.

Web servers are often included as part of a larger package of Internet- and intranet-related programs for serving e-mail, downloading requests for **File Transfer Protocol (FTP)** files, and building and publishing Web pages. FTP, a standard Internet protocol, is the simplest way to exchange files in the electronic commerce model. Like HTTP, which transfers displayable Web pages and related files, FTP is an application protocol that uses the Internet's TCP/IP protocols. Considerations in choosing a Web server include how well it works with the operating system and other servers, its ability to handle server-side programming and publishing, search engines, and enhancements like site-building tools that may come with it.

Typically, the electronic-commerce customer is the client and the business is the server. However, in the client/server model, a single machine can be both a client and a server, depending on the software configuration. The client/server model utilizes a database server in which **relational database management system (RDBMS)** user queries can be answered directly by the server. The client/server architecture reduces network traffic by providing a query response to the user rather than transferring total files, and it improves multi-user updating through a **graphical user interface (GUI)** front end to the shared database. In client/server architectures, client and server typically communicate through statements made in **structured query language (SQL)**.

Two-Tier Architectures

In the **two-tier client/server model**, the user system interface is usually located in the user's desktop environment and the database management services are usually in a server that is a more powerful machine that services many clients. Processing management is split between the user's system interface environment and the database management server environment. The database management server provides stored procedures and triggers. There are a number of software vendors who provide tools to simplify development of applications for the two-tier client/server architecture.

A two-tier client/server application runs the client processes separately from the server processes, usually on a different computer, as shown in Figure 1-6. There are three main factors in the two-tier client/server model:

- The **client** processes provide an interface for the customer, and gather and present data, usually on the customer's computer. This part of the application is the presentation layer, or the user tier.

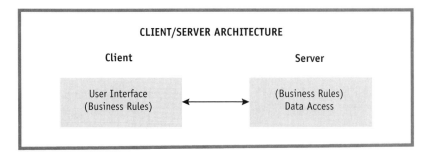

Figure 1-6

Simple Two-Tier Client/Server Architecture

- The **server** processes provide an interface with the data store of the business. This part of the application is the data layer, or the data tier.
- The business logic that validates data, monitors security and permissions, and performs other business rules can be housed on either the client or the server, or even split between the two. The business logic, or business rules, refers to the fundamental units of work required to complete the business process. Business rules can be automated by an application program.

Electronic commerce typically utilizes a two-tier client/server architecture for intranet commerce, Internet retrieval, and decision support. The two-tier model is also used for distributed computing when there are fewer than 100 people simultaneously interacting on a **local area network (LAN)**. A LAN is an acronym used to describe a group of computers and associated devices that share a common communications line. LANs typically share the resources of a single processor or server in a small geographic area, for example, within an office building. Usually, the server in this commerce model has applications and data storage shared by multiple computer users. This commerce model cannot effectively support more than 100 clients. When the number exceeds 100, performance of the commerce model begins to deteriorate. In the two-tier model, the server maintains a connection with each client, even though the client may not be requesting any services at the time. Another limitation of the two-tier architecture is that implementation of processing management services using vendor proprietary database procedures restricts flexibility and choice of RDBMS for applications. The architecture also lacks flexibility in moving program functionality from one server to another.

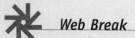

Web Break

Visit Information Technology Support Center's Web site at
http://www.itsc.state.md.us/itsc/techrepts/clntsrvr.html and
explore the trends in client/server technology. Both the traditional database-oriented client/server technology as well as more
recent general distributed computing technologies are discussed.
This site is sponsored by the U.S. Department of Labor.

Three-Tier Architectures

The three-tier commerce model, often referred to as **multitier architecture**, was developed to overcome the limitations of two-tier
architecture. In the three-tier model, a **middle tier** is added
between the client environment and the database management
server environment. There are a variety of ways of implementing the
middle tier, such as **transaction processing (TP) monitors**,
message servers, and **application servers**. The middle tier can
perform queuing, application execution, and database staging.
These internal processes are computer management processes. The
middle tier looks at how objects or other processes line up, or queue,
or how applications are executed, or even how and where databases are staged and maintained. For example, if the middle tier provides queuing, the client can deliver its request to the middle tier
and disengage since the middle tier will access the data and return
the answer from the server to the client. Electronic commerce often
utilizes this client/server architecture model because of the functionality added by the middle tier to the model. The middle tier
allows scheduling and prioritization for work in progress. The **three-
tier client/server model**, as shown in Figure 1-7, has been shown
to improve performance for groups with a large number of users,
even in the thousands, and improves flexibility when compared with
the two-tier approach. Although the early versions of this model
were more difficult to use than the visually oriented development of
two-tier applications, new design approaches to three-tier computing have mitigated such problems.

**Three-Tier Architecture Utilizing Transaction Processing
Monitor** The most basic type of three-tier electronic commerce

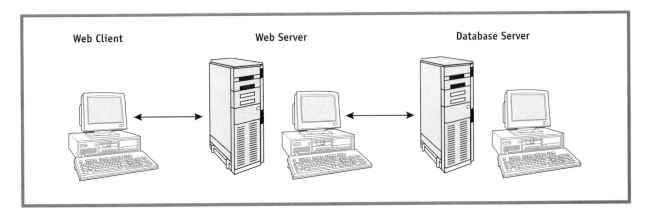

Web Client   **Web Server**   **Database Server**

Figure 1-7
Three-Tier Client/Server Architecture

model has a middle tier consisting of transaction processing (TP) monitor, a technology that involves a type of message queuing, transaction scheduling, and prioritization service where the client connects to the TP monitor of the middle tier instead of the database server. The transaction is accepted by the monitor, which queues it and then takes responsibility for managing it to completion, thus freeing up the client. When this capability is provided by third-party middleware vendors, it is referred to as **TP heavy** because it can service thousands of users. When it is embedded in the **database management system (DBMS)**, it can be considered a two-tier architecture and is referred to as **TP lite** because the performance degrades when more than 100 clients are connected. TP monitor technology also provides several other features:

- The ability to update multiple DBMSs in a single transaction
- Connectivity to a variety of data sources, including flat files and nonrelational DBMS
- The ability to attach priorities to transactions
- Robust security

Electronic commerce models employing a three-tier client/server architecture with TP monitor technology result in an environment that is considerably more scalable than a two-tier architecture with direct client to server connection. For systems like electronic commerce with many thousands of users, TP monitor technology is currently one of the most effective business solutions.

Three-Tier Architecture Utilizing a Message Server Messaging is another way to implement three-tier architecture. Messages are prioritized and processed asynchronously in this model, consisting of headers that contain priority information, the address, and identification number. The message server connects to the RDBMS and other data sources. The difference between TP monitor technology and message server architecture is that the message server focuses on intelligent messages, whereas the TP monitor environment has the intelligence in the monitor, and treats transactions as dumb data packets. Three-tier messaging systems are thus sound business solutions for the wireless infrastructures of M-commerce.

Three-Tier Architecture Utilizing an Application Server Electronic commerce can also utilize the three-tier client/server architecture in the application server model. Three-tier server architecture allocates the main body of an application to run on a shared host rather than in the user system interface client environment. The application server does not drive the GUIs; rather it shares business logic, computations, and a data retrieval engine. The advantages of this approach are that with less software on the client there is less concern with security, applications are more scalable, and support and installation costs are less on a single server than maintaining each on a desktop client. The application server model is particularly desirable when security, scalability, and cost are major considerations.

Three-Tier Architecture with an Object Request Broker Standard The needs of electronic commerce are driving industry and technology to develop standards to improve interoperability and **object request broker (ORB)** standards in the client/server model. ORB support in a network of clients and servers on different computers means that a client program (which may itself be an object) can request services from a server program or object without having to understand where the server is in a distributed network or what the interface to the server program looks like. ORB is the programming that acts as the mediary, or as a broker, between a client request for a service from a distributed object or component and server completion of that request. Components can find out about each other and exchange interface information as they are running. Developing a client/server architecture that supports distributed objects holds great promise for finding solutions to the challenges of interoperability across languages and platforms as well as enhancing maintainability and adaptability of the system. There are currently two prominent distributed object technologies: (1) **Common Object Request Broker Architecture (CORBA)** and (2) **Component Object Model (COM)**, Microsoft's framework for developing and supporting program component objects. The industry is now working on standards to improve interoperability between CORBA and COM as well.

Distributed Enterprise Architecture   The newest electronic commerce model is **distributed enterprise architecture**. Emerging in 1993, this model is based on ORB technology and using shared, reusable business models on a business enterprise-wide scale. The benefit of this approach is that standardized business object models and distributed object computing are combined to give the business greater flexibility. **Enterprise Resource Planning (ERP)**, an industry term used to describe the broad set of activities supported by the distributed enterprise architecture, aids management in overseeing and planning for the important parts of its business, including product planning, parts purchasing, maintaining inventories, interacting with suppliers, providing customer service, and tracking orders. Usually, an ERP system is integrated with an RDBMS and can involve considerable business process analysis, employee retraining, and new work procedures. The model improves enterprise effectiveness organizationally, operationally, and technologically. With the emergence and popularity of ERP software, distributed enterprise architecture promises to enable electronic commerce to extend business processes at the enterprise level.

1.6 The Relationship Between Electronic Commerce and Web Database Constructions

By definition, electronic commerce is dynamic and constantly evolving. It supports—and is supported by—technologies that are constantly changing. Among these technologies, database storage and management is the oldest and currently the most utilized by electronic commerce. As seen in Figure 1-8, when used in the electronic commerce model, database storage and management achieves a new level of applicability.

Figure 1-8
Electronic Commerce: The Web Database Construction

The technologies of electronic commerce have many business uses and implications. The relationship between electronic commerce and Web database construction is heavily rooted in communications systems, payment systems, and organizational support systems. Businesses can implement new sales and marketing channels through the use of the Web, which provides electronic means for businesses to display online materials such as product catalogs, price lists, and brochures. As Internet security issues are resolved, businesses are selling more and more products online, direct to their customers. The use of electronic commerce technologies is an effective way to provide customer support or to create a virtual link between a business and its customer, as shown in Figure 1-9. Many businesses are providing online technical support, allowing their customers to easily find answers to problems and to download needed files and software 24 hours a day, seven days a week, saving the company money on support personnel and mailing costs. Electronic commerce technologies can be used in any environment where documents are exchanged between businesses, including procurement, purchasing, finance, trade and transport, health, law and even revenue and tax collection. Electronic commerce has potential benefits for both suppliers and buyers in reducing paperwork and administrative lead times and allowing agencies to adopt more efficient purchasing practices such as just-in-time, quick response, and direct

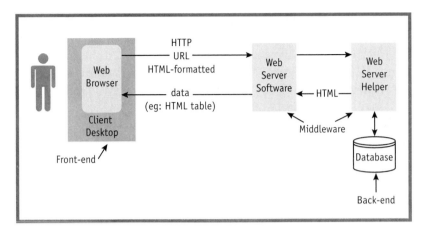

Figure 1-9
A Simple Electronic Commerce Web Database Construction Model

store delivery. Other benefits associated with electronic commerce include reduced paperwork, more accurate and speedy business transactions, quicker and easier access to information, and reduced need to re-key information into computers.

A new era in commerce began when companies began to transact business over the Internet using Web interfaces to interact with back-end relational databases. Electronic commerce was born and its power and reach has only begun to be tapped.

Summary

■ **Define electronic commerce.** Electronic commerce is the paperless exchange of business information, through a variety of technologies—from e-mail and electronic bulletin boards to electronic funds transfer, and electronic data interchange. Electronic commerce seeks to automate business tasks—from the generation, processing, coordination, and distribution of data to the reconciliation of business transactions through the Internet and other electronic media.

■ **Define basic electronic commerce terms.** Electronic commerce is one of the most important aspects of the Internet to emerge. The Internet—often called the Net, the Information Superhighway, or

Cyberspace—is all about connectivity. It is a network of computer networks that is connected to other computers for the purpose of resource and information sharing. One part of the Internet is the World Wide Web, usually just called the Web. This network connects electronic documents, referred to as Web pages, that contain information that may be in the form of basic text or intricate multimedia consisting of graphics, sound, video, and animation. Web pages contain hypertext links, or links, that when selected, connect the user to other Web pages of related information. Each Web page has an address or Uniform Resource Locator (URL). The Web pages on the Web are stored in the computers called Web servers that are connected to and make up the Internet.

■ **Compare traditional commerce with electronic commerce.** Many of the steps are the same, but the way in which the information is obtained and transferred throughout the process is what is different. Many of the media used in the traditional commerce model —for example, the magazines, flyers, and printed catalogs used by traditional commerce to acquire product information—have been supplanted by the Web pages of the electronic commerce process. Requests for items in traditional commerce were made on printed forms or in letters; in electronic commerce, the process uses e-mail. The printed catalogs used to check prices and select products in traditional commerce have now been replaced with online catalogs. Online databases are used in the electronic commerce model to prioritize orders, check inventory at the warehouse, schedule delivery, generate invoices, and even schedule payments. Printed forms and postal mail in traditional commerce were used for checking inventory, scheduling delivery, generating an invoice, confirming a receipt, scheduling a payment from a buyer, and receiving payment from a customer. In electronic commerce these steps are now accomplished by e-mail and electronic data interchange.

■ **Compare electronic commerce to electronic data interchange.** EDI is computer-to-computer transmission of business information from one business computer to another in standard data formats. It is used mostly by large corporations and their satellite suppliers working together over a private network called a value-added network (VAN). The security offered by these VANs sets the benchmark for early electronic commerce on the Internet. VANs offer reliability and security that was difficult to duplicate on business transactions on the public lines of Internet in the early days of electronic commerce. EDI electronic exchange of business documents can be in the form of purchase orders, invoices, or application forms.

■ **Describe electronic commerce strategies and techniques used by businesses.** The business processes and activities that are being supported by electronic commerce are usually in the form of business transactions. There are four broad categories: (1) business and customer, (2) trading partners using electronic data interchange, (3) information gathering, and (4) information distribution with prospective customers. Electronic commerce addresses the need felt by business to cut costs while at the same time improve the quality of goods and services and increase the speed of time to market. Electronic commerce also applies to decision support. Whenever computer networks are used to search and retrieve information to support decision making, that too is electronic commerce. There are five broad information-processing strategies and techniques that are utilized in the electronic commerce model: (1) business-to-business, (2) business-to-consumer, (3) consumer-to-business, (4) consumer-to-consumer, and (5) mobile commerce.

■ **Discuss electronic commerce and client/server architecture.** Electronic commerce is based on client/server architecture, an arrangement that involves client processes requesting service from server processes. The model improves electronic commerce usability, flexibility, interoperability, and scalability. In the electronic commerce model, a client is defined as the requester of the service and a server the provider of service. For example, the user of a Web browser is the client, making requests for pages from servers all over the Web. The browser itself is a client in the relationship. The computer handling the request and sending back the HTML files is the server. The server in the client/server model can also be a computer program that provides services to other computer programs. Generally, in the client/server programming model, a server is a program that waits for and fills client program requests. A given program in a computer may function both as a client sending requests for services and as a server of requests.

■ **Discuss the relationship between electronic commerce and Web database constructions.** The technologies of electronic commerce using Web database constructions have many business uses and implications. Businesses can implement new sales and marketing channels through the use of the Web. The Web provides electronic means for businesses to display online materials such as product catalogs, price lists, and brochures. As Internet security issues are resolved, businesses are selling more and more products online, direct to their customers. The use of electronic commerce technologies is an effective way to provide customer support or to create a virtual link between a business and its customer.

Chapter Key Terms

application servers
Tim Berners-Lee
business-to-business (B2B)
business-to-consumer (B2C)
CERN
client
client/server architecture
common object request broker
    architecture (CORBA)
component object model (COM)
connectivity
consumer-to-business (C2B)
consumer-to-consumer (C2C)
customer relationship
    management (CRM)
database management system
    (DBMS)
disintermediation
distributed enterprise architecture
electronic commerce
electronic CRM (eCRM)

electronic data interchange (EDI)
enterprise resource planning
    (ERP)
file transfer protocol (FTP)
financial EDI
graphical user interface (GUI)
hypertext markup language
    (HTML)
hypertext transfer protocol
    (HTTP)
infomediaries
Internet
Internet information server (IIS)
IR AC IS
local area network (LAN)
marketspace
message servers
middle tier
mobile electronic commerce
    (M-commerce)
multitier architecture

New Economy
object request broker (ORB)
person-to-person commerce (P2P)
relational database management
    system (RDBMS)
server
structured query language (SQL)
three-tier client/server model
TP heavy
TP lite
traditional commerce
transaction processing (TP)
    monitor
two-tier client/server model
Uniform Resource Locator (URL)
value-added network (VAN)
virual marketing
Web server
WebSite
World Wide Web

Review Questions

1. What is electronic commerce?

2. What are the major differences between electronic commerce and traditional commerce?

3. Why is electronic commerce considered one of the most important aspects of the Internet to emerge?

4. Describe the World Wide Web as an enabler of electronic commerce.

5. Who is Tim Berners-Lee? What is his relationship to electronic commerce?

6. What model is used today to create electronic commerce Web database constructions?

7. What are the two major business emphases of electronic commerce?

8. Before the Internet technologies of the Web, information systems were primarily used for what purpose?

9. List and describe the business processes and activities that are being supported by electronic commerce.

10. List and discuss ways in which a weakened connectivity model is a major challenge for electronic commerce in today's business environment.

11. Assess the strengths and weaknesses of electronic data interchange.

12. Which is the most popular of the electronic commerce strategies and techniques? Account for its popularity.

13. What is mobile commerce? What are some specific business uses for mobile commerce?

14. What is a Web server?

15. Within the context of electronic commerce, what is a client? What is a server?

16. Describe three different electronic commerce client/server models. Give a business scenario for each one.

17. Define transaction processing monitor. How are TP lite and TP heavy part of the electronic commerce model?

18. What are the benefits of utilizing a message server in client/server architecture?

19. Describe standardization technology in the client/server model and the impact standardization has on electronic commerce.

20. What is the relationship between electronic commerce and Web database constructions?

Critical Thinking Using the Web

1. Go to Google's Web site at http://www.Google.com and investigate a new technology search engine. Search and retrieve an article on distributive/collaborative enterprise architecture from the Web. Write a brief report summarizing the five main points the article makes about this architecture and its support for the electronic commerce business model.

2. Go to the Infogate Web site at http://www.infogate.com and explore. Write a brief report on Infogate. What is the nature of their business? What type of electronic commerce strategies and techniques are they utilizing? The site has been rated by Nielsen Net-Ratings as the "stickiest-at-work property" on the Internet. What does this rating mean? Do you agree? If so, how did they achieve "stickiness"? If not, what could they do to increase "stickiness"?

3. Visit the SitePoint Web site at http://www.sitepoint.com/ and explore. Write a brief report on how SitePoint could be used to increase the strategic acquisition and aggressive marketing capabilities of electronic commerce for the following businesses:

a. A small cotton textile mill employing 40 people in rural North Carolina

b. An established winery in California's Sonoma County that wants to move into international markets

c. A community newspaper outside of Chicago, IL that has a circulation of 15,000 and whose focus is reporting the news of the local community (no regional or nation news is included in the newspaper)

Chapter Case Study

Albatross Records is a continuing case study that illustrates the process of building electronic commerce with Web database constructions. In Chapter 1, you will get started by investigating the subject on the World Wide Web and creating a proposal for Albatross Records. You will justify the record company's management decision to incorporate electronic commerce into the business. Be *sure to incorporate both the opportunities of electronic commerce as well as the challenges. As you continue through the text, you will complete different facets of electronic commerce Web database constructions, resulting in a complete dynamic Web site for Albatross Records.*

Albatross Records is a small record company located in Freestone, California, about an hour and a half north of San Francisco. Albatross does not specialize in any one type of music, which results in a very eclectic mix of artists and musical styles represented. In the last two years, more "New Wave" artists have been signed than any other type of artist. The company is a small corporation headed by Sam Cooleridge, CEO. His employees just call him "Cool."

Albatross representatives usually find artists to sign one of the following ways:

- They compose 25-, 50-, and 75-word descriptions describing the business to prospective musicians.
- They post index cards on bulletin boards at music businesses—usually record stores, musical instrument stores, college and university music departments, and rehearsal studios.
- They contact local weekly and monthly publications with music coverage to ask if they have a "musicians' referral" section in their classified ads.
- They meet local musicians (on breaks or after shows; at music-related association meetings) to see if they need a recording label, or if they have any side projects.
- They contact the local office of the musicians' union, the American Federation of Musicians (AFM).
- They talk to local club booking agents.
- They post notices in online music newsgroups such as news:place.music.

Tour support—the money that a record company advances to the band to cover any losses incurred on tour—is their largest expenditure. Tours often end up costing more than they earn for newer artists, but because touring is considered by Cool to be necessary to promote clients and to gain exposure for them in new markets, Albatross fronts some money to each touring band to keep it on the tour. Recording con-

tracts generally provide for tour support money that is recoupable against royalties, so ultimately the band will pay the entire cost of the tour.

Albatross also supports their artists working in what are called "sideman performances"—guest performances on other artists' recordings. Albatross recording contracts require their artists to record exclusively for their own labels, but it allows, even encourages, sideman performances because Cool thinks Albatross also benefits from guest appearances.

All electronic commerce Web database constructions should begin with a sound understanding of the task at hand and thorough planning of the design before any code is written or database created. To begin the understanding and planning stages for your design, research the music and record industry on the Internet. Create a one-to-two-page document stating the basic factors or elements you will include in your Web database construction. Also, create a preliminary sketch of your design. Keep in mind that your design will undergo considerable transformation as you continue to understand and plan for your electronic commerce construction design for Albatross Records. So it's your turn to complete a preliminary plan that includes, but is not limited to, the following items:

- Electronic commerce construction benefits to be gained by Albatross Records and value-added from a Web presence
- Estimated Web site audience
- Estimated Web site foot traffic
- Working Web site title
- Justification for design focus
- Content and goals of the site
- Design considerations
- Technical or audience factors that could limit the design goals of the site

2

Introduction to
Web Database Construction

Web applications are becoming more and more popular. This is in part due to the rapid deployment of the tools and technologies for developing them. But mostly because system designers are recognizing the situations where Web applications have very significant advantages over traditional applications.. . . Little attention has been paid to the development process. Current development environments make it so easy to produce simple Web applications that they have the unfortunate side effect of encouraging us to develop and evolve applications in the absence of serious analysis and design. Any system with nontrivial complexity needs to be designed and modeled.

—Jim Conallen, Principal Consultant, Conallen Inc., March 1999

Kanthaka Farms

Kanthaka Farms is a continuing case study in this book that illustrates the process of building electronic commerce with Web database constructions. In Chapter 2, you will continue to investigate the appropriateness of Web database constructions as a methodology for Kanthaka Farms to increase business. You will justify to Kanthaka Farms your suggestions for choosing server-side technologies, client-side technologies, or a combination of both—citing both the benefits and challenges from these technologies to Kanthaka Farms. As you continue through the text, you will complete different facets of electronic commerce Web database constructions, resulting in a complete Web site for Kanthaka Farms.

Continue your electronic commerce plan for Kanthaka Farms utilizing Web database construction and its enabling technologies. Now it's your turn to do the following:

- Plan and discuss the electronic commerce architecture you will use for Kanthaka Farms. Use Visio or another software tool to sketch your plan to show to the Vitas.

The electronic commerce architecture should reflect the designer's understanding of the business. Because Kanthaka Farms is a small business, its architecture will be rather straightforward, consisting of three principal components: (1) a Web server, (2) an electronic commerce Web site, and (3) a client browser. The Web server distributes pages of formatted information to the customer that requests it. The request is made over a network connection and uses the HTTP pro-

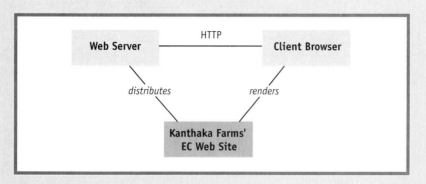

Figure 2-1
Kanthaka Farms Electronic Commerce Model

tocol. Figure 2-1 shows the Kanthaka Farms electronic commerce business model.

- Discuss how Kanthaka Farms' information will move through the electronic commerce model. Be specific as you discuss the components of the Web database design. Use Visio or another software tool to sketch your plan.

The information presented on the Web site will be stored, already formatted, in files on Kanthaka Farms' Web server. Customers will request files by name, and when necessary provide specific path information with their request. These files, also called *pages*, represent the content of the front end of the Kanthaka Farms' Web database construction.

In some instances, information on the Web page will not be stored in a file and will not be assembled until runtime—on the fly—from information stored in the back-end of the Web database construction and in the formatting instructions inside the server-side script file. In other instances, the information will come from the output of a CGI or ISAPI. Kanthaka Farms' Web server will use a page filter to interpret and execute the CGI scripts in the page. Electronic commerce constructions employing this strategy are called *dynamic*. Figure 2-2 shows this dynamic data passing through the Kanthaka Farms' electronic commerce architecture.

- Discuss the integral nature of the Web server to the electronic

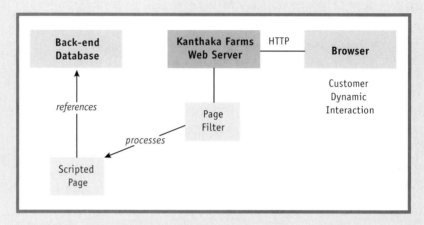

Figure 2-2
Kanthaka Farms' Electronic Commerce Architecture

commerce design. How will this approach be advantageous to the Web database construction designer?

Dynamic Web sites offer certain advantages to Web site designers, making it easy to keep database content fresh and synchronized. The overall look and feel of the business' Web site is defined by a set of pages that contain code executed by the Web server during a request for these pages. In this context the file can be either a plain text file with scripts interpreted by the Web server, or a compiled binary file that is executed by the Web server. In either case the code in the page references and utilizes server resources that include databases, e-mail services, and file services.

■   Discuss HTTP and the client/server interaction in your design using the customer and business in your discussion.

Kanthaka Farms' online customers will access the Web site by clicking on links and requesting pages from the Web server. For example, a customer will interact with Kanthaka Farms using a browser—an application on a client machine that connects to a server on a network and requests a page of information from a business. Once the page request has been fulfilled, the connection terminates. The browser knows how to communicate via HTTP to a Web server, and how to render formatted information from the business returned by the Web server. Most pages of information contain *links* to other pages, or even on other servers, which the browser user may easily request.

2.1 The Web Database Construction

It is difficult to imagine that in 1992 the World Wide Web contained fewer than 100 pages—and these pages were static and allowed no connectivity or interaction between a business and its customer. Today the Web is growing by more than a million pages a day. Visionaries like Tim Berners-Lee, who defined the initial Web specifications and wrote the first Web client and server software, understood the potential power of electronic commerce. A simple electronic commerce Web database construction is shown in Figure 2-3.

The Front-End Introduction: Web Pages

To build an electronic commerce site, two complementary technologies are integrated: the Web and the **relational database management system (RDBMS)**. The Web portion of the construction—called the **front-end**—allows dynamic interchange between the customer and the business. Often, it is the first experience a customer has with a business and is the foundation on which the customer forms attitudes and perceptions. The front-end must be attractive, appealing, concise, and informative—a daunting task for many electronic commerce designers.

The strength of the Web is based on the concept of **hypertext**, a term first coined by Ted Nelson, currently project professor, Keio Shonan Fujisawa Campus, Japan, and invented by Tim Berners-Lee.

Figure 2-3

Simple Electronic Commerce Web Database Construction Model

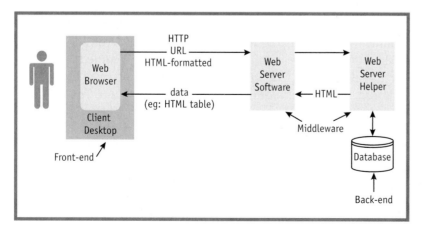

Hypertext is the logical connectivity between computers and text, allowing a computer to interface with text through a system of cross-references to be followed in a nonlinear way. **Hypermedia**, an extension of hypertext, includes graphics, audio, and other multimedia forms. The Web is made up of hypertext and hypermedia that can understand the numerous information-retrieval protocols in use on the Internet. Most important to electronic commerce, the Web provides a single, consistent user interface to both business and customer.

The Back-End Introduction: RDBMS

The **back-end** of the electronic commerce design consists of the database, which must be updated, queried, and modified according to the interaction with the customer and the dynamic data needed by the front-end. The back-end must support three main functions: (1) gathering information, (2) storing information, and (3) processing information. The database, usually an RDBMS, provides an efficient way for the electronic commerce construction to implement these functions.

Middleware Introduction

The key link between the Web and the database is called **middleware**. In the Web database construction, the middleware is the general term used to describe the programming that glues the construction together. **Windows Common Gateway Interface**, or **Windows CGI**, is one type of middleware that defines how a Web server and the external program of the customer communicate with each other. Specifically, CGI determines how information will be transferred between the Web server and the CGI program. It also defines what information will be supplied by the Web server to the CGI program as well as what information can be returned to the Web server. Additionally, CGI will determine the formats used by the Web server to supply the information to the CGI program. The CGI program can be written in any programming language, most often in C++, C#, Perl, Java, PHP, or Visual Basic. CGI programs have been historically the most common way for Web servers to interact dynamically with the customers of a business. The interaction is usually prompted by the completion of **HTML forms** by the client that use a CGI program to process the form's data upon submission. An HTML form is the front-end of the Web database construction used to gather customer input. It is also very common to use CGI to provide dynamic feedback for customers using scripts or programs—Java applets, JavaScripts, VBScripts, or ActiveX controls—that run on the customer's machine rather than the Web server. These technologies are known collectively as client-side, while the use of CGI is a server-side technology, since the processing occurs on the Web server. One limitation is that each time a CGI script is executed a new process is started. For busy Web sites, this can minimize performance of an electronic commerce construction and noticeably slow down the performance of the Web server.

Another popular type of middleware is **Active Server Pages (ASP)**. Like CGI, ASP allows the necessary interaction between the Web front-end and the database back-end. And also like CGI, ASP can generate HTML and pass it to the browser to be viewed by the customer. Created by Microsoft, ASP is easier to code in a Windows environment than CGI. It also provides better solutions for Web database constructions running on Windows platforms. As with CGI, ASP applications can incorporate HTML pages and forms, various scripts, and ActiveX controls. Figure 2-4 shows the interaction between each component in the construction.

Both CGI and ASP are popular forms of middleware used in today's electronic commerce constructions. Speed and the rapid application development environment—crucial to electronic

Figure 2-4

The Interaction of the Three Components of the Electronic Commerce Construction

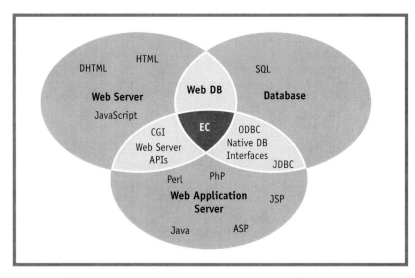

commerce—stand out as important factors in determining the middleware of the construction. The time required for taking an electronic commerce construction from concept to implementation is as critical as the overall efficiency of that construction. Both CGI and ASP support not only rapid application development but an environment of easy debugging and a wealth of technical support. Another benefit of using either CGI or ASP middleware is the minimal capacity needed on the server machine. If that machine is equipped with as little as 64 MB of RAM, the performance demands tend to be negligible when weighed against the overall performance of the electronic commerce construction.

Other types of electronic commerce middleware include standard CGI or Web **server application programming interface (Server API)**. A server API is the method prescribed by the server software by which requests to the construction can be made by various operating systems or application software. Server API, such as *ISAPI* or *NSAPI*, is a more efficient solution than CGI or ASP, but one that is also more difficult to implement. Another increasingly popular solution is to use **Java servlets**. Servlets are small programs that run on the server, as opposed to applets that run on the client.

Another technology used in Web database constructions is **Java Server Pages (JSP)**, a dynamic scripting middleware. It allows special tags to be embedded into the Web file such as HTML or **extensible markup language (XML)**. These tags provide a way to access server-side Java components from the Web pages. JSP is basically an ASP clone and like ASP, is a server-side technology. It does not allow any client-side validation. The suffix of a JSP file traditionally ends with .jsp to indicate to the Web server that the file is a JSP file. Though JSP files actually get compiled into servlets, there are two key benefits to electronic commerce that support the use of JSP:

- *An HTML focus:* JSP adds functionality to HTML used in Web database constructions.
- *Ease of change and modification:* The Web server can compile the JSP into a servlet and run it.

The current debate is over whether electronic commerce developers should use JSP or ASP. Although ASP is complex, it supports multiple scripting languages as well as Microsoft's ActiveX. However, JSP has had the advantage of late arrival to the market and has been able to bypass many of the contrivances and inconveniences associated with ASP. Orion server software tested both JSP and ASP with simple dynamic and static output as well as Session and Application variables. JSP was tested with Orion Web server software; ASP with IIS 5.0 on Windows 2000 Advanced Server. **Web server software**, also called Web servers, are programs that use the client/server model and HTTP to serve files back and forth from the front-end to the back-end of the Web database construction. As seen in Figures 2-5 and 2-6, both were tested for speed—the time to last byte where the time was based on how long an average user would have to wait until the entire page loaded— and capacity—the number of requests the server could serve per second. Orion concluded that JSP outperformed ASP both in speed, measured by response time, and capacity.

New types of middleware in the electronic commerce construction are appearing rapidly. As electronic commerce continues to grow, so will the supporting technologies and ways in which designers build the front-end, middleware, and back-end of the construction.

Figure 2-5

Orion's JSP Versus ASP Performance Benchmarks: Capacity

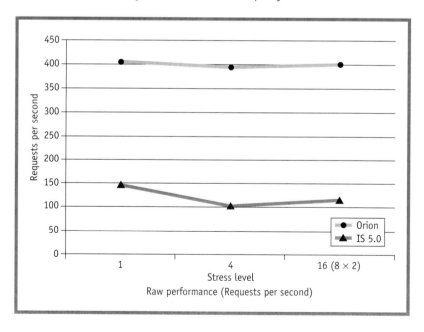

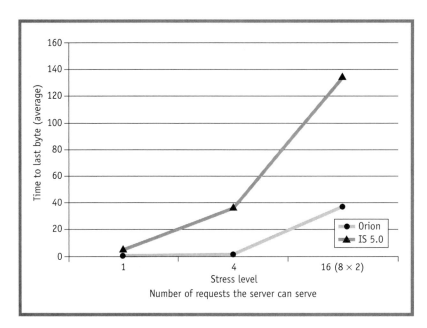

Figure 2-6

Orion's JSP Versus ASP Performance Benchmarks: Speed as Measured by Response Time

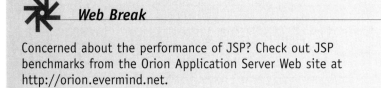

Web Break

Concerned about the performance of JSP? Check out JSP benchmarks from the Orion Application Server Web site at http://orion.evermind.net.

2.2 The Front-End of the Construction and Elements of the Web

The front-end of the electronic commerce construction begins the functionality of the overall design by contributing to the development of the model. Such functionality is not limited to a particular computer hardware or software platform because the elements of the Web, the client and the server, are not. Three communication standards that allow the different hardware and software platforms to communicate with each other enable the interaction between the electronic commerce construction elements to take place: (1) Transmission Control Protocol/Internet Protocol, (2) Hypertext Markup Language, and (3) Hypertext Transfer Protocol. In general terms, the computer-to-computer communication of the Web database construction is handled by the **IP protocol**, the method used to send data from one computer on the Internet to another. In most cases, TCP will move the data from the hardware level to the software level for the software-to-software communication. Once the data have been moved to the software level, the server software and other software packages themselves will provide their own protocols for communication. This is usually handled by HTTP, or in the case of encrypted communication, Secure Sockets Layer.

Figure 2-7 depicts the Web database construction communication standards model. The hardware host opens a TCP/IP connection to exchange data between software programs. Once the TCP/IP connection is opened, the Web server software communicates via HTTP or SSL. The actual data exchanged may or may not be encrypted.

Secure Sockets Layer (SSL) is the industry-standard method for protecting Web communications. Developed by Netscape Communications Corporation, it encrypts data using digital certificates. A digital certificate is similar to a credit card. It is used by crediting authorities to establish identity and authentication. The SSL security protocol provides data encryption, server authentication, message integrity, and optional client authentication for a TCP/IP connection. SSL capability is activated simply by installing a digital certificate because SSL is built into all major browsers and Web servers.

SSL comes in two strengths, 40-bit and 128-bit, which refer to the length of the "session key" generated by every encrypted transaction. The longer the key, the more difficult it is to break the encryption

Figure 2-7

Web Database Constructions Communication Standards

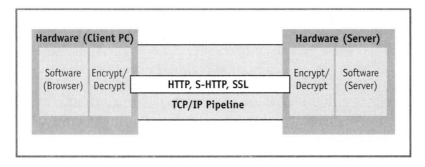

code. Most browsers support 40-bit SSL sessions. However, by using 128-bit sessions, Web database construction developers are able to encrypt transactions trillions of times stronger than the 40-bit sessions. Global businesses that require international transactions for their electronic commerce transactions can use global server certificates program to offer strong encryption to their customers.

 Web Break

Visit Security Center by VeriSign at http://www.verisign.com. The site gives businesses access to a wealth of security resources, products, technologies, and news. Visit their Web site for the latest information about Web security. When it comes to protecting the business and its customers on the Web, you can never be too careful.

TCP/IP

Transmission Control Protocol/Internet Protocol (TCP/IP) is the oldest of these communication standards. TCP and IP were developed by the U.S. Department of Defense in the early 1980s to connect a number of different networks designed by different vendors into a network of networks that later became known as the Internet. By 1983, they were the standard protocol suite. The IP component of TCP/IP provides routing from the local or enterprise network, to regional networks, and ultimately to the Internet. TCP/IP was initially successful because it delivered basic services such as file transfer, electronic mail, and remote logon across a very large number of client and server systems.

TCP ensures that the data are removed from the network-connected computer and delivered to the receiving application in the correct sequence. TCP also ensures that the messages are assembled correctly at the other end of transport. If errors, such as message degradation or the loss of some packets, have occurred during transport, TCP will notify the senders so they will know to resend. Optimization of the network bandwidth is also a TCP task. TCP does this by controlling the flow of information dynamically, slowing it down as network traffic becomes congested.

IP is the **connectionless** protocol that gateways use to identify networks and paths to networks and hosts. It handles the routing of data across the vast network from one computer to another and among the nodes on those networks. The term connectionless refers to "state." It is used to describe communication in which a connection is made and terminated for each message that is sent. IP is connectionless as well as **stateless**. Computers are inherently stateful in operation. Therefore, connectionless and stateless are terms used in the context of a particular set of interactions, not to describe how computers work in general. IP divides Web database construction messages into packets. The numerical counterparts of domain names such as www.aw.com are called *IP addresses*—unique sets of four period delimited octets that represent individual hosts on specific networks. A TCP/IP octet is a number between 0 and 255. An example of an IP address is 28.46.3.77. In this example 77 is the name of the computer that is located on network 3 on host 46 of network 28.

IP is often described as a connectionless protocol because of how it breaks single messages into packets, one is responsible for transversing the network, based on changing traffic congestion and the IP protocol. When a message arrives at an IP router, the router decides where to send it next. There is no concept of a meeting or time period devoted to the messaging activity or even of a preselected path for the message traffic. Routers can send data along the path of least resistance regardless of local network traffic congestion.

HTML

Like TCP/IP, HTML is a standard that enables interaction between electronic commerce components. HTML utilizes markup tags that define a Web document in terms of elements—fundamental components of a text document structure that includes heads, tables, paragraphs, and lists. **HTML tags** are codes that are used used to "mark up" the elements of a file for the client's browser. Elements can contain plain text, other elements, or both. HTML markup tags consist of a left angle bracket (<), a tag name, and a right angle bracket (>). Tags are usually paired (<H1> and </H1>) to start and end the tag instruction. The end tag looks like the start tag except a slash (/) precedes the text within the brackets. Some elements may include an attribute, which is additional information that is included inside the start tag. For example, the alignment of images (top, middle, or bottom) can be specified by including the appropriate attribute with the image source HTML code.

HTML is not case sensitive (it can be in upper or lower case letters), nor is it hardware/software platform dependent, although not all tags are supported by all Web browsers. If a browser does not support a tag, it will simply ignore it; though, any text placed between a pair of unknown tags will still be displayed. Consequently, when building electronic commerce sites, designers often make available different versions, such as a text-only or table-based version, so that their Web pages will accommodate all types of clients. Designers also often include a link on their construction to the public domain versions of Web clients that support the needed HTML enhancements. Appendix A gives a brief overview of HTML tags and techniques to create HTML documents.

 Web Break

To find out more about HTML, check Appendix A, or visit Berkeley Digital Library SunSITE on the Web at http://sunsite.berkeley.edu/Web/basictags.html for a basic set of HTML tags.

HTTP

Hypertext Transfer Protocol (HTTP) is often described as the protocol that enables electronic commerce—having the lightness and speed necessary for dynamic Web database constructions. HTTP sends the data from the software program on one computer, through the network and reassembles it on another computer at the other end. TCP/IP enables Internet communication, whereas HTTP enables Web communication. However, Web browsers and Web servers must transfer more data than is required in network navigation. For example, browser and server software must understand the exchange process necessary for multimedia Web documents. This process can be very complex, and the different types of software must speak their own standard protocols to help them exchange these files as well as understand meta-information about those files. To accomplish this daunting task, Web browsers and servers use the HTTP protocol.

HTTP is a generic, stateless object-oriented protocol that may be used for many similar tasks such as name servers, and distributed object-oriented systems, by extending the commands, or **methods**, used. A stateless protocol is one where there is no record of previous interactions, and each interaction request is handled based entirely on the information accompanying the request. The Internet's basic protocol, IP, is another example of a stateless interaction. With IP, each packet travels entirely on its own without reference to any other packet. A feature of HTTP is the negotiation of data representation, allowing systems to be built independently of the development of new advanced representations. Often a Web server is called an HTTP server. The Web client communicates to the Web server by sending HTTP messages through the TCP/IP requesting specific documents housed on the server. The request is the sending, by the client, of a request message to the server. The response is the sending, by the server, of a response to the client. In this manner, the client may also send an HTTP message to the server with user-specified information.

HTTP uses **Multipurpose Internet Mail Extensions (MIME)** to describe the transfer and format of the software files in order to maintain their format and integrity on the Web, which consists of millions of hyperlinked files, each of which may contain multiple links pointing to other files in the network. However, because the Web is used to deliver files of all types—for example, audio, video, or text—Web browsers and servers need some way of defining what is being linked and transported. The relationship between HTTP and MIME can be seen in Figure 2-8. HTTP uses MIME headers for this task. The header defines the meta-information about the document and the session. MIME type is specified in the content-type field. The header will specify a file's type. Table 2-1 shows MIME type and subtypes.

MIME is the primary mechanism used by HTTP to determine how a Web browser can download and display the content correctly. Providing a standardized way to represent and encode a large vari-

Figure 2-8

The Relationship Between HTTP and MIME

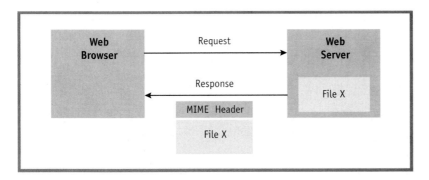

Table 2-1   *MIME Type and Subtype*

MIME Type	MIME Subtype
Application/msword	doc
Application	pdf
Application/postscript	ai eps ps
Application/powerpoint	ppt
Audio/x-pn-realaudio	ram rm ra
Audio	mpeg
Audio/x-wav	wav
Image	gif
Image	jpeg
Image	bmp
Multipart	form-data
Multipart	mixed
Text	html
Text/plain	txt
Video/x-msvideo	avi
Video/x-sgi-movie	movie
X-World/x-vrml	wrl vrml

ety of media or data types, MIME can identify the type of document being sent to the Web browser. Examples of MIME types and subtypes include XML, video/mpeg, video/quicktime, image/gif, text/html, text/plain, or text/richtext.

If a Web server were to send a document of MIME type

```
Content-type: application msword
```

the software would understand to open a Word file and load the document. Other information found in the header is described in Table 2-2.

2.3 HTTP and Client/Server Interaction

HTTP uses the URL standardized addressing method, keeping interaction between the Web server and the client at a minimum. The URL is a unique identifying address that uses the following syntax:

```
protocol://host[:port]/absolute_path
```

Table 2-2   *HTTP Header Information*

Header	Description
Accept	Determines what types of media output the client can handle.
Authorization	Determines whether or not the user has permission to access a secure area.
Content-encoding	Determines that the message body is encrypted, compressed, or encoded.
Content-type	Indicates the media type of the information in the message body.
Content-length	Determines the number of bytes in the message body for requests with a message body.
Date	Indicates the date and time of a request if the request has a message body.
From	Provides the e-mail address of the user using the client if it is available.
If-modified-since	Tells the server not to deal with the request if the document has not been modified since a given time.
MIME-version	Determines the MIME version used to generate the message body.
Pragma	Contains any additional information that the client wishes to specify to the server.
Referer	Indicates the URL of the page from which the request was made. (This request header is misspelled in the protocol itself.)
User-agent	Determines the name and version number of the Web browser making the request.

HTTP defines the communication method needed to access the document with the protocol portion of the URL. The host portion of the URL specifies the Internet host domain name, or IP address, in dotted-decimal form. This form consists of four bytes, each one ranging from 0 to 255, for example 24.28.233.33. A default IP address is 0.0.0.0. The port portion of the URL specifies the host port on which the Web server is listening for requests. Port is the logical connection place specifying the way a client program identifies another computer on the network. This portion is optional if the Web server is listening for client requests on TCP port 80. The absolute path indicates the exact location of the requested document on the host server. Usually, the Web server will identify the absolute path as the directory path leading to the file containing the requested information. Using Web server software mapping features, all of the default location or part of the location can be reconfigured in the Web server's configuration. In the example below, the protocol is http, the host is www.awl.com, and the absolute path is cseng.

http://www.awl.com/cseng/

Client/Server Interaction in HTTP

The client side interaction in HTTP can be seen in the example of requesting a document from the server.

- Link is clicked.
- Client accepts the input.
- Client translates it into an acceptable query to send it to the server.
- Client searches services to find the proper port number at which to contact the server.
- Client encapsulates the query within HTTP packet and sends it to server at the proper port number.

HTTP daemon (httpd) is the generic name given to a Web server. Quite a few are available. Web servers provide several scripting and programming interfaces, the most well known of which is the Common Gateway Interface (CGI).

The server side is prompted to perform the following actions:

- Server httpd is listening to the port.
- httpd server receives the packet and interprets the query.
- httpd server opens and reads the document/file.
- httpd server sends the file back to the client over the network.

The client side performs the following actions upon receiving the document from the server.

- Client reviews the document and caches it in disk or memory.
- Connection between the client and server gets closed.
- Client displays the information to user and may launch viewers to do so.

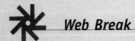 *Web Break*

Visit the World Wide Web Consortium at http://www.w3.org/ Servers.html and explore their list of many varieties of Web server software to serve different forms of data.

HTTP is currently in version 1.1. The major difference between version 1.0 and 1.1 is the latter's support for persistent connections. Either complex HTTP requests or simple messages can be sent by the client to the Web server. The HTTP request method specifies the location of the requested resource. ProtocolVersion is supplied to ensure that the Web server knows how to handle the request. More detailed HTTP requests may also include header fields and customer-entered data that the Web server may need to complete the request. There are three types of request methods generally supported by HTTP Web servers: (1) GET, (2) HEAD, and (3) POST. The HTTP request methods interact with TCP/IP and HTML as shown in Figure 2-9.

The HTTP GET Request Method

The **HTTP GET request method** is the fastest and simplest method for retrieving information specified in the URL absolute path request parameter. The request is sent with a first line containing the method to be applied to the object requested, the identifier of the object, and the protocol version in use, followed by further encoded information in the header. Using this example, the following GET request method will return the Addison-Wesley computer science page (English version) on the www.aw.com host on the default TCP port 80.

```
GET / cseng / HTTP/ 1.1 <ENTER>
```

Figure 2-9

The Interaction Between TCP/IP, HTTP, and HTML in the Electronic Commerce Construction

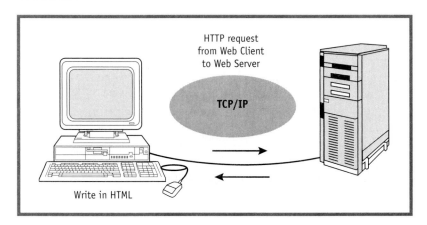

A conditional form of GET can be used to reduce network usage. With this method, the request message will also include an If-Modified-Since header field and a date value, and the Web server will return the specified document only if that document has been modified since the date listed in the header. This conditional request method allows a client to store documents *locally* when they are retrieved for the first time and reload them only if they have changed. This technique is referred to as **document caching**. An early relationship of the Web server, HTTP requests, and electronic commerce can be seen in Figure 2-10.

The HTTP HEAD Request Method

The **HTTP HEAD request method** is most often used by the client to test the validity and availability of an information resource. Although it is similar to the GET method, the Web server will return only the header information, not the actual document.

The HTTP POST Request Method

The **HTTP POST request method** is utilized by a client to interpret existing information resources that reside on a server or to supply supplemental data to a Web server. CGI is a common standard used by many Web servers to make the data transferred by the client

Figure 2-10

The Early Relationship of the Web Server to the Electronic Commerce Construction

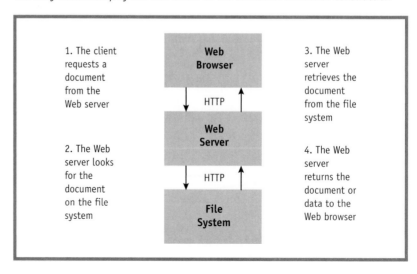

available to an executable script or program. The POST method can also be used to provide keywords for searching databases, for data mining, or for adding or updating database records.

2.4 The Integral Nature of the Web Server to Web Database Constructions

Historically, Web servers allowed clients to serve HTML content over the Internet. This was a static relationship where, upon receipt of a client's request for a Web page, the server would map that URL to a local file on the host server. It would then load the file and serve it to the client across the network, again using HTTP.

Today, Web servers do much more than just serve static content. And though the success, or failure, of an electronic commerce construction is often attributed to the site's content or design, it is often more appropriate to look to the Web server. Keep in mind that Web server is software that is continuously cycling, or looping, waiting for requests by a client for documents over the network. It will categorize and parse the request, classify it, and take appropriate actions. These actions may be executing a script, returning a document, or accessing an RDBMS. There are many Web server softwares available on the market today. The choices range from commercial products that are fully supported to free software, or freeware. Figure 2-11 lists some of the most common Web server software selection criteria used by businesses today.

Figure 2-11

Web Server Software Selection Criteria

- Ease of installation and configuration
- Performance
- Scalability
- Reliability
- Availability of support
- Compatibility with existing technology
- In-house familiarity and expertise
- Documentation

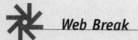
Web Break

Visit the WWW Resource Center on the Web at http://www.
mudhole. spodnet.uk.com/~imp/authoring/resource/servers/.
This site provides an extensive listing with active links to currently available Web server software.

2.5 Web Database Processing Architectures

In any Web environment, change is inevitable and technology is
constantly evolving into new forms and architectures. Interestingly
enough, the Web is a technology that propagates other technologies
that have become a part of the Web itself. Among these Web-related
technologies, the oldest and perhaps the one that is still the most utilized today is database construction.

But why construct a database? The pressures of today's businesses, the pace of data acquisition, continuous quality improvement,
cost containment, and gaining or maintaining competitive edge are
but a few reasons. Today, more than ever, the collection, analysis,
and discerning interpretation of data are essential for businesses to
survive and flourish. A well-designed data system can increase market reach, ensure compliance with regulatory requirements, serve
business interests, help use resources more efficiently, spot emerging
trends, and most importantly, improve customer relations. The combination of data mining, database management, and a Web interface
for connectivity are the essentials needed to harness the power of
electronic commerce.

Over the past few years, a number of competing methods for
building electronic commerce with Web database constructions have
appeared, broadening the number of technologies available for providing active, dynamic content on the Web. These include the
following:

- Web Server APIs, like ISAPI (for Microsoft Internet Information
  Server, Microsoft's Personal Web Servers, and Deerfield's
  WebSite), WSAPI (for Deerfield's WebSite), and NSAPI (for
  Netscape servers).

- Client-side scripts, such as those written in VBScript or JavaScript.
- Server-side includes, which allow special markers to be inserted into an HTML page. When the page is sent to the browser, these markers are replaced with dynamic data.
- Server-side scripts.

Each of these technologies can help a business in reaching the goals of electronic commerce. However, what is most important is that the technology provides a set of features that adequately addresses the needs of the application to be developed and that those features are reasonably accessible given the level of skill or expertise of the designer.

Each of the practical alternatives for developing electronic commerce with Web database constructions must be assessed according to certain criteria. Here are a few of them:

- *Flexibility and power:* The extent to which a Web database construction can accommodate diverse and complex requirements.
- *Developer expertise:* The level of expertise required to learn and master the technology.
- *Development and testing time:* The length of time required to create a fully tested, robust database construction.
- *Adaptability to change:* The ease with which an existing construction can be modified to reflect the changing needs of a business.
- *Life-cycle cost:* The cost of creating, maintaining, and modifying a database construction throughout its lifetime. Such a cost varies directly with the designer's expertise required to create it, the development and testing time needed to deploy it, and its adaptability to change.
- *Operational risk:* The extent to which the construction errors are capable of compromising the server and the entire site.
- *CPU overhead:* The degree to which the construction developed using a particular technology consumes more computer resources than constructions developed with competing technologies.
- *Compatibility:* The extent to which constructions developed for use on a particular server can be run on servers from other vendors that were developed for the same platform.

2.6 The Benefits and Challenges of Web Database Construction

Part of the proliferation of electronic commerce can be attributed to the benefit to business of using Web database constructions as part of a corporate strategy. Once deployed, well-designed database constructions can be immediately accessible from anywhere in the world and can aid businesses in overcoming performance and scalability limitations associated with traditional two-tier client/server applications. Since the RDBMS is centrally located on the business Web or application server, ongoing maintenance and enhancements can be considerably reduced. And since the RDBMS logic resides on the server rather than on the client, the cumbersome and often complex task for the business of deploying information to many clients is significantly reduced in time, and often eliminated completely. In certain business environments, the Web database construction can be run to the business' advantage on **thin clients**, network devices that utilize older and less powerful client workstations reducing hardware and software costs to the company.

Major challenges involved in utilizing Web database constructions include scalability, where businesses can encounter highly variable and potentially huge transaction peak loads. The evolving nature of Web technology is a constant challenge. Developing large, mission critical electronic commerce constructions can be difficult when standards and technology change so rapidly. Most often cited by both customers and businesses alike is the challenge of security. Also, when Web database constructions are needed to work with existing legacy systems, the challenge of creating interfaces can add both complexity and cost to the development process.

2.7 Client-Side Technologies

Client-side computing is run on the client computer rather than the Web server. The functionality of Web database constructions can be extended by executing some code segments directly on the client's computer. Client-side technologies can provide some type of client interface, such as a form with validation or a set of controls. Well-planned and well-designed client-side programs can provide several benefits to electronic commerce, including an improvement in the overall construction's responsiveness and the release of the Web server for other tasks. Limitations of client-side computing include potential security exposure inherent in the script code runtime interpreter engines that are needed to execute Web scripting language programs. A **script** is a synonym for a small portion of a program. Fundamentally, it is a set of instructions that take place automatically when a script is run. Macros, functions, or commands, are other words for scripts.

Typically, client-side computing performs one or more of the following tasks:

- Validates data submitted by the client.
- Performs back-end processing, such as updating a database or a spreadsheet.
- Retrieves data from some source, like a database, to transmit to the client.
- Builds pages on the fly to display on the client's browser.

Examples of client-side computing include VBScript or JavaScript subroutines embedded into an HTML Web page. Such a page will run on the client's computer when the Web page is downloaded. Microsoft's ActiveX can also be used in the model to send programs from the server to the client's browser. **Client-side scripts (CSS)** are an alternative to CGI. Web pages that incorporate CSS that was developed using such languages as VBScript or JavaScript have been offered as at least a partial replacement for CGI. Since client-side scripts consist of static text until they are received and interpreted by the browser, they cannot be used to retrieve remote data from the server or the server's network or to perform back-end processing of the data transmitted by the server. They can, however, be used for data validation as well as building pages on the fly on a client's browser. Overall, client-side programs offer flexibility. They can be written in many languages and run on many platforms. The primary advantages of client-side computing are the abilities to enhance user interfaces, improve performance, and implement solutions using back-end data. See Figure 2-12 for a description of client- and server-side technologies.

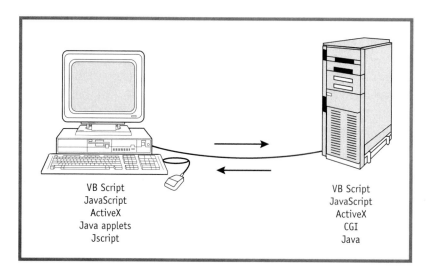

VB Script
JavaScript
ActiveX
Java applets
Jscript

VB Script
JavaScript
ActiveX
CGI
Java

Figure 2-12
Client-side and Server-side Technologies

2.8 Server-Side Technologies

In server-side technologies, the server rather than the client handles the control of the program, or script. When server-side scripts are run, they are executed on the server and standard HTML Web pages are returned from the server to the client's browser, which then only has to display the results. There is no underlying script used to generate the Web pages. Server-side computing can be used to add interactivity to electronic commerce constructions. Because the computing is done server-side or run on the server, it is useful for such tasks as working with a back-end database, providing server authentication, and managing subscriptions.

CGI, ASP, and JSP are examples of server-side computing. Another example is **server side includes (SSI)**, one of the oldest forms of providing dynamic content on the Web. SSI is highly server-dependent and relies on the inclusion of special markers in the HTML document. When the server receives a request, it replaces the markers with the value of variable data before sending the page to the client. One of the advantages of SSI is its relative ease of use. Because of this, it is distinctly a low-end electronic commerce development methodology that relies extensively on the implementation of SSI on the server that a particular Web database construction is using. A number of Web servers, like Microsoft's IIS, do not support

SSI. Version 2.1 of Deerfield's WebSite server offers support for SSI, including full-strength 164-bit encryption technology. SSI is strictly limited in the extent to which it adds active content to Web pages. Depending on the implementation of SSI on a particular server, it can be used for the following:

- *Server state variables:* SSI can be used to retrieve information about the server—for example, the server software, the name of the server, or the current date and time on the server.
- *Client request information:* It can include information, such as the name of the browser or the request method, as well as the request that the browser submitted to the server.
- *Resource information:* It can gather basic file system information—for example, the date an HTML document was last updated or its file size—to include in an HTML page.
- *File contents:* It can insert the entire contents of a file into the HTML text stream. This makes it possible to include a uniform header or footer (or a toolbar) on each of a site's Web pages.
- *Hit counters:* It can maintain a hit counter depicting the number of visitors for a particular page and include its current value within the page.
- *Output from a CGI program:* It can be used to include the output generated by a CGI application within an HTML page; otherwise, if a CGI application runs by itself, it must output an entire page to the client.

A relatively recent development in server-side computing is **server-side scripting (SSS)**. This means that the HTML page contains one or more embedded scripts that are executed at the server, and any output from the script is inserted into the HTML text stream. To this extent, server-side scripts sound very much like server-side includes. However, SSS has greater flexibility and power than CGI and server API applications. Unlike SSI, in which the script is only a marker that indicates where variable text is to be inserted, SSS is an integration tool that, in the case of ASP, can be used to control ActiveX server components. SSS can also be used to access assorted information from the server by using the server's object model. As a result, through the use of assorted add-on components, SSS is very similar in function to CGI applications.

The real potential of electronic commerce lies in the ability of Web servers to run programs behind the scenes and return the results of these programs to the user. CGI has been a common server-side

Identify the challenges Webvan faced doing business the electronic commerce way.

What Web database design considerations of electronic commerce constructions must be considered before moving a business online?

How can businesses best prepare themselves to be ready to meet these challenges of doing business in a virtual environment?

FOCUS ON ELECTRONIC COMMERCE

Can Webvan Deliver the Business?

Webvan was a full-service online retailer. So what made this online business different from any other? Webvan offered customers the ability to shop online and then have their items hand-delivered to their homes or offices at the day and time of their choosing. What were these items? Webvan sold everything from food to Foo Fighter CDs, said Connie Guglielmo of *Inter@ctive Week*.

Webvan entered its first test markets in Atlanta, Chicago, San Francisco, Sacramento, San Diego, Los Angeles, Portland, and Seattle in 2000. Offering groceries, drugstore items, pet items, and books as well as CDs, Webvan had a simple business plan: to deliver anything to anybody any day of the week. However, in order to build the home delivery network that would allow it to reach its $1 billion-per-year sales goal, Webvan first had to raise $1 billion. Another challenge was that it had to become more efficient at warehousing and same-day delivery than any company currently in the market. Webvan's former Chief Executive Officer George Shaheen identified Webvan's single greatest challenge was "to get you out of the brick-and-mortar grocery stores." Shaheen joined Webvan after leaving Andersen Consulting, where he served as president and CEO. Industry observers said Shaheen had vision and no fear. When asked to describe Webvan, he said, "Webvan is the infrastructure backbone for e-commerce." However, for an electronic

commerce business, Webvan was not always Web-savvy, said Guglielmo, who added that some customers had trouble adding items to their orders and others had found that locating goods on the site was cumbersome. "I'd give our Web site a B or B–," Shaheen said. "We know it's not as intuitive as it should be."

Webvan based its grandiose goals on the electronic commerce business model of GroceryWorks, but aimed for better logistics with highly automated megawarehouses stocking 50,000 different products and less handling of goods. The GroceryWorks model had less automation and smaller warehouses closer to customers. Some experts believed that Webvan had little to gain by automating, though an automated system could have made it easier to respond to customer complaints. Still, the operational, capital and mind-set challenges of electronic commerce were not easily dismissed. "The moving parts of this model are huge," Shaheen said. "It's a tremendously complex business. If it were easy, everyone would be doing it. We're changing the way America shops."

So what is the answer to the $1 billion question: Can Webvan deliver? It is, unfortunately, no. Though the company had made significant progress in reducing operating losses and burn rate, as well as improving the economics on each order delivered, the order volume declined considerably during the second quarter, ending June 30,

2001, accelerating the need for even more capital. Robert Swan, Webvan's Chief Executive Officer, said that in light of the tough climate for raising new funds and second-quarter order volume, a difficult decision was made to end all sales and deliveries effective immediately and to wind down the company's operations and sell assets in an orderly manner. After putting up a tough fight to survive, in July 2001, Webvan halted operations and filed for Chapter 11 bankruptcy protection. The company succumbed to the challenges of electronic commerce, laying off all of its 2,000 employees and placing a message on its Web site telling customers they would not be charged for orders already placed but not received. Electronic commerce will survive the failure of Webvan, but growth will come quite a bit slower because of it. The lessons learned by Webvan's failure in online business will become a staple of electronic commerce strategy textbooks for years to come.

Source: Connie Guglielmo, "Can Webvan deliver?" *Inter@ctive Week*, January 31, 2000; Kim Allen, "Webvan no longer bringing home bacon," *eBiz*, Tuesday, July 10, 2001.

computing technique. In the electronic commerce model, CGI is the "gateway" between the customer accessing the Web and the business. CGI's gateway offers a translation between the language the client speaks—usually HTML, DHTML, or XML—and any of the many languages spoken by the resources the client wants to utilize, such as SQL for RDBMS. CGI is neither a language nor an application software program, though typically we say that we write "CGI programs" or "CGI scripts" that perform the functions of the common gateway interface. CGI is a process or an interface that provides well-defined rules for creating these essential electronic commerce partnerships in the Web database construction. CGI scripts include the ability to display the current time or the number of users who have accessed a server. CGI can also include features that allow guest book entries and online questionnaires. In the electronic commerce model, it is used most often in the form of an online bookstore. CGI is often made available to a Web browser by HTML forms. The scripts then process the customer's input and pass the results, usually in the form of an HTML document, back to the Web server, which then sends the results to the Web client. CGI can be written in almost any language, including C++, C#, Perl, AppleScript, PHP, and Visual Basic.

A disadvantage of server-side computing is the toll it takes on server capacity. As electronic commerce continues to grow, the scenario of a Web server running out of memory from many simultaneous form processings and a multitude of dynamic page "hits" asking for returns is common. **Netscape Server Application Programming Interface (NSAPI)** and **Microsoft Internet Server Application Programming Interface (ISAPI)** have developed proprietary technologies to ease the load on Web servers from server-side computing traffic.

Table 2-3 evaluates the six electronic commerce development technologies discussed here. It indicates that despite the emergence of competing technologies CGI is viable as a flexible and powerful tool that at the same time is accessible to large numbers of developers and that permits applications to be developed quickly and efficiently. One of its major strengths is its compatibility across server platforms.

Other Components

An effective and complex Web database construction can be developed with the components discussed here. However, constantly changing technology means that an effective Web database construction designer must continuously assess the environment for new and better electronic commerce components. Some of the latest developments in the electronic commerce design still impact its overall architecture. Examples are scriptlets and extensible markup language (XML). Scriptlets are presently a Microsoft browser exclusive and therefore an option only when it can be guaranteed that all clients are using Internet Explorer 4.0 or a later version. XML is also pushed by Microsoft but is receiving an unusual amount of independent support.

A scriptlet is a cached HTML page, with possible object references, on the client that is used by many pages in a Web database

Table 2-3 *Server-Side Electronic Commerce Development Technologies Evaluated*

	CGI	API	CSS	SSI	SSS	ASP	JSP
Flexibility and Power	High	High	Medium	Low	High	High	High
Developer Expertise	Medium	High	Medium	Low	Medium	Medium	Medium
Development and Testing Time	High	High	Medium	Low	Medium	Medium	Medium
Adaptability to Change	High	Low	High	High	High	High	Medium
Life-Cycle Cost	Medium	High	Medium	Medium	Medium	Medium	Medium
Operational Risk	Low	High	Low	Low	Medium	Medium	Medium
CPU Overhead	High	Low	Low	Medium	High	High	High
Compatibility	High	Low	Low	Low	Low	Medium	Low

construction. Advantages of using scriptlets include reusability and lowered network traffic.

Like HTML, XML is subset of **Standard Generalized Markup Language (SGML)** and defines how related data can be transmitted across the Web in a standardized way. SGML is a standard for specifying the tag set and markup language of a particular document. It is not a language, but only a description of how to specify one. XML is very similar to HTML, using tags to describe the formatting in a Web page and enabling user-defined tags to describe the meta-structure of data with the actual instance data as it is transmitted between server and client.

 Web Break

Visit the World Wide Web Consortium (W3C) on the Web at http://www.w3.org/pub/WWW/TR/WD-xml.html to access the most recent draft of the XML standard. The W3C has developed specifications, guidelines, software, and tools to guide the Web to its full potential.

2.9 Assessment Techniques and Design Considerations

Electronic commerce would not be possible without the Web and the power of Web database constructions that allow the connectivity and reach needed for business and clients to interact. To maximize the power of electronic commerce, it is necessary to have **Web assessment tools** to ensure sound front-ends and design techniques.

Front-end assessment is based on the ability to quantify or measure a design. There are six key measurements, called the Reporter's Measures, that can be used to determine whether a front-end design is "good" or "bad": (1) *who*, (2) *what*, (3) *where*, (4) *when*, (5) *why*, and (6) *how*. Just as a reporter will ask each of these questions to ensure a news story is fully covered, so, too, will the Web site developer to ensure a quality site.

- *Who:* The designer must be sure to ascertain who is the intended audience of a site. Does the front-end of the construction reach the audience? Obviously, electronic commerce sites are built for an audience. Since every measurement of a Web site's success—hits, sales, click-throughs, customer comments, customer complaints, positive community—usually involves the audience then it is imperative that the designer develop a deeper understanding of this group and design a site that accommodates the audience. Understanding who users are, what they want to do, and how they tend to behave doesn't necessarily have to be a complicated process, but it does return the best results when approached systematically and consistently.

- *What:* Of the six Reporter's measurement methods, "what" may be the most crucial element to electronic commerce effectiveness and the construction's design. It is imperative that the Web site contain high-quality content that is designed to generate and hold the customer's attention. A business' Web site is the virtual front door—the first point of contact for potential customers, employees, and investors. The benefit of capturing interest and creating a professional image here should be obvious. Once the construction has captured the customer's attention, the next design consideration is to ensure that the site fully communicates the information and meets the needs of customers allowing them to choose the amount of information they want without being forced to page through, or "drill down through," information that is not of interest to them.

- *Where:* Unfortunately, there can be trade-offs between the goal of capturing attention and the "where" that involves other design considerations. While the creative use of color and images captures attention, inconsistent use of these elements can add confusion and make navigation of a Web site more difficult. Color, size, location standards, and standardization of icons or other images used for navigation make it much easier to navigate a Web site. This type of standardization does not substantially interfere with creative Web page design.

- *When:* There is a more serious trade-off when considering the element of "when"—the process of assessing when to use technology and just how much technology to use. Large and detailed graphic images and video clips can substantially enhance the ability of a Web page to capture a customer's attention and convey information. At the same time, extensive use of these features demands extensive amounts of data that must be sent to a customer's computer. The features that may interest one customer with the hardware and software to accommodate the technology may frustrate other customers with low-speed modems who must wait, perhaps for minutes, for the transfer of data that their browsers may ultimately be unable to display. The level of data that can be incorporated in a Web page without overwhelming older systems is constantly increasing, as hardware, software, and networking resources are upgraded over time. Appropriate "when" decisions require planning and a thorough understanding of the target market of a business. The designer must understand the types of computing resources the business' customers have and the level of sophistication they display in using them.

■ *Why:* The organizational structure of the "why" element of electronic commerce constructions is often complex. What a customer views as one Web site most often consists of a number of linked files. Links can move the customer to other locations within the same file or can transfer the user to other related files. The organization of a Web site is usually a hierarchical one. High-level pages serve as switchboards, allowing the customer to transfer to any of several more detailed pages. However, each Web page may contain multiple levels of detail along with navigational links that allow customers to move quickly to various sections within that one Web page.

A designer will continually be asking "why" during the design process. Theoretically, a Web construction of any degree of complexity could be placed in a single file containing as many links as needed to support navigation. However, this would make for a cumbersome Web site that would be difficult to manage effectively, and would require all customers to download this potentially huge document. So understanding why one location is more advantageous to the designer, customer, or business over another is very important in the process. Typically, each individual file or page in a Web application tends to incorporate about two levels of detail. The portion of the page that appears on the screen when it opens contains a brief discussion of the topic that is to be addressed and an outline of the subtopics addressed in this Web page. These outline items also serve as links to the point in the file where each subtopic is addressed. Of course, some of this information, including possibly the links to subtopics, might be presented in graphic form to stimulate customer interest. Following this introductory screen, the details of the subtopic information are presented in logical order. By scrolling through the document, the customer is able to efficiently read the entire document in logical order. At the same time, the customer who is interested only in a selected topic can quickly move to the detailed information about that topic.

■ *How:* "How" is measured in terms of "how secure" is the Web database construction. Most often cited by both customers and businesses alike is the challenge of security. For a large or complex electronic commerce site, it may be necessary to have substantially more than two levels of hierarchical detail. This can be accommodated by linking the subtopic level items of one file to another Web page, which contains still more detailed information and can, if necessary, link to still more detailed pages. It should be noted that Web page files having only the high-level, outline style information can also be used. Each link in the outline area simply links to another file. This is particularly popular for the highest-level pages of a large Web site encompassing many topic areas.

Table 2-4	*The Reporter's Measures for Web Assessment and Design Considerations*
Measure	Ask Yourself:
Who	*Who is the site's intended audience?* Measuring and preparing for this assessment element allows the designer to measure hits, sales, click-throughs, customer comments, customer complaints, positive community.
What	*What is the content that the site needs to communicate?* The content of the Web site must fully communicate the information to its customers and must capture the customers' attention. It is crucial that the message of the Web site is communicated in a manner that captures the customers' interest.
Where	*Where is the proper placement for each element of the design?* The Web page must be well organized with the information divided into logical categories and subcategories which allow the customer both to read through the full document in a sequential manner, and to selectively drill down into topics of particular interest to them. The location of elements should be standardized if appropriate.
When	*When the customer needs to get to a portion of the site, will the navigation be easy and clear to the customer?* The Web page must have an effective navigation scheme that allows the customer to move through a document sequentially or go directly to more detailed information about a topic of interest. At any level, it should always be possible to link directly back to the opening screen.
Why	*Why is this item necessary to the site?* There should be an economy both in the number of screens that a user must traverse to get to an item of interest and in the amount of data that the site sends to the customer's computer. The designer must remember the successful motto "keep it simple" in the electronic commerce design.
How	*How secure is the site?* All Web sites must have security measures sufficient to ensure that the Web site does not provide a means for hackers to access other organizational data. Passwords, encryption, and firewalls are among the forms of security commonly associated with Web sites.

Summary

- **Define Web database construction.** Web database constructions maximize the power of two complementary technologies that are integrated: the Web and the relational database management system (RDBMS). The Web portion of the construction—called the front-end—allows dynamic interchange between the customer and the business. The portion of the construction that links the Web and the database is called the middleware. There are many methods of creating dynamic electronic commerce Web database constructions. The three that are most commonly used are CGI, ASP, and JSP.

- **Describe the front-end of the construction and the elements of the Web.** The front-end is the first experience a customer has with a business and is the foundation on which the customer forms attitudes and perceptions about the business. The front-end must be attractive, appealing, concise, and informative—a daunting task for many electronic commerce designers. The elements of the Web are communication standards that allow the different hardware and software platforms to communicate with each other. They are TCP/IP, HTML, and HTTP.

- **Describe HTTP and client/server interaction.** HTTP uses the URL standardized addressing method, keeping interaction between the Web server and the client at a minimum. HTTP defines the communication method needed to access the document with the protocol portion of the URL. The HTTP request method specifies the location of the requested resource. There are three types of request methods generally supported by HTTP Web servers: (1) GET, (2) HEAD, and (3) POST.

- **Discuss the integral nature of the Web server to the electronic commerce construction.** Web servers do much more than just serve static content. And though the success, or failure, of an electronic commerce construction is often attributed to the site's content or design, it is often more appropriate to look to the Web server. Keep in mind that Web server is software that is a continuously looping, waiting for requests by a client for documents over the network. It will categorize and parse the request, classify it, and take appropriate actions. These actions may be executing a script, returning a document, or accessing an RDBMS. There are many Web server softwares available on the market today. The choices range from commercial products that are fully supported to freeware.

■ **List and describe the Web database processing architectures.** Over the past few years, a number of competing methods for building electronic commerce with Web database constructions have appeared, broadening the number of technologies available for providing active, dynamic content on the Web. These include the following:

1. Web Server APIs, like ISAPI (for Microsoft Internet Information Server, Microsoft's Personal Web Servers, and Deerfield's WebSite), WSAPI (for Deerfield's WebSite), and NSAPI (for Netscape servers).
2. Client-side scripts, like those written in VBScript or JavaScript.
3. Server-side includes, which allow special markers to be inserted into an HTML page. When the page is sent to the browser, these markers are replaced with dynamic data.
4. Server-side scripts.

■ **Discuss the benefits and challenges of Web database constructions.** The proliferation of electronic commerce can attest to the benefit to business of using Web database constructions as part of a corporate strategy. Once deployed, well-designed Web database constructions can be immediately accessible from anywhere in the world and can aid businesses in overcoming performance and scalability limitations associated with traditional two-tier client/server applications. Since the RDBMS is centrally located on the business Web or application server, ongoing maintenance and enhancements can be considerably reduced. And since the RDBMS logic resides on the server rather than on the client, the cumbersome and often complex task for the business of deploying information to many clients is significantly reduced in time and often eliminated completely. In certain business environments, the Web database construction can be run to the business' advantage on thin clients, network devices that utilize older and less powerful client workstations, reducing hardware and software costs to the company. Major challenges include scalability, where businesses can encounter highly variable and potentially huge transaction peak loads. The evolving nature of Web technology is a constant challenge. Developing large, mission critical electronic commerce applications can be difficult when standards and technology change so rapidly. The security of a

Web database construction is the feature most often cited by both customers and businesses alike. When Web database constructions are needed to work with existing legacy systems, the creation of interfaces can add both complexity and cost to the development process.

■ **Discuss client-side technologies or browser extensions and compiled browser programs.** Client-side computing is run on the client computer rather than the Web server. The functionality of a Web database construction can be extended by executing some code segments directly on the client's computer. Client-side technologies can provide some type of client interface, such as a form with validation or a set of controls. Well-planned and well-designed client-side programs can provide several benefits to electronic commerce, including an improvement in the overall construction's responsiveness and the release of the Web server for other tasks. Limitations of client-side computing include potential security exposure inherent in the script code runtime interpreter engines that are needed to execute Web scripting language programs.

■ **Discuss server-side technologies of scripting languages and compiled server programs.** In server-side technologies, the server rather than the client handles the control of the program, or script. When server-side scripts are run, they are executed on the server, and standard HTML Web pages are returned from the server to the client's browser. The client's browser then only has to display the results. There is no underlying script used to generate the Web pages. Server-side computing can be used to add interactivity to electronic commerce constructions. Because the computing is done server-side or run on the server, it is useful for such tasks as working with a back-end database, providing server authentication, and managing subscriptions. CGI and ASP are examples of server-side computing. Another example of server-side computing is server side includes (SSI), one of the oldest forms providing dynamic content on the Web. SSI is highly server-dependent and relies on the inclusion of special markers in the HTML document.

■ **Discuss Web assessment techniques and design considerations.** Electronic commerce would not be possible without the Web and the power of Web database constructions that allow the connectivity and reach needed for business and clients to interact. To maximize the power of electronic commerce, it is necessary to have sound Web database construction assessment and design techniques. Front-end assessment is based on the ability to quantify or measure a design. There are six key areas, called the Reporter's Measures, in which these electronic commerce constructions can be measured to determine whether the Web site is "good" or "bad": (1) who, (2) what, (3) where, (4) when, (5) why, and (6) how.

Chapter Key Terms

Active Server Pages (ASP)
back-end
client-side scripts (CSS)
connectionless
document caching
Extensible Markup Language (XML)
front-end
HTML tags
HTTP daemon (httpd)
HTTP GET request method
HTTP HEAD request method
HTTP POST request method
hypermedia
hypertext
Hypertext Markup Language (HTML)

Hypertext Transfer Protocol (HTTP)
Internet protocol (IP)
Java Server Pages (JSP)
methods
Microsoft Internet Server Application Programming Interface (ISAPI)
middleware
Multipurpose Internet Mail Extension (MIME)
Netscape Server Application Programming Interface (NSAPI)
relational database management system (RDBMS)
script

Secure Sockets Layer (SSL)
server application software programming interface (Server API)
server-side includes (SSI)
server-side scripting (SSS)
servlets
Standard Generalized Markup Language (SGML)
stateless
thin client
Transmission Control Protocol (TCP)
Web assessment tools
Web server software
Windows Common Gateway Interface (Windows CGI)

Review Questions

1. What is a Web database construction?

2. What elements of the Web interact with the front-end of the construction?

3. How does HTTP work with client/server interaction?

4. What are the three user request methods and how do they work?

5. Discuss several Web database processing architectures. What are advantages and limitations of each?

6. List and explain several benefits for the electronic commerce designer, the customer, and the business when using Web database constructions.

7. List and explain several challenges for the electronic commerce designer, the customer, and the business when using Web database constructions.

8. What are client-side technologies?

9. Discuss how browser extension and compiled browser programs are used in the electronic commerce model.

10. What are server-side technologies?

11. Discuss how scripting languages and compiled server programs are used in the electronic commerce model.

12. What are some other components that can be used in the Web database processing architecture?

13. Why is it important to assess Web design?

14. What are some methodologies used to assess Web design?

15. How can poor design of a Web database construction impact the customer? The business?

16. List and describe the criteria that can be used to assess a designer's alternatives for developing electronic commerce with Web database constructions.

17. What are the determining factors for choosing the middleware of the Web database construction?

18. List and describe Web database construction design alternatives.

19. List and describe some of the most common Web Server software selection criteria used by business today.

20. Define "script" and list some common examples.

Critical Thinking Using the Web

1. It is often said that Web database constructions add synergy to the business/customer relationship. Do you agree or disagree? Visit the following companies from Forbes' Global 500 list. Is there synergy there? Why or why not? Give specific examples from each Web site to justify your opinion.

- Royal Dutch/Shell Group at http://www.shell.com/royal-en/ 0,6091,,00.html

- Volkswagen at http://www.vw.com

- Nippon Telegraph & Telephone at http://www.ntt.co.jp/index_e.html

2. The growth of electronic commerce has been phenomenal. Investigate how governments are trying to handle this exciting new way of conducting business. Go to U.S. Government's electronic commerce site at http://www.ecommerce.gov/. Choose one article to read and write a report of 200 to 300 words describing in what ways the government is focusing on electronic commerce.

3. Browser extensions were introduced in Microsoft Internet Explorer 5.0. This client-side technology allows Web database designers to add functionality to the browser as well as enhance the customer's interface. Visit Microsoft's Web site at http://msdn. microsoft.com/workshop/browser/ext/ extensions.asp. Choose one of the browser extension tutorials listed on the page to work through. Create a step-by-step guide on how to use this technology. Using presentation software, share your step-by-step guide with your class.

Chapter Case Study

Albatross Records is a continuing case study that illustrates the process of building electronic commerce with Web database constructions. In Chapter 2, you will continue to investigate the appropriateness of Web database constructions as a methodology for Albatross Records to increase business. You will justify to Albatross Records your suggestions for choosing server-side technologies, client-side technologies, or a combination of both. Be sure to incorporate both the benefits and challenges from these technologies to Albatross Records. As you continue through the text, you will complete different facets of electronic commerce Web database construction, resulting in a complete Web site for Albatross Records.

Continue your electronic commerce plan for Albatross Records utilizing Web database construction and enabling technologies. Now it's your turn to do the following:

- Plan and discuss the electronic commerce architecture you will use for Albatross Records. Use Visio or another software tool to sketch your plan to show to the business.

- Discuss how information will move through the Albatross electronic commerce model. Be specific as you discuss the components of the Web database design. Use Visio or another software tool to sketch your plan to show to the business.
- Discuss the integral nature of the Web server to the electronic commerce design. How will this approach be advantageous to the Web database construction designer?
- Discuss HTTP and the client/server interaction in your design using the customer and business in your discussion.

3

Getting Started: Web Server Installation and Administration

Learning Objectives

Upon completion of this chapter, you will be able to

- Define Web server software
- Define WebSite Web server components
- Install Web server software
- Configure and maintain Web server software
- Test Web server software installation
- Define and describe Web server software security
- Describe three practical implementations of the electronic commerce theories and techniques discussed in the book

Online retailing is entering a new phase in its evolution. What was once an industry characterized by entrepreneurial dot.coms, targeting the discretionary spending of the Internet-savvy consumer, is fast becoming the domain of traditional retailers, selling both necessities and discretionary items to the broader population.

—Michael Silverstein, Senior Vice President,
Boston Consulting Group, April 2000

3.1 Introduction to Web Server Software

It can be difficult and confusing to understand Web servers—the term itself often being used for both hardware as well as software. When talking about Web server *software*, the designer is referring to the software that enables the electronic commerce construction to communicate between the front-end, middleware, and back-end. Web server software is therefore a major component of the electronic commerce architecture. Specifically, it allows the receipt of requests from the customer and responds to those requests, often allowing the business to serve content over the Internet using Hypertext Markup Language (HTML). Web server software accepts requests from customers' browsers, like Netscape and Internet Explorer, and then returns the appropriate documents. To do this, Web server software can use many types of client-server and server-side technologies including Common Gateway Interface (CGI), Server-Side Includes (SSI), Personal HomePage Tools (PHP), Active Server Pages (ASP), and Java Server Pages (JSP).

Web server software has also been both a catalyst for the astounding growth of electronic commerce and on the leading edge of the Internet revolution. Web servers no longer respond only to a client request, by retrieving static files. Where early Web servers, in most cases, did not read or otherwise process client-requested files, the Web servers of today are very adept at handling numerous simultaneous requests and delivering more quickly on these requests. As with most software, server software's functionality has continued to grow and the lines of just what a Web server does have become blurry and enhanced with other abilities. Web servers are now often marketed as **application servers**, also called **information servers**. Not only can they process extensive information, but they can interact with the client more like an application. Application servers allow dynamic interaction between the client and the server, and they can be integrated with a large number of current technologies. For example, embedded server-side scripting technologies such as ASP and the **open-source PHP** scripting language can be used with a Deerfield WebSite server. PHP is a freely available script language used primarily on Linux servers and is an alternative to Microsoft's ASP. In the most generic sense, this example of an alliance among technologies constitutes an application server. In the marketplace, however, an application server's definition is often more robust. The term is used to describe bundled solutions offered by a vendor, which have been marketed as containing all the component technologies a business would need to successfully implement electronic commerce.

 Web Break

PHP, a project of the Apache Software Foundation, is a server-side, cross-platform, HTML-embedded scripting language. As an open source, PHP can be used for commercial and/or noncommercial use without paying any fees to the Apache. To learn more about PHP and even take a PHP introductory tutorial, visit the PHP Group Web site at http://www.php.net/.

For discussion purposes, Web server software is usually divided into five general areas: (1) launch-related, (2) logging-related, (3) protocol support, (4) security, and (5) miscellaneous. Table 3-1 delineates the applicable subjects in each area.

Businesses decide to use Web server software for many reasons. One of the most common is for publishing information. When information is published on the Web, the ability to change the documents, incorporate multimedia elements, link to other sources of information, update and distribute information quickly, and create dynamic content becomes available where it was not with traditional paper-based publishing. CGI is an electronic commerce technology that, because of its simplicity and universality, continues to have wide appeal for developing dynamic pages. One reason for CGI's

Table 3-1	*The Five Discussion Areas of Web Server Software*			
Launch-related	Logging-related	Protocol Support	Security	Miscellaneous
CGI	VBScript log entries	Access to server state	Access limitations	HTTP proxy server
IP address	Log files	API	Passwords	Direct link to a DBMS
Directory roots	Multiple logs	Image-map handling	S-HTTP	Maintenance
Virtual server	Performance measurement logs		Configurable user groups	HTTP headers
	Tracking individual users		Supports **SSL**	**ISAPI**
				TCP

continued popularity is that most Web servers natively support CGI. Web database constructions implemented with CGI are also relatively easy to port across HTTP software and platforms. CGI was the first popular technology that allowed a Web server to interact with an external computer program. Now, in the evolution of Web servers, embedded server-side scripting technologies like ASP and PHP have appeared where the processing code is inserted directly into the Web page itself. **PHP Hypertext Preprocessor**, like ASP, is a server-side, HTML embedded scripting language created in 1994 by Rasmus Lerdorf. PHP version 3 (PHP3) was written by Zeev Suraski and Andi Gutmans in 1997. The current version of PHP is version 4 Beta. **PHP4** is often shipped standard with Web servers, which support both of the most popular electronic commerce constructions: server-side and client-side technologies.

When Web server software first came on the market, its functionality was limited to serving simple HTML documents and images. At the most basic level, the task of the software is to serve. When the Web server receives a request for a Web page such as

```
http://www.awl.com/index.htm
```

it maps that URL to a local file on the host server. In this case, the file

```
index.html
```

is located on the host file system. The server then loads the `index.htm` file from the host server's disk and serves it out across the network to the client's Web browser. Using HTTP, this exchange is overseen by both the Web browser and Web server software. The Web server's return of a static file to the Web client is shown in Figure 3-1.

However, static pages being served over the Web are not enough for electronic commerce. The power of Web database constructions is in the dynamic communication between client and server. In today's Web database constructions, the Web server runs programs locally and transmits the output through the Web server to the client browser that initiated the dynamic content request. Often, the client does not even realize that the content is dynamic. The middleware—the software that allows the dynamic passing of data from the client to the server and back again—may be as simple as a CGI Web server extension protocol. Figure 3-2 illustrates a simple Web browser request of a dynamically generated page from a CGI program.

Web servers are designed to accept network connections from browsers, retrieve content from servers, run local programs, and transmit data back to clients. The ultimate goal is to perform this networked communication as quickly as possible. However, these tasks are not always compatible. For example, a simple Web server could follow the logic below:

- Accept connection.
- Generate static or dynamic content and return to browser.
- Close connection.
- Accept connection.

Figure 3-1

How Web Server Software Returns a Static File

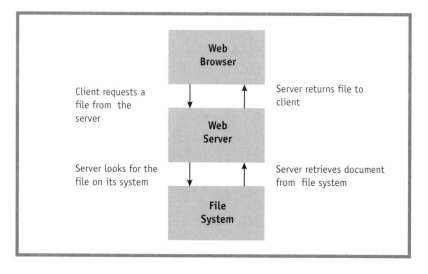

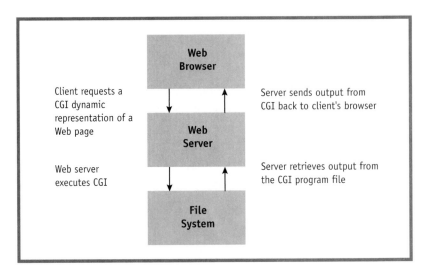

Figure 3-2
How Web Server Software Returns a Dynamic File

Although this would work well for a simple Web database construction, as soon as volume requests for files from multiple clients would begin, the server would start to encounter problems. These problems would be visible to clients when pages would begin to take a long time to generate. Web servers tend to take advantage of two different ways of handling this concurrency: **multithreading** and **multiprocessing**. Multithreading is the software's ability to manage multiple user requests, or threads, at one time. Multiprocessing is the dynamic assignment of the software to one or more computers working in tandem. Multiprocessing is said to be symmetric when multiple processors share memory and the data path. Multiprocessing can also be massively parallel or loosely coupled in this sharing arrangement.

Server-Side Technologies and Web Servers

Server-side programs are launched on the Web server when a browser program requests a Web page. CGI is an example of server-side technology. With this method, the executable program resides on the Web server as either an interpreted script—in VBScript, for example—or as a compiled program. The CGI specification allows for the exchange of data between the Web server and calling browser. One of the major limitations with CGI is that it is inherently slow and

FOCUS ON ELECTRONIC COMMERCE

Web Site Security Breach: Letting Your Customers Know

Electronic commerce has to be just as concerned about security as the brick-and-mortar business is. Part of the planning that has to go into any Web site construction is to decide in advance when and how to communicate with customers and business partners when a security breakdown occurs.

"Online businesses should be careful not to overreact by issuing public statements that could serve to expose them to more break-ins," says Matt Hicks of *eWeek*. However, when customers' information is exposed—and this could be in the form of social security number, credit card numbers, addresses or other records—businesses have a professional and ethical obligation to let their customers know.

Just before Christmas 2000, Egghead.com, an electronic commerce retailer based in Menlo Park, California, faced this dilemma. On December 18 management discovered that their system had been compromised by a hacker who had accessed confidential data including customer credit card information. The president and CEO of Egghead.com, Jeff Sheahan, decided that both customers and key partners had to be informed. By the end of that week, an e-mail from Sheahan to was sent to 3.3 million past and present customers and a press release was issued, precipitating nationwide publicity.

Egghead.com isn't the only company facing the problem of when and what to tell. In January 2001 Travelocity.com LP found that their site accidentally revealed the names and addresses of about 40,000 site visitors who participated in online contests. The Fort Worth, Texas, online travel services company learned of its mistake from media reports and then issued a public statement about the problem. "As a rule, [companies] really don't want this information to get out," said Fred Rica, a partner in global risk management solutions for PriceWaterhouseCoopers, in Florham Park, New Jersey. "They're afraid of eroding customer confidence and afraid that other people may try to exploit that security breach again."

Electronic commerce businesses clearly have a responsibility to notify customers and partners when a security breach has occurred, but when no customer information is compromised, or companies aren't sure of to what extent the security has been breached, then the appropriate action by the company is less clear. But the lesson learned is that electronic commerce businesses can no longer ignore the issue. They must develop policies and procedures for communicating security breaches to customers. Deborah Pierce, a staff attorney for the Electronic Frontier Foundation, an advocacy group in San Francisco, offers this advice: "If companies are serious about wanting to build trust on the Net, then this is one of the key places where they can prove it."

What are some specific strategies electronic commerce businesses can employ to disseminate information to their customers and trading partners that the security of their site has been breached?

Do you think that it is necessary in all cases to inform customers when their data has been compromised?

Justify your answer.

Source: Matt Hicks, *eWEEK*, February 19, 2001 12:00 AM ET.

nonscalable. Each CGI calling launches a new Web server process. To mitigate this limitation, some Web servers, including Deerfield WebSite and Microsoft IIS, offer an optimized application programming interface (API). API, like CGI, also has its limitations, since it is Web-server specific. A new alternative to API is FastCGI—a language-independent and scalable system that provides an open extension to CGI with excellent Web server performance. There are other server-side technologies as well, including application servers, Microsoft Active Server Pages (ASP), and server-side includes (SSI).

Client-Side Technologies and Web Servers

In contrast to server-side technologies, client-side programs actually move the electronic commerce construction closer to the customer. One drawback with server-side technologies has been that they execute browser commands in batch mode. Data entered by the customer cannot be validated ad hoc or on-the-fly by a server-side program and must wait for a completed form to be submitted. This technology moves the construction close to emulating the process of dumb terminal computing. To mitigate this limitation, helper programs were developed that ran client-side. However, helper programs still came with their own problems. They required that the full application for each new content type be installed on every client computer.

Today, there are more efficient client-side technologies, including Java applets, **ActiveX components**, and **dynamic HTML (DHTML)**. Applets are snippets of code that perform on demand from the server to a client, where they execute in the browser's **Java Virtual Machine (JVM)**. Applets are a platform-neutral, language-specific technology. Unfortunately, they have not been widely adopted by the design community due in part to Java's poor performance and the myriad differences between various vendors' JVM implementations.

ActiveX components are also snippets of code sent on demand from server to client, but they execute natively only in Microsoft's Web browser. They are a platform-specific, language-neutral technology. A serious limiting factor is that ActiveX components have numerous major security problems because, unlike Java, which executes in a protected memory space called a **sandbox**, ActiveX has broad access to the customer's machine resources.

The popularity and use of DHTML is on the rise. This technology utilizes event-driven scripting languages such as JavaScript that add client-side functionality independent of platform or browser. For these reasons scripting is currently the most prevalent client-side programming technique.

Partitioned Web Technologies and Web Servers

Partitioned Web technologies share the processing duties between the server and the client. With partitioned Web technology, scripts are allowed to validate input on the client before sending data to a back-end of the construction where business logic resides. Electronic commerce designers can optimize performance, network traffic and reliability, and client complexity, utilizing traditional client/server partitioning with **distributed Web constructions**.

The future of electronic commerce seems to lie somewhere between the fat clients and dumb terminals of the past. The rise of XML as a complementary markup language to HTML implies that client-side technologies will continue to grow, while business logic and back-end repositories become increasingly accessible via HTTP, JDBC, ODBC, OLE-DB, Native Database Access and other access protocols.

3.2 Web Server Software Components

All electronic commerce constuctions created in this book will use WebSite for the Web server software. This book's companion Web site contains an evaluation copy of WebSite server software. The link for the companion Web site is http://www.aw.com/nelson. WebSite is one of the top three Web Servers on the market today and is supported by Windows operating systems. Its popularity is due in part to scripting flexibility, ease of installation and use, and excellent documentation for the electronic commerce designer as well as its variety of add-on tools, including HTTP Web services, **HomeSite** 2.5 HTML editor for image map editing, WebView for site management, WebIndex for site indexing, and **QuickStats** for site traffic analysis. WebSite deserves serious consideration from businesses considering a Windows-based Web database construction.

WebSite has provided a great deal of scripting support for designers. It supports standard CGI, Windows CGI, API for both WebSite (WSAPI) and Microsoft (ISAPI) servers. Netscape (NSAPI) is not supported at this time. Though ASP support requires installing a Microsoft Web Server, such as IIS, on the same box, ASP can be created using VBScript, Jscript, Perl, and Python. WebSite also supports server-side Java technologies such as servlets written to JavaSoft's servlet API. Most importantly, security is one of WebSite's greatest strengths. WebSite supports full-strength 128-bit encryption SSL, native Windows NT authentication, and NTLM authentication.

 Web Break

The evaluation copy of WebSite that accompanies this book does not contain all of the add-ons available in the full version of **WebSite Professional.** After evaluating WebSite, you may want to investigate the full commercial Web server software. A free 30-day evaluation copy of WebSite can be obtained at the Deerfield Web site as a download at http://www.deerfield.com. You may also purchase the Web server at this site.

IIS Info

Instructions on Internet Information Server (IIS), Microsoft's Web server, will be highlighted in tip boxes to show you how you can implement the same electronic constructions using another Windows platform Web Server software. IIS 5.0 comes with Windows 2000 Server operating system. It is good as a first-time Web server for Windows-based electronic commerce constuctions and for designers who are comfortable with the Windows operating systems. IIS 4.0 is available for the Server edition of Windows NT 4.0, and it is also a free download as part of the Windows NT 4.0 Option Pack. Microsoft's Personal Web Server (PWS), designed for Windows 95 and Windows NT Workstation users, can also be used with the Web database constuctions created in this book. It is packaged with IIS as part of the freely downloadable Windows NT 4.0 Option Pack. PWS is a scaled-down version of the commercial IIS versions 4.0 and 5.0. It is Microsoft's entry-level Web server that makes it easy to publish personal home pages, serve small Web sites, and share documents via a local intranet. Many electronic commerce designers use PWS for testing Web sites for validity of links, scripts, applications, and functionality on Windows NT Workstation clients before hosting them on the Internet.

WebSite Features

WebSite provides the electronic commerce designer with a large array of tools to manage the server and develop a Web database construction for a business. These tools will be discussed here.

WebSite Server WebSite is a full 32-bit, multithreaded HTTP server that is supported by the Microsoft Windows operating systems. WebSite utilizes Windows Registry and **multithreading** and can run as an application or as a system production service. Usually the server icon appears on the taskbar with the status shown as either idle or busy.

Server Properties The **server properties** administration utility program is accessed by right-clicking on the server icon on the taskbar and choosing Server Properties. It can also be accessed by double-clicking on the icon. When accessed, the utility program window will look like Figure 3-3. This admin program lets you configure the WebSite server to meet the needs of your business. Mapping, identities for **virtual servers**, automatic directory listings, access control, and logging parameters are set through this utility.

Mapping Support WebSite supports document, redirect, CGI, association, directory icon, and content mapping. These features will help you manage both your documents and the capabilities of your server. With **document mapping**, a URL path can be mapped to a physical directory on the server. **Redirect mapping** allows the redirection of one URL to another URL, most often on a different server. **CGI mapping** allows the association of a URL to a specific type of script or other executable program. To describe documents in MIME format, **content mapping** can be used to allow appropriate display of a document. In accordance with HTTP standards, Web servers must include a media content type with every document returned to the browser. The browser must be able to identify the content type and display the document as appropriate for the type. Content types can require an external viewer or plug-in, such as Acrobat Reader for a Portable Document Format (PDF) file. Content types can be defined for applications such as Microsoft PowerPoint, Word, or Excel. **Directory icon mapping** supports the special use of content types mapped to icons used in directory listings. For example, content type text/html can be mapped to the icon html.gif.

Figure 3-3
WebSite Properties Admin Utility Program

Virtual Servers WebSite allows multiple virtual servers, or Web
identities, to be assigned. Each of the many home pages will each
have its own IP address, assigned through the graphical admin utility.

Logs WebSite is programmed to record each request it tries to serve
in an access log. If the server is configured with multiple Web identities, separate log files will be recorded. You can create separate
access logs for virtual servers. Access logs can be generated in one
of three formats. The first is the older **National Center for Supercomputing Applications (NCSA)/Centre pour Européenne
Recherche du Nucléaire (CERN) format**, which is used in earlier
versions of WebSite, includes basic information. If an error is generated while it is processing a request, WebSite will make an entry in

a separate error log. The second is the combined NCSA/CERN format, which includes fields for the referring URL and the browser type. Access log data can be imported directly to many Windows programs for processing and analysis. The third is the combined W3C and NCSA access logs, which is the most common format used today. Access logs contain the Internet address of the user requesting the document, the date/time/type of the request, the document being requested, the server's response to that request, and the amount of data transferred in response to a request.

Map This! WebSite contains Map This!—an image map editor that works with both NCSA file-based and client-side image maps. These image maps are a very powerful way of presenting location-based information and are processed by the client's browser. Some of the most common uses of Map This! are to create attractive menus for customers' selection purposes or to simulate a zoom facility to present portions of an image in more detail.

Site Security WebSite offers a great deal of security to the electronic commerce construction. Through mapping, WebSite controls the Web browser. A client's browser does not have unlimited access to the server; it can view only those documents that are part of the document tree, beginning with the document root. WebSite also gives security control through class restrictions and user authentication. These can be applied to the whole Web or any URL in the Web. With class restrictions, WebSite gives the server the ability to allow or deny access based on the Internet address or hostname of the Web browser—a feature called IP or hostname filtering. WebSite also allows user authentication based on a user name and password. These are specific to the server and are not related to user names and groups established on the system.

Server-Side Includes WebSite supports SSI technology, which allows data from various sources to be dynamically inserted into an HTML document. WebSite has built-in SSI directives, such as counters and current date and time. CGI variables and the output of external CGI programs can be inserted using SSI.

WebView This tool aids in the building and managing of the Web site by graphically depicting it. It includes a high-level view of a business site, including all virtual servers, mappings, and subfolders.

The tool allows adding, changing, and deleting of current mappings from WebView. It also shows hypertext links between and within documents including internal, external, broken, and virtual.

WebFind and WebIndex These tools provide search capability. WebIndex is a wizard that walks the developer through the steps of creating a new index, reconfiguring an existing one, or deleting an old one. It can also create searchable indexes. WebFind is a CGI program that searches the indexes created by WebIndex.

QuickStats This statistics program reads log formats and gives the developer activity reports. It can report the number of various types of requests on any URL path, virtual server, or specific document.

HomeSite HTML Editor From Allaire Corporation, this editor simplifies coding with its templates, tag references, and quick search capabilities.

WebSite Java Servlet SDK This development kit is a framework for creating Java servlets to run on the WebSite server. It also includes a copy of the Java Runtime Environment (JRE).

Active Server Page (ASP) Support This tool allows built-in support of Microsoft's Active Server Page technology. It allows dynamic, cross-platform ASP pages from Chili!Soft. Chili!Soft ASP is a complete platform for the rapid development of sophisticated Web-based applications.

IP-less Servers Sharing a single IP address, **IP-less virtual servers** are multiple virtual servers. The developer can use both IP-less virtual servers with IP-bound ones. This gives the developer the ability to provide entire electronic commerce solutions for different businesses, or different groups within one business, each with its own domain name from one server.

ECMerchant This tool allows the creation of a fully functional storefront including sophisticated shipping options, real-time credit card processing, and browser-based store management. Using ECMerchant's Remote Management Console allows developers to be able to update the store anytime, from anywhere, using a secure, feature-packed management site without the need for FTP programs.

Server-Side Java Allaire's JRun is an easy-to-use Java application server. It has an integrated development environment for building and deploying server-side Java applications. JRun Server includes an EJB and JMS server, support for JavaScript as the JSP server-side scripting language, and an extensible JSP custom tag library.

iHTML Professional and iHTML Merchant iHTML is a powerful scripting language that allows the addition of dynamic functions and graphics to the Web pages. It also supports creation of ODBC database access on the fly and back-page processing technologies. iHTML Merchant, from Inline Internet Systems, is a merchant server that simplifies the setup and administration of online stores. It is built entirely with iHTML and completely customizable through HTML document editing.

3.3 Installation of WebSite Web Server Software

Before you install WebSite, verify that the following hardware and software requirements have been met. These are necessary in order to install and run the server software successfully.

Hardware Requirements

While allowing high-performance levels, the hardware requirements of WebSite are minimal compared with other commercial Web servers. WebSite performance is impacted not only by hardware choice but by RAM. Web server performance increases substantially with increased amounts of RAM. A wise electronic commerce designer will be aware that WebSite is as powerful and rugged a Web server as the hardware and connection to the Internet permit. WebSite also supports multiple processors in a single computer, or symmetric multiprocessing used for processing-intense electronic commerce constructions.

Hardware
- Pentium 166 (Pentium 500 or higher recommended).
- 96 MB RAM for Windows NT, or Windows 2000 (128 MB or higher recommended); 64 MB RAM minimum with Windows 98 or Windows Me (128 MB recommended).

- 30 MB of free hard disk space with 100 MB required for installation.
- VGA video display adapter; SVGA recommended.
- CD-ROM drive.
- Network card or modem (28.8 KB or higher recommended).

Software Requirements

WebSite runs under the Windows operating system platform. It is supported by Windows 2000 (Advanced Server, Server, or Professional), Windows NT 4.0 (Workstation or Server), Windows 98, or Windows Me. Under Windows NT, WebSite can run on either a **FAT** file system or **NTFS**; under Windows 2000, the server can run on either a FAT or FAT32 filesystem, or NTFS. A file allocation table (FAT) is a table located on the hard disk, maintained by the computer's operating system, that maps files to the cluster in which they are stored. A cluster is the basic unit of logical storage on a hard disk. The NT file system (NTFS) is the Windows NT equivalent to the FAT. However, NTFS offers performance, extendability, and security improvements over FAT.

A Web browser is also necessary to run Web server software and to be able to utilize online technical support, resources, and capabilities.

Software

- For Windows 4.0, Service Pack 6a must be installed. This can be obtained from the Microsoft Web site at http://www.microsoft. com.
- For Windows 2000, Service Pack 1 must be installed.
- Web browser.
- Visual Basic 6.0 or Visual Basic.NET.
- Microsoft Access 2000.
- Connectivity.
- TCP/IP stack installed and running.
- An IP address in the dotted-decimal format.
- Fully Qualified Domain Name (FQDN) for the server.
- Internet e-mail address for WebSite server administrator.
- Domain Name System (DNS) server (optional, but highly recommended).
- WebSite server registered with DNS (optional, but highly recommended).

In addition to a unique IP address, a computer that is on a TCP/IP network, whether on an intranet or the Internet, may also have a domain name. For example, www.aw.com is a domain name used to identify computers connected to the Internet at Addison-Wesley. For WebSite, you must know the **fully qualified domain name (FQDN)** for your Web server. An FQDN includes the hierarchical name of the computer and is written from the most specific to the least specific address. In the electronic commerce scenario, FQDNs are often called **fully qualified host names (FQHN)**. Both FQDN and FQHN refer to the same name, and they are used interchangeably.

Other

- System Date/Time set to the correct date, time, and time zone.
- Administrator or Backup privileges for installing WebSite as a service (NT only).
- Add-ons and Application Development Tools (optional).
- Chili!Soft ASP requires Windows NT or Windows 2000. It will not install or run under Windows 98 or Windows Me.

Connectivity Requirements

There are several connectivity issues that must be addressed. The TCP/IP protocol stack must be installed and running, even if the Web server is not connected to any TCP/IP network.

TCP/IP As discussed in Chapter 2, the IP component of TCP/IP provides routing from the enterprise network to regional networks and ultimately to the Internet. However, you can install TCP/IP without any knowledge of either the corporate or regional network. Three pieces of information are required:

1. The IP address assigned to the Web server.
2. The part of the IP address (the subnet mask) that distinguishes other machines on the same LAN (messages can be sent to them directly) from machines in other departments or elsewhere in the world (which are sent to a router machine). Subset masks identify the network part of the IP address.
3. The IP address of the router machine that connects this LAN to the rest of the world.

TCP/IP capability is built into the Windows operating systems, and no additional software is needed. If you are on an intranet, verify with the network administrator or Internet service provider that connectivity requirements for WebSite have been met. If you are installing WebSite on a personal computer, you can set up TCP/IP through the Network option of the Control Panel. This must be done prior to WebSite installation. For more information on installing and configuring TCP/IP on your computer, see the operating system's documentation.

Connectivity of your WebSite server will be addressed either as part of an intranet, on the Internet, or as a development system for Web applications with no physical connection to the Internet or a network.

IP Address An important piece of information you need to know about your TCP/IP setup is the IP address assigned to your server. The IP address is in a dotted-decimal format—a set of four bytes, with each set consisting of one to three digits. In the dotted-decimal format, each set of numbers is separated by periods (or dots). The IP address is needed for testing the Web server.

TCP/IP Connection to an Internal Network If WebSite is used as an electronic commerce construction running on an intranet, the network must still be running TCP/IP. The computer on which WebSite is installed must be configured with a connection to that network. If on a network, the IP address is needed and can be obtained from the network administrator.

TCP/IP Connection to the Internet If you want your Web to be reachable by other computers on the Internet, you need a connection that puts your computer "on the Net."

Add-ons and Application Development Tools

There are several optional add-ons and application development tools associated with WebSite. Depending on the electronic commerce needs of the business, these may or may not be needed for the Web database construction. Add-ons allow enhancement of the Web site with specialized elements and functionality. Application development tools are essential for writing CGI programs or using **WebSite Application Programming Interface (WSAPI)**. Add-ons can be used to incorporate graphics, video, and/or audio into your electronic commerce construction. They can also be used to add forms processing and conferencing tools to increase the efficiency and effectiveness of the constructions. Add-ons and application development tools to consider include the following:

- PolyForm, a Web forms construction kit
- Web Board, a Web conferencing system
- Graphics editor/viewer such as Lview Pro, Paint Shop Pro, Adobe Photoshop, or Corel Photopaint
- Audio editor/player such as RealAudio, Sound Recorder, or Gold Wave
- Video editor/player such as QuickTime or MPEGPlay
- Adobe Acrobat Exchange and/or Distiller (available in Acrobat Pro)
- Visual Basic development environments
- Java Developers Kit (JDK)
- Active Server Pages development environment
- POSIX Shell and tools from the Windows Resource Kit

Web Break

The list of add-ons and application development tools is by no means comprehensive. Web technology is continuously changing. Use your favorite search engine to look for new tools on the Web that will add interest and functionality to your electronic commerce Web database constructions.

Kanthaka Farms is a continuing case study in this book that illustrates the process of building electronic commerce with Web database constructions. In Chapter 3, you will install and set your administration properties for WebSite, your Web server software. As you continue through the text, you will complete different facets of electronic commerce Web database construction, resulting in a complete Web site for Kanthaka Farms.

Kanthaka Farms
Installing WebSite Server
Software

WebSite's Setup program, which can be found on this book's companion Web site, can be installed as follows:

1. Navigate to the Web site installation program at http://www. aw.com/nelson.

2. Start the WebSite Set Wizard by running the WebSite executable program designated WebSite.exe.

3. Click on Yes to confirm the installation of the Web service software process. Select the folder destination for installing the WebSite server software. It is recommended that the default C:\WebSite be chosen to match the paths used as examples in this book and in Figure 3-4. If you want to change the destination folder, click on the Browse button to locate the destination where you will install the Web server files. Once the destination has been selected, click on the Next button to continue the installation wizard.

4. The installation of the Web server software can back up all replaced files. You have the choice to either back up or not as shown in Figure 3-5. If you choose yes, you must select the directory where the replaced files will be copied. The default is C:\WebSite\BACKUP. If you choose to back up and want to use another directory, click on the Browse button to find and select the Backup folder. Once you have completed this screen, press the Next button.

5. You will now need to create your initial Web server software settings. This can be changed after the installation process is completed and the Web server is running. For now, you must communicate to the Web server software the fully qualified domain name (FQDN)

Figure 3-4
Select Destination for WebSite Server Software

Figure 3-5
Backup Files Screen of the Installation Process

of your system—for example, www.awl.com. If you plan to use multiple domain names, enter the primary name in the first text box. You will add the others at a later time. If you are unsure what to use, enter "localhost."

6. WebSite requests the Internet e-mail address for the server administrator as shown in Figure 3-6. This address includes a name and a domain name—for example, nelson@awl.com. The e-mail address can be for any location. It does not have to be the system on which the WebSite server resides. Also, the e-mail address is for the WebSite server administrator, not the system administrator. In smaller businesses like Kanthaka Farms, the system administrator and the Web server administrator may often be the same person. The e-mail address you set here will be used in a few WebSite documents, such as search forms.

7. WebSite includes a default administrator named Admin, a user who has access to all document and program locations used by the Web server. As the electronic commerce designer, you have an obligation to protect the business' information and the Web server's content and programs. To do so, enter the password password for the user Admin. *Be sure to write this down!* You will need the Admin password to reach protected areas of the Web server. The screen on which you will create the Admin user and password is seen in Figure 3-7.

Figure 3-6
Creating the Initial Web Server Settings

Figure 3-7
Creating the Administrator Password

8. You will next use the installation wizard to assign settings for a Remote Manager, a utility that lets you administer the WebSite server using a browser. Before you can use Remote Manager, you must specify a port number for it as shown in Figure 3-8. Be sure to use a number that is not already in use. It is recommended that a number above 8192 and below 32768 be used. These numbers are unlikely to conflict with other TCP/IP applications on your system. The default is 9999. You can change the default setting should you need to at a later time. For now, accept the default by pressing the Next button.

9. You have now completed the Web server installation wizard and are ready to install the software. Click Next to begin the installation or Back to change any installation information that you may have entered incorrectly. The installation wizard creates folders and files on the destination you selected as shown in Figure 3-9. Upon clicking Next, the installation process will begin. You will need to restart your system and log back in under the name you were using when you installed the Web server software. After you have done this, open the WebSite folder on your hard disk drive. Locate the application file, httpd32.exe. This is the WebSite server software executable. Should your installation not add the WebSite choice to your Start/Programs selection, then you can double-click on this file to launch the WebSite program.

10. Check to verify that upon completed installation, your hard drive file hierarchy is similar to Figure 3-10.

Figure 3-8
Setting the Remote Manager Port

Figure 3-9
Ready to Install Web Server Software Screen

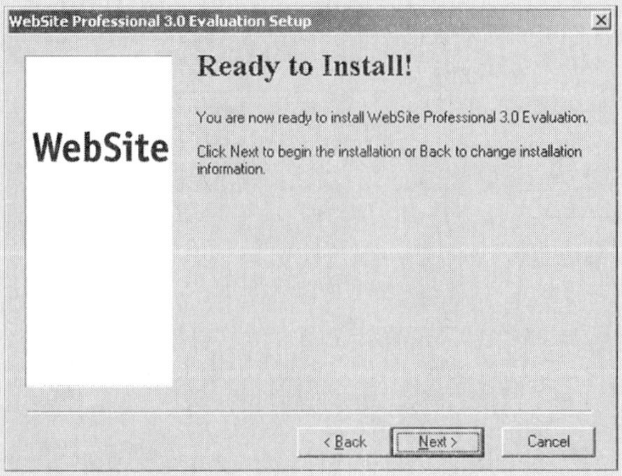

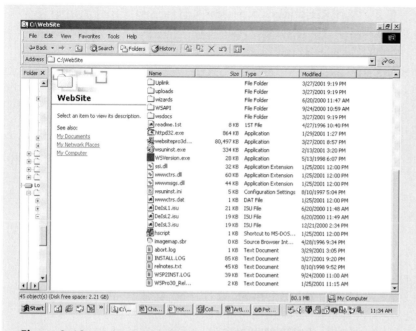

Figure 3-10
Viewing Installed Files and Folders from Windows Explorer

IIS Info

IIS 5.0 is installed on a Windows 2000 Server by default. Use your Add/Remove Programs application in Control Panel to remove IIS or select additional components.

To install IIS on computers running other Windows operating systems, do the following:

1. Choose Start, Settings, Control Panel, and start the Add/Remove Programs application.
2. Choose Configure Windows, Components, and follow the on-screen instructions to install, remove, or add components to IIS.

It should be noted that if you upgraded to Windows 2000, IIS 5.0 will not be automatically installed unless it was installed on your previous version of Windows.

3.4 WebSite Web Server Software Configuration and Maintenance

To verify that the installation of the WebSite server software is functioning correctly, you should see the cloud icon in the tray on the right side of the Windows taskbar. If your Web server software does not start, you will usually not receive an error message. You may, however, see the cloud icon momentarily flash in the tray of the taskbar and then disappear. If the cloud icon flashes in the tray and then disappears upon running WebSite, the first step is to look in the server log, which is usually located at C:WebSite\logs. Here are some common start-up problems followed by a solution code number.

- Failed to change password on wspro_anon (code = 5)
- Failed to log into account wspro_anon (code 1314)
- Failed to log into account wspro_anon (code 1326)
- Failed to log in anonymous account wspro_anon (code 1792)

Another solution can be to update the registry key for the wspro_anon account. To do so, use **regedit** or **regedt32**. (*Note:* If you do not know where to locate either regedit or regedt32, you can use your operating systems' search tool to find the executable file. For this solution you will edit HKEY_LOCAL_MACHINE\SOFTWARE\Denny\WebServer\CurrentVersion as shown in Figure 3-11. It is always wise to back up the Denny registry key *before* you work on it.)

Right-click AnonUserName and select Modify. Delete the Value DataL wspro_anon and press OK. If you are multihomed you will also have to edit HKEY_LOCAL_MACHINE\SOFTWARE\Denny\WebServer\CurrentVerson\MultiHome\AnonAccount. Repeat the process you used above to delete the Value Data for each IP address. Now start WebSite. You should see the cloud icon on the taskbar tray. You may be prompted to enter a Key Ring password. If so, press Cancel and No Key Ring.

Now view the Server Properties Admin utility. Double-click on the cloud icon to open the utility. You will know that your Web server is running if you see a large box with large green letters reading "Running." If it is not, "Stop" will appear in red letters.

The WebSite server can be run as either a system service or an application. A system service is a production Web server that can be accessed by anyone who is connected to the Internet. In functional-

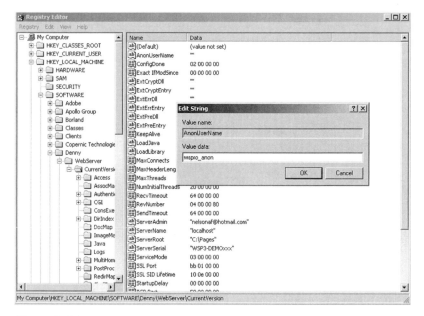

Figure 3-11
Editing the Registry

IIS Info

To verify that IIS is running, as with WebSite, the icon will appear in your tray on your taskbar on your Windows desktop. If it is not displayed, from Windows Explorer, go to the Windows\System\Inetsrv folder for Windows 98 and Windows Me users. For Windows 2000 users, go to the Winnt\ Systems32\Inetsrv folder. Double-click the IIS executable file to start the server software. If this file is not on your computer, it means that the server software is not installed on your computer.

ity and performance of the server and its tools, there really is no difference between a system service and an application. If you choose to run your server software configured to a desktop application, it can be started manually or automatically whenever you log in. Simply place it in the startup group for automatic startup. The advantage of running WebSite as a production Web server is that when it is set up as a system service, it continues to be available even when no one is logged onto the network. This is a strong security feature. Also, if you experience a power failure, WebSite can restart automatically without someone having to log in and launch it. If you will run the server software in a heavy traffic environment or full-time and are familiar with the operating system and its services, it is best to consider running WebSite as a service. However, if you choose desktop application, it is easier to start and stop. To leave the system running while you are away from your computer, simply lock your screen to prevent unauthorized use. If you are not familiar with your operating services and identity issues are involved, it is best to begin with WebSite as a desktop application. It is easier to initially set up and can be switched to a service at a later date. Running WebSite as an application is an excellent environment for setting up a personal Web server, for participating in an intranet, for learning about Web server administration, or for testing electronic commerce constructions prior to moving them to a production Web server. If you are already running multiple services on your computer and are familiar with how they work, then you may prefer to run WebSite as a service from the beginning.

IIS Info

View the manager utilities for IIS by double-clicking on the icon or by right-clicking and choosing Start Service.

Setting WebSite to a System Service

To change WebSite from an application server to production server requires only a few steps.

Kanthaka Farms
Setting WebSite Server
Software to a System Service

To run Kanthaka Farms' Web server software as a system service rather than a desktop application, complete the following steps:

1. Shut down the WebSite server if it is running. To do so, double-click on the WebSite icon in the tray on your taskbar. Open the Server Properties utility and choose the General tab. Click on the Stop button on the top left under Server Control. The word "Stop" in large red letters should now be displayed.

2. Choose the Run Mode pulldown list on the General tab. Select System Service.

3. Close Server Properties.

4. Now start the server from your operating system. This is done differently depending on your operating system:

- If you are running Windows 2000, choose Start, Settings, Control Panel to open the Control Panel. Choose Administrative Tools and Services (this is a shortcut icon). Scroll until you see Web server. Right-click Web server and choose Start as shown in Figure 3-12. You can also choose Properties, General tab, and Start. The server icon should now appear on your taskbar.
- If you are running Windows NT, from the Control Panel, open Services. Scroll through the services listed until you see Web Server. Highlight Web Server and click Start. The server icon should now appear on your taskbar.
- If you are running Windows 98 or Me, start the server from the WebSite Start menu folder. The server is now running.

Figure 3-12

Setting the Server to a System Production Server

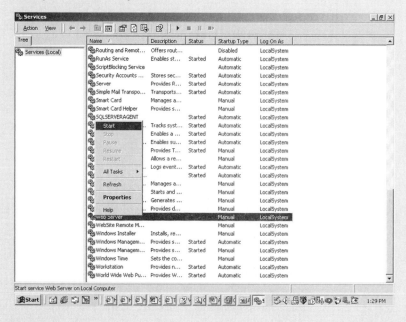

5. If you want WebSite to start automatically when you start your system, then click Startup on the Services window and complete the necessary information. You may need to refer to the operating system guide for more help in setting up services.

6. To switch from a production service back to a desktop application, simply stop the service from your operating system, reset the Run Mode in the Server Properties, and start the server as an application.

Note: The evaluation copy of WebSite may not allow you to change from an application server to a production server. You may need to upgrade to the full server software program.

Testing the WebSite Server Software

You must perform a test on the server software to verify that your installation is operating properly. The verification will consist of four parts:

1. Verify that the server software starts properly.
2. Verify that you can view an HTML document from a local computer using both localhost and the fully qualified domain name (FQDN) or the IP address.
3. Verify that you can view an HTML document from a remote computer using the fully qualified domain name (FQDN) or IP address.
4. Verify that you can run both the server self-test and the demonstration from WebSite Pro Resources.

You should have completed Step 1 earlier in the chapter to ensure your Web server starts properly. This is the first test you should perform after installation. When WebSite is running, the icon will appear in the tray on your taskbar. Passing the cursor over the icon indicates the status of the server in a tip box. It will either be Starting, Idle, Busy, or Paused. For this test, the status should say WebSite Idle.

Locally Viewing an HTML Document   The easiest way to test whether the server software is configured and installed properly is from a Web browser.

Test Kanthaka Farms' configuration and installation by viewing an HTML document from the local computer. To do so, follow these steps:

1. Verify that your TCP/IP is running. If you are on a TCP/IP network or have a dedicated connection to the Internet, the protocol may not be visible to you. If you are on a standalone computer and receive the connectivity with a dial-up SLIP or PPP account using Dial-Up Networking, then make sure that you have a live connection.

2. Ensure that your WebSite server is running.

3. From the Start menu, choose Programs, WebSite Professional, WebSite Pro Resources. Your screen should look like the one depicted in Figure 3-13.

4. From the left pane of the Resources window, choose the Server Self-Test link.

5. You should now be at the Server Self-Test and Demonstration page. Your server software has a self-test and demonstration that lets you check out various features of the software to ensure you have a proper and full installation. There are two benefits of running the

Kanthaka Farms
Testing WebSite Server Software's Configuration and Installation

Figure 3-13

WebSite Pro Resources

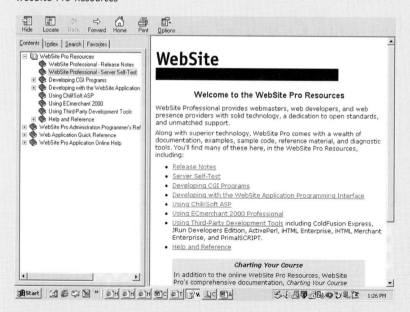

test: you can ensure that your server is configured correctly and that all the features are working; second, the test will introduce you to many of the WebSite server capabilities.

6. To begin the WebSite Pro self-test and demonstration, ensure that the server is running. Open the URL http://localhost/~wsdocs/ 32demo/ in a browser. If prompted, supply the Admin username and password you set up during the installation process. Your screen should look like Figure 3-14. Note the checklist near the beginning of the self-test. If you are unable to meet all these requirements, you should still complete the self-test although some features will not work correctly.

7. Test the server using the server's domain name. In the URL field in the browser, type in the URL for the WebSite Pro Resources Welcome page for your server, using the following format:

```
http://your.server.name/~wsdocs/
```

8. The next task is to test whether a remote computer, either one on your internal network or one connected to the Internet, can view

Figure 3-14
The WebSite Server Self-Test and Demonstration Page

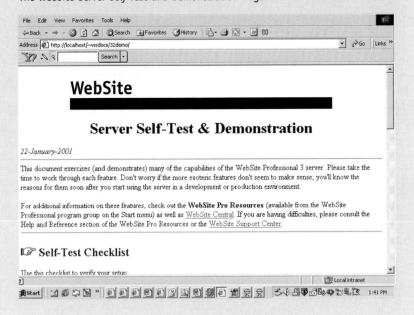

a document on your WebSite server. You must have access to another computer that has a working Web browser to complete this test. To do so, on another computer, specify the URL for your server using the same format you used in the previous step.

If your test failed, try again. Heavy Internet traffic can cause connections to time out. If you still cannot make a connection after several attempts, verify the TCP/IP connections on both computers. Verify that the server is running. Also, recheck that your server's name is a fully qualified domain name and that it is registered with DNS. If you continue to have difficulties, contact your Internet service provider (ISP).

If you have completed 1 through 8 successfully for Kanthaka Farms, you have seen the server running and you have verified that it can serve documents locally and that the host name is resolving correctly. Now you must really put your server through its paces by running the server self-test. This test will provide you with examples that you may wish to implement in your Kanthaka Farms electronic commerce construction. Some of the features that you will see during the self-test are more advanced features. If at this point, you do not understand them, don't worry. You will learn about them later in the text as you build your electronic commerce Web site.

9. To start the self-test and demonstration in your Web browser, open the URL http://localhost/~wsdocs/32demo. Be sure to record the server's responses to each item in the self-test on a copy of the checklist document.

 Web Break

There are many ways to discover your computer's IP address. One interesting way is to perform a privacy analysis of your computer and your Internet connection. Go to the Privacy.net/anonymizer Web site at http://privacy.net/anonymizer and see what information can be collected about you when you visit a Web site.

3.5 Web Server Software Security

From the first time you run your Web server software, WebSite is enabled for cryptographic enhanced security. However, until the server has a public key certificate, it is not secure. An alert box will appear to inform you that the key/certificate database cannot be opened and secure transactions are impossible. If you plan to use this enhanced security feature of WebSite server, you must apply for your server's certificate as soon as possible.

Enabling WebSite Key Ring Security

The WebSite server's certificate key ring—which holds the public/private key pairs, signed certificates, and trusted roots for using the server's cryptographic security—requires a password. The key ring is a part of WebSite's Server Properties. Every time you open the Server Properties utility or start the server, you will be queried to provide the password. WebSite can be set to remember the password. Although you can also open the property sheet without a password, the key ring is not available when you do this.

Kanthaka Farms
Creating WebSite Server
Software Password Security

Create Kanthaka Farms' Key Ring password to ensure cryptographic security for your electronic commerce design. To create the password, follow these steps:

1. Open Server Properties by double-clicking on the WebSite icon on your taskbar. A message appears telling you that no password exists and that WebSite will help you create one now. Click on OK to continue.

2. Enter the new password twice in the New WebSite Key Ring dialog box. This will verify that you typed the password correctly. It will not be displayed for security reasons. You can check the box to have the server software remember the password. Click OK to create the password.

Keep this password safe so that the Kanthaka Farms electronic commerce Web site is not compromised. The password is an important part of ensuring security of information for Kanthaka Farms as well as their customers.

Note: The evaluation copy of WebSite may not allow you to activate this security feature. You may need to upgrade to the full-server software program.

Another security feature supported by WebSite is the TLS/SSL security protocol defined for Internet usage. This protocol requires a Digital ID or public key certificate (sometimes also called cert) for your server. These can be obtained from certification authorities (CAs). Your WebSite server comes with built-in support for the major CAs and provides the ability to add them as they become available. Until you have generated a public-private key pair, sent the public key to a Certification Authority, and received a signed certificate, you cannot use SSL.

Setting Up the Administrator Account

The default user account for WebSite is Admin. This account has no password and belongs to no groups by default. Another security feature is to activate the Administrator account, assign it a password, and add it to at least the Administrators group. This account is used for restricting certain URLs and server functions to a single account. It is also used for the **wsauth** server feature, a utility that lets you manage users and groups from a browser or the command line, including adding users from a flat-file database, providing a mechanism for self-registration, and allowing users to change their own passwords via the browser.

Kanthaka Farms
Creating an Administrator Account for the WebSite Server Software

Create the Administrator account for Kanthaka Farms. To activate the account, you must first select a password. Harris Vita has asked you to use the word *iggy* for the Kanthaka Farms Administrator account password. To activate the account, follow these steps:

1. From the Start menu, choose Programs, WebSite Professional, WebSite Pro Server.

2. Choose the Users tab.

3. In the Users field, select the user Admin from the pulldown list. Click Password. The Change Password dialog box will appear.

4. Type in the old password, *password*. Using your Tab key, navigate to the next textbox and type in *iggy*, the new password. Type the new password again. Press OK.

5. In the Group Membership section, select Administrators in the Available Groups list and click Add. It will move to the right pane of the window. Repeat for the group Users. Your Users window should look like Figure 3-15.

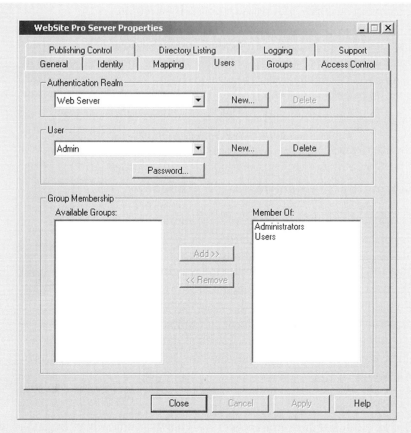

Figure 3-15
Activating the Administrator Account for Kanthaka Farms

6. Click OK to update the server and finish the activation of the Admin account for Kanthaka Farms.

3.6 Installation of Web Applications Provided on This Book's Companion Web Site

This book's companion Web site contains sample applications that will be discussed in later chapters. You must install these applications onto your hard disk drive. These applications include three examples of electronic commerce Web database constructions: (1) a guestbook application, (2) an online questionnaire, and (3) a shopping cart. You will use these applications for both Kanthaka Farms and Albatross Records. These Web database constructions are designed to provide a practical implementation of the electronic theories and techniques discussed in this book.

The Guestbook Application

The **guestbook application** allows a dynamic interaction between customer and business, enabling the business to find out more about its customers and for obtaining their feedback. Often this information is appended to an ASCII file and a link through which that file can be viewed. The guestbook application provided with this book uses a back-end database for the storage of the customer's information, rather than an ASCII appended file. The guestbook performs the following functions:

- Displays entries with customer name, e-mail, date, and text comments.
- In Administration mode, deletes entries.
- In Navigation mode, jumps to first page, last page, previous page, next page, discrete pages.

An example of a simple guestbook application is seen in Figure 3-16.

The guestbook application provided with this book is ready-to-use. HTML formatting has been limited in order to keep the sample clear. However, some students may choose to modify the application

Figure 3-16

Guestbook Application Example

by changing the language of the application, adjusting the design to meet the needs of the electronic construction they are creating, or extending the functionality of the application.

The Online Survey Application

The online survey application takes advantage of the dynamic interchange between customer and business with Yes and No questions. It can be used to accept customer feedback and as an analysis tool for the business. This is a more advanced Web database construction than the guestbook application. Like the guestbook, the online survey stores the customer's feedback in a back-end database. The query feature of the RDBMS can be used to dynamically generate the feedback analysis. An example of a simple online survey application is seen in Figure 3-17.

Figure 3-17

Online Survey Application Example

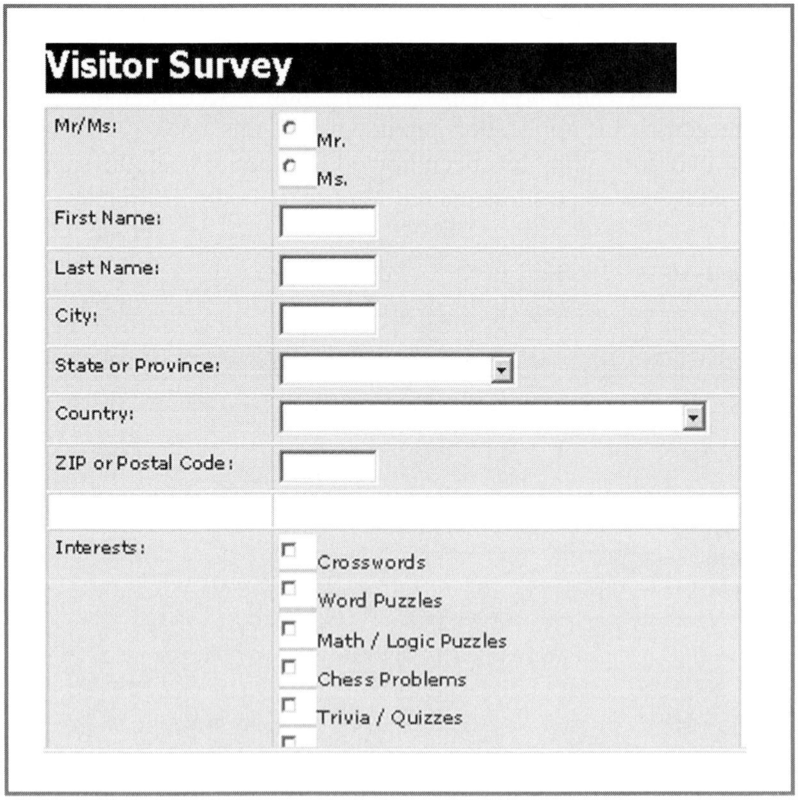

The Shopping Cart Application

The shopping cart application is the most complex of the electronic applications included on the companion Web site. This is a feature-rich Web application that simulates an online store using the shopping cart metaphor, one with which today's customers are familiar. The shopping cart application has the capability of accepting payments and orders online. The application has a keyword and concept search feature. This feature uses a word-indexing technique to add speed and flexibility to the Web database construction.

Summary

- **Define Web server software.** Web server software enables the electronic commerce construction to communicate between the front-end, middleware, and back-end. Web server software is a major component of the electronic commerce architecture. Specifically, it allows the receipt of requests from the customer and responds to those requests, often allowing the business to serve content over the Internet using HTML. Web server software accepts requests from customers' browsers, like Netscape and Internet Explorer, and then returns the appropriate documents. To do this, Web server software can use many types of client-server and server-side technologies including CGI, SSI, SSL, and ASP.

- **Define WebSite Web server components.** Deerfield WebSite is a brand of Web server software that is supported by Windows operating systems. It is one of the three most popular Web servers available today. Components of WebSite include WebSite Server, Mapping Support, Virtual Servers, Logs, Map This!, Site Security, Server-Side Includes, WebView, WebFind, WebIndex, QuickStats, HomeSite HTML Editor, WebSite Java Servlet SDKL, ASP Support, IP-less Servers, ECMerchant, Server-Side Java, iHTML Professional, and iHTML Merchant.

- **Explain the steps involved in Web server software installation.** Before installing WebSite, verify that the proper hardware and software requirements have been met. These are necessary in order to install and run the server software successfully. There are several connectivity issues that must also be addressed. The TCP/IP protocol stack must be installed and running, even if the

Web server is not connected to any TCP/IP network. The steps that are necessary for the installation process include the following:

1. Navigate to the Web site installation program at http://www. aw.com/nelson.

2. Start the WebSite Set Wizard by running the WebSite executable program designated WebSite.exe.

3. Click on Yes to confirm the installation of the Web service software process. Select the folder destination for installing the WebSite server software. It is recommended that the default C:\WebSite be chosen to match the paths used as examples in this book. If you want to change the destination folder, click on the Browse button to locate the destination where you will install the Web server files. Once the destination has been selected, click on the Next button to continue the installation wizard.

4. Continue to follow the installation wizard, accepting the defaults of the software. Set the host's domain name to *localhost*. Set the administrator's e-mail address to your own.

■ **Discuss configuration and maintenance of Web server software.** The WebSite server can be run as either a system service or an application. A system service is a production Web server that can be accessed by anyone who is connected to the Internet. In functionality and performance of the server and its tools, there really is no difference between a system service and an application. If you choose to run your server software configured to a desktop application, it can be started manually or automatically whenever you log in. Simply place it in the startup group for automatic startup. The advantage of running WebSite as a production Web server is that, when it is set up as a system service, it continues to be available even when no one is logged onto the network. This is a strong security feature. Also, if you experience a power failure, WebSite can restart automatically without someone having to log in and launch it. If you will run the server software in a heavy traffic environment or full-time and are familiar with the operating system and its services, it is best to consider running WebSite as a service. However, if you choose desktop application, it is easier to start and stop. To leave the system running while you are away from your computer, simply lock your screen to prevent unauthorized use. If you are not familiar with your operating services and identity issues are involved, it is best to begin with WebSite as a desktop application.

■ **Describe what is needed to test the Web server software installation.** After installation, four tests must be performed on the server software to verify that the installation is operating properly. The verification will consist of four parts: (1) verify that the server software starts properly; (2) verify that you can view an HTML document from a local computer using both localhost and the fully qualified domain name (FQDN) or IP address; (3) verify that you can view an HTML document from a remote computer using the fully qualified domain name (FQDN) or IP address; and (4) verify that you can run both the server self-test and the demonstration from WebSite Pro Resources.

■ **Define and describe Web server software security.** The WebSite server's certificate key ring—which holds the public/private key pairs, signed certificates, and trusted roots for using the server's cryptographic security—requires a password. The key ring is a part of WebSite's Server Properties. Every time you open the Server Properties utility or start the server, you will be queried to provide the password. WebSite can be set to remember the password. Although you can also open the property sheet without a password, the key ring is not available when you do this. Another security feature supported by WebSite is the TLS/SSL security protocol defined for Internet usage. This protocol requires a Digital ID or public key certificate. You should also set up a new password and assign user accounts to your Admin login to better secure your server.

■ **Describe three practical implementations of the electronic theories and techniques discussed in the book.** There are three sample applications that must be installed from the companion Web site onto your hard disk drive. These applications include three examples of electronic commerce Web database constructions: (1) a guestbook application, (2) an online questionnaire, and (3) a shopping cart. You will use these applications for both Kanthaka Farms and Albatross Records. These Web database constructions are designed to provide a practical implementation of the electronic theories and techniques discussed in this book.

Chapter Key Terms

ActiveX components
application server
association mapping
CGI mapping
content mapping
directory icon mapping
distributed Web constructions
document mapping
Dynamic HTML (DHTML)
File allocation table (FAT)
fully qualified domain name
    (FQDN)
fully qualified host names
    (FQHN)

guestbook application
HomeSite
information server
IP-less virtual servers
Java Virtual Machine
multithreading
multiprocessing
native database format
NCSA/CERN format
NT file system (NTFS)
ODBC
OLE-DB
open-source PHP
partitioned Web technologies

PHP Hypertext Preprocessor
PHP4
QuickStats
redirect mapping
regedit
regedt32
sandbox
server properties
WebSite Application
    Programming Interface
    (WSAPI)
WebSite Professional
wsauth

Review Questions

1. Why is it said that Web server software has been both a catalyst for the astounding growth of electronic commerce as well as on the leading edge of the Internet revolution?

2. Describe a new alternative to API.

3. List and describe some of today's client-side technologies.

4. How do partitioned Web technologies share the processing duties between the server and the client?

5. List three of the scripting support designers provided by WebSite server. What are the benefits of these to the electronic commerce designer.

6. WebSite server is supported by what operating systems?

7. What does CGI mapping do?

8. How is content mapping used?

9. What do the access logs contain? How might these logs be used by an electronic commerce site administrator?

10. Describe the Map This! feature and how it might be used.

11. What are the hardware requirements for installation of WebSite server software?

12. What are the software requirements for installation of Deerfield's WebSite server software?

13. What connectivity information must you know prior to installation of WebSite server?

14. It is recommended that when assigning a port number for Remote Manager that a number above 8192 and below 32768 be used. Why?

15. Describe using WebSite as a desktop application and as a system production service. What will you use for Kanthaka Farms? Justify your answer.

16. What are the four tests that should be performed to ensure that the Web server is installed and working properly?

17. What is WebSite's key ring feature? How is it used? How is the password changed?

18. Describe three practical implementations of the electronic theories and techniques discussed in this book.

Critical Thinking Using the Web

1. Go to http://www.alltheweb.com or your favorite search engine to find out more about "smurf"—a type of network security breach. Write a 200 to 300 word essay explaining your findings and answering the following questions: What steps can the electronic commerce designer take to protect the Web site from smurf attacks? What companies have been troubled by smurf attacks?

2. Go to AntiOnline.Com's Web site at http://www.antionline.com/ and explore their security-related information. How might an electronic commerce administrator use a site like Antionline.com to stay current on Web site security issues? Use the Web site to find specific ways you can fight back against Web site intruders and computer hackers. Write a 200 to 300 word essay discussing your findings.

3. Guestbook applications are a very common Web database construction. Visit the Application Rental Guide's Web Site at http://guestbook.find-apps.com. They boast that they have "thousands of Web-based apps at your fingertips." Search for Guest Book application and bookmark this page for reference later. Read several of the guestbook reviews. Using Excel, list three guestbook applications that you may be able to utilize in your Kanthaka Farms electronic commerce construction. Beside each name, use other cells for a brief description, the type of interface, reported errors, price, and noted advantages. Save the Excel worksheet as Kanthaka_Farms_guestbook_ideas.xls.

Chapter Case Study

Albatross Records is a continuing case study that illustrates the process of building electronic commerce with Web database constructions. In Chapter 3, you will install and set your administration properties for Web-Site, your Web server software. As you continue through the text, you will complete different facets of electronic commerce Web database construction, resulting in a complete Web site for Albatross Records.

- Plan for your installation of Albatross Records Web server software. Write out notes that you will use for your meeting with Cool to justify to him why you have chosen WebSite for the Web server.

- Define the Web server components that you will use with the Albatross Web database construction.

- List the steps that you will take to install the Web server software for Albatross.

- How will you configure and maintain the Web server software?

- What tests will you perform after your Web server software installation before you begin to use the software?

- Will you use WebSite as a desktop application or as a system production server? Justify your decision in a memo to Cool.

- Define and describe the Web server software security features included in WebSite.

- Describe three practical implementations of the electronic theories and techniques discussed in this book. Which will you use for your Albatross Records design? Why?

4

Electronic Commerce Business Models

Learning Objectives

Upon completion of this chapter, you will be able to

- Define the most common types of electronic commerce business models used today
- Discuss the differences between pull versus push technology
- List the necessary steps in planning an electronic commerce business
- Describe the fundamental elements of the guestbook model
- Describe the fundamental elements of the survey model
- Describe the fundamental elements of the job listing service model
- Discuss the use of metrics to assess the success of an electronic commerce model

American kids who are wired into the online world tend to be heavier consumers of all media when compared to their non-online peers. Unlike the online adult population, which consumes less TV than their non-user counterparts, online kids are eager to gobble up every type of media from television to magazines to movies.

—Simmons Market Research Bureau Study, August 2000

4.1 Building Electronic Commerce Business Models

Electronic commerce is here to stay. On a daily basis, some form of electronic commerce already permeates our lives. The most commonly used **electronic commerce business models** include **guestbooks**, **online surveys** and questionnaires, **online job-listing services**, and most certainly, the **online shopping cart**. Consumers use electronic commerce to purchase a variety of goods and services online, including books, flowers, cars, food, banking, music and other forms of entertainment. Businesses also use these models to improve internal communication, help manage supply chains, conduct technical and market research, and locate potential customers and business partners.

Several sample electronic commerce business models are on this book's companion Web site. Two are elementary Web database constructions: the guestbook and the online survey. A job-listing model is included as an example of a more advanced Web database construction. The job-listing service demonstrates how successful electronic commerce models use Web-based mediators to replace the traditional middleman. This job-listing model is a Web database construction for pairing job applicants with businesses with job openings. The job seeker initiates the connection by utilizing a Web front-end. The job seeker is then connected through VBScript to potential employers stored in a back-end Access database.

The last electronic commerce business model that is on this book's companion Web site is the online shopping cart, a feature-rich Web database construction that simulates an online virtual store with the capability of accepting orders and payments online. This model will be discussed separately in a later chapter in the book. The online shopping cart includes a powerful keyword and concept search feature, using a word-indexing technique to achieve both effectiveness and efficiency. It can be modified for use by many different types of businesses, as a Web-based mediator in order to eliminate the middleman and help the business save money and improve customer service as well as capture sales.

 Web Break

The U.S. Census Bureau of the U.S. Department of Commerce Web site is an excellent example of an organization using many of these electronic commerce business models. Visit the site at http://www.census.gov and see them in action. You'll find a job-listing service, a survey, and a shopping cart model all in use on the same site.

Determining the Appropriate Business Model

Fundamentally, a business model is the way a business conducts business to sustain itself, in other words, a plan for how the business generates revenue. The business model sets the parameters for how a company makes money by determining where it is positioned in the value chain. One of the first steps in building successful Web database constructions is to determine the appropriate business model to use. A thorough business analysis must be made to determine which form of electronic commerce best suits the needs and goals of the business. It is important that the choice of business model depict the business processes that will be supported by the Web database construction. During this analysis phase, the following questions should be asked:

- What are the current opportunities, current problems, and/or current customers' needs?
- What is the business mission?
- What is the mission of the proposed Web database construction?
- What are the business objectives?
- What is the construction scope?

The first step in choosing an electronic commerce business model is to determine whether the business is selling a product or a service. If the business is selling a product, then the electronic commerce model is **brand-centric** and will usually result in lower fixed costs and wider profit margins. An electronic commerce business model for selling products can take advantage of sales generated when third parties create related applications. However, this may also require a sales force in the field, which could significantly add to the cost of doing business.

If the business is selling a service, then the model is **customer-centric** and would eliminate manufacturing and distribution costs and generate a recurring revenue stream. This model would also attract customers because of lower up-front capital expenditures and a shorter deployment process. Electronic commerce models for services can be expensive to build and deploy because the fixed costs to run a network for customers increase as the business grows. These models are also easily replicated by the competition.

Push versus Pull Technology

To best determine the appropriate business model, it is also important to understand what electronic commerce can and cannot do for the business. Electronic commerce is a **pull technology** medium. The information that is available on the Web is downloaded on command, or "pulled," by the customer. Compare this to other media. Broadcast, for example, is sent, or pushed, to customers. It is not yet as dynamic or interactive as electronic commerce. Initially, the act of a customer requesting information from an electronic commerce business is similar to tuning in a TV or radio broadcast. With electronic commerce, however, customers can use a dynamic business model, such as a guestbook or shopping cart, not only sending information to the business, but also requesting that information be sent back, thus making the medium interactive. The traditional way to reach a customer has been to use push marketing to deliver information about the business and its goods or services. Direct mail marketing uses the post office. Telemarketers use telephones. The brick-and-mortar business generally uses push marketing, while the click-and-mortar uses pull. What has laid the foundation for this generalization? Typically, the market pushes and technology pulls. With technology and pull marketing, the identification of an interesting technology or a product is made first, then consumers are sought.

Think of traditional **push technology** as a sales pitch in which the salesperson "pushes" the customer to buy. In contrast, pull marketing does just the opposite. Pull marketing is based on first identifying consumers' needs and then developing a new product to meet those needs. In the electronic commerce pull model, customers must discover purchasing sources by searching the Web using a search engine like Google or Alltheweb or by going to Web portals, such as Yahoo or Excite. The business must also employ strategies to motivate customers to visit the site and make purchases. One consideration in determining the appropriate business model is for the business to understand which methodologies can be used to make its Web site the customer's first choice. Strategies must be developed for enhancing the business' publicity on the Internet.

Web Break

Want to increase the visitor traffic? Consider ensuring your business is the first one returned in a Web search to bring more customers to your site. Visit ZDNet and read PC Magazine Editor's Choice for Web Portals at http://www.zdnet.com/pcmag/stories/reviews/0,6755,2327801,00.html. Find out what they say about which portal is best and why.

The possibilities include the use of **banner advertisements**, where businesses advertise their products or services on other popular Web sites. The use of links in other business databases and Web sites is also a strategy that can be employed. Also, consideration should be given to purchasing the top ranking from a heavily used search engine. The first return in a search will bring more viewers and, in turn, more business. Even choosing the business' name comes into play. Some businesses intentionally use "A" words in the business title to move it up in alphabetical listings. The use of metatags in the HEAD section of the company's homepage can also be used. Often businesses use these metatags to repeat words many times in type that is masked from the customer's view by formatting the text in the same color as that of the page. The search engine will then read these "invisible words" and use them in its ranking, thus increasing the site's relevance to the search. For example, some sites use words such as "Buy Our Widgit" dozens of times in hidden fonts. The search engine will count the words "buy" and "widgit" and rate the site favorably. This form of marketing is similar to using the alphabet to move the business higher in order in the Yellow Pages.

Today, push technology is not limited to disseminating static information about a business to customers—it is emerging as a marketing alternative for electronic commerce. Information push can be used to attract customers with the results of intensive datamining or computation that might trigger consumer-buying action. For example, businesses can subscribe to an agent that processes large datastores in the background and uses the results of its analysis to create interest profiles of users tailored to particular products or services. An example of this type of technology is **Webcasting**. In this model users locate relevant sites and register their interest profiles. The business stores the data from these profiles, and the information server itself sends relevant information, at suitable times, to users without waiting for additional requests. Businesses have used Webcasting to send information regarding new product lines, sales, or items of interest based on database profile queries. PointCast and Netscape's Inbox direct service are two examples of Webcasting services. PointCast requires users to download and, without cost, install client software that communicates over a proprietary TCP/IP-based protocol with PointCast servers. Users register their interest profiles with the PointCast client, which then initiates requests on the users' behalf and displays the results. Netscape's Inbox direct service is not client based. With Inbox, interest profiles are registered on the server. The server filters Web data and sends relevant information to users via electronic mail based on their profiles. Another example of the use of push marketing in electronic commerce business models is the use of **SPAM**, junk e-mail. Not only is this not effective, but applications have been developed to aid the consumer in avoiding, or even eliminating, SPAM.

4.2 Planning a Successful Electronic Commerce Business

Once the business goals have been analyzed and the appropriate electronic commerce business model has been determined, the plans for the site can begin. Sound planning, following the analysis, and setting realistic goals can help a business control Web database construction costs and is worth the time invested.

Plan Considerations

The main steps in planning a successful electronic business are the following:

- Identify the customers and/or potential customers
- Identify the customers' needs
- Determine the site's content
- Determine the organization of the site's contents

To identify the potential customers and their needs, the use of a **dynamic feedback form** is useful. This allows direct user feedback and can be used in shaping the focus of the electronic commerce site. Building a feedback form is similar to building a guestbook. Both are simple Web database constructions.

Your plan must also consider content and should include a physical drawing of the layout of the site. How many pages are there? How do they link to one another? Who will maintain the Web site? How much time-sensitive material will be included? Remember that the business' Web site will be viewed not only by customers, but also by potential customers, prospects, suppliers, potential employees, loan officers, and the Web community members around the globe. Once you have identified the business' most important audience, focus the electronic commerce model and the business' message on them.

The plan should directly address brand- or customer-centricity. The brand-centric model is one that contains little beyond outbound

Figure 4-1
Determinants in Planning Electronic Commerce Web Database Constructions

- Improve business image
- Improve customer service
- Increase sales
- Identify potential customers
- Increase visibility
- Expand markets
- Reduce costs
- Meet and exceed customers' expectations
- Gain and/or maintain competitive advantage

information about the product, company, and purchasing details. To construct a successful electronic commerce model, it is necessary to establish a balance between actively selling the product and providing customers reasons to enjoy their visit. The customer-centric site is aware of the existing customers, the potential customers, and the browsers. A successful model moves the potential customers and browsers to the customer category. One strategy for enabling this move is to allow visitor interaction with the business and other visitors. E-mail, discussion groups, and chat rooms have all been proven to increase visitor interaction.

Examples of Successful Web Database Constructions

Figure 4-2 shows the Hellmann's Web site at www.mayo.com. The site does not simply give information about their products or deliver a hard sell. Instead, Hellmann's has created a site filled with engaging colors, whimsy, humor, and a high level of customer interaction. Customers can enter contests, send feedback, join chat rooms, and even send a cyber sandwich to a friend.

Another customer-centric site is the BMW North America Web site at http://www.bmwusa.com, shown in Figure 4-3. The site allows visitors to build their own dream car, join an owners' newsgroup, or visit the virtual BMW center. Visitors can also view short videos, such as *The Follow*, by acclaimed director Wong Kar-Wai, or Guy Ritchie's *Star*. To increase customer interest and awareness, BMW has fea-

Figure 4-2

Hellmann's Web Site Utilizes Visitor Interaction

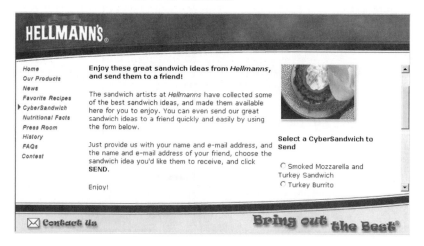

Figure 4-3
*BMW North America's Web Site Uses Video Streaming Technology to Entertain and
Capture Interest*

tured international personalities like Mickey Rourke and Madonna.
The BMW Interactive Film Player on the site allows visitors to play
enhanced Quick Time films, automatically checking on availability of
new films and trailers each time they connect to the Internet.

The Disney Web site at www.disney.com (Figure 4-4) also gains
customer interaction in a variety of ways. From the Disney Web site
visitors can plan vacations, send electronic greeting cards, play
games, and hear stories.

Figure 4-4
Disney's Web Site Gains Customer Interaction in a Variety of Ways

An excellent example of an online survey can be seen at the Louvre Museum's Web site at http://www.louvre.fr/louvrea.htm (Figure 4-5). Visitors can take a virtual tour of the museum. To view their QuickTime Virtual Reality images of the museum, visitors need the QuickTime plug-in provided by the museum.

From http://www.levi.com/ view the Levi's jeans Web site. Levi's is another site that makes excellent use of customer engagement and interactions. Customers cannot only view hilarious karaoke, but also create a custom pair of jeans by working with the interactive software, Original Spin, to modify an existing style or put a new twist on an old one.

Several sites have created a loyal customer base through interaction with and among customers and in the process have won awards for best Web site on the Internet. These include The Hunger Site (http://www.thehungersite.com) for public activism and awareness, Joe Cartoon (http://www.joecartoon.com/) for animation, The Void (http://www.thevoid.co.uk/) for Web site design, MediaConsult (http://www.mediaconsult.ch/) for health care, the Motley Fool (http://www.fool.com/) for financial and money information, Atom Films (http://www.atomfilms.com/) for movies, Spinner (http://www.spinner.com) for music, PBS TV (http://www.pbs.org/) for television, and Discovery Kids (http://kids.discovery.com/) for kidssites. Each is a model of successful electronic commerce Web database construction.

Figure 4-5

The Louvre Museum's Web Site Includes a Virtual Tour

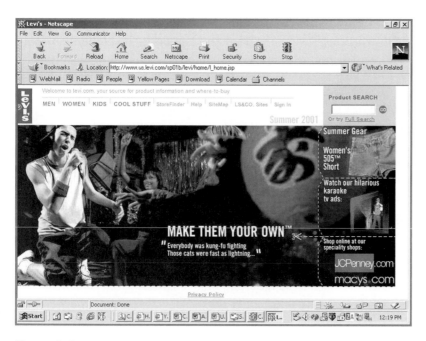

Figure 4-6
Create Your Own Jeans at the Levi's Web Site

4.3 The Online Guestbook Model

The guestbook is simple electronic commerce Web database construction that enables customer interaction with businesses. A guestbook gives the business the ability to gather information from its visitors. Visitors can post a public message that may include name, e-mail, URL, home page, or comments about the site. With a guestbook, the business can also easily collect visitor feedback on the business or the site. Creating an online guestbook gives visitors to the site a user-friendly format to provide valuable feedback and, at the same time, reduces the effort involved in collecting and recording this information.

This book's companion Web site contains the sample electronic commerce business models discussed in this chapter and throughout the book. You will need to install these sample models on your hard drive. The folders on the Web site should be placed in the WebSite folder on your hard drive so that at the conclusion of the installation, you have ...WebSite\cgi-win, ...WebSite\htdocs, and ...WebSite\lib. Verify that all folders and files have read/write permission after the copy process has been completed. If they do not have this access, the interaction between the front-end and back-end of the Web database construction will not be completed.

Kanthaka Farms
Exploring the Sample
Guestbook Electronic
Commerce Business Model

Kanthaka Farms is a continuing case study in this book that illustrates the process of building electronic commerce with Web database constructions. In Chapter 3, you installed and set your administration properties for WebSite, your Web server software. Now you will explore the sample guestbook electronic commerce business model as you determine the appropriate business model for Kanthaka Farms Web database construction.

To run the guestbook business model that accompanies this book, verify that your Web server software is installed and that you have installed the sample applications from this book's companion Web site to your WebSite directory as explained earlier in this chapter.

1. Launch your Web server software. Click on Start, Programs, WebSite Professional, WebSite Pro Server. Your server icon should now appear in the taskbar tray.

2. Start your **Web client.** A Web browser is also referred to as a Web client. The main purpose of the Web client is to pass the user's request to the Web server and pass any user data related to this request to the Web server. The Web client is also responsible for showing the results of the request returned by the Web server in a format that is understood by the user.

3. From your Web client, type the following URL to display the main menu of the electronic commerce guestbook business model:

`http://localhost/book/ch04/ch04.htm`

4. Your main menu of the electronic commerce guestbook business model should look similar to Figure 4.7. Notice the symbol of the gryphon on the far right of the taskbar tray. This symbol is the WebSite server software logo and indicates that the program is running.

5. Click the link that reads "Click here to SIGN our guestbook."

6. The link takes you to a dynamic Web page that allows user input. This is the dynamic front-end of the Web database construction. This screen is an HTML form that you will work with in Chapter 6 of this book.

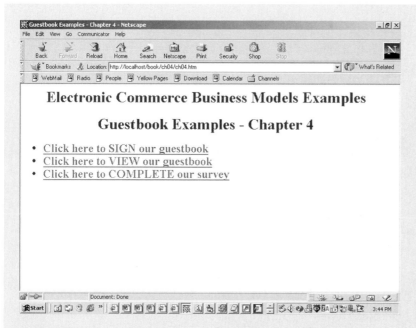

Figure 4.7
The Main Menu of the Electronic Commerce Guestbook Business Model

7. Complete the form by typing in your name, e-mail address, date of birth, and a comment or two. Be sure that you type in the date in the XX/XX/XX format.

8. Once you have completed the form, click on the Enter button at the bottom of the form to submit your text to an Access back-end database.

If your Web client displays a message box that informs you that any information you submit is insecure and could be observed by a third party while in transit, just click on Continue. The middleware that will be used for this example is a Microsoft Visual Basic program. Within seconds, the middleware will submit your text to the database where the data will be saved, and a new HTML form will be completed ad hoc. An **ad hoc form** is one that is "improvised" or created from the means at hand. Often, these types of forms are created on the return trip from back-end to front-end by the middleware and are referred to as having been created "**on the fly.**"

You will also note that the middleware program returned your day of birth. The code in the Visual Basic program enables this field to

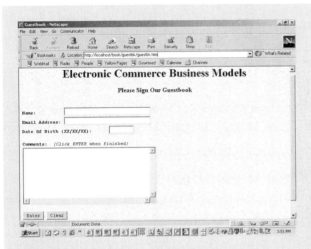

Figure 4-8

The Dynamic Front-End HTML Form

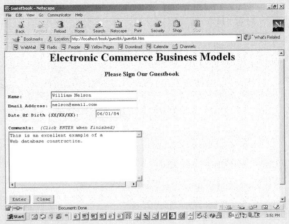

Figure 4-9

A Sample HTML Form Submission

be used to pass a page with the correct day to the browser. Part of the code in the CGI program is shown below:

```
Set rs = db.OpenRecordset("tblGuestbook_Entries")
rs.AddNew
rs!Name = Name
rs!Email = Email
rs!BirthDate = BirthDate
rs!Remarks = Remarks
rs.Update
Send ("<H1 ALIGN=CENTER>Electronic Commerce Business
  Models</H1><P><H2 ALIGN=CENTER>Thank you for signing our
  guestbook. You will be receiving more information from
  us by email soon!")
If Not IsNull(BirthDate) Then
 txtBirthDate = Format(BirthDate, "Long Date")
 DayOfBirth = Left(txtBirthDate, InStr(txtBirthDate, ",")
  - 1)
 Send ("<BR><BR>From the birthdate that you submitted our
  records indicate that you were born on " & DayOfBirth &
  ".")
End If
Send ("<BR><BR>At this point, <A HREF = " & QT &
  CGI_ExecutablePath & "/ViewGuestBook" & QT & ">you can
  view the guest book.</A></H2>")
End Sub
```

9. You will note that in the ad hoc HTML form there is an active Web link. As you move your pointer over the words "you can view the guestbook," your pointer will turn into a hand, indicating the link.

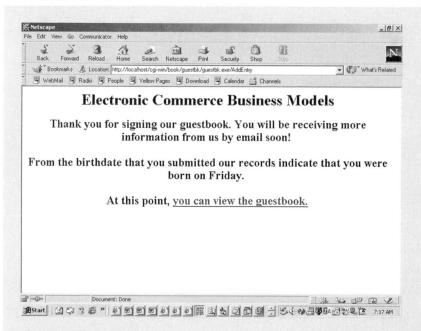

Figure 4-10
The Ad Hoc HTML Form

Note that the link URL is http://localhost/cgi-win/book/guestbk/ guestbk.exe/ ViewGuestBook. Either click on the link, or type this URL directly into your browser.

10. Your screen should look similar to Figure 4-11 and should display a listing of the guestbook's entries.

Consider how the display of the guestbook would look if your business had ten entries, or even 110 entries. As the guestbook grows it is important to have a mechanism in place to manage the growth. Most visitors would not want to see all the guestbook entries; more likely, they will want to view only the most recent visitors to the site.

Using SQL, the Web database construction can be built to search the back-end database for entries made after a specified date. View the ViewGuestBook page (Figure 4-12) to see how it would add to this electronic commerce business model.

11. In your Web client, open the following page:

```
http://localhost/book/guestbk/view.htm
```

12. Enter a valid date in the Enter Starting Date field. Click on the View button.

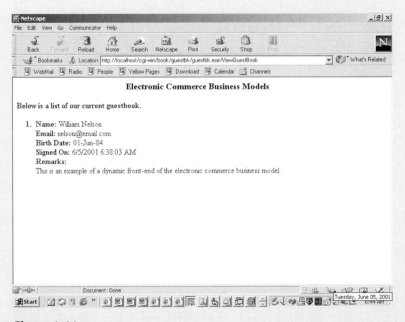

Figure 4-11
Display of the Guestbook Entries

13. The Web database construction will return the entries in the back-end database that are on or before the date you entered, as shown in Figure 4-13.

The code in the middleware Visual Basic program allows the back-end database to be searched for any entries that meet your criteria. The list is another example of an ad hoc form created "on the fly" from the information being passed back and forth through the Web database construction. Below is partial code in the middleware that enables the visitors on specified dates to be returned to the user.

```
Sub APP_ViewWithDate()
    Dim StartingDate As Variant
    StartingDate = EmptyToNullField("StartingDate")
    'Check For Required Fields
  If IsNull(StartingDate) Then
    StartingDate = Date
  End If
    Set rs = db.OpenRecordset("Select * From
    tblGuestbook_Entries Where SignedOn >= #" &
    StartingDate & "#")
```

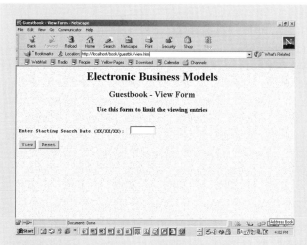

Figure 4-12

The View HTML Form of the Guestbook

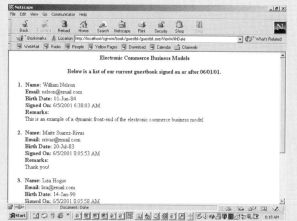

Figure 4-13

The ViewWithDate HTML Form of the Guestbook

```
If rs.EOF Then
   Send ("<H4>There are no entries in our guestbook that
   were made on or after " & StartingDate & ".</H4>")
   Exit Sub
End If
Send ("<H4 ALIGN=CENTER>Electronic Commerce Business
 Models</H4><p> <H4 Align=CENTER> Below is a list of our
 current guestbook signed on or after " & StartingDate &
 ".</H4>")
Send ("<OL>")
Do Until rs.EOF
   Send ("<B><LI>Name: </B>" & rs!Name)
   Send ("<BR><B>Email: </B>" & rs!Email)
   Send ("<BR><B>Birth Date: </B>" & Format(rs!BirthDate,
   "Medium Date"))
   Send ("<BR><B>Signed On: </B>" & rs!SignedOn)
   Send ("<BR><B>Remarks: </B><BR>" & rs!Remarks)
   Send ("<P><P>")
   DoEvents
   rs.MoveNext
Loop
Send ("</OL>")
rs.Close
End Sub
```

4.4 The Online Survey Model

Another dynamic Web database construction is the online survey. Businesses use online surveys to determine customer opinion and increase customer–business interaction. Although online surveys are a relatively inexpensive and simple business model to construct, their rewards can be high. They often provide quick and beneficial results; however, like guestbook projects, require planning for maximum effectiveness. Careful attention should be given to their development. The key steps for creating successful online surveys are the following:

Key Steps
- Identify the business' survey objectives
- Determine what information is needed
- Develop the survey questions
- Conduct the survey
- Analyze the customer responses
- Recommend and plan a course of action

Kanthaka Farms
Exploring the Sample Online
Survey Electronic Commerce
Business Model

To run the online survey business model that accompanies this book, verify that your Web server software is installed and that you have installed the sample applications from this book's companion Web site to your WebSite directory as explained earlier in this chapter.

1. Verify that your Web server software is running, and from your Web client display the following file:

http://localhost/book/ch04/ch04.htm

2. Click on the link that reads "Click here to COMPLETE our survey." The screen shown in Figure 4-14 should appear.

3. Examine the online survey. There are four different ways in which this survey gathers user information. The first is with the use of **option buttons**, also called radio buttons. Notice that you are only allowed one choice with this type of input. Option buttons are used to capture user input in a way that presents several mutually exclusive choices to the user, meaning that a user can select only one option at any one time. For instance, in this survey, users are not permitted to be satisfied and dissatisfied at the same time (Figure 4-15).

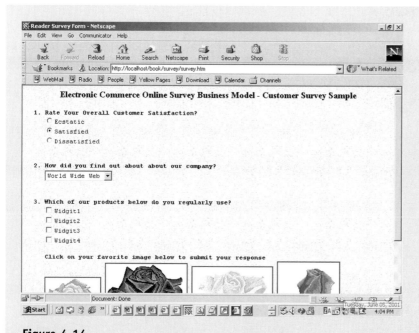

Figure 4-14

The Online Survey Business Model—Customer Survey Sample

The next type of input on the survey is the **list box**, as shown in Figure 4-16. Like option buttons, list boxes can be used by visitors to the Web site to answer questions or select options. List boxes can also be used in broader ways, however, and they are an excellent tool to limit user and data input error.

Figure 4-15

Option Button as Customer Input Type

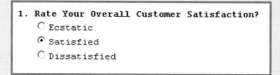

Figure 4-16

List Box as Customer Input Type

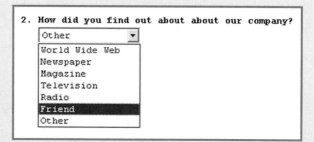

Check boxes, like option buttons and list boxes, also allow customers to interact with your Web database construction. Unlike option button, with check boxes customers are not limited in the number of selections they can make. However, each check box displays a choice that has two clearly distinguishable states, for example, on and off. In this case, the check boxes allow customers to check yes or no to the use of a particular company product. Since check boxes are typically used in a group to provide a multiple-choice field, in our example the user may check all that apply (Figure 4-17).

The last input type is the **submit button**. Figure 4-18 displays an example of how a business' products might be displayed and the images used to effect the interaction.

4. Click on an image. Once the image is clicked, the customer's input is sent from the front-end HTML to the middleware Visual Basic program. There the program parses the data onto the back-end Access database. An HTML ad hoc form is created, thanking the customer for their input and offering yet another link as shown in Figure 4-19.

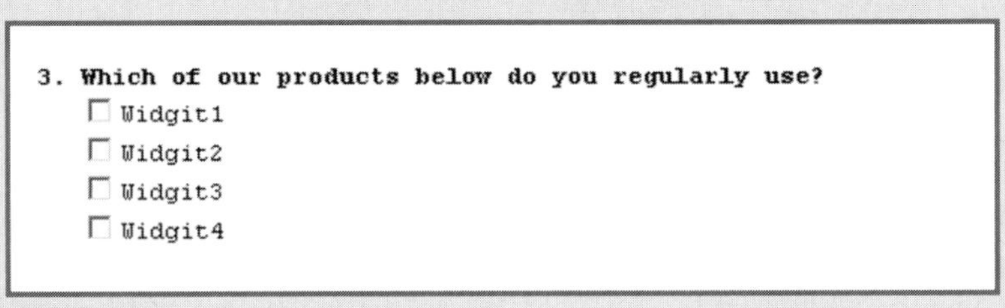

Figure 4-17
Check Box as Customer Input Type

Figure 4-18
Images as Customer Input Type

5. Click on the link to view the analysis. The analysis page is the .../cgi-win/book/survey/survey.exe/GetStat page that is delineated in the Visual Basic program. With help from Access queries, the Visual Basic program mines the back-end database for information gathered from customers submitting the survey. Responses have been totaled, and appropriate percentages have been calculated to make the analysis more meaningful to both the customer and management. This type of analysis can be very useful in management's decision-making processes (Figure 4-20).

Figure 4-19

Online Survey Ad Hoc Response Form

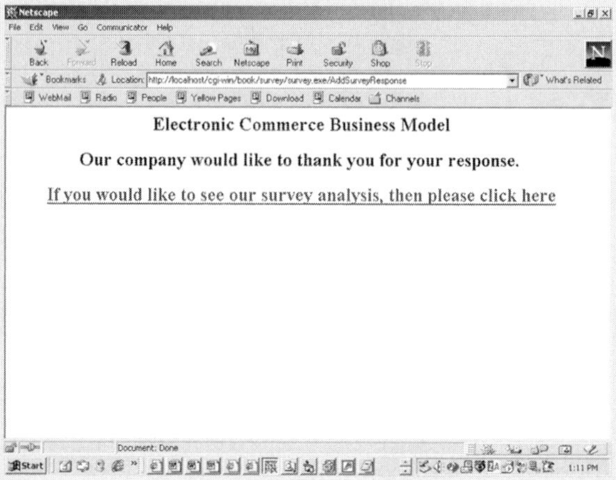

Figure 4-20

Data Analysis Performed through Back-End Database Queries

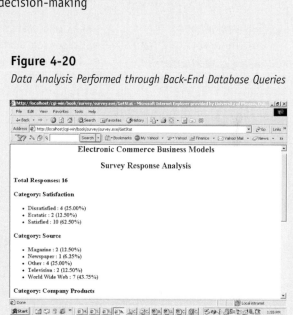

4.5 The Online Job Listing Service Model

The online job listing service is another type of business model commonly used in electronic commerce. The interaction between the customer and the business in this model is handled similarly to that of the online survey. The front-end Web interface is an HTML form. Visual Basic is used for the middleware in this example, and the back-end is an Access database.

FOCUS ON ELECTRONIC COMMERCE

Managing the Content Infrastructure: The Foundation for Successful Business Sites

The focus of this piece was on a business-to-customer relationship, but what happens when the interaction is not B2C?

What are some problems that are associated with businesses exchanging data in a B2B scenario?

How can systems such as content management applications help businesses overcome these challenges?

The success of the online business is rooted in its Web content infrastructure. Its real power is in the dynamic content and customer interaction. The challenge is in the business' ability to move new and ever-changing information to the customer in near-real time and to customize the information to the individual customer's preferences.

The infrastructure has typically involved a Web site manager's creation of an HTML form Web page, called a template. New information is then poured directly into the page many times as it passes from front-end to middleware to back-end and back again. Because of this dynamic Web page generation, Web technicians are able to create an overall template once, with fields for customer-specific information. Web servers can then complete each template with specific data in ad hoc, individualized pages.

Software applications, called Web **content management software**, are designed to speed the delivery of Web content by pushing it closer to the customer and end-user. Web **content management** is needed to keep the infrastructure intact for the massive amounts of recycled, or **"repurposed" data** available today. Web content management software is similar to a word processor's mail-merge function, which has the ability to mass-mail myriad form letters with customer-specific data. What Web content applications do is match Web page templates to a content server, add a back-end database, and attach the complete package to a Web server.

Martin Brauns, President and CEO of Interwoven, Inc., recently opened an enterprise content-management conference for the Association for Information and Image Management International in Silver Springs, MD. He said that the old model of a centralized Web development team is not enough in today's competitive business environment and added that with reduced IT spending, content management is crucial to a business' success. Electronic commerce responsibility must be spread throughout the company.

Brauns offered "five slices" of **content infrastructure** for the electronic commerce business to focus on: content aggregation, content collaboration, content management, content intelligence, and content distribution. "We need to give people the tools, systems, and processes to put stuff on the Web themselves," Brauns said. "We need to democratize and decentralize the job of content distribution."

Content management systems usually support tagging structures like HTML or XML that allow content reuse without manual reformatting. They also generally employ scripting languages like VBScript, JavaScript, or Tool Command Language.

The downside is that content management is often both difficult and expensive to implement and use. Each new Web page requires new templates and scripting. Standardized templates can become detrimental to business and customer innovation. Even effective content management applications may have difficulty handling large infrastructures with specialized needs for expert customization, building scripts for massive data transfer, or constructing effective and efficient templates.

But the benefits certainly outweigh the challenges. Content management systems are a critical component in personalizing the electronic commerce business experience and enabling business–customer interaction. Managing the content infrastructure is the foundation for successful business sites.

Sources: Stacy Cowley, IDG News Service, "Web content infrastructure: What businesses need," *ComputerWorld*, May 1, 2001; James Cope, "Web content delivery competition increases," *ComputerWorld*, September 4, 2000; Cynthia Morgan, "Web content management," *ComputerWorld*, April 24, 2000.

 Web Break

XML is a tagging system that, in the electronic commerce model, allows content to be reused without reformatting. Many of the standards built around XML are still in flux. The Information and Content Exchange (ICE) protocol, first introduced to the WWW Consortium in 1998, is specifically designed to alleviate many of these XML problems. To learn more about ICE, visit http://www.w3.org/TR/1998/NOTE-ice-19981026.

This type of application is more advanced in many ways than the previous two electronic commerce examples. Though this example is not as robust as a commercial site would be, it is easy to see how this model depends on the efficient storage and retrieval capability of the back-end database to match job seekers with potential employers across the great expanse of the World Wide Web. For the job listing service to work, every job in the database must have an associated company. As you investigate the example, try to notice which forms have been created by the middleware "on the fly."

Kanthaka Farms
Exploring the Sample Job
Listing Service Business Model

Kanthaka Farms is a continuing case study in this book that illustrates the process of building electronic commerce with Web database constructions. In Chapter 3, you installed and set your administration properties for WebSite, your Web server software. Now you will explore the sample job listing service electronic commerce business model as you determine the appropriate business model for Kanthaka Farms Web database construction.

To run the online job listing service business model that accompanies this book, verify that your Web server software is installed and that you have installed the sample applications from this book's companion Web site to your WebSite directory as explained earlier in this chapter.

1. Launch your Web server software. Click on Start, Programs, WebSite Professional, WebSite Pro Server. Your server icon should now appear in the taskbar tray.

2. From your Web client view the following URL:

```
http://localhost/book/job/joblist.htm
```

The Web page in Figure 4-21 below should now be displayed.

3. Click on the first Web link that will allow the user to add a new business to your online job listing service. The Web client will then display the form to add a business as in Figure 4-22.

Figure 4-21
Start Page for the Sample Job Listing Service

Figure 4-22
Add Business Form

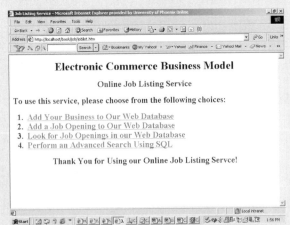

4. Using the information below, complete the HTML form:

```
Business Name:        Prairie Paper
Address:              Post Office Box 2000
City:                 High Point
State:                NC
Zip:                  27262
Phone:                800-111-1111
Fax:                  800-111-1112
Email:                Prairie@email.com
Web Address:          http://prairie.net
Description:          Prairie Paper is a new age company
                      that manufactures paper not from
                      trees, but from inorganic sources.
```

5. Click on Add. Your returned ad hoc HTML form should look like Figure 4-23. The information in your Web front-end HTML form was directed in the source code to the Visual Basic middleware program. The middleware program then parsed the information to the back-end database and referenced another file located on the server. A message was then returned to you indicating that your information had been added to the database. Notice that two interactive links are also displayed. The first link allows you to view the information that

Figure 4-23

Added Business Ad Hoc HTML Form

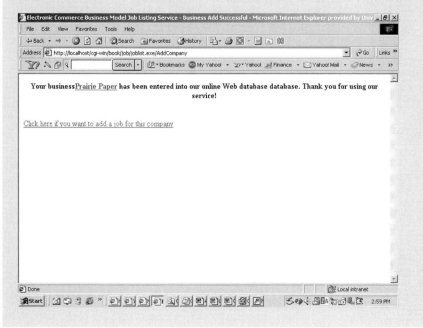

has been added to the database about your business. By clicking on second link, a specific job opening can be associated with the new business just added to the database.

6. Click on the second link and add the following data:

```
Job Title:              Web developer
Contact Name:           Clancey Nolan
Search Keywords:        ASP, JSP, CGI-WIN, SSI
Estimated Salary:       80000
Job Reference Code:     CAT1
Job Description:        Web developer for progressive start-
                        up with strong financing
Job Requirements:       College degree in CIS or MIS with
                        minimum 3 years in the field.
                        Programming experience in Visual
                        Basic and Java. Knowledge of WebSite
                        and IIS Web server software. Strong
                        communication and organization skills
                        a MUST!
```

7. Click on the Add Job button to enter the information to the back-end database. Figure 4-24 below shows the returned page created on the fly. There are three links, providing more opportunity for user

Figure 4-24

Ad Hoc Form Returned after Job Submission

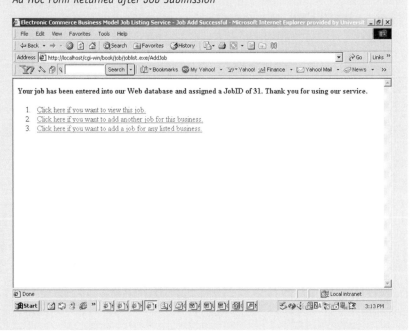

interactivity with the job listing service: The first allows you to view the job that was just entered; the second allows you to add another job for Prairie Paper; and the last allows you to add a job for any business that exists in the database.

8. Spend some time interacting with the online job listing service. Make notes on the URL displayed on your Web client. See whether you can identify the front-end, middleware, and back-end components of the Web database construction. You will learn how to build this business model later in the book.

4.6 Measuring the Success of the Electronic Commerce Business Model

Though success can often be defined in many ways, in the electronic commerce business model success is measured in customer interaction. A business can measure success in the number of visitors to its Web site. As the Web server receives a request for information these **hits** on the server can be counted and used as a measurement for success. Hits can be measured historically—how the company has done in the past—or they can be measured against similar companies. Hits are also measured against industry averages.

Businesses can also use sophisticated Web management software that will aid in the analysis of the Web page traffic and guide the users more effectively through the business' site. These Web management applications can also provide another level of customer interactions. The applications can offer suggestions to users to go to certain areas of the Web site and view other information. Information gathered about the customer can be used later to continue the interaction in an **asynchronous** delivery. Asynchronous means not synchronized. Asynchronous delivery describes objects or events that are not coordinated in time, or not real-time delivery, like e-mail.

The most common way in which businesses measure success is in the bottom line. An electronic commerce public Web site often will use incremental sales revenue produced from the site as a measure of success. This reinforces the need for planning in Web site design. The more intuitive the site is to the user, the more customer interaction that is available, and the more user-friendly the site is, the more successful the electronic commerce design, no matter how it is measured.

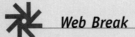

Web Break

Java Server Pages, JSP, give the programmer the ability to define their own JSP tags, also called custom tags. These can be added to tag libraries and reused in any number of JSP files. Custom tags allow complex programming logic to boil down to a set of simple tags, which JSP developers can then easily use to interact with the asynchronous processing of Java Messaging Service, JMS. To learn more about how to add the power of asynchronous processing to JSPs, visit JavaWorld at http://www.javaworld.com/.

Understanding the Online Job Listing Business Model

This electronic commerce business model has a great deal of customer interaction built into the construction. And though the process of navigating the forms is fairly intuitive, a better understanding of the communication among the model components is appropriate. First, note that there are both mandatory and optional fields. Mandatory fields are specified both in text and in format. If mandatory fields are not completed by the user, the construction will return an ad hoc form notifying the user which fields are empty and must be completed. Optional fields, such as salary and job description, are helpful when a user performs a job search, but are not necessary to the completion of the Web interaction process.

Drop-down lists are used to increase the efficiency of the interaction. It is possible that a user might not realize that a business must be added to the database before a job can be added. If they go directly to the form to add a job, the business that is associated with the job must be chosen from a drop-down list rather than typed directly into the database. If the user does not find the company name on the list, the Add button is conveniently located next to the list. This is an example of sound Web database design. These types of controls used in the design add efficiency to the construction and an element of user-friendliness.

As you investigate the online job service, you will note that the back-end database, Job.mdb, has two tables. These tables are related by the common field CompanyID. This relationship is discussed at greater length in Chapter 5. The CompanyID uniquely identifies each company in the database. In the job listings table, the JobID is the unique identifier for each record. The back-end database works most efficiently when you specify a key for a table. The value of the key field, or the combined values of a group of key fields, must not be found in more than one record.

There are several advantages to setting a unique identifier for a table. First, the key is automatically indexed, which makes information retrieval faster. Second, a table is opened, and the records are automatically sorted in order by this key. Finally, a key prevents entry of duplicate data because the back-end database does not allow duplicates in the primary key field.

Searching the Online Job Service

As electronic commerce grows, the back-end databases used for search and retrieval will increase in size, and the power to seek, index, and retrieve information must also grow. The Web database design must be structured so that the typical customer has no trouble browsing and locating information on topics in the business' Web database.

The online job service business model shown here has three search features to enable Web users to quickly find jobs of interest. The user can use a **keyword search**. This search uses pertinent words that appear in different fields to find information for the user in the back-end database. **Drill-down searches** use a hierarchical form of exploring to narrow down the search for the user. Both keyword and drill-down searches usually limit the user to a limited number of fields. The **SQL search** uses structured query language to find data by specifying valid SQL criteria. This type of search does not limit the user by fields; however, users are expected to know SQL syntax to complete their search.

The Role of the Web Server

The Web server, using the client/server model and HTTP, serves the files that form Web pages to the Web client. Web server software is often part of a larger application for serving e-mail, downloading requests for FTP files, and building and publishing Web pages. When your Web browser requests the URL http://localhost/ book/job/joblist.htm, the Web server delivers the file C:\WebSite\ HTDOCS\BOOK\Joblist.htm. Web servers also act as gateways to external programs. It does so by *pointing*, or directing the server to an executable file or scripting program. This interaction often uses CGI programs to point the server to the appropriate file. How effectively and efficiently the Web server performs its responsibilities can have a direct impact on the success of a site.

Summary

▣ **Define the most common types of electronic commerce business models used today.** The most commonly used electronic commerce business models include guestbooks, surveys and questionnaires, job listing services, and most certainly, the shopping cart. Consumers use electronic commerce business models to purchase a variety of goods and services online. The business model is the way a business conducts business to sustain itself, in other words, a plan for how the business generates revenue. The business model sets the parameters for how a company makes money by determining where it is positioned in the value chain. One of the first steps in building successful Web database constructions is to determine the appropriate business model to use. A thorough business analysis must be made to determine which form of electronic commerce best suits the needs and goals of the business. It is important that the choice of business model depict the business processes that will be supported by the Web database construction.

▣ **Discuss the differences between pull versus push technology.** Electronic commerce is a pull medium. The information that is available on the Web is downloaded on command, or "pulled," by the customer. The traditional way to reach a customer has been to use push marketing to deliver information about the business and its goods or services. Pull marketing is based on first identifying consumers' needs and then developing a new product to meet those needs. In the electronic commerce pull model, customers must discover purchasing sources by searching the Web using a search engine like Google or Alltheweb or by going to Web portals, such as Yahoo or Excite.

▣ **List the necessary steps in planning an electronic commerce business.** Once the business goals have been analyzed and the appropriate electronic commerce business model has been determined, the plans for the site can begin. Sound planning, following the analysis, and setting realistic goals can help a business control

Web database construction costs and is worth the time invested. The main steps in planning a successful electronic business are the following:

1. Identify the customers and/or potential customers
2. Identify the customers' needs
3. Determine the site's content
4. Determine the organization of the site's contents

■ **Describe the fundamental elements of the guestbook model.** The guestbook is a simple electronic commerce Web database construction that enables customer interaction with businesses. A guestbook gives the business the ability to gather information from its visitors. Creating an online guestbook gives visitors to the site a user-friendly format to provide valuable feedback, and, at the same time, reduces the effort involved in collecting and recording this information.

■ **Describe the fundamental elements of the survey model.** The online survey is another dynamic Web database construction. Businesses use online surveys to determine customer opinion and increase customer–business interaction. Although online surveys are a relatively inexpensive and simple business model to construct, their rewards can be high. They often provide quick and beneficial results. The key steps for creating successful online surveys are the following:

1. Identify the business' survey objectives
2. Determine what information is needed
3. Develop the survey questions
4. Conduct the survey
5. Analyze the customer responses
6. Recommend and plan a course of action

■ **Describe the fundamental elements of the job listing service model.** Like the first two models, the online job listing service uses a front-end Web interface to connect to a back-end database. This type of application is a more advanced electronic commerce design that depends on the efficient storage and retrieval capability of the back-end database to match job seekers with potential employers across the World Wide Web.

■ **Discuss the use of metrics to measure the success of the electronic commerce business.** Businesses measure success in many ways.

In the electronic commerce business model, success is often measured in customer interaction. A business can measure success in the number of visitors to its Web site. As the Web server receives a request for information, these hits on the server can be counted and used as a measurement for success. Hits can be measured historically—how the company has done in the past—or they can be measured against similar companies. Hits are also measured against industry averages. Sophisticated Web management software can also be used to aid in the analysis of the Web page traffic and guide the users more effectively through the business' site. The most common way in which businesses measure success is in the bottom line. An electronic commerce public Web site often will use incremental sales revenue produced from the site as a measure of success. This reinforces the need for planning in Web site design. The more intuitive the site is to the user, the more customer interaction that is available, and the more user-friendly the site is, the more successful the electronic commerce design, no matter how it is measured.

Chapter Key Terms

ad hoc form	dynamic feedback form	on-the-fly form
asynchronous	electronic commerce business	option buttons
banner advertisement	models	pull technology
brand-centric	guestbook	push technology
check boxes	hits	repurposed data
content infrastructure	keyword search	SPAM
content management	list box	SQL search
content management software	online job-listing service	submit button
customer-centric	online shopping cart	Web client
drill-down search	online survey	Webcasting

Review Questions

1. List and describe the steps that should be taken to determine the appropriate electronic commerce business model to use.

2. Define pull technology. Describe how electronic commerce can use pull technology to meet its goals.

3. What is push technology? How is it used in the electronic commerce model?

4. What is a banner ad? Are banner ads an example of push or pull technology? Justify your answer.

5. How is SPAM used by businesses to reach customers? Discuss the negative elements of using SPAM.

6. Why is planning for an electronic commerce site directly related to its success?

7. What are the key steps in planning for a successful electronic commerce business?

8. What is customer-centricity? How does the electronic commerce plan address customer-centricity?

9. What is a guestbook? How can this model be used to increase customer interactivity with the business?

10. What is a Web client? What is its role in the electronic commerce model?

11. Define ad hoc. How is this characteristic relevant to Web database construction?

12. What are the key steps for creating successful online surveys?

13. List four different input types used to allow dynamic customer interaction in Web database constructions. How is each used?

14. What is content management software? Why is it used and what is its relationship to repurposed data?

15. Discuss the advantages of the job listing service business model over the other two models.

16. What are some metrics that can be used to measure the success of the electronic commerce model?

17. What is asynchronous delivery? How can it be used in the electronic commerce business model?

18. List three different types of searches used to enable customer–business interactivity. Describe how each is used in the electronic commerce model.

Critical Thinking Using the Web

1. We have discussed both synchronous and asynchronous uses of electronic commerce. Plesiochronous delivery is also used in the electronic commerce model. It describes communication that is almost, but not quite, synchronized. Use the Web to find out more about plesiochronous digital hierarchy (PDH), a widely used system in which the transmissions from one continent, such as North America, are interconnected with transmissions from other continents, such as Europe, by making small adjustments in the differing data rates between the systems. What is replacing PDH and why?

2. Visit the Electronic Commerce Reading Room at http://www.wilsonweb.com/research/. This site offers many resources to better understand the intricacies of electronic commerce. The site boasts "the largest collection of articles, links and resources on e-commerce to be found at any single place on the planet." Use the link to Example Stores to view many examples of well-designed Web stores. Also click on other links for more information about how to attract customers to your store, marketing strategies, exploiting the medium, promotion strategies, service, brands and branding, and using banner ads. After exploring the site, write a 200- to 400-word essay describing new "tricks of the trade" that you gleaned from the site. Use presentation software to bullet your main points to share with other members of the class.

3. Shoutcasting is an easy and affordable alternative to corporate Webcasting technologies. Shoutcast is based on a plug-in and server software that allows you to Webcast from your desktop. Shoutcast can broadcast even over limited bandwidths. For the moment, it is a total free-for-all. On any given night on the Shoutcast Web site, you can find around 450 eager Shoutcasters happily producing personal radio stations with truly innovative names. Although the growing Shoutcasting community is still struggling with questions of legality and licensing, many are describing it as the first time that broadcasting has truly been available to the public. Visit the Shoutcast Web site at http://www.shoutcast.com/ and learn more about the technology. Write a 200- to 400-word essay describing the challenges and opportunities of this technology. How can electronic commerce utilize Shoutcasting in its model? Be prepared to discuss your findings.

Chapter Case Study

Albatross Records is a continuing case study in this book that illustrates the process of building electronic commerce with Web database constructions. In Chapter 3, you installed and set your administration properties for WebSite, your Web server software. Now you will continue to plan your Web database construction and begin to determine the appropriate business model for Albatross Records.

■ Define the most common types of electronic commerce business models used today. What techniques might each of these models employ to increase business–customer interaction? Describe each model in detail.

■ Discuss the differences between pull versus push technology. How will each be used in the Albatross Records Web site?

■ List the necessary steps in planning the Albatross Records electronic commerce business.

■ Describe the fundamental elements of the guestbook model. Give a specific example of how Cool could incorporate this model in his site.

■ Describe the fundamental elements of the survey model. Give a specific example of how Cool could incorporate this model in his site.

■ Describe the fundamental elements of the job listing service model. Give a specific example of how Cool could incorporate this model in his site.

■ Discuss the use metrics that measure the success of the electronic commerce business. How will you measure the success of your design for Albatross Records? How will Cool measure the success of your electronic commerce design for his company? Describe instances where the two metrics might be different and explain the differences in the chosen measures.

5

Relational Database Concepts

Learning Objectives

Upon completion of this chapter, you will be able to

- Understand database terms, types, and structures
- Build a back-end database using Microsoft Access 2000 or Access 2002
- Design advanced queries and analyze data through the use of total queries and nested queries
- Create parameter-based queries, which are heavily used for designing the advanced electronic commerce constructions described in the book

Chapter Outline

Data has become the lifeblood of our Internet information economy. Please note that by "Internet information economy," I am referring not only to dot-coms, but to any industry that expects to survive and prosper in the e-business age.

—Curt Hall, "2001: A Data Odyssey," *Business Intelligence Advisor,* Volume V, No. 1, January 2001

5.1 Understanding Relational Databases

The strength of electronic commerce is rooted in the **database**. In business, databases are generally used to automate business forms, for example, invoicing, bookkeeping, and employee records. Business databases are also used to track shipping, inventory, and billing. The search capabilities of a database make it easy for businesses to locate documentation, and the report features of databases make it easy to produce summaries. Databases also allow businesses to make new use of their existing data. For example, a business may take a database containing a customer list and easily create a mailing list or suggestion list.

The Web database construction allows businesses to share information, maintain customer and partner relationships, and conduct business transactions through telecommunication channels, typically the Internet, using databases. Databases are used to store and keep track of the prolific digital information used today by customers and businesses alike. The types of databases used in electronic commerce vary. Typically, the business will use one of the four main types of databases: **flat-file**, **relational**, **object-oriented**, or **hybrid**.

Flat-File Databases

The oldest and simplest form of database is the flat-file database. File-file databases perform some of the most common business duties: bookkeeping, generating mailing labels, and handling personal productivity tasks, such as scheduling appointments. These databases are usually referred to as **spreadsheets**. They use **columns** and **rows** to organize small **pieces of data** into a **list**. These pieces of data are called **elements**. The list is called a **table**. Columns are generally referred to as **fields** or **attributes** and rows are referred to as **records** or **tuples**. Every database consists of records, and each record contains a set of data, often organized as a form. For instance, in the flat-file database storing employee data in Figure 5-1, each complete set of information (name, age, salary, date of employment, and employee number) is a record. In each field there is a single piece of information, such as one employee's name or age. The information in the field appears in a specific place on the record. It is the structure of fields that organizes each record and makes a flat-file database different from other collections of information, such as a business policy manual or pictorial representations.

Flat-file databases do little more than house the business data. They have minimal structure. No **metadata** is stored by the flat-file database structure. The generally accepted definition of the prefix "meta" is "an underlying definition or description." Therefore, metadata is a definition or description of data and **metalanguage** is a definition or description of language. Meta derives from Greek meaning "among, with, after, change." There is also minimal **overhead**, that is, non-data contents, in the flat-file database structure. Examples of overhead are file storage parameters or other coding issues.

Flat-file databases can store information in one long text file, called a **tab-delimited file**. A special character separates each entry in the tab-delimited file. Often a vertical bar (|) is used as a separator. Each entry in the flat-file database contains fields of multiple pieces of information. These fields are organized around a particular object or person and grouped together as a record.

The flat-file database can also be viewed as a table that stores all the data in the flat-file database. The table can be very simple or extremely complex. Closely examine the employee data in Figure 5-1. In a table structure the same data looks like Figure 5-2.

The structure of the text file makes it difficult for the business to search for specific information or to create reports that include only certain fields from each record. For instance, suppose that the business has both a human resources department and an after-hours intramural softball team. The human resources department keeps track of the employee number, name, date of employment, and salary information. The employee who is captain of the company softball team needs to know the names of all employees, their

```
Lname, FName, Age, Monthly_Salary,
Date_of_Employment, Employee_Number|Nelson,
William, 45, $5000, 06/01/1989, 0001|Fulcher,
Cleo, 50, $4500, 11/31/1989, 0002|Nolan, Patricia,
29, $3000, 04/12/1990, 0003|Fowkes, Kate,20,
$2000, 01/19/1993, 0004|Medlar, Stephanie, 22,
$1500, 09/21/1996, 0005
```

Figure 5-1

An Example of a Flat-File Database Storing Employee Data in a Tab-Delimited File

departments, their e-mail addresses, and team positions (if they play) in order to keep them informed about the company softball games. Human resources keeps the information in six fields. The team captain keeps her information in a separate flat-file database with five fields. The last name (Lname) and first name (Fname) fields are the same for both company databases. However, there are fields that are unique to each, too. For example, human resources does not need to know the team position that the employees play. Therefore, this field is unique to the team captain's database. The team captain does not need to know the salary of each employee, so salary-related fields are unique to the human resources database. Each department must inform the other when changes are made to their database in order to keep the two database tables synchronized with the most current information. If the human resource department fails to inform the team captain of a change in an employee name or the addition of a new employee, then the team captain will have poor-quality data. Every time information is recorded in the separate data-

Figure 5-2

Flat-File Database Table for Employee Data

LName	FName	Age	Monthly_Salary	Date_of_Employment	Employee_Number
Nelson	William	45	$5000	06/01/1989	0001
Fulcher	Cleo	50	$4500	11/30/1989	0002
Nolan	Patricia	29	$3000	04/12/1990	0003
Fowkes	Kate	20	$2000	01/19/1993	0004
Medlar	Stephanie	22	$1500	09/21/1996	0005

bases, the opportunity for data errors and redundancies increases. For small businesses, flat-file databases may be sufficient but the larger the file, the more cumbersome it is to process. Also, flat-file databases can contain data anomalies and redundancies.

Flat-file databases do have their strengths. Operating on flat-files can be extremely fast, because there is only data in the file and nothing to slow the processing speed. Many flat-file databases on the market are specialized products containing prearranged tables with relevant information for a particular industry, making start-up time and training less of an issue. These prepackaged databases also have built-in sorting, filtering, and reporting capabilities. Some examples of flat-file database products currently on the market are Microsoft Excel, Intuit Quicken, Microsoft Money, and Datatel Colleague.

Relational Databases

The relational database was born in 1970 when E. F. Codd, a researcher at IBM, wrote a paper outlining the theory. In 1979, Oracle delivered the first commercial SQL relational database management system (RDBMS). Since then, relational databases have grown in popularity to become the business standard. SQL, or structured query language, is an ANSI (American National Standards Institute) standard language for accessing databases that was developed by IBM and was adopted as an industry standard in 1986. SQL can be used to access, define, and manipulate the data in many database systems, among them Oracle, Access, DB2, Sybase, Informix, Microsoft SQL Server, and Corel Paradox.

Relational databases grew quickly in popularity because they solved the major weakness of the flat-file database. In flat-file databases, businesses had to search sequentially through the entire file in order to gather related information. This could be both time-consuming and costly. Relational databases use tables to store information and can share tables. These **relations** are actually two-dimensional tables. Relations reduce data redundancy, duplication of entry effort, and storage space. The relational database model takes advantage of uniformity to build completely new tables out of required information from existing tables. In other words, it uses the relationship of similar data to increase the speed and versatility of the database.

The "relational" part of the name comes into play because of the other tables. A typical relational database can have anywhere from just a few to more than 1,000 tables. Each table contains a column

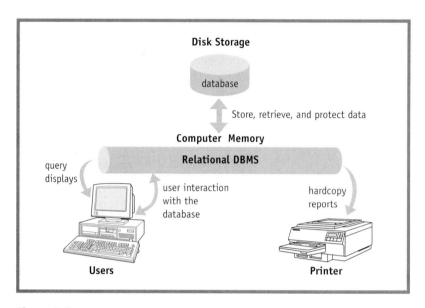

Figure 5-3

The Relational Database Management System Model

or columns that other tables can key on to gather information from
that table so that specific information is easily found.

The flat-file database in Figures 5-1 and 5-2 can be stored in a
relational database and eliminate many of the problems associated
with the flat-file setup. In the example with flat-file databases,
shared by human resources and the softball team, their tables can be
consolidated into one comprehensive relational database. Since
human resources is the department that will first record employee
information, it will have the responsibility of keeping track of the
employee information that was kept by both departments. In this
new model, human resources records changes only once, and the
information is accessible to both departments. When human
resources adds a new employee, the team captain does not also need
to add the new employee to her database.

Remember that there is information that is only relevant to one
individual department. To store this in a relational database, the
business asks three questions about the data:

- What data is only relevant to human resources?
- What data is only relevant to the softball team?
- What data is needed by both departments?

Human resources is responsible for the first and last set of data, and it will be housed in one relational database table, which is shown in Figure 5-4.

To eliminate the duplication of data and the necessity of the team captain sharing a table with human resources, another table can be created. It will not contain the employee data fields Lname, Fname, Age, Date_of_Employment, or Monthly_Salary. To create a relationship between the two tables, a key, or linking column, is identified. A key is the one column that will be repeated in both tables and will be the reference for all the data associated with a record. In this example, the Employee_Number will be used as a key. It is a unique identifier for each employee record. The team captain can look up the Employee_Number in the human resource table to see the related information about the employee that is not stored in the Softball Team table.

The data in relational databases can be sorted on any field. Reports can be generated that contain only certain fields from each record. Not only does the related database structure reduce data redundancy and increase data integrity, but also the new relational structure makes querying the data easier than in the flat-file structure. The word **query** comes from the Latin *quaere*, meaning to ask or seek. Queries are used to search databases. A database query can be either a **select query** or an **action query**. A select query is used to simply retrieve data from the database. An action query is used to ask for additional operations on the data, such as insertion, updating, or deletion. Languages that are used to interact with databases are called **query languages**, one example of which is SQL. In the

Figure 5-4

The Relational Database Table

LName	FName	Age	Monthly_ Salary	Date_of_ Employment	Employee_ Number	Dept	Email	Team_ Member?	Team_ Position
Nelson	William	45	$5000	06/01/1989	0001	3	nelson@email.com	Yes	Pitcher
Fulcher	Cleo	50	$4500	11/30/1989	0002	1	fulcher@email.com	No	
Nolan	Patricia	29	$3000	04/12/1990	0003	6	nolan@email.com	Yes	Short stop
Fowkes	Kate	20	$2000	01/19/1993	0004	4	fowkes@email.com	No	
Medlar	Stephanie	22	$1500	09/21/1996	0005	4	medlar@email.com	Yes	First base

Human Resources Table

Employee_ Number	LName	FName	Age	Monthly_ Salary	Date_of_ Employment	Dept	Email	Team_ Member?	Team_ Position
0001	Nelson	William	45	$5000	06/01/1989	3	nelson@email.com	Yes	Pitcher
0002	Fulcher	Cleo	50	$4500	11/30/1989	1	fulcher@email.com	No	
0003	Nolan	Patricia	29	$3000	04/12/1990	6	nolan@email.com	Yes	Short stop
0004	Fowkes	Kate	20	$2000	01/19/1993	4	fowkes@email.com	No	
0005	Medlar	Stephanie	22	$1500	09/21/1996	4	medlar@email.com	Yes	First base

Softball Team Table

Employee_ Number	Dept	Email	Team_ Member?	Team_ Position
0001	3	nelson@email.com	Yes	Pitcher
0002	1	fulcher@email.com	No	
0003	6	nolan@email.com	Yes	Short stop
0004	4	fowkes@email.com	No	
0005	4	medlar@email.com	Yes	First base

Figure 5-5

The Completed Relational Database Table

electronic commerce model, both select queries and action queries are used.

In the earlier example, by storing the information in separate tables, the business' database can be used for a variety of purposes. As the business grows, new tables can be added to the database, linked together with common keys. A typical large electronic commerce Web database may contain hundreds or thousands of tables linked together so that the business can quickly find the exact information needed at any given time.

While the strength of relational databases resides in their ability to reduce duplication of information, storage requirements, and data entry time, and increase data integrity, they do have some weaknesses. These software applications are typically more costly than flat-file databases and require more RAM and storage capacity.

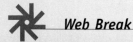

Web Break

To learn more about SQL, visit SQLCourse's Web site at http://sqlcourse.com and take part in a unique SQL Tutorial. The tutorial is easy to follow and provides SQL practice with immediate online feedback. You will be able to create your own unique tables as well as perform Select, Insert, Update, Delete, and Drop SQL commands on your tables. This SQL tutorial currently supports a subset of ANSI SQL. The basics of each SQL command are covered in SQLCourse's introductory tutorial.

Object-oriented Databases

The third type of database is the object-oriented database. Object-oriented databases are based on object-oriented programming properties. **Object-oriented programming (OOP)** is organized around objects rather than actions and around data rather than logic. Historically, a computer program was conceived from the logical perspective. It was seen as a procedure that took input data, processed it, and produced output data. The programming challenge became how to write the logic, not how to define the data. Object-oriented programming was revolutionary in that it no longer concentrated on manipulating the logic, but focused rather on manipulating the objects. Examples of objects may be a person who is described by name, address, height, weight, or a building described in terms of ceilings, floors, and walls.

Object-oriented programming first identifies all the objects to be manipulated and their relations to one another. This process is termed **data modeling**. Objects are then generalized as classes of objects, and the data is identified by data type. Any logic sequences that can manipulate the data are also identified. Each distinct logic sequence is called a **method**. Simply put, the object is what is executed on the computer. The methods provide instructions to the computer and the class object characteristics provide relevant data.

In an object-oriented database, all the data are assigned to categories called **classes**. Just like relational databases, each table in the object-oriented model has rows and columns. Each separate piece of data is called an **object** and each object has one instance of a particular class or **subclass**. The concept of class is unique to object-oriented programming. Object-oriented databases follow the following rules:

- In an object-oriented database, the concept of a data class sub-classes of data objects enables them to share some or all of the main class characteristics to be defined. This is called **inheritance**.
- In an object-oriented database, the concept of data classes enables the creation of new data types that are not already defined in the language itself.

Even relational databases have classes. All data in relational databases are either numbers, text, or dates. Each class has its own rules and functions. For instance, in the relational database model, text classes cannot perform mathematical calculations. The concept of classifying data, or objects, is taken a step further in the object-oriented model. An **object-oriented database management system**, or OODBMS, is a database management system that supports the modeling and creation of data as objects and support for classes of objects, as well as the inheritance of class properties and methods by subclasses and their objects. OODBMS, and OODBMS products, are considered to be still in their infancy. An industry group, the **Object Data Management Group** (ODMG), is developing an object-oriented database interface standard. The Object Management Group, in their acclaimed paper, The Object-Oriented Database Manifesto, defines an OODBMS as follows:

> An object-oriented database system must satisfy two criteria: it should be a DBMS, and it should be an object-oriented system, i.e., to the extent possible, it should be consistent with the current crop of object-oriented programming languages. The first criterion translates into five features: persistence, secondary storage management, concurrency, recovery and an ad hoc query facility. The second one translates into eight features: complex objects, object identity, encapsulation, types or classes, inheritance, overriding combined with late binding, extensibility and computational completeness.

Object-oriented databases have limited query capabilities. In today's business environment of multimedia exchange, object-oriented databases are often used for their expanded classifications of nontext data, such as pictures or other multimedia files. One of the strengths of object-oriented databases is their capability for storing **binary large objects**, or BLOBs, efficiently. A BLOB is a large file, usually an image or sound file. Because they work with the storage of large multimedia objects, films and television programming software are examples of applications that handle BLOBs. GOODS is an example of an object-oriented, fully distributed database management system using an active client model.

 Web Break

Visit The Object-Oriented Management Group at http://www. odmg.org. The Object-Oriented Management Group is an organization engaged in database and tools development and in consulting or deploying object technology. The Group is on the cutting edge of the object-oriented database market and is the standards organization for object storage. Visit their Web site to learn what's new in OODMS, find industry links, or sit in on an OOPs users' forum.

The Hybrid Database

The needs of today's businesses and the rapid growth of electronic commerce have led to the emergence of the hybrid database, which is a combination of the relational database model and the object-oriented model. A hybrid database has a thin object layer above the relational structure. This type of architecture provides for a syntax and semantics that is closer to the object-oriented design while making it easier to build the data layer. Theoretically, object-oriented databases are a better fit for the kind of complex queries that modern businesses need. Often these hybrids are referred to as **object-relational systems**. Hybrid databases handle nontext data, such as pictures or XML, as easily as do object-oriented databases. They also handle text well. Like relational databases, they have the capability of processing complex data quickly using SQL. An example of a hybrid database is the Jasmine Object database. Oracle's relational database, though not considered a hybrid database, handles multimedia objects within its relational structure with both efficiency and speed.

5.2 Building Back-End Databases

Back-end databases are the key to the success and exponential growth of electronic commerce. Using a Microsoft Access 2000 or Access XP version 2002 database, it is easy to directly store, mine, and manipulate the back-end database with a Web front-end. Databases in this book and its supporting figures will be built using Access 2000; however, tip boxes will point out differences, helpful hints, and screen shots for those using a Microsoft Access 2002 release. Step-by-step instructions for creating databases and tables using Access are beyond the scope of this book. It is assumed that the reader has a basic understanding of Access. The focus will be on table- and query-type database objects, the only database components that will be used in our electronic commerce business models. The first step in creating an electronic commerce business model is to create a new database that can be used to store the business-related information.

Kanthaka Farms
Creating a New Database
for the Back-end of the
Electronic Commerce
Construction

Kanthaka Farms is a continuing case study in this book that illustrates the process of building electronic commerce with Web database constructions. In this chapter, using Microsoft Access 2000 or XP version 2002, you will build the back-end database for your Web database construction. As you continue through the text, you will complete different facets of electronic commerce Web database construction, resulting in a complete Web site for Kanthaka Farms. Harris and Anicca want their customers to be able to keep track of dogs that they have bred and now sold by accessing the business' back-end database. In this exercise you will create a database to house information about dogs from Kanthaka Farms now at other kennels. We will begin by creating a new database in Microsoft Access to store information for Kanthaka Farms. If you have not done so already, launch Access.

1. The first step in creating the back-end relational database for Kanthaka Farms is to create an INVENTORY subdirectory under the C:\WebSite\cgi-win\BOOK directory. From within Access, create a new, blank database named KANTHAKA as shown in Figure 5-6.

2. Choose the table object, select New, and Import two pre-existing tables. The tables that you will need to import to your database are located at C:\WebSite\cgi-win\BOOK\EXAMPLES\CH05_K.mdb. One is titled tblDOG_Listings and the other is tblDOG_Kennels. If you cannot find the CH05_K.mdb database, please review the instructions in Chapter 4 for copying files located on this book's companion Web site to your WebSite folder. Upon completion of importing, your database table object should look similar to Figure 5-7.

3. Establish a relationship between the two tables and enforce the referential integrity. To do so, click on the Relationships icon on the Tools menu. Click on the Add button to add each table to the Relationships window. Click on the KennelsID field in the tblJDOG_Kennels table and drag and drop on the field of the same name in the tblDOG_Listings table. In response, Access will display a dialog box from which you will enforce the referential integrity. Select the Enforce Referential Integrity check box as well as the Cascade Update Related Fields options. Access will now display a one-to-many relationship between the two tables as shown in Figure 5-8.

Figure 5-6

Creating the INVENTORY Database for Kanthaka Farms

Figure 5-7

Importing Two Pre-existing Tables into the Database

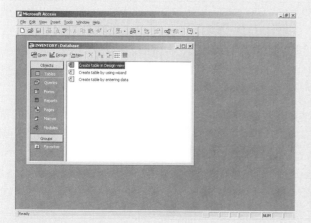

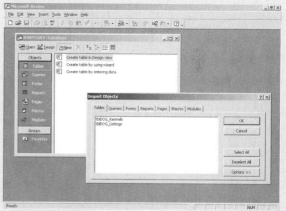

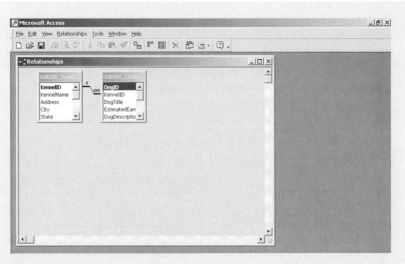

Figure 5-8

A One-to-Many Relationship Between the Two Tables

FOCUS ON ELECTRONIC COMMERCE

Visit the Eddie Bauer Web site. Discuss the Web database construction from a customer interaction point of view. How would you rate the site after reading the ratings from Gomez.com?

Do you agree or disagree with the Gomez ratings?

Justify your answer.

The Key to Online Success? Utilizing the Back-End for Personalized Product Information at Eddie Bauer

How do you measure success? If you are Eddie Bauer, you might just count your awards. Named the "Best Apparel Web Site" on Gomez.com's Summer Internet Scorecard™ for the second consecutive time, Eddie Bauer received top rankings in the "Ease of Use" and "First-Time Buyer" categories. More importantly, they also received high scores in the Customer Confidence category. Gomez.com's evaluation also praised the site's live chat and real-time inventory status features.

What does that mean? The praise from Gomez is really praise from the customers and users of the Eddie Bauer site. And Gomez is the leading provider of e-commerce customer experience measurement, benchmarking, and customer acquisition services. Many businesses use Gomez to help build successful e-businesses and guide consumers in transacting business online.

So what did Eddie Bauer do to receive all the praise? Eddie Bauer recently deployed a newly revamped electronic commerce Web site utilizing Servicesoft 2001, MicroStrategy, Microsoft Windows NT Server, and Microsoft Internet Information Server software. The new site builds on the strength of the Web database construction. With Web database constructions, Eddie Bauer is able to provide proactive customer service via the Internet. The interactive, dynamic site enables Eddie Bauer to give its customers complete, Web-based customer service around the clock. It integrates self-service, e-mail, and live interaction capabilities based on a shared, sophisticated knowledge platform.

According to Sally McKenzie, director of merchandising and operations at Eddie Bauer Inc.'s interactive media division in Redmond, Washington, the electronic commerce site allows visitors to customize their shopping experience by storing their addresses for faster checkout, setting up wish lists, and offering a special event reminder service. All of these new personalization services allow customers to interact with Eddie Bauer's back-end database.

"Our original goal was e-commerce-driven—to sell goods online," said Judy Neuman, divisional vice president of interactive media at Eddie Bauer headquarters in Redmond, Washington. "E-commerce is still key to our Web efforts, of course, but equally important are the opportunities for branding and the ability to develop one-to-one and one-to-mass communications with our customers. The Web is a very powerful medium and has become our third sales channel for expanding our business while complementing and enhancing the retail store and print catalog channels."

Sources: http://www.Gomez.com; http://www.eddiebauer.com/eb/default.asp; Carol Sliwa, "Web sites strive to personalize, attracting, not repelling, users a delicate balance," *ComputerWorld*, April 17, 2000; David Drucker, "Online customer support doesn't come in a wrapper," *InternetWeek Online*, June 5, 2000.

5.3 Designing Advanced Queries and Analyzing Data

The Simple Query

Electronic commerce Web databases contain aggregations of business data records and files. These often include such data as sales transactions, product catalogs and inventories, and customer profiles. But what benefit is derived from a well-designed database if it can't be queried or mined by customers, business partners, or management? The aim of electronic commerce database querying is to find information in the back-end databases and deliver it to the customer quickly and efficiently. Traditional techniques work well for databases with standard, single-site relational structures, but databases containing more complex and diverse types of data demand advanced query processing and optimization techniques. Today's databases typically contain much nonstructured data such as text, images, video, and audio—often distributed across computer networks. In this complex Web environment, efficient and accurate querying can become quite challenging. In this exercise, you will create queries in Access to better understand their importance to the Web database construction. You will use the K_Inventory.mdb database constructed earlier in this chapter. This database is stored at C:\WebSite\cgi-win\BOOK\INVENTORY.

Kanthaka Farms
Designing Access Queries

In this exercise you will create a query to mine your Kanthaka Farms database. The Vitas will analyze this data to make management decisions about Kanthaka Farms' dogs that are now with other kennels. Harris is very interested in seeing what types of royalties and breeding fees dogs that were formerly with Kanthaka Farms are expected to earn for other kennels. For instance, he has asked to you locate any dogs that are expected to earn $40,000 or more during their lifetimes. To quickly accomplish this task, you design a query that extracts those dogs from the tblDOG_Listings.

1. Open the C:\WebSite\Book\INVENTORY\K_Inventory.mdb database file in Microsoft Access.

2. Choose Queries, Objects and click on the New button.

3. Choose the Design View option. Access will display a query design window and display a list of tables present in the INVENTORY database as shown in Figure 5-9.

4. Select the tblDOG_Listings table from the displayed table list, and click on the Add button. Click on the Close button to hide the table list. Access adds the tblDOG_Listings table to the query design window. Double-click the asterisk (*) symbol in the DOG_Listings table. Access adds the symbol to the first cell of the Field row. It also lists the table name in the first cell of the Table row and automatically selects the first Show check box.

5. Add the EstimatedEarnings field to the second cell of the Field row. Deselect the Show check box and in the Criteria cell, type >=40000 as shown in Figure 5-10.

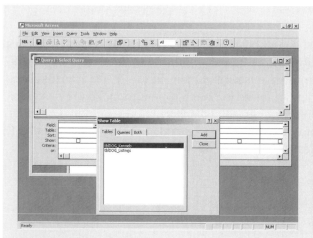

Figure 5-9

Adding a Query in a Design Window

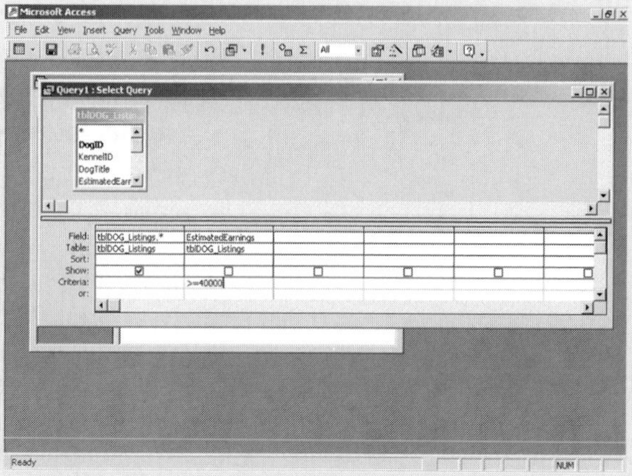

Figure 5-10

Adding the EstimatedEarnings Field to the Field Row

6. Now run the query. Click on the Run option from the Query menu. Access executes the query and returns a list of eight dogs, each with an estimated lifetime earning of $40,000 or greater.

7. Save your query as qry_DOG_HighEarnings and close the query window.

Figure 5-11

Results of the Select Query for Estimated Earnings of $40,000 or More

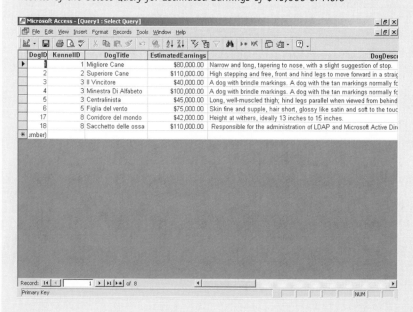

Sorting Data

In order to make sound business decisions, management often uses information returned from queries. In this way, databases act as simple **decision support systems**. Often, however, data needs to be viewed in a variety of forms for management to make the best decisions. Table records are typically displayed in the primary key order. To display records in a different sort order, only a small change is needed in the design of the original query.

Kanthaka Farms
Sorting Records

In this exercise you sort the qryDOG_HighEarnings with the highest earning dog listed first.

1. Select the qryDOG_HighEarnings query from the database and view in Design view.

2. Click in the Sort area of the EstimatedEarnings Field and from the drop-down list, choose Descending.

3. Run the Query and Save the results as qryDOG_HighEarnings_ Sorted. Your results should be similar to those displayed in Figure 5-12.

Figure 5-12
Results of qryDOG_HighEarnings_Sorted

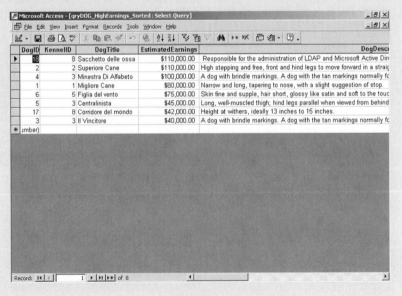

Filtering Data

Filtering is another way to manipulate the data to increase the functionality of the database query. A **filter** is a set of criteria that describes the sequence of the records in a database. It is very similar to a query; however, it only applies to the current datasheet. It cannot be saved as a filter. If you want to use a filter at another time, you must save the filter as a query. The Advanced Filter/Sort in Access allows multiple selection criteria to be specified.

In this exercise you will filter the query qryDOG_HighEarnings to return information about the dogs sold during the month of May 2001. This will require a limiting criterion on the dog listing table's DateSold field, which stores each dog's date of sale. The month of May can be described as any date falling between 5/1/2001 and 5/31/2001. A Between...And operator will be specified to complete this filter.

Kanthaka Farms
Filtering Records

1. Select the qryDOG_HighEarnings query from the database and view in Design view.

2. Position your pointer at the top of the EstimatedEarnings Field and, when the pointer symbol changes to a black, downward-pointing arrow, Click. Your entire field should now be selected. Press delete to remove the contents of the field selection.

3. Click on the downward-pointing arrow in the field cell and choose DateSold.

4. In the Criteria cell of the DateSold field add the filter date parameters. You can type it in as >=#5/1/2001# AND <=#5/31/2001# or BETWEEN #5/1/2001# AND #5/31/2001#.

5. Run the Query and Save the results as qryDOG_HighEarnings_Filtered. Your results should be similar to those displayed in Figure 5-13.

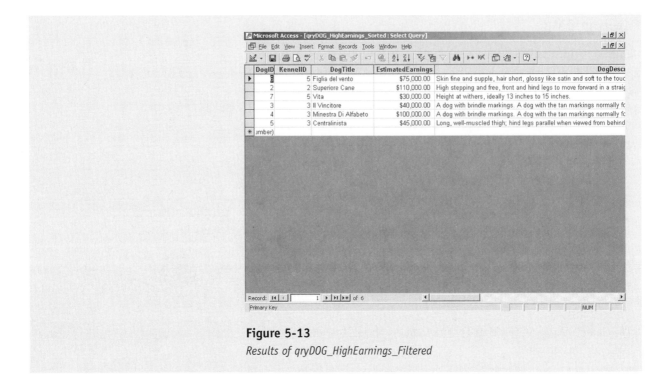

Figure 5-13
Results of qryDOG_HighEarnings_Filtered

Using Expressions and Calculated Fields

Sound database design does not include **calculated fields** within the table itself. Calculated fields are added through queries, and the results run and displayed for management to use in the decision-making process. A calculated field is a field that shows the results of an **expression**. An expression contains a combination of fields, constants, and operators. Usually, the data types of the fields must be number, currency, or date/time for numeric expressions where the constants are numbers such as 0.10 for 10%. Operators can be **arithmetic operators** (+ − × /) or other specialized operators. When creating complex expressions, calculations are enclosed in parentheses to indicate which one should be performed first. Access calculates expressions without parentheses in the following order: multiplication and division before addition and subtraction. Operators that have equal precedence are calculated by Access in order from left to right. A calculated field is calculated by Access at query runtime and displays the resulting values in the datasheet.

In this exercise you will create a calculated field to retrieve the month's information from the DateSold field and compare it against all dogs sold in the month of May, irrespective of the year. The Month function in Access will be used for this task. This function takes a date expression as a parameter and returns its month as a number between 1 and 12.

Kanthaka Farms
Using Expressions and Calculated Fields

1. Open a new query in the query design window with the tblDOG_Listings table as the data source.

2. Type the following in the first column of the Field row:

```
Month Sold: Month[(DateSold])
```

3. In the second column, add the asterisk field.

4. In the Criteria cell of the calculated field in the first column, type 5.

5. Run and save the query as qryDOG_Listings_May. The results will show all the dogs sold in May regardless of the year in which they were sold. Your results should look similar to those shown in Figure 5-14.

Figure 5-14
Results of qryDOG_Listings_May

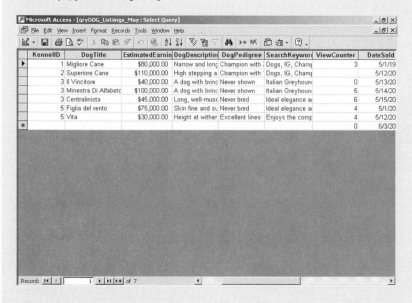

Creating a Multiple-Table Query

Access supports **multiple-table queries**. Edits and changes are updated directly to the underlying tables as with single-table queries.

Kanthaka Farms
Creating a Two-Table Query

In this exercise, you will create for the Vitas a two-table query for Kanthaka Farms using both tables in the INVENTORY database, the tblDOG_Kennels and the tblDOG_Listings. They have asked you to provide them with a listing of all high-earning dogs by kennel name that they have placed in Florida.

1. Open a new query in the query design window and add both tables as data sources for the query. Note that Access not only adds both tables, but also displays the one-to-many relationship.

2. Add the following fields to the query: KennelName, tblDOG_Listings.*, State, and EstimatedEarnings. Note that in the cell directly under the field name, Access displays the table to which each field belongs.

Figure 5-15
Results of qryDOG_Listings_Florida_HighEarnings

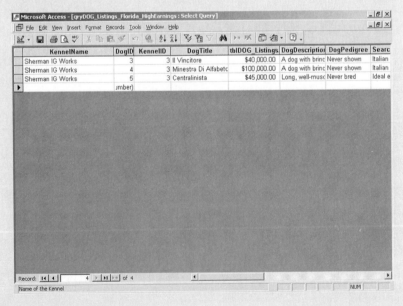

3. Type the following criterion for the State field:

```
Like "FL"
```

4. Type the following criterion for the EstimatedEarnings field:

```
>=40000
```

5. Run the query and save it as qryDOG_Listings_Florida_ HighEarnings. Your results should look similar to Figure 5-15.

Working with Inner and Outer Joins

Joins allow you to work with the data from multiple tables. An **inner join** is a join where the records from two tables are only selected by Access when the records have the same value in the common field that links the tables. For example, in the Kanthaka Farms database, an inner join would show all dogs that have a matching kennel record and all the kennels that have a matching dog record. There are two main types of **outer joins**. A **right outer join** is a join where all records from the second, or right table, and only those records from the first table that have matching common field values are selected. Alternatively, a **left outer join** would select all records from the first, or left, table and only those records from the second table that have matching common field values.

For the first part of this exercise, you will work with an inner join to better understand how it works.

1. Open a new query in the query design window and add the tblDOG_Kennels table and the tblDOG_Listings table to this query.

2. Now add the KennelName Field from the tblDOG_Kennels table and the asterisk field from the tblDOG_Listings table.

3. Run the query and save it as qryDOG_Kennels_Listings_InnerJoin. Your results should look similar to those shown in Figure 5-16.

4. Close the query design window.

5. Open the tblDOG_Kennels table and add the following record for a dog that Anicca just sold today to CrossCreek Kennels. The entire information is:

Kanthaka Farms
__Working with Inner and__
__Outer Joins__

KennelID: 9, KennelName: CrossCreek Kennels, Address: 2341
Clocktower Lane, City: Madison, State: WI, Zip: 34566,
Phone: 555-555-2345, Fax: 555-555-4567, Email:
ccreek@email.com, ReferenceURL: http://crosscreek.uk,
KennelInformation: World Class Igs, Champions: Yes

6. Close the tblDOG_Kennels table, and reopen the qryDOG_Kennels_Listings_InnerJoin. Notice that Access does not include the name of the newly added kennel in its query result. This is because the new kennel does not have any associated dog record in the tblDOG_Listings table.

The Vitas have asked you to provide them information about the kennels in the database and the dogs sold to them. They want to see the new CrossCreek Kennel displayed even though it does not have the associated dog listed yet (the Vitas haven't decided which of their new puppies they will be sending to CrossCreek). This will require you to create an outer join of the two tables. To do so, follow the steps below:

7. In Design View, open the inner join query you just created. Double-click on the link representing the inner join between the two

Figure 5-16
Results of qryDOG_Kennels_Listings_InnerJoin

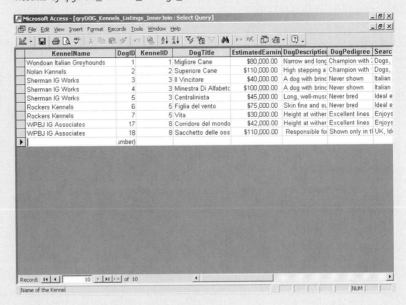

tables. Access will display the join properties window. Select the second option where all records from the tblDOG_Kennels and only those records from tblDOG_Listings where the join fields are equal will be displayed. Click on OK.

8. Run the query and save it as qryDOG_Kennels_Listings_OuterJoin. Notice that this time Access will return CrossCreek Kennels in the results.

5.4 Creating Advanced Queries

Queries have much more power than just finding and organizing the information stored in back-end databases. They can perform specified tasks and make managing the business' data a great deal easier. As you learned earlier, queries that perform specific jobs are known as action queries because they do things with or to the information stored in the database tables. A query can look for and modify records that have an unmatched field between two related tables, update records stored in the tables, delete specified records from one or more tables, create a new table, or even add records to an existing table. All of these jobs would be an onerous task to perform manually, but a carefully designed query can accomplish them in a matter of seconds.

As we have discussed earlier in this chapter, SQL is the standard language used in querying relational databases. Much of what Access does behind the scenes is accomplished with SQL. For example, when you create a query in Design View, Access automatically creates an equivalent SQL statement transparent to you. When you save the query, Access also saves the SQL statement version of the query. You can easily view the SQL statements when you are in Design View by clicking on the SQL View button or by selecting SQL View from the View menu.

Creating a Total Query

Earlier in the chapter you worked with several types of queries and discovered that the strength of the Web database construction is rooted in the ability to query the database and mine the data. The results of these queries are often used by management in the decision-making process. In addition to inner join and outer join queries, the ability to create a **total query** is very important in the electronic commerce business model. Total queries allow **aggregate functions** such as sum, average, count, or other totals on a set of records to be performed.

Kanthaka Farms
Creating a Total Query

Anicca has asked for some information on dogs that Kanthaka Farms has sold to other kennels. She is primarily looking for a listing of the names of each kennel that Kanthaka Farms has an association with and also the total number of dogs the kennel has purchased from the farm. As you assess her instructions, you decide that a total query will return to you the information you need.

1. Open a new query in the query design window and add the tblDOG_Kennels table and the tblDOG_Listings table. Verify that the two tables have been linked with an inner join.

2. Add the KennelName field of the tblDOG_Kennels table and the DogID field from the tblDOG_Listings table.

3. Click on the Totals icon on the Tools menu. Access adds a new row called Total to the query design. The Total displays Group By function by default under both fields.

Figure 5-17
Results of qryDOG_Kennels_DogCount

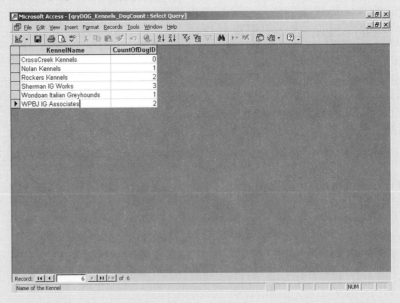

4. Change the Group By function of the DogID field to the Count function so that you can give Anicca the total information she wants. To do so, click on the Group By cell. Using the downward-pointing arrow, select the Count function.

5. Run the query and save it as qryDOG_Kennels_DogCount. Your query results should be similar to those shown in Figure 5-17.

Using Multiple Aggregate Functions

As you learned earlier, aggregate functions perform arithmetic operations on the selected records in the database. The word "aggregate" comes from the Latin *aggregare* meaning to add to. Therefore, an aggregate function is used to collect things together. Often you will need to apply several aggregate functions at one time on a single total query to extract the needed information from the database.

Kanthaka Farms
Using Multiple Aggregate Functions

The Vitas are finding the information you have been providing very useful. Now they would like to perform more in-depth data analysis regarding the placement of their dogs. They have asked you five questions:

- *What are the maximum earnings of a Kanthaka Farms dog by state?*
- *By state, what are the average earnings of a Kanthaka Farms dog?*
- *How many Kanthaka Farms dogs belong to the kennels in each state?*
- *How many kennels that have purchased Kanthaka Farms dogs have won championships?*
- *How many Kanthaka Farms dogs are there in each state?*

As you inspect their questions, you will find that it is possible to return the answers with one query to the database. Each of their questions pertains to the state. Therefore, the state will be your common grouping field.

1. Open a new query in the query design window and add the tblDOG_Kennels table and the tblDOG_Listings table.

2. Select the Total function from the Tools menu.

3. Add the State field from the kennels table to the Field row.

4. Calculate the job count by state. Add the DogID field from the tblDOG_Listings table to the Field row and set the aggregate Count function in the Total row.

5. To find the kennels who have purchased their dogs and who have won championships, you will create a calculated field as follows:

```
ChampionCount: Iif([Champions],1,0)
```

The calculated field returns a 1 if the Champions field of the kennel record is True, or Yes. If No, then it returns 0.

6. To add these, set the Total row for this calculated field to the aggregate Sum function. The query will now return the total dogs owned by kennels listed by state.

7. To find the average and maximum earnings for the dogs organized by state, add the EstimatedEarnings field of the tblDOG_Listings table to the query and set the Total cell to the aggregate function of Avg. Also, add the EstimatedEarnings field again, and this time set the Total cell to the aggregate function Max.

8. Run the query and save it as qryDOG_Analysis_ByState. The results are displayed in Figure 5-18.

Now your task is to analyze the data returned from the query. What does it tell you? You should be able to tell the Vitas how many dogs they have in each state, how many kennels (by state) whose dogs have won championships, and the average and maximum earnings of their dogs by state.

- In California, there are three Kanthaka Farms dogs in kennels without championships. These dogs have average earnings of $71,666 and maximum earnings of $110,000.
- In Florida, there are three Kanthaka Farms dogs and all three kennels have won championships. These dogs have average earnings of $61,666 and maximum earnings of $100,000.
- In North Carolina, there is one Kanthaka Farms dog in a kennel without a championship. This dog has average and maximum earnings of $80,000.
- In New York, there are two Kanthaka Farms dogs in kennels without championships. These dogs have average earnings of $76,000 and maximum earnings of $110,000.

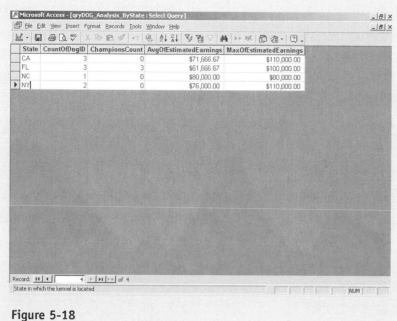

Figure 5-18
Results of qryDOG_Analysis_ByState

Using a Crosstab Query

A **crosstab query** also performs aggregate function calculations. This type of query presents a large amount of summary information in an easily understandable format, usually a spreadsheet, and makes comparisons and data analysis easy. This useful query is often the basis for a report that groups and totals your data.

The Vitas are interested in knowing how many dogs have been sold in any given year and to what state they have been shipped. Using a Crosstab query, you can return the information so that it will be easily grouped by year and state.

1. To include fields from more than one table, you must begin by creating a query with all the fields you need, and then you can use the Crosstab Query Wizard to make the crosstab query. To do so, create a new query with the State field from the tblDOG_Kennels. Add

Kanthaka Farms
Using a Crosstab Query

a calculated field that extracts the year from the DateSold field and is based on the following expression:

```
Year: Year([DateSold])
```

2. Run the query and save it as qryDOG_forCrosstab. You will now use it to build your crosstab query.

3. To build the crosstab query, from the query object window, click on the New object button. Select the Crosstab Query Wizard to help in the process.

4. From the Crosstab Query Wizard, select the query you just created for the crosstab query results. To do so, click on the Queries option button in the middle. The window will now display a list of queries from which you can choose. Click on qryDOG_forCrosstab then click on Next.

5. Select the State field as the value you want to use for your row headings. Click on the right-pointing symbol to move the State field from the Available Fields column to the Selected Fields column. Click on Next.

6. Select the Year field as the value you want for the column headings and Click on Next.

Figure 5-19
Results for qryDOG_forCrosstab_Crosstab

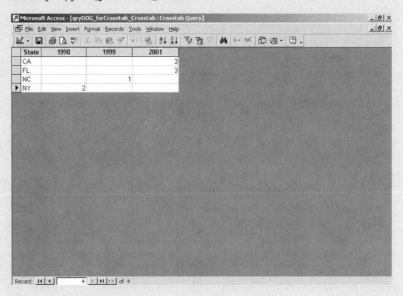

7. Select the field DogID and the aggregate function Count. The DogID field will now be counted by State and by Year and returned in your new crosstab query. Uncheck the summary box. Do not include or summarize each row. Click on Next.

8. Accept the default name for the query. It should read qryDOG_forCrosstab_Crosstab. Click on Finish to View the query results. Your results should look similar to Figure 5-19.

Parameter Queries

A **parameter query** displays one or more predefined dialog boxes that prompt the user for the parameter value, or criteria. A parameter query prompts the user to provide data or information before it is run. For example, a database could be queried to display the number of sales generated in a given month. Each time the query is run, the user is prompted to identify the month. When Access runs the parameter query, it displays a dialog box and prompts the user to enter the pertinent information. Access then creates the query results just as if the criteria had been modified in the query's Design view.

Web Break

Parameter queries are commonly used in Web database constructions. An excellent example of a parameter query in use is in the electronic commerce model at the Environmental Protection Agency's Air Data Web site. At http://www.epa.gov/aqspubl1/parameter.html, the EPA utilizes a parameter query to mine their Air Quality database and to generate reports based on pollutant categories, codes, and descriptions. The visitor's query output is either returned as an ASCII file for downloading or displayed on the screen, as per the visitor's request.

The strength of the parameter query is that one query can be set to different criteria by having Access prompt the user for input when the query is run. You may wish to run the same query several times, but with different values for the conditions. It is the interactivity that makes the parameter query so useful to electronic commerce. The parameter query interactively specifies one or more criterion values. However, a parameter query is not, strictly speaking, a separate kind of query; instead, it extends the flexibility of select queries, including crosstab queries.

A parameter is defined by anything between square brackets, for example [Enter Dog Name]. It does not matter what is between the brackets. If instead of [Enter Dog Name] the parameter had read [Dog], the result would have been the same. The alphanumeric prompt enclosed within the brackets can include spaces, but it cannot match any field name of the underlying tables. What is in the brackets becomes the name of the parameter.

Kanthaka Farms
Using a Parameter Query

The Vitas want to see an example of a general-purpose query that can be used when their Web database construction is deployed over the Internet. You have talked with them about the usefulness of parameter queries in Web-based database searches. You will create for them a parameter query to list the dogs sold to any kennel by specifying the dog's name at the time the query is run. Follow the steps below:

1. Create a new query in the query design window. Add both tables from your database to the query.

2. Add the KennelName field from the kennel table and the asterisk field from the listing table.

Figure 5-20

Running the Parameter Query

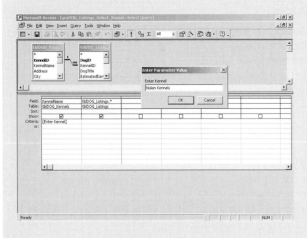

Figure 5-21

Results of the qryDOG_Listings_Select_Kennel

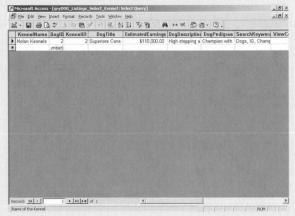

3. Use the following criterion in the Criteria cell of the KennelName field:

```
[Enter Kennel]
```

4. Run and save the query as qryDOG_Listings_Select_Kennel. Figure 5-20 displays the parameter query running. Figure 5-21 displays the results of the qryDOG_Listings_Select_Kennel.

Parameter queries can also be designed so that less typing is required in the interaction. For instance, instead of typing the full kennel name, you may want to design the parameter to accept only the first few letters of the kennel name. To do so, the criterion would change to:

```
Like [Enter Kennel Name Starts With] & *
```

The wildcard characters in the syntax above allow the user to limit typing input. For instance, in the exercise above, the letters "Nol" could be entered in the parameter now, and the results returned would be the same as before.

The same parameter name can also be repeated at different places in a query. Access will recognize that there are multiple occurrences of the same parameter and only prompt the user once for the value. It will then substitute the value wherever the parameter name appears in the query.

Kanthaka Farms
Using Multiple Occurrences of the Same Parameter Query

Harris has asked whether you can create a query that prompts for a search keyword and finds all the kennels that have that search keyword in either the DogDescription field or the SearchKeywords field. You answer yes, and to do so, you will use two occurrences of the same parameter in your query.

1. Create a new query in the query design window. Add the tblDOG_Listings table to the query.

2. Add the asterisk, DogDescription, and SearchKeywords fields to the Field row.

3. Verify that the Show check boxes of the DogDescription, and the SearchKeywords fields are unchecked.

4. Add the following criterion in the Criteria cell of the DogDescription and the Or cell of the SearchKeywords fields:

```
Like * & [Search for these words] & *
```

Figure 5-22 displays the parameter query running.

Figure 5-22

Query with Two Occurrences of the Same Parameter

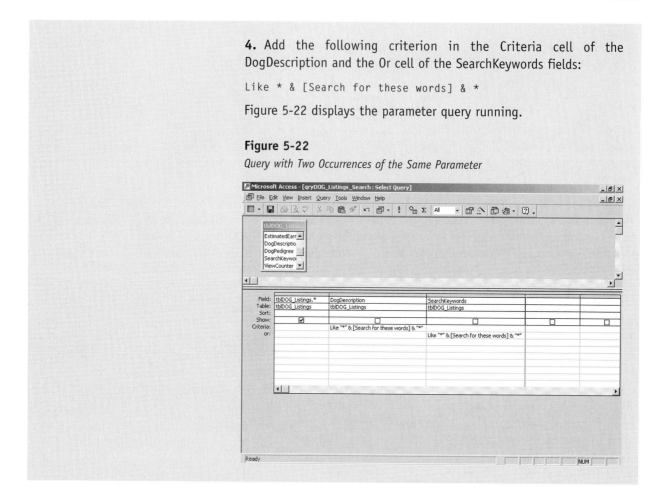

Nested Queries

Another example of a complex query is a **nested query**. A nested query is a query that includes more than one type of operator. Often in nested queries, parentheses are used as **scope of operation delimiters**. If you are familiar with algebra, you will recognize the use of these delimiters as a way to establish the scope of a particular mathematical operation. In a query, parentheses can delineate the range of terms that a particular operator influences, or control the order in which operations within the query are evaluated.

As you begin to work more with mining your back-end database and find that many of the queries you are building have common fields, consider using nested queries. The first step is to build a query that computes the common part, and then base other queries on the first query.

Avoid calculated fields in nested queries. Access allows you to use a query as a table source for a query, this produces nested queries. Calculated fields in the nested queries will slow performance considerably. Instead, place them at the top level.

As you review the queries you have created for the Vitas, you notice that most are based on an inner join between the tblDOG_Listings table and the tblDOG_Kennels table. To avoid the possibility of error and the duplication of effort, use the strength of nested queries to simplify and add functionality to your task.

Kanthaka Farms
Using Nested Queries

1. Create a new query in the query design window. Add both tables to the query. This will become your common query on which the nested query will be based. To it add both the asterisk fields of both the tables to the first two field rows. Save the query as qryDOG_Kennels_Dogs_InnerJoin.

2. To create a nested query that will count dogs by kennels, you can build a total query using the qryDOG_Kennels_Dogs_InnerJoin as the common query. The first step is another new query in the query design window.

3. Instead of adding tables, choose the Queries tab and select the qryDOG_Kennels_Dogs_InnerJoin from the list. Click Add.

4. Add two fields to your query: KennelName and DogID.

5. Click on the Total function button on the Tools menu. In the DogID field, change Group By to the aggregate function of Count.

6. Run and save the query as qryDOG_Kennels_DogCount_UsingNestedQuery. Your results should be similar to those displayed in Figure 5-23.

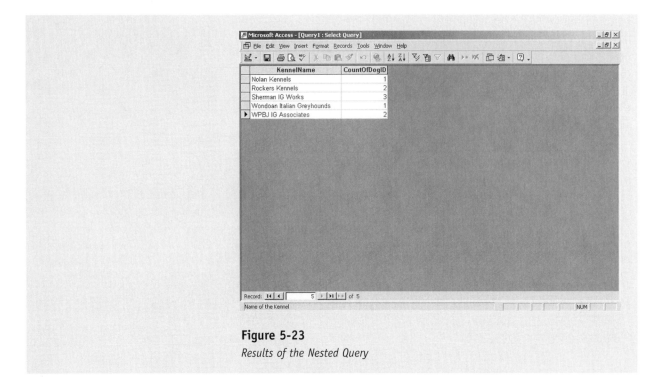

Figure 5-23
Results of the Nested Query

Optimizing the Performance of a Query

Optimizing the performance of queries is essential to optimizing Web database construction performance. To maximize gains in query performance, look beyond simple syntactic changes in the query, but also review the overall database design and database indexing issues. Often maximization comes even from simply taking a completely different approach to building a query.

One way to make queries run more efficiently is to be sure to choose the smallest data type appropriate for a field during the table design. The data type determines what field values can be entered for the field and what other properties the field will have. The initial field's size property should be based on the largest value that you expect to store in that field; however, Access processes smaller data sizes faster by using less memory. Just ensuring that the table's data type field sizes have been correctly chosen can optimize a query's performance. When creating queries, only add the fields that are necessary to answer the question posed to the data. Clear the Show check boxes for fields only used to set criteria. Avoiding restrictive query criteria on calculated and nonindexed fields is also beneficial to query performance.

Avoiding calculated fields in subqueries can also optimize query performance. If you add a query that contains a calculated field to another query, the expression in the calculated field may slow performance in the top-level query. For greater speed, use Group By on as few fields as possible. Also, if a total query includes a join, consider grouping the records in one query and adding this query to a separate query that will perform the join. This improves performance in some queries.

Lastly, optimization can be gained by compacting the database. Compacting can speed up queries because it reorganizes a table's records so that they reside in adjacent database pages ordered by the table's primary key. This will improve the performance of sequential scans of a table's records because the minimum number of database pages will have to be read to retrieve all of the records. After compacting the database, run each query to compile it using the updated table statistics.

Summary

- **Understand databases terms, types, and structures.** The Web database construction allows businesses to share information, maintain customer and partner relationships, and conduct business transactions through telecommunication channels, typically the Internet, using databases. Databases are used to store and keep track of the prolific digital information used today by customers and businesses alike. The types of databases used in electronic commerce vary. Typically, the business will use one of the four main types of databases: flat-file, relational, object-oriented, or hybrid.

- **Build a back-end database using Microsoft Access 2000 or Access 2002.** Back-end databases are the key to the success and exponential growth of electronic commerce. Using a Microsoft Access 2000 or Access 2002 database makes it easy to directly store, mine, and manipulate the back-end database with a Web front-end. The focus in electronic commerce constructions is on table- and query-type database objects. The first step in creating an electronic commerce business model is to create a new database that can be used to store the business-related information.

■ **Design advanced queries and analyze data through the use of total queries and nested queries.** The aim of electronic commerce database querying is to find information in the back-end databases and deliver it to the customer quickly and efficiently. Information mined from the databases is also useful in the managerial decision-making process. Traditional techniques work well for databases with standard, single-site relational structures, but databases containing more complex and diverse types of data demand advanced query processing and optimization techniques. The ability to create a total query is very important in the electronic commerce business model. Total queries allow aggregate functions such as sum, average, count, or other totals on a set of records to be performed. A nested query is a query that includes more than one type of operator. Often in nested queries parentheses are used as scope of operation delimiters. If you are familiar with algebra, you will recognize the use of these delimiters as a way to establish the scope of a particular mathematical operation. In a nested query, parentheses can delineate the range of terms that a particular operator influences, or control the order in which operations within the query are evaluated.

■ **Create parameter-based queries, which are heavily used for designing the advanced electronic commerce constructions described in this book.** Optimizing the performance of queries is essential to optimizing Web database construction performance. One way to make queries run more efficiently is to be sure to choose the smallest data type appropriate for a field during the table design. When creating queries, only add the fields that are necessary to answer the question posed to the data. Clear the Show check boxes for fields only used to set criteria. Avoiding restrictive query criteria on calculated and nonindexed fields is also beneficial to query performance, as is avoiding calculated fields in subqueries. Use Group By on as few fields as possible. Also, if a Total query includes a join, consider grouping the records in one query and adding this query to a separate query that will perform the join. Finally, compact the database.

Chapter Key Terms

action query	attributes	class
aggregate function	binary large object (BLOB)	columns
arithmetic operators	calculated field	crosstab query

data modeling
database
decision support system
elements
expression
fields
filter
flat-file database
hybrid database
inheritance
inner join
join
key
left outer join
list
metadata
metalanguage

method
multiple-table query
nested query
object
object data management group
   (ODMG)
object-oriented database
object-oriented database
   management system
   (OODBMS)
object-oriented programming
   (OOP)
object-relational system
outer join
overhead
parameter query

pieces of data
query
query language
records
relational database
relations
right outer join
rows
scope of operation delimiters
select query
sort
spreadsheet
subclass
tables
tuples
total query

Review Questions

1. Why is it said that the strength of electronic commerce is rooted in the database?

2. List and describe the elements of a database.

3. How does the structure of a text file make it difficult for a business to search a database for specific information? What other limitations does a text file put on reaping information from a database?

4. How do partitioned Web technologies share the processing duties between the server and the client?

5. Describe a strength of a flat-file database. List an appropriate use for a flat-file database in a business scenario.

6. How does the relational database model take advantage of uniformity to build completely new tables out of existing tables?

7. How are keys used in the relational database model?

8. Describe the difference between action and select queries.

9. List and describe the strengths of the relational database.

10. What are the rules that object-oriented databases must follow?

11. What are BLOBs? How are they used in databases? What type of database uses BLOBs?

12. Describe the hybrid database and how it meets today's business needs.

13. In what ways do databases and queries support decision support systems and managerial decision-making?

14. What is a sort filter? How is it used?

15. Describe how expressions are used in calculated fields.

16. What are joins? Discuss the differences between inner joins, outer joins, right outer joins, and left outer joins.

17. What is a total query? How are aggregate functions used in their creation?

18. Discuss how complex crosstab, parameter, and nested queries are created and used.

19. List five ways to optimize the performance of a query. Discuss the benefits derived from database and query optimization.

Critical Thinking Using the Web

1. Rushmore technology is a data-access technology that was borrowed from Microsoft's FoxPro PC database engine for use in Access. It improves the performance and processing of queries. A query must be constructed in a certain way to benefit from Rushmore, because the technology can be utilized only when certain types of expressions are included in the query criteria. Visit Microsoft's Web site at http://www.microsoft.com and search their database for more information on this technology. Write a 200–400 word essay summarizing your findings.

2. When querying databases, the use of operators is limited by data types. Visit the USDA National Cooperative Soil Survey National Soil Information System (NASIS) Web Site at http://nasis.nrcs.usda.gov/docu-ments/help/Data_typ.htm and view their information about the use of data types and comparison operators. Print out their data types and comparison operators table. Note that the table is very useful for determining which data types are allowed by query programs, which are not, and which, when used, result in meaningful information. Summarize the table findings. Do you agree or disagree with their assessment? Justify your answer.

3. Using your favorite search engine, search the Web for examples of each type of databases discussed in this chapter. Create a listing of database type, brand, and a short review of the product. Insert your table into Microsoft PowerPoint and be prepared to report your findings to the class using presentation software.

Chapter Case Study

Albatross Records is a continuing case study in this book that illustrates the process of building electronic commerce with Web database constructions. In Chapter 5, you will create a back-end database for the business' electronic commerce construction. Appropriate queries will be built to mine the database for useful information. Cool and the gang at Albatross Records will use the information from your queries to make managerial decisions.

■ Using Access, create a back-end relational database for Albatross Records and save it in the C:\WebSite\cgi-win\BOOK\INVENTORY folder on your hard drive. Name your database A_Inventory.mdb. Your database must contain two tables. The tables should include the following fields and can be imported from c:\WebSite\cgi-win\BOOK\EXAMPLES\CH05_A.mdb.

tblARTIST Listings

ArtistID—Primary key used for uniquely identifying the artist

Fname—Artist's first name

Lname—Artist's last name

Address—Artist's address

City—City artist lives in

State—State artist lives in

Zip—Artist's zip code

Phone—Artist's phone number

Type—Category of music the artist performs

DateSigned—Date the artist joined Albatross Records

tblARTIST Advertising

AdType—Type of advertising used to promote the artist

Date—Run date of the ad

Place—Location the ad ran

Responses—Any responses from the ad

Cost—Cost of the advertising

Contact—Name of advertising contact

Repeat—Has the ad run multiple times? Yes/No

ArtistID—Used for uniquely identifying the artist and link tblARTIST_Advertising to the tblARTIST_Listings

The tables can be imported from the Ch05_A.mdb located in your C:\WebSite\cgi-win\BOOK\EXAMPLES folder.

- Establish a relationship between the two tables and enforce the referential integrity.
- Mine the database using appropriate types of queries to answer the following questions Cool has posed to you:

1. Cool is very interested in seeing what advertising costs are associated with individual artists. He has asked to see a list of artists on whom his company has spent in excess of $1,000 on advertising. Save the query as qryARTIST_Listings.

2. Sort the qryARTIST_Listings query to show the artists in descending order by the advertising dollars spent. Save the query as qryARTIST_HighAds.

3. Filter the qryARTIST_Listings query to return the artists signed in the month of December 2001. This will require a limiting criterion on the artist listing table's DateSigned. Use a "Between...And" operator to perform this filter. Save the query as qryARTIST_HighAds_Filtered.

4. Create a query with a calculated field to retrieve the month information from the DateSigned field and compare it against all artists signed in the month of December, irrespective of the year. Use the Month function in Access for this task. Save the query as qryARTIST_Listings_December.

5. Create a two-table query to provide a listing of all advertising expenditures in descending order that have been placed on the Internet in descending order by the artist's name. Save the query as qryARTIST_Listings_ Internet_ HighAds.

6. Create a query that lists the type of advertising and the total number of ads by artists. Use a Total query to return the information that you need. Save the query as qryARTIST_AdType_ArtistCount.

7. Using multiple aggregate functions, create a query regarding artists' advertising. The query should answer the following questions:
    a. What is the maximum advertising expenditure for an Albatross artist by ad type?
    b. By ad type, what is the average advertising cost for an Albatross artist?
    c. How many artists have advertised in the same place using the same ad type?
    d. How many ad types have been repeated?
    e. How many artists have used each type of ad?

   You will use AdType field as the common grouping field. Save the query as qryARTIST_Analysis_ ByAdType. Discuss your findings.

8. Create a query to show how many artists have been advertised in any given year and by what ad type has been advertised. Use a crosstab query to group by year and type. Save the query as qryARTIST_forCrosstab_Crosstab.

9. Create a parameter query to list the artist advertising with any ad type by specifying the artist's name when the query is run. Save the query as qryARTIST_Listings_Select_AdType.

6

Client-Side Technologies

Learning Objectives

Upon completion of this chapter, you will be able to

- Discuss the purpose of hypertext links and hypermedia in the canonical model
- Discuss how HTML forms are used to create dynamic Web interactions
- Build HTML forms
- Use cookies for state management in the hidden HTML form fields
- Use cascading style sheets (CSSs) to display HTML elements
- Discuss the uses of XHTML in the electronic commerce model
- Describe the fundamentals of DHTML and uses in the electronic commerce model

6.1 Hypertext and Hypermedia

Hypertext is the name given to the organization of units of data into connected associations. These associations are called **hypertext links**, or just links. The creation of hypertext has been credited with leading to the invention of the World Wide Web, which is, after all, an enormous number of information associations connected by millions and millions of hypertext links.

Ted Nelson first used the term hyperlink in describing his **Xanadu** system. Nelson has described Xanadu as "an instantaneous electronic literature" and "perhaps the ultimate" hypertext system. Conceived in the 1960s, Xanadu was a software design project for a universal system of electronic information storage and access based on hypertext. In many ways, Xanadu anticipated the concepts of the Web with such ideas as groupware, group writing, and virtual organizations.

The hypertext link allows the user to select a connection from one medium, such as a word, picture, or information object, to another. In a multimedia environment such as the Web, hypertext links can

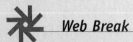

Web Break

To learn more about Ted Nelson's new vision for the Web, visit the Xanadu project at http://www.xanadu.net. To clean up much of the Web's coding environment, the Xanadu project proposes a new file type for virtual content, tentatively called .XVF.

even include sound and motion video sequences. Links to these types of media are called **hypermedia**. Hypermedia can also connote a higher level of user interactivity than the interactivity already implicit in hypertext. The most common form of hypertext link is the highlighted word or picture, called an **anchor**, that can be selected by the user, usually with a mouse click. The click event results in the immediate delivery and view of another file. The anchor reference and the object referred to constitute the hypertext link.

Hypertext markup language (HTML) is a simple data format used to create hypertext documents that are **portable** from one platform to another. A portable document is one that is usable on many different types of computers without modification. **Portability** is an important concept for electronic commerce where myriad platforms are present. HTML is an application of the ISO Standard 8879:1986 information processing text and Office Systems standard generalized markup language (SGML). The HTML **document type definition (DTD)** is a formal definition of the HTML syntax in terms of SGML. HTML is a subset of SGML with generic semantics that are appropriate for representing information from a variety of domains. This specification also defines HTML as an **Internet media type (IMEDIA)** and MIME content type, called text/html. The text/html was specified in documents located in C:\WebSite\cgi-win\Book\Job\ used in the online job service electronic commerce business model introduced in Chapter 4. This text/html specification defines the semantics of the HTML syntax and how that syntax should be interpreted by Web clients and user agents. HTML markup can represent hypertext news, mail, documentation, and hypermedia. It can also be used to represent menus of options, database query results, simple structured documents with in-line graphics, and hypertext views of existing bodies of information.

Understanding **HTML forms** is the first step in understanding the Web database construction process, where an HTML form, a client browser, a Web server, and the HTTP protocol work together to become electronic commerce. Web clients display hypertext documents written in HTML, and they can also display HTML forms. HTML forms are a dynamic component of the front-end of the Web database construction that allows users to interact with the business' back-end database. By using these dynamic forms, Web clients can collect, as well as display, business and customer information.

To understand this Web database construction interaction, it is first necessary to understand how Web clients and Web servers work together to deliver an HTML document that is *not* a dynamic form.

This **canonical Web activity** is an example of a standard Web interaction task. An understanding of the passing of a simple HTML document between Web client and Web server, as well as how scripts in the middleware are executed in the Web environment without mediating forms, builds the foundation for understanding electronic commerce.

Canonical Web Interaction

When information is collected by a Web client, it is usually sent via HTTP to a Web server that has been specified in the HTML form. In the business scenario, the Web server then starts a program, also denoted in the HTML form, that can process the customer information. One example of these programs is CGI scripts. During a typical exchange, the Web client requests a document from a Web server and displays that document on the customer's computer. If that document contains a hyperlink to another document, on a click event, the Web client will obtain and return the linked document.

Figure 6-1 depicts the canonical Web interaction in which the Web client is running on a customer's computer.

Figure 6-1

Canonical Web Interaction

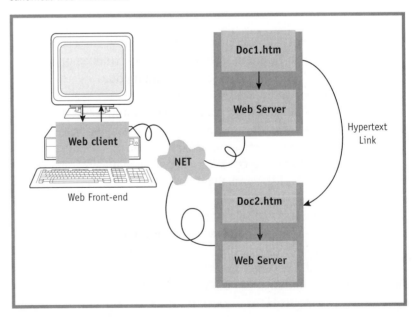

In the figure, the Web client obtains a document that is stored in a file named doc1.htm from the business' Web server. This document contains a link to another document stored in a file named doc2.htm on another Web server. An example of the URL for the hyperlink could be:

```
http://Businesscomputer.domain/doc2.htm
```

When the customer begins the click event by activating the link, the Web client retrieves the file from the second Web server and displays it on the customer's computer. In this scenario, HTTP defines the communication between the Web client and the Web server.

6.2 Building HTML Forms for Dynamic Web Interaction

Basic Form Elements

The only difference between the HTML canonical model and the dynamic model is the presence of input fields, buttons, and other resources for customer interaction. An HTML form is an area that can contain **form elements**, which allow the customer to enter information into the form. These elements, or **controls**, can be text fields, text area fields, drop-down menus, option buttons, and check boxes. Creating an HTML form typically involves two independent steps: creating a layout for the form and creating a script program on the server side. This script program is used to process the information returned from the HTML form and will be discussed in detail in later chapters of this book. HTML form programming does not require an extensive understanding of HTML, because only two **HTML elements**, or tags, are needed to create a basic form: the **FORM** and **INPUT** tags. The FORM tag denotes a form, and the INPUT tag defines a visual interface element, such as the textbox or option button that allows dynamic Web interaction. The following tags can be used in the simple HTML form:

- <FORM> </FORM> A form is defined with the <form> tag.
- <INPUT> </INPUT> The most used form tag is the INPUT tag. The type of INPUT is specified with the TYPE attribute. The most commonly used input types are text fields, option buttons, and checkboxes.

- <TEXTAREA> </TEXTAREA>
- <SELECT> </SELECT>
- <OPTION>

These tags shown in Table 6-1, when combined in the syntax below, begin the following simple form:

```
<FORM ACTION=url METHOD=get-post TARGET=window>
```

In this example, the **ACTION** attribute denotes which URL of the HTTP server should process the form. If the URL is not specified, then the base URL of the document is used. The **METHOD** in the example determines how the form will be submitted: HTML forms are either submitted by the **POST method** or the **GET method**. POST is the most common method used to send information from an HTML form to an information-processing program or function. POST is used when sending form information to Visual Basic script programs or JavaScript functions. Most CGI programs are written to accept information with the POST method, and some are written to *only* accept the POST method, for the reason that the POST method can send much more information than the typical GET method. Today, most Web clients and Web servers limit the amount of POST information to 32K. If the POST method is specified, then the form is submitted to the server using an HTTP post transaction. The GET method can send only a limited amount of information. The limitation depends on the Web server from which the Web page is

Table 6-1	HTML Form Tags		
Start Tag	IE	N	Description
<form>	3.0	3.0	Form for user input
<input>	3.0	3.0	An input field
<textarea>	3.0	3.0	A text-area (a multiline text input control)
<label>	4.0		A label to a control
<fieldset>	4.0		A fieldset
<legend>	4.0		A caption for a fieldset
<select>	3.0	3.0	A selectable list (a drop-down box)
<optgroup>		6.0	An option group
<option>	3.0	3.0	An option in the drop-down box
<button>	4.0		A push button

Web browser: IE, Internet Explorer; N, Netscape.

fetched, or retrieved, and the Web client where the information is returned. The limitation can be as little as 256 bytes, but is usually 1K or more. When the GET method is used, data from the form controls is appended as arguments to the action URL. The Web client then opens the form as an anchor. The **TARGET** has the results loaded into a specific Web client window:

```
<FORM TARGET="viewer"
    ACTION= "http://cseng.aw.com/catalog/comingsoon/
    0,3838,,00.html">
</FORM>
```

Here, the Web client fetches the Web page from a Web server by a standard HTTP request containing a page address. The page address in the example above is http://cseng.aw.com/catalog/comingsoon/0,3838,,00.html. The Web client is able to display the pages because all Web pages contain instructions on how to be displayed. The Web client displays the page by reading these instructions, the most common of which are the HTML tags. HTML forms, however, do not actually process the Web client information; they are only a means of collecting information from the Web client. For the information to be processed, it must be sent somewhere. Information-processing destinations can be CGI programs, JavaScript functions, "mailto:" links, or even a Web page that directs the browser to load the page at the specified URL.

Adding Customer Interaction

Text Fields To add the capacity for interaction between customer and business by allowing the customer to type letters, numbers, or symbols into a form, **text fields** are used in the HTML form. The code for a text field is the following:

```
<FORM> First Name: <INPUT TYPE="TEXT" NAME="FIRSTNAME">
<BR>
Last Name: <INPUT TYPE="TEXT" NAME="LASTNAME">
</FORM>
```

When viewed by a Web client, the HTML form will look like Figure 6-2. You will notice that the form itself is not visible and that the width of the text field is 20 characters by default.

Option Buttons When you allow the customer to select one choice from among a limited number of choices, **option buttons** are used. Each choice is mutually exclusive of the other. The following code is

Figure 6-2

Example of a Text Field

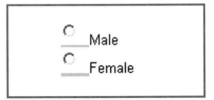

Figure 6-3

Example of Option Buttons

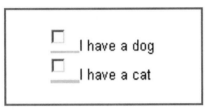

Figure 6-4

Example of Check Boxes

used for option buttons:

```
<FORM>
<INPUT TYPE="RADIO" NAME="SEX" VALUE="MALE"> MALE
<BR>
<INPUT TYPE="RADIO" NAME="SEX" VALUE="FEMALE"> FEMALE
</FORM>
```

When viewed by a Web client, the HTML form will look like Figure 6-3.

Check Boxes To allow the customer to select one or more options of a limited number of choices, **check boxes** are used. These choices, unlike the option buttons, are not mutually exclusive. The following code is used for check boxes:

```
<FORM>
<INPUT TYPE="CHECKBOX" NAME="BIKE" VALUE="YES"> I have a dog
<BR>
<INPUT TYPE="CHECKBOX" NAME="CAR" VALUE="YES"> I have a cat
</FORM>
```

When viewed by a Web client, the HTML form will look like Figure 6-4.

The HTML Action Attribute and Submit Button The HTML form's action attribute defines the name of the file where the information will be sent. Upon receipt, the file processes the information defined in the ACTION attribute. A submit button is most often used to send the information to the file. When the customer clicks on the Submit button, this causes a click event to occur, and the content of the form is sent to the other file. The code for the Submit button is shown below. In the example, upon the Submit click event, the customer input will be sent to a page called nelson_form_action.asp.

```
<FORM NAME="INPUT" ACTION="Nelson_Form_Action.asp"
    METHOD="GET">
Customer Name: <INPUT TYPE="TEXT" NAME="USER">
<INPUT TYPE="SUBMIT" VALUE="SUBMIT">
</FORM>
```

When viewed by a Web client, the HTML form will look like Figure 6-5.

Figure 6-5

Example of a Submit Button

Kanthaka Farms is a continuing case study in this book that illustrates the process of building electronic commerce with Web database constructions. In this chapter you will learn to create different client-side technologies to use in your electronic commerce model. First, you will create the HTML form for the guestbook electronic commerce model. As you continue through the text, you will complete different facets of electronic commerce Web database construction, resulting in a complete Web site for Kanthaka Farms.

Kanthaka Farms
Creating an HTML Form

1. Launch your Web server software and verify that it is running.

2. From Start, Programs, Accessories, launch Notepad text editor. You may use any HTML or text editor, however, if you prefer not to use Notepad.

3. In your text editor, type the following HTML code to create the title of the HTML form:

```
<HTML>
<HEAD>
<TITLE>Guestbook</TITLE>
</HEAD>
<BODY BACKGROUND="bk.jpg">
<H1 ALIGN=CENTER>Electronic Commerce Business Models</H1><P>
<H3 ALIGN=CENTER>Please Sign Our Guestbook</H3><P>
```

4. Next, type the PRE tag to align the form fields and specify the beginning of preformatted text:

```
<PRE>
```

5. Your HTML form must now be initialized using the FORM tag. Type the following code under the PRE tag:

```
<FORM METHOD=POST ACTION="/cgi-win/book/guestbk/guestbk.exe/
   AddEntry">
<STRONG>Name: </STRONG><INPUT NAME="Name" TYPE="TEXT"
   MAXLENGTH=50 SIZE=30>
<STRONG>Email Address: </STRONG><INPUT NAME="Email"
   TYPE="TEXT" MAXLENGTH=50 SIZE=30>
<STRONG>Date Of Birth (XX/XX/XX): </STRONG><INPUT
   NAME="BirthDate" TYPE="TEXT" MAXLENGTH=8 SIZE=8>
<STRONG>Comments: </STRONG><EM>(Click ENTER when
   finished)</EM>
<TEXTAREA NAME="Remarks" ROWS=8 COLS=45></TEXTAREA>
```

Note: You will insert spaces between the labels' colons and the </STRONG> tag to align the text.

6. Now you will add a submit button to allow your customer to send the information in your form.

```
<INPUT NAME="Submit" TYPE="SUBMIT" VALUE="Enter">
```

7. Add a reset button that will clear the input.

```
<INPUT NAME="Reset" TYPE="RESET" VALUE="Clear">
```

8. To finish your HTML form, you must close the tags that are still open. These are the FORM, PRE, BODY, and HTML tags. The code to enter is:

```
</FORM>
</PRE>
</BODY>
</HTML>
```

9. Save the HTML form as Exercise1_K.htm in C:\WebSite\HTDOCS\ BOOK\CH06.

10. View the page in your Web client by typing in the following URL in your browser:

```
http://localhost/book/CH06/Exercise1_K.htm
```

Your HTML form should look like the one shown in Figure 6-6.

Figure 6-6

Guestbook HTML Form

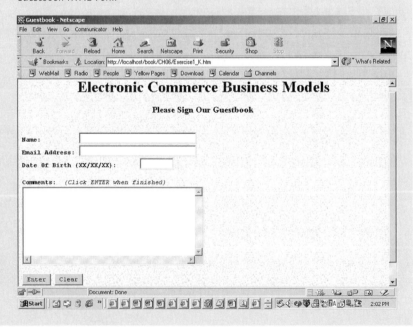

Using Passwords for Added Security in the Electronic Commerce Model

Input fields can be used to parse data to the back-end database to add more security to your site. Text boxes can be used for user name and password inputs, and the submit button can be used to send the content of the form to the back-end. The **ENCTYPE attribute** is used to set or retrieve the MIME encoding for the form. The code for the ENCTYPE is the following:

```
<FORM ENCTYPE = sType... >
```

The **sType** is a string that specifies or receives the format of the data being submitted by the form. The Web client sends the form data using the ENCTYPE attribute. This attribute is optional, and when not used the URL-encoding scheme is automatically applied. This scheme follows these syntax rules:

```
scheme://host.domain:port/path/filename
```

The scheme defines the type of Internet service, the most common type being HTTP. The domain defines the Internet domain name, such as cseng.aw.com/catalog/comingsoon/0,3838,,00.html/. The host defines the domain host. If omitted, the default host for http is www. The :port defines the port number at the host, which is normally omitted. The default port number for http is 80. The path defines a path, in this case a subdirectory, at the Web server. If the path is omitted, the document must be located at the root directory of the Web site. The filename defines the name of a document. The default filename might be default.asp, or index.html, or in this case comingsoon/0,3838,,00.html. These URL schemes are shown in Table 6-2.

Web Break

Today, the distinctions among various forms of information, such as documents and databases, are quickly disappearing. New query languages are being created to better search these new forms of information. Xquery is a new query language for XML. Visit the W3C Web site at http://www.w3.org/TR/2001/WD-xquery-20010215 and work with a prototype that allows you to formulate Xqueries.

Table 6-2 *URL Schemes*

Schemes	Access	Syntax Example
file	a file on your local PC	<A NAME="C:\My_File.htm">My File</A>
ftp	a file on an FTP server	<A HREF="ftp://www.myprogram.exe">Program Name</A>
http	a file on a Web server	<A HREF="http://www.myfile.htm">File Name</A>
gopher	a file on a Gopher server	<A HREF="gopher://www.myfile.htm">Gopher Name</A>
news	a Usenet newsgroup	<A HREF="news:myfile.html">News Name</A>
telnet	a Telnet connection	<A HREF="telnet:myfile.html">Telnet Name</A>
WAIS	a file on a WAIS server	<A HREF="wais:myfile.html">Wais Name</A>
mail system	a link to a mail system	<A HREF="mailto:myemail.com">My Email</A>

Kanthaka Farms
Adding Security to the Design

In this exercise you will add security to the HTML form for the guestbook electronic commerce model you created in the previous exercise.

1. Verify that your Web server is launched and running.

2. From Start, Programs, Accessories, launch Notepad text editor. You may use any HTML or text editor, however, if you prefer not to use Notepad.

3. Type the following code:

```
<HTML>
<HEAD>
<TITLE>Security</TITLE>
</HEAD>
<BODY BACKGROUND="bk.jpg">
<CENTER>
<H1 ALIGN=CENTER>Electronic Commerce Business Models</H1><P>
<H1 ALIGN=CENTER>Please Sign In</H3><P>
<FORM METHOD=POST ACTION=/cgi-win/book/
    SECURITY/Security.exe/>
<B>Username:</B><INPUT NAME="UserName" MAXLENGTH=20
    SIZE=20><BR>
<B>Password:</B><INPUT TYPE="Password" MAXLENGTH=20
    SIZE=20><BR>
<BR><BR>
<INPUT NAME="Login" TYPE="SUBMIT" VALUE="Login">
<INPUT NAME="Reset" TYPE="RESET" VALUE="Clear">
</CENTER>
</BODY>
</HTML>
```

4. Save your document as C:\WebSite\HTDOCS\BOOK\CH06\ Exercise2_K.htm.

5. In your browser, request the following page:

`http://localhost/book/CH06/Exercise2_K.htm`

6. Enter *Test* as the user name and *password* for the password as in the form shown in Figure 6-7. Click on the Login button to submit your HTML form. Your form data is received by Security.exe, which then returns the associated URL-encoded string as shown in Figure 6-8.

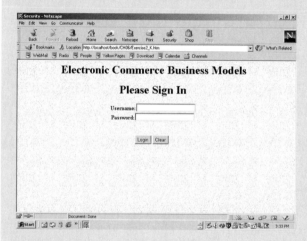

Figure 6-7
Security Login Form

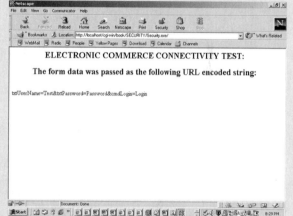

Figure 6-8
URL-Encoded String for Login Form Data

IIS Info

Windows 2000 Internet Server Security Configuration Tool makes it easy to secure a Web server running IIS 5.0. It conducts an interview to determine what services you want to provide and the general way that you would like the server to operate. It then generates and deploys a policy to configure the server appropriately. For more information on this tool, visit http://www.microsoft.com/technet/security/ tools.asp.

6.3 Using Cookies for State Management in the Hidden HTML Form Fields

INPUT tags can also be used to create **hidden form fields**. When a hidden form field is used in the business' Web page, no field is presented to the customer, but the content of the field is sent with the submitted HTML form. Even though the **HIDDEN VALUE** is not displayed in the form, the user can see the hidden text by viewing the HTML source of the document, just like in a **PASSWORD** field. The syntax of the field is the following:

```
<INPUT TYPE= "HIDDEN" NAME= "Hidden_Field_Name"
   VALUE= "Hidden_Value"
```

Hidden fields serve three purposes: they define script functionality, specify script parameters, and embed state information within a form. Specifically related to the electronic commerce model, this hidden field value is useful for transmitting state information about client–server interaction.

Understanding State Management Systems

A **state management system** includes at least three elements: **data**, **name**, and **persistence**.

The data element is the major component of a state management system. For electronic commerce, the environment is a Web database environment. The back-end database easily allows for the storage of the following:

- The name and access rights of the customer
- A description of the customer's most recent inquiries
- A set or named selection with the results of a customer's inquiries
- Historical information about the customer's past behavior at the business' Web site
- The customer's preferred language
- The customer's e-mail address and other contact information

The name element is used to coordinate access to the stored state data. Both the Web database system and the Web client need to participate in this coordination process. There are many ways to build a name for the process. The only requirement is that you use the name to find the correct state information. If you use an electronic com-

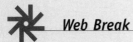

Web Break

Are you concerned about your computer privacy and cookies being written to your hard drive? Many browsers only give you the ability to either accept everything or be prompted each time a cookie tries to be written to your computer. Cookie Jar (version 2.01 released in May 2001) is software that will allow you to control which sites you will allow to write cookies to your computer. It will also stop the browser from sending any revealing information to Web servers. Find out more about this software and other computer security and protocol issues at http://www. lne.com/ericm/cookie_jar/.

merce Web site, then the URLs that embed information allowing the Web database system to coordinate the Web client's activity with the state information will be stored on the server. For example:

```
http://shop.mystore.com/Shop/cart.asp?userid=18SRFU8VOB&mscssid
    =ABCDEFGHI001234L&srefer=&xt=Y&direct_to_summary=false
```

By default, Web servers do not keep information about past requests. The Web server merely receives the request and responds to the request—the request information has no persistence. The purpose of building a state management system into a Web database construction is to add persistence to the model. The state system maintains information about a customer's requests to session actions. This is used in the electronic commerce shopping cart model. The shopping cart model is coded so that the business may "remember" a customer's account information or past purchases. A consideration in state management system design is to consider what will persist and the length of time for each persistence.

State information can be stored on the Web client in the form of **cookies**, or hidden fields, or on the Web server machine in the business' database.

Storing State Information in Cookies

Cookies are a way in which server-side connections, like JSP, ASP, or CGI scripts, can both store and retrieve information on the client side of the connection. The addition of a simple, persistent, client-side state significantly extends the capabilities of the Web-based client/server electronic commerce model. Cookies are similar to records or variables in that a cookie has both a name and a value called a name-value pair. A cookie is introduced to the Web client by including a Set-Cookie header as part of an HTTP response. The syntax of the Set-Cookie HTTP response is the following:

```
Set-Cookie: NAME=VALUE; expires=DATE; path=PATH;
    domain=DOMAIN_NAME; secure
```

A cookie is associated with an HTML document and is referenced using the **Cookie property**, Document.Cookie. Cookies are always stored as text strings and the only required attribute on the Set-Cookie header is the NAME=VALUE. This string is a sequence of characters excluding semicolons, commas, and spaces. A sample client/server exchange that illustrates the use of cookies follows:

Client requests a document and receives in the response:
```
Set-Cookie: CUSTOMER=JOHN_Q_PUBLIC; path=/;
expires= Saturday, 01-Jun-02 13:13:40 GMT
```

When client requests a URL in path "/" on this server, it sends:
```
Cookie: CUSTOMER= JOHN_Q_PUBLIC
```

Client requests a document and receives in the response:
```
Set-Cookie: PART_NUMBER=BUSINESS_WIDGET0001; path=/
```

When client requests a URL in path "/" on this server, it sends:
```
Cookie: CUSTOMER= JOHN_Q_PUBLIC; PART_NUMBER=
BUSINESS_WIDGET0001
```

Client receives:
```
Set-Cookie: SHIPPING=UPS; path=/here
```

When client requests a URL in path "/" on this server, it sends:
```
Cookie: CUSTOMER= JOHN_Q_PUBLIC; PART_NUMBER=
BUSINESS_WIDGET0001
```

When client requests a URL in path "/here" on this server, it sends:
```
Cookie: JOHN_Q_PUBLIC; PART_NUMBER= BUSINESS_WIDGET0001;
SHIPPING=UPS
```

Developers who do not have access to a back-end database on the Web server often use client-side cookies. Cookies are also used in the Web database construction and are stored server-side in the back-end database. In the earlier security example, a cookie would store the user login name and password entered in the HTML form. In the example, there is one cookie variable named "UserName" that stores the value Test and a second cookie variable named "pass-

Figure 6-9

Storing State Information on a Web Client with Cookies

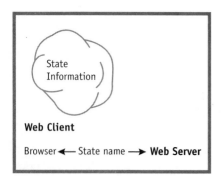

State Information

Web Client

Browser ◄— State name —► **Web Server**

word" that stores the value password. This information would be stored in the cookie in two **name=value pairs**:

```
username=Test; password=password;
```

It is important to keep track of the number of name=value pairs used. A single cookie can only store 20 of these pairs, or a maximum of 4096 characters. Should the pair limit be reached before the maximum character limit, the oldest pairs are dropped. If the character limit is reached first, then the cookie values cannot be read within the script procedure.

There are two types of cookies used in the electronic commerce model: session and persistent. **Session cookies**, also called **temporary cookies**, are only stored in memory and are deleted when the session with the Web browser is terminated. The Web browser keeps track of temporary cookies as long as it is running, but deletes them when it is shut down. Temporary cookies are used to pass information between Web pages during a single visit. Online shopping carts often use temporary cookies.

Persistent cookies, or **permanent cookies**, are stored in a text file on the user's computer. The Web browser saves permanent cookies as tiny files to maintain settings or data between multiple visits. Persistent cookies are actually set to expire at some time in the future, usually between 30 days and a year from their creation dates, and are automatically deleted from the system at that time.

In this exercise you will add a cookie to the HTML form for the guestbook electronic commerce model you created in the first exercise in this chapter.

Kanthaka Farms
__Creating a Session Cookie__

1. Verify that your Web server is launched and running.

2. From Start, Programs, Accessories, launch Notepad text editor. You may use any HTML or text editor, however, if you prefer not to use Notepad. Open Exercise2_K.htm HTML.

3. You will create a script within the Exercise2_K.htm HTML form. This will be used to add functionality to the security form. The customer will be required to enter a user name and password before submitting it to a Web server. The submit button will also be modified so that on click, it will call the script code associated with the click event. Scripts will be discussed in more detail in Chapter 7. Modify your form so that it contains the following code:

```
<HTML>
<HEAD>
<TITLE>Security</TITLE>
<SCRIPT LANGUAGE="VBSCRIPT">
Option Explicit
Function ValidateUserName(ByVal strUserName)
  If strUserName = "" Then
    MsgBox "Please enter your User Name.", vbCritical,
    "Missing User Name"
    ValidateUserName = False
  Else
    ValidateUserName = True
  End If
End Function
Sub cmdLogin_Click
  If ValidateUserName(Document.frmLogin.txtUserName.Value)
  Then
  Document.Cookie = "username=" &
  Document.frmLogin.txtUserName.Value & ";"
  MsgBox Document.Cookie, vbInformation, "Cookie Alert"
  End If
End Sub
</SCRIPT>
</HEAD>
<BODY BACKGROUND="bk.jpg">
<CENTER>
<H1 ALIGN=CENTER>Electronic Commerce Business Models</H1><P>
<H1 ALIGN=CENTER>Please Sign In</H3><P>
<FORM NAME=frmLogin METHOD=POST ACTION=
    /cgi-win/book/SECURITY/Security.exe/>
<B>Username:</B><INPUT TYPE="TEXT" NAME="txtUserName"
    MAXLENGTH=20 SIZE=20><BR>
<B>Password:</B><INPUT TYPE="PASSWORD" NAME="txtPassword"
    MAXLENGTH=20 SIZE=20><BR>
<BR><BR>
<INPUT TYPE=BUTTON NAME="cmdLogin" ONCLICK=cmdLogin_Click
    VALUE="Login">
<INPUT NAME="Reset" TYPE="RESET" VALUE="Clear">
</CENTER>
</BODY>
</HTML>
```

4. Save your document as C:\WebSite\HTDOCS\BOOK\CH06\ Exercise3_K.htm.

5. In your browser, request the following page:

```
http://localhost/book/CH06/Exercise3_K.htm
```

6. Again, enter *Test* as the user name and password for the *password*. Click on the Login button to submit your HTML form. The client-side script in your form causes the message box shown in Figure 6-10 to be displayed. In the message box you should see the cookie variable name and the value you typed for the user name.

Figure 6-10
Message Box Created with Client-Side Script Displaying a Session Cookie

6.4 Using Cascading Style Sheets to Display HTML Elements

Basic Elements of Cascading Style Sheets

Learning **cascading style sheets** is similar to learning HTML. HTML elements were originally designed to define the contents of the HTML document; for instance, different tags declared the header, the title, or a paragraph. Web browsers were supposed to determine the layout of the document without using any formatting tags. However, as the two major browsers, Netscape and Internet Explorer, added new HTML tags and attributes to the original HTML specifications, it became more and more difficult to separate the content from the presentation layout. In an effort to resolve this problem, the World Wide Web Consortium (W3C) created cascading style sheets (CSSs), styles that define how to display HTML elements. A **style** is simply a collection of information about displaying and positioning attributes that a Web author defines. These styles are normally stored in style sheets. For example, a style could specify 12-point, bold, red, sans serif font with a 3-point black border, beginning 10 pixels down from the top of the screen. Every style is uniquely named—the style described above could be named P1 or references or TopDownRed. Should a style be named the same as a valid HTML element, then the style is automatically applied to every instance of that element. When a style is given a name for which there is no corresponding HTML tag, then it must be applied manually wherever it is to appear. This is done by modifying an existing tag in the document or by creating a new tag. For instance, to apply a references style, a paragraph tag could be modified to read <P CLASS="references">.

Styles consist of two parts: a **selector** and a **declaration**.

```
.selector { declaration }
```

Curly braces always follow the selector, and the declaration consists of everything between the curly braces. The selector is also usually used as the style name. The declaration consists of a series of properties and their associated values, separated by semicolons.

```
.Iggy { size:small; runs:reallyfast; sings:caninechorus;
fur-decoration:sleek; }
```

Not all values work with all properties. In the example above, the property "size" can never take the value "brown," although "sings" could take the property "reallyfast."

External Style Sheets

Styles in HTML 4.0 define how HTML elements are displayed, just like the font tag and the color attribute in HTML 3.2. Styles are normally saved in files external to the HTML documents. **External style sheets** enable both the appearance and layout of Web pages to be changed just by editing a single CSS document. This allows developers to control the style and layout of multiple Web pages all at one time by defining a style for each HTML element.

Styles cascade into a new virtual style sheet by the following rules, where the highest number has the highest priority:

- Browser default
- External style sheet
- Internal style sheet (inside the <head> tag)
- Inline style (inside HTML element)

Therefore, an inside HTML element has the highest priority. This means that the inside element will override every style declared inside the HEAD tag, in an external style sheet and in a browser. An external style sheet is extremely useful when the style is applied to many pages. Each page must link to the style sheet using the LINK tag, which must be positioned inside the head section:

```
<HEAD>
<LINK REL="stylesheet" type="text/css" HREF="mystyle.css" />
</HEAD>
```

In the code above, the Web browser will interpret the style definitions from the file mystyle.css and format the document accordingly. As with HTML, an external style sheet can be written in any text editor. However, the external style sheet file should not contain any HTML tags and should be saved with a .css extension. Examine the style sheet file shown below:

```
hr {color: green}
p {margin-left: 10px}
body {background-image: url("Kanthaka/kanthaka_logo.gif")}
```

Internal Style Sheets

An **internal style sheet** is used when a single document has a unique style. Internal styles are defined in the head section by using the STYLE tag:

```
<HEAD>
<STYLE TYPE="text/css">
hr {color: green}
p {margin-left: 10px}
body {background-image: url("Kanthaka/kanthaka_logo.gif")}
</STYLE>
</HEAD>
```

In this exercise you will install Style Master 1.9 CSS Editor and create a cascading style sheet for your electronic commerce design for Kanthaka Farms.

1. Verify that your Web server is launched and running.

2. From Start, Programs, Accessories, launch Notepad text editor. You may use any text editor, however, if you prefer not to use Notepad.

3. If you have not installed the cascading style sheets editor Style Master 1.9 from this book's companion Web site, do so now. An examination of Style Master 1.9 can also be obtained from http://www.westciv.com/style_master/. To install Style Master 1.9, simply run the application Setup_Style_Master1.9.exe and follow the instructions. To uninstall Style Master, use the Add/Remove Programs control panel. Launch Style Master 1.9. Notice that when the application is launched, a new untitled window opens. Choose to create a new style sheet based on the basic.css template.

Kanthaka Farms
Installing a CSS Editor
and Creating a Cascading
Style Sheet

4. To create a new style sheet, choose File New from the Style Master application.

5. From the Statement menu, choose Comment and click OK. In the comment editor window, type *Kanthaka Farms* and click OK.

6. Save the style sheet by choosing File, Save from the menu bar. Save the files as Exercise4_K.css in your CH06 folder. Even though it only contains a comment, you have created your first style sheet. Notice that unlike HTML documents, a style sheet does not display header information or special code to identify its type to the browser.

7. To view the source codes of your style sheet, choose Style Sheet Text from the Windows menu. A separate window will open displaying your CSS source code as shown in Figure 6-11.

Figure 6-11

Displaying CSS Source Code

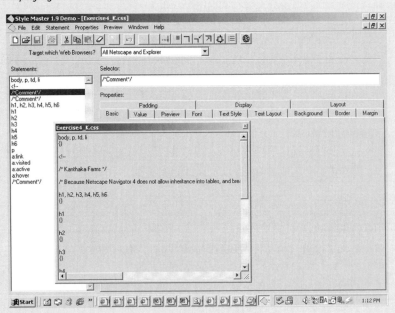

8. Now, using your Notepad or another text editor, create the following Web page. This page will be used for previewing our style sheet. In the text editor, type in the following code:

```
<HTML>
<HEAD>
<TITLE>Kanthaka Farms CSS</TITLE>
<LINK REL=STYLESHEET TYPE="text/css" HREF="Exercise4_K.css">
</HEAD>
<BODY>
<H1>Kanthaka Farms Welcomes You!</H1>
<H2>Buying an Italian Greyhound Companion</H2>
<P>Buying any pet must never be an impulse decision. An
    Italian Greyhound will become an intimate family member
    despite its age or gender. This relationship can never
    be casual. <A HREF="IG1.jpg"></A> These dogs have a long
    life span and need a stable environment with plenty of
    affection and responsible care. This must include the
    best possible standards of canine nutrition, health care,
    exercise and sanitation including mental health.<P>
<H3>Description</H3>
<P>The Italian Greyhound is very similar to the Greyhound,
    but much smaller and more slender in all proportions and
    of ideal elegance and grace.</P>
<H3>Head</H3>
<P>Narrow and long, tapering to nose, with a slight
    suggestion of stop.</P>
<H3>Body</H3>
<P>Of medium length, short coupled; high at withers, back
    curved and drooping at hindquarters, the highest point
    of curve at start of loin, creating a definite tuck-up
    at flanks.</P>
<H1>For More Information</H1>
<P>to contact Kanthaka Farms, email us at
<A HREF="mailto:kanthaka@email.com">
    kanthaka@email.com</A></P>
<P>to download a full description of the Italian Greyhound
    standard in acrobat format,
<A HREF="ftp://ftp.kanthaka.com.pdf">click here</A></P>
<P>for more information about Italian Greyhounds, visit the
    Italian Greyhound Club of America at
<A HREF="www.italiangreyhound.org/">
    www.italiangreyhound.org/ </A></P>
</BODY>
</HTML>
```

9. Save your file as Exercise4_K.htm in your CH06 folder. Notice the line in the HEAD that reads:

```
<LINK REL=STYLESHEET TYPE="text/css" HREF="Exercise_4.css">
```

This means that this Web page is linked to your CSS named Exercise_4.css. Make sure that both files are located in the CH06 folder since this is a relative reference.

10. Now you need to add some rules to your style sheet. Remember that a style sheet is just a set of rules that are used to determine which elements will be affected by the rule and to define how many affected elements should appear. Our first rule will be to affect the appearance of the BODY tag of the page. When creating a rule, the first step is to create a selector, which will specify to which elements the rule applies. To create a statement and its selector, choose Statement, New Statement from Exercise4_K.css menu.

11. In the window that opens, verify that HTML Element Selector is shown and click OK. The HTML Element Selector will appear.

12. From the list of HTML elements, choose BODY(document body) and click on OK.

13. In the style sheet window, click the Background Properties tab. Click the downward-pointing arrow to the left of the color field to display keywords. Choose the keyword "transparent." Notice the box to the right changes to display the color transparent. Click on the box. Notice that it displays a pallet to allow you to customize your background color.

14. Now preview your first rule. To do so, choose Preview, Preview in Browser, Edit Preview Browser List from the menu bar. Click Add Browser and locate the browser you want to add to the list of preview browsers. You may repeat this process to add multiple browsers. When have added all the browsers, click OK. This list of preview browsers will now appear as a submenu of the Preview in Browser.

15. The next step is to set up the preview documents. To do so, from the Preview menu choose Preview Using Document, Edit Preview Document List. Click the Add Document button and add CH06\Exercise4a_K.htm and click OK.

16. The style sheet must be previewed using the chosen browser and the chosen document. To preview the style sheet, choose Preview, Preview Now from the Menu or click the Preview button that looks like a green globe on the far right of the toolbar. Your browser will display the Kanthaka Farms Web page similar to the one shown in Figure 6-12.

17. Let's assume that Anicca has asked us to set a background image for the page. This is easily done in the style sheet. To set the image, click the list box arrow to the right of the Image field. Choose Locate. From the window, choose the sketch.jpg file in the CH06 folder. The Style Master editor will place the link from the style sheet to the sketch.jpg image in the text field. You should always specify a background color when using a background image. This ensures that if the image becomes unavailable, the foreground text colors do not blend with the text, making it illegible.

18. You have now created a rule that gives the body of a page a transparent background with a sketch of an Italian greyhound. Save the style sheet and preview again in the browser. The page should look like Figure 6-13.

Figure 6-12

Previewing the Kanthaka Farms Web Page in the CSS Editor

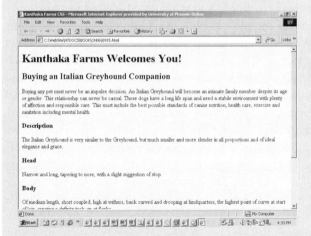

Figure 6-13

Using a Background Image in the CSS

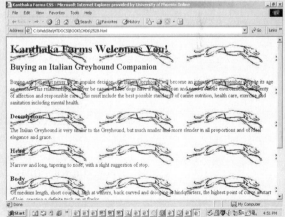

6.5 Using XHTML in the Electronic Commerce Model

Extensible Hypertext Markup Language (XHTML) is a combination of HTML and XML (Extensible Markup Language). The "X" in XHTML is the same as that in XML. XML is a markup technology that lets you define your own markup language and data formats for new applications. XHTML consists of all the elements in HTML 4.01 combined with the syntax of XML. XML imposes strict syntax rules that result in well-formed documents and will ultimately replace proprietary Web file formats such as portable document format files, Flash, and other multimedia formats. XML is preferable to HTML, and with its emergence the distinctions among various forms of information, such as documents and databases, are quickly disappearing. It was designed to describe data, whereas HTML was only designed to display data. XHTML is currently in version 1.0 and is the first step toward a modular and extensible Web-based XML. Modularity will be important in the future of electronic commerce: electronic commerce, increasingly, will become M-commerce. Many devices, such as cell phones, will only need a subset of XHTML because modules will automatically filter the XHTML to include only what the device needs.

XHTML meets the demands of today's business market. There are different Web browser technologies, some of which are used on computers and some on mobile phones and hand-held computers. By the year 2002, it is estimated that as much as 75 percent of Internet access could be carried out on non-PC platforms. These include televisions, refrigerators, even automobiles. In most cases these devices will not have the computing power of a desktop computer and will not be designed to accommodate poorly structured HTML as do current browsers. Therefore, by combining the strengths of both HTML and XML, XHTML is a markup language that not only is ready to meet today's computing needs, but also is positioned to handle those of the future. Support for client-side standards like XHTML will extend the role of the application server on a daily basis.

XHTML pages can be read by all XML-enabled devices, and they comply with the following rules:

- XHTML elements and attributes are almost identical to HTML.
- XHTML tags are all lowercase.

- XHTML is a stricter, more structured version of HTML.
- Pages written in XHTML are compatible with most browsers.
- All XHTML tags, including empty elements, must be closed.

In this exercise you will create an XHTML Web page.

Kanthaka Farms
Creating an XHTML Web Page

1. Verify that your Web server is launched and running.

2. From Start, Programs, Accessories, launch Notepad text editor. You may use any HTML or text editor, however, if you do not prefer to use Notepad.

3. Type the following code:

```
<!DOCTYPE html PUBLIC "-//W3C//DTD XHTML 1.0
   Transitional//EN" "DTD/xhtml1-transitional.dtd">
<html xmlns = "http://www.w3.org/1999/xhtml">
<head>
  <title>XHTML Example</title>
</head>
<body>
<h1>XHTML Example
</h1>
<a href = "http://validator.w3.org/check/referer">
<img src = http://validator.w3.org/images/vxhtml10 height=
   "31" width = "88" border = "0" hspace   = "16" align =
   "left" alt = "Valid XHTML 1.0!"/></a>
<p>That wasn't that bad was it?
</p>
<p>Note that the layout in this example (with tabs and
   alignment) is purely for readability - XHTML does not
   require it.
</p>
</body>
</html>
```

4. Save your document as C:\WebSite\HTDOCS\BOOK\CH06\ Exercise5_K.htm.

5. In your browser, request the following page:

```
http://localhost/book/CH06/Exercise5_K.htm
```

Figure 6-14 should be displayed in your Web browser.

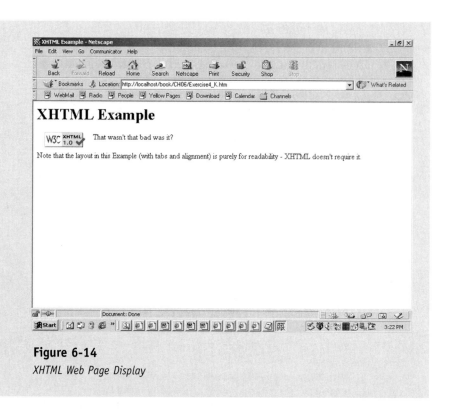

Figure 6-14
XHTML Web Page Display

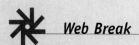 **Web Break**

Want to take that first step in the process to clean up your HTML pages? Take a look at Dave Raggett's **HTML Tidy** at http://www.w3.org/People/Raggett/tidy/. HTML Tidy is an excellent tool for converting your untidy (not well-formed) HTML to well-formed documents. It can also be used to convert HTML to XHTML and XML.

FOCUS ON ELECTRONIC COMMERCE

M-Commerce and XHTML: Partners in the Future of Computing

The mobile communications and content industries are getting primed for the future of computing. How are they doing it? M-commerce is throwing its support to XHTML as the format for the future evolution of mobile services. In March 2001, Nokia Corp., Motorola Inc., LM Ericsson AB, and Siemens AG not only publicly embraced XHTML, but expressed their focus for XHTML-based product development, content, and services.

XHTML is the natural evolution of the **wireless application protocol (WAP)**. The great advantage of WAP is that it frees people from their PCs—even their laptops. WAP phones allow users to read news, check football scores, or monitor stock prices wherever they are. Receiving television and theater listings, ATM locations, and even information about traffic congestion are other uses. E-mail is the next big goal for WAP. WAP is perfect for tiny screens and users on the move. On-phone shopping will use WAP, and there are countless possibilities for businesses, for example, giving salespeople instant mobile access to inventory data. WAP will be using XHTML, and it will be used to create all content regardless of whether it is for the fixed Internet or the mobile phone world. A number of mobile operators, including Vodafone Group PLC, Sonera Corp., Telenor ASA, Netcom AB, Deutsche Telekom AG's T-Mobil, and Telecom Italia SpA's TIM, have also announced plans to offer XHTML-based services. Interwoven, a provider of enterprise-class content management software, has joined with Nokia to enable enterprises to create, preview, and deploy Web content and applications to wireless devices more easily and quickly—and is no surprise that they are using XHTML to deliver it.

It's time to start planning for the M-commerce arena, even if businesses don't want to start wireless information delivery right now, says Christopher Lindquist of *CIO Magazine* in his predictions for mobile electronic commerce and online transactions. "By 2004, 74 million people—or one-third of wireless users—will have access to the wireless Web, according to a report by Boston-based Aberdeen Group," said Lindquist. "That growth presents a tremendous opportunity for enterprises looking to take competitive advantage of the medium."

Sources: David Cotriss, "Interwoven mobilize content management," *MBizCentral*, April 12, 2001; "Mobile leaders endorse XHTML," *AFX News Limited*, March 21, 2001; Christopher Lindquist, "Mobilize," *CIO Magazine*, October 15, 2000.

What are some other strategies businesses can use to be prepared for the M-commerce revolution?

Given that HTML and other Internet technologies have worked well without a consistent software platform like XHTML, do you think XHTML is the answer for M-commerce?

Justify your answer.

6.6 Exploring the Fundamentals of DHTML in the Electronic Commerce Model

Dynamic HTML, or **DHTML**, is one of the most exciting and useful technologies to be introduced to the Web recently. Enabled by a number of other technologies, including VBScript, JavaScript, the Document Object Model (DOM) layers, and CSSs, DHTML is a collective term typically used to describe the combination of these technologies to create animated Web pages. With DHTML, a Web page can be changed after it is loaded into the Web browser without any communication with the Web server. For example, a section of text can change from 12-point, sans serif, blue type to 14-point, serif, green; or a graphic can move from one location to another in response to a user's action, such as a button-click event. Much of DHTML is specified in HTML 4.0 standards. Often called **animated HTML**, DHTML allows Web documents to look and act like desktop applications or even multimedia productions.

The major components of DHTML include the following:

- *Cascading style sheets and the layering of content* that let developers specify the stylistic attributes of the typographic elements of the Web page such as color, size, or style of the text. There is no waiting for the screen to refresh to see the changes.
- *Content positioning and dynamic content programming* that can address all or most page elements.
- *Dynamic fonts* that let developers enhance the appearance of the text by packaging the fonts with the Web page.
- *Data Binding* that increases interactivity by allowing connection to the information needed to ask questions, change elements, and get results without interacting with the Web server.
- *Scriptlets* that let developers author content once, then reuse the content in other Web pages or applications. Scriptlets are Web pages authored with DHTML.

In the DHTML model, each page division or section, such as heading, paragraph, image, or list, is viewed as an object. This model is called the **Dynamic HTML Object Model** by Microsoft, the **HTML Object Model** by Netscape, and the **Document Object Model** by the W3C. Regardless of which name the model is called, each heading on a page can be given attributes of text style and color, named, and addressed by that name in a small program or *script* included on the Web page. This heading can then be changed by events such as a mouse passing over the object or a button being clicked or even time passing. Images can also be moved from one place to another on the Web page simply by dragging and dropping the image object with the mouse. Because all variations of all elements, or objects, on the Web page have been sent from the Web server to the Web client as part of the same page, any changes are instantaneous. Although JavaScripts, Java applets, and ActiveX controls were present in previous levels of Web pages, DHTML provides an increased amount of programming in Web pages since more elements of a page can be addressed by a program. The DOM is the real core of DHTML because it is what makes HTML changeable.

Dynamic HTML is client-side scripting. The growing use of DHTML new elements on business and entertainment sites can be attributed to DHTML's offer of more engaging and interactive Web pages for users. In addition to getting faster access to database information, businesses use DHTML to give customers a more attractive Web layout and a more functional GUI interface. Businesses have found the use of DHTML creates Web sites with more appeal to their customers and eliminates lengthy download times for multimedia experiences.

 Web Break

If you want to see sophisticated DHTML in action, check out these DHTML games available on the Internet. The first is Star Blaster at http://www.dansteinman.com/dynduo/demos/starthruster2. The second game is an interactive puzzle found at http://www.dansteinman.com/dynduo/demos/puzzle/puzzle.html. Both show what DHTML offers by demonstrating the increased user interactivity and the elimination of lengthy download times associated with multimedia experiences.

Summary

■ **Discuss the purpose of hypertext links and hypermedia in the canonical model.** The hypertext link allows the user to select a connection from one medium, such as a word, picture, or information object, to another. In a multimedia environment such as the Web, such hypertext links can include even sound and motion video sequences. Links to these types of media are called hypermedia. Hypermedia can also connote a higher level of user interactivity than the interactivity already implicit in hypertext. The most common form of hypertext link is the highlighted word or picture that can be selected by the user, usually with a mouse click. The click event results in the immediate delivery and view of another file. The highlighted object is referred to as an anchor. The anchor reference and the object referred to constitute the hypertext link.

■ **Discuss how HTML forms are used to create dynamic Web interactions.** An HTML form uses input fields, buttons, and other resources for customer interaction. An HTML form is an area that can contain form elements. Form elements allow the customer to enter information into the form. These elements, or controls, can be text fields, text area fields, drop-down menus, option buttons, and checkboxes. Creating an HTML form typically involves two independent steps: (1) creating a layout for the form and (2) creating a script program on the server side. This script program is used to process the information returned from the HTML form and will be discussed in detail in later chapters of this book. HTML form programming does not require an extensive understanding of HTML, because only two HTML elements, or tags, are needed to create a basic form: the FORM and INPUT tags. The FORM tag denotes a form, and the INPUT tag defines a visual interface element, such as the textbox or option button that allows dynamic Web interaction.

■ **Build HTML forms.** A simple text editor can be used to build HTML forms. The following tags can be used to create an HTML form:

1. <FORM> </FORM> A form is defined with the <form> tag.
2. <INPUT> </INPUT> The most used form tag is the INPUT tag. The type of INPUT is specified with the TYPE attribute. The most commonly used input types are text fields, option buttons, and checkboxes.
3. <TEXTAREA> </TEXTAREA>
4. <SELECT> </SELECT>
5. <OPTION>

- **Use cookies for state management in the hidden HTML form fields.**
  State information can be stored on the Web client in the form of
  cookies, or hidden fields, or on the Web server machine in business' database. Cookies are a way in which server-side connections, like JSP, ASP, or CGI scripts, can both store and retrieve
  information on the client side of the connection. The addition of
  a simple, persistent, client-side state significantly extends the
  capabilities of Web-based client/server electronic commerce
  model. Cookies are similar to records or variables in that a cookie has both a name and a value. A cookie is introduced to the
  Web client by including a Set-Cookie header as part of an HTTP
  response.

- **Use cascading style sheets (CSSs) to display HTML elements.**
  Cascading style sheets, (CSSs) are styles that define how to display HTML elements. A style is simply a collection of information
  about displaying and positioning attributes that a Web author
  defines. These styles are normally stored in style sheets. For
  example, a style could specify 12-point, bold, red, sans serif font
  with a 3-point black border, beginning 10 pixels down from the
  top of the screen. Every style is uniquely named. For instance,
  the style described above could be named P1 or references or
  TopDownRed. Should a style be named the same as a valid
  HTML element, then the style is automatically applied to every
  instance of the HTML element. When a style is given a name for
  which there is no corresponding HTML tag, then it must be
  applied manually wherever it is to appear. This is done by modifying an existing tag in the document or creating a new tag. For
  instance, to apply a references style, a paragraph tag could be
  modified to read <P CLASS="references">. Styles consist of two
  parts: a selector and a declaration.

- **Discuss the uses of XHTML in the electronic commerce model.**
  Extensible Hypertext Markup Language (XHTML) is a combination of HTML and XML (Extensible Markup Language). The "X"
  in XHTML is that same as that in XML. XML is a markup technology that lets you define your own markup language and data
  formats for new applications. XHTML consists of all the elements
  in HTML 4.01 combined with the syntax of XML. XML is a
  markup language that imposes strict syntax rules that result in
  well-formed documents and will ultimately replace proprietary
  Web file formats such as portable document format files, Flash,
  and other multimedia formats.

■ **Describe the fundamentals of DHTML and uses in the electronic commerce model.** Dynamic HTML, or DHTML, is one of the most exciting and useful technologies to be introduced to the Web recently. Enabled by a number of other technologies, including VBScript, JavaScript, the Document Object Model (DOM) layers, and cascading style sheets (CSSs), DHTML is a collective term typically used to describe the combination of these technologies to create animated Web pages. With DHTML, a Web page can be changed after it is loaded into the Web browser without any communication with the Web server. For example, a section of text can change from 12-point, sans serif, blue type to 14-point, serif, green, or a graphic can move from one location to another in response to a user's action, such as a button-click event. Much of DHTML is specified in HTML 4.0 standards. Often called animated HTML, DHTML allows Web documents to look and act like desktop applications or even multimedia productions. There are five major components of DHTML: cascading style sheets and the layering of content, content positioning and dynamic content programming, dynamic fonts, data binding, and scriptlets.

Chapter Key Terms

ACTION
animated HTML
canonical Web activity
cascading style sheet
check boxes
client-side technologies
cookie
Cookie property
declaration
data
Document Object Model (DOM)
Document Type Definition (DTD)
Dynamic HTML (DHTML)
Dynamic HTML Object Model
ENCTYPE attribute
Extensible Hypertext Markup
    Language (XHTML)
external style sheet
Fetch
FORM

form elements
GET method
hidden form fields
HIDDEN VALUE
HTML elements
HTML forms
HTML Object Model
HTML Tidy
hypermedia
hypertext
hypertext links
INPUT
input fields
internal style sheet
Internet media type (IMEDIA)
METHOD
name
name=value pair
option buttons
PASSWORD

permanent cookie
persistence
persistent cookie
portability
portable
POST method
selector
session cookie
state data
state management system
state name
state persistence
style
sTYPE
TARGET
temporary cookie
text fields
wireless application protocol
    (WAP)
Xanadu

Review Questions

1. What is client-side computing? Why are these technologies beneficial to business?

2. What are the two types of Web interaction? Which is better for electronic commerce? Why?

3. Describe the two methods used by HTML forms to submit data. Which is most often used by business? Why?

4. How is customer interaction added to the HTML form?

5. How are input fields used to add security to the electronic commerce model?

6. How are hidden form fields used in the electronic commerce model? What are the benefits of the use to the customer? to the business?

7. What is state management? What are the three elements of state management systems? How is each used?

8. What are cookies? List and define the major types of cookies used today.

9. Why do businesses store cookies on customers' computers?

10. What benefits does business gain from the use of client-side cookies?

11. Why are customers often concerned about cookies written to their hard drives by businesses?

12. Define cascading style sheets and describe their use in business Web database constructions.

13. What are two types of CSSs? How are they alike? How do they differ?

14. What is XHTML? Compare and contrast XHTML with HTML.

15. How does XHTML meet the demands of today's businesses?

16. What are the rules that XHTML must follow?

17. What is DHTML? How does DHTML animate Web pages?

18. What are the major components of DHTML? Describe each.

19. To what can the growing use of DHTML be attributed? Justify your answer.

Critical Thinking Using the Web

1. Use your favorite search engine and search the Web for information on the world's first treaty against cyber crime to tighten provisions protecting online privacy. Initiated by The Council of Europe, a 43-country human rights watchdog, the treaty wants to ensure that police respect privacy rights when they follow digital trails to fight online crimes such as hacking, spreading viruses, using stolen credit card numbers, or defrauding banks. Write a 200–400 word essay describing your findings. Be prepared to discuss whether you believe such a treaty is necessary and justify your opinion.

2. Go to Cookie Central at http://www.cookiecentral.com. Click the Cookie tab at the top of the Web page and explore more about this client-side technology. Examine some of the sample code available at the site. Which would be useful in your Kanthaka Farms business model? Why would you incorporate them? What benefits do they offer Kanthaka Farms? Prepare your answer in a 200–400 word essay and be prepared to present your findings.

3. It has been noted that XHTML and DHTML will eliminate the use of Flash technology on the Web. Using your favorite search engine, find information about Flash. How is it used in business? What benefits are gained by the business with the use of Flash technology? Is Flash a client-side technology? After your investigation of the technology, be prepared to discuss whether you think the new HTML technologies will replace Flash. Prepare your answer in a 200–400 word essay and be prepared to present your findings.

Chapter Case Study

Albatross Records is a continuing case study in this book that illustrates the process of building electronic commerce with Web database constructions. In Chapter 6, you will install the CSS editor and use client-side technologies in the Albatross Records electronic commerce model. As you continue through the text, you will complete different facets of electronic commerce Web database construction, resulting in a complete Web site for Albatross Records.

■ Plan for your inclusion of client-side technologies in the Albatross Records site. Consider the importance of interactivity in the model. In your plan, list which you will include, with which other technolo-

gies they will interact, and what benefits the business will receive from their inclusion in the model.

■ Using at least two of the technologies discussed in this chapter, create Web pages for Albatross Records. You may use any editor you choose to complete this assignment.

■ Upon completion of your Web pages, press Print Screen of each Web page and paste the screen capture into a word document. Also, include in the word document the associated source code with a copy-and-paste method. Be prepared to turn in your document as well as demonstrate your pages in a Web client.

7

Windows Common Gateway Interface Server-Side Technologies

Learning Objectives

Upon completion of this chapter, you will be able to

- Define server-side computing and list different server-side technologies
- Define Common Gateway Interface (CGI) and the three different types of CGI
- Discuss input and the CGI environmental variables
- Discuss CGI output: returning and redirecting
- Create a CGI application using Visual Basic

It don't mean a thing if you can't get that Ping . . .

—Duke Ellington, 1932

7.1 Server-Side Technologies

The Web uses Hypertext Markup Language (HTML), or a successor of HTML, to create Web pages or documents. In the electronic commerce model, these HTML documents allow the customer to jump from page to page through the use of hyperlinks. However, while HTML development allows the customer to retrieve information from Web pages, it does not provide for the interactive, dynamic exchange of information so important for successful electronic commerce constructions. With HTML alone it is not possible for the customer to submit data to the business with an HTML form or search the business' back-end database. To obtain these types of interaction, businesses must look beyond HTML and use extending technologies that allow the Web server to interact with external applications or databases.

Electronic commerce is based on the **client–server model**, where the Web browser is the client and the Web server is the server. Client-side technologies include HTML forms, Cascading Style Sheets (CSS), Extensible HTML (XHTML), and Dynamic HTML (DHTML). Client-side computing has been extended to include **plug-ins**. Plug-ins are code modules used to enhance the Web browser, allowing it to view specific file types. Examples of plug-ins include **Flash** and **Shockwave** technology. Another client-side extending technology is the **Java applet**. These applets, or small Java program modules, are downloaded to the Web client from the server. The Web client then runs the program. It is not desirable or practical, however, to run all-extending applications on the client side.

Server-side technologies enhance HTML Web pages and are used to increase customer interactivity with the business. In the

230

server-side model, the Web server uses an interface program to communicate with an external program or database. The most widely used of these interface programs is **Common Gateway Interface (CGI)**. Other server-side technologies include **proprietary plug-ins** such as ASP, ISAPI or NSAPI, and Java servlets.

7.2 Common Gateway Interface

The Common Gateway Interface (CGI) is an interface for running external programs, called **gateways**, using an information server. Currently, the supported information servers are HTTP servers. In fact, CGI is part of the Web HTTP. Gateways are programs that handle information requests from the Web client and return the appropriate document or generate an HTML ad hoc document on the fly. With CGI, Web servers can serve information that is not in a form readable by the Web client, such as an SQL database. CGI acts as a gateway between the unreadable information and the Web client, converting the information into something that the Web client can use. Some examples of the uses of CGI include the following:

- Converting Web pages into HTML on the fly and sending the HTML result to the Web client
- Interfacing with WAIS and other back-end databases (WAIS is the acronym for wide-area information servers and is an Internet system where databases created for specialized subjects are housed on multiple server locations and made accessible for searching by users with WAIS specialized Web client programs)
- Converting the results of back-end interaction to HTML and sending the result to the Web client
- Allowing front-end customer feedback about the business' Web server through an HTML form and an accompanying CGI decoder

These gateway programs are written as scripts and compiled as executable programs that can be run under different platforms. They can even be run independently, though this would serve no useful purpose. The **CGI executable** provides a consistent way for data to be passed from the Web client on request to the Web server and back-end of the electronic commerce construction. This means that a business that has an application program written in one language, or for a specific platform, can make sure it gets used no matter which operating system the Web client is using. CGI is simply a basic way for information about the client's request to be passed from the Web server and back again.

Because the gateway interface is consistent, CGI applications can be written in a variety of languages. Gateways can be written in any language that produces an executable file, including shell scripts. Some of the more popular languages to use include the following:

- Visual Basic
- C and C++
- PERL
- Tcl and TclBlend, a version of Tcl that can access certain Java language facilities
- Unix C Shell
- Unix Bourne Shell
- DOS command interpreter or third-party enhanced interpreters such as Norton NDOS

Notice that Java was not included in the list of CGI languages. CGI is a protocol for running programs on a Web server. Although Java can also be used for that, and even has a standardized API, the major role of Java on the Web is for client-side scripting. In certain instances the two may be combined in a single application; for example, Kanthaka Farms might use a Java script to define a region on a map showing where it had placed Italian greyhounds. The Java script, or applet, together with a CGI script would be used to process a query for the area defined.

How Does CGI Work?

CGI is not a language, but a simple protocol that can be used to communicate between the Web client and the Web server. Remember that a plain HTML document that the **Web daemon** retrieves is static, which means it exists in a constant state. A static document allows for no interaction between the customer and the business. The HTTP daemon (httpd) waits in attendance for Web client requests. This daemon is a program that forwards the requests as they come into other processes as appropriate. A CGI program, on the other hand, is executed in real-time, so that it can output dynamic information and customer interaction to the electronic commerce model. Through the use of FORM tags in an HTML form, the name of the application that the CGI will control will be specified in the URL:

```
<FORM NAME=frmLogin METHOD=POST ACTION=
   /cgi-win/book/SECURITY/Security.exe/>
```

In this example, the server at Kanthaka Farms would pass control to the CGI application called Security.exe to record the customer's login data. The CGI would then return a confirmation message to the customer's Web client. During the interchange, the data are passed between the Web server and the CGI program through **temporary input** and **output files**. Typically, scripts must be placed in the base of the CGI folder; for example, if the /cgi-bin folder is defined as C:\WebSite\cgi-bin, then CGI scripts must be placed in this folder. They cannot be placed in a child folder like C:\WebSite\cgi-bin\child\folder. This, however, does not prevent scripts from storing their own information in child folders, often for their temporary input and output files. Upon completion of the Web client's request, the Web server deletes all of the temporary files created during the processing of the request unless the server's API is set to retain the files. A schematic representation of CGI is shown in Figure 7.1.

Types of CGI

Windows CGI server-side technologies benefit a large class of Web applications, such as business applications, that are best implemented using external programs controlled by a Web server. However, these business applications are subject to frequent

Figure 7-1

How Does CGI Work?

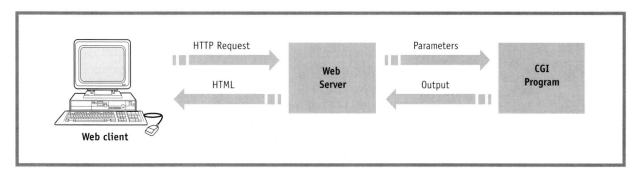

changes in business rules. The broad acceptance of **rapid application development (RAD)** tools such as Visual Basic and Delphi have given rise to the need to use these tools to Web-enable many kinds of business applications. RAD techniques are well suited to the widely used CGI. However, with CGI, a different sort of interface is needed to support these common Windows RAD tools, and **Windows CGI** provides this interface between business applications and Windows RAD tool technologies. Windows CGI was invented by Robert Denny, a former CEO turned software developer, who invented a 16-bit shareware product, Winhttpd. Denny has also partnered with Deerfield to offer WebSite Web server and utilities.

With Windows CGI (WCGI) the data that are passed between the Web server and the CGI application are passed using temporary files. Input is sent to the CGI application via a CGI initialization file (**CGI.INI file**) and a content file. The CGI.INI file name is sent over the applications command line and contains information about the Web server environment, the Web client, and the CGI request. Upon request, the Web server places the data to be passed to the **primary input file**, termed the **CGI profile file**. To get input from the .INI file, the Win32 API function GetPrivateProfileString is used. This file contains the name and path of the file where the Web server will look for the Windows CGI application to write its result. The file in which the result is written is called the **CGI output file**. After the CGI program has been executed, the Web server will wait for the CGI program to terminate. The Web server may even process other Web client requests while waiting. Upon execution of the CGI application, three files with the same name, but with different extensions, are created and assigned names in incremental value. Both the .INI input file and the .OUT output file are created during the interaction between the Web server and the CGI application. The .INP file is the **content file**. It holds the data that are passed by the Web server that appears after the question mark symbol in the URL through the **Query_String CGI variable**. A separate file is created by the Web server for any data enclosed in the body of the HTTP request. In both cases, the Web server delivers the URL-encoded string without making any modifications. In Windows CGI, these data are decoded by the Web server if passed as a URL-encoded string using the POST method. It then passes the decoded data back to the CGI application in addition to providing the raw data. Before terminating, the CGI program writes a response to the CGI output file, the location of which is listed in the profile file. Upon receiving the termination signal, the Web server will read the CGI output file, determine whether the output data need any packaging, and send the final data back to the Web client. At this point, all temporary files created during the process are usually deleted.

Kanthaka Farms is a continuing case study in this book that illustrates the process of building electronic commerce with Web database constructions. In Chapter 7, you will use server-side technologies as you continue to build your Kanthaka site. As you continue through the text, you will complete different facets of electronic commerce Web database construction, resulting in a complete Web site for Kanthaka Farms.

Kanthaka Farms
Locating CGI Temporary
.INI, .OUT, and .INP Files

1. Launch your Web server software. Verify that the server icon is running and in the tray.

2. Open the Admin utility, by double-clicking on WebSite's icon in the tray. Your WebSite server properties window should appear.

3. Click on the Logging tab. From the Tracing Options, check the API/CGI Execution option. Your settings should look like Figure 7-2.

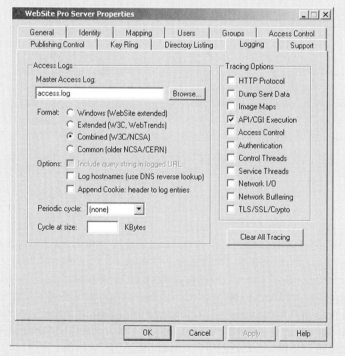

Figure 7-2

Changing the Tracing Options of the Web Server

4. When prompted, click Yes for the server to be updated for your tracing option change.

5. From your Web client, go to the following URL:

`http://localhost/cgi-win/book/job/joblist.exe`

The Web server will execute the Joblist.exe CGI program.

6. In Windows Explorer, view the temporary files created during the Windows CGI operation. Open C:\WebSite\cgi-temp. Compare your files to those in Figure 7-3.

7. In Notepad, open the most recent input file created in the cgi-temp folder. You will notice it has the .INI extension. Examine the contents. Notice how the data appears in the key=value pairing with each pairing listed on a separate line. The contents of your file should be similar to those shown in Figure 7-4.

Figure 7-3

Displaying the Contents of the CGI-Temp Folder

Figure 7-4

Examining the Contents of a CGI Input File

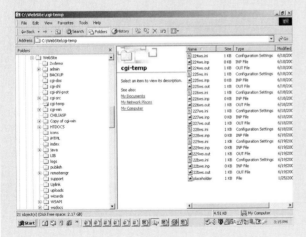

Standard CGI The main difference between **Standard CGI** and Windows CGI is in how the input and output files are sent between the Web server and the CGI application. With Standard CGI, the input data are sent with environment labels and the standard input rather than temporary input/output files. To get input from environment labels, either the Win32 API function GetEnvironmentVariable or the ANSI C function *getenv* is used. The CGI output is sent to standard output, usually writing to the "ostream" (output stream) cout, which is automatically made by including the iostream.h header file. Though converted to be used with Windows-based servers, Standard CGI (stdCGI) is generally used only on UNIX servers.

Fast CGI A server-side, language-independent program, **FastCGI** manages multiple CGI requests within a single process, saving many program instructions for each request. FastCGI, just as its name implies, speeds up CGI interface processing. It is credited with handling customer requests three to thirty times faster than Windows CGI. FastCGI is a Web server plug-in that requires only small changes to existing server applications to reap the performance benefits. Without FastCGI, each Web client request initiates the opening of a new process on the Web server. Each process gets control, performs the service, and is then closed. Unlike Windows or Standard CGI, with FastCGI a process shares the overhead with other processes of the Web server, isolating it and thus providing more security. FastCGI was developed and is copyrighted by Open Market, Inc. It can be obtained from Open Market, without cost, and as an open standard for use across platforms and on any Web server.

Evaluation of the CGI Model

CGI and **Server-Side Includes** (SSIs) are often interchangeable. The following guidelines will help you better understand which to use:

- CGI is a common standard supported by all major httpds. On the other hand, SSIs are not a common standard, but an innovation of NCSA's httpd. CGI has the greatest portability, if this is an issue in your electronic commerce construction.
- SSIs do not evoke executable files. They represent a variable value that a server can include in an HTML file before it sends it to the Web client.
- HTML forms are more complex applications and usually require an executable program, often making CGI the best choice.
- SSIs are not usable when the transaction returns a response that is not an HTML page.

CGI is an older technology, and there are limitations to its use. For instance, the cgi-bin interface dictates that the **HTML form handler** start and terminate each interaction. Therefore, in the model, the form handlers do not have state, though state can in fact be passed through the form interface using information in hidden fields. For large applications, this starting and stopping can be very inefficient. Although Web servers can send and receive data, the server itself has limited functionality. The most basic Web server can only send the requested file to the requesting Web browser. The Web server typically will not know what to do with any additional input. Unless the Web provider tells the server how to handle that additional information, it is most likely to be ignored. Many of the limitations of CGI are limitations of HTML or HTTP, and as the standards for the Web in general evolve, so does the capability of CGI.

Probably the best-known variation on SSIs is **PHP**. PHP embeds server-side scripting in a pre-HTML page and ASP, which is Microsoft's version of a similar interface. **ASP**s are also an alternative to CGI. With ASPs, like PHP, a script is embedded in a Web page and executed at the server before the page is sent. Whether to use CGI or ASP in the electronic commerce construction is usually a matter of the developer's preference. ASP, however, is proprietary, whereas CGI is not and CGI is both versatile and portable. A CGI application can be written using almost any programming language on any platform. Some of the alternatives, such as server APIs, restrict you to certain languages and are much more difficult to learn. However, server APIs tend to be more efficient than CGI programs. Many servers now include a programming API that makes it easier to program direct extensions to the Web server as opposed to separate CGI applications. Other servers include built-in functionality that can handle special features without CGI, such as database interfacing. Finally, some applications can be handled by new client-side, rather than server-side, technologies.

 ### *Web Break*

It was not too long ago that the Web database construction was the latest technological innovation. Another new technology, set to come out commercially in bulk around 2002, is Bluetooth. It promises to significantly change the way we use machines. For more information about this cable-replacement technology visit http://www.bluetooth.com.

WebSite Web server supports both standard CGI and the Windows variant of CGI, which is well suited to the Windows environment. In addition, the Web server comes with a framework module for Visual Basic that allows the rapid development of sophisticated CGI programs. Because Visual Basic can access a wide variety of information sources, such as Access and SQL server databases, the WebSite-CGI development environment flexibility is almost unlimited.

7.3 Understanding Input and the CGI Environmental Variables

One of the methods that the Web server uses to pass information to a CGI application is through **environmental variables**, named parameters that pass the information from the server to the CGI application. These environmental variables are not necessarily variables in the operating system's environment, although that is the most common implementation. Environmental variables are read-only variables and are set automatically when the CGI script is called. They can be accessed like any other environmental variable and contain the important information needed to correctly pass data between Web client and Web server. For example, these variables store the Web browser type that is being used to process the Web client's request as well as the relevant IP addresses.

Environment variable names are case-insensitive. There cannot be two different variables whose names differ in case only. In Table 7-1 the environmental variables show the canonical representation of capitals plus underscore ("_"). However, the actual representation of the names is system defined. Depending on the system in use, the representation may be defined differently than that in Table 7-1. A missing environmental variable is equivalent to a zero-length, null value.

The CGI Test Program

Many resources are available to developers using WebSite server software because it provides electronic commerce developers with solid technology and open standards. A wealth of documentation, examples, sample code, reference material, and diagnostic tools is easily accessed from the Start menu. One such resource is the

Table 7-1	*The CGI Environmental Variables*
CGI version	The version of CGI spoken by the server
Request protocol	The server's info protocol (e.g. HTTP/1.0)
Request method	The method specified in the request (e.g., "GET")
Request keep-alive	If the client requested connection re-use (Yes/No)
Executable path	Physical pathname of the back-end (this program)
Logical path	Extra path info in logical space
Physical path	Extra path info in local physical space
Query string	String following the "?" in the request URL
Content type	MIME content type of info supplied with request
Content length	Length (bytes) of info supplied with request
Request range	Byte-range specification received with request
Server software	Version/revision of the info (HTTP) server
Server name	Server's network hostname (or alias from config)
Server port	Server's network port number
Server admin	E-mail address of server's admin. (config)
Referrer	URL of referring document
From	E-mail of client user (rarely seen)
User agent	String describing client/browser software/version
Remote host	Remote client's network hostname
Remote address	Remote client's network address
Authenticated username	Username if present in request
Authenticated password	Password if present in request
Authentication method	Method used for authentication (e.g., "Basic")
Authentication realm	Name of realm for users/groups

Windows CGI test program usage. The CGI test program is a Visual Basic 6.0 32-bit application that returns dynamically generated documents that report on various aspects of the CGI interface. It also serves as an example of using the Visual Basic CGI interface that is included with WebSite. This resource allows exploration of CGI environmental variables as well as system variables and headers. More information on the CGI test program usage may be obtained from the Deerfield WebSite Web site.

In this exercise, you will investigate the CGI variables from WebSite Resources and CGI test examples.

Kanthaka Farms
Investigating CGI Variables

1. Verify that your Web server software is launched. The server icon should be visible in the tray.

2. From the Start menu, choose Programs, WebSite, WebSite Resources. Your window will look similar to the one shown in Figure 7-5.

3. In the right-hand frame of the WebSite Resources window, click on the URL http://localhost/~wsdocs/32demo/ to open in a browser window. You may also type the URL directly into a browser to open the file. If prompted, supply the Admin username and password you provided during installation. Your browser window should look similar to Figure 7-6.

4. Scroll down and click on the link that reads, "WebSite's Two CGI Interfaces." The corresponding URL is http://localhost/~wsdocs/32demo/st-int.html.

5. Click on the sample test program link (http://localhost/~wsdocs/cgi-win-samples/cgitest32.exe). The test program produces various reports from the Web server about the CGI environment. The reports are in HTML format. Note that the sources of this test program, as well as those of all of the other WebSite resource samples, are in the C:/WebSite/cgi-src folder with a usage page in the server document root. The usage page is returned if no test selector is specified as

Figure 7-5
The WebSite Resources Window

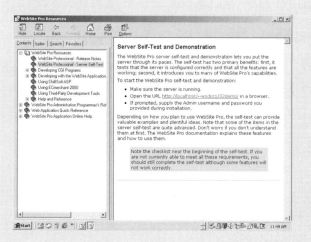

Figure 7-6
WebSite's Server Self-Test and Demonstration

extra path information. The direct URL to the usage page is http://localhost/~wsdocs/cgi-win-samples/cgitest32.exe.

This CGI test program is a Visual Basic 6.0 32-bit application that returns dynamically generated documents to the Web client. These documents report on various aspects of CGI server-side scripting and serve as an example of using the Visual Basic CGI interface that is included with WebSite.

6. To generate a particular report, it is necessary to add extra path information to the URL. The test program will then interpret the added information as a selector for the report and return the selected report to the Web client. Valid selectors are the following:

- **CGI:** Reports the values of the environmental and system variables as passed by the Web server to the CGI program.
- **Headers:** Reports the MIME Accept:types and any extra headers that were received from the Web browser.
- **Form:** Reports the keywords and fully decoded contents of each of the form's fields.
- **Transparent:** Returns a short document directly from the Visual Basic program to the Web browser without interpretation by the Web server. This is an illustration of the server's "transparent return" feature.
- **Empty—no extra path:** Causes the document to be returned by sending a one-line response from the test program to the server that consists of Location:/cgitest32.html.

Click on the first example link (/~wsdocs/cgi-win-samples/cgitest32.exe/CGI) to generate a report. Your browser should display a document similar to the one pictured in Figure 7-7.

This test simply accesses Visual Basic's associative environmental array to display the values of the environmental variables. Possibly the most useful of these environmental variables is the QUERY_STRING variable. In the test, this was the empty string; however, it can be appended. This is accomplished by adding a ? onto the end of the URL. The string after the ? is then added into the environmental variable QUERY_STRING.

7. Open the second test URL (/~wsdocs/cgi-win-samples/cgitest32.exe/CGI?Query+Info+Here). This test has the string Query+Info+Here appended to the QUERY_STRING environmental variable as seen in Figure 7-8.

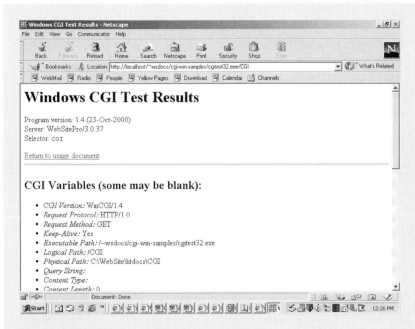

Figure 7-7

Windows CGI Test Results

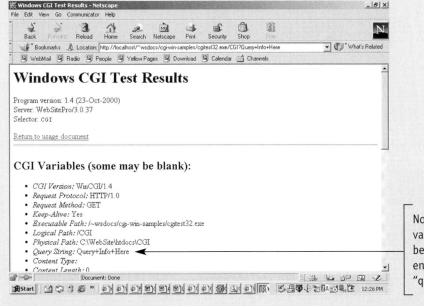

Notice the environmental variable "Query_String" has been appended with the text entered in the URL after the "question mark" symbol

Figure 7-8

Appending the Query_String Environmental Variable

8. Remember that adding "headers" to your URL will produce a report of the MIME Accept:types and any "extra" headers that were received from your browser. Click on the header's test to view this report.

9. The last test creates a short document to be returned directly from the Visual Basic program to your browser, without interpretation by the Web server. Add the word "transparent" to the URL, and view an illustration of the server's "transparent return" feature.

7.4 Understanding CGI Output: Returning and Redirecting

Data are passed back and forth from the Web server and Web client using input and output files, with a goal of minimizing programming efforts and keeping the interface simple. The CGI program returns its results to the Web server as a data stream representing the goal of the request, either directly or indirectly. The Web server is then responsible for packaging the data according to HTTP, which is also used to transport the data to the requesting Web client. Generally, the Web server will add the needed HTTP headers to the CGI script's results.

The data consist of two parts: the **header** and the **body**. The header is separated from the body by a blank line and is made up of one or more lines of text. The MIME-conforming data whose content type must be reflected in the header are contained in the body. The Web server does not interpret or modify the body in any way. The Web client must receive the exact data that were generated by the back-end in the electronic commerce model.

Special Header Lines

The Web server recognizes the following header lines in the results data stream:

- *Content-type:* Indicates that the body contains data of the specified MIME content type. The value must be a MIME content type/subtype.

The Web Database Construction Aids Businesses in the Race for Web Customers

Businesses are eager to increase their market share. But that's an age-old story. What *is* new is that online users are growing by astounding rates. According to *CIO Magazine*, the online population in the United States alone is estimated to nearly double between 2000 and 2005, adding 85 million new online users. Businesses are vying for their share of this market and want to win online customer loyalty before their competitors.

According to *CIO Magazine*, the demographic breakdowns show the heaviest online use for the ages between 35 and 55 and over 55. The first group is categorized as "in their peak earning and spending years" and represents the largest group of new users. The over-55 crowd is also very attractive to businesses for their spending potential.

CIO Magazine shared some other large numbers: By the year 2005, $8.5 trillion worth of transactions using the B2B model and Internet commerce will occur, and. 995 million units of Bluetooth-enabled equipment shipments are projected for the same year.

Bluetooth is the cable-replacement technology that promises to significantly change the way we use our computers.

Businesses will spend $2.8 billion on streaming video technology in 2005 to enhance the electronic commerce model. It is estimated that the $80 billion U.S. businesses spent in 2000 on technology products, services, and personnel specifically for Internet activities to support electronic commerce will reach almost $200 billion by 2004.

Plug-in technologies will continue to be popular in Web database construction. Tool sets that tie both front-end and back-end will also be commonplace. Macromedia Inc. (and their newly acquired Allaire Corporation) and Microsoft are just two of the businesses positioned to support the Web site design and the back-end application development tool market. Integrating products of the future will give developers more control and power over the back-end, writes Lee Copeland Gladwin of *Computer-World*.

What are some specific strategies businesses are employing to be ready to reach the large online markets?

How will new technologies help them reach their goal?

Will there be a place for server-side technologies in the electronic commerce model of the future?

Justify your answers.

Sources: Lee Copeland Gladwin, "Customers optimistic after Macromedia/Allaire merger," *ComputerWorld*, January 22, 2001; Anonymous, "Department of big, scary numbers," *CIO Magazine*, June 15, 2001; Molly Upton, "Race for first impressions," *CIO Magazine*, June 15, 2001.

- *URL:* <VALUE> The value is enclosed in angle brackets like HTML. The value is either a full URL or a local file reference. It points to an object to be returned to the Web client in lieu of the body. If the value is a local file, then the Web server sends it as the results of the request, as though the Web client issued a GET method for that object. If the value is a full URL, then the Web server returns a "401redirect" to the Web client to retrieve the specified object directly.
- *Location:* This is treated the same as URL, but this form is now deprecated. The value will not be enclosed in angle brackets with this form.
- *Other headers:* Any other headers in the result stream are passed unmodified by the Web server to the Web client. The CGI program must avoid including headers that clash with those used by HTTP.

There are several advantages to using redirection as a CGI response. If the data to be returned to the Web client do not have to be created ad hoc, then a redirection-type CGI response is beneficial. If data are being sent that have been created by another program or a utility, redirect-type should be used. By redirecting rather than generating the output, the CGI application can be more efficient in its duties in the electronic commerce model.

7.5 Creating a CGI Application Using Visual Basic

Earlier it was discussed that the input file is in the .INI file format. Retrieving the information from this file can be quite complicated. Without the very powerful API calls of Windows, the process would probably also be unacceptably slow. These **API calls** allow data to be read from the .INI files quickly and easily. The GetPrivateProfileString API call is used for this purpose.

Distributed with the WebSite server is a Visual Basic module that easily handles all file input and output using these API calls. Bob Denny, inventor of Windows CGI, created this module, which is located in the LIB folder on the textbook Web site as Cgi32.bas. It can also be obtained from the Internet at the Deerfield WebSite Web site. You will call this module from the Visual Basic projects created in the electronic commerce model and use the procedures stored in it.

Common **Windows CGI libraries** are also available from the Internet for other programming environments, such as Borland Delphi and Microsoft Visual C++. A framework for MSVC++ is distributed with the WebSite Web server software and can be found in the \cgi-src\cppsample folder upon installation of the WebSite server.

The Windows CGI application is based on a Windows executable file. This file is designed to run primarily in a noninteractive mode. The first CGI application you will create for Kanthaka Farms will allow the business to request a customer's e-mail address and return an ad hoc form, showing that the customer's address has been successfully added to the Kanthaka database. The control structure of your Windows CGI Kanthaka e-mail project is shown in Figure 7-9. The sequence for creating the CGI application will be the following:

■ Create the HTML form for the front-end of the electronic commerce model, which will allow customer input.
■ Using Visual Basic, write code to return the ad hoc form showing that the customer's data have been successfully submitted to the back-end of the model.
■ Create the Windows executable file for the CGI program by compiling the Visual Basic project.
■ Test the electronic commerce model.

Figure 7-9

Control Structure of the WCGI E-mail Project

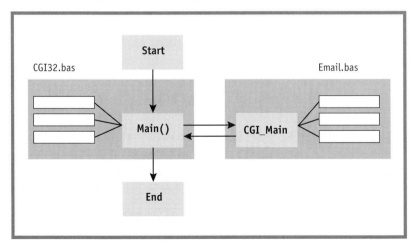

Kanthaka Farms
Creating a CGI Program

In this exercise, you will create a CGI application for Kanthaka Farms that will allow the customer to submit an e-mail address to the business.

1. Verify that your Web server software is launched. The server icon should be visible in the tray.

2. From the Start menu, launch Visual Basic by choosing Programs, Microsoft Visual Basic 6.0, Microsoft Visual Basic 6.0.

3. Create a new folder on your hard drive called C:\WebSite\cgi-win\book\Email.

4. Open the Template.vbp Visual Basic project located in the C:\WebSite\cgi-win\book\Template folder by double-clicking on it in Windows Explorer. From the File menu, choose Save Project As. Rename your project Email.vbp. Also from the File menu, choose Save Template.bas. Rename your .bas file Email.bas. Now compile the project, naming the executable file Email.exe. All of these files should now be stored in the new C:\WebSite\cgi-win\book\Email folder.

5. Add Visual Basic code to the CGI_Main procedure of the Email.bas module to generate the e-mail message. Type the following code under the Sub CGI_Main():

```
Send ("Content-type: text/html")
Send ("")
Send ("<HTML>")
Send ("<HEAD>")
Send ("<TITLE>Kanthaka Farms Email Request</TITLE>")
Send ("</HEAD>")
Send ("<BODY>")
Send ("<H1>Kanthaka Farms Email Request</H1>")
Send ("</BODY>")
Send ("</HTML>")
```

6. From the File menu, choose Save Email.bas to save the Email.bas module.

7. Compile your CGI program. From the File menu, choose Make Email.exe.

8. Test the CGI program. Specify the following URL from your Web client:

```
http://localhost/cgi-win/book/email/email.exe
```

The Web browser should display the message from Kanthaka Farms as shown in Figure 7-10.

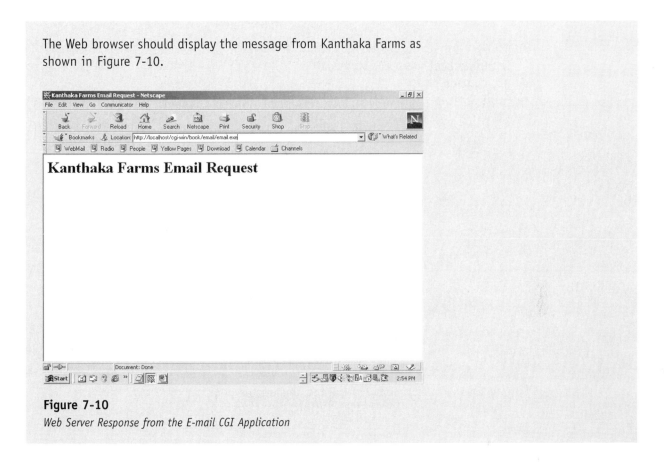

Figure 7-10
Web Server Response from the E-mail CGI Application

Examining the Guestbook CGI Application

The **CGI_Main procedure** code writes the HTML text for the Kanthaka Farms e-mail message to the CGI output file using the Send procedure provided in the Cgi32.bas module. For all Windows CGI applications that utilize the **Cgi32.bas library module**, the program's entry point must be set to the Sub Main procedure. Never add a form to a CGI application. The CGI application relies on input and output files and never needs to open a window during execution; a form will slow down execution of the CGI application.

Kanthaka Farms
Changing the
CGI Application's
Entry Point Setting

In this exercise, you will assign your Sub Main as an entry point for your CGI program.

1. Verify that the Email.vbp project is running.

2. From the Project menu, choose properties. Your project may be named Project1 at this point. When the Project Properties window opens, it should look similar to Figure 7-11.

3. With the General tab selected, select the Startup Object as Sub Main, if necessary. This will set the program's entry point to the CGI_Main procedure. This also implies that the CGI program will automatically terminate when the control reaches the end of the procedure.

4. Your project should be named Email. If necessary, type Email in the Project Name text box. Click OK.

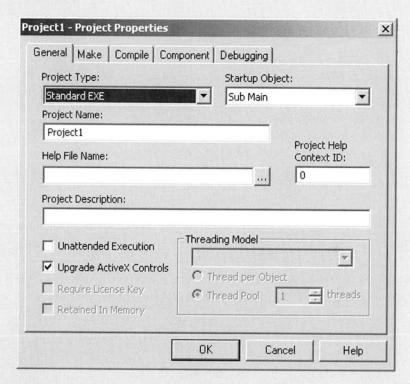

Figure 7-11
The Project Properties Window

Examining the CGI32.bas Library Module

The Cgi32.bas module supplied with this book's Web site is version 1.8. It contains common procedures needed to establish a Visual Basic environment for your Windows CGI programs that run behind the WebSite Web server. The Cgi32.bas module will be used in all of your Windows CGI applications. In principle, you never need to edit this file.

The CGI version 1.1 specifies a minimal set of data that is made available to the back-end application by an HTTP Web server. It also specifies the details for passing this information to the back-end. The latter part of the CGI specification is specific to Unix-like environments. The NCSA httpd for Windows supplies the data items specified by CGI 1.1; however, it uses a different method for passing the data to the back-end. Because the WebSite Web server requires any Windows back-end program to be an executable image, the Visual Basic applications used for CGI must be compiled into executable programs before they can be tested with the Web server. The WebSite Web server executes the CGI script requests by doing a CreateProcess with a command line in the following form:

```
prog-name cgi-profile
```

The **Main() procedure** for the CGI application is in the Cgi32.bas module. It handles all of the setup of the Visual Basic CGI environment. The Main() procedure calls the Sub_Main procedure. Because of the coding of the Cgi32.bas, the Sub_Main must be called CGI_Main(). If the CGI program is started without command-line arguments, the code assumes that it must run interactively. This is useful for providing a setup screen for the business in the electronic commerce model. Instead of calling CGI_Main(), it calls Inter_Main(). The CGI module must also implement this function. If an interactive mode is not needed, an **Inter_Main() procedure** can be created with a one-line call to MsgBox alerting the user that the program is not meant to be run interactively. However, this procedure can be modified to perform other tasks as needed in interactive mode. If a Visual Basic runtime error occurs, it will be trapped and result in an HTTP error response being sent to the client. Upon program finish, be sure to code RETURN TO MAIN() to point back to the Cgi32.bas module.

The Main() procedure in the Cgi32.bas module is the entry point for the Visual Basic middleware. The **error handling** is very carefully set up. If any errors occur during the execution of the CGI application and no other error-trapping routine is set to preempt the error, the control goes to the line labeled "ErrorHandler." This ensures that the CGI program will always terminate properly.

The Cgi32.bas also contains **global variables** and **global arrays**. These hold the data listed in various sections of the CGI profile file, and, since they are declared global, they are accessible from every procedure of your CGI application. The global arrays used in the Cgi32.bas are one-dimensional. Their purpose is to hold the data parsed in the Accept, Extra Headers, and other form-related sections of the CGI profile file.

Kanthaka Farms
*Modifying the CGI_Main
Procedure in the Email.vbp to
Display Global Variables
and Arrays*

In this exercise, you will modify the CGI_Main procedure in the Email.vbp project to output the values of a selection of the global variables and arrays made available by the Cgi32.bas library module.

1. Verify that the Email.vbp project is running.

2. In the CGI_Main procedure of the Email.bas module, modify the CGI_Main procedure to appear as follows:

```
Sub CGI_Main()
  Send ("Content-type: text/html")
  Send ("")
  Send ("<HTML>")
  Send ("<HEAD>")
  Send ("<TITLE>Kanthaka Farms Email Request</TITLE>")
  Send ("</HEAD>")
  Send ("<BODY>")
  Send ("<H1>Kanthaka Farms Email Request</H1>")
  Send ("<B>Selection of CGI32.bas Global Variables</B>")
  Send ("<PRE>")
  Send ("<BR>CGI_ServerSoftware : " & CGI_ServerSoftware)
  Send ("<BR>CGI_RequestMethod : " & CGI_RequestMethod)
  Send ("<BR>CGI_AcceptTypes(1).key : " &
  CGI_AcceptTypes(1).key)
  Send ("<BR>CGI_AcceptTypes(1).value : " &
  CGI_AcceptTypes(1).value)
  Send ("</PRE>")
  Send ("</BODY>")
  Send ("</HTML>")
End Sub
```

3. From the File menu, choose Save Email.bas to save the Email.bas module.

4. Compile your CGI program. From the File menu, choose Make Email.exe.

5. Test the CGI program. Specify the following URL from your Web client:

```
http://localhost/cgi-win/book/email/email.exe
```

The Web browser should display the message from Kanthaka Farms as shown in Figure 7-12.

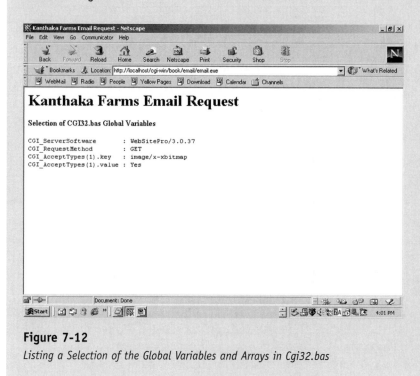

Figure 7-12
Listing a Selection of the Global Variables and Arrays in Cgi32.bas

Adding Customer Interactivity to the Electronic Commerce Model

Creating the Front-End with HTML Forms It is the interactivity of the electronic commerce model that demonstrates the true capability of the CGI application. To add this functionality to your CGI project, you will first determine what method the customer will request when the CGI script is launched. The **request method** can be accessed using the **CGI_RequestMethod variable**. This method, as discussed earlier, is either **GET** or **POST**. You need to decide what to do on receipt of each of these requests. The GET method is used when the CGI script is accessed for the first time. In this case, the customer will be sent a form to request that they type in an e-mail address along with other pertinent information. The guestbook HTML form created earlier in the book will be used as the front-end of the electronic commerce model since it captures customer information, including e-mail addresses.

Kanthaka Farms
Adding Customer Interaction
to the CGI Application—
Creating the Front-End

In this exercise, you will use the previously created guestbook HTML form as the front-end of Kanthaka Farms' electronic commerce Web database construction. The guestbook front-end data will be stored in the Guestbk.mdb. A CGI request for a specific guestbook will list the path of the guestbook directly in the extra logical path portion of the URL as follows:

```
http://localhost/CGI_Request_Path/DirectoryPath
```

To add an entry to a guestbook, a POST request will be made to a Windows CGI program named GBADD.exe as follows:

```
http://localhost/cgi-win/book/gbx/gbadd.exe/DirectoryName
```

To list the entries from a guestbook, a request will be made to a Windows CGI program named GBLIST.exe and it will contain a hidden field listed in the guestbook entry return form to return a customized response. The URL will be as follows:

```
http://localhost/cgi-win/book/gbx/gblist.exe/DirectoryPath
```

Note that two Windows CGI applications will be used for the front-end of the Web database construction: gblist.exe and gbadd.exe, using an extra logical path to specify the folder holding the guestbook. To meet the needs of the Kanthaka Farms Web database construction, you will need two guestbook front-end HTML forms with the necessary input fields for submitting an entry. Each form will update the back-end database. The construction will also need two guestbook listing forms. This will contain the start date input fields and will allow the listing of the entries from the guestbooks to be entered after a customer-specified date. Finally, a main menu screen will be needed that provides links to the preceding forms.

1. Verify that your Web server software is running and the WebSite icon is visible in the tray.

2. In Windows Explorer, create the following folders to hold your new electronic commerce model:

```
C:\WebSite\HTDOCS\BOOK\GUEST1
C:\WebSite\HTDOCS\BOOK\GUEST2
C:\WebSite\cgi-win\BOOK\GUESTX
```

3. Copy the Kan_Logo.gif from the C:\LIB folder to both the GUEST1 and GUEST2 folders.

4. Using the FirstPage 2000 HTML editor found on this book's Web site, or any text editor, create a new text file. Name the file GBADD1_K.htm in the C:\WebSite\HTDOCS\BOOK\GUEST1 folder. It should contain the following HTML code:

```
<HTML>
<HEAD>
<TITLE>Guestbook</TITLE>
</HEAD>
<BODY BACKGROUND="bk.jpg">
<H1 ALIGN=CENTER>Kanthaka Farms</H1><P>
<P align="center"><IMG SRC="KAN_LOGO.gif" width="121"
   height="97"></P>
<H3 ALIGN=CENTER>Please Sign Our Guestbook</H3><P>
<PRE>
<FORM METHOD=POST ACTION="/cgi-
   win/book/GUESTX/guest.exe/book/guest1>
<STRONG>Name: </STRONG><INPUT NAME="Name" TYPE="TEXT"
   MAXLENGTH=50 SIZE=30>
<STRONG>Email: </STRONG><INPUT NAME="Email" TYPE="TEXT"
   MAXLENGTH=50 SIZE=30>
<STRONG>Date Of Birth (XX/XX/XX): </STRONG><INPUT
   NAME="BirthDate" TYPE="TEXT" MAXLENGTH=8 SIZE=8>
<STRONG>Phone Number: </STRONG><INPUT NAME="PhoneNumber"
   TYPE="TEXT" MAXLENGTH=50 SIZE=30>
<STRONG>Comments: </STRONG><EM>(Click ENTER when
   finished)</EM>
<TEXTAREA NAME="Remarks" ROWS=8 COLS=45></TEXTAREA>
<BR><BR>
<INPUT NAME="Response" TYPE="HIDDEN" VALUE="Entry added to
   GUEST1">
<INPUT NAME="Submit" TYPE="SUBMIT" VALUE="Enter"> <INPUT
   NAME="Reset" TYPE="RESET" VALUE="Clear">
</FORM>
</PRE>
</BODY>
</HTML>
```

5. Again, using the FirstPage 2000 HTML editor or any text editor, create another new text file. Name this file GBADD2_K.htm in the

C:\WebSite\HTDOCS\BOOK\GUEST2 folder. It should contain the following HTML code:

```
<HTML>
<HEAD>
<TITLE>Guestbook</TITLE>
</HEAD>
<BODY BACKGROUND="bk.jpg">
<H1 ALIGN=CENTER>Kanthaka Farms</H1><P>
<P align="center"><IMG SRC="KAN_LOGO.gif" width="121"
   height="97"></P>
<H3 ALIGN=CENTER>Please Sign Our Guestbook</H3><P>
<PRE>
<FORM METHOD=POST ACTION=/cgi-win/book/guestx/guest.exe/
   book/guest2>
<STRONG>Name: </STRONG><INPUT NAME="Name" TYPE="TEXT"
   MAXLENGTH=50 SIZE=30>
<STRONG>Email: </STRONG><INPUT NAME="Email" TYPE="TEXT"
   MAXLENGTH=50 SIZE=30>
<STRONG>Comments: </STRONG><EM>(Click ENTER when
   finished)</EM>
<TEXTAREA NAME="Remarks" ROWS=8 COLS=45></TEXTAREA>
<BR><BR>
<INPUT NAME="Response" TYPE="HIDDEN" VALUE="Entry added to
   GUEST2">
<INPUT NAME="Submit" TYPE="SUBMIT" VALUE="Enter"> <INPUT
   NAME="Reset" TYPE="RESET" VALUE="Clear">
</FORM>
</PRE>
</BODY>
</HTML>
```

Figure 7-13
Viewing GUEST1\GBADD1_K.htm in the Web Browser

Figure 7-14
Viewing GUEST2\GBADD2_K.htm in the Web Browser

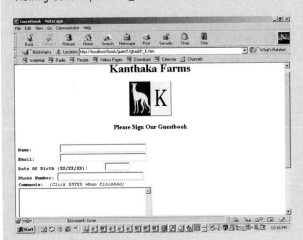

There is a hidden field in each of these HTML forms named Response that will be used to hold the custom response of the back-end.

6. Test each HTML form in the Web browser by specifying the following URLs :

```
http://localhost/book/guest1/gbadd1_k.htm
http://localhost/book/guest2/gbadd2_k.htm
```

The Web browser should display the message from Kanthaka Farms as shown in Figures 7-13 and 7-14.

Continuing the Front-End by Creating the HTML Main Menu and Listing Forms Separate forms will be required in the Kanthaka Farms electronic commerce Web database construction to list the entries of each guestbook. Each HTML form will contain an input control for a starting date field. As with the Job Listing Service model, this will allow the customer to list entries in the back-end database by specifying a date in the front-end of the construction. The main difference between these two forms will be the **ACTION attributes**, each of which will identify what should happen to the data when the HTML form is submitted from the Web client to the Web server.

In this exercise, you will create the main menu and listing HTML forms for the Kanthaka Farms Web database construction.

Kanthaka Farms
Creating the Main Menu and Listing HTML Forms

1. Verify that your Web server software is running and that the icon appears in the tray.

2. Using the FirstPage 2000 HTML editor or any text editor, create a new HTML file named GBLIST1_K.htm in the C:\WebSite\HTDOCS\ BOOK\GUEST1 folder. It should contain the following HTML code:

```
<HTML>
<HEAD>
<TITLE>Guestbook</TITLE>
</HEAD>
<BODY BACKGROUND="bk.jpg">
<H1 ALIGN=CENTER>Kanthaka Farms</H1><P>
<P align="center"><IMG SRC="KAN_LOGO.gif" width="121"
    height="97">
<H3 ALIGN=CENTER>Our Guestbook Listings:</H3><P>
```

```
<FORM METHOD=POST ACTION=/cgi-win/book/guestx/guestlist.exe/
   book/guest1>
<STRONG><BR><B>Enter Starting Date (XX/XX/XX): </STRONG></B>
<INPUT NAME="StartingDate" TYPE="TEXT" MAXLENGTH=8 SIZE=8>
<BR>
<INPUT NAME="Submit" TYPE="SUBMIT" VALUE="View">
<INPUT NAME="Reset" TYPE="RESET">
</FORM>
</BODY>
</HTML>
```

3. Using the FirstPage 2000 HTML editor or any text editor, create a new HTML file named GBLIST2_K.htm in the C:\WebSite\HTDOCS\BOOK\GUEST2 folder. It should contain the following HTML code:

```
<HTML>
<HEAD>
<TITLE>Guestbook</TITLE>
</HEAD>
<BODY BACKGROUND="bk.jpg">
<H1 ALIGN=CENTER>Kanthaka Farms</H1><P>
<P align="center"><IMG SRC="KAN_LOGO.gif" width="121"
   height="97"></P>
<H3 ALIGN=CENTER>Our Guestbook Listings:</H3><P>
<FORM METHOD=POST ACTION=/cgi-win/book/guestx/guestlist.exe/
   book/guest2>
<B>Enter Starting Date (XX/XX/XX): </B>
<BR><INPUT NAME="StartingDate" TYPE="TEXT" MAXLENGTH=8
   SIZE=8>
<BR>
<INPUT NAME="Submit" TYPE="SUBMIT" VALUE="View">
<INPUT NAME="Reset" TYPE="RESET">
</FORM>
</BODY>
</HTML>
```

4. Using the FirstPage 2000 HTML editor or any text editor, create a new HTML file named GUESTMM.htm in the C:\WebSite\HTDOCS\BOOK\GUEST1 folder. It should contain the following HTML code:

```
<HTML>
<HEAD>
<TITLE>Guestbook Main Menu</TITLE>
</HEAD>
<BODY BACKGROUND="bk.jpg">
<H1 ALIGN=CENTER>Kanthaka Farms</H1><P>
<P align="center"><IMG SRC="KAN_LOGO.gif" width="121"
   height="97"></P>
```

```
<H3 ALIGN=CENTER>Our Guestbook Main Menu:</H3><P>
<H2>
<UL>
<LI><A HREF="/book/guest1/gbadd1_K.htm">
Add an entry to the first guestbook</A>
<LI><A HREF="/book/guest2/gbadd2_K.htm">
Add an entry to the second guestbook</A>
<LI><A HREF="/book/guest1/gblist1_K.htm">
Display entries from the first guest book</A>
<LI><A HREF="/book/guest2/gblist2_K.htm">
Display entries from the second guestbook</A>
</UL>
</H2>
</BODY>
</HTML>
```

5. Test each HTML form in the Web browser by specifying the following URLs :

```
http://localhost/book/guest1/gblist1_k.htm
http://localhost/book/guest2/gblist2_k.htm
http://localhost/book/guest1/guestmm.htm
```

Your display in the Web browser should look similar to Figures 7-15 and 7-16.

Figure 7-15

Viewing GBLIST1_K.htm in the Web Browser

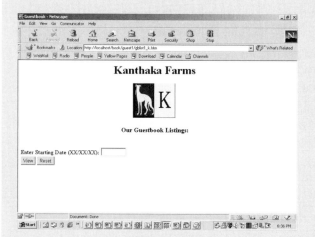

Figure 7-16

Viewing GUESTMM.htm in the Web Browser

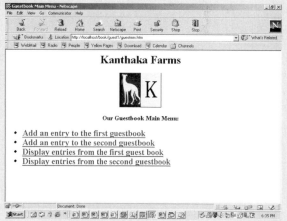

Creating the Middleware CGI Application in Visual Basic The first step in coding the middleware CGI application is to create two new folders in your cgi-win folder located on C:\WebSite. Name the folders GUEST and GUESTX. The middleware of the Web database construction will be responsible for passing information from the Web client to the Web server and back again.

Kanthaka Farms
Creating the CGI Guest Application in Visual Basic

In this exercise, you will create the CGI application in Visual Basic. This program's executable file will act as the middleware of Kanthaka Farms Web database construction.

1. Verify that your Web server software is running and that the icon appears in the tray.

2. Verify that the GUEST and GUESTX folders were added to the C:\WebSite\cgi-win\book folder. If not, add them now.

3. In Windows Explorer, locate the Cgi32.bas module in the C:\WebSite\Lib folder and copy to the C:\WebSite\cgi-win\book\guest folder.

4. Also using Windows Explorer, copy the Template.bas and Template.vbp files to the GUEST folder and rename the Template.vbp as Guest.vbp.

5. Launch Visual Basic from your Start menu. Choose Programs, Microsoft Visual Basic, Microsoft Visual Basic.

6. Choose to open an existing project and locate the .vbp project file you just moved to the C:\WebSite\cgi-win\book\guest folder. Open the project. In the Project Explorer window, verify that both the Template.bas and the Cgi32.bas modules are visible. You may need to expand the project Modules folder to do so.

7. Double-click on Module 1 (Template.bas) to view in code view. Maximize your window if necessary.

8. From the menu bar, click on Project, Template properties. In the Project properties window, make your Startup Object the Sub Main procedure. Change your project name to Guest by typing it in the appropriate text box. Click on OK.

9. In the Declaration section of the Module1(Template.bas) module, declare the following variables:

```
Dim Name As String
Dim Email As String
```

```
Dim PhoneNumber As String
Dim Remarks As String
Dim BirthDate As Variant
Dim Response As String
Dim DataBaseFile As String
Dim ErrorMessage As String
```

10. Use the Procedure selector of the Module1(Template.bas) to go to the CGI_Main procedure. Add the following code:

```
  On Error GoTo Err_CGI_Main
  ErrorMessage = ""
  ReadFormData
  CheckDataValidity
  AddDataToGuestbook
  GenerateResponse
Exit_CGI_Main:
  Exit Sub
Err_CGI_Main:
  HandleError
  Resume Exit_CGI_Main
```

11. Insert a new procedure by clicking on the Tools menu and choosing Add Procedure. When the Add Procedure window appears, type ReadFormData in the Name text box. Verify that the procedure type is a public sub. If not, click the appropriate option buttons. Your Add Procedure window should look like Figure 7-17. Click OK.

12. Add the following code to the ReadFormData procedure:

```
Public Sub ReadFormData()
  On Error Resume Next
  Name = GetSmallField("Name")
  Email = GetSmallField("Email Address")
  PhoneNumber = GetSmallField("Phone Number")
  BirthDate = GetSmallField("Date of Birth")
  Remarks = GetSmallField("Remarks")
  Response = GetSmallField("Response")
End Sub
```

13. Using the steps described above, add a new public sub procedure named CheckDataValidity. Add the following code to the procedure:

```
Public Sub CheckDataValidity()
If Name = "" Then
    ErrorMessage = "Please specify your name."
    Error ERR_BAD_REQUEST
  End If
If BirthDate <> "" And Not IsDate(BirthDate) Then
  ErrorMessage = "Please specify a valid date of birth."
```

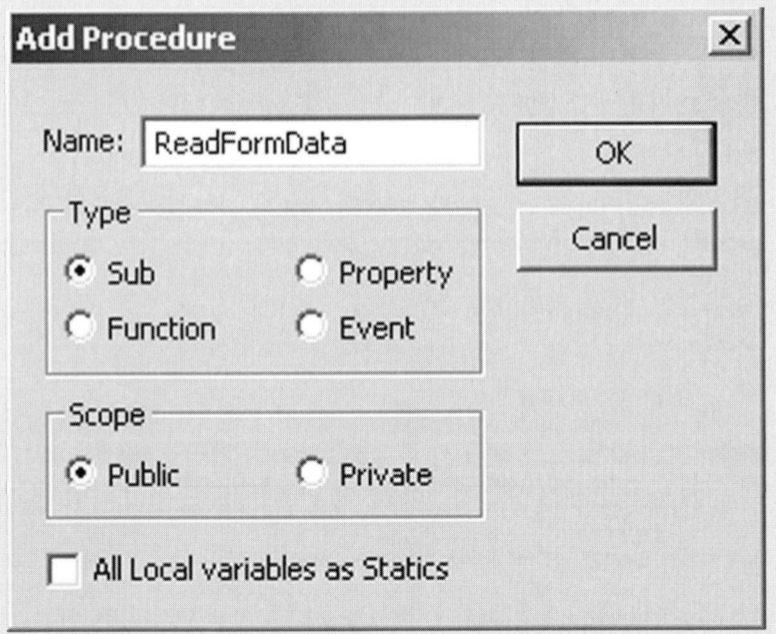

Figure 7-17
The Add Procedure Window

```
     Error ERR_BAD_REQUEST
   End If
End Sub
```

14. Add the AddDataToGuestbook procedure to the module. The code to the new procedure will be added in Chapter 9 as you explore the necessary steps to connect the CGI application to the back-end of the electronic commerce construction. Your new procedure at this point should look like the following:

```
Public Sub AddDataToGuestbook()
DataBaseFile = CGI_PhysicalPath & "\Guestbk.mdb"
'In Chapter 9, the code for this procedure will be added
   here
End Sub
```

15. Insert a new procedure named GenerateResponse in your Module1(Template.bas) module and add the following code:

```
Public Sub GenerateResponse()
  Send ("Content-type: text/html")
  Send ("")
  Send ("<HTML>")
  Send ("<HEAD>")
  Send ("<TITLE>Guestbook Entry Added</TITLE>")
  Send ("</HEAD>")
  Send ("<BODY>")
  If Response = "" Then
    Send ("<H1>Thank you for adding your name to our
    mailing list at Kanthaka Farms!</H1>")
  Else
    Send (Response)
  End If
  Send ("<H3>Temporary Output</H3>")
  Send ("Name: " & Name)
  Send ("<BR>Email: " & Email)
  Send ("<BR>Phone#: " & PhoneNumber)
  Send ("<BR>BirthDate: " & BirthDate)
  Send ("<BR>Remarks: " & Remarks)
  Send ("<BR>Database File: " & DataBaseFile)
  Send ("</BODY>")
  Send ("</HTML>")
End Sub
```

16. The last procedure that needs to be added to your CGI application is the HandleError procedure. Add this procedure to the Module1(Template.bas) module and add the following code:

```
Public Sub HandleError()
  Send ("Content-type: text/html")
  Send ("")
  Send ("</TITLE></HEAD><BODY>")
  Send ("Error")
  Send ("</TITLE></HEAD><BODY>")
  If ErrorMessage = "" Then
    Send ("<H2>" & Error$ & "</H2>")
  Else
    Send ("<H2>" & ErrorMessage & "</H2>")
  End If
  Send ("</BODY>")
  Send ("</HTML>")
End Sub
```

17. The last step in creating the CGI Guest application is to make the executable file. From the menu bar, choose File, Save Project and File, Make Guest.exe. Be sure to choose to place the compiled executable file in the Guestx folder on C:\WebSite\cgi-win\book.

Kanthaka Farms
Creating the CGI Guestlist
Application in Visual Basic

In this exercise, you will continue to create the CGI application in Visual Basic. The Guestlist will allow the customer to view the guestbook entries after a specified date. As with the Guest CGI application, the code to connect to the back-end database will be added in Chapter 9. This program's executable file will act as the middleware of Kanthaka Farms Web database construction.

1. Verify that your Web server software is running and that the icon appears in the tray.

2. Verify that the Guest and Guestx folders were added to the C:\WebSite\cgi-win\book folder. If not, add them now.

3. In Windows Explorer, locate the Cgi32.bas module in the C:\WebSite\Lib folder and copy to the C:\WebSite\cgi-win\book\guestx folder.

4. Also using Windows Explorer, copy the Template.bas and Template.vbp files to the GUESTX folder and rename the Template.vbp as Guestlist.vbp.

5. Launch Visual Basic from your Start menu. Choose Programs, Microsoft Visual Basic, Microsoft Visual Basic.

6. Choose to open an existing project and locate the .vbp project file you just moved and renamed as Guestlist.vbp to the C:\WebSite\cgi-win\book\guestx folder. Open the project. In the Project Explorer window, verify that both the Template.bas and the Cgi32.bas modules are visible. You may need to expand the project Modules folder to do so.

7. Double-click on Module 1 (Template.bas) to view in code view. Maximize your window if necessary.

8. From the menu bar, click on Project, Template properties. In the Project properties window, make your Startup Object the Sub Main procedure. Change your project name to Guestlist by typing it in the appropriate text box. Click on OK.

9. In the Declaration section of the Module1(Template.bas) module, declare the following variables:

```
Dim StartingDate As Variant
Dim DataBaseFile As String
Dim ErrorMessage As String
```

10. In the CGI_Main procedure of the Module1(Template.bas) add the following code:

```
On Error GoTo Err_CGI_Main
  ErrorMessage = ""
  ReadFormData
  CheckDataValidity
  SelectDataFromGuestbook
  GenerateResponse
Exit_CGI_Main:
  Exit Sub
Err_CGI_Main:
  HandleError
  Resume Exit_CGI_Main
```

11. Add the following new procedures to the Module1(Template.bas) module of the Guestlist.vbp project and their corresponding code:

```
Public Sub ReadFormData()
  StartingDate = GetSmallField("StartingDate")
End Sub
```

```
Public Sub CheckDataValidity()
  If Not IsDate(StartingDate) Then
    ErrorMessage = "Please specify a valid starting date."
    Error ERR_BAD_REQUEST
  End If
End Sub
```

```
Public Sub SelectDataFromGuestbook()
  DataBaseFile = CGI_PhysicalPath & "\GUESTBK.MDB"
  'The code to connect to the back-end of the Kanthaka
   Farms construction will be added here
End Sub
```

```
Public Sub GenerateResponse()
  Send ("Content-type: text/html")
  Send ("")
  Send ("<HTML>")
  Send ("<HEAD>")
  Send ("<TITLE>Guestbook Listing")
  Send ("</TITLE>")
  Send ("</HEAD>")
  Send ("<BODY>")
  Send ("<H2>The following entries were added at Kanthaka
   Farms after ")
  Send (StartingDate & "</H2>")
  Send ("<H3>(Kanthaka Farms Entries Listed Here)</H3>")
  Send ("<H3>Temporary Output</H3>")
  Send ("Database File: " & DataBaseFile)
```

```
      Send ("</BODY>")
      Send ("</HTML>")
End Sub

Public Sub HandleError()
    Send ("Content-type: text/html")
    Send ("")
    Send ("<TITLE>")
    Send ("<HEAD>")
    Send ("<BODY>")
    Send ("Error")
    Send ("</TITLE>")
    Send ("</HEAD>")
    Send ("<BODY>")
    If ErrorMessage = "" Then
        Send ("<H2>" & Error$ & "</H2>")
    Else
        Send ("<H2>" & ErrorMessage & "</H2>")
    End If
    Send ("</BODY>")
    Send ("</HTML>")
End Sub
```

12. Save and compile the Guestlist.vbp to create the Guestlist.exe. The executable file should be placed in the GUESTX folder.

Testing the CGI Application The next step is to test the customer interface of the Web database construction and make any necessary changes in your code. Though the connection to the back-end database will not be completed until Chapter 9, you can still test that the data is being handled between the Web client and the Web server as expected. When testing, it is important to test with valid data, invalid data, and empty fields. If your application does not work as expected, use the CGI Profile file created in the cgi-temp folder to aid in debugging.

Kanthaka Farms
Testing the CGI Application

In this exercise, you will test your Web database construction for the expected interaction between the Web client and the Web server.

1. Verify that your Web server software is running and that the icon appears in the tray.

2. From your Web client, display the following URL:

`http://localhost/book/guest1/guestmm.htm`

3. Click on the first link and add entry test data. Your filled form will look similar to the one displayed in Figure 7-18.

4. Click on the Enter button to submit the data to the Web server. The middleware will pass the data to the back-end of the construction. It should also return the expected ad hoc response shown in Figure 7-19.

5. Return to the main form and continue the process, leaving text boxes blank as well as putting invalid data in text boxes. As you check for coding errors with these tests, modify your front-end or middleware as needed so that you have a professional Web database construction for Kanthaka Farms.

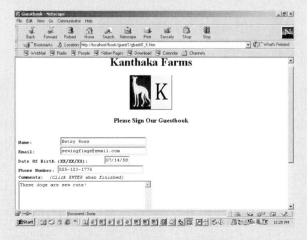

Figure 7-18
Kanthaka Farms New Guestbook Entry with Data

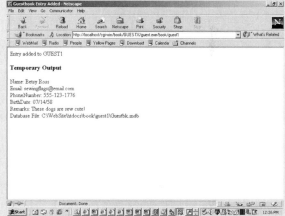

Figure 7-19
The Web Server's Response to the Web Client as Created in the CGI Application

Summary

■ **Define server-side computing and list different server-side technologies.** Server-side technologies enhance HTML Web pages and are used to increase customer interactivity with the business. In the server-side model, the Web server uses an interface program to communicate with an external program or database. The most widely used of these interface programs is Common Gateway Interface (CGI) scripts. Other server-side technologies include proprietary plug-ins such as ASP, ISAPI or NSAPI, and Java servlets.

■ **Define Common Gateway Interface (CGI) and the three different types of CGI.** The CGI is an interface for running external programs, called gateways, using an information server. Currently, the supported information servers are HTTP servers. In fact, CGI is part of the Web HTTP. Gateways are programs that handle information requests from the Web client and return the appropriate document or generate an HTML ad hoc document on the fly. With CGI, Web servers can serve information that is not in a form readable by the Web client, such as an SQL database. CGI acts as a gateway between the unreadable information and the Web client, converting the information into something that the Web client can use. There are three types of CGI: Windows, Standard, and Fast.

■ **Discuss input and the CGI environmental variables.** One of the methods that the Web server uses to pass information to a CGI application is through environmental variables, named parameters that pass the information from the server to the CGI application. These environmental variables are not necessarily variables in the operating system's environment, although that is the most common implementation. Environmental variables are read-only variables and are set automatically when the CGI script is called. They can be accessed like any other environmental variable and contain the important information needed to correctly pass data between Web client and Web server. For example, these variables store the Web browser type that is being used to process the Web client's request as well as the relevant IP addresses.

■ **Discuss CGI output: returning and redirecting.** Data are passed back and forth from the Web server and Web client using input and output files, with a goal of minimizing programming efforts and keeping the interface simple. The CGI program returns its results to the Web server as a data stream representing the goal of the request, either directly or indirectly. The Web server is then responsible for packaging the data according to HTTP, which is also used to transport the data to the requesting Web client. Generally, the Web server will add the needed HTTP headers to the CGI script's results using two parts: the head and the body.

■ **Create a CGI application using Visual Basic.** The Windows CGI application is based on a Windows executable file. This file is designed to run primarily in a noninteractive mode. The first CGI application you will create for Kanthaka Farms will allow the business to request a customer's e-mail address and return an ad hoc form, showing that the customer's address has been successfully added to the Kanthaka database. The sequence for creating the CGI application is (1) create the HTML form for the front-end of the electronic commerce model, which will allow customer input; (2) using Visual Basic, write code to return the ad hoc form showing that the customer's data have been successfully submitted to the back-end of the model; (3) create the Windows executable file for the CGI program by compiling the Visual Basic project; and (4) test the electronic commerce model.

Chapter Key Terms

API calls	gateways	rapid application development
ASPs	GET method	(RAD)
body	global arrays	request method
CGI executable	global variables	server-Side Includes (SSIs)
CGI_Main procedure	header	server-side technologies
CGI_RequestMethod variable	HTML form handler	Shockwave
Cgi32.bas library module	Inter_Main() procedure	standard CGI
client-server model	Java applet	temporary input file
Common Gateway Interface (CGI)	Main() procedure	temporary output file
content file	PHP	Web daemon
environmental variables	plug-ins	Windows CGI
error handling	POST method	Windows CGI libraries
FastCGI	proprietary plug-ins	Windows CGI test program usage
Flash	Query_String (CGI) variable	

Review Questions

1. Define server-side technology. What is its place in the electronic commerce model?

2. List and describe two server-side technologies.

3. How are server-side technologies different from client-side technologies?

4. What are plug-ins? How do plug-ins extend the electronic commerce model?

5. What is a gateway? How does the gateway work?

6. In what language must CGI be written? Why is it not considered a language itself?

7. Describe the process CGI uses to pass data back and forth from the Web client to the Web server.

8. What is a daemon? How is it used by the Web server? by the Web client?

9. Who invented Windows CGI? What is its purpose?

10. Describe the three types of CGI and discuss the similarities and differences between them.

11. Discuss alternative technologies to CGI. Discuss their advantages and disadvantages in comparison to CGI.

12. What are environmental variables? How can they be accessed?

13. What is the CGI data stream? Define the two parts of the data stream and how each is used.

14. What are the advantages of using redirection as a CGI response? Are there disadvantages? Discuss.

15. What are API calls? How are they used to simplify the process of returning information from the .INI file?

16. Describe the purpose of the Cgi32.bas library module. What is the entry point for the Visual Basic CGI application of the module?

17. What are global variables and arrays? How are they used in the CGI application?

18. How can the ACTION attribute create differences among HTML forms?

19. Discuss the importance of the cgi-win folder in your Web database construction.

Critical Thinking Using the Web

1. Lifeclinic.com offers visitors to its site a plethora of opportunities for customer interaction. Visit them at http://www.lifeclinic.com/ and investigate their Health Calculators based on the Web database construction. They have the body mass index, ideal body weight, ideal calorie intake, ideal cholesterol level, calories burned, sleep, and stress calculators. After visiting the site and experimenting with their calculators, determine how these models are constructed. Can you determine whether they are using server-side, client-side, or another technology to pass data from the Web client to the Web server and back? Write a 200–400-word essay on your analysis. Be prepared to report your findings to the class.

2. AudioBasket is an easy-to-use service for any content-driven Web site looking to increase repeat visitation and strengthen user loyalty. The AudioBasket service can be added quickly and easily to a Web site. It gives customers a custom-made package of relevant audio programming. It continually updates the business' Web site with the newest programming from leading global media sources. Request more information from AudioBasket's CoolSite by sending an e-mail to audiobasket@coolsiteoftheday.com. Evaluate the information. Can this be used to enhance your site for Kanthaka Farms? for Albatross Records? What are the advantages of using AudioBasket? What are the disadvantages? Determine the advantages from the point of view of both the customer and the business. Write a 200–400-word report of your findings. Be prepared to report your findings to the class.

3. One way to increase your site's visibility is to add it to the most popular search engines. Investigate how to have your site in the first 10 listings of top search engines like Alta Vista, Northern Lights, Euroseek, DirectHit, Google, Excite, Lycos, MSN, NBCi, Fast, HotBot, Webcrawler, and/or Yahoo! (Yahoo search, Google database) using single or multiple keywords. Visit http://www.submitplus.com/ and prepare a 200–400-word report of your findings. Be prepared to report your findings to the class.

Chapter Case Study

Albatross Records is a continuing case study in this book that illustrates the process of building electronic commerce with Web database constructions. In Chapter 7, you will use server-side technologies as you continue to build your Albatross site. As you continue through the text, you will complete different facets of electronic commerce Web database construction, resulting in a complete Web site for Albatross Records.

Using Windows Common Gateway server-side technology, create a two-form Web database construction as you did for Kanthaka Farms earlier in the chapter.

Do not worry about completing the database connection at this time, but do ensure that your data are coded to pass successfully from the front-end to the back-end of your electronic commerce model. The following general steps should be followed in your construction:

- Create a CGI application using Visual Basic.
- Change the CGI application's entry point setting.
- Add the CGI32.bas library module to your Visual Basic project.
- Add customer interactivity to the electronic commerce model.
- Create the front-end with HTML forms for listing, adding, and a Main Menu.
- Create the middleware CGI application in Visual Basic using a minimum of two CGI executable files.
- Test the CGI application.

Be prepared to demonstrate your design for Albatross Records in class.

8

Processing CGI Template Files with Server-Side Technology

These numbers do not tell the full story. We are witnessing an explosive increase in innovation. Using open standards, people around the world are creating new products and services that are instantly displayed to a global audience. We are witnessing myriad new forms of business activity, such as electronic marketplaces linking buyers and sellers in seamless global bazaars and changes in business processes from customer service to product design that harness the new technologies to make businesses more efficient and responsive.

—William M. Daley, U.S. Secretary of Commerce, *Digital Economy 2000*, the Commerce Department's third annual report on the information-technology revolution and its impact on our economy, June 2000

8.1 Benefits of Using CGI Template Files with Server-Side Technology

HTML provides some flexibility to Web page developers, but HTML by itself is static. In the electronic commerce model, once written, HTML Web pages are not able to interact with the customer other than by presenting hyperlinks. CGI applications, which run on Web servers, have made it possible for businesses to actually interact with their customers over the Internet. For example, CGI applications can collect sets of data from an HTML form and validate the data for completeness and correctness before sending them to the Web server. This can greatly improve the performance of the browsing session, because customers are not restricted by models that send unverified data to the server. CGI applications can also help to reduce network bandwidth, either over the Internet or an intranet, by performing the data checks locally.

The benefits of using CGI as middleware to connect the front-end of a Web database construction to the back-end are evident. CGI is not only portable, but can be written in numerous languages. However, there are disadvantages to the choice of CGI in the electronic commerce model using Visual Basic and the Cgi32.bas library module. As you begin to develop large-scale Web database constructions, two limitations will become apparent: **String expressions** are required for sending any CGI output. Visual Basic handles all text processing with strings and string-related functions. For instance, if you want to return information about the customer's IP address, the Send statement would read:

```
Send ("Customer's IP address: " & CGI_RemoteAddr)
```

The quotation marks must be included in the code. Suppose, however, that you want to include quotation marks within your response—for instance, if you want to return that the Italian greyhound is 10" in height, then your code would be written in one of two ways:

```
Send ("The Italian greyhound is: 10""".")
```

or

```
Send ("The Italian greyhound is: 10" & Chr$34) & ".")
```

Figure 8-1

Comparison of the Template File and SSI Approaches

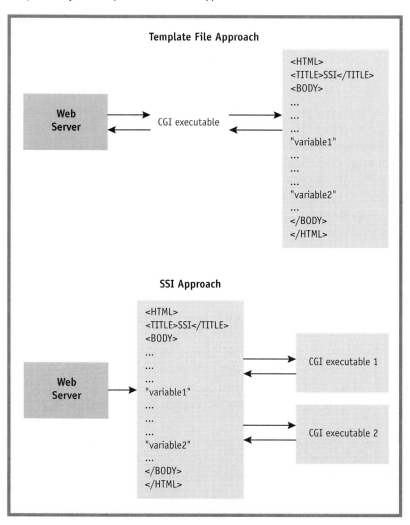

A second limitation is the necessity of recompiling the CGI executable file every time a change is made to the CGI output. Because Windows CGI is a **binary executable file**, when even a slight change is made to the application's CGI output, the program must be recompiled. This limitation is frequently a nuisance, and often can become an insurmountable obstacle, should you want to customize the format and contents of the Web server responses generated by the CGI application. To overcome this limitation, **Server-Side Includes (SSIs)** can be used as shown in Figure 8-1. A server-side include is a variable value that a Web server can include in an HTML file before it sends it to the requestor. Another solution is to use **template files** with the CGI application. This chapter will address the latter. Server-side includes will be addressed later in the book.

8.2 Sending Output Using a CGI Template File

A template file is built for output, requiring less **hard-coded HTML**. This makes it easier to create CGI programs and easier to make changes to the Web page design later on. The httpd server expects a CGI program to produce output known as **standard output (stdOUT)**. This output is basically a stream of output data that can then be processed either as a dynamic HTML document, or a pointer to a file in the form of a location header containing a URL to the desired file. Remember, a dynamic HTML document is an ad hoc document that is created on the fly by a CGI program. This document can be created in one of three ways:

- Hard-coded into the CGI program as described in Chapter 7.
- As HTML template files, residing on the server. These files can be filtered by the CGI program, substituting special codes with program variables and writing the result to stdOUT.
- Static HTML Files that can be read by the CGI program and written directly to stdOUT with no processing. This method could be implemented using a location header, although the file would have to be accessible via the Web to do this.

When template files are used for sending output, the output is based on external files. Special instructions are included in the template files to allow more functionality and flexibility in the Windows

CGI application. These special instructions are preprocessed *before* sending the final output file to the Web server. The process usually consists of using a CGI module to create CGI form processing executable files. **Location headers** and **header lines** are used in processing template files.

Location Headers

The location header can be returned from a CGI program, causing the referenced URL to be returned to the browser. The location header has the following form:

```
"Location: <URL>\x\x" seen as "Location: http://
    www.aw.com/cseng/\x\x"
```

In the example, the <URL> tag can be either a fully qualified or a relative URL. The location header must be followed by a blank line. This is ensured by the trailing "\x\x" in the example above.

The document pointed to can be created by the CGI program at run time and saved to disk, facilitating the ability to create custom-made HTML responses to form submissions. This practice is generally avoided though, because the same functionality can be realized by returning the document dynamically. In this way no disk storage space is required, instead of saving to disk and then returning the URL.

Location headers are most useful when the required form response comes from template forms, or a set of stock HTML documents that already exists. The CGI program then decides on which response URL to return on the basis of the input.

 Web Break

Have you ever wanted to visit Australia, but haven't found the time? Or how about Thailand? Want to make friends around the world? Need a forum to share your travel stories and pictures? Then visit the Virtual Tourist Web site at http://www.virtual tourist.com. In addition to providing a wealth of travel information and creating a virtual travel community, the site is an excellent example of a Web database construction that utilizes the power of CGI template files.

Header Lines

The dynamic HTML response may contain header fields such as **Content-type**, which must be placed at the very top of the returned document and separated from the document body by a blank line. This allows the CGI program to return document types other than HTML documents. Examples of these would include pictures stored as .GIF or .JPG files, or even sound files.

8.3 Designing and Testing a CGI Template File

When creating template files, each **embedded instruction** in the file must begin with a **backquote (`)** character. The instruction may end with a variety of terminating characters based on the type of instructions found in the template file. If the template file does not contain any embedded instructions, then the contents of the files are simply returned to the calling procedure.

To better understand the template file, the Job Listing Service electronic commerce model and the Utilities.bas library module that are located on this book's Web site will be explored. The Utilities.bas module contains code for sending data based on embedded instructions in external template files.

Reviewing the Design of the Job Listing Service

The Job Listing Service model uses only one Windows CGI application for handling all Web client and Web server dynamic interactions. This CGI application is named Joblist.exe. Its function is to examine the value listing in the extra logical path portion of the URL and determine which function is being requested.

The front-end of the construction has some functions that call the CGI application through its HTML forms using the **POST request method**. This is shown in Figure 8-2. In other instances, the CGI application is referred through a hypertext link, as shown in Figure 8-3. The Web server calls the CGI program by creating a new process. When calling by the **GET request method**, the **query string parameters** are passed as command line parameters to the main program. The query string is any data after the question mark character, (?). This is where the **form data** are located on a GET request. When calling a CGI application through a hypertext link, the CGI request must always use the GET method.

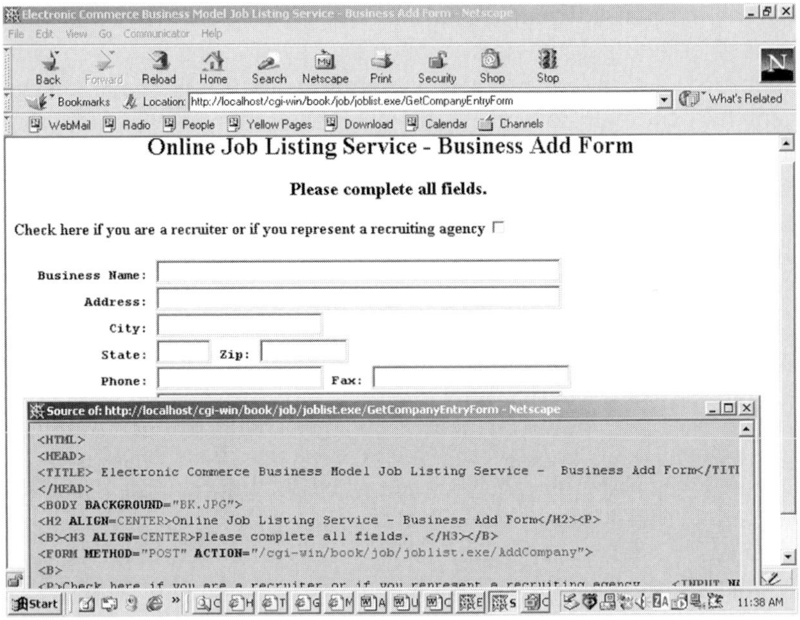

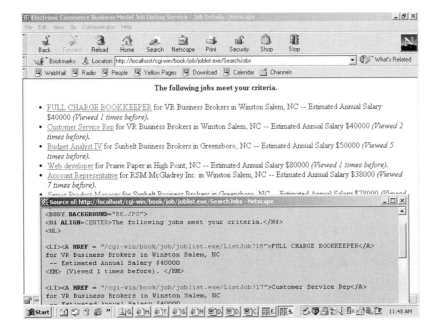

Figure 8-2

Calling a CGI Application

Figure 8-3

Referencing a CGI Application

The main disadvantage of using the GET request method in template files and passing data through the query string in a Web form is restrictions on length. Most operating systems have limits on the length of the path to a file. A length of 256 characters is common, though some operating systems may even be much shorter. The Web server treats the local portion of the URL, including the query string, as a substitute file path. This limits the amount of data that can be passed using this method. Another disadvantage is that the URL, including the query string, is often collected in the **access logs** main-

IIS Info

IIS logs can include information such as who has visited your site, what the visitor viewed, and when the information was viewed last. You can monitor attempts, either successful or unsuccessful, to access your Web sites, virtual folders, or files, including events such as reading the file or writing to the file. To enable logging on a Web site, follow these steps:

- Open IIS. To do this, click Start, point to Programs, point to Administrative Tools, and then click Internet Services manager. (In Windows 2000 Professional, Administrative Tools is located in Control Panel.)
- Click the plus sign (+) next to your server name.
- Right-click the Web site or FTP site, and click Properties.
- On the Website or FTP site tab, select Enable Logging.
- In the Active log format list, select a format. By default, Enable Logging is selected, and the format is W3C Extended Log File Format, with the following fields enabled for logging: Time, Client IP Address, Method, URI Stem, and HTTP Status. Select the items that you want to monitor in the log, leaving the defaults unless you want to customize your monitoring.

Note: If the format you select is ODBC logging, click Properties and then type the data source name and the name of the table that is within the database in the text boxes. If a user name and password are required to access the database, type these also and click OK.

- Click Apply, then click OK.

tained by most Web servers. In WebSite, access logs can be viewed from the Log folder located on C:\WebSite. The WebSite server has an extended logging format that supports WebTrends W3C/IIS for Web site analysis. Also, WebSite access logs include both the query string and the Cookie: header. To add more security, the WebSite server's access log cycling can be set automatically by time of day or file size. In addition, the server log is now time-stamped whenever an entry is written to the log, assisting in better, quicker debugging of problems. These are important features. When access logs are public, there is probably no objection to the number of hits or other data recorded; however, the form data might contain information the business or customer may prefer not to be so easily exposed.

Kanthaka Farms is a continuing case study in this book that illustrates the process of building electronic commerce with Web database constructions. In Chapter 8, you will learn how to use and process template files with a CGI server-side application. As you continue through the text, you will complete different facets of electronic commerce Web database construction, resulting in a complete Web site for Kanthaka Farms.

Kanthaka Farms
Review a Job Listing Service Web Database Designed with Template Files

1. Launch your Web server software, and verify that it is running by observing the server icon in the tray.

2. Launch Visual Basic. Open the Joblist.vbp project file located in the C:\WebSite\cgi-win\book\Job folder.

3. Notice that the project contains three modules: the Cgi32.bas library module, an application-specific Joblist.bas module, and the Utilities.bas library module. The Utilities.bas, like the Cgi32.bas modules, is designed to be shared by many programs.

4. Open the **CGI_Main procedure** in the Joblist.bas module. List the main control flow of the program as shown in Figure 8-4.

The CGI_Main procedure begins by assigning the **TaskSelector variable** to the task name specified in the **CGI_LogicalPath variable.** Before assigning the variable, any leading forward slashes (/) are removed from the logical path value. The remaining characters of the logical path are converted to uppercase letters.

The next step performed by the CGI_Main procedure is to examine whether the TaskSelector variable is empty. If it is empty, the CGI_Main processes a template file named NADDA.TXT by calling the

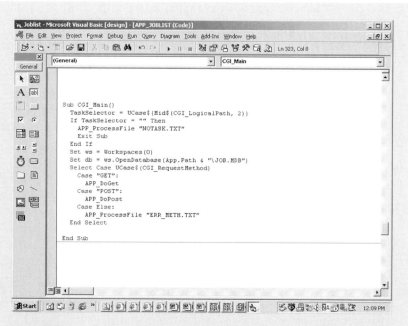

Figure 8-4

The Main Control Flow of the CGI Application

APP_ProcessFile procedure and passing this file name as a parameter. Once the NADDA.TXT template file is called, the procedure terminates. This is an alternative to hard-coding the HTML form response. The template file gives the electronic commerce design greater flexibility and provides an opportunity for the business to create a custom response for this situation.

If the TaskSelector is not empty, then the CGI_Main procedure opens the back-end database, Job.mdb. The database is opened using the Workspace object's OpenDatabase method. This method is explored in detail in the next chapter. Note that the Job.mdb file resides in the same folder in which the CGI application is located. By locating the database in the same folder, its path is easily determined from the value of the App.Path property.

After the Job.mdb database is opened, the CGI_Main procedure inspects the value of the CGI_RequestMethod variable to choose between the APP_DoGet or the APP_DoPost procedures. The error message, listed in the ERROR_MTHD.TXT template file, is sent if the request method is neither a POST or a GET request method. Figure 8-5 shows the contents of the ERROR_MTHD.TXT template file.

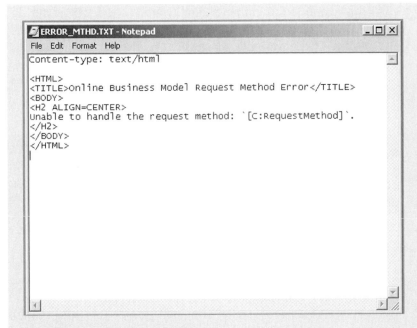

Figure 8-5
The Contents of the ERROR_MTHD.TXT Template File

Notice how the APP_DoGet procedure acts as a task delegator. It simply uses a large Case statement to call the appropriate procedure based on the value of the TaskSelector variable. The APP_DoPost also acts as a task delegator, except it calls procedures that expect data from CGI requests made by the use of the POST request method. Both of these procedures use the APP_SendMsg procedure with only slightly different modifications. The APP_SendMsg is fired when a task name is encountered that the procedure is not coded to handle.

8.4 Listing CGI Application Variables in a CGI Template File

CGI application variables located in templates files can be listed using embedded instructions that instruct specific processing and functions to be performed on designated portions of the file. To display CGI variables, the following code is inserted into the appropriate position within the file:

```
`[C:VariableName]`
```

In this example the VariableName refers to the name of the CGI variable as declared in the Cgi32.bas library module without the CGI_prefix. If the variable for *version* needed to be listed, then Version would replace VariableName in the syntax.

Another example of a template file that uses CGI referencing is the ERROR_MTHD.TXT template file. The code of this file is found in Figure 8-5.

Referring to Form Fields in a Template File

Form fields may also be referenced within a template file. The syntax used takes on one of the following two forms:

```
`[F:VariableName]`
`[V:VariableName]`
```

FieldName refers to the name of the form field currently available to the CGI application. The only difference between these two instructions is in what value they return when a field within the specified name does not exist or contains an empty string. Should the `[F:VariableName]` instruction find that a field within the specified name does not exist, it will return a Null value. The `[V:VariableName]` will return an empty string ("") instead.

Referring to User-Defined Variables in a Template File

User-defined variables are treated as special form fields that are not passed by a Web client but are created internally by the CGI application. In the job listing service, the AssignField function is used. The syntax of this function is the following:

```
AssignField FieldName, FieldValue
```

The FieldName and **FieldValue** refer to the name and value of the form field to be created. Again examine the Joblist application. The APP_SendMsg procedure is called by the APP_DoGet and the APP_DoPost procedures of the job listing service application. The code for the APP_SendMsg procedure is as follows:

```
Public Sub APP_SendMsg(Msg, Title)
  UTILITIES_AssignField "Msg", Msg
  UTILITIES_AssignField "Title", Title
  APP_ProcessFile "MESSAGE.TXT"
End Sub
```

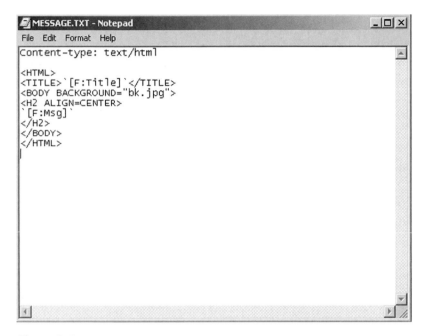

Figure 8-6
The Contents of the MESSAGE.TXT Template File

This procedure uses the AssignField procedure to create two new form fields named Msg and Title, whose values are set on the basis of the arguments passed to this procedure. The SendMsg procedure then processes the MESSAGE.TXT template file that refers to these two fields from within the HTML text. Figure 8-6 shows the content of the MESSAGE.TXT template file.

In this exercise, you will test the SendMsg procedure of the Job Listing Service and review the template file and its output.

1. Launch your Web server software, and verify that it is running by observing the server icon in the tray.

2. From your Web client, enter the following URL:

```
http://localhost/cgi-win/book/job/joblist.exe/list
```

The CGI application returns an error message based on the MES-SAGE.TXT file, as shown in Figure 8-7.

Kanthaka Farms
Testing a Template File

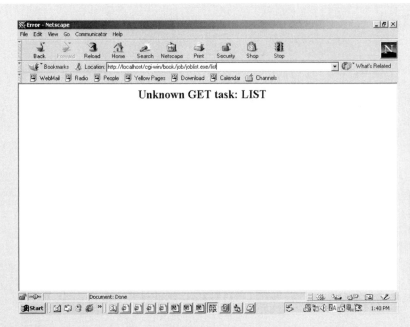

Figure 8-7
Testing the Output of a Template File

In this example the form field did not exist, and an error message was returned. If the FieldName argument of the AssignField procedure had referred to an exiting form field, however, the AssignField procedure would have overwritten the previous value of that existing form field with the new value.

Referring to Query String Parameters within a CGI Template File

Parameters are passed through the query string portion of a URL in the GET CGI request method. This query string is not decoded by the Web server; it is passed as it is to a Windows CGI application through the CGI_QueryString variable. If the query string contains multiple parameters, the parameters must be separated.

The library module of the Job Listing Service Web database construction uses the plus sign (+) character as a method for separating the parameters. Should the following data need to be passed to the Web server through the query string portion of the GET request

114+alpha+07/04/58

then each parameter can be referred to by its parameter number in the template file using the following syntax:

```
`[Q:ParameterNumber]`
```

In the previous example, `[Q:1]` will be replaced by 114, `[Q:2]` by alpha, and `[Q:3]` by 07/04/58 when the template file containing these codes is processed. Multiple parameters may also be passed through the query string using the standard **URL-encoding method**. This encoding method would list name=value string pairs delimited by the & character.

Remember, not only can data be transmitted, but also the CGI application can acquire data. As the data are acquired, the CGI application interprets the data. Web clients often bundle the data with special encoding. Form data consist of a number of distinct items, each with a name and a value, which are packaged into a single string or stream, so the CGI application must unpack it into distinct items and differentiate the names and the values. As in the example below, a Web form may contain text input tags to allow for customer/business interaction.

```
<input type=text name="user_name" value = "">
<input type=text name="user_personality" value = "">
```

In the example, in the front-end of the construction, blank text entry fields will appear on the form where the customer can type in name and personality data. When the customer submits the form, the CGI application must be told that form data called user_name and user_personality were submitted with values "John Q. Public" and "ready to buy," for example.

The Web client will bundle the data being passed into a single string using the rules of URL encoding:

- All submitted form data will be concatenated into a single string of ampersand (&) separated name=value pairs, one pair for each form tag.
- Any spaces occurring in a name or value will be replaced by a plus (+) sign. URLs cannot have spaces in them, and under the GET request method the form data are supplied in the query string in the URL.
- Other punctuation characters, for example, equal signs and ampersands, occurring in names or values will be replaced with a percent sign (%) followed by the two-digit hexadecimal equivalent of the punctuation character in the ASCII character set. This

rule exists to help distinguish these characters *inside* a form variable from those *between* the form variables in the first rule above.

8.5 Evaluating Expressions in a CGI Template File

The CGI application uses Visual Basic variable nomenclature. All variables are of the type **variant**, which means that they can be used for any of the supported data types. Constants in Visual Basic, called **literals**, are similar to variables and can also be of any type. In the CGI applications, literals are treated the same as variables. The only difference lies in how the Web database developer uses them. The variables can hold **Boolean data**; one-, two-, or four-byte integers; four- or eight-byte real numbers; dates; strings; and a few specialized types such as objects and error numbers. The following are some of the types of data supported:

- Integers: These types can be 1, 2, or 4 bytes in length, depending on how big they are.
- Floating-point: VB Script supports single- and double-precision floating-point numbers.
- Strings: Strings can represent words, phrases, or data; and they are set off by double quotation marks.
- Boolean: Booleans have a value of either true or false.

Expressions can also be evaluated within a template file. An expression is anything that can be evaluated to get a single value. Expressions can contain string or numeric literals, variables, operators, and other expressions; and they can range from simple to quite complex. The syntax is:

```
`expression`
```

For example, a 9 would be substituted for the expression `4 + 5` when the template file is processed. By comparison, a 45 is not 12 would be substituted for the expression ` "4" + "5"` when the template file is processed, because the double quotes signify string characters.

Expressions can refer to any of the program variables. For example, if the program contains two form fields named UnitPrice and Quantity that contain the values of 4 and 5, respectively, then the following expression

```
`[F:UnitPrice]` * `[Q:Quantity]`
```

would be substituted with the value of 20. This expression could also add up to a value of 20 if the UnitPrice and Quantity fields contained text strings "4" and "5". This is because the ProcessFile of the library module converts their values to a numeric data type before evaluating the expression. If, however, the field UnitPrice contained the data "$2/pound", then the preceding expression would produce an error.

Locating Errors in an Expression

Expressions must be based on terms that belong to compatible types. Examine the code below in the ProcessFile procedure of the Utilities module, paying careful attention to the **error handlers**.

```
Public Function UTILITIES_ProcessFile(ByVal InputFileNum As
    Integer) As Variant
  Const INPUT_PAST_EOF = 62
  Dim Char As String
  Dim TokenOutput As String
  Dim OutputChars As String
  Dim TokenChars As String
  Dim TokenResult As Variant
  Dim Result As String
  Dim NumCharsRead As Variant
  Dim ErrValue As Integer
  Dim ErrString As String
  Dim RecordsetNumber As Integer
  Dim MaxLoops As Variant
  Dim LoopCount As Variant
  On Error GoTo Err_UTILITIES_ProcessFile
  UTILITIES_Error = 0
  Result = ""
  Seek #InputFileNum, 1
  TokenChars = UTILITIES_InputUpto(InputFileNum, Chr(0), 0,
  Char, NumCharsRead)
  Result = Result + UTILITIES_ProcessString(TokenChars, "`")

Exit_UTILITIES_ProcessFile:
  On Error Resume Next
  If UTILITIES_Error <> 0 Then
    Result = Result & ErrString
  End If
  UTILITIES_ProcessFile = Result

Err_UTILITIES_ProcessFile:
  UTILITIES_Error = Err
  ErrString = "<!--UTILITIES_ProcessFile: " & Error$ & " -->"
  Resume Exit_UTILITIES_ProcessFile
End Function
```

Note that in the ProcessFile function the following expressions are considered invalid:

```
`"abc" + 6`
`Kanthaka`
`[F:UnitPrice] + 6`
```

In all these cases, the ProcessFile function would substitute the expression with an HTML comment that indicates the reason why the expression does not display the error. The HTML source code must be viewed to get the error.

For the efficiency of the Web database construction, there should be, at a minimum, an error handler around each entire routine, something like the following:

```
Sub DoSomething()
 On Error Goto DoSomething_Error
  .  .  .
DoSomething_Exit:
  Exit Sub
DoSomething_Error:
  Resume DoSomething_Exit
End Sub
```

Be sure to append "_Exit" and "_Error" to the name of the procedure. Within the body of the procedure, regions can be created where different error handling is required. A more sophisticated technique is to temporarily disable the **error trapping**, or error handlers, and test for errors using in-line code:

```
DoThingOne
DoThingTwo

On Error Resume Next

  DoSomethingSpecial

  If Err Then
    HandleTheLocalError
  End If

  On Error Goto ThisProcedureName_Error
```

Yet, another technique is to set **flag variables**. Flag variables indicate the location in the body of the procedure and then write logic in the error handler to take different actions on the basis of where the error occurred.

In this exercise, you will experiment with a few valid and invalid expressions to see how the expressions are processed and what kind of error messages are returned. For this experiment you will use the Test action of the Job Listing Service. This action returns the response based on a template file named TEST.TXT.

Kanthaka Farms
Locating Errors in
an Expression

1. Launch your Web server software, and verify that it is running by observing the server icon in the tray.

2. Using Windows Explorer, locate the TEST_EXP.TXT in the C:\WebSite\cgi-win\BOOK\JOB folder. Double-click on the TEST_EXP.TXT file to open it.

3. From the File menu, choose Save As. When prompted for a name, name the file TEST.TXT. You will be informed that a file by that name already exists and asked if you would like to overwrite it. Click on Yes.

4. The TEST.EXE file contains the following code:

```
Content-type: text/html
<HTML>
<HEAD>
<TITLE> Electronic Commerce Business Model Job Listing
   Service - Testing</TITLE>
</HEAD>
<BODY BACKGROUND="BK.JPG">
<H1 ALIGN=CENTER>The Online Job Listing Service - Expression
   Test</H1>
<PRE>
4 + 6 = `4+6`
"4" + "6" = `"4" + "6"`
"dog" + 5 = `"dog" + 5`
`Kanthaka`
</PRE>
</BODY>
</HTML>
```

5. Enter the following URL and display from the Web client:

```
http://localhost/cgi-win/book/job/joblist.exe/test
```

Your browser display should be similar to that shown in Figure 8-8.

6. Notice that the first two expressions are evaluated and returned by the template file correctly. The result of the last two expressions does not appear in the browser's window. However, the underlying HTML source of the response can be viewed to see the errors and their corresponding error messages. To view the HTML source, click on Source from the View menu. Your display should be similar to Figure 8-9.

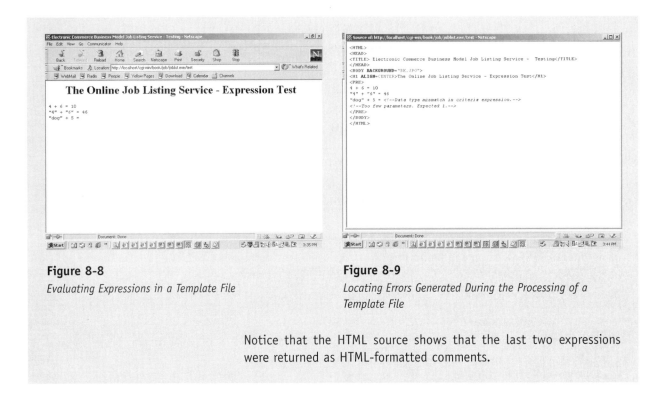

Figure 8-8

Evaluating Expressions in a Template File

Figure 8-9

Locating Errors Generated During the Processing of a Template File

Notice that the HTML source shows that the last two expressions were returned as HTML-formatted comments.

Using Built-In Functions in an Expression

Built-in Visual Basic functions can also be used in an expression. Visual Basic and VBScript provide a fairly complete set of **built-in functions** and commands, enabling math calculations to be performed, sounds to be played, new windows and URLs to be opened, and user input to the business' Web forms to be accessed and verified.

Code to perform these actions can be embedded in the template file and executed when the template file is loaded. Functions can also be written that contain code that is triggered by events the developer specifies. For example, a method can be written that is called when the customer clicks the Submit button on the business' front-end HTML form or, alternatively, that is activated when the customer clicks a hyperlink on the active Web page. When working with functions, lowercase letters should be used to specify the function name. Do not use your own user-defined functions in an expression. User-defined functions cannot be called directly from template files.

Visual Basic and VBScript can also set the attributes, or properties, of OLE controls or Java applets running in the Web browser. This way, the behavior of plug-ins or other objects can be easily changed without having to delve into their coding.

8.6 Assigning Variables in a CGI Template File

User-defined variables are treated as special form fields that are created in the CGI application. New form fields can also be defined from within the template file using the following syntax:

```
`A:FieldName=FieldValue`
```

In the syntax, FieldName refers to the name of the form field, and FieldValue can be any valid expression. Some examples include the following:

```
`A:InterestRate=.185`
`A:Currency=$`
`A:Profit=[F:Revenue] - [F:Expenses]`
```

Notice that there is no backquote character before the expression representing the field value.

In this exercise, you explore assigning variables in a template file using the Test option of the Job Listing Service.

1. Launch your Web server software, and verify that it is running by observing the server icon in the tray.

2. Using Windows Explorer, locate the TEST_VAR.TXT in the C:\WebSite\cgi-win\BOOK\JOB folder. Double-click on the TEST_VAR.TXT file to open it.

3. From the File menu, choose Save As. When prompted for a name, name the file TEST.TXT. You will be informed that a file by that name already exists and asked if you would like to overwrite it. Click on Yes.

4. The TEST.EXE file contains the following code:

```
Content-type: text/html
<HTML>
<HEAD>
<TITLE> Electronic Commerce Business Model Job Listing
    Service - Testing</TITLE>
```

Kanthaka Farms
Assigning Variables in a
Template File

```
</HEAD>
<BODY BACKGROUND="bk.JPG">
<H1 ALIGN=CENTER>The Online Job Listing Service - Variable
   Test</H1>
`A:Currency="$"`  `A:Revenue=5000`  `A:Expenses=3000`
`A:Profit=[F:Revenue] - [F:Expenses]`
<H2>
In January, Kanthaka Farms generated `[F:Currency]`
   `[F:Revenue]` revenues (in thousands) and associated
   costs for that time period were `[F:Currency]`
   `[F:Expenses]`.
<BR>
<BR>
`[F:Currency]` `[F:Revenue]` less `[F:Currency]`
   `[F:Expenses]` equals `[F:Currency]` `[F:Profit]`.
</H2>
</BODY>
</HTML>
```

5. Enter the following URL from your Web browser:

```
http://localhost/cgi-win/book/job/joblist.exe/test
```

Your Web browser display should be similar to the one shown in Figure 8-10. If it is not, refresh your Web browser display and re-enter the URL.

Figure 8-10

Assigning Variables in a CGI Template File

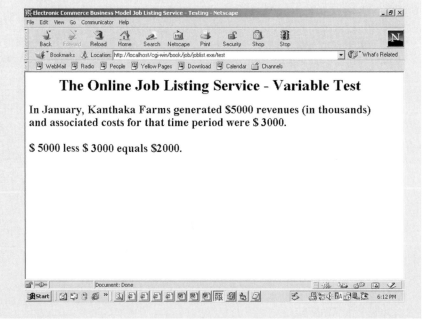

8.7 Specifying Conditions in a CGI Template File

Conditional statements allow a program to decide on a course of action on the basis of the result of a condition. These conditions are commonly divided into two general classifications. In the first class, the course of action is typically limited to one or two paths, without nesting statements. The first path is executed when the condition evaluates to true. The second path, also known as the alternate or else part, is executed when the condition evaluates to false. For example, the following conditions in a template file would print "Pass" when the variable average is greater than or equal to 60, otherwise, it prints "Fail."

```
if average >= 60 then
  print "Pass"
else
  print "Fail"
end if
```

In the second condition classification, multiple courses of action may be specified. These structures allow a problem to be divided into several cases that are handled differently. Visual Basic supports a labeled case statement that is more flexible than an unlabeled case statement. In particular, the labeled case statement allows values other than integers to be used to determine between the cases. For example, the code below displays a message based on a student's grade.

```
select case grade
  case "A"
    print "Two Thumbs Up!"
  case "B"
    print "Looking Good!"
  case "C"
    print "Better Than Nothing"
  case "D", "F"
    print "Not What I Expected"
end select
```

Sections of a template file can be conditionally processed based on the value of an expression. The syntax to specify conditions is:

```
`?Condition^TextIfTrue^TextIfFalse^
```

The condition must be a valid expression. **TextIfTrue** is the text that is processed if the condition evaluates to a "true-type" value. The **TextIfFalse** is the text that is processed if the condition evaluates to a "false-type" value. The syntax calls for the condition instruction to begin with the backquote character, but it ends with the ^ character. This ^ character is used by the ProcessFile function in the Job Listing Service to correctly determine the scope and boundaries of the condition instructions.

A condition can be either a string or numeric expression. It is considered to be a false-type if it evaluates to any of the following values:

```
"0", 0, "False", "No", "", "<!<--Null-->"
```

Otherwise, the value of the condition is considered to be a true-type. In the example below, the template file condition would produce the text Zero:

```
`?^0^Zero^Non-Zero^
```

As with program variables, expressions can also be embedded in any part of the condition instruction. The following condition ensures that a bonus is only calculated if the profit is a positive number.

```
`?^[F:Profit]>0^Bonus is `[F:Profit]*[F:CommissionRate]^
```

The false section of the condition instruction is empty in the example above. Therefore, no text will be substituted if the profit field is zero or a negative.

In the above condition instructions, the ^ character acts as a **delimiter**. A delimiter is a character that marks the beginning or end of a unit of data. This character identifies three separate sections. The delimiter character does not have to be the ^ character; however, it cannot be replaced by the backquote. Nesting conditions can be used as long as a different delimiter is used with each condition instruction.

Kanthaka Farms
Examining Conditions in a
Template File

In this exercise, you explore how conditions are specified in a CGI template file.

1. Launch your Web server software, and verify that it is running by observing the server icon in the tray.

2. Using Windows Explorer, locate the TEST_IF.TXT in the C:\WebSite\cgi-win\BOOK\JOB folder. Double-click on the TEST_IF.TXT file to open it.

3. From the File menu, choose Save As. When prompted for a name, name the file TEST.TXT. You will be informed that a file by that name already exists and asked if you would like to overwrite it. Click on Yes.

4. The TEST.EXE file contains the following code:

```
Content-type: text/html
<HTML>
<HEAD>
<TITLE>Electronic Commerce Business Model Job Listing
    Service - Testing</TITLE>
</HEAD>
<BODY BACKGROUND="bk.jpg">
<H1 ALIGN=CENTER>The Online Job Listing Service - Condition
    Test</H1>
<H2>
`A:DogPrice=0`
Item's current price:
    `?^[F:DogPrice]=0^Free^$`[F:DogPrice]`^
<BR>
`A:DogPrice=15,000`
A Kanthaka Farms IG is currently priced at:
    `?^[F:DogPrice]=0^Free^$`[F:DogPrice]`^
<BR>
`A:TestResult="False"`
Test result: `?&[F:TestResult]&Success&Fail&
</H2>
</BODY>
</HTML>
```

Figure 8-11

Experimenting with Condition Instructions in a Template File

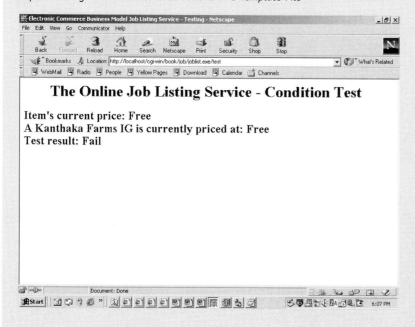

5. Enter the following URL from your Web browser:

```
http://localhost/cgi-win/book/job/joblist.exe/test
```

Your Web browser display should be similar to the one shown in Figure 8-11. If it is not, refresh your Web browser display and re-enter the URL.

8.8 Creating Loops in a CGI Template File

Sometimes the CGI applications are very simple and execute the same way each time they are loaded. An example of this type of CGI script in a typical Web database construction would be used to display a graphic animation. In order to write a CGI application that will perform different functions depending on different customer inputs at the front-end or in response to other changes in conditions, more sophistication is needed. One way to achieve this is to create **loops** for controlling the execution of the CGI programs based on a variety of inputs. A loop is a series of instructions that is repeated until a terminating condition is reached.

The control structures used in the CGI application include the following:

- *Testing conditions:* Conditions can be tested using If...Then...Elseif...Else...End structures. In use, these would look something like the following code:

```
if (sngX> sngY) then
  blnTest = TRUE
  intCount = intCount + 1
else
  blnTest = FALSE
  intCount = 0
end if
```

- *Repeated actions:* CGI applications can use several looping constructs, including For...Next, For Each...Next, While...end, Do While...End, and Do...Until. Each of these loops performs similar actions. An example of a Do...Until loop is the following:

```
intCount = 1
do
  document.write "Count is " & CStr(intCount) & "<BR>"
  intCount = intCount + 1
until (intCount = 101)
```

CRM's Place in the Electronic Commerce Model

Health Plan of Nevada found that process reengineering was needed to maintain its competitive advantage. Until the late 1990s, Health Plan not only had competitive advantage, but also was the only game in town. Since then, however, the competition has been entering the market at a fast and furious pace. Big-time players like UnitedHealthCare and Aetna Inc. increased their territories to include that of Health Plan of Nevada.

Looking for a solution to the problem of declining market share, the parent company of Health Plan of Nevada, Sierra Health Service Inc., turned to **customer relationship management (CRM)** to retain its current customers and to begin to build back its market share.

Robert Church, Sierra's electronic data interchange manager of Information Systems, found that one of the first places to start in this daunting task was to take a hard look at the practices of the company's commercial sales group that works with health services brokers, because 70 percent of the company's business is sold through brokers.

It was necessary for each functional area of the company to keep its information safe from the others and in its own legacy database system. A CRM package of software and consulting services was implemented by Sierra.

Sierra chose a suite of Web-based CRM software, Onyx Front Office. This software can also include Onyx Software's Onyx Customer Portal and Onyx Partner Portal. The Onyx Front Office CRM software enables a business to relate the information that an agent views onscreen to the customer's particular inquiry. The software runs on Windows NT and Solaris servers, and also with Microsoft's SQL server and Oracle's database server.

Customer-centric electronic commerce is the next evolution of CRM. It merges traditional CRM capabilities with **e-CRM** capabilities to enable the business' employees to share information more effectively with partners and customers, analyze the overall health of the business, build greater customer loyalty, and gain a competitive edge.

Sierra's executives fully supported the system implementation, which took about four months at a cost in excess of $1 million spent on consulting services, implementation, and training. Sierra uses e-CRM technology to enhance not only the sales and marketing function areas, but also customer service departments. Has it been a success? The competition hasn't gone away, but more than two years since the initial implementation, Health Plan of Nevada is still the largest HMO in the state.

Source: Gina Fraone, *eWEEK*, June 3, 2001, 9:00 p.m. PT

How can business products help companies achieve a competitive advantage?

Customer-centric electronic commerce is the convergence of traditional CRM capabilities with e-CRM. List several traditional CRM capabilities.

What are the new online customer interaction capabilities enabled by e-CRM?

A section of a template file can be repeatedly processed by enclosing that section within a loop instruction. The syntax of the loop instruction follows:

```
`N@IndexVariableName,MaxLoops,TextToProcess@
```

The IndexVariableName is the name of the form field that acts as the loop index. MaxLoops is a numeric expression that defines the maximum value of the loop index field. TextToProcess is the section of the template file that is processed for each loop iteration. For example,

```
`N@I,3,`[F:I]`@
```

in which the value of the index variable automatically starts at 1 and is incremented by 1 after every loop iteration. It will produce the text 123. It is possible to start with a value other than 1. To do so, the index variable is pre-assigned to one number less than the desired start value with the assignment instruction, and then the loop instructions are listed. For example, the following set of instructions produces the text 78:

```
`A:I=6 `N@I,8,`[F:I]`@
```

In the example, the first assignment instruction presets the value of the index variable *i* to 6. This is one less than the desired and expected 7 and causes the loop instructions to run through two loop iterations, one with *i* = 7 and the other with *i* = 8.

Kanthaka Farms
Creating Loops in a
Template File

In this exercise, you will explore how loops are created in a CGI template file. You will use delimiter characters in a loop instruction in the exercise below.

1. Launch your Web server software, and verify that it is running by observing the server icon in the tray.

2. Using Windows Explorer, locate the TEST_FOR.TXT in the C:\WebSite\cgi-win\BOOK\JOB folder. Double-click on the TEST_FOR.TXT file to open it.

3. From the File menu, choose Save As. When prompted for a name, name the file TEST.TXT. You will be informed that a file by that name already exists and asked if you would like to overwrite it. Click on Yes.

4. The TEST.EXE file contains the following code:

```
Content-type: text/html
<HTML>
<HEAD>
<TITLE>Electronic Commerce Business Model Job Listing
    Service - Testing</TITLE>
</HEAD>
<BODY BACKGROUND="BK.JPG">
<H1 ALIGN=CENTER> The Online Job Listing Service - Loop
    Test</H1>
`N@i,3,Italian Greyhounds are the best! @
<BR>
<BR>
`A:n=3`
`N@n,8,
9 x `[F:n]` = `9 * [F:n]` <BR>
@
<BR>
`N@i,3,Visit Kanthaka Farms and see! @
</BODY>
</HTML>
```

Notice the delimiter character used in the code above. Just like in the condition instruction, the @ delimiter character of a loop instruction can be replaced with another character, and you can create nested loops or add conditions within a loop by using different delimiter characters. Commas are used to separate the various parameters of a loop instruction. These cannot be substituted with another character, but commas can be added in the text portion of the loop instruction.

5. Enter the following URL from your Web browser:

```
http://localhost/cgi-win/book/job/joblist.exe/test
```

Your Web browser display should be similar to the one shown in Figure 8-12. If it is not, refresh your Web browser display and re-enter the URL.

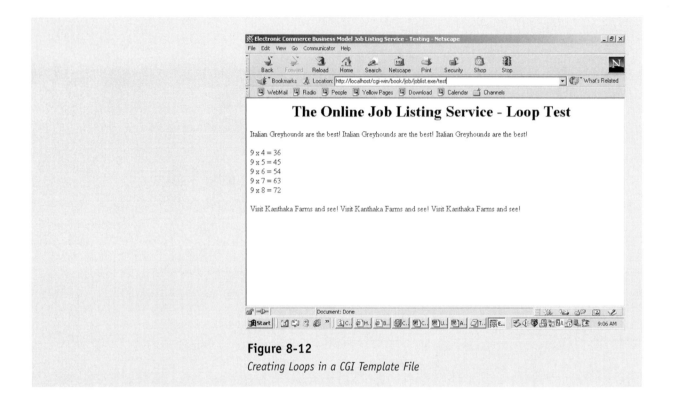

Figure 8-12
Creating Loops in a CGI Template File

8.9 Including the Contents of Another File in a CGI Template File

The contents of another file can be included in a template file. The syntax is the following:

```
`[I:FilePathName]`
```

FilePathName refers to the absolute path and name of the file whose contents are to be inserted. Remember that an absolute path will always be called for in a variable that is referencing a data file, data directory, send mail, or the location of a language interpreter on the Web server. Relative paths are used often in HTML documents for links to sites, links to programs, links to sound files, links to images or movies, and links to e-mail forms. Relative paths are used in the call for a server-side include. An example of including the contents of another file in a template file can be seen in the code below:

```
`[I:C:\WebSite\cgi-win\book\job\another_file.txt]`
```

The inserted file is not treated like another template file. Its contents are not processed. This technique is useful in inserting headers and footers or other information that is common to many files.

In this exercise, you will learn how to include the contents of another file in a template file.

Kanthaka Farms
Including the Contents of
Another File in a Template File

1. Launch your Web server software, and verify that it is running by observing the server icon in the tray.

2. Using Windows Explorer, locate the TEST_FIL.TXT in the C:\WebSite\cgi-win\BOOK\JOB folder. Double-click on the TEST_FIL.TXT file to open it.

3. From the File menu, choose Save As. When prompted for a name, name the file TEST.TXT. You will be informed that a file by that name already exists and asked if you would like to overwrite it. Click on Yes.

4. The TEST.EXE file contains the following code:

```
Content-type: text/html
<HTML>
<HEAD>
<TITLE>Electronic Commerce Business Model Job Listing
   Service - Testing</TITLE>
</HEAD>
<BODY BACKGROUND="bk.JPG">
<H1 ALIGN=CENTER>The Online Job Listing Service - Insert
   File Test</H1>
<H2 ALIGN=CENTER>KANTHAKA FARMS ITALIAN GREYHOUNDS</H2>
<BR>
`[I:C:\WEBSITE\CGI-WIN\BOOK\JOB\TEST_INS.TXT]`
</BODY>
</HTML>
```

5. Enter the following URL from your Web browser:

```
http://localhost/cgi-win/book/job/joblist.exe/test
```

Your Web browser display should be similar to the one shown in Figure 8-13. If it is not, refresh your Web browser display and re-enter the URL.

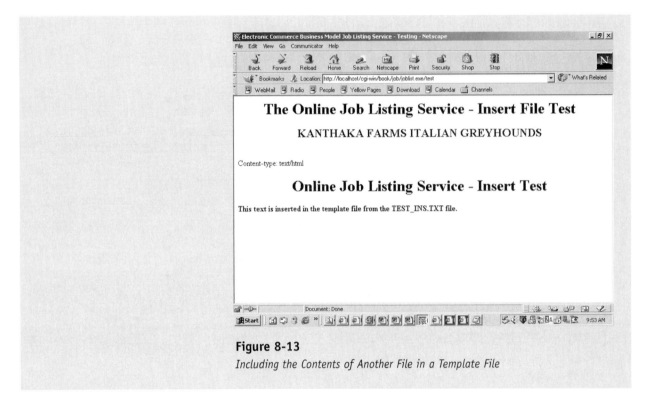

Figure 8-13
Including the Contents of Another File in a Template File

Note that typically, loops will continue to be processed until the index variable exceeds the specified MaxLoops value. The only exception is when an error is generated while processing the loop. Then, the error is returned, and the loop is terminated. The error will only terminate the current loop, then the remainder of the template file will be processed.

Summary

■ **Discuss the benefits of using template files with server-side technology.** Template files are commonly used by Web developers to overcome the CGI limitation of recompiling the CGI executable file every time a change is made to the output. Because Windows CGI is a binary executable file, when even a slight change is made to the application's CGI output, the program must be recompiled. This limitation is frequently a nuisance, and often can become an insurmountable obstacle, should you want to customize the format and contents of the Web server responses generated by the CGI application. SSIs can be used to overcome the need to recompile the CGI executable file. Another solution is to use template files with the CGI application.

- **Send output using a template file.** When template files are used for sending output, the output is based on external files. Special instructions are included in the template files to allow more functionality and flexibility in the Windows CGI application. These special instructions are preprocessed *before* sending the final output file to the Web server. The process usually consists of using a CGI module to create CGI form processing executable files. Location headers and header lines are used in processing template files.

- **Design and test a template file.** When creating template files, each embedded instruction in the file must begin with a backquote (`) character. The instruction may end with a variety of terminating characters based on the type of instructions found in the template file. If the template file does not contain any embedded instructions, then the contents of the files are simply returned to the calling procedure.

- **Evaluate expressions in a template file.** Expressions can also be evaluated within a template file. An expression is anything that can be evaluated to get a single value. Expressions can contain string or numeric literals, variables, operators, and other expressions; and they can range from simple to quite complex. Expressions can refer to any of the CGI program variables, and they must be based on terms that belong to compatible types. Error trapping and flag variables are used to evaluate expressions and increase the efficiency of the CGI template file and Web database construction design.

- **Specify conditions in a template file.** Conditional statements allow a program to decide on a course of action on the basis of the result of a condition. These conditions are commonly divided into two general classifications: (1) the course of action is limited to one or two paths or (2) the course of action is executed when the condition evaluates to false. The latter is known as the alternate or else part. Delimiters using special characters, such as the ^ character, are used to mark the beginning or end of a unit of data. This character identifies separate sections. The delimiter character does not have to be the ^ character; however, it cannot be replaced by the backquote. Nesting conditions can be used as long as a different delimiter is used with each condition instruction.

- ■ **Create loops in a template file.** Loops are necessary when a CGI application is needed that will perform different functions depending on different customer inputs at the front-end or in response to other changes in conditions. Loops control the execution of the CGI programs based on a variety of inputs. A loop is a series of instructions that is repeated until a terminating condition is reached.

- ■ **Include the contents of another file in a template file.** The contents of another file can be included in a template file to add increased functionality and customization to the Web database construction. When the contents of another file are inserted into a template file, the inserted file is not treated as another template file. Its contents are not processed. This technique is useful in inserting headers and footers or other information that is common to many files.

Chapter Key Terms

access logs
backquote (`)
binary executable file
Boolean data
built-in functions
CGI application variables
CGI_LogicalPath variable
CGI_Main procedure
conditional statements
content-type
customer relationship
    management (CRM)
delimiter
e-CRM
embedded instruction

error handlers
error trapping
expressions
FieldName
FieldValue
flag variables
form data
form fields
GET request method
hard-coded HTML
header lines
literals
location headers
loop

POST request method
query string parameters
repeated actions
Server-Side Includes (SSIs)
standard output (stdOUT)
string expressions
TaskSelector variable
template files
testing conditions
TextIfFalse
TextIfTrue
URL-encoding method
user-defined variables
variant

Review Questions

1. What are the benefits of using CGI template files with server-side technology?

2. What are location and header lines? How are location and header lines used in template files?

3. How is the backquote (`) special character used in template file coding?

4. Discuss the POST and GET request methods in the construction of the Job Listing Service electronic

commerce model. What are the benefits each affords the Web database construction?

5. Discuss the importance of access logs. How are they viewed if the Web server software is WebSite? What information can they tell you?

6. What are form fields? How are they referenced within a template file? Why is this important to the Web database construction?

7. What are user-defined variables? How are they treated in a CGI template file?

8. What is URL encoding? Discuss how multiple parameters are used with this methodology. Why is URL encoding used?

9. List and describe the Visual Basic variable types that can be used in the CGI application.

10. What are expressions? How can they be evaluated within a template file?

11. How can errors be located in an expression? Why is this important to the Web database construction?

12. How are flag variables used in CGI template files?

13. Discuss how built-in Visual Basic functions can be used in an expression.

14. What are conditional statements? How can they aid a CGI program in the decision-making process?

15. Describe the two condition classifications.

16. What is a delimiter? How is it used in a CGI template file?

17. What are loops? Why are they used in CGI template files? How are they beneficial to the Web database construction?

18. Discuss a situation in which including the contents of another file in a CGI template file would be beneficial. How is this accomplished?

Critical Thinking Using the Web

1. Most access logs, as well as other server software logs, can be set for hourly, daily, weekly, or monthly cycles. Discuss how these options are set using Web-Site server software. Using the Web, visit Microsoft's Web site at http://www.microsoft.com and find how these options are set using IIS server software. Discuss when each option is used and why it would be used.

2. This chapter began with a quotation of William M. Daley, U.S. Secretary of Commerce, from *Digital Economy 2000*, the Commerce Department's third annual report on the information-technology revolution and its impact on our economy (June 2000). Locate this report on the Web and print it out. Find a section of interest to you. After reading, write a 200–400-word essay discussing your findings. Be prepared to present your report in class.

3. A recent ECTalk discussion focused on screen-scraping. Screen-scraping is a way of automatically retrieving information from Web sites for deposit into another location, such as a database or another Web site. Use the Web and search for specific tools that provide a means of screen-scraping. In a report, list three of the tools you found. Evaluate each by using at least four different metrics, such as cost, reliability, and ease-of-use. Be prepared to present your findings in class.

Chapter Case Study

Albatross Records is a continuing case study in this book that illustrates the process of building electronic commerce with Web database constructions. Chapter 8 demonstrates how to use and process template files with a CGI server-side application. In your template files, you will use expressions, specify conditions, create *loops, and include the contents of at least one other file. As you continue through the text, you will complete different facets of electronic commerce Web database construction, resulting in a complete Web site for Albatross Records.*

- Using the job listing service as a model, create a series of CGI template files for Albatross records.
- Your design should use only one Windows CGI application for handling all Web client and Web server dynamic interactions.
- Use both POST and GET request methods.
- Using `[F:VariableName], list CGI application variables in a CGI template file.
- Create user-defined variables using the following syntax:

  `AssignFieldName, FieldName`

- Pass parameters through the query string portion of a URL in the CGI GET request method.
- Locate errors in your expressions using error handlers.

- Assign variables in special form fields.
- Use conditional statements to allow your CGI application to decide on a course of action based on the results of your condition.
- Create at least one loop in a template file. Use the loop to control the execution of your CGI application.
- Include the contents of at least one other file in a CGI template file.
- Print the access logs after your application has run successfully.
- Be prepared to demonstrate your application and justify your choice of Web design techniques and tools.

9

Connectivity: Databases, Visual Basic, and CGI

The increasing demand for digital information will bring about a "Content Big Bang" and usher in a new wave of IT growth. In the next three years, almost three times as much information will be created as has been created by man since the beginning.

—Joseph M. Tucci, President and CEO, EMC Corporation, *Oracle OpenWorld*, Berlin, June 20, 2001

9.1 Using a Database in a CGI Application for Connectivity

Businesses today understand the importance of electronic commerce and are moving their business processes to the Web at an astronomical rate. However, the success of electronic commerce depends on the scalability of the back-end of the application that it implements. Web database architecture success is equated with high traffic, often measured by volume capacity. Many businesses face a daunting task as they decide to put customer-oriented, interactive processes on the Web. To capture user preferences and then respond with order-entry or other information, they need to move beyond ordinary Web pages to Web database constructions with high-capacity database applications.

Databases represent significant infrastructure for the electronic commerce model. Web database designs require rapid access to large amounts of data passing between the Web client and the Web server. For instance, an electronic commerce shopping cart model for an online bookstore must track the entire product line of the operation as well as keep track of customer information and customer preferences. Online airline reservation systems must be able to simultaneously place passengers from around the world on numerous flights on different dates. Online libraries store millions of entries and access citations from hundreds of publications stored in back-end databases. Transaction-processing systems in online banks and online brokerage houses keep the accounts that generate international flows of capital. Web search engines scan thousands of Web pages to produce quantitative responses to queries almost instantly.

Hundreds of thousands of businesses and organizations use databases to track everything from inventory and personnel to DNA sequences and pottery shards from archaeological digs.

Web Break

Visit Canada's Electronic Commerce Strategy at http://e-com.ic. gc.ca/english/ to see how Canada has outlined the various initiatives that are helping make them a world leader in the adoption and use of electronic commerce. Working in close collaboration with the private sector, the federal government has concentrated on creating the most favorable environment possible in areas that are critical to the rapid development of electronic commerce.

Creating the Database File

The main considerations when designing the back-end of a Web database construction are capacity and front-end/middleware application specifications. To create a database that can be used for multiple electronic commerce models, often a generic database file is created that can simply be copied to different Web server directories. The structure of a generic database must accommodate every entry field and CGI application variable, even though some of these applications may not use all of the optional fields in the back-end database.

Consider the Web database construction created for Kanthaka Farms in Chapter 7. Their electronic commerce model allowed customers to submit their names, e-mail addresses, and comments to the business' back-end database. Customers could also view entries in the database and query the back-end with SQL statements. It is possible to create a **generic back-end database** to meet the electronic commerce demands of Kanthaka Farms. The first point of investigation must be the fields that will be necessary in the back-end database. To make this determination, the input fields used in the front-end of the construction must be evaluated. You will need to carefully review the HTML forms located in the GUEST1 and GUEST2 folders on C:\WebSite\HTDOCS\Book and the CGI application Visual Basic projects located in the GUESTX and GUEST folders on C:\WebSite\cgi-win\Book. Be sure to look carefully at spelling and capitalization of the field names. Your field determination for the back-end database should correspond to the information in Figure 9-1 below.

Even though you will be creating a generic database, a suitable primary key must be chosen that uniquely identifies each record in the database table. The primary key can only contain non-null data values, so optional fields that are not used by all components in the Web database construction must be ruled out. An AutoNumber could be assigned that would be generated by the back-end database. However, Kanthaka Farms business logic precludes the use of an AutoNumber as a primary key. It will be important to the business that a customer not be allowed to submit duplicate entries to the database. A composite primary key that combines fields, or attrib-

Figure 9-1

Field Needs Determination for the Back-End Database

Field Needs Determination for the Back-End Database			
Application	Location	Field Names	Type
Front-end	C:\WebSite\HTDOCS\Book\Guest1\GBAdd1_K.htm	Name	Text
Front-end	C:\WebSite\HTDOCS\Book\Guest1\GBAdd1_K.htm	Email	Text
Font-end	C:\WebSite\HTDOCS\Book\Guest1\GBAdd1_K.htm	BirthDate	Date
Front-end	C:\WebSite\HTDOCS\Book\Guest1\GBAdd1_K.htm	PhoneNumber	Text
Front-end	C:\WebSite\HTDOCS\Book\Guest1\GBAdd1_K.htm	Comments	Text
Front-end	C:\WebSite\HTDOCS\Book\Guest1\GBAdd1_K.htm	Response	Text
Front-end	C:\WebSite\HTDOCS\Book\Guest1\GBList1_K.htm	StartingDate	Text
Front-end	C:\WebSite\HTDOCS\Book\Guest2\GBAdd2_K.htm	Name	Text
Front-end	C:\WebSite\HTDOCS\Book\Guest2\GBAdd2_K.htm	Email	Text
Front-end	C:\WebSite\HTDOCS\Book\Guest2\GBAdd2_K.htm	Comments	Text
Front-end	C:\WebSite\HTDOCS\Book\Guest2\GBAdd2_K.htm	Response	Text
Front-end	C:\WebSite\HTDOCS\Book\Guest2\GBList2_K.htm	StartingDate	Text
Middleware	C:\WebSite\cgi-win\BOOK\GUESTX\Guestlist.vbp	StartingDate	String
Middleware	C:\WebSite\cgi-win\BOOK\GUEST\Guest.vbp	Name	String
Middleware	C:\WebSite\cgi-win\BOOK\GUEST\Guest.vbp	Email	String
Middleware	C:\WebSite\cgi-win\BOOK\GUEST\Guest.vbp	PhoneNumber	String
Middleware	C:\WebSite\cgi-win\BOOK\GUEST\Guest.vbp	Remarks	String
Middleware	C:\WebSite\cgi-win\BOOK\GUEST\Guest.vbp	BirthDate	Variant
Middleware	C:\WebSite\cgi-win\BOOK\GUEST\Guest.vbp	Response	String

utes, can accomplish this goal. Name, combined with the PhoneNumber and Email fields, would permit only one entry from each customer.

Kanthaka Farms is a continuing case study in this book that illustrates the process of building electronic commerce with Web database constructions. In Chapter 9, you will connect to the back-end of Kanthaka Farms Web database construction using Microsoft Access. As you continue through the text, you will complete different facets of electronic commerce Web database construction, resulting in a complete Web site for Kanthaka Farms.

Kanthaka Farms
Creating the Back-End
Database Shell

1. Launch Microsoft Access and choose the "Create a New Database Using Blank Database" option.

2. Select the C:\WebSite\cgi-win\book\guestx folder and name the new database Guestbk_k.mdb. Click on the Create button. You now have an empty database container that will be used for the back-end of the front-end and middleware components of the electronic commerce model you created for Kanthaka Farms in Chapter 7.

3. Choose the Table object and click on New. Choose Design View.

4. Using the identified fields needed from Figure 9-1, create table fields and their properties.

5. Move your pointer to the gray area to the left of the field names. When your pointer turns into a black pointing arrow, select the Name, Email, and PhoneNumber fields while holding down the Ctrl key as shown in Figure 9-2. From your tools bar, click on the Primary Key icon to create the composite key for the table. This composite key will permit only one entry from each user.

6. Save the table as tblGuestbook_Entries.mdb by selecting the Save option from the File menu.

7. Close the GUESTBK_K.MDB database and exit Access.

8. From Windows Explorer, copy the database to the GUEST1 and GUEST2 folders on C:\WebSite\HTDOCS\book.

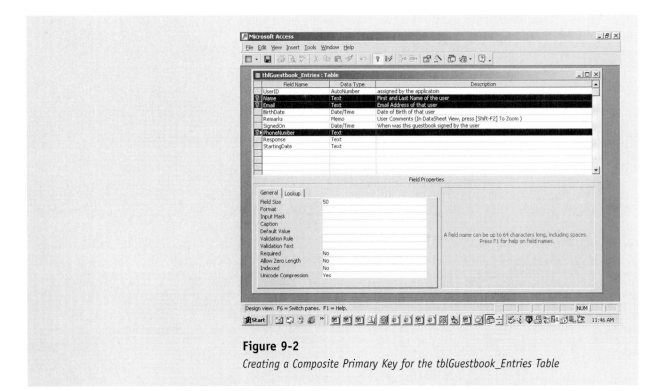

Figure 9-2

Creating a Composite Primary Key for the tblGuestbook_Entries Table

9.2 Understanding the Database Objects

The database model behind the Microsoft Access database and other Structured Query Language (SQL)-oriented databases is quite different from the database model behind traditional PC databases such as dBASE, FoxPro, or Paradox. Traditional PC databases are **record-oriented database systems**. SQL databases are **dataset-oriented systems**. This understanding proves important in optimizing the Web database construction and back-end database programs in Visual Basic.

In record-oriented database systems, database operations are performed one record at a time. The most common programming construct in record-oriented systems is the loop. The following code example shows how to increase the price field in the Kanthaka Farms Champion Dogs table in a record-oriented database:

```
ReadLoop:
  If EndOf File
    Goto EndLoop
  Else
```

```
Read Record
    If Record.SireLine = `Figorella' Then
      Price=Price*1500
      Write Record
    End If
  EndIf
Goto ReadLoop
EndLoop
End Program
```

Processing in record-oriented systems usually involves creating a procedure that reads a single data record, processes it, and returns to read another record until the job is completed. These record-oriented databases use **indexes** to speed the process of locating records in data tables. Indexes also help speed processing by allowing the databases to access the data in sorted order, for instance, by Name, Email, BirthDate.

In data-oriented systems, such as Microsoft Access or Oracle, the database operations are performed one set at a time, not one record at a time. The most common programming construct in dataset-oriented systems is the SQL statement. Instead of using program code to loop through single records, SQL databases can perform operations on entire tables from just one SQL statement. The following code example demonstrates this process on the price field in the same Kanthaka Farms Champion Dogs table in a dataset-oriented database:

```
UPDATE Dogs SET Price=Price*1500 WHERE Dogs.SireLine=
  "Figorella"
```

Much as keywords behave in Visual Basic programs, so the **UPDATE SQL command** behaves with SQL databases. In the example, UPDATE tells the database that it wants to update an entire Dogs table. The **SET SQL command** changes the value of a data field, in this example, the Price data field. The **WHERE SQL command** is used to perform a logical comparison of the Sireline field to the value Figorella. A single statement is used to select only the records needed to perform the database operation on dataset-oriented databases. In dataset systems, indexes are used more to maintain database integrity than to speed the location of specific records.

Every Visual Basic program that accesses database tables uses **data objects**. There are a number of object types that are used in Visual Basic. The most common objects and their corresponding type tags are shown in Table 9-1.

Table 9-1	*Visual Basic Object Types*
Visual Basic Prefix	Visual Basic Object
db	Database
ds	Dynaset
fld	Field
idx	Index
qdf	QueryDef
qry	Query
rpt	Report
rs	Recordset
ss	Snapshot
tbl	Table
tdf	TableDef
wrd	Word object
ws	Workspace
xl	Excel object

Data objects are used within a Visual Basic program to manipulate databases, as well as the data tables and indexes within the database. The data objects are the program code representations of the physical database, data tables, fields, and indexes. The primary data object used in Visual Basic programs is the **Recordset object**, which holds the collection of data records used in the Web database construction. There are three different types of Recordset objects:

- **Dynaset-type Recordset objects**
- **Snapshot-type Recordset objects**
- **Table-type Recordset objects**

Access can be gained to an existing table in a database using any one of these three Recordset object types; however, each has its own unique properties and can behave quite differently at times. The Visual Basic table-type Recordset object performs record-oriented processing very effectively. The Visual Basic dynaset- and snapshot-type Recordset objects do not perform well on record-oriented processes.

Another object, the **database object**, is used by the middleware to access and retrieve information about the connected database.

Visual Basic database objects are dataset-oriented. Often Web database developers will use Visual Basic as the middleware and assume a record-oriented database model. This assumption can result in the electronic commerce model's being slow to perform on large data tables and slow to return a specific record of data. The model's poor performance can usually be attributed to the middleware's sluggishness from improper use of Visual Basic data objects. Often Web database developers will create a middleware environment in which entire data tables are opened when only a small subset of the data is needed to perform the Web client/Web server required tasks.

The Dynaset-type Recordset Data Object

The most frequently used data object in the middleware is the Visual Basic dynaset Recordset data object. Its name, dynaset, is derived from the fact that it is used to dynamically gain access to part or all of an existing data table in a database. A dynaset Recordset object is a dynamic set of records that can contain fields from one or more tables or queries in a database and may be updateable. When the DatabaseName and RecordSource properties of a Visual Basic data control are set, a Visual Basic dynaset Recordset is created. You can also create a dynaset Recordset by using the **CreateDynaset method** of the Database object.

When a dynaset Recordset object is created, it is not necessary to create a new physical table in the database. A dynaset Recordset object exists as a virtual data table, usually containing a subset of the records in a real data table. Because creating a dynaset Recordset object does not create a new physical table, it does not add to the size of the back-end database. However, when a dynaset Recordset object is used, RAM capacity on the Web server running the application can be a concern. Depending on the number of records in the dynaset Recordset object, temporary disk space can also be used on the Web client requesting the dataset. Also, the dynaset Record object stores only the primary key for each record, instead of the actual data. In this manner the dynaset Record object is updated with changes made to the source data.

There are several reasons to use dynaset Recordset objects to access data in the Web database construction: They require less memory than other data objects and provide the most update options, including the capability to create additional data objects from existing dynaset Recordset objects. They are also the default data objects for the Visual Basic data control, and they are the only updateable data object that can be used for databases connected through Microsoft's **Open Database Connectivity (ODBC)** model. Dynaset Recordset objects use relatively little Web client memory, even for large datasets. When the object is created, the back-end application performs several tasks. First, the records requested by the Web client are selected. Next, temporary index keys are created to each of these records. The complete set of keys is then sent to the Web client along with enough records to fill out any bound controls such as text boxes and/or grid controls that appear on the Web client's form.

The DB Engine, ODBC, and the Microsoft Jet Data Engine The top level object in the **Data Access Object (DAO)** model is the **DBEngine object**. The DAO is a programming interface to access and manipulate database objects. In the hierarchy of DAO objects, the DBEngine object contains and controls all other objects. Additional DBEngine objects cannot be created and the DBEngine object does not belong to any collection. When an ODBC data source is referenced directly through DAO, it is called an **ODBCDirect workspace**. This nomenclature distinguishes it from an ODBC data source that is referenced indirectly through the **Microsoft Jet database engine**, using a **Microsoft Jet workspace**. When a workspace object is first referred to or used, it must be declared, and a default workspace is created with the following code:

```
Dim ws As Workspace
Set ws = DBEngine.Workspaces(0).
   OpenDatabase(DatabaseFilePath)
```

ODBC is an open standard **application programming interface (API)** for accessing a database. In the electronic commerce model, back-end database files in a number of different databases, including Access, dBase, DB2, Excel, and Oracle, can be accessed by using ODBC statements in the middleware program. The Microsoft ODBC API provides the electronic commerce model with the ability to connect to a variety of different client/server and mainframe databases. However, connecting to a back-end database requires a product-specific **ODBC driver** written to ODBC specifications. DAO has always supported access to remote data using the Jet database engine, but since the introduction of DAO version 3.5, access to remote data using ODBCDirect has also been supported. With ODBCDirect, the Jet database engine can be bypassed and DAO used to access remote data directly. ODBCDirect establishes a connection directly to an ODBC data source, without loading the Microsoft Jet database engine into memory, and is useful in situations where specific features of ODBC are required.

Visual Basic uses the Microsoft Jet data engine as the actual data request engine. In pure SQL systems, all requests for data result in a set of data records. Data requests to the Microsoft Jet data engine result in a set of keys that point to the data records. By returning keys instead of data records, the Microsoft Jet data engine is able to limit network traffic in the Web database design and speed back-end performance. The Microsoft Jet database engine can be thought of as a data manager component with which other data access systems, such as Microsoft Access and Microsoft Visual Basic, are built.

Dynaset Recordset Object and Connectivity

The **OpenRecordset method** of opening a database is used to create a dynaset Recordset object. When a dynaset Recordset object is opened using Visual Basic code instead of using the data control, two Visual Basic objects must be created: a Database object and a Recordset object. The code is as follows:

```
Dim db As Database ` the database object
Dim rs As Recordset ` the recordset object
```

These objects must be initialized with values before they can access the data in the back-end. To initialize the values, two variables that correspond to the DatabaseName and RecordSource properties of the data control are created. The code below demonstrates this process:

```
Dim db As Database ` the database object
Dim rs As Recordset ` the recordset object

Dim DBName As String ` a local variable
Dim RSName As String ` a local variable

DBName = App.Path & "\..\book\Guestx\GUESTBK_K.mdb" `
    initializes the variable
RSName = "tblGuestbook_Entries"
```

To open the database and create the dynaset Record object, the following code can be used:

```
Dim db As Database ` the database object
Dim rs As Recordset ` the recordset object

Set db = DBEngine.OpenDatabase(DBName) ` creates the objects
Set rs = db.OpenRecordset(RSName, dbOpenDynaset)
```

If the type is not specified in the OpenRecordset code, a Table Recordset is returned if the source is a single table. If the source is a query or an SQL string, then a dynaset Recordset object is returned by default.

This is all the code that is needed to open an existing Microsoft Access database and create a dynaset Recordset object ready for update. However, more code is needed to perform more sophisticated actions on the data. A variable can be used to hold the record count. The MoveLast method can be used to move the record pointer to the last record in the Recordset. Example of code is shown below:

```
Dim db As Database ` the database object
Dim rs As Recordset ` the recordset object

Dim DBName As String
Dim RSName As String
Dim Records As Integer

DBName = App.Path & "\..\ book\Guestx\GUESTBK_K.mdb"
RSName = "tblGuestbook_Entries"

Set db = DBEngine.OpenDatabase(DBName)
Set rs = db.OpenRecordset(RSName, dbOpenDynaset)

rs.MoveLast ` move to end of list to force a count
Records = rs.RecordCount ` get count
MsgBox RSName & " :" & CStr(Records), vbInformation, "Total
    Records in Set"
```

The OpenRecordset command can also be used on an existing Recordset to create a smaller subset of the data. This is often done when the Web client is allowed to create a record selection criterion. If the dataset returned is too large, the customer at the front-end of the construction is allowed to further qualify the search by creating additional criteria to apply to the back-end dataset. This can be accomplished by creating a new Recordset object and a new variable called **Filter variable** to hold the criteria for selecting records. The code below demonstrates how to add the object and variable to the existing **snippets**, or small portions, of code:

```
Dim db As Database ` the database object
Dim rs As Recordset ` the recordset object
Dim rs2 As Recordset ` add another recordset object

Dim DBName As String
Dim RSName As String
Dim Records As Integer
Dim Filter As String ` add the filter
```

```
DBName = App.Path & "\..\ book\Guestx\GUESTBK_K.mdb"
RSName = "tblGuestbook_Entries"
Filter = "StartingDate>01/01/01" ` set filter

Set db = DBEngine.OpenDatabase(DBName)
Set rs = db.OpenRecordset(RSName, dbOpenDynaset)

rs.Filter = Filter
Set rs2 = rs.OpenRecordset

rs.MoveLast ` move to end of list to force a count
Records = rs.RecordCount ` get count
MsgBox RSName & " :" & CStr(Records), vbInformation, "Total
   Records in Set"
```

In many cases, it is important that the back-end database be updateable by the Web client. However, the dynaset Recordset object may not be updateable if:

■ There is not a unique index on the ODBC or tables.
■ The data page is locked by another customer.
■ The record has changed since it was last read.
■ The customer does not have permission to update.
■ One or more of the tables or fields are read-only.
■ The database is opened as read-only.
■ The Recordset object was either created from multiple tables without a JOIN statement or the query was too complex.

The Snapshot-Type Recordset Data Object

Snapshot-type Recordset objects are very similar to dynaset Recordset objects in both their behavior and properties. However, a snapshot Recordset object is a static set of records that is used to examine data in an underlying table or tables. There are two major differences between snapshot Recordset objects and dynaset Recordset objects:

■ Snapshots are stored entirely in Web client memory.
■ Snapshots are read-only, non-updateable objects.

Snapshot Recordset objects are generally faster to create and access than dynaset Recordset objects because their records are either in memory or stored in temporary disk space. In addition, the Microsoft Jet database engine has no need to lock pages or handle multiuser issues with the snapshot Recordset object. However, snapshot Recordset objects use more resources than dynaset Recordset objects, because the entire record is downloaded to local memory.

FOCUS ON ELECTRONIC COMMERCE

MetalSite Shows Just What the Steel Industry Is Made of

How has Bethlehem Steel redefined the metals supply chain?

Describe Bethlehem Steel's electronic commerce strategy. What kind of benefits have they achieved by conducting business over the Internet?

What business processes can companies integrate by using or implementing an online exchange like MetalSite?

How do you help an ailing business? Bethlehem Steel found moving to the Internet to be their needed shot in the arm. In 2000, falling prices and consolidation of overseas steel manufacturers had left the company with a reported net loss of over $115 million on revenues of $4.2 billion. Like many businesses founded in the industrial age, the move to the information age and the New Economy was not an easy one and not one of first resort. It was not until Bethlehem Steel acquired an equity stake in MetalSite, an online exchange for the steel industry, that they began to investigate the benefits of electronic commerce.

Bethlehem Steel, the world's fifth-largest steel producer, shipped 8.5 million tons of steel in 2000 and today employs more than 14,000 people. But as little as a year ago, they were still faxing information to potential customers and waiting for replies via phone or fax.

Now, with the tools of electronic commerce, the company's MetalSite Web site (http://www.metalsite.net/) has become the enabler of strategic partnerships, customer growth, customer service, and even employee information. Bethlehem Steel uses the site to create buyer, seller, and industry connections.

MetalSite bills themselves as the "number one in metals electronic commerce... the Internet's premier site for buying and selling metals." The site has increased the ease with which its partners can now access, buy, and sell metals through advanced Internet tools like their fast, comprehensive, and secure back-end database, MetalSite Catalog. The site also supports more than just buying and selling, with online information and news sources, state-of-the-art electronic commerce integration capabilities, and other services that meet the business needs of the metals community.

Bethlehem Steel has not stopped with MetalSite in their pursuit of electronic commerce. They have also streamlined internal processes via the Web. An electronic procurement system from Ariba that lets employees buy supplies for maintenance, repair, and operations was rolled out with a goal of driving down unauthorized spending. A new human resources portal where employees can access information on health benefits and even get reimbursed for travel has been implemented.

"We're still feeling our way on all of this [electronic commerce], but we're committed to using the Internet where it makes sense," said Mike Ippoliti, the company's electronic commerce manager. "For us, the risk of experimenting with this technology is small compared to building a billion-dollar steel plant. But the payoffs down the road could be tremendous."

Source: Sarah L. Roberts-Witt, *PCMagazine*, May 21, 2001.

The following code is used to open and set a snapshot Recordset object:

```
Dim db As Database
Dim rsSnapshot As Recordset

Set rsSnapshot = .OpenRecordset(Name, dbOpenSnapshot)
```

Because the snapshot Recordset object is a static set of records, it is often used to create calculated reports or graphical displays.

Web Break

Although the total number of Americans going digital increases each day, there are still large segments of our society that are being passed by in the information age. Digital Divide, a production by Studio Miramar for the Independent Television Service (ITVS) with funds provided by the Corporation for Public Broadcasting, explores four major gaps in technology usage: schools, gender, race, and the workplace and why many people are having to play "catch-up" for very different reasons. Explore more on this subject at http://www.pbs.org/digitaldivide/themes.html.

The Table-Type Recordset Data Object

A table-type Recordset object can be used to add, change, or delete records from a table. It represents a base table view of the data. A **base table**, the physical data table, is a table in a Microsoft Jet database. The structure of a base table can be manipulated by using the DAO objects or data definition SQL statements. Its underlying data can be manipulated using Recordset objects or action queries. With table Recordset objects, only the current record is loaded into memory. A predefined index determines the order of the records in the Recordset object. The Table object can be used to directly open a table defined by Data Manager or some other database definition tool.

A table Recordset object is created by using the OpenRecordset method of an open Database object. Table-types cannot be created from an ODBC or linked table. Unlike dynaset or snapshot Recordset objects, table Recordset objects cannot refer to more than one base table nor be created with an SQL statement that filters or sorts the data.

One advantage to using the table Recordset object is that Index objects can be specified for Web client use in searching for specific records in the table. The use of indexes can be beneficial to the Web database construction to order the data table for displays and reports and to speed searches.

9.3 Adding a Table Record Through a Visual Basic Recordset Object

Recordset objects are used to access and manipulate database records. This object can be used in a table, an SQL statement that returns records, or a query. The following generic syntax, using the database object's OpenRecordset method, is used to create the object:

```
Set rs = db.OpenRecordset(source[, type[, options]])
```

In the code example above, source refers to the table name, SQL statement string, or query name. Type is the Recordset object type, and the options are set to restrict the front-end users' ability to view and edit records while the back-end database's Recordset is active.

Kanthaka Farms
Using AddNew and Update Methods with a Recordset Object

In this exercise, you will add a new record to the underlying record source in the CGI template file.

1. Launch Visual Basic and open the Guest.vbp project located in the C:\WebSite\cgi-win\Book\Guest folder.

2. Make sure the Module 1 (Template.bas) module is active and modify the AddDataToGuestbook procedure as follows:

```
Public Sub AddDataToGuestbook()
  Dim ws As Workspace
  Dim db As Database
  Dim rs As Recordset
  DataBaseFile = CGI_PhysicalPath & "\Guestbk_k.mdb"
  Set ws = DBEngine.Workspaces(0)
  Set db = ws.OpenDatabase(DataBaseFile)
  Set rs = db.OpenRecordset("tblGuestbook_Entries")
  rs.AddNew
```

```
   rs!Name = Name
   rs!Email = Email
   rs!PhoneNumber = PhoneNumber
   rs!BirthDate = BirthDate
   rs!Remarks = Remarks
   rs.Update
End Sub
```

3. From the Project menu, select References. Visual Basic will display a list of references as shown in Figure 9-3.

4. Select the Microsoft DAO 3.6 Object Library option by scrolling down until it is visible and clicking in the check box. Click OK.

5. From the File menu, choose Save Project and Make Guest.exe to recompile the project.

6. Test the updated CGI application by submitting a Web client request to the Web server. Launch your Web server. In your browser window, specify the following URL:

```
http://localhost/book/guest1/gbadd1_k.htm
```

Figure 9-3

List of Available Library References

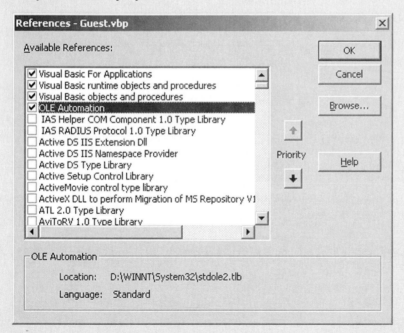

7. Submit the following test entry:

```
Name: Marion Davies VanZandt
Email: mdvz@email.com
PhoneNumber: 555.234.2345
BirthDate: 03/04/62
Remarks: This is a test entry.
```

8. The CGI application Guest.exe should return the response shown in Figure 9-4 to the Web client.

9. Verify that the entry was added to the back-end database. Open the Guestbk_K.mdb from the Guest1 folder in C:\WebSite\HTDOCS\ Book\Guest1. Open the tbl_Guestbook_Entries and verify that the record you submitted from the Web client was added to the back-end database. If so, your screen should look similar to Figure 9-5.

10. Verify that the composite primary key will limit the number of entries a customer can enter to one. Using your browser's Back button, resubmit the data. The composite primary key should prevent the CGI application from adding a duplicate entry for the same user and return an error message as shown in Figure 9-6.

Figure 9-4

Web Client Response from Web Server via CGI Application

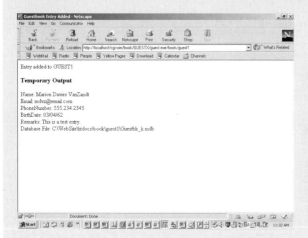

Figure 9-5

Updated tblGuestbook_Entries

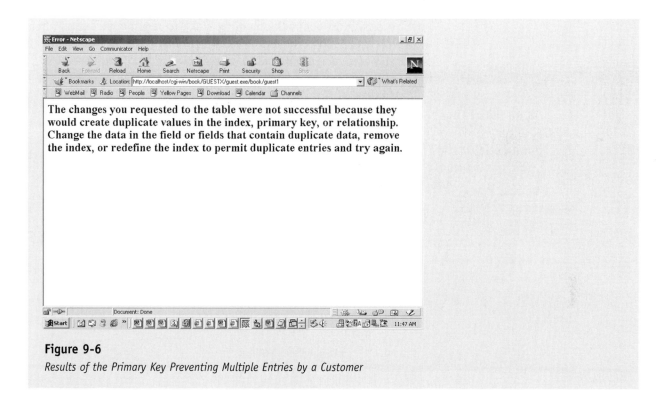

Figure 9-6

Results of the Primary Key Preventing Multiple Entries by a Customer

9.4 Trapping Database-Related Errors

The error message that was returned in the previous exercise is an excellent example of how the back-end of the Web database construction can use error handlers to maintain the integrity of the construction. When trapping a primary key violation, the CGI application, through Visual Basic, sets an **Err variable** with that error code before passing content to the currently active error-handling procedure. The Err object is a built-in object that exists in all Visual Basic programs. This object contains several properties and two methods. Each time an error occurs in the program, the Err object properties are filled with information you can use within your program. **Error** is a second Visual Basic built-in object. The Error object is a child object of the DBEngine. It can be used to obtain additional details on the nature of the database errors that occur in a program. It should be noted that Visual Basic does allow the use of a global error handler. Typical of most object-oriented languages, after Visual Basic travels up the procedure stack to locate the error handler, it cannot travel back down the stack to resume execution after the error has been corrected. It is for this reason that the use of local error handlers is recommended in the CGI application.

Kanthaka Farms
Adding Error Handling
Procedural Code to the
CGI Application

In this exercise, you will modify your CGI application so that the output value of the Err variable will be displayed when a duplicate entry by the same customer is submitted, violating the primary key data integrity rules.

1. Launch Visual Basic and open the Guest.vbp project located in the C:\WebSite\cgi-win\Book\Guest folder.

2. Make sure Module1 (Template.bas) module is active and modify the HandleError procedure as follows:

```
Public Sub HandleError()
  Send ("Content-type: text/html")
  Send ("")
  Send ("</TITLE></HEAD><BODY>")
  Send ("Error")
  Send ("</TITLE></HEAD><BODY>")
  If ErrorMessage = "" Then
    Send ("<H2>" & Error$ & "</H2>")
    Send ("<BR>Err = " & Err)
  Else
    Send ("<H2>" & ErrorMessage & "</H2>")
  End If
  Send ("</BODY>")
  Send ("</HTML>")
End Sub
```

3. Save the project and recompile the executable file.

4. Verify that your Web server software is running.

5. Test the updated CGI application by resubmitting the same Web client request to the Web server as in the previous exercise. The returned response should now display a 3022 error code value associated with the primary key violation as shown is Figure 9-7.

6. Now modify the HandleError procedure with the following code:

```
Public Sub HandleError()
  Send ("Content-type: text/html")
  Send ("")
  Send ("<HTML>")
  Send ("<HEAD>")
  Send ("<TITLE>Error</TITLE>")
```

```
    Send ("</HEAD><BODY>")
    Select Case Err
      Case 3022
        ErrorMessage = "<H2>Thank you for sending us your
    information earlier. It has already been added.</H2>"
    End Select
    If ErrorMessage = "" Then
      Send ("<H2>" & Error$ & "</H2>")
      Send ("<BR>Err = " & Err)
    Else
      Send (ErrorMessage)
    End If
    Send ("</BODY>")
    Send ("</HTML>")
End Sub
```

7. Save the project and recompile the executable file.

8. Again, test the updated CGI application by resubmitting the same Web client request to the Web server as in the previous exercise. The returned response should now display a user-defined error code value associated with the primary key violation, as shown in Figure 9-8.

Figure 9-7

Results of Err Variable Error Handling

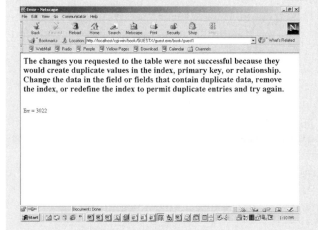

Figure 9-8

Results of User-Defined Error Message

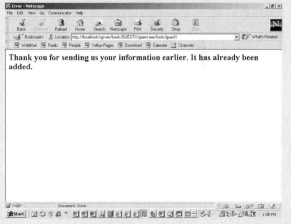

9.5 Listing Existing Back-End Records

The first record in the underlying record source is set as the current record of the Recordset when a Recordset object is created. When using a dynaset Recordset object, virtual tables are created in memory from physical tables. As needed for the electronic commerce model, they are dynamic, not static, copies of the data table. When a customer alters the underlying data table by modifying, adding, or deleting records from the front-end of the Web database construction, the changes in the Recordset can be seen as soon as it is refreshed. Refreshing the Recordset can be done using the **Refresh method**, by moving the record pointer using the arrow keys of the data control (which refreshes only the records read, not the entire Recordset), or by using one of the **Move methods**. The following syntax is used for the Move method:

```
rs.Move rows[,start]
```

where the start parameter is defined in terms of a **bookmark**. This bookmark is a unique string assigned by the Jet Database Engine to every record in the Recordset.

The Move methods offer the most basic form of record searching. There are four methods you can apply to the Recordset object:

- *MoveFirst:* This method moves the record pointer to the first record in the dataset. It is the same as clicking the double-headed arrow on the left side of the data control.
- *MovePrevious:* This method moves the record pointer to the record just before the current record. It is the same as clicking the single-headed arrow on the left side of the data control.
- *MoveNext:* This method moves the record pointer to the record just after the current record. It is the same as clicking the single-headed arrow on the right side of the data control.
- *MoveLast:* This method moves the record pointer directly to the last record in the dataset. It is the same as clicking the double-headed arrow on the right side of the data control.

In this exercise, you will explore how to list back-end database entries from the Web client using the Move method.

Kanthaka Farms
Listing Entries in the
Kanthaka Farms Database
from the Web Client

1. Launch Visual Basic and open the Guestlist.vbp project located in the C:\WebSite\cgi-win\Book\Guestx folder.

2. Make sure the Module1(Template.bas) module is active and add the following variable declarations in the Declaration section of the module:

```
Dim ws As Workspace
Dim db As Database
Dim rs As Recordset
```

3. Create a Recordset object for the tblGuestbook_Entries by modifying the SelectDataFromGuestbook procedure in the same module. The code for the procedure should be written as follows:

```
Public Sub SelectDataFromGuestbook()
  DataBaseFile = CGI_PhysicalPath & "\GUESTBK_K.MDB"
  Set ws = DBEngine.Workspaces(0)
  Set db = ws.OpenDatabase(DataBaseFile)
  Set rs = db.OpenRecordset("tblGuestbook_Entries")
End Sub
```

4. Modify the GenerateResponse procedure in the same module to list the back-end database table entries. The code needed to perform this task is:

```
Public Sub GenerateResponse()
  Send ("Content-type: text/html")
  Send ("")
  Send ("<HTML>")
  Send ("<HEAD>")
  Send ("<TITLE>Guestbook Listing")
  Send ("</TITLE>")
  Send ("</HEAD>")
  Send ("<BODY>")
  If rs.EOF Then
    Send ("<H2>Kanthaka Farms has no entries for you to
  view.</H2>")
    Exit Sub
  End If
  Send ("<H2>The following entries were added at Kanthaka
   Farms after ")
  Send ("<OL>")
  Do Until rs.EOF
    Send ("<LI><B>Date Added: </B> " & rs!StartingDate)
    Send ("<BR><B>Name: </B> " & rs!Name)
    Send ("<BR><B>Email: </B> " & rs!Email)
```

```
    If Not IsNull(rs!PhoneNumber) Then
       Send ("<BR><B>PhoneNumber: </B> " & rs!PhoneNumber)
    End If
    If Not IsNull(rs!BirthDate) Then
       Send ("<BR><B>BirthDate: </B> " & rs!BirthDate)
    End If
    If Not IsNull(rs!Remarks) Then
       Send ("<BR><B>Remarks: </B> " & rs!Remarks)
    End If
    Send ("<P>")
    rs.MoveNext
  Loop
  Send ("</OL>")
  Send ("</BODY>")
  Send ("</HTML>")
End Sub
```

5. Ensure that your Web server is running. Open the following URL location:

http://localhost/book/guest1/gblist1_k.htm

Request to view entries with a starting date after 6/1/01 and click on the View button.

6. The current contents of the back-end database will be returned to your Web client and will look like that shown in Figure 9-9.

Figure 9-9

Accessing Back-End Records from a Front-End Web Client

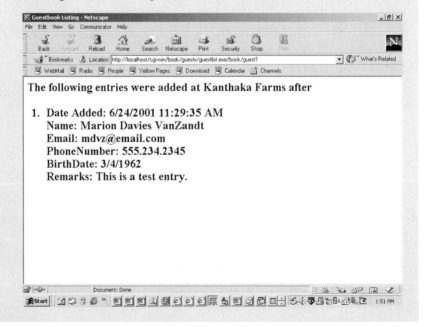

9.6 Locating Records in the Back-End Database That Meet Specific Criteria

The fastest way to locate a specific record is to use the **Seek method** on a table object. The Seek method performs an indexed search for the first occurrence of the record that matches the index criteria. First, it prompts the Web client to enter a value for which to search. Second, the code confirms that the customer, through the Web client, entered a value, and then performs the Seek operation. After performing the Seek operation, the code uses the **NoMatch method** to get the results of the Seek operation. The results of the search can then be posted in a message box or returned as an ad hoc form. However, if the search was successful, the new record is often loaded into the form controls.

The following code can be used for the Seek procedure:

```
rs.Index = "Index Name"
```

It should be noted that while the Seek method is the fastest search method, it can only be applied to Recordset objects opened as table objects. To locate a specific record in a dynaset or snapshot Recordset object, one of the Find methods should be used.

Using the Find Method of a Dynaset Recordset Object

Dynaset and snapshot Recordset objects do not use indexes; therefore, the Seek method cannot be used to search for specific records within them. The **Find method** is used to locate specific records in non-table objects. The Find method performs a sequential search, starting at the beginning of the dataset and looking at each record until it finds one that matches the search criteria. Obviously, this method will not be as fast as the Seek method; however, it is still faster than using the Move methods to handle this operation within the middleware code.

The Find methods are specified as follows:

```
rs.{FindFirst|FindPrevious|FindNext|FindLast} Criteria
```

The syntax is almost identical to a SQL WHERE clause. Note that there are four Find methods: **FindFirst**, **FindPrevious**, **FindNext**, and **FindLast**. The FindFirst method starts its search from the beginning of the file. The FindLast method starts its search from the end of the file and works its way to the beginning. The FindPrevious and FindNext methods are used to continue a search that can return more than one record.

Kanthaka Farms
Using the Find Method to
List Records from the
Back-End Database

In this exercise, you will explore how to use the Find method to retrieve records in the Kanthaka Farms back-end database.

1. Launch Visual Basic and open the Guestlist.vbp project located in the C:\WebSite\cgi-win\Book\Guestx folder.

2. Make sure the Module1(Template.bas) module is active and modify the Recordset object in the SelectDataFromGuestbook procedure of the project:

```
Set rs = db.OpenRecordset("tblGuestbook_Entries",
   dbOpenDynaset)
```

3. Modify the GenerateResponse procedure so that it is coded as follows:

```
Public Sub GenerateResponse()
  Dim Criteria As String
  Send ("Content-type: text/html")
  Send ("")
  Send ("<HTML>")
  Send ("<HEAD>")
  Send ("<TITLE>Guestbook Listing")
  Send ("</TITLE>")
  Send ("</HEAD>")
  Send ("<BODY>")
  If rs.EOF Then
    Send ("<H2>Kanthaka Farms has no entries for you to
  view.</H2>")
    Exit Sub
  End If
  Criteria = "StartingDate >= #" & StartingDate & "#"
  rs.FindFirst Criteria
  If rs.NoMatch Then
    Send ("<H2>There are no entries to Kanthaka Farms added
  since " & StartingDate & ".</H2>")
    Exit Sub
  End If
  Send ("<H2>The following entries were added at Kanthaka
   Farms on or after " & StartingDate & ".</H2>")
  Send ("<OL>")
  Do Until rs.NoMatch
    Send ("<LI><B>Date Added: </B> " & rs!StartingDate)
    Send ("<BR><B>Name: </B> " & rs!Name)
    Send ("<BR><B>Email: </B> " & rs!Email)
    If Not IsNull(rs!PhoneNumber) Then
      Send ("<BR><B>PhoneNumber: </B> " & rs!PhoneNumber)
    End If
```

```
        If Not IsNull(rs!BirthDate) Then
          Send ("<BR><B>BirthDate: </B> " & rs!BirthDate)
        End If
        If Not IsNull(rs!Remarks) Then
          Send ("<BR><B>Remarks: </B> " & rs!Remarks)
        End If
        Send ("<P>")
        rs.FindNext Criteria
      Loop
      Send ("</OL>")
      Send ("</BODY>")
      Send ("</HTML>")
End Sub
```

4. Ensure that your Web server is running. Open the following URL location:

`http://localhost/book/guest1/gblist1_k.htm`

Request to view entries with a starting date after today's date and click on the View button.

5. The current contents of the back-end database will be returned to your Web client and will look like that shown in Figure 9-10.

Figure 9-10

Viewing the Back-End Database with Specific Find Criteria

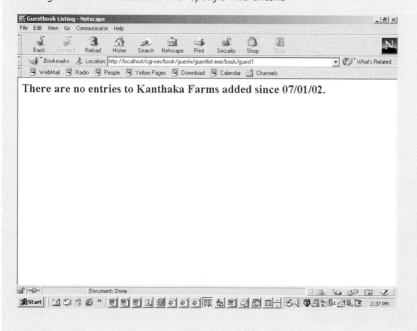

9.7 Applying Analyzing and Filtering Techniques to the Back-End Database

The Seek and Find methods are excellent resources to use to search for records after a Recordset has been created. Finding records with specific criteria can also be accomplished by specifying a query or an SQL string as the source of the Recordset in the OpenRecordset method. Visual Basic–stored queries must be used, however, when the source query contains one or more parameters in either the search criteria or a calculated field. **QueryDef objects** are the collection of SQL queries stored in the database. These stored queries, or QueryDefs, can also be used as replacements for the complete SQL statement on either side of a UNION keyword. The QueryDef object contains information about a stored SQL query. SQL queries can be used as record sources for the Visual Basic data control or as the first parameter in the Recordset object. QueryDef objects run faster than inline SQL queries because Visual Basic must go through a processing step before executing an SQL query. Stored queries, or QueryDef objects, are stored in their processed format. Using QueryDef objects means there is one less processing step to go through before the customer at the front-end of the Web database construction sees the business' back-end data. They can be created so that the QueryDef is not added to the QueryDefs collection by executing the CreateQueryDef method with an empty name:

```
set qd = db.CreateQueryDef("")
```

The SQL property of the query is then completed and executed to return the resulting dataset. When the query is closed, it is destroyed rather than being saved to the QueryDefs collection. This is extremely important in a Web database construction where it is important to execute dynamic SQL statements; however, it is inefficient to create and delete QueryDefs at runtime.

There are two basic methods for obtaining results from QueryDefs: Execute and OpenRecordset. The **Execute method** is used to perform an **SQL action query**. Action queries are SQL statements that perform some action on the data table. Examples of action queries are SQL statements that

■ Add, modify, or remove table records
■ Add indexes or relationship rules
■ Add, modify, or remove tables from the database

The OpenRecordset method is also used with QueryDefs. This method is used to retrieve data from the tables into a programming object for manipulation. **Parameter queries** are most often used when filtering records based on a criterion that varies in its condition values, as in the Kanthaka Farms starting date guestbook entries. These parameter queries are efficient in the Web database construction since they eliminate the elaborate steps of constructing an SQL statement, while giving flexibility in modifying the query design without changing the CGI source code. The code to use the QueryDef data access object with a parameter-based Recordset is as follows:

```
Declare qd As QueryDef ` declares a variable for the QueryDef
   object

Set qd = db.QueryDefs![ParameterQueryName] ` sets the variable
   to point
Set qd = db.QueryDefs("ParameterQueryName") ` definition of
   the parameter query

qd![ParameterQueryName] = ParameterValue ` assigns specific
   values
qd("ParameterQueryName") = ParameterValue ` parameter query

Set rs = qd.OpenRecordset() ` creates the recordset
```

In this exercise, you will explore how to use the QueryDef object to filter records through a parameter query.

Kanthaka Farms
Filtering Records with the
QueryDef Object

1. Open the Guestbk_K.mdb in the C:\WebSite\HTDOCS\BOOK\ GUEST1 folder.

2. Design a parameter query containing the starting date parameter in its criteria as shown in Figure 9-11. The SQL View should read:

```
SELECT DISTINCTROW tblGuestbook_Entries.*
FROM tblGuestbook_Entries
WHERE ((([tblGuestbook_Entries].[StartingDate])>=[Starting
   Date]));
```

Save the query as qryGuest_BegDate.

3. Open the Guestlist.vbp project if it is not running. Make sure the Module1(Template.bas) module is active and modify the Recordset object in the SelectDataFromGuestbook procedure of the project:

```
Public Sub SelectDataFromGuestbook()
   Dim qd As QueryDef
```

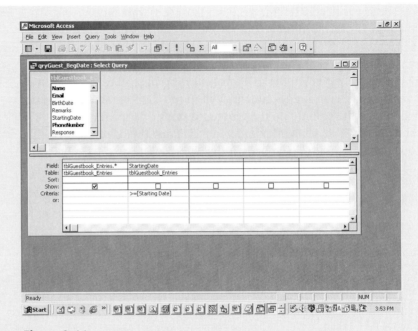

Figure 9-11

Designing the Parameter Query for the QueryDef Object

```
DataBaseFile = CGI_PhysicalPath & "\GUESTBK_K.MDB"
Set ws = DBEngine.Workspaces(0)
Set db = ws.OpenDatabase(DataBaseFile)
Set qd = db.QueryDefs![qryGuest_BegDate]
qd![Starting Date] = StartingDate
Set rs = qd.OpenRecordset()
End Sub
```

4. Ensure that your Web server is running. Open the following URL location:

`http://localhost/book/guest1/gblist1_k.htm`

Request to view entries with a starting date after today's date and click on the View button. Now request a starting date before today's date and click on View button. Verify that the results were returned to the Web client from the Web server correctly.

Summary

▪ **Use a database file for connectivity.** The primary data object used in Visual Basic programs is the Recordset object, which holds the collection of data records used in the Web database construction. There are three different types of Recordset objects: (1) the dynaset-type Recordset object, (2) the snapshot-type Recordset object, and (3) the table-type Recordset object. Access can be gained to an existing table in a database using any one of these three Recordset object types; however, each has its own unique properties and can behave quite differently at times. The Visual Basic table-type Recordset object performs record-oriented processing very effectively. The Visual Basic dynaset- and snapshot-type Recordset objects do not perform well on record-oriented processes.

▪ **Add a table record through Visual Basic.** Recordset objects are used to access and manipulate database records. This object can be used in a table, an SQL statement that returns records, or a query. The following generic syntax, using the database object's OpenRecordset method, is used to create the object:

```
Set rs = db.OpenRecordset(source[, type[, options]])
```

where source refers to the table name, SQL statement string, or query name. Type is the Recordset object type, and the options are set to restrict the front-end users' ability to view and edit records while the back-end database's Recordset is active.

▪ **Trap database related errors.** When trapping a primary key violation, the CGI application, through Visual Basic, sets an Err variable with that error code before passing content to the currently active error-handling procedure. The Err object is a built-in object that exists in all Visual Basic programs. This object contains several properties and two methods. Each time an error occurs in the program, the Err object properties are filled with information you can use within your program. Error is a second Visual Basic built-in object. The Error object is a child object of the DBEngine. It can be used to obtain additional details on the nature of the database errors that occur in a program. It should be noted that Visual Basic does allow the use of a global error handler.

■ **List existing records.** The first record in the underlying record source is set as the current record of the Recordset when a Recordset object is created. When using a dynaset Recordset object, virtual tables are created in memory from physical tables. As needed for the electronic commerce model, they are dynamic, not static, copies of the data table. When a customer alters the underlying data table by modifying, adding, or deleting records from the front-end of the Web database construction, the changes in the Recordset can be seen as soon as it is refreshed. Refreshing the Recordset can be done using the Refresh method, by moving the record pointer using the arrow keys of the data control, or by using the MoveFirst, MoveNext, MovePrevious, and MoveLast methods. Moving the pointer refreshes only the records read, not the entire Recordset. The following syntax is used for the Move method:

```
rs.Move rows[,start]
```

■ **Find records meeting specific criteria.** Dynaset and snapshot Recordset objects do not use indexes; therefore, the Seek method cannot be used to search for specific records within them. The Find method is used to locate specific records in non-Table objects. The Find method performs a sequential search, starting at the beginning of the dataset and looking at each record until it finds one that matches the search criteria. Obviously, this method will not be as fast as the Seek method; however, it is still faster than using the Move methods to handle this operation within the middleware code. The Find method is specified as follows:

```
rs.{FindFirst|FindPrevious|FindNext|FindLast} Criteria
```

■ **Analyze and filter records.** The Find is an excellent resource to use to search for records after a Recordset has been created. Finding records with specific criteria can also be accomplished by specifying a query or an SQL string as the source of the Recordset in the OpenRecordset method. Visual Basic–stored queries must be used, however, when the source query contains one of more parameters in either the search criteria or a calculated field. QueryDef objects are the collection of SQL queries stored in the database. These stored queries, or QueryDefs, can also be used as replacements for the complete SQL statement on either side of a UNION keyword. The QueryDef object contains information about a stored SQL query. SQL queries can be used as record sources for the Visual Basic data control or as the first parameter in the Recordset object. QueryDef objects run faster than inline SQL queries, because Visual Basic must go through a processing step before executing an SQL query. Stored queries, or QueryDef objects, are stored in their processed format. Using QueryDef objects means there is one less processing step to go through before the customer at the front-end of the Web database construction sees the business' back-end data. They can be created so that the QueryDef is not added to the QueryDefs collection by executing the CreateQueryDef method with an empty name:

```
set qd = db.CreateQueryDef("")
```

■ **Filter records through a parameter query.** The OpenRecordset method is also used with QueryDefs. This method is used to retrieve data from the tables into a programming object for manipulation. Parameter queries are most often used when filtering records based on a criterion that varies in its condition values, as in the Kanthaka Farms starting date guestbook entries. These parameter queries are efficient in the Web database construction since they eliminate the elaborate steps of constructing an SQL statement, while giving flexibility in modifying the query design without changing the CGI source code.

Chapter Key Terms

Application Programming
  Interface (API)
base table
bookmark
CreateDynaset method
Data Access Object (DAO)
data objects
database object
datset-oriented database systems
DBEngine object
dynaset-type Recordset objects
Err variable
Error object
Execute method
Filter variable
Find method

FindFirst method
FindLast method
FindNext method
FindPrevious method
generic back-end database
indexes
Microsoft Jet database engine
Microsoft Jet workspace
Move methods
MoveFirst method
MoveLast method
MoveNext method
MovePrevious method
NoMatch method
ODBC driver
ODBCDirect workspace

Open Database Connectivity
  (ODBC)
OpenRecordset method
Parameter query
QueryDef object
record-oriented database systems
Recordset object
Refresh method
Seek method
SET SQL command
snapshot-type Recordset objects
snippets
SQL action query
table-type Recordset objects
UPDATE SQL command
WHERE SQL command

Review Questions

1. What is a generic database? Why is it suggested that the back-end database be created as a generic database?

2. How does a composite primary key help in checking duplicate front-end Web client submissions?

3. What are data access objects? How are they used in the Web database construction?

4. Are Visual Basic Database objects dataset-oriented or record-oriented? Explain your answer.

5. What is the most common Visual Basic data object?

6. Do dynasets use a relatively large amount or small amount of workstation RAM? Why?

7. What are the weaknesses of using a dynaset object?

8. What are the main advantages of using the table data object?

9. What is the difference between a snapshot and a dynaset data object?

10. Which data object do you use to extract table and field names from a database definition?

11. What does the DBEngine object represent? What is its function in the electronic commerce model?

12. What is a workspace? What is a Recordset? What are the commonalities between the two?

13. What is the relationship between an object variable and the object it represents?

14. Discuss disadvantages to performing a sequential search to find selective records in a back-end database. What is an alternative to this method?

15. How are the Seek method and Find method approaches different? How are they similar?

16. What kinds of queries can be opened with the OpenDatabase method of the database object? What is the purpose of using these queries in the electronic commerce model?

17. What is an easy and efficient way to construct an SQL statement? Give an example.

18. How can back-end database records that have been produced by a parameter query be accessed by the Web client?

Critical Thinking Using the Web

1. Today Wells Fargo is one of the most Internet-savvy businesses in the financial services industry. One of their initiatives that utilizes the Web database construction model married with voice technology is their Talking ATMs. Talking ATMs are part of their commitment to provide services to diverse groups of customers, including those who are blind or have low vision. Wells Fargo has enhanced the ATM access for its vision-impaired customers in the state of California. Through voice instructions, the new Talking ATMs tell users who cannot read information on an ATM screen how to perform various transactions. Visit Wells Fargo at http://www.wellsfargo.com/ and learn more about this new technology. In a 200–400-word essay, discuss your findings and relate the importance of the technology to all sectors in the electronic commerce spectrum.

2. Should more businesses be concerned with meeting the needs of the disabled in their click-and-mortar businesses? There are many commendable efforts to champion the cause of improving Internet accessibility for the over half-billion people in the world who are disabled. Using your favorite search engine, explore some of the initiatives to address Internet Accessibility launched by governments, individuals, organizations, and companies. Write a 200–400-word essay discussing your findings. Be prepared to present your report in class.

3. There are different approaches to Web page design for the disabled. Awareness of the potential barriers and possible solutions should help Web page designers employ practices that will lead to the inclusion of all potential customers and visitors to a business' Web site. Investigate these areas:

- Improving the customers' access with browser preferences and other strategies
- Providing Web access for people who encounter vision, hearing, learning, or cognitive barriers to the click-and-mortar business
- Assistive devices and software to overcome physical barriers to the Web site

- Minimizing economic barriers to the Web site

Write your findings in a 2–4-page paper. Include specific techniques and tools in your report. How might your findings be included in the Kanthaka Farms Web site? Albatross Records?

Chapter Case Study

Albatross Records is a continuing case study in this book that illustrates the process of building electronic commerce with Web database constructions. In Chapter 9, you will connect to the back-end of Albatross Records Web database construction using Microsoft Access. As you continue through the text, you will complete different facets of electronic commerce Web database construction, resulting in a complete Web site for Albatross Records.

- Create a database back-end for Albatross Records. Be sure to review both your front-end and middleware variables to determine what fields will be required in the back-end of the Web database construction.
- Add 25 table records using Visual Basic. Do so by creating a Recordset object representing the table

in your database. Add the new record entry to this Recordset. Trap any primary key violation errors generated when adding the entry.

- List existing records using Move and Find methods.
- Analyze and filter records using either nonparameter queries or parameter queries. Query for the total entries in the database, the date of the oldest entry, and the date of the most recent entry. Be sure that if a parameter query is used, the variable for a QueryDef object is declared.
- Be prepared to demonstrate your Web database construction in class and justify your choice of design.

10

Active Server Pages
Server-Side Technologies

I think the opportunities for developers in this next decade will be phenomenal, not only taking the existing applications and doing them in a much better way with Web services, but enabling new applications, business efficiency, business communications, notifications when you need them, dealing in rich media types, taking knowledge workers and their efficiency to a whole new level. So it's distributed computing, the dream of distributed computing delivered across the Internet.

—Bill Gates, keynote speaker at Tech Ed 2001,
Atlanta, Georgia, June 19, 2001

10.1 Understanding Active Server Pages Server-Side Technology

As the electronic commerce business model developed, the need for dynamic interaction between customer and business resulted. Common Gateway Interface (CGI) and Internet Server Application Programming Interface (ISAPI) were designed to meet this need by enabling Web clients using HTML forms to send requests to executable programs running on the Web server. These gateway programs generate ad hoc HTML output that is sent back to the Web client. **Active Server Pages**, better known as ASP, a technology developed by Microsoft, is another server-side technology designed to meet the need for dynamic interaction between customer and business in the electronic commerce model. Primarily developed in VBScript, JavaScript, or PerlScript, ASP is integrated into the Hypertext Markup Language (HTML) of front-end Web pages. Conditional logic, loops, math, and string functions can be embedded into the HTML in ASP using these scripting languages. Initiated by the Web client, the Web server compiles the ASP code ad hoc, and the resulting output is standard HTML. By using ASP, Web pages can be dynamic, full of ever-changing content, and browser independent, all necessary components of successful electronic commerce designs.

ASP, like CGI, is a server-side technology. And like CGI, ASP allows Web database developers to create server-side, scripted templates that generate dynamic, interactive Web server applications. By embedding special programmatic codes in standard HTML pages, the customer can access data in a back-end business database, interact with ActiveX controls or Java components, or even create other types of dynamic output available from the business' Web site. The HTML output by ASP is also browser independent, which means that it can be read equally well by whichever Web client a customer may choose. Unlike CGI, however, ASP runs in the same processes as the Web server, and they are multithreaded, meaning ASP is generally faster than CGI applications and can handle larger numbers of users.

ASP can also be used with Extensible Markup Language (XML). XML is similar to HTML in that it contains markup symbols to describe the contents of a page or file. However, unlike HTML, which only describes the content of a Web page in terms of how it should be displayed by the Web client, XML is "extensible." This means that the markup elements of XML are self-defining and unlimited. Both XML and HTML are subsets of the Standard Generalized Markup Language (SGML), the standard for how to create a document structure. Though XML is simpler and easier to use than HTML, it is expected that both HTML and XML will be used together in ASP Web applications for some time.

The key concept behind ASP is to use the scripting language to access the methods and properties of objects. ASP provides a core set of objects, called the **Five Intrinsics**, which includes the **Application**, **Request**, **Response**, **Server**, and **Session objects**. These Five Intrinsics, together with their parent object, the **ScriptingContext object**, form the **ASP object model**, as seen in the simple ASP object model in Figure 10-1.

The ScriptingContext Object

The ScriptingContext object is the primary object in the ASP model. It exposes the interaction of the Web client to the electronic commerce model. Because the ScriptingContext object is always available to ASP applications, there is no need to explicitly reference it. This object contains the Five Intrinsics, the primary ASP built-in objects, and the **ObjectContext object**. Whenever a block of ASP code is run, the ScriptingContext object is automatically created, making the ASP Five Intrinsics available to the scripting host along with the scripting objects. At completion, when the scripting host finishes parsing an ASP page, it destroys the instance of ScriptingContext automatically. In Visual Basic, an instance of the ScriptingContext object is created to access the ASP object model. In the new Microsoft.Net environment, the WebClass feature performs this task.

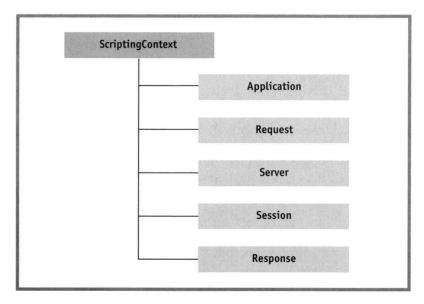

Figure 10-1
The Simple ASP Object Model

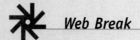 **Web Break**

The first Web server for Windows products was actually developed and sold by O'Reilly in 1995: WebSite. It was an extension of Bob Denny's original freeware httpd for Windows. At that time, 90 percent of the Web browsers were on Windows, but there were no Windows Web servers. For more information on the history of Web servers, visit the leading site for in-depth information on Web server software at http://webcompare.iworld.com/.

ObjectContext Object

The ObjectContext object is part of the **Component Object Model** (COM). ASP technology has evolved into an open technology framework and compile-free application environment that can take advantage of COM and Distributed Component Object Model (DCOM) objects with minimum effort. COM, like Common Object Request Broker Architecture (CORBA), is a framework for the inter-operation of distributed objects in a network. COM is Microsoft's framework for developing and supporting program component objects and provides the underlying services of client/server interface negotiation, determination of when an object can be removed from a system, and object event services. COM also includes **COM+**, DCOM, and ActiveX interfaces and programming tools. COM+ adds to COM a set of new system services for application components while they are running. For instance, COM+ can notify applications of significant events or ensure the application is authorized to run. As both an object-oriented architecture and a set of operating system services, COM+ is intended to provide a model that makes it relatively easy for electronic commerce developers to create business applications that work well with Microsoft Component Services, formerly Microsoft Transaction Server (MTS), in a Windows system. COM+ is seen by the electronic commerce industry as Microsoft's answer to the Sun Microsystems-IBM-Oracle approach known as Enterprise JavaBeans (EJB). Figure 10-2 shows an ASP model that includes the ObjectContext object as well as the Five Intrinsics' most used methods.

The ObjectContext object represents the scope under which an ASP script runs and is used to control ASP transactions that are managed by the Component Services. As such, it returns the built-in ASP objects and provides methods used to commit (complete) or abort transactions in the transaction processing.

In order to use the ObjectContext object, the **@Transaction directive** must be on the first line of the ASP page. The @Transaction directive causes a transaction to run to competition unless an abort occurs. The following methods and events are used with the ObjectContext object.

Methods Two methods are used with the ObjectContext object: the **SetAbort method** and the **SetComplete method**. The SetAbort method is used to declare that a transaction has not been completed and resources should not be updated. The SetComplete method declares that the transaction has been completed and resources can be updated.

Events The **OnTransactionAbort event** and the **OnTransactionCommit event** occur with the ObjectContext object. The SetAbort method explicitly aborts the transaction. The OnTransactionAbort event occurs when a transaction has been aborted because of a processing error. The signal of this event will run a handler script in the same file, if it exists. The OnTransactionCommit event occurs when a transaction has been successfully completed. The signal of this event will run a handler script in the same file, if it exists.

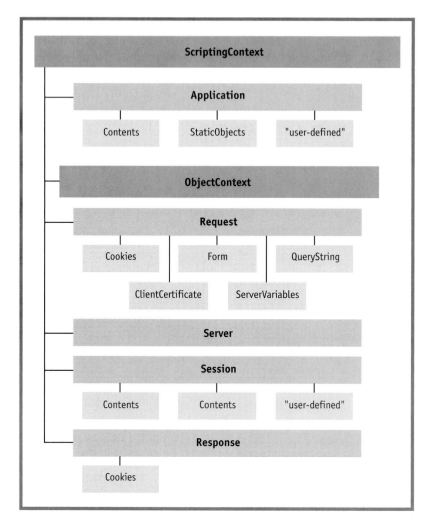

Figure 10-2
The ASP Object Model

Response Object

The Response object is used to send output to the Web client. Its vital capabilities include the following:

- Response.write
- Response.write alternate syntax <%= %>, which allows ASP to be placed in HTML
- Response.end, which effectively halts a script
- Response.redirect, which transfers control to another page

The syntax for the Response object is:

```
Response.collection|property|method
```

The Response object writes information into the HTML stream and sends that information to the Web client browser. It also supports a collection of cookies, where each cookie object contains information that can be written to the Web client system for later reading by the Request object.

Request Object

The Request object retrieves the values that the Web client has passed to the Web server during an HTTP request. It can receive all the data on the HTML form, as well as information about the current user. The Request object contains several collections, each of which represents a different set of information that can be returned to the Web client. The **ClientCertificate collection** retrieves the certification fields from a request issued by the Web browser. Each ClientCertificate object in the ClientCertificate collection represents a certificate field that the Web client returns and that identifies the client. Before the ClientCertificate collection can be used, the Web server must be configured to request client certificates.

The **Cookies collection** contains a set of Web cookies, where each cookie contains a small amount of information about the Web user. The Forms collection contains a set of Form objects, and each object represents an HTML form. The **QueryString collection** contains a set of added URL arguments, and the **ServerVariables collection** contains a set of server environment variables.

The syntax for the Request object follows:

```
Request.collection|property|method|(variable)
```

If the specified variable is not in the ClientCertificate, Cookies, Form, QueryString, or ServerVariables collections, then the Request object returns "empty."

Application Object

The Application object stores information that persists for the entire lifetime of an ASP application, generally the entire time that the Web server is running. It is used by all active Web sessions to share information among all users of an ASP application. The Application object contains the **Contents collection** and the **StaticObjects col-**

lection. Each Contents object in the Contents collection contains all the items used in ActiveX script commands and adds them to the Web application. The StaticObjects collection contains all the objects used in the HTML <Object> tag and adds them to the Web application. In addition, the Application object can contain user-defined objects that the Web application creates, and multiple users can share it.

Specifically, an ASP-based application is defined as all the .asp files in a virtual directory and associated subdirectories. All the variables created with Application object have application level scope, meaning that they are accessible to all the users. All .asp pages in a virtual directory and its subdirectories come under the application scope. Therefore, more than one user shares application level variables at a time. Because more than one user can share the Application object, **Lock** and **Unlock methods** are provided to ensure that multiple users do not try to alter a property simultaneously.

The syntax for the Application object follows:

```
Application.method
```

Server Object

The Server object provides access to methods and properties on the Web server. Most of these methods and properties serve as utility functions. The syntax for the Server object follows:

```
Server.property|method
```

The Server object contains four miscellaneous methods that the server performs; the most used of which is CreateObject, which allows an instance of an ASP component to be created.

The methods and their properties for the Server object are shown in Table 10-1.

Session Object

Like the Application object, the Session object provides the virtual memory for a Web application to run correctly and retain state. In addition, it maintains information that relates to the current Web session. Though the Session object is much like the Application object, the Application object pertains to all Web users, whereas the Session object refers only to the current Web session. The collection of **Contents objects** in the Session object contains all the items used for script commands to be added to the Web session. The

Table 10-1	Server Object Methods and Properties
Methods	Properties
CreateObject	Creates an instance of the object, a component, application, or a scripting object. By giving its *CLSID* or *ProgID* in the *Server.CreateObject* method, the component can be instantiated.
Execute	Executes the given *.asp* page and then returns the control to the page called the method. This method is used to execute another *.asp* page without leaving the current page, and then control is passed back to the calling page.
GetLastError	Returns an *ASPError* object, which can be used to retrieve information about the last error that occurred in the ASP script.
HTMLEncode	Provides HTML encoding to a given string. All nonlegal HTML characters are converted to their equivalent HTML entity.
MapPath	Maps the specified virtual or relative path into the physical path of the Web server.
Transfer	Transfers the control of the page to another page specified in the URL. Control of the page is not returned to the page calling the *Server.Transfer* method, unlike *Execute*.
URLEncode	Provides URL encoding to a given string. For example: *Server.URLEncode "http://www.psacake.com"* returns *http%3A%2F%2Fwww%2Epsacake%2Ecom*.

ObjectContext object provides access to the current object's context. It typically **instantiates** MTS objects or controls database transactions. To instantiate is to create a particular realization of an abstraction, such as a class of object or a computer process, by defining one particular variation of object within a class, giving it a name, and locating it in some physical place.

ASP and Connectivity

Powerful electronic commerce constructions can be built with ASP scripting languages and these built-in objects. In addition, for complex business logic or connectivity pointers, custom objects can be used. These custom objects can be built in a variety of languages, including Visual Basic, Delphi (Pascal), C++, and Java on a Windows NT platform, or C++ and Java on a Unix platform. With simple scripting languages and language choices for building components, the ASP environment maximizes the productivity of Web database construction development resources.

The fact that ASP processes at the Web server allows connectivity to other server services and function libraries. Like CGI, ASP can connect to any ODBC-compliant back-end database such as Access, Paradox, Microsoft SQL Server, FoxPro, or Oracle. ASP makes database interaction easy through another object, the **ActiveX Data Objects** (ADO). ADO is a powerful, yet standard **application program interface** from Microsoft for accessing a wide variety of relational and nonrelational databases. As part of ActiveX, ADO is also part of Microsoft's overall COM. ADO evolved from an earlier Microsoft data interface, **Remote Data Objects (RDO)**, which works with Microsoft's ODBC to access relational databases, but not nonrelational databases such as IBM's ISAM and VSAM.

ADO is an object-oriented programming interface and part of Microsoft's overall data access strategy called **Universal Data Access** for universal access to all kinds of existing and future databases. Universal Data Access works with a **bridge program** between the database and Microsoft's **OLE DB**, the low-level interface to databases. OLE DB is the underlying system service that a programmer using ADO is actually using. To conform to Microsoft's vision of a Universal Data Access model, electronic commerce developers are being encouraged to move from **Data Access Objects** (DAO), still widely used, to ADO and its low-level interface with databases, OLE DB.

DAO is an application program interface available with Microsoft's Visual Basic that lets a programmer request access to a back-end Microsoft Access database. DAO was Microsoft's first object-oriented interface with databases. DAO objects include, or **encapsulate**, Access's Jet functions. Through Jet functions, DAO can also access other Structured Query Language (SQL) databases, like Oracle. ADO and OLE DB offer a faster interface that is also easier to program.

In addition to the Intrinsic objects and ADO, ASP includes several other important objects. For example, the **FileSystem object** provides access to the server's file system, and the **BrowseCap object** lists the capabilities of a user's browser.

10.2 Installing Chili!Soft ASP

Chili!Soft ASP is ASP technology with server-side, object-oriented components to provide an integrated Web development environment. Chili!Soft ASP allows the use of any scripting language supported by the Web server and gives Web database developers the technology to easily build powerful database and component-driven applications. Web database constructions can be created by combining HTML, server-side scripting, and server components with Chili!Soft ASP. The Five Intrinsic Objects are included to eliminate much of the overhead associated with low-level programming in the electronic commerce design, allowing developers the freedom to focus on the task of creating interesting, interactive Web content. However, for Web database constructions requiring more powerful programming, COM objects can be created to process data and deliver output with Chili!Soft ASP scripts. The Chili!Soft ASP environment also allows the use of JavaBeans, EJBs, and CORBA objects in the same manner.

To easily manipulate Web applications without specific knowledge of a particular Web server's ISAPI or CGI interface, the Chili!Soft ASP engine provides Web developers direct interaction with the Web server. Chili!Soft ASP is the exact functional and syntactic equivalent of Microsoft's ASP, which is included with the Internet Information Server (IIS). Using Chili!Soft ASP, ASP applications can be developed to run on nearly every Web server under Sun Solaris, IBM AIX, Hewlett Packard HP-UX, Linux, and Windows platforms. In addition, applications developed with Chili!Soft ASP are portable across enterprise servers.

Installation of Chili!Soft ASP on Windows Systems

To install Chili!Soft ASP on a Microsoft Windows operating system, you must be using Windows NT 4.0, SP 3 or higher, or Windows 2000 Professional or Server, SP 1 or higher. Numerous Web servers can be used with Chili!Soft ASP including WebSite, Netscape Enterprise, Apache, or Lotus Domino. Other installation requirements include the following:

Hardware

- 128mb RAM (256 recommended)
- Pentium class processor ($\times$86)
- 100mb free hard drive space

Database

- Any database for which you have an ODBC driver

FrontPage support

■ FrontPage 2000 Server Extensions are supported

Other

■ Administrator privileges

Before installing Chili!Soft ASP, verify that all Web servers have been stopped. The Setup program cannot properly configure Chili!Soft ASP if any Web servers are running. Running applications using ODBC or OLE DB can also prevent the proper installation.

A newer version of **Microsoft Data Access Components (MDAC)** must be installed, because it contains ADO and ODBC drivers, which are required for database connectivity. In order to have the Chili!Soft ASP installer install a newer version of MDAC, select to install the Chili!Soft ASP samples and confirm that the newer version of MDAC is desired.

Kanthaka Farms
Install Chili!Soft ASP Software
and Change Web Server
Mappings

Kanthaka Farms is a continuing case study in this book that illustrates the process of building electronic commerce with Web database constructions. In Chapter 10, you will install Chili!Soft ASP software and create ASP server-side files. As you continue through the text, you will complete different facets of electronic commerce Web database construction, resulting in a complete Web site for Kanthaka Farms.

1. Access the secure Web site for this book and locate the software folder in which Chili!Soft ASP is located. The installation executable is casp30.exe. Double-click on the file.

2. Follow the instructions of the installation wizard. If prompted, choose to install the software to C:\Website. Upon completion, click on Finish and restart your computer.

3. Verify that your installation has been fully completed. From Windows Explorer, you should see a new folder named CHILIASP in the C:\WebSite folder.

4. Once the software has been installed, you must add two new mappings to your WebSite Server Properties. From the Start menu, choose Programs, WebSite, Server Properties.

5. Choose the Mapping tab at the top of the Server Properties window. Verify that the Documents option button of the Mapping Types is selected. Create a mapping to the Kanthaka Farms .asp files that you will create later in this chapter. To do so, in the Document URL path text box type:

`/kasp/`

and in the Directory (Full local path or UNC) text box type:

`C:\WebSite\CHILIASP\Samples\Kanthaka`

6. Click on Add and repeat the process to add a mapping for Albatross Records. To do so, in the Document URL path text box type:

`/aasp/`

Figure 10-3

Web Server Mapping after Chili!Soft Installation

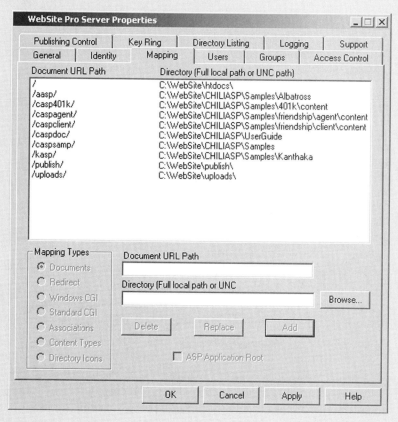

and in the Directory (Full local path or UNC) text box type:

```
C:\WebSite\CHILIASP\Samples\Albatross
```

7. Click on Add.

8. Verify that the Web server mapping matches that shown in Figure 10-3.

10.3 Exploring the ASP Code

Creating an ASP application is similar to creating a CGI application. It begins with an HTML file. With ASP, however, there is some additional code, separated from the HTML markup by a different delimiter:

```
<% ASP Code evaluated here %>
```

A sample page might look something like this:

```
<%@ Language=VBScript %>
<HTML>
<HEAD>
<TITLE>ASP Sample</TITLE>
</HEAD>
<BODY>
<P> </P>
<% Response.Write("A Sample ASP Page!") %>
</BODY>
</HTML>
```

ASP code looks a lot like HTML tags. However, instead of starting and ending with lesser than (<) and greater than (>) brackets, it typically starts with <% and ends with %>. The <% is called an **opening tag**, and the %> is called a **closing tag**. In between these tags are the server-side scripts, which can be inserted anywhere in the Web page, even inside HTML tags.

Remember that ASP uses **server-side scripts**. A server-side script is a program, or sequence of instructions, that is interpreted or carried out by another program rather than by the computer processor. Languages like Practical Extraction and Reporting Language, the IBM mainframe language Restructured Extended Executor, JavaScript, and Tcl/Tk were created with the express purpose of being scripting languages. In the electronic commerce model, Perl and VBScript are often written to handle HTML forms input or other services for a business' Web site and are processed on the Web server. JavaScript script, however, is not server-side. In a Web page, JavaScript runs client-side on the customer's Web browser.

Script languages are generally easier to learn and faster to code in than the more structured and compiled languages and are ideal for programs of very limited capability or those that can reuse and tie together existing compiled programs. A script takes longer to run than a compiled program, since each instruction is being handled by another program first rather than directly by the basic instruction processor, requiring additional instructions and more time.

10.4 Creating an ASP Application

In this exercise, you create a simple ASP file to display a time and welcome greeting on the Kanthaka Farms Web site.

1. From Windows Explorer, create a new folder named Kanthaka in the C:\WebSite\CHILIASP\Samples.

2. In a text editor like Notepad, write the following code:

```
<HTML><HEAD>
<TITLE>Step 1 ASP</TITLE>
</HEAD>
<BODY BGCOLOR="#00FF00">
<P ALIGN="CENTER"><IMG SRC="KAN_LOGO.gif" width="121"
    height="97"></P>
<H1 ALIGN=CENTER>
Today is <%=now%> and all is well<br>
<%if hour(now())>=12 THEN%>
Good Afternoon from Kanthaka Farms!
<%ELSE%>
Good Morning from Kanthaka Farms!
<%END IF%>
</H1>
</BODY></HTML>
```

Notice that the background color will be green and that the Kanthaka Farms logo is inserted into the ASP. Be sure that the KAN_LOGO.gif file is in the same folder as your ASP file, or the picture will not appear on the Web client's browser.

3. Launch your Web server software. In a browser window, type in the following URL:

```
http://localhost/kasp/time.asp
```

Your ASP should look similar to Figure 10-4.

Kanthaka Farms
Creating Your First Active Server Page

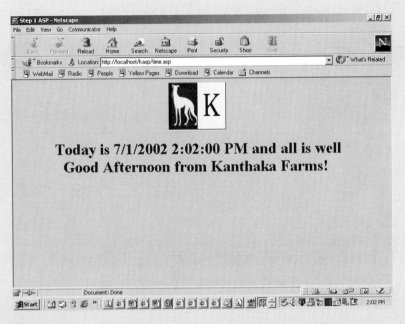

Figure 10-4
A Simple Time ASP for Kanthaka Farms

In the time.asp file, upon request, the Web Server finds the file and processes all the ASP code between <% and %> before handing back the page. The code between <% and %> never arrives at the browser. The ASP compiler retrieves the ASP page and interprets all the <% %> markers before the browser sees the page. If the time is before 12 P.M., the Kanthaka Farms customer at the browser receives a "Good Morning from Kanthaka Farms!" message. If the time is 12 o'clock or after, then the Kanthaka Farms customer at the browser receives a "Good Afternoon from Kanthaka Farms!" message.

10.5 Creating an ASP Page with Banner Ads

If you have visited any business on the Web recently, you have seen those horizontal rectangular banners that urge customers to "click here" for a FREE offer. Banner advertising is almost as new as the Web itself and has become nearly as ubiquitous. HotWired ran the first banner in 1994, with outstanding results: a nearly 50 percent **click-through rate** (CTR). CTR is a measurement based on the number of customer Web responses, called clicks. Clicks are commonly

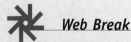

Web Break

Case-Based Reasoning (CBR) is a way of solving new problems by using solutions that have worked in the past. It is both a methodology to model human reasoning and thinking and a way for building intelligent computer systems. It is especially applicable to electronic commerce, because it enables businesses to increase efficiency and reduce costs by substantially automating processes such as diagnosis, scheduling, and design. Electronic commerce is touted as "currently the hottest commercial application field for CBR," particularly in the areas of intelligent search and customer support. Discover more about CBR incorporation into electronic commerce applications at http://www.cbr-web. org/CBR-Web/?info=fields&menu=f.

used to count the number of customers who click on the banner and are transferred to the advertiser's site. The click-through rate is the percentage of click-throughs to banner views; for example, a 1 percent CTR indicates that 1 percent of each 1000 banner views, or 10 customers, has clicked through.

Today's Web customers seem to be less enamored of banners as an advertising medium than they were in 1994. Today, if a banner gets a 1 percent click-through rate, it is considered a top performer. Despite their decline in performance, banner ads remain the most widely used form of online promotion. Other programs and media are now competing directly with banner ads for online marketing dollars and click-throughs. While the CTR has greatly declined since the medium's inception, the number of businesses using banner advertising continues to increase. One recent study by Forrester Research predicts that online advertising spending will increase nearly sixfold in the next four years, rising from 1.3 percent of all advertising spending to over 8 percent of total spending. If the study is correct, banner ads will account for $22 billion per year.

Types of Banner Advertising

There are three types of banner advertising: **click-through**, **brand-awareness**, and **sell-through**. Each type of banner advertising can be equally effective at building brand awareness, generating click-throughs, and boosting sales. However, although individual banners often accomplish all three objectives, the most effective are designed and implemented to accomplish only one of these major goals at a time.

Click -Through Banners Click-through banners are measured on a **cost per click** (CPC) basis. With CPC, advertisers only pay when a customer actually clicks on the banner. Though it has high advertiser appeal, CPC is not the type of banner ad most widely used. Businesses often choose not to incorporate banner ads from other businesses because they do not meet their design and quality standards. The cost of CPC ranges from $0.01 per click up to $0.75. Businesses measure their **return on investment** (ROI) on click-through banners by dividing the value of the customer traffic that the banner ad brings to the site by the total cost of the advertising.

Brand-Awareness Banners The purpose of brand-awareness banners is to build positive awareness for the business. Brand-awareness is a marketing strategy to identify the business' products with a name, phrase, design, or symbol to distinguish them from those of the competitors. The business' brand can elicit an immediate image or emotion from customers.

It is difficult to measure ROI for brand-awareness banners. Businesses often use before-and-after surveys to quantify the success of brand-awareness banners; however, this approach has not met with much success. Instead, most brand-awareness banner success is measured on a **cost per thousand** (CPM, or cost per mille) basis. Using CPM, businesses pay either a site or advertising network a set amount for the banners. The price may range from $1 to $200 for each 1,000 displays or impressions of its banner. If Kanthaka Farms were to buy 100,000 impressions on a Web site that charges a $100 CPM, they would pay $10,000. The $100 CPM is multiplied by the 100,000 impressions to arrive at the total cost. When ROI is calculated on brand-awareness banners, the value placed by the business on the increased awareness of its brand is divided by the cost of the brand-awareness banners.

Sell-Through Banners Sell-through banners result in immediate sales and are used to generate revenue quickly. They use ploys to induce customers to come and buy. **Loss-leader pricing** is used to deliberately sell a product below its customary price to attract attention to it and the business. The purpose of loss-leader pricing is not to increase sales of the item, but to attract customers to the business with the intent that once there, they will buy other products as well. However, the loss-leader approach *only* works when the business is also able to sell high-margin items.

Sell-through campaigns are measured on a **cost per action** (CPA) basis. With CPA, the advertiser only pays when a specific action, in this case the completion of a sale, occurs. CPA provides excellent accountability, but is very costly. ROI on sell-through banners is calculated by dividing the total sales generated by the total cost of the sell-through banners.

An ASP Banner Strategy

One example of an ASP banner ad strategy is to show different ads each time customers access the business' page from its Web server. An effective ASP banner system is based on a randomizer that will ensure that the banners appear in random order.

In this exercise, you will use ASP server-side scripting to create banner ads for Kanthaka Farms. The ads will be limited to a maximum number of 10.

Kanthaka Farms
Using ASP Server-Side Scripting to Create Banner Ads

1. Launch your Web server software. Verify that it is running by viewing it in the tray.

2. Using a simple text editor, create a file named Ban_Demo.asp with the code below. Save the file in the C:\WebSite\CHILIASP\ Samples\Kanthaka folder.

```
<HTML>
<BODY BGCOLOR="#FFFFFF" TEXT="#000000">
<H1 ALIGN=CENTER>Kanthaka Farms</H1><P>
<P align="center"><IMG SRC="KAN_LOGO.gif" width="121"
    height="97"></P>
<CENTER>
<!--#INCLUDE FILE="banner.asp"-->
</CENTER>
<BR><BR>
<H2 Align=Center><A HREF="Ban_Demo.asp">Click here to reload
    this page</A>. Watch the Banner Ad Change!<BR>
</H2>
<H3 Align=Center>The random value is: <%=RandomNumber%>
</H3>
</BODY></HTML>
```

This code is used to generate a random value, so the site can display random banners. A built-in random function generates a random number used to select one of the 10 banners. Notice that the RANDOMIZE must come first, because it ensures that the value generated is truly random. This is important to Kanthaka Farms, because they do not want their site to repeatedly display only one banner ad. The LowestNumber is set to the lowest value desired, in this case 1, and the HighestNumber to the highest value, in this case 10. Coded in this fashion, the RandomValue variable will retrieve one of the following values: 1, 2, 3, 4, 5, 6, 7, 8, 9, or 10.

3. The next task is to select a banner ad. To accomplish this, the code will use the SELECT CASE function to select a banner. In a simple text editor, create a new file and type in the following code:

```
<%
RANDOMIZE
LowestNumber = 1
HighestNumber = 10
RandomNumber = INT((HighestNumber-
    LowestNumber+1)*Rnd+LowestNumber)
SELECT CASE RandomNumber
CASE "1"%>
<A HREF="link1.htm"><IMG SRC="banner1.gif" BORDER=0></A>
<%CASE "2"%>
<A HREF="link2.htm"><IMG SRC="banner2.gif" BORDER=0></A>
<%CASE "3"%>
<A HREF="link3.htm"><IMG SRC="banner3.gif" BORDER=0></A>
<%CASE "4"%>
<A HREF="link4.htm"><IMG SRC="banner4.gif" BORDER=0></A>
<%CASE "5"%>
<A HREF="link5.htm"><IMG SRC="banner5.gif" BORDER=0></A>
<%CASE "6"%>
<A HREF="link6.htm"><IMG SRC="banner6.gif" BORDER=0></A>
<%CASE "7"%>
<A HREF="link7.htm"><IMG SRC="banner7.gif" BORDER=0></A>
<%CASE "8"%>
<A HREF="link8.htm"><IMG SRC="banner8.gif" BORDER=0></A>
<%CASE "9"%>
<A HREF="link9.htm"><IMG SRC="banner9.gif" BORDER=0></A>
<%CASE "10"%>
<A HREF="link10.htm"><IMG SRC="banner10.gif" BORDER=0></A>
<%END SELECT%>
```

Save the file as banner.asp in the C:\WebSite\CHILASP\Samples\ Kanthaka folder.

4. To see the page in action, use the link.htm files provided; however, as you prepare your Kanthaka Farms Web database construction, you may want to replace these files. To do so, just replace the "link" with the URLs you wish to use. Also, create banners that link to the IMG tag.

5. Open the "link" files provided in the CHILIASP\Samples\Kanthaka folder. Since your banner program uses Server Side Includes (SSI), the following line of code must be coded on all the pages where you want your banners to appear:

```
<!-#INCLUDE FILE="banner.asp"->
```

6. In your Web browser, view the Ban_Demo.asp file from the following URL:

```
http://localhost/kasp/Ban_Demo.asp
```

Test the links. Click on each banner. Modify any code as necessary to make your banner system free of error. Your finished Ban_Demo.asp page should look like the one shown in Figure 10-5.

Figure 10-5

Kanthaka Farms' Banner Ad System

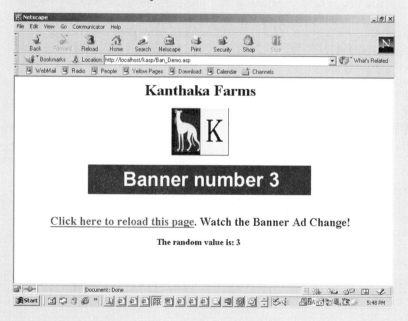

FOCUS ON ELECTRONIC COMMERCE

Canada: A Most Favorable Environment

Industry Canada believes that Canada is the perfect place to grow an electronic commerce business. The list of telecommunications and information technology breakthroughs that have come out of Canada in recent years is impressive. How does innovation play an important role in electronic commerce growth and Canada's position of competitive strength?

Justify your answer.

Electronic Commerce connects computers in order to accomplish tasks like selling products, invoicing, controlling inventories, and communicating with suppliers and customers that have traditionally drained time and money from businesses. Canada has been quick to recognize the benefits of electronic commerce and is determined to be a world leader in the adoption and use of electronic commerce. Working in close collaboration with the private sector, the Canadian federal government has concentrated on creating the most favorable environment possible in areas that are critical to the rapid development of electronic commerce.

If you find it hard to believe that Canada has become the perfect hothouse for growth in the field of electronic commerce, Industry Canada, Canada's business and government initiative, stresses 10 reasons why it is so: (1) access, (2) location, (3) cost advantage, (4) skilled workers, (5) research facilities, (6) tax breaks, (7) export opportunities, (8) great domestic markets, (9) first-rate banking system, and (10) innovation.

One of Canada's electronic commerce success stories is Critical Mass in Calgary. Critical Mass began as a producer of interactive solutions, including promotional CD-ROMs, in 1995. In 1996, the company founder, Ted Hellard, offered to build a Web

site on speculation for Mercedes-Benz USA, which became Critical Mass' first major account. Hellard offered Mercedes-Benz a deal: if you like the site, you pay for it. If you don't like it, don't pay.

In 2001, Critical Mass employs 240 persons in Calgary with satellite offices in Chicago, New York, and Toronto as well. Not only did Mercedes-Benz approve of the Canadian company's Web work, but so also has its list of other impressive clients including Nike, Proctor and Gamble, and Smirnoff Vodka.

In the words of Senior Vice President of the Critical Mass Calgary Headquarters, Dan Evans, the "world is full of consultants who can tell you what to do, but we've positioned ourselves as the company that can do it for you. It's all about the speed at which you're able to function, how fast your time to market, being able to stay up on the leading edge of an industry that seems to turn over every seven days."

Canada's solid business environment in information and communication technologies has given companies like Critical Mass a strong base from which to become world leaders in electronic commerce. Canada's business and government leaders seem to understand the key to electronic commerce success. According to Evans, "The Internet is not solely a marketing tool. It's a whole other business chan-

nel. You have to approach it that way. | much bigger part of the word than the
What people forget is commerce is a | 'e' is in e-commerce."

Sources: Critical Mass at http://www.criticalmass.com; Industry Canada at http://
www.ic.gc.ca/

Using a server-side include (SSI) file can make a banner system
easier to maintain. To use an SSI, it is necessary to modify the ban-
ner.asp file; once modified, however, all the pages on the Kanthaka
Farms site will be updated. Just make sure that banner.asp is in the
same directory as the script. If you want to include banner.asp in
scripts that are located in subfolders, you must place banner.asp in
the root of the Kanthaka Farms site and use this "include" statement
instead:

```
<!-#INCLUDE VIRTUAL="banner.asp"->
```

The use of the word *virtual* in the header indicates to ASP that the
file to be included is located in the root folder of the Web server. If the
word *file* were to be used in place of the word *virtual* in the code, the
SSI would not work, because it would indicate to ASP that the file to
be included is located in the same directory as the ASP file in which
the include statement appears. It is also important that the include
statement appear at the top of the file in order for it to run properly.

10.6 Creating an ASP Guestbook

As you learned with CGI, the guestbook is a popular and suitable
use for server-side scripting. As with the CGI guestbook, the ASP
guestbook will have an HTML form on the front-end of the Web
database construction. The ASP file will include a write script that
will add the contents of the input control on the form to a text file.
This text file can be easily modified to be used as a log file by the
Web site manager. Rather than use the text file for the back-end of
the construction, a database instead of text files could be used to
store customer input. In Chapter 11, you will learn how to connect
your ASP files to the back-end database. The last process in this ASP
guestbook Web database construction is for an ad hoc form to be
created and returned to the customer upon submission of customer
input to the Web server.

Kanthaka Farms
Creating an ASP Guestbook

In this exercise, you will use ASP to create a guestbook for Kanthaka Farms. Instead of storing the customer input in a back-end database, you will use a text file. The script must be stored in a folder where there is write access to the file. For this exercise, store your guestbook.txt in the cgi-win folder on C:\WebSite. You will store your ASP files in your C:\WebSite\CHILIASP\Samples\Kanthaka folder.

1. Launch your Web server software. Verify that it is running by viewing it in the tray.

2. Using a simple text editor, create a file named guest.asp with the code below. Save the file in the C:\WebSite\CHILIASP\Samples\Kanthaka folder.

```
<%
%>
<HTML><BODY BGCOLOR="#FFFFFF" TEXT="#000000">
<P align="center"><IMG SRC="KAN_LOGO.gif" width="121"
    height="97"></P>
<H2 Align=center><B>Welcome to Kanthaka Farms—Please sign
    our Guestbook!</B><BR>
</H2>
<FORM METHOD="POST" ACTION="sign.asp">
<INPUT NAME="new_line" TYPE="TEXT" SIZE=75>
<INPUT TYPE="SUBMIT" VALUE="Submit Message">
</FORM>
<BR><BR>
<%
MyFile = "C:\WebSite\cgi-win\guestbook.txt"
Set MyFileObj=Server.CreateObject
    ("Scripting.FileSystemObject")
IF MyFileObj.FileExists(MyFile) THEN
Set MyTextFile=MyFileObj.OpenTextFile(MyFile)
WHILE NOT MyTextFile.AtEndOfStream
%>
<HR>
<%=MyTextFile.ReadLine%>
</HR>
<%
WEND
MyTextFile.Close
END IF
%>
<HR>
</BODY>
</HTML>
```

3. You will need a second file for the ASP guestbook. Again, in a text editor, type in the following code:

```
<%
MyFile = "C:\WebSite\cgi-win\guestbook.txt"
Set MyFileObj=Server.CreateObject
   ("Scripting.FileSystemObject")
Set MyOutStream=MyFileObj.OpenTextFile(MyFile, 8, TRUE)
New_line = Request.Form("new_line")
New_line = Server.HTMLEncode(New_line)
New_line = "<I>Posted: " & NOW & "</I><BR>" & New_line
MyOutStream.WriteLine(New_line)
MyOutStream.Close
Response.Redirect "guest.asp"
%>
```

Save this file as sign.asp in the Kanthaka folder of C:\Website\ CHILISOFT\Samples.

4. Launch your Web server software. In a browser window, type in the following URL:

```
http://localhost/kasp/guest.asp
```

Figure 10-6

An ASP Guestbook with Text File

5. To test the guestbook ASP application, type in the word "test" in the input box at the Web client. Submit your greeting. After the ad hoc form has been returned to the Web client, verify that the text file information has been inserted at the bottom left of your screen. Open your guestbook.txt file and verify that the correct information was returned to the Web client. Your ad hoc ASP should look similar to Figure 10-6.

10.7 Creating an ASP Page for Login Security

ASP pages can also be used for adding security to the electronic commerce model. In this example the name and password are hard-coded into the script. This type of script becomes more useful and manageable when the login name and password values are compared to those stored in a back-end database or some other source of customer information rather than hard-coding them into the actual ASP code. In Chapter 11, a database will be added to the ASP to make a more robust application.

Kanthaka Farms
Using ASP to Add Security to
the Business Web Site

In this exercise, you will create a login page for Kanthaka Farms. This page will be used to add security to the electronic commerce model. In this example, the ASP will not be connected to a back-end database. Instead of storing the customer login name and password information in a back-end database, it will be hard-coded into the script. In Chapter 11, you will add connectivity to your ASP and add a back-end database to make this application more robust and functional. For this exercise, store your finished ASP files in the Kanthaka folder on C:\WebSite\CHILIASP\samples.

1. Launch your Web server software. Verify that it is running by viewing it in the tray.

2. Using a simple text editor, create a file named login.asp with the code below. Save the file in the C:\WebSite\CHILIASP\Samples\Kanthaka folder.

```
<%
%>
<%
If Request.Form("login") = "Guest" AND
   Request.Form("password") = "Chien" Then
Response.Write "<H1 Align=Center>Welcome to Kanthaka Farms!
   <BR>You are a Registered User of Our Site!</H1>"
Else
Response.Write "<H3 Align=Center>Access to Kanthaka Farms is
   Denied - Please Try Again</H2>"
'Response.End
End If
%>
<P align="center"><IMG SRC="KAN_LOGO.gif" width="121"
   height="97"></P>
<FORM ACTION="login.asp" METHOD="post">
<TABLE BORDER=0>
<TR>
<TD ALIGN="center">Login:</TD>
<TD><INPUT TYPE="text" NAME="login"></INPUT></TD>
</TR>
<TR>
<TD ALIGN="center">Password:</TD>
<TD><INPUT TYPE="password" NAME="password"></INPUT></TD>
</TR>
<TR>
<TD ALIGN="center"></TD>
<TD><INPUT TYPE="submit" VALUE="Login"></INPUT>
<INPUT TYPE="reset" VALUE="Reset"></INPUT>
</TD>
</TR>
</TABLE>
</FORM>
<BR><BR>
<H5 Align=Center>Sample Hint: The Login = Guest and
   Password = Chien. Both are case sensitive.<BR></H5>
```

3. In your Web browser, view the login.asp file from the following URL:

```
http://localhost/kasp/login.asp
```

Login both with the correct login name and password and with an invalid combination to verify that your ASP application is working properly. A successful login will display an ASP that looks similar to Figure 10-7.

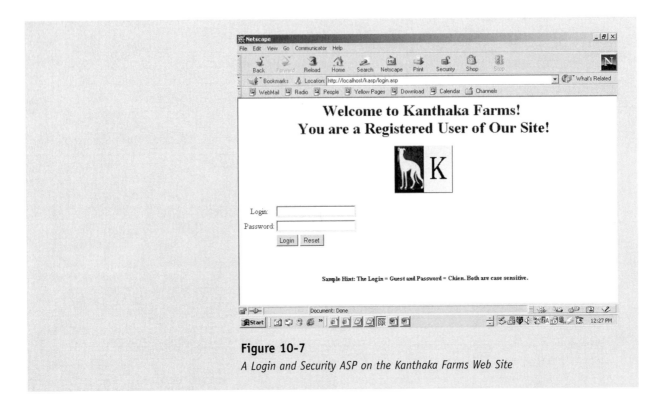

Figure 10-7
A Login and Security ASP on the Kanthaka Farms Web Site

Summary

■ **Discuss Active Server Pages server-side technology.** Microsoft developed Active Server Pages (ASP) technology, which, like CGI, is a server-side technology designed to meet the need for dynamic interaction between customer and business in the electronic commerce model. Primarily developed in VBScript, JavaScript, or PerlScript, ASP is integrated into the Hypertext Markup Language (HTML) of front-end Web pages. Conditional logic, loops, math, and string functions can be embedded into the HTML in ASP using these scripting languages. Initiated by the Web client, the Web server compiles the ASP code ad hoc, and the resulting output is standard HTML. By using ASP, Web pages can be dynamic, full of ever-changing content, and browser independent, all necessary components of successful electronic commerce designs.

■ **Describe the ASP object model and the Five Intrinsics.** The key concept behind ASP is to use the scripting language to access the methods and properties of objects. ASP provides a core set of objects, called the Five Intrinsics, which includes the Application, Request, Response, Server, and Session objects. These Five Intrinsics, together with their parent object, the ScriptingContext object, form the ASP object model.

■ **Install Chili!Soft ASP software and add document mapping.** Chili!Soft ASP is the exact functional and syntactic equivalent of Microsoft's ASP, which is included with the Internet Information Server (IIS). Using Chili!Soft ASP, ASP applications can be developed to run on nearly every Web server under Sun Solaris, IBM AIX, Hewlett Packard HP-UX, Linux, and Windows platforms. In addition, applications developed with Chili!Soft ASP are portable across enterprise servers. Chili!Soft ASP is ASP technology with server-side, object-oriented components to provide an integrated Web development environment. It allows the use of any scripting language supported by the Web server and gives Web database developers the technology to easily build powerful database and component-driven applications. Web database constructions can be created by combining HTML, server-side scripting, and server components with Chili!Soft ASP. The Five Intrinsic Objects are included to eliminate much of the overhead associated with low-level programming in the electronic commerce design, allowing developers the freedom to focus on the task of creating interesting, interactive Web content.

■ **Describe the necessary components of ASP code.** Like CGI, ASP begins with an HTML file. With ASP, however, there is some additional code, separated from the HTML markup by a different delimiter. ASP code looks a great deal like HTML tags. However, instead of starting and ending with lesser than (<) and greater than (>) brackets, it typically starts with <% and ends with %>. The <% is called an opening tag, and the %> is called a closing tag. In between these tags are the server-side scripts, which can be inserted anywhere in the Web page, even inside HTML tags.

■ **Create an ASP application.** When an ASP file is created, upon request, the Web Server finds the file and processes all the ASP code between <% and %> before handing back the page. The code between <% and %> never arrives at the browser. The ASP compiler retrieves the ASP page and interprets all the <% %> markers before the browser sees the page.

- **Create an ASP page with banner ads.** Banner advertising is almost as new as the Web itself and has become nearly as ubiquitous. HotWired ran the first banner in 1994, with outstanding results: a nearly 50 percent click-through rate (CTR). CTR is a measurement based on the number of customer Web responses, called clicks. Clicks are commonly used to count the number of customers who click on the banner and are transferred to the advertiser's site. The click-through rate is the percentage of click-throughs to banner views. There are three types of banner advertising: click-through, brand-awareness, and sell-through. Each type of banner advertising can be equally effective at building brand awareness, generating click-throughs, and boosting sales. Although individual banners often accomplish all three objectives, the most effective are designed and implemented to accomplish only one of these major goals at a time. One example of an ASP banner ad strategy is to show different ads each time customers access the business' page from its Web server. An effective ASP banner system is based on a randomizer that will ensure that the banners are appearing in random order.

- **Create an ASP guestbook.** Like CGI, the ASP guestbook is a popular and suitable use for server-side scripting and has an HTML form on the front-end of the Web database construction. The ASP file includes a write script that will add the contents of the input control on the form to a text file. This text file can be easily modified to be used as a log file by the Web site manager. Rather than use the text file for the back-end of the construction, a database instead of text files could be used to store customer input. The last process in an ASP guestbook Web database construction is for an ad hoc form to be created and returned to the customer upon submission of customer input to the Web server.

- **Adding security to the electronic commerce model with ASP.** ASP pages can also be used to add security to the electronic commerce model. One way to accomplish this is to add the name and password of the customer. This type of script becomes more useful and manageable when the login name and password values are compared to those stored in a back-end database or some other source of customer information rather than hard-coding them into the actual ASP code. Chapter 11 will introduce database–ASP connectivity.

Chapter Key Terms

@Transaction directive
Active Server Pages
ActiveX Data Objects
Application object
application program interface
ASP object model
brand-awareness
bridge program
BrowseCap object
Case-Based Reasoning
Chili!Soft ASP
click-through
click-through rate
ClientCertificate collection
closing tag
Com+
Component Object Model (COM)
Contents collection

Contents objects
Cookies collection
cost per action
cost per click
cost per thousand (CPM)
Data Access Objects (DAO)
encapsulate
FileSystem object
Five Intrinsics
instantiates
Lock method
loss-leader pricing
Microsoft Data Access
    Components
ObjectContext object
OLE DB
OntransactionAbort event
OntransactionCommit event

opening tag
QueryString collection
Remote Data Objects (RDO)
Request object
Response object
return on investment
ScriptingContext object
sell-through
Server object
server-side scripts
ServerVariables collection
Session object
SetAbort method
Setcomplete method
StaticObjects collection
Universal Data Access
Unlock method

Review Questions

1. How are Active Server Pages used in the electronic commerce model?

2. What are the Five Intrinsics? How do they and their parent object make up the ASP model?

3. When is the ObjectContext object created? What is its primary use?

4. Define COM. For what is COM used in the Web database construction?

5. Discuss the ObjectContext object's two methods and their uses.

6. How does the Request object interact with the Web server?

7. What collections are associated with the Request object?

8. What level scope do variables created with Application object have? Discuss the meaning of this level of scope.

9. Through which objects can ASP create database connection to the back-end of the electronic commerce construction?

10. What is Chili!Soft ASP? How is it used?

11. What is a delimiter? What delimiter is a necessary component of ASP code?

12. How is a scripting language different from a language?

13. Define Case-Based Reasoning and discuss how it is used to enhance electronic commerce.

14. How is the success of an ASP banner campaign measured?

15. What are the types of banner advertising? Discuss the benefits of each.

16. How is a randomizer used in an effective ASP banner system? Why is this important to the banner ad campaign's success?

17. If you want to include ASP pages to scripts that are located in subdirectories, what must be present in the root of the business' site? Why?

18. How can ASP be used to create a guestbook? to add security to a Web site?

19. What is a loss-leader? How is it used in electronic commerce?

20. You recently used your ASP skills to create banner ads for Anne's Web site. After going over the effectiveness of the campaign with her CIO, she isn't sure she got her money's worth from your design. Anne's Web site spends $10 to show its banner ads to 1000 people. The click through rate has been measured to be 2 percent. The percentage of shoppers in Anne's online store who actually make a purchase is only 0.05 percent. If the cost per customer = CPM/1000 × CTR, and the cost per sale = cost per customer/conversation rate, then how effective are your designs at Anne's Web site?

Critical Thinking Using the Web

1. A casual look at PHP leads many to believe that it will effectively replace the server-side scripting aspects of ASP. Use your favorite search engine and make a comparison of PHP and ASP. Consider PHP's support for using databases. After your investigation, write a 200–400-word essay stating your opinion on the future of PHP and ASP. Justify your position. Be prepared to present your findings to the class.

2. When Microsoft crippled the TCP/IP stack in NT Workstation 4.0 so that no more than 10 simultaneous TCP/IP connections could be made, many in the industry saw this not only as a corruption of what up to then had been an industry-standard protocol, but as an example of using unfair practices to gain an advantage in the Web server software market. Microsoft's response was that NT Workstation was not up to the task of running a Web server. The Web server industry responded by demonstrating that it was possible to turn NT Workstation into NT Server simply by changing a few Registry entries. Review some historical documents relating to this controversy at the following sites or find other sites on your own:

■ ftp.ora.com/pub/examples/windows/win95/update/ntwks4.html

■ ftp.ora.com/pub/examples/windows/win95/update/ntwk4.html

■ ftp.ora.com/pub/examples/windows/win95/update/ntnodiff.html

Using your favorite search engine, see what other information you can find to support a 200–400-word position essay, siding either with the Web server industry or with Microsoft in this action. Be prepared to justify your opinions to the class.

3. Although there are those who measure a banner campaign's effectiveness based on click-throughs or ROI, direct marketers firmly support the CPM banner metrics. RightNow Technologies, a leading provider of Web-based customer service solutions for the Internet and Intranet environments, offers yet another measurement tool, RightNow Metrics, a closed-loop customer service tool. RightNow Metrics builds a real-time dialog with customers, delivering information and automatically asking for feedback enabling businesses to fine-tune their customer service organization to increase customer satisfaction and build loyalty. Visit RightNow at http://www.rightnow.com/ and take the virtual Quick Tour. In a 200–400-word essay, discuss how RightNow uses CRM to help electronic commerce businesses retain customers and provide top service. Be prepared to present your answer in class.

Chapter Case Study

Albatross Records is a continuing case study in this book that illustrates the process of building electronic commerce with Web database constructions. In Chapter 10, you will create ASP server-side files. As you continue through the text, you will complete different facets of electronic commerce Web database construction, resulting in a complete Web site for Albatross Records.

Using your knowledge of ASP, add several ASP pages to the Albatross Records electronic commerce constructions.

- Much more can be displayed than random banners with the banner ad system ASP code. Using the banner ad model, create ASP that displays a "Tip of the day," "News flash," or a "Random link" on the Albatross Web site.

- Code an ASP guestbook that allows customers, musicians, and promoters to sign the guestbook and write a greeting. The data should be coded to a text file. Be sure to store the text file in a folder that has read–write properties.

- Cool has asked that you begin to add some degree of security to the business' site. Create an ASP page where a customer login name and password are required. He has asked that you use the password "BigBird."

11

Connectivity: Databases, Visual Basic, and ASP

The computer can't tell you the emotional story. It can give you the exact mathematical design, but what's missing is the eyebrows.

—Frank Zappa, 1981

11.1 Utilizing a Database in an ASP Application for Connectivity

In the electronic commerce model, the importance of the back-end database cannot be overstressed. It is this connectivity between the Web client and the Web server with previously recorded data that brings the economic power to the Web database construction. One method of connection is to use **ActiveX Data Objects (ADO)**, the object-oriented programming application program interface (API) from Microsoft that allows access to relational or nonrelational databases from both Microsoft and other database providers. ADO uses the **connection string**, the database access layer used in ASP, to pair the code to the database. The connection string code and syntax will vary with database provider. ADO is also part of an overall data access strategy from Microsoft called Universal Data Access that provides connections between the database and Microsoft's **OLE DB**, Microsoft's strategic low-level API for access to different data sources. Though these meanings are no longer ascribed to OLE DB by Microsoft, OLE once stood for "Object Link Embedding" and DB for "database."

The SQL capabilities of the Microsoft-sponsored standard data interface **Open Database Connectivity** (ODBC) are included in OLE DB as well as access to data other than Structured Query Language (SQL) data. A feature of ADO, the **Remote Data Service** (RDS) ActiveX control, is often used by Web developers to move data from the Web server to the Web client, manipulate the data on the Web client, and return updates to the Web server. RDS also supports *data-aware* ActiveX controls in Web pages for efficient Web client caching. As part of ActiveX, ADO is also part of Microsoft's overall Component Object Model (COM), the framework for developing and supporting program component objects.

ODBC is an API that allows for **datamining**, or data extraction, from a back-end database through a unified source. Historically, it was difficult to mine data from a variety of back-end databases, because each database had its own language that had to be coded. If a customer wished to extract back-end data from multiple databases, it would be necessary for the Web server to run a program that had been recoded in order to allow this switching. Now, the task of accessing several different databases is simplified. Web database developers must only program in the ODBC language that is a combination of the ODBC API function calls and SQL. Today, most databases support the SQL standard, and all that is needed for the front-end of the construction to interact with various databases is the correct ODBC driver for the database and knowledge of SQL.

VBScript and the Database

VBScript is readable by Web browsers as ASP files using a variety of Web servers. However, instead of index.html as is often used with CGI, with ASP, the top-level page is index.asp. Upon request, these ASP files are executed and their information returned to the Web browser in HTML form. None of the scripting language source is viewable by the customer on the front-end when it is sent, only the HTML.

This first line of the ASP file must begin with the code <%@ LANGUAGE="VBScript" %>. This denotes that the language that will be used within ASP is VBScript. The script part of this page is contained within the <% %> brackets with the remainder of the code being written in HTML. The value of the variable *i* is printed in HTML by using the <%=*i*%> command. Note that in VBScript, all variables are variants.

As is true for creating CGI database connectivity, one of the great strengths of Visual Basic is its ability to work with databases. VBScript is also very easy to set up to access and perform database operations. The initial code to allow VBScript connection to back-end databases is the following:

```
<%@ LANGUAGE="VBScript" %>

<%
Option Explicit

Dim Connection
Dim RS
Dim SQLStmt
Dim SSN, Fname, Lname

Set Connection = Server.CreateObject("ADODB.Connection")

Connection.Open "DSN=Dogs; UID=da"
```

FOCUS ON ELECTRONIC COMMERCE

"May I Take Your Order, Please?" Web Database Constructions Take Packaged Foods to the Internet

How does electronic commerce create an even more competitive playing field, with small businesses able to compete alongside larger ones?

What were some of the advantages E.G. Forrest gained by moving part of their business to the Web?

What new challenges were presented?

Use SWOT analysis to further explore E.G. Forrest's move to electronic commerce.

In Winston-Salem, North Carolina, ASP and the Internet are the future for an 81-year-old, family-owned packaged food company. E.G. Forrest, a company with 100 employees and $50 million in sales in 2000, is looking to extend its business with Web database constructions. The company's management sees electronic commerce as a way to increase current customer service and move its packaged food products farther than the current tri-state area of Virginia, North Carolina, and South Carolina that it now covers.

George Witter, information systems manager, used efficient, economical, dynamic Web site design to meet the company objective to be the best food-service distributor in the business. The company uses electronic commerce to reach its wide range of customers, which include day care centers, summer camps, local restaurants, and nursing homes.

"Our goal was to have our site be dynamic and professional," said Witter. "But food distribution is generally a low-margin business, so we had to do a lot with a little." He and his associate, Mike Shelton, built the company's site last year in under three months. Web clients are not only able to view the usual Web information of company history, location, and products, but also place an order, download coupons, or view company specials. A product guide and an industry news feed are also offered courtesy of a free syndication service.

The front-end of the Web database construction was built in-house by Witter and Shelton, but, the back-end systems are hosted by eFoodusa, a Chicago-based application service provider for the food industry. Orders are retrieved by connecting daily to eFoodusa's systems and downloading the day's orders into the company's IBM AS/400 server.

In addition to Web database constructions, E.G. Forrest has embraced technology in other ways. Sales representatives in the field can submit orders using a modem and software from Sales Partner Systems. This Web-based order-entry system was added to E.G. Forrest's Web page at the request of one of their nursing-home clients.

E.G. Forrest has also been using Global Food Exchange, a B2B online exchange where distributors and wholesalers bid on food items online. Web-based Global Food Exchange enables food industry retailers, whole-salers, food-service distributors, man-ufacturers, and suppliers to profitably manage the sourcing, procurement, and transport of perishable and non-perishable products.

Jeff Holderfield, president of E.G. Forrest, sees electronic commerce and Web database constructions as a way to create competitive advantage for his company: "As younger folks come into the work force, we'll be dealing with more and more people who are comfortable with technology. However, we feel strongly that there's always going to be a need for human contact alongside these new tools—people still want that personal touch."

Sources: Sarah L. Roberts-Witt, "Hot Food Online," *PC Magazine*, May 22, 2001, 12:00 A.M. ET; Global Food Exchange: http://www.globalfoodexchange.com/index.php; E.G. Forrest: http://www.egforrest.com/

In the preceding example, the Connection variable is set to the ADO Connection type object. Once it has been set, the connection can be opened through a **Data Source Name (DSN)**. The DSN is configured after the correct ODBC driver for the database is installed. Microsoft Access, dBase, FoxPro, and SQL Server drivers are the standard drivers installed with Windows servers. Drivers for various other databases such as Oracle, Sybase, Informix, and Lotus Approach are easily attainable. The DSN must be configured for the database, or databases, that will be accessed, and it must be set to a System DSN or a User DSN. If set to a User DSN, only the creator of the DSN is allowed to access the database through the data source. A System DSN will allow all users of a particular machine to access the database through that data source.

To set a System DSN in Windows, the Administrative Tools, Data Sources ODBC control panel must be accessed. Once in the ODBC control panel, the database is added through the System DSN tab. The datasource will also be set in the ODBC panel. With ASP, Web pages never increase in size, though the back-end database will ulti-mately grow. In the dynamic electronic commerce model, data can change and the pages returned to the Web client will change, but the original ASP files will remain constant. Also, as server-side scripts, ASP can be used on various platforms. As long as the Web browser can read the HTML, there is no limit on operating system or machine. Also, since all the ASP files are generally in one location, all the files can be updated easily, so there are no patches or version updates that need to be released to customers.

 Web Break

Learn more about how to use Front Page in your ASP files. Visit the Tecumseh Group Web site at http://www.tek-tips.com/ gthreadminder.cfm/lev2/4/lev3/31/pid/256. There you will find cutting-edge forums to foster dialogue among professionals on work-related topics in a noncommercial environment.

ASP Database Connectivity

One method for connecting the ASP to the back-end database is to use a connection string. Connection strings are string variables that contain database connection information. These string variables are passed to ADO, which in turn interprets them and follows their instructions. The format of a standard connection string will contain several arguments, each set to equal its associated values and separated by semicolons. The format is as follows:

```
argument1=value1; argument2=value2; argument3=value3;
```

ADO recognizes the following arguments:

- Provider
- File Name
- Remote Provider
- Remote Server

The **File Name argument** is used to point to a **Universal Data Link (UDL)** file that can be used to provide all the other parameters. UDL files can simply be created by creating an empty text file with a .udl extension. They are normally stored in a special folder located at Programs Files\Common Files\System\OLE DB\Data Links. Another method to create a UDL file is to navigate using Windows Explorer to the Data Links folder and choosing the New Microsoft Data Link option from the context-sensitive menu.

The File Name argument usually only contains one parameter such as the following:

```
File Name=C:\path\filename.udl;
```

The Provider argument instructs ADO what provider should be used for connecting and for access to the back-end database. If not coded, the default provider is **MSDASQL**, Microsoft's OLE DB Provider for ODBC. The three most commonly used in ASP are MSDASQL, **Microsoft.Jet.OLEDB.4.0**, and **SQLOLEDB**.

The last two are only used with RDS.

Microsoft.Jet.OLEDB.4.0 The OLE DB provider for Access is Microsoft.Jet.OLEDB.4.0. The syntax for an OLE DB Provider for Jet connection string is the following:

```
Provider=Microsoft.Jet.OLEDB.4.0; Data
    Source=C:\path\filename.mdb;
User ID=admin; Password=iggy;
```

The parameters User ID and Password are also used to specify user authentication values.

SQLOLEDB Microsoft OLE DB Provider for SQL Server is SQLOLEDB. It communicates with network software through the SQL Server Library interface, requiring a **dynamic-link library (DLL)**. The DLL is a collection of small programs that are dynamically linked to larger programs as needed. They allow the larger program to communicate with a specific device such as a scanner or printer and are often packaged as DLL programs, similar to library routines provided with Visual Basic and other programming languages. SQLOLEDB also uses the Data Source parameter; however, the name or address of Microsoft's SQL Server is indicated. SQL Server has the ability to run multiple databases. It uses the **Initial Catalog parameter** to indicate the database to which the connection string will be associated and the **Network Library parameter** to specify the network library of choice. The default network library is **Named Pipes** and can also be changed through the SQL Server Client Network Utility. Named Pipes is appropriate if the client and the server are on the same network and is coded Network Library=dbnmpntw. In the electronic commerce model, however, to force the client to use TCP/IP to connect, a value of *dbmssocn* will be specified for the Network Library parameter. The syntax for SQLOLEDE is:

```
Provider=SQLOLEDB; Data Source=server_name_or_address;
Initial Catalog=database_name; User ID=username;
   Password=password;
Network Library=dbmssocn;
```

It is important that the Win32 SQL Server driver-defined data sources always reference a Win32 network library and the Win16 SQL Server driver-defined data sources always reference Win16 network libraries. The available network libraries are listed in Table 11.1.

 Web Break

Microsoft's vision for the future of ASP is ASP.NET. ASP.NET files will end with the .aspx extension. Existing .asp files will also work in the ASP.NET environment. Microsoft promises that ASP.NET will improve browser compatibility with HTML server-side controls and offer easier configuration and application deployment, as well as cleaner code and ease of use. For more information about ASP.NET, visit the Microsoft Developers Network (MSDN) Show at http://msdn.microsoft.com/theshow/Episode009/default.asp and hear what two developers, Mark Anders and Scott Guthrie, have to say about the architecture of ASP.NET. CodeJunkies.Net developers also discuss their experiences with developing Web sites that use ASP.NET, and how important a role they think this will play in their future Web development.

Table 11-1 *Network Libraries*

Type	Driver	Network Library	Library Name
Win32	SQLSRV32	TCP/IP	dbmssocn
Win32	SQLSRV32	NWLink IPX/SPX	dbmsspxn
Win32	SQLSRV32	Banyan VINES	dbmsuinn
Win32	SQLSRV32	Multiprotocol (RPC)	dbmsrpcn
Win32	SQLSRV32	AppleTalk	dbmsadsn
Win32	SQLSRV32	Named Pipes	dbnmpntw
Win16	SQLSRVR	TCP/IP	dbmssoc3
Win16	SQLSRVR	NWLink IPX/SPX	dbmsspx3
Win16	SQLSRVR	Banyan VINES	dbmsvin3
Win16	SQLSRVR	Mulitprotocol (RPC)	dbmsrpc3
Win16	SQLSRVR	Named Pipes	dbnmp3

MSDASQL One of the oldest forms of connection is MSDASQL, also known as ODBC. When ASP was first released by Microsoft, it was the only option available to electronic commerce developers. This contributed to its becoming the default connection. The ODBC connection string can be set so that it utilizes a DSN or not, in which case it is called a **DSN-less connection**. In either a DSN or DSN-less connection, the parameters used in the syntax are the same. They are differentiated by where and how they are stored and specified.

DSN and DSN-less Connection Because DSN connections store their connection information in the Windows Registry, the ODBC Data Sources applet is the most useful tool to use to create these connections. The applet provides a user-friendly interface and can be accessed from the Control Panel Administration Tools folder. When creating DSN connections for ASP, use System DSNs to ensure their availability for all users. The syntax for a DSN connection is the following:

```
Provider=MSDASQL; DSN=data_source_name; UID=username;
   PWD=password;
```

Because the default provider is MSDQSQL, the syntax could also be coded in the following way:

```
DSN=data_source_name; UID=username; PWD=password;
```

The Driver parameter identifies which driver will be used and is required by all ODBC connection strings. Each driver requires the information found in Table 11-2.

Table 11-2	Driver Parameter Requirements		
Type	Provider	Driver	DBO
Microsoft Access	Provider=MSDASQL:	Driver={Microsoft Access Driver (*.mdb)};	DBQ=C:\path\filename.mdb;
Microsoft Excel	Provider=MSDASQL;	Driver={Microsoft Excel Driver (*.xls)};	DBQ=C:\path\filename.xls;
Microsoft Text	Provider=MSDASQL;	Driver={Microsoft Text Driver (*.txt; *.csv)}	DBQ=C:\path\; Note: The filename is not included here, but will be specified when opening the recordset.
Microsoft SQL Server	Provider=MSDASQL;	Driver={SQL Server};	Server=server_name_or_address; Database=database_name; UID=username; PWD=password;

11.2 Viewing Table Records with VBScript and ASP

The simplest ASP database connectivity is for the Web client to read back-end data. Although the Web client is only reading the business' data, this is still a very useful connectivity in the electronic commerce model. For example, not only can the viewed data be written to a page, but data can be used in variables, expressions, and as the arguments for other functions.

In the first ASP database connectivity exercise in this chapter the randomizer discussed in Chapter 10 will be revisited. In this example, however, the randomizer will be used to display the names of Kanthaka Farms' championship dogs. The dog names are records in the back-end database rather than in a text file.

> ### IIS Info
> If you are working on IIS, you have access to the settings of your Windows OS and can set your own DSN by selecting the 32-bit ODBC from the Control Panel and following the steps in the wizard.

Kanthaka Farms
Creating an ASP to Randomly
Display Database Records

Kanthaka Farms is a continuing case study in this book that illustrates the process of building electronic commerce with Web database constructions. In Chapter 11, you will explore ASP database connectivity. This connectivity will be made by utilizing VBScript in the ASP. As you continue through the text, you will complete different facets of electronic commerce Web database construction, resulting in a complete Web site for Kanthaka Farms.

1. From the Start menu, choose Programs, WebSite to launch your server software program. Verify that it is running by viewing the icon in the tray.

2. Launch Microsoft Access and create a new database. Save the database as randomizer.mdb in your C:\WebSite\CHILIASP\Samples\Kanthaka folder.

3. In Design View, create a new table and save it as RandomDog. The table should look like the one in Figure 11-1.

RandomDog : Table

Field Name	Data Type
dogid	AutoNumber
listing	Text

Figure 11-1

The RandomDog Table Design View

RandomDog : Table

dogid	listing
1	Realmente Veloce Cane
2	Graziosa Piccola Ragazza
3	Mela del Mio Occhio
4	Piacere dei Corridori
5	Sole e Sorrisi
(AutoNumber)	

Figure 11-2

The RandomDog Table Datasheet View

4. In Datasheet View, add the records of the championship dogs as shown in Figure 11-2.

5. Create an ASP file. Copy the following code into the file and save it as random.asp in the C:\WebSite\CHILIASP\Samples\Kanthaka folder.

```
<%
Option Explicit
Response.Buffer = True
%>
<HTML>
<HEAD>
<BODY BGCOLOR="#FFFFFF" TEXT="#000000">
<H1 ALIGN=CENTER>Kanthaka Farms</H1><P>
<P align="center"><IMG SRC="KAN_LOGO.gif" width="121"
   height="97"></P>
<H3 ALIGN=CENTER>Meet Our Championship Dogs:</H3><P>
<CENTER> <STYLE>
p { font-family:arial; font-size:20px; }
</STYLE>
</HEAD>
<BODY>
<BR><p align="center">
<%
Const adCmdText = &H0001
Dim query, connStr
```

```
query = "select listing from RandomDog"
connStr = "Provider=Microsoft.Jet.OLEDB.4.0; Data Source=" &
    Server.MapPath("randomizer.mdb")
Dim rs
Set rs = Server.CreateObject("ADODB.Recordset")
rs.Open query, connStr, 3, , adCmdText
Dim intRnd
Randomize Timer
intRnd = (Int(RND * rs.RecordCount))
rs.Move intRnd
Response.Write "<b>" & rs("listing") & "</b>"
rs.Close
Set rs = Nothing
%>
<H3 ALIGN=CENTER>For more information, please contact us at
    India Trails Road, Chapel Hill, NC 27514</H3><P></p>
</BODY>
</HTML>
```

Note that the ASP uses the Microsoft.Jet.OLEDB.4.0 provider connection string. Also, the ASP uses an intRnd variable to hold the random record number. The Randomize Timer statement is used to initialize the random-number generator, and the RND Function is used to generate a random number between 1 and the total number of records in the table. This is obtained with the Recordset.RecordCount property.

The Recordset Cursor location must be set to adOpenKeyset 3 in order to randomize the timer and generate a random number. The re.Move intRnd moves from record to record and the Response Write shows the random records. The database connection is closed and the Recordset object removed with the rs.Close and Set rs = Nothing code.

6. Note that both the database and the ASP files have been saved to the same folder. Test the application by viewing the ASP file from the following URL:

```
http://localhost/kasp/random.asp
```

Click on the browser Refresh button several times. Notice that each time the screen is refreshed, a random statement is displayed with the name of a different championship Kanthaka Farms dog. Your screen should look similar to the one displayed in Figure 11-3.

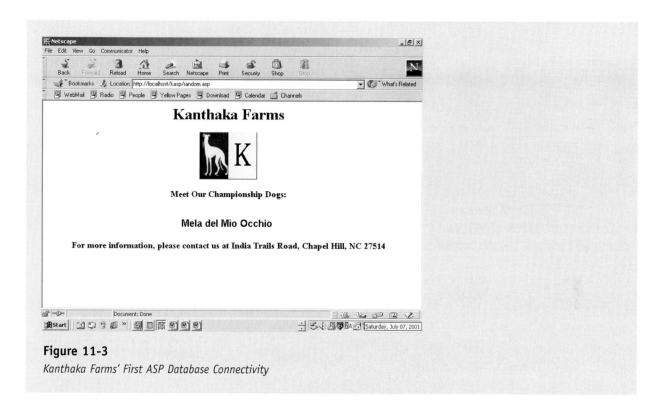

Figure 11-3
Kanthaka Farms' First ASP Database Connectivity

11.3 Querying and Sorting a Back-End Database with VBScript and ASP

The strength of the Web database construction comes from the ability of the back-end data to be manipulated by the front-end of the model. In this exercise, you will learn to query and sort records in the back-end database in an ASP file. The ASP code will allow a search for a group of records in the database. Rather than SQL statements, this file uses the Recordset object properties of Filter and Sort.

Filter allows the database to be queried for a specific group of records, and Sort performs sorts based on the criteria in the ASP code. Note that a DSN-less connection is made in this file rather than using a DSN connection string as the argument. The connection string used includes Provider and Data Source fields and their values to establish the connection to the database.

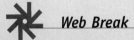

✳ *Web Break*

ODBC is one of Microsoft's earliest technologies for connecting to databases; it is very popular and widely used. Learn more about how to set up and use ODBC from a PHP perspective at http://php.weblogs.com/discuss/msgReader$52?mode=topic.

Kanthaka Farms
Creating an ASP to Query and
Sort a Back-End Database

In this exercise, you will create an ASP to query and sort your back-end database. The information mined from the database will be used by the Vitas to make sound management decisions.

1. From the Start menu, choose Programs, WebSite to launch your server software program. Verify that it is running by viewing the icon in the tray.

2. Launch Microsoft Access and create a new database. Save the database as dogfilter.mdb in your C:\WebSite\CHILIASP\Samples\Kanthaka folder.

3. In Design View, create a new table and save it as soldto. The table should look like the one in Figure 11-4.

4. In Datasheet View, add the records of the dogs and the kennels to which they have been sold as shown in Figure 11-5.

5. Create an ASP file. Copy the following code into the file and save it as query.asp in the C:\WebSite\CHILIASP\Samples\Kanthaka folder.

```
<% Option Explicit %>
<%
Sub ShowRec(qc1, qc2, qc3)
Response.Write "<TABLE width=500 border=0 cellpadding=0
    cellspacing=0" & vbcrlf
Response.Write "<TR>"
Response.Write "<TD width=100>"
Response.Write qc1
Response.Write "</TD><TD width=200>"
Response.Write qc2
Response.Write "</TD><TD width=200>"
Response.Write qc3
Response.Write "</TD></TR></TABLE>"
End Sub
Const adCmdTableDirect = &H0200
Const adLockReadOnly = 1
```

Field Name	Data Type
🔑 dogid	AutoNumber
listing	Text
kennel	Text

soldto : Table

Figure 11-4

The soldto Table in Design View

soldto : Table

dogid	listing	kennel
1	Relmente Veloce Cane	Tribecca Kennels
2	Graziosa Piccola Ragazza	Alfalfa Farms
3	Mela del Mio Occhio	Tribecca Kennels
4	Piacere dei Corridor	Tribecca Kennels
5	Sole e Sorrisi	India Farms
6	Fairy Veloce	Tribecca Kennels
7	Come per Mangiare Cioccolato	Alfalfa Farms
8	Bella Signora Cane	Alfalfa Farms
9	Signora Della Valle	India Farms
10	Primo Cane di il Nostro	Tribecca Kennels
(AutoNumber)		

Figure 11-5

The soldto Table Datasheet View

```
Const adOpenStatic = 1
Const adUseClient = 3
%>
<HTML>
<HEAD>
<STYLE>
body { font-family : arial; font-size : 10pt; }
</STYLE>
</HEAD>
<BODY>
<%
Dim connStr
connStr = "Provider=Microsoft.Jet.OLEDB.4.0; Data Source=" &
    Server.MapPath("dogfilter.mdb")
Dim rs
Set rs = Server.CreateObject("ADODB.Recordset")
rs.CursorLocation = adUseClient
rs.Open "soldto", connStr, adOpenStatic, adLockReadOnly,
    adCmdTableDirect
If Not rs.EOF Then
Response.Write "<B>Records Found!</B>" & "<BR><BR>" & vbcrlf
```

```
Response.Write "Showing all records in the back-end
    database: " & rs.RecordCount & "<BR><BR>" & vbcrlf
While Not rs.EOF
ShowRec rs("dogid"), rs("listing"), rs("kennel")
rs.MoveNext
Wend
rs.MoveFirst
rs.Sort = "listing"
Response.Write "<BR><BR>Sorting by the database field titled
    ""listing"" to show the Kanthaka Farms dogs: " &
    rs.RecordCount & " <BR><BR>" & vbcrlf
While Not rs.EOF
ShowRec rs("dogid"), rs("listing"), rs("kennel")
rs.MoveNext
Wend
rs.MoveFirst
rs.Sort = "kennel"
Response.Write "<BR><BR>Sorting by field ""kennel"" to show
    the kennels in ascending alphabetical order to which
    Kanthaka Farms' dogs have been sold: " & rs.RecordCount
    & "<BR><BR>" & vbcrlf
While Not rs.EOF
ShowRec rs("dogid"), rs("listing"), rs("kennel")
rs.MoveNext
Wend
rs.MoveFirst
rs.Sort = "Kennel Desc"
Response.Write "<BR><BR>Sorting by field ""kennel"" and
    arranging the kennels in descending order : " &
    rs.RecordCount & "<BR><BR>" & vbcrlf
While Not rs.EOF
ShowRec rs("dogid"), rs("listing"), rs("kennel")
rs.MoveNext
Wend
rs.MoveFirst
rs.Sort = ""
rs.Filter = "kennel = 'Tribecca Kennels'"
Response.Write "<BR><BR>Now <B>querying </B> the records and
    showing only dogs sold to Tribecca Kennels: " &
    rs.RecordCount & "<BR><BR>" & vbcrlf
While Not rs.EOF
ShowRec rs("dogid"), rs("listing"), rs("kennel")
rs.MoveNext
Wend
rs.MoveFirst
rs.Filter = ""
rs.Filter = "listing like '%cane%'"
Response.Write "<BR><BR>Now <B>querying </B> the records and
    showing only dogs whose name contains the word ""cane""
    which is Italian for ""Dog"": " & rs.RecordCount &
    "<BR><BR>" & vbcrlf
```

```
While Not rs.EOF
ShowRec rs("dogid"), rs("listing"), rs("kennel")
rs.MoveNext
Wend
rs.MoveFirst
rs.Filter = ""
rs.Filter = "listing like '%cane%'"
rs.Sort = "kennel"
Response.Write "<BR><BR>Now <B>querying</B> for the records
    and showing only where dog's name contains word
    ""Cane"": " & rs.RecordCount & "<BR>" & vbcrlf
Response.Write "And then sorting the records by kennel name
    in ascending alphabetical order.<BR>"
Response.Write "Note this example uses both <B>Query</B> and
    <B>Sort</B> together :<BR><BR>"
While Not rs.EOF
ShowRec rs("dogid"), rs("listing"), rs("kennel")
rs.MoveNext
Wend
Else
Response.Write "No records Found!"
End If
rs.Close
Set rs = Nothing
```

Figure 11-6

Querying and Sorting Database Records with ASP

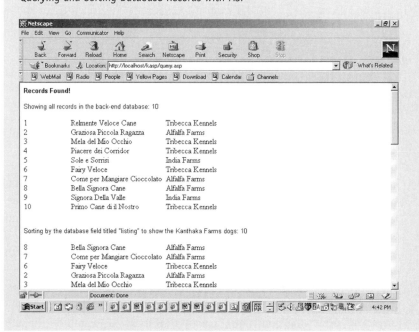

```
%>
<BR><BR>
</BODY>
</HTML>
```

6. Note that both the database and the ASP files have been saved to the same folder. Test the application by viewing the ASP file from the following URL:

```
http://localhost/kasp/query.asp
```

Your screen should look similar to the one displayed in Figure 11-6.

11.4 Building Advanced Queries Using ASP Database Transactions

An ASP page, which uses database transaction objects to either execute all of the queries or none of the queries, is very useful in the electronic commerce model. A **transaction** is a logical atomic unit of work that contains one or more SQL statements. The outcome of the SQL statements in a transaction can be either all **committed**, applied to the database, or all **rolled back**, undone from the database.

Three Connection Object methods can be used to produce these results:

- Connection.BeginTrans
- Connection.CommitTrans
- Connection.RollbackTrans

A transaction begins with the first executable SQL statement and ends when it is committed or rolled back, either explicitly with a **Connection.CommitTrans** or **Connection.RollbackTrans** statement or implicitly when a **Data Definition Language (DDL)** statement is issued. The DDL is the part of SQL that is used to create, change, or destroy the basic elements of a relational database such as tables, views, or schemas.

To illustrate the concept of a transaction, consider a Kanthaka Farms database. When a customer purchases a dog collar online, the transaction might consist of three separate operations: decrement the dog collar inventory, increment the Kanthaka Farms revenues account, and record the transaction in the transaction journal.

If all three SQL statements can be performed, the effects of the transaction can be applied to the database. However, if something such as insufficient inventory or a hardware failure prevents one or two of the statements in the transaction from completing, the entire transaction must be rolled back.

An SQL statement that executes successfully is different from a committed transaction. When a statement has been executed successfully, the single statement was parsed and found to be a valid SQL construction, and the entire statement executed without error as an atomic unit. In the Kanthaka Farms example, if an SQL statement was executed successfully, then all rows of a multi-row update are changed. However, until the transaction that contains the statement is committed, the transaction can be rolled back, and all of the changes in the statement can be undone. A statement, rather than a transaction, executes successfully. For a statement to be committed, a customer has said either explicitly or implicitly that the changes should be made permanent. Upon commit, the changes made by the SQL statement of the transaction become permanent and visible to other customers. Only other customers' transactions that started after the commit will see the committed changes.

Other Connection Objects that are useful in the ASP database query include the following:

- **Connection.State.** This property indicates whether the connection to the database is open or not. In the Kanthaka Farms example, if the connection is open, then it is equal to 1, and if closed, then it is equal to 0.
- **Connection.Errors.Count.** In the Kanthaka Farms example, if any errors occur, then this error count will be greater than 0. Therefore, a non-zero error count will iterate through the Connection.Errors collection and show all the information about the error.

In this exercise, you will create an advanced ASP to query and sort your back-end database. You will be able to execute all of your SQL queries; or, if some error occurs, roll back all the actions, and no query will be executed. You will also build a very useful Function to track database errors and show them to the Kanthaka Farms customer if some error occurs. You will use this Function to see whether there have been any errors in executing any query; if not, then commit the transaction, otherwise roll back to the original database state.

Kanthaka Farms
Creating Advanced Queries
Using Database Transactions

1. From the Start menu, choose Programs, WebSite to launch your server software program. Verify that it is running by viewing the icon in the tray.

2. Launch Microsoft Access to open the database dogfilter.mdb that you created in the previous exercise. It is located in your C:\WebSite\CHILIASP\Samples\Kanthaka folder.

3. In Design View, open the soldto table. Change the primary key from the dogid field to the listing field for the purposes of this example. Your table should look like the one shown in Figure 11-7.

4. In Datasheet View, verify that you have 10 records of the dogs and the kennels to which they have been sold.

5. You are now ready to build the ASP database error-tracking Function. Create an ASP file. Copy the following code into the file and save it as query2.asp in the C:\WebSite\CHILIASP\Samples\ Kanthaka folder.

```
Function ErrorsFound(mycon)
Dim myError
If mycon.State <> 1 Then
eStr = "<TABLE border=1 width=""85%"" align=""center""
    bordercolor=""#E2EAEE""" & " style=""font-family:arial;
    font-size:10pt;"" cellpadding=3>" &
    "<TR><TD>Error</TD><TD>Database not found.</TD></TR>" &
    "<TR><TD>Page</TD><TD>" &
    Request.ServerVariables("SCRIPT_NAME") &
    "</TD></TR><TR><TD>Date &amp; Time</TD><TD>" &
    FormatDateTime(Date, 1) & " " & Time &
    "</TD></TR></TABLE><BR>"
ErrorsFound = True
ElseIf mycon.Errors.Count > 0 Then
For Each myError in mycon.Errors
If myError.Number <> 0 Then
eStr = "<TABLE border=1 width=""85%"" align=""center""
    bordercolor=""#E2EAEE""" & " style=""font-family:arial;
    font-size:10pt;"" cellpadding=3>" & "<TR><TD
    width=100>Error Property</TD><TD>Contents</TD>" &
    "</TR><TR><TD>Number</TD><TD>" & myError.Number &
    "</TD></TR><TR><TD>Native Error</TD><TD>" &
```

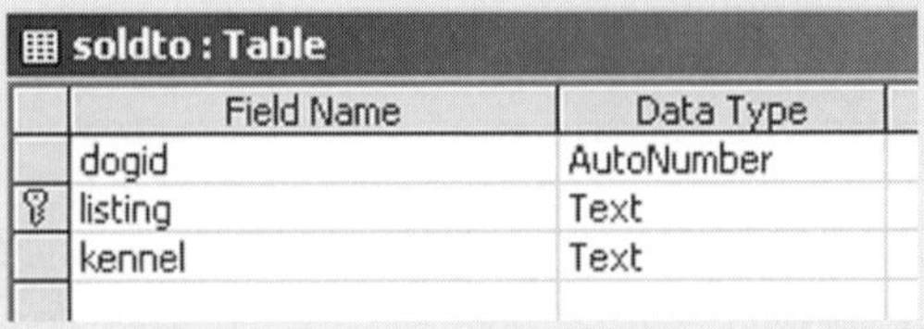

Figure 11-7

The Modified soldto Table Design View

soldto : Table		
Field Name	**Data Type**	
dogid	AutoNumber	
🔑 listing	Text	
kennel	Text	

```
      myError.NativeError & "</TD></TR>" &
      "<TR><TD>SQLState</TD><TD>" & myError.SQLState &
      "</TD></TR><TR><TD>Source</TD><TD>" & myError.Source &
      "</TD></TR>" & "<TR><TD
      valign=""top"">Description</TD><TD>" &
      myError.Description & "</TD></TR>" &
      "<TR><TD>Page</TD><TD>" &
      Request.ServerVariables("SCRIPT_NAME") &
      "</TD></TR><TR><TD>Date &amp; Time</TD><TD>" &
      FormatDateTime(Date, 1) & " " & Time &
      "</TD></TR></TABLE><BR>"
ErrorsFound = True
End If
Next
Else
ErrorsFound = False
End If
End Function
```

The Function you have just created will track the back-end database errors and report them to the Web client. As you review the
Function, notice that it will return True if an error is found and False
if no error is found. It can also detect the error if you remove or
rename the database.

6. In the same ASP, add the following code *before* the Function. Save
your ASP.

```
<%
Option Explicit
Response.Buffer = True
On Error Resume Next
Dim connStr, eStr
connStr = "Provider=Microsoft.Jet.OLEDB.4.0; Data Source=" &
    Server.MapPath("dogfilter.mdb")
```

7. Now in the same ASP, add the following code *after* your Function.
Save your file.

```
%>
<HTML>
<HEAD>
<STYLE>body, p, td { font-family : arial; font-size : 10pt;
    }</STYLE>
</HEAD>
<BODY>
<%
Dim con
Set con = Server.CreateObject("ADODB.Connection")
con.Open connStr
```

```
Response.Write "Opening ASP to Database
    Connection...<br><br>"
con.BeginTrans
Response.Write "Beginning Transaction Called...<BR>"
con.Execute("insert into soldto(listing, kennel) values
    ('Cane Che Mangia Gatti', 'Alfalfa Farms')")
Response.Write "Trying to insert records .no1...<BR>"
con.Execute("insert into soldto(listing, kennel) values ('I
    Corridori Si Vantano', 'India Farms)")
Response.Write "Trying to insert records .no2...<BR>"
con.Execute("insert into soldto(listing, kennel) values
    ('Prnotare Intorno Alla Terra', 'Tribecca Kennels')")
Response.Write "Trying to insert records .no3...<BR>"
If ErrorsFound(con) = False Then
con.CommitTrans
Response.Write "Committing Transaction...<BR>"
Response.Write "Records added successfully...<BR><BR>"
Else
con.RollbackTrans
Response.Write "Rolling back transaction...<BR>"
Response.Write "Records were not added...<BR><BR>"
End If
con.Close
Response.Write "Closing Connection...<BR>"
Set con = Nothing
Response.Write "Setting Con = Nothing...<BR><BR><BR>"
If Len(eStr) Then
Response.Write eStr
End If
Const adCmdText = &H0001
Const adCmdTableDirect = &H0200
Dim rs, query
query = "soldto"
Set rs = Server.CreateObject("ADODB.Recordset")
rs.Open query, connStr, , , adCmdTableDirect
If Not rs.EOF Then
Dim i, j
Response.Write "<TABLE align=""center"" border=""1""
    width=""105%"" cellspacing=""1"" cellpadding=""3""
    bordercolor=""silver"">" & vbcrlf
Response.Write "<TR>"
Dim Item
For Each Item in rs.Fields
Response.Write "<TD bgcolor=""silver"">" & Item.listing &
    "</TD>"
Next
Response.Write "</TR>"
Dim ds
ds = rs.GetRows
End If
rs.Close
Set rs = Nothing
```

```
If IsArray(ds) Then
For i = 0 To UBound(ds, 2)
Response.Write "<TR>" & vbcrlf
For j = 0 To UBound(ds, 1)
If ds(j, i) = False Then
Response.Write "<TD style=""color:red;font-size:7pt;"">"
ElseIf ds(j, i) = True Then
Response.Write "<TD style=""color:green;font-
    weight:bold;"">"
Else
Response.Write "<TD>"
End If
Response.Write ds(j, i)
Response.Write "</TD>"
Next
Response.Write "</TR>" & vbcrlf
Next
Response.Write "</TABLE>"
Set ds = Nothing
End If
%>
</BODY>
</HTML>
```

Though this is quite a bit of code, what it does is not very complicated. After opening the database, the **Connection.BeginTrans** method is executed to start the transaction. Two SQL queries are then executed to enter dog listings and their corresponding kennels into the database. Because you set the listing field as the primary key, it will not allow two identical dogs to be added to the database.

Next, the ErrorsFound Function will check to see whether any errors occurred. If not, the transaction is committed; otherwise, a rollback is performed. The connection is then closed, and if any error messages were indicated, they will be shown to the Web client.

8. Test the application by viewing the ASP file from the following URL:

```
http://localhost/kasp/query2.asp
```

The first time you run the application, your screen should look similar to the one displayed in Figure 11-8.

As you scroll the browser, the two dogs and their corresponding kennels should be shown on your screen as they were added to the database.

9. Open the dogfilter.mdb database and verify that the records have been added.

10. Now test the application again viewing the ASP file from the following URL:

http://localhost/kasp/query2.asp

Because you are now running the application for a second time, the dog listings and their corresponding kennels have been added to your database, and the ASP Error Function will now prevent you from duplicating these entries in your database. This time, your screen should look similar to the one displayed in Figure 11-9.

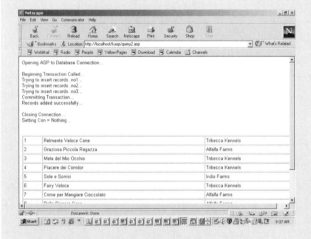

Figure 11- 8
Adding Records and Using Advanced Queries with ASP

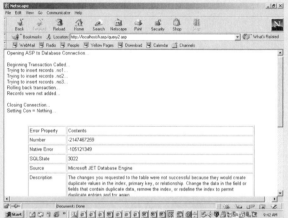

Figure 11- 9
Error Function and Advanced Queries with ASP

Summary

■ **Utilize a database in an Active Server Pages (ASP) application for connectivity.** One method of connection is to use ActiveX Data Objects (ADO), the object-oriented programming application program interface from Microsoft that allows access to relational or nonrelational databases from both Microsoft and other database providers. ADO uses the connection string, the database access layer used in ASP, to pair the code to the database. The connection string code and syntax will vary with database provider. The SQL capabilities of the Microsoft-sponsored standard data interface Open Database Connectivity (ODBC) are included in OLE DB as well as access to data other than Structured Query

Language (SQL) data. A feature of ADO, Remote Data Service (RDS) ActiveX control, is often used by Web developers to move data from the Web server to the Web client, manipulate the data on the Web client, and return updates to the Web server. RDS also supports data-aware ActiveX controls in Web pages and efficient Web client caching. As part of ActiveX, ADO is also part of Microsoft's overall COM. ODBC is an API that allows for data-mining, or data extraction, from a back-end database through a unified source. Historically, it was difficult to mine data from a variety of back-end databases, because each database had its own language that had to be coded. If a customer wished to extract back-end data from multiple databases, it would be necessary for the Web server to run a program that had been recoded in order to allow this switching.

■ **From the Web client, view table records with VBScript and ASP.** The simplest ASP database connectivity is for the Web client to read back-end data. Although the Web client is only reading the business's data, this is still a very useful connectivity in the electronic commerce model. For example, not only can the viewed data be written to a page, but data can be used in variables, expressions, and as the arguments for other functions. To accomplish this, ASP can use the Microsoft.Jet.OLEDB.4.0 provider connection string. Another technique for viewing table records with VBScript and ASP is for ASP to use an intRnd variable to hold the random record number. The Randomize Timer statement is used to initialize the random-number generator and the RND Function is used to generate a random number between 1 and the total number of records in the table. This is obtained with the Recordset.RecordCount property.

■ **Query and sort a back-end database with VBScript and ASP.** The strength of the Web database construction comes from the ability of the back-end data to be manipulated by the front-end of the model. Querying and sorting can be accomplished in the ASP code to allow a search for group of records in the database. SQL statements or Recordset object properties of Filter and Sort can be used. Filter allows the database to be queried for a specific group of records, and Sort performs sorts based on the criteria in the ASP code. Note that a DSN-less connection is made in this file rather than using a DSN connection string as the argument. The connection string used includes Provider and Data Source fields and their values to establish the connection to the database.

■ **Build advanced queries using ASP database transactions.** An ASP page, which uses database transaction objects to either execute all of the queries or none of the queries, is very useful in the electronic commerce model. A transaction is a logical atomic unit of work that contains one or more SQL statements. The outcome of the SQL statements in a transaction can be either all committed, applied to the database, or all rolled back, undone from the database. The three Connection Object methods can be used to produce these results. They are Connection.BeginTrans, Connection.CommitTrans, and Connection.RollbackTrans. A transaction begins with the first executable SQL statement and ends when it is committed or rolled back, either explicitly with a Connection.CommitTrans or Connection.RollbackTrans statement or implicitly when a Data Definition Language (DDL) statement is issued. The DDL is the part of SQL that is used to create, change, or destroy the basic elements of a relational database such as tables, views, or schemas. Other Connection Objects that are useful in the ASP database query include the Connection.State and the Connection.Errorrs.Count.

Chapter Key Terms

ActiveX Data Objects (ADO)
committed
connection string
Connection.BeginTrans
Connection.CommitTrans
Connection.Errors.Count
Connection.RollbackTrans
Connection.State
Data Definition Language (DDL)

Data Source Name (DSN)
datamining
DSN-less connection
dynamic-link library (DLL)
File Name argument
Initial Catalog parameter
Microsoft.Jet.OLEDB.4.0
MSDASQL
Named Pipes

Network Library parameter
OLE DB
Open Database Connectivity
   (ODBC)
Remote Data Service (RDS)
rolled back
SQLOLEDB
transaction
Universal Data Link (UDL)

Review Questions

1. What techniques can be used for ASP to connect to a back-end database?

2. How is SQL used in ASP?

3. What is the DSN? How is it used in the ASP electronic commerce model? Describe how to configure the DSN.

4. What is a connection string? How does it work within ADO?

5. What arguments are recognized by ADO? Discuss each.

6. What is the dynamic-link library? What is its significance to ASP database connectivity?

7. What is one of the oldest forms of database connection? Discuss its use in ASP database connectivity today.

8. Describe DSN and DSN-less connections. What are the benefits and constraints of each.

9. How are filters and sorts used in ASP database connection? Give specific electronic commerce business examples of each.

10. What is the transaction object? How is it used in ASP database connectivity?

11. Discuss the purposes of (1) Connection. BeginTrans, (2) Conection.CommitTrans, and (3) Connection.RollbackTrans.

12. What is a Data Definition Language? Discuss its use in the ASP database connectivity model.

13. Why is SQL incorporated in ASP? How can it be used by customers in an electronic business environment?

14. Discuss the uses of Connection.State and Connection.Errors in the ASP database connectivity model.

15. What is the purpose of the Error Function in the Kanthaka Farms example? How else might it be used in an electronic commerce application?

Critical Thinking Using the Web

1. There is much discussion about which technique is best to use for ASP connectivity to a back-end database. Many say that because a System DSN is for ODBC data sources, it causes OLE DB to wrap an ODBC driver within itself, adding to the electronic commerce model overhead and reducing the Web database construction performance. Using your favorite search engine to search the Web, investigate connection techniques. Create a report detailing the pros and cons of each in a table. Insert your table into presentation software. Be prepared to present your findings to the class.

2. Explore how a Native OLE DB Provider is used. How is it set up? Why is it necessary to replace the name of the system DSN with the string that has been produced in order to connect to the data store using the Native OLE DB Provider? Investigate the subject on the Web with your favorite search engine. Create a 200–400-word essay and discuss your findings. Be sure to list the steps needed to create the UDL file in this process. What can you do if you do not have a .udl? Be prepared to discuss your findings with the class.

3. Microsoft Data Access Components includes ADO, OLE DB, and every component needed for getting your databases out on the Internet. Learn more about MDAC at the Microsoft Web site at http://www.microsoft.com/data/. Prepare a 200–400-word essay of your findings and be prepared to discuss them with the class.

Chapter Case Study

Albatross Records is a continuing case study in this book that illustrates the process of building electronic commerce with Web database constructions. In Chapter 11, you will explore ASP database connectivity. This connectivity will be made by utilizing VBScript in the ASP. As you continue through the text, you will complete different facets of electronic commerce Web database construction, resulting in a complete Web site for Albatross Records.

■ Create an ASP page that utilizes a database for connectivity.

■ From the Web client, add code that will allow table records to be viewed. Your ASP should allow this connectivity using the Microsoft.Jet.OLEDB.4.0 provider connection string.

■ Create a Randomize Timer state in an ASP page to initialize a random-number generator and a RND Function. These should be used to move from record to record as the Web client clicks on Refresh. Your records should display Albatross Records artists with comments from reviewers and short biographical items.

- Create an ASP with database connectivity to filter and sort the database records of Albatross Records artists.

- Create an ASP with database connectivity to query the database using transaction objects. Include an Error Function to prevent multiple updates of the primary key reference.

12

Server-Side Development
with ASP Template Files

I do not fear computers. I fear the lack of them.

—Isaac Asimov (1920–1992)

12.1 The Importance of Template Files in the ASP Electronic Commerce Model

As with Computer Gateway Interface (CGI), Active Server Pages (ASP) can utilize **template files** in Web database constructions to add development ease and Web site standardization. Using an ASP template file requires the electronic commerce developer to use less hard code in the construction. This makes it easier not only to create global ASP applications, but also to make changes in the Web page design at a later date.

ASP template files share a similar interface to provide a consistent customer experience throughout the business Web site. This makes the site more maintainable, as updates can be propagated to the entire site by updating a single template file. The decision to switch to a dynamically generated site is usually based on a business' desire to ensure a consistent look and feel throughout the Web site and by observing the duplication of tasks in the process of updating the site. Each time a business updates a Web site, the following steps must be performed:

- Create a document representing the new content.
- Find the logical breaks in the multiple pages.
- Organize the content into multiple pages.
- Open an existing page and copy the existing Web client interface.
- Paste and modify the Web client interface to fit the new page.

The last two steps of the process are iterative and need to be frequently revisited to ensure the Web client interface is consistent and up to date. Without templates, each document must be examined when the appearance of the business' Web site changes. With a template-based electronic commerce model, modifying the template modifies the entire Web site.

Understanding Necessary Components of the Template File

Often, the starting point for creating ASP template files begins with a thorough understanding of the site, the customers, and their preferences. This area receives the bulk of the business' traffic and is where the majority of the updates occur. Before building the template, it is necessary to understand the needs of the Web client interface. The developer must fully understand what information each customer who visits the site needs and how to generalize this information to reach the largest audience. Upon careful inspection, trends will appear. These trends usually are in the following areas and can be used for site generalization development:

- Include current date.
- Include site category or location.
- List pages or site map.
- List related material, links, sites.
- Target areas most frequently visited by the Web browser.

Planning the Template File Design

ASP template files use code that formats pages of the business' Web site dynamically, basing the layout, colors, and formatting contained in the template file on **custom tags**. Located at the top of all content

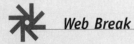

Web Break

Electronic commerce has even moved into the database management field! Today there are software solutions for remote database administration that give Oracle, Microsoft SQL Server, and db2 Universal Database data managers the freedom to manage the business' databases from a standard Internet browser. To learn more about database management through your browser visit http://www.bmc.com/webdba.

pages is code used to reference which template should be used for a particular Web client. This code can point to a page based on customer selection, browser detection, or entry page. These pages also contain formatting HTML code to be inserted in each dynamically produced page, around the main page content. This code is inserted by a Response.Write, a statement above and below the content of the normal site pages. Though pages are created dynamically, the template file must be static. ASP code within it will not run. In order to incorporate ASP code, it must be included in a referenced page that is added into each page by replacing a custom tag code that has been added to the template. **Server-side include (SSI) files** also cannot be used within the template. A server-side include is a variable value that a Web server can include in an HTML file before it is sent to the Web client. However, SSI files can be included in the referenced ASP, if required.

12.2 The Use of the Cookies Collection in ASP Template Files

Often **cookies** are used when Web browsers are routed to other ASP pages using template files. The name cookie derives from UNIX objects called **magic cookies**. These magic cookies, or tokens, are attached to a user or program and change depending on the areas entered by the user or program. In ASP, a cookie is information that the Web site puts on the customer's hard disk for later use. It is simply a set of printable ASCII pairs in the form of **key-value pairs**. There must be at least one such pair that gives the name of the cookie and its value. Key-value pairs, which are optional in cookies, include the following:

- *Expires*. This pair sets the date/time after which this cookie will be deleted. If omitted, the default is the current "browser session." This means that the cookie is not written to disk. The date/time string must be in Internet-standard format, referred to the GMT time zone: for example: "Mon, 01-Jun-2051 14:28:57 GMT"
- *Domain*. This pair controls the domains to which the cookie will be sent, for example, cseng.aw.com. Very strict rules regulate what domain specifiers are valid. If omitted, the default will be the Web server that set the cookie.
- *Path*. This pair is used to control to which programs the cookie will be sent.

- *Secure.* This pair, if present, informs the Web browser that this cookie should only be sent over secure, or encrypted, communications channels.

A cookie is stored by the Web server on the client side of a client/server communication. Typically, a cookie records customer preferences at a business's site. The location of the cookies depends on the Web browser. For example, Internet Explorer stores each cookie as a separate file under a Windows subdirectory; Netscape, however, stores all cookies in a single cookies.txt file. Opera, yet another brand of browser, stores cookies in a single cookies.dat file. In the ASP template file, a cookie is set so that the customer can return to the previous template page. The cookie will tell the function that formats this page to use another template. The customer will be viewing this same page, but it will be formatted using a different template. The content will be the same, but the page layout, colors, and fonts will be different.

In Chapter 9, banner ads were created. Cookies can be used rather than a randomizer to ensure that the customer does not repeatedly view the same banner ads. Cookies rotate the banner ads that the Web site sends so the same ad is not sent with a succession of requested pages. They can also be used to customize pages on the basis of browser type or other information that may have been provided to the Web site. Customers must agree to let cookies be saved for them, but, in general, cookies help Web sites to better serve the customer.

ASP sites that use sessions and any nonstatic Web site can make use of cookies. It is also possible to set and read cookies using client-side code; however, in this chapter, server-side cookies will be discussed using ASP built-in **Request and Response objects**. The cookies collection is a part of the Request and Response objects. They support the standard key-value pairs of all ASP collections, as well as a few additional methods and properties. Cookies must be set before any HTML code is sent to the Web client, because it uses the Response object. The following code can be used to write a cookie:

```
Response.Cookies Properties and Methods:
Response.Cookies("myCookie").Expires = "June 6, 2051"
Response.Cookies("myCookie")("myValue1") = 1
Response.Cookies("myCookie")("myValue2") = 2
Response.Cookies("myCookie")("myValueN") = N

Request.Cookies Properties and Methods:
Response.Write Request.Cookies("myCookie")("myValue1")
```

What were the changing markets that drove Longs Drug Stores to outsource?

List benefits associated with moving the electronic commerce component of the business to a third party.

Is there a down side to outsourcing a company's electronic commerce? Longs mentions that they used a third party to manage the company's Web site as well as several enterprise applications. What could these applications be?

Why would they be outsourced along with the Web site?

Q & A: Outsourcing May Be the Answer to Electronic Commerce Questions

Longs Drug Stores, a recognized leader in the chain drug industry, has grown steadily since it began in 1938. Once privately owned by brothers Joe and Tom Long, Longs has been publicly held since 1961 and traded on the New York Stock Exchange since 1971.

In 2001, with their competition moving to the World Wide Web, Longs Drug Stores saw their market changing and the advent of electronic commerce as a major challenge to the future of their business. Longs' vision was to move their business to the Internet to complement their over 400 brick-and-mortar stores in California, Hawaii, Nevada, Colorado, Washington, and Oregon. They wanted their Web presence to continue their reputation for customer service with Web customization based on a customer's health concerns. Like their competitors, Longs also wanted the ability to accept orders for prescriptions over the Internet and provide health-related information to their customers.

The trick was to make the move to electronic commerce seamless, meet all the identified goals, protect customer personal information, and integrate new technology with that already in place.

A daunting task? Linda Rossi, Longs' director of Internet technology, and Brian Kilcourse, Longs' senior vice president and chief information officer, noted there were significant technical and administrative hurdles to overcome. "Our world is gravitating towards a 24 by 7 computing environment," Kilcourse said. "People are accessing our Web site and ordering prescriptions at all hours." Rossi also noted the significant technical and administrative challenges associated with managing an around-the-clock data center.

After a thorough cost analysis, outsourcing was determined to be the answer to Longs' electronic commerce questions. Intira was chosen to host a personalization engine from BroadVision and manage Longs' Web site as well as several enterprise applications.

Rossi said the decision to outsource the company's Web site and several key applications was the right one. The multimillion-dollar partnership meets drivers affecting the drug retailing business' new market. Rossi added that Longs has an advantage over its competitors, because they don't have to spend the kinds of dollars its competitors do to get the new Web customers. With outsourcing the Web database construction, Longs has personalized technology—a major sales and customer service tool—and gives customers new reasons to shop in their stores. For Longs, outsourcing electronic commerce was the right answer to their question.

Sources: Mel Duval, *Interactive Week,* March 27, 2001, 4:38 P.M. ET; http://www.longs.com; http://www.intira.com/

Developers often check to see whether the cookie has been set with IsNull. If so, then

```
If IsNull(Request.Cookies("myCookie")
```

If the business only needs to retain customer cookie data for a short period of time, the cookies can be created to expire when the customer closes their browser. This is one way developers tie together user state without forms, querystrings, or a Session variable. To accomplish this task, the Expires field can be set to a relative time in the future, for instance one week away, and the VB's DateAdd() function used as in the following code:

```
Response.Cookies("Example").Expires = dateadd("d",1,now)
```

The **cookies object collection** does not have to have a series of key-value pairs. It is possible to give the cookie a single value. However, without the key-value pairs, it is easy to overwrite all of the data in the cookie. One method to check to see whether a cookie is scalar or a collection is to use the Count method to return the number of items it holds.

Kanthaka Farms is a continuing case study in this book that illustrates the process of building electronic commerce with Web database constructions. In Chapter 12, you will explore the use of cookies and template files in ASP server-side technology. As you continue through the text, you will complete different facets of electronic commerce Web database construction, resulting in a complete Web site for Kanthaka Farms.

Kanthaka Farms
Learn How to Use Cookies in Your ASP Page

1. From your Start Programs menu, launch your server software. Verify that it is running by observing the icon in the tray.

2. The first file you will set is a cookie called cookie_return.asp with the value Request.Form("name"). The expiration date is set to the first day of June, 2051. Failure to set an expiration date will cause the cookie to expire when the user closes the browser. In a text editor, write the following code. Save your file in the C:\WebSite\CHILIASP\Samples\Kanthaka folder.

```
<%
Response.Cookies("Name")= Request.Form("name")
Response.Cookies("Name").Expires="Jun 1, 2051"
%>
```

```
<HTML>
<BODY BGCOLOR="#FFFFFF" TEXT="#000000">
<H1 ALIGN=CENTER>Kanthaka Farms</H1><P>
<P align="center"><IMG SRC="KAN_LOGO.gif" width="121"
   height="97"></P>
<P>
Thank you for submitting this information. Please click on
   the link below...
<P>
<P>
<P><a href="http://localhost/kasp/cookie_read.asp">View the
   Stored Data</a></p>
</BODY>
</HTML>
```

3. Next you will create another ASP file to read your cookie. Using a text editor, code the following to a new file:

```
<%
Name = Request.Cookies("Name")
%>
<HTML>
<BODY BGCOLOR="#FFFFFF" TEXT="#000000">
<H1 ALIGN=CENTER>Kanthaka Farms</H1><P>
<P align="center"><IMG SRC="KAN_LOGO.gif" width="121"
   height="97"></P>
<P>
<H2 align=center>Hello to <%=name%> from Kanthaka Farms!
   Thank you for visiting our site!
</H2></BODY>
</HTML>
```

Save the file as cookie_read.asp in the same folder as cookie_return.asp. Notice that the value the cookie is set to read is Request.Cookies("Name"). The above code will return the value that the Kanthaka Farms customer places in the name variable.

4. Your next step is to create a user-interface with the Kanthaka Farms customer to allow him or her to enter data in the name variable. To do so, create a new file in a text editor named cookie_ask.asp in the C:\WebSite\CHILIASP\Samples\Kanthaka folder. Use the following code:

```
<%
%>
<HTML>
<BODY>
<FORM ACTION="cookie_return.asp" METHOD="POST">
```

```
<BODY BGCOLOR="#FFFFFF" TEXT="#000000">
<H1 ALIGN=CENTER>Kanthaka Farms</H1><P>
<P align="center"><IMG SRC="KAN_LOGO.gif" width="121"
   height="97"></P>
Kanthaka Farms would like to know you better.
Please type in your name so that we may call you by name!
<P>
<INPUT TYPE="TEXT" NAME="name">
<INPUT TYPE="SUBMIT" VALUE="Submit">
</FORM>
</BODY>
</HTML>
```

5. Test your cookie application by viewing the ASP cookie_ask.asp
file from the following URL:

```
http://localhost/kasp/cookie_ask.asp
```

Your screen should look similar to the one displayed in Figure 12-1.

6. Type in your name and press the Submit button to send the front-
end data. Your screen should now look like Figure 12-2.

7. To read the cookie, you can either type in the localhost URL for
the file, or click on the hyperlink displayed on the cookie_return.asp
screen. Your cookie_read.asp screen should look like the one shown
in Figure 12-3.

Figure 12-1	**Figure 12-2**
The cookie_ask.asp Screen	*The cookie_return.asp Screen*

Figure 12-3
The cookie_read.asp Screen

Alternatives to Cookies

Remember that not all browsers support cookies. If the business' application is in contact with browsers that do not support cookies, alternatives for passing information from page to page in the application must be used in the electronic commerce model. One alternative to cookies is to pass the information through added parameters in a query string. The following code is an example of added parameters in a query string:

```
http://www. http://cseng.aw.com/guest.asp?userid=Nelson
```

Hidden controls can also be used to accomplish the same task as cookies. Using hidden controls, the form passes a user id value, in addition to the rest of the information, as in the following example:

```
<FORM method="post" action="guest.asp">
First Name: <INPUT type="text" name="fname" value="">
Last Name: <INPUT type="text" name="lname" value="">
<INPUT type="hidden" name="userid" value="Nelson">
<INPUT type="submit" value="Send">
</FORM>
```

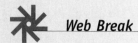

Web Break

Some new data-warehousing techniques, as well as a new set of data standards, are proving to be the customer profiling and tracking breakthrough that have Customer Relationship Management (CRM) specialists salivating. The **Common Warehouse Metamodel (CWM)** will allow different data warehouse systems, databases, and other data repositories to exchange data automatically. The Object Management Group's Common Warehouse Metamodel is an attempt to define and explain different data sets in a universal format. The following is a list of what CWM does:

- Opens a path between isolated, modern software object modeling and data warehouse.
- Implements eXtensible Markup Language as a tagging method for moving data between dissimilar sources.
- Allows data from multiple sources to be related to each other and used in business intelligence systems.

To find about more about CWM, read the CWM Interchange Specifications at http://xml.coverpages.org/omg-cwmi.html.

12.3 Creating ASP Template Files

Template files are used to add consistency to the business Web site, and, since changes and modifications are often necessary, they add ease to the change process. Template files are usually ASP pages that retrieve some of the content from a text file. They can also employ HTML forms for editing the content of that text file. In the electronic commerce model, businesses often use these types of applications for breaking news, updating price lists, or disseminating information about special offers. Remember that the template file itself must be static, or the ASP code within it will not run. In order to incorporate ASP code, it must be run in a separate ASP file and added into the page by replacing custom tags in the templates. Cookies are incorporated into the ASP template model: The customer's Web browser is re-routed with another ASP page where a cookie is set, and the customer is returned to the first page. The cookie will tell the code Function that formats the first page to use another template. Though the customer will be viewing the same page, it will be formatted using a different template. The content will remain the same, but the page layout, colors, and fonts will have been changed.

Kanthaka Farms
Creating ASP Template Files
to Add Consistency
to the Web Site

In this exercise, you will create several ASP files, cookies, and HTML forms to use as templates for later updating of the business's Web site. The hierarchy shown in Figure 12-4 depicts the positions of folders and files in the template creation for this example.

Figure 12-4
The Template Hierarchy

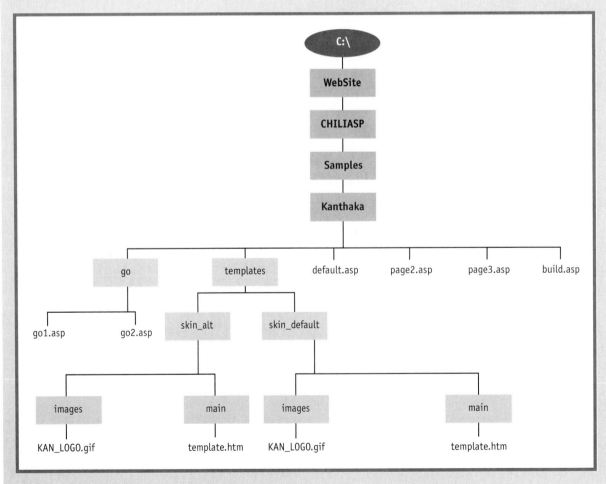

1. From your Start Programs menu, launch your server software. Verify that it is running by observing the icon in the tray.

2. Create the necessary folders as shown in Figure 12-4. Be very careful to place your folders as they are depicted in the figure.

3. Using a text editor, create the two templates that will be used by Kanthaka Farms. Both files will be named template.htm; however, one file will be stored in the C:\WebSite\CHILIASP\Samples\ Kanthaka\templates\skin_default\main folder and the other will be stored in the C:\WebSite\CHILIASP\Samples\Kanthaka\templates\ skin_alt\main folder. Use the following code for the skin_default\ main\template.htm:

```
<HTML>
<HEAD>
<STYLE>
<!-
.small          { font-size: 7.5pt; font-family:
  Verdana,Arial; font-weight: normal }
.smallbold      { font-size: 7.5pt; font-family:
  Verdana,Arial; font-weight: bold }
.medium         { font-size: 9pt; font-family: Verdana,Arial;
  font-weight: normal }
.mediumbold     { font-size: 9pt; font-family: Verdana,Arial;
  font-weight: bold }
.largebold      { font-size: 14pt; font-family:
  Verdana,Arial; font-weight: bold }
a:link          { color: blue; text-decoration: underline; }
a:visited       { text-decoration: underline; color:blue; }
a:hover         { text-decoration: underline; color:red; }
->
</STYLE>
<TITLE>ASP Template Demo 1</TITLE>
</HEAD>
<BODY>
<TABLE border="0" cellpadding="2" cellspacing="0"
  width="600">
<TR>
<TD width="600" colspan="2"><img border="0"
  src="../images/KAN_LOGO.gif" width="180"
  height="86"></TD>
</TR>
<TR>
<TD width="600" colspan="2" class="smallbold">
  <A HREF="../../../default.asp">Page 1</A> |
<A HREF="../../../page2.asp"> Page 2</a> |
  <A HREF="../../../page3.asp">Page 3</A></TD>
</TR>
<TR>
```

```
<TD width="150" class="small"
   valign="top">xxxDATESTAMPxxx</TD>
<TD width="450" valign="top">xxxPAGECONTENTxxx</TD>
</TR>
</TABLE>
</BODY>
</HTML>
```

Save the file as template.htm. Using Windows Explorer, verify that this file is in the skin_default\main folder.

4. Your next step is to create the skin_alt\main\template.htm. This will be the alternate template file. Create the file in a text editor using the following code:

```
<HTML>
<HEAD>
<STYLE>
<!-
.small      { font-size: 7.5pt; font-family: Arial;
   font-weight: normal; color: black; }
.smallbold   { font-size: 7.5pt; font-family: Arial;
   font-weight: bold; color: black; }
.medium     { font-size: 9pt; font-family: Arial;
   font-weight: normal; color: black; }
.mediumbold { font-size: 9pt; font-family: Arial;
   font-weight: bold; color: black; }
.largebold   { font-size: 14pt; font-family: Arial;
   font-weight: bold; color: black; }
a:link      { color: #9999FF; text-decoration: underline; }
a:visited   { text-decoration: underline; color:#9999FF; }
a:hover     { text-decoration: underline; color:red; }
->
</STYLE>
<TITLE>ASP Template Demo 2</TITLE>
</HEAD>
<BODY bgcolor="#00FF00">
<TABLE border="0" cellpadding="2" cellspacing="0"
   width="90%" bgcolor="#00FF00">
<TR>
<TD class="mediumbold" valign="top" colspan="1">This second
   ASP template looks very different...
<P>Use this template for easier printing or to meet the
   needs of the disabled on the Internet.
It's your call how you will code this for Kanthaka Farms.
<P>You can go back to the first template by clicking Page 1
   on the menu (right hand side of page now!) and then
   clicking the bottom link on that page.</P>
<P> </P>
</TD>
```

```
</TR>
<TR>
<TD valign="top">xxxPAGECONTENTxxx</TD>
<TD valign="top" class="medium" width="300" align="center">
<P><A HREF="../../../default.asp">Page 1</A></P>
<P><A HREF="../../../page2.asp">Page 2</A></P>
<P><A HREF="../../../page3.asp">Page 3</A></P></TD>
</TR>
<TR>
<TD class="smallbold" colspan="2"
   align="right">xxxDATESTAMPxxx</TD>
<IMG border="0" src="../images/KAN_LOGO.gif" width="90"
   height="40"></TR>
</TABLE>
</BODY>
</HTML>
```

5. Copy the KAN_LOGO.gif from the Kanthaka folder to the images folders in both the skin_alt and the skin_default folders.

6. Now you need to create the cookies files. These will be stored in the Go folder. Using a text editor, create the first file as go1.asp using the following code:

```
<%
response.cookies("templatesample")("templatepath") =
   "templates/skin_default/"
response.redirect("../default.asp")
%>
```

7. Following the same procedure as in step 6, create the go2.asp file. This file will also be saved in the Go folder. Use the following code:

```
<%
response.cookies("templatesample")("templatepath") =
   "templates/skin_alt/"
response.redirect("../default.asp")
%>
```

8. The last files you will create will be stored directly in the Kanthaka folder. Using a text editor, create the build.asp file using the following code:

```
<%
strTemplateLocation =
   request.cookies("templatesample")("templatepath")
If request.cookies("templatesample")("templatepath") =""
   then
strTemplateLocation="templates/skin_default/"
response.cookies("templatesample")("templatepath") =""
```

```
End if
strDateStampHTML = Ucase(day(now()) & " " &
   monthname(month(now())) & " " & year(now()))
Function
   ReadFromTemplate(strTemplateLocation,aryPageTemplate,
   strDateStampHTML)
Set FileObject =
   Server.CreateObject("Scripting.FileSystemObject")
BodytextFile = Server.MapPath(strTemplateLocation &
   "main/template.htm")
Set InStream= FileObject.OpenTextFile (BodytextFile, 1,
   False, False)
While not InStream.AtEndOfStream
strPageBaseText = strPageBaseText & InStream.ReadLine &
   vbcrlf
Wend
Set Instream = Nothing
strPageBaseText =
   Replace(strPageBaseText,"../images",strTemplateLocation &
   "images")
strPageBaseText = Replace(strPageBaseText,"../","")
strPageBaseText = Replace
   (strPageBaseText,"xxxDATESTAMPxxx",strDateStampHTML)
aryPageTemplate = split(strPageBaseText,
   "xxxPAGECONTENTxxx",-1)
ReadFromTemplate = aryPageTemplate
END Function
%>
```

9. Create the default.asp file in a text editor using the following code:

```
<%@ LANGUAGE="VBSCRIPT" %>
<!-#include file="build.asp"->
<%
Call ReadFromTemplate(strTemplateLocation,aryPageTemplate,
   strDatestampHTML)
response.write(aryPageTemplate(0))
%>
<TABLE border="0" cellpadding="5" cellspacing="0"
   width="100%">
<TR>
<TD class="largebold">Kanthaka Farms Template Page 1 </TD>
</TR>
<TR>
<TD class="medium"><P>Place your template text for Kanthaka
   Farms here...</P>
<P><A HREF="go/go2.asp">Click here to view using the
   alternative template</A></P>
<P>Or if you prefer the first template...</P>
<P><A HREF="go/go1.asp">Click here to view the first
   template</A> </TD>
</TR>
</TABLE>
```

```
<%
response.write(aryPageTemplate(1))
%>
```

10. The next file you will need to create is the page2.asp file. Use a simple text editor and enter the following code:

```
<%@ LANGUAGE="VBSCRIPT" %>
<!--#include file="build.asp"-->
<%
Call ReadFromTemplate(strTemplateLocation,aryPageTemplate,
    strDatestampHTML)
response.write(aryPageTemplate(0))
%>
<TABLE border="0" cellpadding="5" cellspacing="0"
    width="100%">
<TR>
<TD class="largebold">Kanthaka Farms Template Page 2</TD>
</TR>
<TR>
<TD class="medium">Place your template text for Kanthaka
    Farms here... </TD>
</TR>
</TABLE>
<%
response.write(aryPageTemplate(1))
%>
```

11. The last file you will need to create to complete this exercise is the page3.asp. Create this file with the following code:

```
<%@ LANGUAGE="VBSCRIPT" %>
<!--#include file="build.asp"-->
<%
Call ReadFromTemplate(strTemplateLocation,aryPageTemplate,
    strDatestampHTML)
response.write(aryPageTemplate(0))
%>
<TABLE border="0" cellpadding="5" cellspacing="0"
    width="100%">
<TR>
<TD class="largebold">Kanthaka Farms Template Page 3</TD>
</TR>
<TR>
<TD class="medium">Place your template text for Kanthaka
    Farms here...</TD>
</TR>
</TABLE>
<%
response.write(aryPageTemplate(1))
%>
```

12. You are now ready to test your template application by viewing the ASP default.asp file from the following URL:

http://localhost/kasp/default.asp

Your screen should look similar to the one displayed in Figure 12-5.

13. Click on the link at the bottom of the page to go to your alternate template. Notice on your screen and in Figure 12-6 how different the alternate template looks from the default template.

14. Click on the different pages. Your Page 3 of the default template should be similar to Figure 12-7 shown below.

15. Add appropriate text to your three Kanthaka Farms pages and the template HTML files.

Figure 12-5

The Default ASP Template for Kanthaka Farms

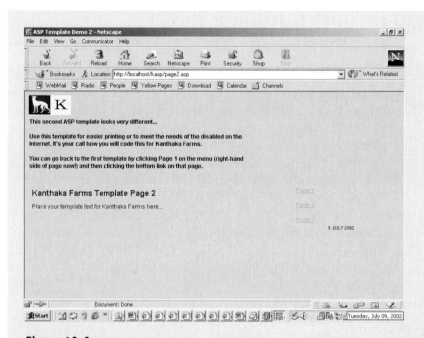

Figure 12-6

The Alternate ASP Template for Kanthaka Farms

Figure 12-7

Page 3 of Kanthaka Farms' Default Template Files

12.4 Using Functions to Modify Template VBScripts

It is often necessary for the developer to modify scripts to meet the ever-changing needs of the business. The solution to making this task easier is to use the VBScript functions. For example, in an earlier example, customer information was collected from a form using the Request.Form("name") command, where "name" was the name of the form field. Remember that the Request.Form command has been used earlier in the Web database construction. It was used to collect the values in a form with the POST method in CGI. There, information sent from a form with the POST method was invisible to others, and since the POST method has no limits, it was used to send a large amount of information. The Request.Form command with ASP can be used to modify the template VBScripts. Examine the following code:

```
<%
Form_LName = Request.Form("lname")
Form_FName = Request.Form("fname")
Form_Email = Request.Form("email")
Form_comment = Request.Form("comment")
%>
```

In this example, the customer information has been collected using VBScript variables. Before validating the customer information, it may be necessary to remove unwanted extra space characters from the form. Often, these are added by the customer; however, they are sometimes also added by the browser. The **Trim() Function** returns a string without leading and trailing spaces and can be used to remove them. In the following script, notice the use of the Function:

```
<%
Form_LName = Trim(Request.Form("lname"))
Form_FName = Trim(Request.Form("fname"))
Form_Email = Trim(Request.Form("email"))
Form_comment = Trim(Request.Form("comment"))
%>
```

In addition to Trim, the **LTrim** and **RTrim Functions** are also available in VBScript. The LTrim() Function returns a string without leading spaces and the RTrim() Function returns a string without trailing spaces.

The **Len() Function** is useful to check for empty fields. Minimum can also be incorporated into the code to increase data integrity. In the following example, the comment field is optional and an IF THEN statement is used to check the length:

```
<%
IF len(Form_LName)<20 THEN
    Validated_Form = false
ELSE Validated_Form = true
END IF
%>
```

To check whether a field contains a character, use the **InStr() Function** to return a 0 if the string does not contain the search string. Now the Lname code looks like the following:

```
<%
IF len(Form_LName)<20 OR InStr(Form_LName,"@")=0 THEN
 Validated_Form = false
ELSE
 Validated_Form = true END IF
%>
```

The developer may also want to check for returned values containing special characters such as the double quote (") or the single quote ('). The double-quote symbol marks the beginning and the end of a VBScript string. The single quote marks the beginning and end in a database string. The **Replace() Function** can be used to replace all the double and single quotes in the returned values with double double quotes (" ") and double single quotes (' '). This signals to VBScript and the back-end database that the symbol is not marking a beginning or end of a string, but is actually a part of the string. The following code will accomplish this task:

```
<%
Form_LName = Replace(Form_LName,"""","""""")
%>
```

Summary

■ **Describe the importance of template files in the Active Server Pages (ASP) electronic commerce model.** ASP can utilize template files in Web database constructions to add development ease and Web site standardization. Using an ASP template file requires the electronic commerce developer to use less hard code in the construction. This makes it easier not only to create global ASP applications, but also to make changes in the Web page design at a later date. ASP template files share a similar interface to provide a consistent customer experience throughout the business Web site. This makes the site more maintainable, as updates can be propagated to the entire site by updating a single template file. The decision to switch to a dynamically generated site is usually based on a business' desire to ensure a consistent look and feel throughout the Web site and by observing the duplication of tasks in the process of updating the site.

▪ **Create cookies for use in ASP template files.** In ASP, a cookie is information that the Web site puts on the customer's hard disk for later use. It is simply a set of printable ASCII pairs in the form of key-value pairs. A cookie is stored by the Web server on the client side of a client/server communication. Typically, a cookie records customer preferences at a business' site. The location of the cookies depends on the Web browser. For example, Internet Explorer stores each cookie as a separate file under a Windows subdirectory. However, Netscape stores all cookies in a single cookies.txt file. Opera, yet another brand of browser, stores cookies in a single cookies.dat file. In the ASP template file, a cookie is set so that the customer can return to the previous template page. The cookie will tell the function that formats this page to use another template. The customer will be viewing the same page, but it will be formatted using a different template. The content will be the same, but the page layout, colors, and fonts will be different. One alternative to cookies is to pass the information through added parameters in a query string. Hidden controls can also be used to accomplish the same task as cookies.

▪ **Create ASP template files.** Template files are used to add consistency to the business Web site and, since changes and modifications are often necessary, they add ease to the change process. Template files are usually ASP pages that retrieve some of the content from a text file. They can also employ HTML forms for editing the content of that text file. In the electronic commerce model, businesses often use these types of applications for breaking news, updating price lists, or disseminating information about special offers. Remember that the template file itself must be static, or the ASP code within it will not run. In order to incorporate ASP code, it must be run in a separate ASP file and added into the page by replacing custom tags in the templates. Cookies are incorporated into the ASP template model: the customer's Web browser is re-routed with another ASP page where a cookie is set, and the customer is returned to the first page. The cookie will tell the code Function that formats the first page to use another template. Though the customer will be viewing the same page, it will be formatted using a different template. The content will remain the same, but the page layout, colors, and fonts will have been changed.

■ **Use functions to modify template VBScripts.** It is often necessary for the developer to modify scripts to meet the ever-changing needs of the business. The solution to making this task easier is to use the VBScript functions. For example, customer information can be collected from a form using the Request.Form("name") command, where "name" is the name of the form field. The most common functions used to modify VBScripts are the Trim(), Len(), InStr(), and the Replace() Functions.

Chapter Key Terms

Common Warehouse Metamodel (CWM)	InStr() Function	Request objects
cookies	key-value pairs	Response objects
cookies object collection	Len() Function	RTrim Function
custom tags	LTrim Function	server-side include files
hidden controls	magic cookies	template files
	Replace() Function	Trim() Function

Review Questions

1. What are template files? How are they used with ASP?

2. Compare and contrast the uses of ASP and CGI template files.

3. What steps must a business perform in order to update its Web site if it is not using template files?

4. What are custom tags? How are they used in template files?

5. What is a cookie?

6. Are cookies client-side or server-side technology?

7. How do cookies use the Request and Response objects?

8. What are key-value pairs? How are they used in template files?

9. Discuss the process of creating template files using ASP. What is the hierarchy that should be used? Why is this type of organization important to the efficiency of the model?

10. Why is it often necessary for the Web database construction developers to modify previously written and deployed scripts?

11. How is customer information collected in the Web database construction using VBScript variables?

12. Explain the use of the Trim() Functions. Be sure to include LTrim and RTrim in your discussion.

13. For what is the InStr() Function used? Write a snippet of code for Kanthaka Farms that would use this function in the electronic commerce model.

14. When would it be necessary for a Web database developer to use the Replace() Function?

15. What signals to VBScript and the back-end of the database that quote symbols are not marking the beginning or end of a string, but are actually part of the string?

Critical Thinking Using the Web

1. More and more businesses are looking to increase their internal efficiency. The evolution of business to electronic business demands such efficiencies. The rapid emergence and phenomenal growth of Web-based applications in general and electronic commerce applications in particular are changing the IT landscape. Software now *supports* a traditional business model, but in electronic commerce software applications *are the business*. Organizations are facing new challenges in the electronic commerce world, but they are not all related to dealing with new technology. Using your favorite search engine, choose one of the points below and find specific examples on the Web of how today's businesses are meeting this challenge.

- Supporting legacy applications and databases in an electronic commerce environment
- Meeting the high-availability, high-quality, and rapid-change implementation requirements dictated by electronic commerce
- Managing the increasing size and complexity of databases required to support electronic commerce applications

Write a 200–400-word essay of your findings and be prepared to present your report in class.

2. Cookies are one method companies use to collect customer data. Wal-Mart and many other companies are reassessing the customer data they share. In some cases, more open communication of data is occurring, whereas in others sharing is being discontinued. As data collection techniques become more sophisticated, so do the ways in which the data are shared. Visit Wal-Mart's Web site at http://www.walmartstores.com as well as two other companies of your choice. What are the companies' strategies regarding data collection and data sharing? Prepare a 200–400-word essay on your findings. Be prepared to present your essay in class.

3. The back-end of the construction, the database, stores a wealth of valuable information in today's business environment. However, many businesses are not getting the most out of the customer-profiling data that they have spent a large amount of resources (both time and money) to collect. One way for businesses to evaluate whether they are efficiently using the profiling data that have been collected is to use the Personalization Index (PI). PI is calculated by taking the number of profile elements used in customer interactions and dividing that figure by the total number of profile elements collected. A PI of less than 0.03 indicates that the business is collecting much more data than it is using. A PI of 0.75 or higher means that there is an efficient use of data-collecting resources. Explore other methods your electronic commerce design can use to benefit from analytic solutions to improve the company's performance. Visit NetGen's Web site at http://www.netgen.com/. Write a 200–400-word report on the company, its offerings, and electronic commerce solutions. Be prepared to present your findings in class.

Chapter Case Study

Albatross Records is a continuing case study in this book that illustrates the process of building electronic commerce with Web database constructions. In Chapter 12, you will explore the use of template and cookie files in ASP server-side technology. As you continue through the text, you will complete different facets of electronic commerce Web database construction, resulting in a complete Web site for Albatross Records.

- Create three templates to use in the Albatross Records Web database construction. One template should be print-friendly, one disability-friendly, and one designed for those customers with high-speed capabilities.
- Create a Cookie collection for Albatross Records to record the customers' preferences. Set your cookie to expire on June 6, 2005.
- Add Functions to your VBScript to modify your templates. Use the Trim(), Len(), InStr(), and Replace() Functions in your code.

13

Browser Programs and Other Server-Side Technologies

Learning Objectives

Upon completion of this chapter, you will be able to

- Discuss the basic components of JavaScript
- Discuss the basic components of Java Server Pages (JSP)
- Use JavaScript and JSP in the electronic commerce model
- Use ActiveX in the electronic commerce model
- Create compiled browser programs using ActiveX
- View a dynamically linked ActiveX document in a Web page

13.1 The Basic Components of JavaScript

JavaScript is another electronic commerce tool that is used in the Web database construction to create the dynamic interaction between the customer and the business. In a Hypertext Markup Language (HTML) page, JavaScript is simply a series of instructions that the Web browser understands and uses to perform various actions. The JavaScript code can either be part of the Web page file or, in much the same way that cascading style sheets (CSS) can be used, JavaScript can be referenced from the Web page by using a link to another file. It allows the electronic commerce developer to provide the customer at the front-end of the electronic commerce model interaction with both the business and its Web site content, rather than merely to present a static or fixed Web page. In more advanced JavaScript applications, the actions taken by the Web client can directly affect the Web page content, presentation, or site navigation methods.

JavaScript is not **Java**. Java is a **compiled language** that must be transformed into machine language before it can communicate with a computer. JavaScript is an **interpreted language**, which means it is transformed into machine language *on* the computer. There are similarities, however, between JavaScript and Java: The coding in JavaScript looks very similar to Java, but it is much less restrictive. For example, in JavaScript variables may be assigned any type of value, but Java will not allow such freedom. Netscape originally developed JavaScript independent of Java under the name of **LiveScript**. The name was later changed to JavaScript as a result of an agreement with **Sun Microsystems**, the developer of Java.

JavaScript is the originating technology for the **ECMA Standard** proposed by Netscape in 1996. The **Electrotechnical Commission Management Association (ECMA)** is an international industry association, headquartered in Geneva, Switzerland, that was founded in 1961 and dedicated to the standardization of information and communication systems. In the Standard, **ECMAScript** is defined as object-oriented programming language for performing computations and manipulating objects within a **host environment**. A Web server provides a different host environment for server-side computations, including objects representing requests, clients, and files, and mechanisms to lock and share data. By using browser-side and server-side scripting together in the electronic commerce model, it is possible to distribute computations between the Web client and Web server and at the same time provide a customized user interface for the Web database construction. The ECMA Standard also formalized the definition of a **scripting language** as a programming language used to manipulate, customize, and automate the facilities of an existing system. In these systems, useful functionality is already available through the user interface, and the scripting language is simply a mechanism for exposing that functionality to the electronic commerce model. In this way, the existing system is said to provide a host environment with objects and facilities that complete the capabilities of the scripting language. ECMAScript was originally designed to be a **Web scripting language**, defined by the ECMA Standard as a mechanism used to "enliven" Web pages in browsers and to perform Web server computation as part of the Web-based client–server architecture.

JavaScript will also run on Microsoft's Internet Explorer browsers. Internet Explorer also supports Microsoft's **Jscript**. Jscript, the Microsoft implementation of the ECMA Standard, is very similar to JavaScript, with only a few minor exceptions to maintain backwards compatibility.

Just like HTML, JavaScript is coded as text and therefore loads quickly from the Web server to the Web client. There are no additional applications to download and run with JavaScript, since it is actually executed on the client's computer. The HTML tag combination <SCRIPT> </SCRIPT> can be used to identify JavaScript. Unlike HTML, however, the JavaScript language is case sensitive. Careful attention must be paid to keywords, variables, and function names when coding in JavaScript.

FOCUS ON ELECTRONIC COMMERCE

Red Robin Is Serving up Fresh Data Daily

How has the Web database construction aided Red Robin in adding value to its value chain?

What are specific ways that management information systems and the electronic commerce model have paired to bring synergy to Red Robin?

How has easy and efficient access to data been the key to Red Robin's success?

Red Robin, an international leader in casual dining, is well known for frequent "Food and Beverage Celebrations." The management of Red Robin says that that these celebrations are recognized as some of "the most hip and cool in the industry."

Founded in 1969 in Seattle, Red Robin has always embraced innovation and now boasts over 175 restaurants. Today, their innovative philosophy has moved from food delivery to data delivery and state-of-the-art Management Information Systems (MIS). In an intense market for information service workers, Howard Jenkins, Red Robin's Vice President of Management Information Systems, uses a "contract-to-hire" strategy. Jenkins explains this innovative approach to hiring as one of "hiring for values and training for skills." He believes that you can't teach the attitude and culture of innovation.

His department is also responsible for managing Red Robin's Web site at http://www.redrobin.com. The company's innovative approach is seen in the electronic commerce techniques and tools employed by Jenkins and his team. Red Robin uses the latest version of Aloha by Ibertech point-of-sales software running on Javelin Systems terminals. Back-office Windows NT servers are used with Hewlett-Packard and Compaq computers in a thin-client environment.

Sales, inventory, marketing, and other operational data had been housed on separate and aging legacy databases when Jenkins joined Red Robin in 1996. They made it difficult, if not sometimes impossible, for regional managers to get up-to-the-minute reports on what was selling well and where. Jenkins, along with Rob Jakoby, Red Robin's Director of Restaurant Systems, decided it was time to push for some innovation in how Red Robin managed and housed its data. They trashed the old reporting systems and brought in a Web-based business intelligence (BI) system that consolidated the company's data and spawned new decision support systems, executive systems, and expert systems to support management in the decision-making process.

The innovative move has paid off. In three short years, Red Robin, now headquartered in Greenwood Village, Colorado, has reduced food and sales expenses by over $1 million—directly attributable, according to Jackoby and Jenkins, to the new data systems. The data warehouse is managed on computers running Microsoft SQL Server and Power Play by Cognos and polls regional Access databases. Store-level polling is accomplished using XcelleNet and dial-up connections. To complement the system, spreadsheet application software by Deterministics and Visual Basic programming language are used.

BI is the new backbone of the successful Red Robin management information systems. Jenkins said that it provides "a cost-effective way to connect the restaurant locations to corporate headquarters with a higher speed solution." He added that they are constructing an experimental lab to better understand the use of the thin-client environment in their restaurants and how best to take advantage of the new electronic commerce model.

When asked whether all this investment had been a success, Jakoby said that now regional managers can better engineer menus by looking at what is selling and can even track purchasing rebates. But the proof is in the pudding as they say in the restaurant business. The savings are being re-invested in technology and management information systems to track even more data in other areas of the business. Jackoby added that providing Red Robin's managers and sales directors with the ability to quickly access data from anywhere in the world at any time continues as a top priority. Even a single percentage point reduction in Red Robin's operation costs can save the chain millions of dollars. Dinner and data are now being served.

Source: Valarie Rice, "House Specialty: Fresh Data," *eWeek*, July 10. 2001, 11:27 A.M. PT; Ron Ruggles, "Red Robin's Jenkins Keeps Chain's MIS Operations Bobbin' Along," *Nation's Restaurant News*, May 29, 2000; http://www.redrobin.com.

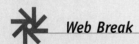
Web Break

Both Internet Explorer and Netscape have online resources for JScript and JavaScript, respectively. JScript resources are available at http://msdn.microsoft.com/scripting/default.htm. View the Netscape JavaScript Guide Version 1.2 at http://developer. netscape.com/docs/manuals/communicator/jsguide4/index.htm or their JavaScript Reference Guide at http://developer.netscape. com/docs/manuals/communicator/jsref/index.htm.

13.2 Exploring JavaScript Code

JavaScript code can be included anywhere in the BODY section of HTML code. With the use of a Function, it can even be placed in the HEAD section of HTML code. Examine the following JavaScript embedded in an HTML file:

```
<HTML>
<HEAD></HEAD>
<BODY>
```

```
<SCRIPT LANGUAGE="JavaScript">
alert("Thank you for shopping at Kanthaka Farms!");
</SCRIPT>
</BODY>
</HTML>
```

Figure 13-1 shows the output message box with alert function from this JavaScript code.

JavaScript can use three message boxes: **alert**, **confirm**, and **prompt**. The code above could be modified to use the other message boxes simply by substituting *confirm* or *prompt* for *alert*. Figure 13-2 shows the variations among the three message boxes.

Variables can also be used with message boxes. First, the variable must be declared using the **var statement**. In the following example code, the variable *a* will have either a true or a false result. A **condition statement** (*if-else*) is then used to allow two script paths, depending on the variable's result. If the customer at the Kanthaka Farms' Web site clicks OK, then the result is true and a "Thank you for visiting" message box appears in the Web browser window. If the customer clicks Cancel, then the result is false and a "Thank you for remaining" message will appear instead. Examine the code below:

```
<HTML>
<HEAD></HEAD>
<BODY>
<SCRIPT LANGUAGE="JavaScript">
var a=confirm("Please click on OK if you are certain you want
   to exit Kanthaka Farms Web site");
if (a)
   alert("Thank you for visiting Kanthaka Farms");
else
   alert("Thank you for remaining at Kanthaka Farms");
```

Figure 13-1

JavaScript Message Box Using Netscape Navigator

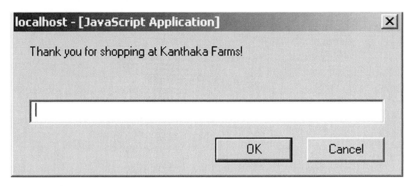

Figure 13-2
The Alert, Confirm, and Prompt Message Boxes

```
</SCRIPT>
</BODY>
</HTML>
```

Message boxes can be used to obtain customer information in the Web database construction. For example, the following code will allow a customer to enter a name into the message box:

```
<HTML>
<HEAD></HEAD>
<BODY>
<SCRIPT LANGUAGE="JavaScript">
var a=prompt("Please enter your name");
alert(a)
</SCRIPT>
</BODY>
</HTML>
```

JavaScript message boxes can also be used to redirect customers to a URL. In the following code snippet, if Cancel is clicked, then the code redirects the customer to the Addison-Wesley Computer Science Web address. The code **if (!a)** is translated by the program as *if click Cancel.* Clicking OK simply continues to load the current page. In JavaScript, the exclamation mark (!) is translated as *none.*

```
<HTML>
<HEAD></HEAD>
<BODY>
<SCRIPT LANGUAGE="JavaScript">
var a=confirm("Are you sure you want to quit?");
if (!a)
location="http://www.aw.com/cseng/";
</SCRIPT>
</BODY>
</HTML>
```

To render the date and time from JavaScript code, the following code can be added to the script above. For the date and time to appear on the screen after the message box appears, the code would be placed directly above the </SCRIPT> tag.

```
var today = new Date()
document.write(today)
```

The first var today = new Date() line initializes a **date object**. The **document.write** code is a method of the **document object**. In order to output text in JavaScript, either the **write()** or **writeln() method** must be used. The write() method will only output text where the writeln() method can output text and a line break. Since JavaScript is case sensitive, the document object is coded in lowercase. When the file is saved and run from a Web browser using localhost, the screen display is similar to that shown in Figure 13-3.

 Web Break

Jolibean.com creates modular electronic commerce solutions for electronic commerce development using the power of Java, JavaScript, Java Servlets, and Java Server Pages. Businesses can remotely manage their entire Web site content with the powerful, flexible, and secure capabilities of the Jolibean Server. Visit Jolibean at http://www.jolibean.com/ to use a demo of the Jolibean Server or browse through live examples of their customers' sites using Jolibean modules at Le Sauze Ski Resort, France (http://www.skipass-sauze.com/) or City of Praloup, France (http://www.skipass-praloup.com/).

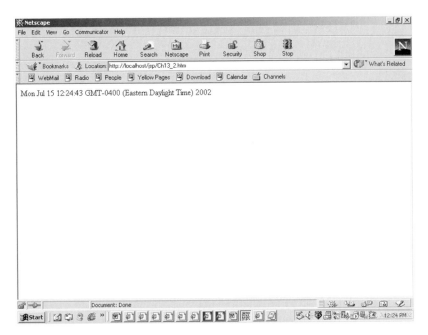

Figure 13-3

JavaScript Date and Time Display

All text between the two HTML tags used to identify JavaScript (<SCRIPT language="JavaScript"> and </SCRIPT>) is interpreted as JavaScript code by the browser. Though there are a few Web browsers in use that are unable to run JavaScript, most today have some version of JavaScript built-in. The browser will properly execute JavaScript even when the attribute is omitted. The <SCRIPT> tag will be ignored and the text between the tags displayed. Therefore, it is possible to omit these tags when coding, though not recommended, because the attribute identifies the code as JavaScript to the user. The use of the <SCRIPT> tag ensures that old browsers that do not support JavaScript do not display the JavaScript. Though this is optional, it is considered good practice. Future browsers may require that this attribute be defined to distinguish it from other languages. To prevent the <SCRIPT> tag from being ignored and the text between the tags displayed, JavaScript code should be enclosed by a combination of the HTML comment tag <!— —> and the double slash (//), which is used in JavaScript to identify a comment. The result looks like this: <!— //—>. Examine the following JavaScript code:

```
<HTML>
<HEAD>
<TITLE>A JavaScript Example</TITLE>
</HEAD>
<BODY>
<CENTER>
<H1 ALIGN=CENTER>KANTHAKA FARMS</H1>
<P align="center"><IMG SRC="KAN_LOGO.gif" width="121"
    height="97"></P>
<SCRIPT LANGUAGE="JavaScript"><!-
// Will and Anne Nelson, June 2001, NMA, Inc.
alert("Thank you for shopping at Kanthaka Farms!");
// added code for second script
var today=new Date()
document.write(today)
//->
</SCRIPT>
</BODY>
</HTML>
```

When rendered in a Web browser from localhost, the JavaScript code displays a screen similar to the one shown in Figure 13-4.

The use of a **Language attribute** is also optional in JavaScript, but recommended. A particular version of JavaScript may be specified as shown in the code snippet below:

```
<SCRIPT LANGUAGE="JavaScript1.2">
```

Figure 13-4

The Completed JavaScript File

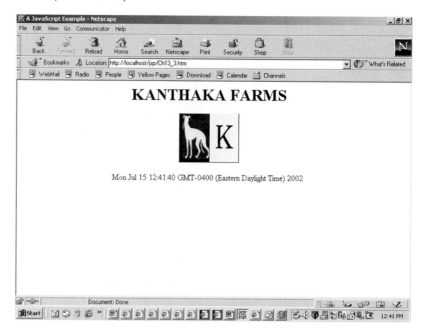

To change the background colors with JavaScript, **bgcolor** and **fgcolor** are incorporated into the code. Examine the following code:

```
<HTML>
<HEAD>
<TITLE>A JavaScript Example</TITLE>
</HEAD>
<BODY>
<CENTER>
<BODY BGCOLOR="#000000" TEXT="#FFFFFF">
<H1 ALIGN=CENTER>KANTHAKA FARMS</H1>
<P align="center"><IMG SRC="KAN_LOGO.gif" width="121"
    height="97"></P>
<SCRIPT LANGUAGE="JavaScript"><!-
document.bgColor="black"
document.fgColor="#FFFFFF"
// Will and Anne Nelson, June 2001, NMA, Inc.
alert("Thank you for shopping at Kanthaka Farms!");
// added code for second script
var today = new Date()
document.write(today)
//->
</SCRIPT>
</BODY>
```

As shown in Figure 13-5, this code will render a reversal of the screen shown in Figure 13-4.

Figure 13-5

Reversing the Background and Text Colors of the JavaScript File

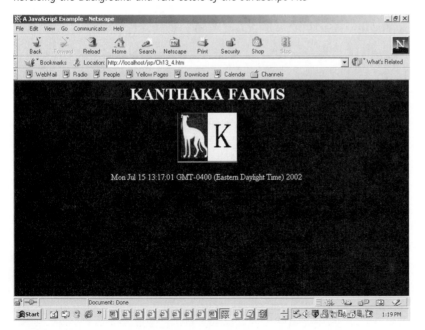

13.3 Working with JavaScript Errors

Microsoft's Internet Explorer and Netscape's browsers handle JavaScript errors differently. In Internet Explorer the JavaScript Error dialog box is activated from the Advanced tab of Tools, Internet Options. From there it is necessary to verify that the check box *Display a notification about every script error* has been checked. In Netscape browsers, **javascript**: can be typed into the Location box and the Enter key pressed before any JavaScript development. This will bring up **Netscape's Communicator Console**. Leave the console open while developing JavaScript so errors can be displayed. Another method for displaying errors in Netscape is to modify the **prefs.js file**. The prefs.js file is the JavaScript user's preference file and is located in the Netscape\Users directory. For example, on Windows 2000, the prefs.js file is found in the following location:

```
<Netscape path>\Users\<user name>
```

To modify the preference file to display JavaScript errors, add one of the following lines to the prefs.js file:

- To automatically open the console when a JavaScript error occurs, add the following line to prefs.js:

  ```
  user_pref("javascript.console.open_on_error", true);
  ```

- To open a dialog box each time an error occurs, add the following line to prefs.js:

  ```
  user_pref("javascript.classic.error_alerts", true);
  ```

Kanthaka Farms
Write JavaScript Code

Kanthaka Farms is a continuing case study in this book that illustrates the process of building electronic commerce with Web database constructions. In Chapter 13, you will learn about browser programs and server-side technologies to enhance the Kanthaka Farms Web site. As you continue through the text, you will complete different facets of electronic commerce Web database construction, resulting in a complete Web site for Kanthaka Farms.

1. From the Start, Programs menu, launch your Web server and verify that it is running.

2. Double-click on the Web server icon to display the Server Properties. Click the Mapping tab. In the Document URL path, type the following path:

```
/jsp/
```

In the Directory (Full local path or UNC) text box, type the following path:

```
C:\WebSite\java\
```

Your mapping will look similar to that shown in the Server Properties window displayed in Figure 13-6.

Click on Add and exit the utility. This mapping will allow you to type the URL http://localhost/jsp for your JavaScript files. They will be mapped to the C:\WebSite\java folder.

Figure 13-6

Mapping to the Java Folder Using the Server Properties Utility

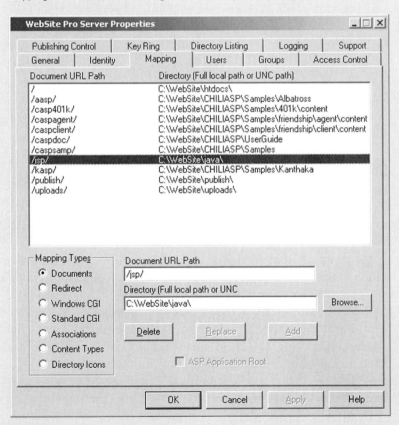

3. Copy the KAN_LOGO.gif from the C:\WebSite\HTDOCS\BOOK\ Guest1 folder to the C:\WebSite\java folder.

4. Using a text editor, copy the JavaScript code shown in the previous examples in the text to create a JavaScript appropriate for Kanthaka Farms. You should modify or change the code as needed to meet the requirements of the business' Web site.

5. Save your file(s) in the java folder in C:\WebSite.

6. Test your files using localhost. Use the JavaScript console to help you eliminate any errors in your JavaScript code.

Web Break

The JavaScript Source has put together a collection of hundreds of free JavaScripts that are available for use on your Web pages. The scripts are available via a user-friendly interface, which includes a working JavaScript example of all the scripts and a text box with the complete actual JavaScript code used. Electronic commerce developers can simply cut and paste these samples into their applications. Visit JavaScript Source on the Web at http://javascript.internet.com/.

13.4 Writing Cookies with JavaScript

Like ASP, JavaScript can utilize cookies to retain customer information for use during subsequent customer visits or for use by other pages on the business' Web site. All JavaScript cookie data remain on the computer that created it, and the computer is not capable of sending these data back to the Web server. In JavaScript, a cookie has one required attribute, **name**, and four optional attributes: **expires**, **domain**, **path**, and **security**. The optional attribute *expires* is used to make a cookie, written to a customer's hard drive, available for future visits. The *domain* and *path* optional attributes enable additional directories and servers to be specified for access to a customer's cookies. The *security* attribute determines how a cookie is transmitted over a network, and it is set to "insecure" by default.

In Netscape's cookies.txt file, each line contains one name–value pair. An example cookies.txt file may have an entry similar to the following:

```
.Kanthaka.com TRUE / FALSE 142857142 KANTHAKA_ID 265208
```

Each line represents a single unit of stored data with a tab inserted between each of the fields. The following attributes for each field are read from left to right as follows:

- *Domain*: This represents the domain that created the variable as well as the domain that can read the variable.
- *Flag*: A TRUE/FALSE value is rendered, indicating whether all machines within a given domain can access the variable. The Web browser, depending on the value that has been set for the domain, sets this value automatically.
- *Path*: This is the path within the domain that the variable is valid for.
- *Secure*: A TRUE/FALSE value is rendered, indicating whether a secure connection with the domain is needed to access the variable.
- *Expiration*: The UNIX time on which the variable will expire is indicated. UNIX time is defined as the number of seconds since Jan 1, 1970 00:00:00 GMT.
- *Name*: This is the name of the variable.
- *Value*: This is the value of the variable.

Internet Explorer stores cookies in various locations, depending on the version. In Explorer 5.x, cookies are located in C:\Windows\ Temporary Internet Files. Although the location varies with version, the storage format is the same. Each domain's cookies are stored in separate files with the username that accessed the Web site. For example, a customer named Will Nelson visiting Kanthaka Farms' Web site would store a cookie in the file Cookie:wnelson@ Kanthaka_Farms.com.

JavaScript supplies a built-in object called **document.cookie** to handle cookie interaction. This object will store all the valid cookies for the page on which the script is running. An example is the code below:

```
<SCRIPT LANGUAGE="JavaScript">
function setCookie (name, value, expires, path, domain,
   secure) {
```

```
document.cookie = name + "=" + escape(value) +
   ((expires) ? "; expires=" + expires : "") +
   ((path) ? "; path=" + path : "") +
   ((domain) ? "; domain=" + domain : "") +
   ((secure) ? "; secure" : "");
}
</SCRIPT>
```

This function requires that name and value data are passed. The other cookie parameters in the code are optional. The code following is an example of a sample use of this function:

```
<SCRIPT LANGUAGE="JavaScript">
setCookie("KF", "test", "Mon, 06-June-2051 00:00:00 GMT",
   "/");
</SCRIPT>
```

Kanthaka Farms
Create Cookies
With JavaScript

In this exercise, you will learn to create cookies with JavaScript for use in the Kanthaka Farms' Web site.

1. From the Start, Programs menu, launch your Web server and verify that it is running.

2. Using a text editor, type the following code:

```
<HTML>
<HEAD>
<TITLE>A JavaScript Example</TITLE>
</HEAD>
<BODY>
<CENTER>
<H1 ALIGN=CENTER>KANTHAKA FARMS</H1>
<P align="center"><IMG SRC="KAN_LOGO.gif" width="121"
   height="97"></P>
<FORM name="formjs">
<INPUT type="text" length=20 name="textjs">
<P>
<INPUT type="button" value="Set Cookie" name="set1"
onClick='document.cookie="Cookie="+document.formjs.textjs.
   value'>
<INPUT type="button" value="Get Cookie Data" name="get1"
onClick='alert(document.cookie="Thank you for the data!")'>
</FORM>
</HTML>
</HEAD>
```

3. Save the file as CH13_5.htm in the java folder in C:\WebSite.

4. In your browser, type the following URL to test your code:

```
http://localhost/jsp/Ch13_5.htm
```

Type your name in the text box and click on the button to set the cookie. Now click the button to get the cookie data. Your screen display should be similar to the one shown in Figure 13-7.

Figure 13-7

Setting a Cookie with JavaScript

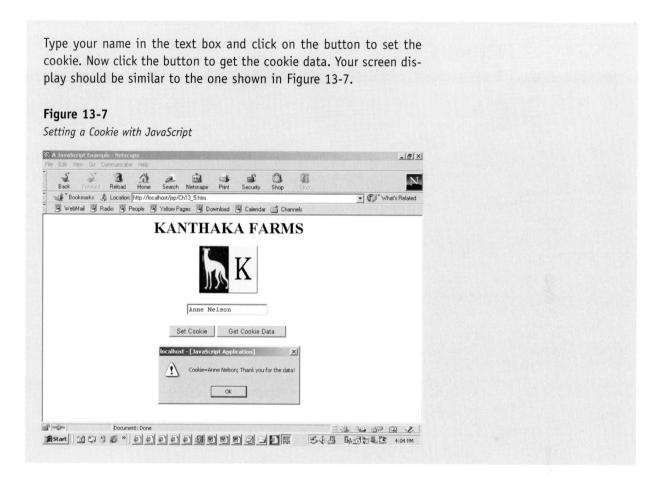

13.5 Understanding Java Server Pages

Java Server Pages (JSP) technology is an alternative to ASP (which is costly to use and often ties up with the Windows platform) or CGI (which has portability issues and the disadvantages of non-object-oriented development). JSP is an extension of the **Java servlet** technology. Servlets are platform-independent Java server-side modules that are incorporated into the electronic commerce model and can be used to extend the capabilities of a Web server with minimal overhead, maintenance, and support. Java servlets are downloaded, on demand, to the part of the system that needs them. As seen in Figure 13-8, JSP technology and servlets together provide an attractive alternative to other types of dynamic Web scripting and programming.

```
<%!
int dayOfWeek = 3;
String message;
%>
<%
switch (dayOfWeek)

        {
        case 1:
        message = "Happy Monday from the world's leader in superior quality Italian
                greyhounds, Kanthaka Farms!";
        break;

        case 2:
        message = "Kanthaka Farms reminds you that a healthy dog is a happy dog. Be sure
                your dog has annual visits to the vet.";
        break;

        case 3:
        message = "This Wednesday make sure your dog has the bed he deserves. Visit our
                large selection of indoor and outdoor monogrammed dog beds.";
        break;

        case 4:
        message = "Thursday is an excellent day to buy your dog a new dog collar from
                Kanthaka Farms. Check out our excellent variety of types and styles.";
        break;

        case 5:
        message = "Have a happy and healthy weekend from your friends at Kanthaka Farms.";
        break;

        default:
        message = "Sorry, Kanthaka Farms is closed for the weekend";
        break;

        }

out.println(message);                                    .jsp file
%>
```

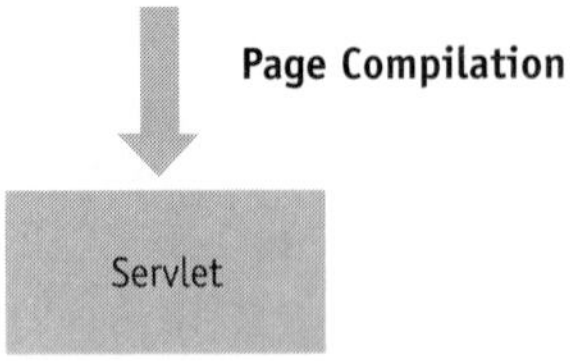

Page Compilation

Servlet

Servlet container

Figure 13-8

The JSP Process

The focus of JSP is data—JSP is data-driven. Like CGI and ASP, with JSP Web sites become dynamic and allow customer interactivity. JSP looks very similar to HTML with embedded Java. It uses XML-like tags and scriptlets in the Java programming language to generate Web page content and separate page logic from design and display, supporting a reusable, component-based design. This makes building Web database constructions with JSP faster and easier than with competing technologies. Learning JSP also means understanding HTML and **Java Beans**. Also from Sun Microsystems, Java Beans is an object-oriented programming interface. With Java Beans re-useable applications or program building blocks can be built. These building blocks, called **components**, can be deployed in a business' network on any major operating system platform. Java Beans, like **Java applets**, can be used to add interactive capabilities to the electronic commerce model. An **applet**, as the suffix "-et" implies, is a little program. Before the advent of the Web, built-in programs that came with Windows were sometimes called applets. On the Web, applets are usually sent with a Web page to the Web client and can perform interactive tasks without having to send a Web client request back to the Web server. Java Beans are developed with a **Beans Development Kit (BDK)** from Sun Microsystems and are operating system independent. They can also run on many application environments, called containers, including Web browsers, word processors, or other applications. Like **ActiveX**, Java Beans technology gives JSP applications the **compound document capability**, meaning many applications or containers can use it. ActiveX is Microsoft's answer to the Java technology and is roughly equivalent to a Java applet.

JSP Tags

JSP uses tags in the programming language to create page content. The following are the most common tags:

- Declaration tag
- Expression tag
- Comment tag
- Scriptlet tag
- Forward tag
- Include tag

Declarations Tag The JSP declaration tag is used to declare a variable or method. The syntax for this tag is the following:

```
<%! declarations %>
```

With this tag, variables and methods must be declared using standard Java syntax, and each is followed by a semicolon. As with Visual Basic and VBScript, each variable or method must be declared before it is referenced. The following is an example of a JSP declaration tag:

```
<%! Sting day = "Monday" ;
String message;
%>
```

Expression Tag The JSP **expression tag** is used to put data into an output buffer and can be used anywhere on a JSP page. Expression tags are evaluated as a Java expression and converted into a string. The string is then inserted into the generated HTML. The syntax for the tag is the following:

```
<%= Java expression %>
```

Expression tags never terminate with a semicolon.

Comment Tag Because JSP resides on an HTML page, this type of JSP output tag can be created using HTML. These **comment tags** may include only HTML or be combined with Java. The following syntax is used for the tag:

```
<!- your comment and/or [<%= a Java expression %>] ->
```

Any text coded between the <!— and —> comment tags will appear in the generated HTML. When a comment is combined with Java, the brackets shown in the code above are optional. A **hidden comment tag** can also be used in JSP. A hidden comment tag is a comment that is included in the JSP code, but is not a part of the HTML returned from the container to the Web server. This is a useful technique for keeping comments from being viewed by the browser. Because hidden comments are not part of the JSP process, however, expressions cannot be used. The syntax for hidden comments is:

```
<%- your hidden comment-%>
```

Unlike output comments, hidden comments cannot be dynamic.

Scriptlet Tag The majority of the Java code in JSP is included in this type of tag. Java language rules apply to code within the scriptlet tag, and each ends with a semicolon. The syntax for the scriptlet tag is the following:

```
<% scriptlet %>
```

Forward Tag The JSP **forward tag** is used to transfer control to a different location on the server. This may be a servlet, ASP, CGI, or any other document. The syntax for the tag is:

```
<jsp:forward page="relativeURL">
```

The following is an example of JSP with a forward tag:

```
<!- Pass control to kanthaka.jsp->
<HTML>
<BODY>
<jsp:forward page="kanthaka.jsp" />
</BODY>
</HTML>
```

Include Tag The JSP **include tag** is used to allow the incorporation of JSP, HTML, or text into the JSP page. It facilitates the reuse of code and modularity. The include tag is coded at the point where the file that is to be reused will be added. The syntax for the include tag is the following:

```
<%@ include file="relative.url"%>
```

13.6 Using JRun Java Application Server for Windows

An electronic commerce tool included on this book's companion Web site is Allaire Corporation's **JRun Java application server**. This Java server provides a development and deployment platform for building and delivering **Java 2 Platform Enterprise Edition (J2EE) applications**. Designed by Sun Microsystems, the J2EE applications are based on the Java platform and are developed for the thin client n-tiered business environment. JRun upholds the programming philosophy of creating standardized, reusable modular components by enabling the n-tier to handle many aspects of programming automatically. Typical use of the JRun tool includes Web database constructions that may be constrained by budget, time-to-market schedules, or limited resources. JRun easily integrates into an existing electronic commerce infrastructure by connecting into all major Web servers and platforms.

JRun supports any of the J2EE technology specifications and can be installed as separate modules, including:

- JSP
- Java servlets
- Enterprise Java Beans (EJB)
- Java Transaction API (JTA)
- Java Messaging Service (JMS)

JRun functions as both a standalone Java application server and as a plug-in module that adds Java application support to an existing Web server, such as IIS or WebSite.

Kanthaka Farms
Install and Explore JRun
Application Server
for JSP Support

In this exercise, you will install the JRun Java application server for use in the Kanthaka Farms Web site.

1. In order to connect your JRun Java application server to your Web server, you must first stop your Web server if it is running.

2. Exit all currently running Windows applications.

3. On this book's companion Web site, locate and double-click on the JRun installation file *jr302.exe*. This file can also be downloaded as a free 30-day evaluation copy at http://www.allaire.com.

4. Click on the Windows version of JRun to install. Your screen should look similar to the one shown in Figure 13-9.

5. Follow the JRun installation and setup wizard as it prompts you for information. When prompted, select the following destination folder for JRun installation and click Next:

```
C:\Program Files\Allaire\JRun
```

6. As shown in Figure 13-10, since you are installing the Developer edition of the Java server, you will not need a serial number.

7. Just click Next to progress through the wizard installation process. You may choose to install the minimal required option. This includes servlet, JSP, EJB, and JMS support; however, documentation and samples are not installed with a minimal installation. This installation is not recommended for deployment servers.

8. During setup you will be asked to select a Java runtime. Because **Java Runtime (JRE)** from Sun Microsystems is included with the Windows version of JRun, you are not required to provide your own JRE. The current JRE, Java 2 Runtime Environment v 1.2.2_008, consists of the **Java virtual machine**, the Java platform core classes, and supporting files. It is the runtime part of the Java 2 SDK, but without the development tools such as compilers and debuggers. The Microsoft Windows version of the current JRE is packaged with the **Java Plug-in software**. These plug-ins enable Web browsers to use the JRE 2 to run applets and enterprise customers to direct applets or Java Beans on intranet Web pages to run instead of the Web browser's default virtual machine. The virtual machine is Java's terminology for describing software that acts as an interface between compiler Java binary code and the hardware platform that actually performs the program's instructions.

You will find references to the virtual machine made by companies other than Java. When you do, it is usually meant as either an operating system or any program that runs a computer.

9. When prompted, enter a unique port number that you will use to access JRun's administrative Web application on the **JRun Web Server (JWS)** and click Next. The JWS listens on this port to provide

Figure 13-9
Allaire JRun Installation Window

Figure 13-10
Request for Serial Number

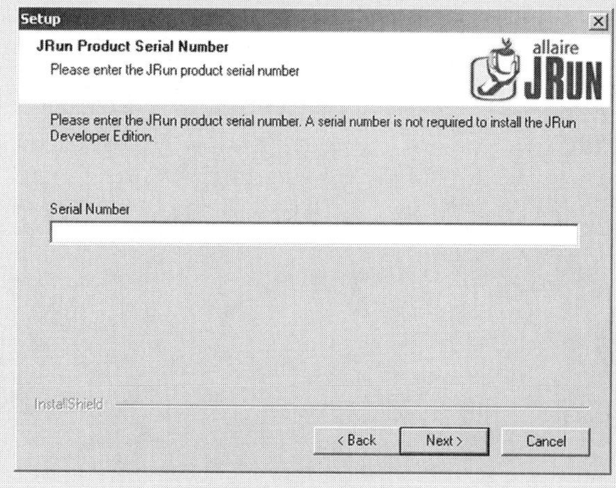

access to the **JRun Management Console (JMC).** The default port is 8000. Do not, however, select a port number between 8100 and 8199, because JRun uses ports in this range for the default JRun server JWS.

10. When prompted to enter a JMC password, use the word *password*.

11. When you get to the last screen, which asks whether you want to configure an external Web server, select Yes. This will launch the connector wizard. After you log in, select *JRun Default Server* for the JRun Server Name, *WebSite Pro* for the Web Server type, and *Win-intel* for the Web Server Platform. Enter *127.0.0.1* for the JRun Server IP Address and *5321* for the JRun Server Connector Port. Click Next twice to complete the process of connecting to an external server.

12. Now stop the JRun Admin server and the JRun Default server and restart them after you use the connector wizard.

13. From Windows Explorer, locate the server and connector folders located in C:\Program Files\Allaire\JRun. Copy both to a new folder created on C:\WebSite\JRun\

14. From the Start, Programs, WebSite menu choose Server Properties. Click on the Mapping tab and add the following mappings:

```
Document Mapping:
/demo/
C:\WebSite\JRun\servers\default\demo-app

Associations Mapping:
.jsp
C:\WebSite\JRun\connectors\wsapi\intel-win\jrun.isa

Content Types:
.jsp
wwwserver/isapi

Document Mapping:
/demo/servlet/
C:\WebSite\JRun\connectors\wsapi\intel-
    win\jrun.isa\demo\servlet
```

Your completed document mappings should look like the ones shown in Figure 3-11.

15. Test your JRun server. From the Start menu choose Programs, JRun, JRun Admin Server. You can also use the JRun command-line utility. Note that if you installed JRun as a service and try to launch JRun from the program group by selecting it from the Start menu when the service is already running, you will get a *JRun exited abnormally* error. To stop the server as an application, open the JRun Application Manager by double-clicking the JRun server's icon in your system tray. Then click the Stop button. JRun stops only that JRun server. If you are running JRun as a service, use the Services Control Manager utility found in the Control Panel to stop the server.

Figure 13-11

WebSite Mappings

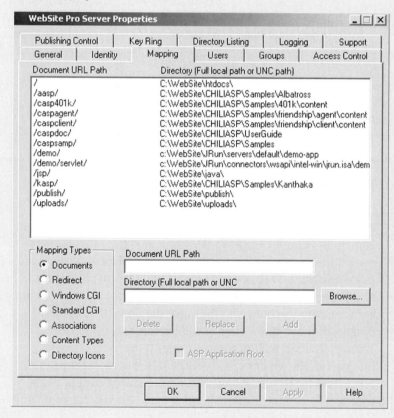

Though JSP and ASP may seem very similar in function and features, they are fundamentally different technologies, as shown in Table 13-1.

	ASP	JSP
Platform Support	Is fully supported under Windows. Deployment on other platforms is cumbersome due to reliance on the Win32-based component model.	Platform independent. Runs on all Java-enabled platforms.
Web Server Support	Native support only within Microsoft IIS or Personal Web Server. Support for select servers using third-party products like Chili!Soft.	Most popular Web servers, including WebSite, Apache, Netscape, and Microsoft IIS, can be easily enabled with JSP.
Component Model	Uses the Win32-based COM component model.	Relies on reusable, cross-platform components like Java Beans, Enterprise Java Beans, and custom tag libraries.
Scripting	Supports VBScript and JScript for scripting.	Can use the Java programming language or JavaScript.
Customizable Tags	Cannot use custom tag libraries and is not extensible.	JSP is extensible with custom tag libraries.
Security	Can work with the Windows NT security architecture.	Works with the Java security model.
Database Access	Uses Active Data Objects for data access.	Uses JDBC for data access.

Table 13-1 *Comparing JSP with ASP*

IIS Info

IIS cannot execute Java servlets and JSP without a JSP engine. Many electronic commerce developers use the Jakarta Tomcat or Alliare JRun with IIS. Tomcat is the official reference implementation for the servlet and JSP technologies and is a standalone Web server. Tomcat and IIS, just like JRun and WebSite, will install and configure together easily. It will be necessary to configure IIS to use the Tomcat redirector plug-in that will allow IIS to send servlet and JSP requests to Tomcat. Tomcat will then serve them to the Web clients. This first part of the process is to get the JDK and Tomcat running. Since Tomcat works well as a standalone application, begin with it. Tomcat can be downloaded from the Jakarta Tomcat Web site at http://jakarta.apache.org/tomcat/.

For this installation, <tc_home> will be designated as the root directory of the Tomcat Web server. Your Tomcat installation should have the following subdirectories:

- <tc_home>\conf. This is where various configuration files will be placed.
- <tc_home>\webapps. This folder will contain the application example.
- <tc_home>\bin. This is where Web server plug-ins will be placed.

In all the examples in this IIS Info box <tc_home> will be C:\jakarta-tomcat. The isapi_redirect.dll should be placed in C:\jakarta-tomcat\bin\win32\i386\ and properties files should be in C:\jakarta-tomcat\conf. To complete the process, follow these steps:

- In the registry, create a new registry key named "HKEY_LOCAL_MACHINE\SOFTWARE\Apache Software Foundation\Jakarta Isapi Redirector\1.0"
- Add a string value with the name extension_uri and a value of /jakarta/isapi_redirect.dll
- Add a string value with the name log_file and a value pointing to where you want your log file to be (for example C:\jakarta-tomcat\logs\isapi.log).
- Add a string value with the name log_level and a value for your log level (can be debug, info, error, or emerg).
- Add a string value with the name worker_file and a value, which is the full path to your workers.properties file (for example C:\jakarta-tomcat\conf\workers.properties).
- Add a string value with the name worker_mount_file and a value that is the full path to your uriworkermap.properties file (for example c:\jakarta-tomcat\conf\uriworkermap.properties).
- Using the IIS management console, add a new virtual directory to your IIS/PWS Web site. The name of the virtual directory must be jakarta. Its physical path should be the directory where you placed isapi_redirect.dll. While creating this new virtual directory, assign it with execute access.
- Using the IIS management console, add isapi_redirect.dll as a filter in your IIS/PWS Web site. The name of the filter should reflect its task, such as jakarta, and its executable must be C:\jakarta-tomcat\bin\win32\i386\isapi_redirect.dll. For PWS, you will need to use regedit and add/edit the "Filter DLLs" key under HKEY_LOCAL_MACHINE\System\

> CurrentControlSet\Services\W3SVC\Parameters. This key contains a "," separated list of dlls (full paths). You will need to insert the full path to isapi_redirect.dll.
>
> ■ Restart IIS (stop + start the IIS service), make sure that the jakarta filter is marked with a green upward-pointing arrow. Windows NT/2000 users should note that the stop/start feature of the Microsoft Management Console does not actually stop and start the IIS service. You will need to use the services control panel to stop and start the World Wide Web Publishing Service.

Review the JSP code in Figure 13-8. This code uses a *switch* command to create the JSP cookie messages. It offers more flexibility than the *if* or the *if-else* constructs seen in CGI and the ASP cookies created earlier in this book and is used when the code must handle more than two possibilities. The JSP in the figure uses the day of the week to decide which cookie message to display. A numeric *dayOfWeek* variable is used with the switch construct. The *break* keyword is used to isolate the switch statement block and move immediately to the lines that follow it. The *default* keyword is used to execute the default statement set when the *dayOfWeek* variable passed does not meet the conditions listed in the statement block. In the code following, compare the switch construction with the if-else. Both JSP files can be used effectively to create a separate cookie message for each day of the week.

```
<%!
String day = "Monday";
String message;
%>
<%
// check day and set message
if (day.equals("Monday"))
{
message = "Happy Monday from the world's leader in superior
    quality Italian greyhounds, Kanthaka Farms!";
}
else if (day.equals("Tuesday"))
{
message = "Kanthaka Farms reminds you that a healthy dog is a
    happy dog. Be sure your dog has annual visits to the vet.";
}
else if (day.equals("Wednesday"))
{
```

```
message = "This Wednesday make sure your dog has the bed he
   deserves. Visit our large selection of indoor and outdoor
   monogrammed dog beds.";
}
else if (day.equals("Thursday"))
{
message = "Thursday is an excellent day to buy your dog a new
   dog collar from Kanthaka Farms. Check out our excellent
   variety of types and styles.";
}
else if (day.equals("Friday"))
{
message "Have a happy and healthy weekend from your friends at
   Kanthaka Farms.";
}
else
{
message = "Sorry, Kanthaka Farms is closed for the weekend.";
}
// print output
out.println(fortune);
%>
```

13.7 Using ActiveX in the Electronic Commerce Model

Microsoft's ActiveX was unveiled at a developer's conference in the spring of 1996. Like Java applets, ActiveX can provide functionality to the electronic commerce architecture of programmable components. An ActiveX control is the third version of **Object Linking and Embedding (OLE) controls**, known as **OCX**. OLE was originally used for **compound documents**. Compound documents are those that incorporate more than one type of application in a single document, for example, a spreadsheet included in a word-processing document. **ActiveX documents**, the second version of OLE, was the result of Microsoft reworkings to enable links to live documents on the Web. **OLE Automation**, a COM-based macro programming technique used primarily for writing Visual Basic scripts that controlled Office applications, was built into Microsoft's browser and had the ability to store automation scripts on HTML pages and run them in the same way Visual Basic did. The result became known as **ActiveX Scripting**.

Both OLE and ActiveX controls are part of the Component Object Model (COM) and are among the many types of components that use COM technologies to provide interoperability with other types of

COM components and services to support electronic commerce. ActiveX is specifically designed to integrate the distribution of components into the Web database design with such features as incremental rendering and code signing, which enable users to identify the authors of controls before allowing them to execute on the Web client.

An ActiveX component includes three parts:

- An ActiveX executable (.exe)
- An ActiveX data link library (.dll)
- An ActiveX control

Though the ActiveX controls may seem strange or complex at first, they have already been used in the CGI and ASP electronic commerce models created earlier in this book. For instance, when the Text property of a Text Box was set, an ActiveX control was utilized. When the Click event of a submit button was processed or the MoveNext method of the Data control was run, ActiveX controls were being used.

 Web Break

A variety of freeware and shareware ActiveX controls is available to the electronic commerce developer from Download.com. One of the most popular ActiveX downloads at the site is ActiveX Manager, a software interface that enables Web database developers to view registered controls, remove misbehaving controls, or even register new controls with a pop-up menu. Another popular download featured at Download.com is Shockwave and Flash Player ActiveX Controls. This software allows developers to experience animation and entertainment on the Web with Microsoft Internet Explorer. New in the current release is Shockwave Remote for use in deployed applications. Visit the ActiveX page of Download.com at http://download.cnet.com/downloads/0-10081.html.

In this exercise, you will create an ActiveX document with both a visual interface and Visual Basic code to process customer inputs and actions for the Kanthaka Farms Web database construction.

1. Create a new folder named AX on C:\WebSite. From this book's companion Web site, copy the contents of the AX to the newly created AX folder on your hard drive. After the copy process is complete, verify that your AX folder on your hard drive contains the following files:

- dogfilter.mdb (copied from C:\WebSite\CHILIASP\Kanthaka\ dogfilter.mdb)
- KAN_LOGO.gif (copied from C:\WebSite\CHILIASP\Samples\ Kanthaka)
- frmList.frm (copied from the AX folder on the companion Web site)
- List.vbp (copied from the AX folder on the companion Web site)

2. Launch Microsoft Visual Basic from the Microsoft Windows Start menu. When prompted from the New Project window, verify that the New tab is active, and choose ActiveX Document Exe. Click OK.

3. In the Project Explorer, open the User Document folder, and double-click UserDocument1. It may be necessary to expand the User Documents folder by clicking on the plus (+) symbol in order to view UserDocument1.

4. Display the Properties window, if necessary. In the Properties window, change the Name property to ListAX.

5. Save both the ActiveX document as ListAX.dob and the ActiveX document project file as ListAX.vbp in the C:\WebSite\AX folder. The .dob extension designates an ActiveX document.

6. A sample Visual Basic form named frmList.frm was created and placed in the AX folder on this book's companion Web site and should now be copied to C:\WebSite\AX. Add the form to your ActiveX document by clicking Add Form from the Visual Basic project menu bar. Click the Existing tab and, if necessary, navigate to the AX folder. Select frmList.frm and then click Open. The form has now been added to your ActiveX document.

7. Right-click on the User Document. From the short-cut menu that appears, choose View Code. Type the code as seen in Figure 13-12.

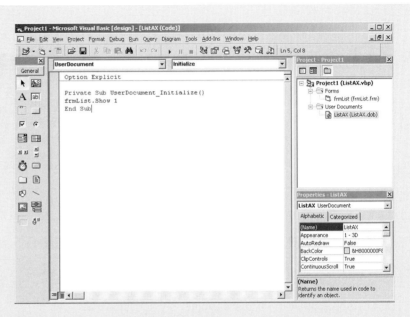

Figure 13-12
ActiveX vbModal Code

The code you added to your ActiveX document will initialize the user document event and display the List form using the Show method. The code will allow the form to be shown as a **modal** form with the vbModal parameter being replaced by the number 1.

A modal form is one that uses modality in its coding logic. It will contain provisions as to the mode of procedure. The forms and dialog boxes you create in Visual Basic are either modal or **modaless**. Either type of form must be closed before the rest of the application can be developed or modified. For instance, you must click on OK or Cancel before you can switch to another form or dialog box if the form you are working on is modal. It is important to remember that dialog boxes that display important messages should always be created as modal forms.

8. From the Project menu, choose References and from the available references list, check the Microsoft ActiveX Data Objects 2.1 Library check box. Click OK. Re-save your project.

9. Create an executable ActiveX document file by choosing Make ListAX.exe from the File menu bar. Be sure to create the executable file in the AX folder.

10. Using Windows Explorer, navigate to the AX folder. Notice that you now have a ListAX.exe, ListAX.vbp, ListAX.dob, and ListAX.vdb. The last file is a Visual Basic document, which associates the ActiveX executable with its container. This container is needed to display the ActiveX document.

11. Exit Visual Basic and test your ActiveX document by entering the following file URL and clicking Enter:

```
C:\WebSite\AX\ListAX.vbd
```

When prompted, choose the "Open this file from its current location" option button and click on OK. Be sure to use Microsoft's Internet Explorer as your browser for this exercise. The container that is associated with this ActiveX document is Microsoft Internet Explorer. Your ActiveX document should look similar to the one shown in Figure 13-13.

Figure 13-13
The ActiveX Document Displayed Using Internet Explorer

13.8 Creating ActiveX Installation Packages with ActiveX Documents

Executable files are very useful in the electronic commerce model because they can be run independently of other applications. To run executables, however, individual users must have dynamic link libraries and system Registry entries on their individual computers.

A problem arises when all users do not have these libraries or Registry entries. A solution to this is for the developer to create an **ActiveX installation package** for ActiveX documents. The package will contain the files that are necessary for the individual user to install an application. Installation packages can be created with the Visual Basic Package and Deployment Wizard.

Kanthaka Farms
Create an ActiveX
Installation Package

In this exercise, you will create an ActiveX installation package for your ActiveX document.

1. From the Start menu, choose Programs, Microsoft Visual Basic, Microsoft Visual Basic Tools, and Package and Deployment Wizard.

2. From the wizard, click on Browse to locate the ListAX.vbp in the C:\WebSite\AX folder. Your screen should look similar to the one shown in Figure 13-14.

Figure 13-14
The Package and Deployment Wizard

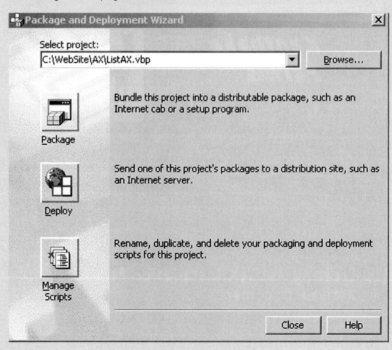

3. Choose the Package button to bundle the ListAX.vbp package into a distributable installation package.

4. When prompted, click Yes to recompile the file. This may take a few minutes, so be patient.

5. Upon completion, you will be prompted to choose the type of package you want. Choose Internet Package to create a .cab-based installation package that can be downloaded from a Web site or posted to a Web server. Click on Next.

6. If necessary, navigate to your AX folder in C:\WebSite and click Next. You will be prompted to create the Package folder. Click on Yes. Because the application will be used as a **Remote Automation (RA) Server**, special files will have to be added to the package. When prompted to include these special files in your package, click on Yes. (Note: if you are informed that a .dll file is missing, click OK in each message box for each instance to continue.)

7. You will be shown a list of files that will be included in your package. Click Next to continue.

8. When the File Source dialog box is displayed, verify that the *Include in this cab* option button under File Source is selected. If not, select it and click Next. This will specify where the application can locate the needed files.

9. In the Safe for Scripting and Safe for Initialization columns, click to activate the list box and choose Yes as shown in Figure 13-15. When you are finished, click Next.

10. Enter the name ListAWPackage as the name under which to save the session settings. Click Finish to create the package. Upon completion you will receive a packaging report that may state the following:

The cab file for your application has been built as 'C:\WebSite\AX\Package\ListAX.CAB'.

There is also a batch file in the support directory (C:\WebSite\AX\Package\Support\ListAX.BAT) that will allow you to re-create the cab file in case you make changes to some of the files.

11. Click Close twice to exit the wizard. You now have an installation package for Kanthaka Farms' ActiveX document that will install needed dynamic link libraries, create Registry entries, and enable multiple users to run the application.

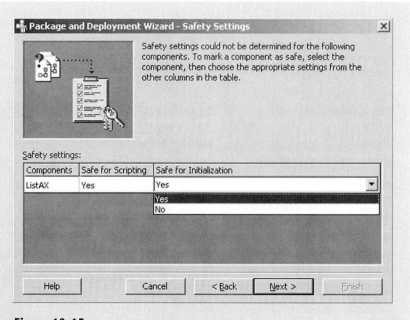

Figure 13-15
The Safety Settings of the Package and Deployment Wizard

12. Test the installation package by adding a reference to it in one of the Web pages you previously created for Kanthaka Farms. To do so, using Windows Explorer, first open the HTML file in the Internet package you created with the Package and Deployment Wizard. This file contains a command for a hyperlink that references your ActiveX document .vbd file. Using Windows Explorer, locate the ListAX.htm file at C:\WebSite\AW\Package\ListAX.htm and copy it to C:\WebSite\HTDOCS\BOOK\GUEST1 folder so that a relative reference can be used in later coding.

13. In Notepad, open the ListAX.htm file. Copy the line of code that reads

```
<a href=ListAX.VBD>ListAX.VBD</a>
```

and insert it in the GUESTMM.htm file also located in the GUEST1 folder. Insert the line of code *before* the </UL> tag. Add a <P> tag above the newly inserted line. Change the hyperlink that the customer will view to read *View our List of Dogs Currently Available*. Your finished file should include the code seen in Figure 13-16.

14. To test the hyperlink that will display your ActiveX document, launch your Web server software and in a browser window, type in the following URL:

http://localhost/BOOK/GUEST1/GUESTMM.htm

Click the new link to display your ActiveX document. When prompted, select *Open this file from its current location*. You should see the dynamic Kanthaka Farms current dog listing as shown in Figure 13-13.

Figure 13-16
Displaying an ActiveX Document Using a Hyperlink

Summary

■ **Discuss the basic components of JavaScript.** JavaScript is an interpreted language, which means it is transformed into machine language *on* the computer. JavaScript is another electronic commerce tool that is used in Web database constructions to create the dynamic interaction between the customer and the business. In a Hypertext Markup Language (HTML) page, JavaScript is simply a series of instructions that the Web browser understands and uses to perform various actions. The JavaScript code can either be part of the Web page file or, in much the same way that cascading style sheets (CSS) can be used, JavaScript can be referenced from the Web page by using a link to another file. It allows the electronic commerce developer to provide the customer at the front-end of the electronic commerce model interaction with both the business and its Web site content, rather than merely being presented with a static or fixed Web page. In more advanced JavaScript applications, the actions taken by the Web client can directly affect the Web page content, presentation, or site navigation methods. JavaScript code can be included anywhere in the BODY section of HTML code. With the use of a Function, it can even be placed in the HEAD section of HTML code.

■ **Discuss the basic components of Java Server Pages (JSP).** The focus of JSP is data—JSP is data-driven. JSP technology is an alternative to ASP (which is costly to use and often ties up with the Windows platform) or CGI (which has portability issues and the disadvantages of non-object-oriented development). JSP is an extension of the Java servlet technology. Servlets are platform-independent Java server-side modules that are incorporated into the electronic commerce model and can be used to extend the capabilities of a Web server with minimal overhead, maintenance, and support. Java servlets are downloaded, on demand, to the part of the system that needs them. JSP looks very similar to HTML with embedded Java. It uses XML-like tags and scriptlets in the Java programming language to generate Web page content and separates page logic from design and display, supporting a reusable, component-based design.

■ **Use JavaScript and JSP in the electronic commerce model.** Both JSP technology and JavaScript provide an attractive alternative to other types of dynamic Web scripting and programming. Like CGI and ASP, with JSP, Web sites become dynamic and allow customer interactivity.

■ **Use ActiveX in the electronic commerce model.** ActiveX technology gives applications compound document capability, meaning many applications or containers can use it. ActiveX is Microsoft's answer to the Java technology and is roughly equivalent to a Java applet. Both Object Linking and Embedding (OLE) and ActiveX controls are part of the Component Object Model (COM) and are among the many types of components that use COM technologies to provide interoperability with other types of COM components and services to support electronic commerce. ActiveX is specifically designed to integrate the distribution of components into the Web database design with such features as incremental rendering and code signing, which enable users to identify the authors of controls before allowing them to execute on the Web client. An ActiveX component includes three parts: An ActiveX executable (.exe), an ActiveX data link library (.dll), and an ActiveX control.

■ **Create compiled browser programs using ActiveX.** To create compiled browser programs using ActiveX, Microsoft Visual Basic must be launched and a new ActiveX Document .exe project created. The code in the ActiveX document will initialize the user document event and is often used to display modal forms using the Show method. A modal form is one that uses modality in its coding logic. It will contain provisions as to the mode of procedure. The forms and dialog boxes you create in Visual Basic are either modal or modeless. Either type of form must be closed before the rest of the application can be developed or modified. For instance, you must click on OK or Cancel before you can switch to another form or dialog box if the form you are working on is modal. It is important to remember that dialog boxes that display important messages should always be created as modal forms.

■ **View a dynamically linked ActiveX document in a Web page.** ActiveX installation packages must be created to view a dynamically linked ActiveX document in a Web page. These executable files are very useful in the electronic commerce model because they can be run independently of other applications. To run executables, however, individual users must have dynamic link libraries and system Registry entries on their individual computers. A problem arises when all users do not have these libraries or Registry entries. When created, the installation package will contain the files that are necessary for the individual user to install an application. Installation packages can be created with the Visual Basic Package and Deployment Wizard.

Chapter Key Terms

ActiveX	alert message box	comment tag
ActiveX documents	applet	compiled language
ActiveX installation package	Beans Development Kit (BDK)	components
ActiveX Scripting	bgcolor	compound document capability

compound documents
condition statement
confirm message box
date object
declaration tag
document object
document.cookie
document.write
domain attribute
ECMA Standard
ECMAScript
Electrotechnical Commission
    Management Association
    (ECMA)
expires attribute
expression tag
fgcolor
forward tag
hidden comment tag
host environment
if (!a)

include tag
interpreted language
Java
Java 2 Platform Enterprise Edition
    (J2EE) applications
Java applets
Java Beans
Java Plug-in software
Java Runtime (JRE)
Java Server Pages (JSP)
Java servlet
Java virtual machine
JavaScript
javascript:
JRun Java application server
JRun Management Console (JMC)
JRun Web Server (JWS)
Jscript
Language attribute
LiveScript
modal

modaless
name attribute
Netscape's Communicator
    Console
Object Linking and Embedding
    (OLE) controls
OCX
OLE Automation
path attribute
prefs.js file
prompt message box
Remote Automation (RA) Server
scripting language
scriptlet tag
security attribute
Sun Microsystems
var statement
Web scripting language
write() method
writeln() method

Review Questions

1. What is JavaScript? How is it similar to Java? How is it different?

2. Describe the importance of the ECMA Standard to JavaScript technology.

3. Define scripting language and Web scripting language.

4. What is Jscript? Discuss its use in the electronic commerce model.

5. What are the three message boxes that can be used in JavaScript? What is the benefit of using a message box in the electronic commerce model? Give two specific examples of a message box in the Web database construction.

6. What methods must be used to output text in JavaScript? Discuss the syntax of their use in code.

7. Between what tags must JavaScript be placed?

8. Discuss two ways that JavaScript errors can be displayed. Which way do you prefer? Why?

9. What are the JavaScript cookie attributes? How are they used with JavaScript?

10. Discuss the use of the built-in document.cookie object in JavaScript.

11. Compare how cookies are created in JavaScript with how you created them in CGI and ASP. Which of the methods provides the most functionality to the electronic commerce model? Why? Which of the methods is the easiest for the developer to create? Why?

12. What is JSP? Compare and contrast JSP technology to ASP and CGI.

13. JSP seems to be quickly gaining industry acceptance. What is your opinion about what is facilitating this acceptance?

14. Discuss each of the six JSP tags. How are they used in the electronic commerce model? Why are they used?

15. What is the purpose of the JRun Java application server?

16. Discuss the switch and if-else code choices for creating JSP cookies. Which do you prefer? Why?

17. What is ActiveX? Give two examples of ActiveX technology.

18. Discuss the history of the development of ActiveX technology.

Critical Thinking Using the Web

1. By utilizing ActiveX data link libraries to centralize database code, three-tiered Web database constructions can be created. However, the database functionality must be separated from ASP pages to minimize the changes needed within the ASP code. Tools used to create this three-tier construction utilizing ActiveX include DAO, Visual Basic or VBScript, and Microsoft Data Access Components (MDAC). Microsoft Transaction Server (MTS) or COM/COM+ can also be used. Using your favorite search engine, explore the Web for more information on how to utilize ActiveX .dlls. Prepare a 200–400-word essay on using ActiveX.dlls. If you find code snippets, append them and their sources to your essay. Be prepared to discuss your findings in class.

2. Did you know that you can write ActiveX in Java? Use your favorite search engine to investigate on the Web how this is done. Find how to use Java language to write an ActiveX component for IIS Web server. Save your findings and sources and be prepared to share with the class.

3. The JGuru at http://www.jguru.com/faq/home.jsp?topic=JSP writes that "Few technologies are as effective as JSP in facilitating the separation of presentation from dynamic Web content. JSP pages are secure, platform-independent, multithreaded, and best of all, make use of Java as a server-side scripting language." Visit his site on the Web and learn more about JSP technology. There you will find code snippets and forums, as well as JSP news. Summarize an interesting learning point from your visit to JGuru in a 200–400-word essay. Be prepared to present your findings to the class.

Chapter Case Study

Albatross Records is a continuing case study in this book that illustrates the process of building electronic commerce with Web database constructions. In Chapter 13, you will learn browser programs and server-side technologies to enhance the Kanthaka Farms Web site. As you continue through the text, you will complete different facets of electronic commerce Web database construction, resulting in a complete Web site for Albatross Records.

- Create a JavaScript message box for use in your Albatross Records Web database construction. You may use the alert, confirm, or prompt message box.
- Using JavaScript, add cookies to the electronic commerce model. Plan for their use so they add functionality to the model as well as collect useful user information. Be able to justify your decision.
- Create a dynamic ActiveX document with both a

visual interface and code to process Albatross customer inputs and actions for the business.

- Create an executable ActiveX document file and be sure that a .vdb file is created to associate your file with its container. This will be needed to display the ActiveX document.
- Create an ActiveX installation package for your ActiveX document using the Visual Basic Package and Deployment Wizard.
- Create a new link on another of your previously created Albatross Records HTML documents that will dynamically display your ActiveX document. The document that displays must be a dynamic document that will display records from an Albatross Records database. Customers must also be able to add records to the database from the document.

14

Enhancing the Electronic
Commerce Business Model

If you put tomfoolery into a computer, nothing comes out of it but tomfoolery. But this tomfoolery, having passed through a very expensive machine, is somehow enabled and no one dares criticize it.

—Pierre-MarieGallois, 1996, General, French Air Force, author of essays on strategy and geopolitics and the books *Le soleil d'Allah aveugle l'Occident* (1995) and *Le sang du pétrole: Bosnia* (1996)

14.1 Factors That Affect the Success of Electronic Commerce

Just as e-business *is* business, electronic commerce is the fundamental infrastructure for commerce, communication, and communities in the New Economy. Basic technological advancements are generating new applications to extend the use of computers and networking with Web database constructions into all aspects of economic, social, and political activities.

Many factors affect the success of electronic commerce. The first lies in the exponential growth of the Internet. As few as 50 Web pages were available in 1992, whereas today the Web boasts multimillions of pages, and the number is growing rapidly. As the size of the infrastructure increases, congestion and bandwidth have the potential to drag the pace of electronic commerce to a halt. Though greatly tightened in the last few years, security issues also remain a challenge to electronic commerce. Each day, the news media report more cases of identity fraud or theft. Many of these cases are associated with the nature of the Internet's open network; and, without a continued increase in comfort level with online purchasing, consumers may find reason to revert to more traditional means of trade.

Electronic commerce also faces legal uncertainties such as reinterpretation of copyright laws and laws addressing intellectual property theft and taxation. However, as businesses and customers become more accustomed to the intricacies of the digital age and its New Economy, electronic commerce will continue to transform the world of business and emerge as a viable model of a perfectly competitive market.

Kanthaka Farms is a continuing case study in this book that illustrates the process of building electronic commerce with Web database constructions. In this last chapter, the factors that affect the success of the electronic commerce model will be assessed, and enhancements will be added to the design to increase its efficiency and effectiveness. In this chapter, you will complete the electronic commerce Web database construction for Kanthaka Farms.

Many tools are available to today's developers that can gauge the success of a Web site. As you have learned, the challenges facing businesses that employ the electronic commerce model are great. Take the time to assess your design and note challenges that affect the online success of Kanthaka Farms. Strategies must be devised to overcome each of the challenges you identify.

Kanthaka Farms
Identify the Challenges Facing the Electronic Commerce Design

1. Analyzing your design is critical for a Web site's success. Go to Web Site Garage at http://websitegarage.netscape.com and click on the Improve Your Site tab near the top of the page. This site provides many tools for maintaining and improving your Web site. With them you are able to automate site maintenance checks, optimize your graphics, and analyze your traffic.

2. From the list of services offered on the page, click on the first one, Tune Up. This tool will help you measure the Kanthaka Farms' Web site performance, so critical to the Web site's success. Tune Up will provide you with comprehensive, automated diagnostics on your Kanthaka Farms design. Web Site Garage offers a free one-page tune up. Choose one page of your Kanthaka Farms design. Type in the URL and your e-mail address at the Web Site Garage site. The Web Site assessment will include the following:

- Browser compatibility: to verify that your Web site is able to display properly in different browsers and browser versions.
- Readiness: to ensure your site is ready to be indexed and submitted to the top search engines and directories.
- Load time check: to report your site's load time.
- Dead link check: to detect links that may no longer be active or are using relative references to files not available in the folder.
- Link popularity check: to ascertain the number of sites to which you are linking.
- Spell check: to spot misspelled words on your Web page.

■ HTML check: to compare your design to some of the best in the industry.

Use the assessment to modify your design. Print the assessment and be prepared to share the assessment in class.

14.2 Speed

Though **speed** is an obvious element that can either enhance or detract from the Web site design, it may be the most abused. The single most important predictor of site success is the perspective from which the site has been designed. The site should be customer-centered—not designer-centered—and designed for those customers with the lowest capacity components. Be responsive to the typical Web user on a 56K modem. Even if it has been determined that the business' site is used primarily by high-end technology users, speed and download times must still be major design considerations. It has been estimated that the maximum response time before customers lose interest is eight seconds. Table 14-1 shows the estimated download speed of a Web page by a typical customer.

This must be kept in mind as well as the fact that bandwidth is getting worse and not better, as the Internet adds users faster than the infrastructure can support them. One design approach is to create two versions of the business' Web site, one that can be chosen by customers with limited hardware and software capabilities and another for those with cutting-edge or even bleeding-edge technology.

Speed is also affected by the use of graphics in the Web design. Use graphics sparingly to convey the business' message. For each graphic, the Web client must make a trip the Web server. Design considerations include consolidating neighboring graphics. The use of cascading style sheets (CSS) text or table cells with formatted colors can look attractive and greatly speed display. The use of CSS can aid efficiency by controlling the overall site appearance rather than changing fonts and appearance on every page. Remember that size matters in Web site design: The typical customer will use a screen that is a maximum of 465 to 532 pixels wide. Create the business' Web site for the typical customer.

When tables are used, consider breaking them vertically for a cascading load. This will enhance the speed and make the site appear

Table 14-1	Web Page Download Time (in Seconds) for Typical Customers
Modem Speed	**Expected Load Time**
14.4K Modem	11.5 Sec
33.6K Modem	7.5 Sec
56K Modem	5.2 Sec
Cable/DSL Modem	2.2 Sec
T1 and Above	0.8 Sec

to be more responsive to the customer. Smaller, stacked tables demand less time to load than one large table.

In continuous-toned images, use .jpg files to optimize graphic file size for Web display. A limit of 20 KB per graphic should be included in the planning of Web design enhancements. Width and height attributes can also be used to increase page display speed and, if the image has no function, use the alternate text tag set to equal nothing, for instance:

```
<IMG SRC="KAN_LOGO.gif" ALT="">
```

Limit the use of color, and, in addition to limiting color, the actual palette size should be reduced to optimize file size for viewing. Remember that a 256-color image consists of an 8-bit palette. If the palette is reduced from 8 to 6 bits, the number of colors will be reduced from 256 to 64, and the file size reduced by 25 percent. Table 14-2 shows a palette bit number table with the maximum number of colors allowed and the comparison for the associated palette. By changing the site's design to accommodate minimized color depths, speed and efficiency can be increased. Text alternatives to graphics should also be available for low-bandwidth and disabled customers.

It can be confusing to decide when it is best to use .gif files and when to use .jpg files in your Web site design. Use .gif files when the Web site incorporates small images such as icons and thumbnails on the Web pages or when using low-density images with a small spectrum of colors no greater than 256; .gif files are also better when the site uses clipart images that do not have great detail. On the other hand, .jpg files are the better choice when the Web site uses large images such as photographs, high-resolution quality images, and high-density images with a large spectrum of colors.

Table 14-2   *Two-Color Palette Bit Number Table*

Color Palette Bit Depth	Number of Colors
1	2
2	4
3	8
4	16
5	32
6	64
7	128
8	256 (GIF maximum) (JPEG minimum)
24	16.8 million (JPEG only)

Kanthaka Farms
Check the Download Speed
of Your Web Site and
Optimize Graphics

Test the download speed of your Kanthaka Farms Web site design with a free evaluation from Web Site Garage. The same tool can also help you optimize your Web page graphics.

1. Go to Web Site Garage at http://websitegarage.netscape.com and click on the Gif Lube hyperlink on the Improve Your Site tab.

2. GIF Lube can decrease the Web page load time by optimizing your graphics.

3. Click on the Sign Up! button and enter the Kanthaka Farms URL on which you wish to use GIF Lube. Click on Next.

4. From this page, you have the choice to upload a file from your hard drive, type in the URL of your site, or choose an image to optimize. Web Site Garage will immediately compress the image and give you back the results. Make your choice and click on Start.

5. If you have chosen an image to optimize, then the tool will return the compressed image for you to compare to your original. Choose the image that will best optimize your site and click the Compare to Original button next to your selection. To save the compressed, optimized image, click on download and add to your site.

This tool is free and can be used for all images on your site as often as you need it. The GIF Lube tool is completely Web based, so neither downloading nor installing is necessary.

Web Break

A tool to increase the speed of efficiency of your Web site is OptiView. This Web site design software can reduce graphics such as .gif, .jpg, and .bmp files up to 90 percent without sacrificing quality. It can also be used to crop, resize, rotate, adjust colors, and compress in one integrated online editor. To learn more about OptiView, visit the Web site at http://www.optiview.com/.

Another method for increasing speed is to reduce or eliminate unnecessary HTML code, JavaScripts, and other Web components. All comments on Web pages can be stripped away to add speed to the electronic commerce model. Each line of code that does not have to be sent to the Web customers can result in significant bandwidth savings. Closing tags for <BR>, <LI>, and <OPTION> tags can also be stripped away because they are unnecessary. Unneeded white space, returns, and tabs should also be removed from the Web pages to increase speed in the design.

Remember that HTML headers must be read first. Until they are read, no content can be displayed. Moving all JavaScripts to the bottom of the Web pages and shortening excess META tags will add efficiency to the design. Though client-side DHTML adds robustness and functionality to the Web site, it does so at the cost of adding drag to a Web site. Consider Flash as an alternative.

Web Break

Macromedia Flash is one method to add speed and efficiency to your Web site design. Macromedia Flash can deliver low-bandwidth animations and presentations as well as offering scripting capabilities and server-side connectivity, Web interfaces, and training courses. Learn more about Macromedia Flash and try their evaluation software by visiting their Web site at http://www.macromedia.com/software/flash/. The Macromedia Flash Player can also be downloaded at the site for seamless viewing of content created with Macromedia Flash.

14.3 Layout

Layout is another factor that affects the success of the electronic commerce design. Successful Web database constructions are well organized. The degree of **hyperization**, the number of levels within the site, must be balanced with page length to decrease the display and scrolling time required of the customer. A very effective way to increase **stickiness** at the Web site is to minimize scrolling. A business' Web site is said to be "sticky" if a customer tends to stay for a long time and to also make return visits.

Common approaches to stickiness include the following:

- Using appropriate and timely user content
- Providing site personalization and interactivity
- Offering membership in discussion groups and virtual communities
- Encouraging customer feedback and contact
- Using hypertext indexing within the business' Web site to promote ease of navigation within the site

It is important that **orphan pages** be eliminated. These are pages that do not have a link to the business' home page and do not contain some indication of where they fit within the structure of the Web site. Because customers may access Web pages directly without entering through the home page, make sure that all pages have a clear indication of the Web site to which they belong.

The inclusion of **frames** in the Web site design can also negatively affect the success of the electronic commerce model. Frames, originally created by Netscape as an HTML extension and now part of the HTML 4.0 specifications, were an attempt to present multiple views of an information space of task domain. Frames incorporate multiple, independently controllable sections on a Web site by building separate HTML file sections with one master HTML file identifying all of the sections. They do not work well with many browsers, however, and actually have added to the problem they were designed to address. Frames violate a fundamental model of building a successful electronic commerce Web site: When frames are used, customers cannot bookmark the current page and return to it because the bookmark will point to another version of the frameset. Often URLs will not work properly with frames or will just stop working altogether. Printouts from the business' site are even more difficult and challenging for the customer. Sites that use frames should create an alternative scheme of pages for customers who prefer non-frame versions or who have browsers that do not support frames.

Other layout factors that minimize the success of a Web site include the use of scrolling text, blinking text, and animated graphics. Though movement on the site can be seductive, it can also be distracting; in fact, in most cases the movement will draw the customer's attention away from the site content and will degrade performance and possibly comprehension.

14.4 Change

A constantly **changing** Web site can also affect the success of the electronic commerce model. Be consistent throughout the Web site. Similar concepts should be incorporated by utilizing identical terminology in the narrative of the Web site and in the choice of graphics. The layout should be uniform throughout the site, as should the formatting and choice of type fonts.

When change is necessary, minimize the discomfort customers may feel by increasing site interactivity. Dynamic sites engage the user and make the visit to the business more memorable. Maximize the use of the Web as an interactive hypermedia communication medium. Involve the customer and incorporate a sense of adventure and fun. Sites that do maximize interactivity get more hits and return visits. When this happens, the business can charge more for advertising space on its site.

 Web Break

Not only can customers at Slashdot customize the Web site to their preferences, but the site is actually a user-driven site. Visit Slashdot at http://www.slashdot.org, a news site for "nerds" that posts short stories submitted by users and allows them to easily append comments to each story.

Dynamic sites also have an added benefit: they produce **self-generating content**. Include script-driven customer surveys and allow visitors to the site to share information with the business. The use of these electronic business models will increase interactivity and produce customer-generated content from ad hoc forms and code. Chat rooms, forums, and discussion threads are other useful techniques for increasing the dynamic interaction between the customer and the business.

Do not avoid change at too high a cost to the Web site, however. The Web site must provide valuable and timely information to the customer and be updated regularly. The site must also be well edited for dead links (links that go nowhere). Add the content learned from your customers through the dynamic model to the Web site. Customers will then know that the time they take to share and interact with the business is valued by the business.

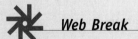

Web Break

Know your customer. To build the most effective site, this rule is paramount. Visit StatMarket at http://www.statmarket.com/ for in-depth statistics on a wide variety of Internet topics and a sharp interface. StatMarket provides free global Internet usage statistics gathered from tens of thousands of Web sites and millions of daily visitors.

14.5 Searchability

Searchability is a broad term used to describe the capability for searching and tracking within the site. Allow customers to search the business' Web site with search tools for Web servers. Be careful when incorporating search engines into your site that they do not take customers to other sites on the Web. A well-designed Web site will utilize myriad techniques to increase stickiness and keep customers within its own online business pages.

Searchability also includes speaking the customer's language. Be careful to write with the site's audience in mind by using words, phrases, and concepts that are familiar to the customer. The business' information should be presented in an order that will seem both natural and logical to the customer. Information technology is awash with jargon and acronyms. Use these on the business' Web site in a judicious manner, spelling out any initials or acronyms on first reference, even when it seems that the term is part of the vernacular. A site that is designed explicitly for the high-level user who

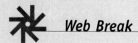

Web Break

Add some Swish to your site. Swish lets you create Flash animations without Flash and include text effects, images, audio, and interactivity. Swish exports the same animation format as Macromedia Flash. Visit Swish at http://www.swishzone.com/ and download a free trial version or view an assortment of demos.

will be familiar with a given task domain may employ specialized vocabulary, whereas a site designed for the general public must use a more accessible vocabulary.

Another aspect of searchability is **automation**. Incorporating automated tools into the electronic commerce design can greatly affect the success of the Web site. Large Web sites can be difficult to maintain. **Local spiders** can be used to search the site for old and dead URLs. Local spiders, also known as **crawlers** or **bots**, search the Web site and read the page. The name "spider" comes from the fact that their virtual legs span large areas of the site, or in the case of **Web spiders**, the Web. Spiders crawl through the site by following all the hypertext links in each page until all the pages have been read.

One measure of searchability is through counting Web site **hits** and revisits. A "hit" is a single file request that can be viewed in the Web server's access logs, and it serves as a meaningful measure of site traffic. Advertising agencies also use **impressions**, or **views**, to quantify the success of a Web site. Unlike hits, impressions are logged in a separate log that can be read by special programs that extract meaning from the log and generate a report about customer usage of the Web site. Examples of these types of programs include Web Trends and Central Ad.

Use Web Site Garage to add a hit counter to begin tracking your visitors to the Kanthaka Web site by inserting a few lines of HTML code into your page. Daily, weekly, and monthly hits will be reported in an online and e-mail format.

Kanthaka Farms
Add a Hit Counter to Your Design

1. Go to Web Site Garage on the Web at http://websitegarage. netscape.com. Verify that the Improve Your Site tab is active and click on Hitometer. Hitometer is a free service and offers a complete tracking and reporting system to help you better understand and analyze your Web site traffic.

2. If necessary, sign in for the service.

3. Once in the service, select the style of Hitometer that best complements the Kanthaka Farms' Web site you have designed throughout the exercises in this book by clicking on the appropriate option button. You can choose an **invisible counter**. This is a stealth-tracking device that will keep the same statistics as the other counters, yet the Kanthaka Farms customers will not see it on your page. Like all the Web Site Garage counters, you will still need to add some HTML to your page for this to work. Another choice is the **transparent counter**. The transparent counter has a clear background and blends in with the site background color or image on the Web page. When the Web page background is very dark, it is difficult to read numbers in a transparent counter.

4. Complete the remaining questions on the form and choose Next.

5. Choose the Free version of the Hitometer and click on Next.

6. Web Site Garage will now generate the HTML code necessary to add the hit counter to your design. You can copy and paste the code into your Web page. If you have created a frames-based site for Kanthaka Farms, it will be necessary for you to copy the Hitometer code into the page that serves as your main frame, not the page that contains all the <FRAME SRC=...> directives.

7. Launch your Web server and visit your site several times to test your Hitometer.

FOCUS ON ELECTRONIC COMMERCE

The Personalized Touch at Land's End Online

Land's End, a leading direct merchant of traditionally styled, casual clothing for men, women, and children, has found that there is a correlation between its increased sales and their online, personalized touch. And the touch is definitely high-tech at Land's End.

With their introduction of a new Web feature, "My Virtual Model," virtual reality meets Web site personalization. A "virtual" you is created at Land's End with just a series of clicks and answers to simple questions posted by the site's model wizard and "Quick Questionnaire" to determine the way your Virtual Model should look. This cutting-edge technology allows Web customers to "try on" clothing and accessories of all types online before making a purchase.

Bill Bass, Land's End's senior vice president of electronic commerce and international comments, "The Internet is nothing but good news for us." To back up that statement, all you need to do is look at sales for the year 2000. The Web site logged $138 million that year, making it more profitable than the catalog business. The first half of 2001, Web sales continued to rise and are up 70 percent from the previous year. And if revenues weren't enough proof that Land's End is an electronic commerce success, they have also received national accolades. The National Retail Federation has ranked the Land's End Web site as the 15th largest electronic commerce site overall and the largest online retail site.

But this success didn't come overnight. The Web site, launched in 1995, has tweaked and tried many tools to successfully deliver the perfect online shopping experience for its customers. In 1998, My Personal Model, a forerunner of the Virtual Model product, was launched. Both products use software from a Canadian company called My Virtual Model. The software engine that creates the model is built on a marketing theory called **conjoint analysis**. Conjoint analysis is the application of design of experiments to obtain individual customer preferences. The output of the Land's End Quick Questionnaire is the quantified preference of a customer for a set of attributes of style, color, and appearance. McKinsey & Co., a New York–based consulting firm, partnered with Land's End to create outcomes that would simulate the model, clothing, and adaptive suggestions. For instance, if a customer receives a score of 2.5, indicating a preference for conservative, dark clothing, the software engine will continue to suggest items in the 2.5 range. If the customer begins consistently choosing clothing with a score of 3, however, then the software adapts, and suggestions for more items come from the 3 range of categories.

Karen Johnson, a project leader in the Land's End Internet Group, says that "each time a person comes back, we want it to be more like that in-store experience. But you don't have to do any of this personal-model or personal-shopper stuff. It's just one more choice we offer."

So what is Land's End looking at to increase the online customer personalization? There's talk of integrating My Personal Shopper with My Personal Model. They also plan to license the software on which My Personal Shopper runs to Quickdog, a provider of electronic commerce services for both consumers and merchants. There's no doubt about it: Land's End is walking the talk—as a virtual model on a virtual runway

Conjoint analysis was used to help personalize the Web site. How could this marketing theory be applied to other areas of electronic commerce to create more dynamic customer interaction?

If you used similar technology at your business site, who should own the model?

How would you handle diversity?

What steps should be taken to protect customers' privacy and data?

Justify your answers.

Source: Sarah L. Roberts-Witt, "Try This on for Size," *PC Magazine*, December 4, 2000 9:00 P.M. PT; http://www.landsend.com/cd/frontdoor/; http://www.myvirtualmodel.com/mvmhome/pages/en/

14.6 Database Structure

Sound structure of relational databases will lead to more successful electronic commerce designs. **Normalization** is the key to meeting this objective. Normalization is a refinement technique of database design that suggests certain criteria be used when constructing table columns and creating the key structure. The purpose of normalization is to eliminate data redundancy of non-key data across tables. Normalization is usually referred to in terms of **forms**. In this book, only the first three will be discussed, even though the more advanced forms, such as fourth, fifth, and Boyce-Codd, are more commonly used.

First Normal Form

First Normal Form is the "basic" level of normalization and generally refers to moving data into separate tables where the data in each table are of a similar type, or kind. Each table is given a unique identifier called a **primary key**. Databases are considered to be in this form when they meet the following requirements:

- The database is made of two-dimensional tables with rows and columns.
- Each column corresponds to an **attribute**, or an inherent characteristic, of the object represented by the entire table.
- Each row is a unique representation of the attribute and contains no duplications.
- All column entries belong together and are representative of a single "kind."

Second Normal Form

In **Second Normal Form**, any column, or **field**, that does not determine the contents of another column must itself be a function of the other columns in the table. When creating this form, the data that are only dependent on a part of the key are removed to other tables. For example, the names of the dog owners in a Kanthaka Farms table would not be in Second Normal Form because that data would be redundant. The owner's name would be repeated for each dog owned, and as such, for sound database structure, the names would be removed and be placed in a table of their own. The names themselves do not have anything to do with the dogs; they refer only to the identities of the buyers and sellers. To better demonstrate function, consider that in a Kanthaka Farms table with three columns containing customer ID, dog sold, and price of the dog when sold, the price would be a function of the customer ID and the specific dog.

Third Normal Form

Third Normal Form involves eliminating table data that does not depend solely on the unique identifier (the primary key). In this form, tables are divided, and their data tracked separately. Only information dependent on the key remains, and data independent of the primary key are moved to independent tables, with new primary keys created for the new tables.

To increase the soundness of the database structure, data should be arranged so that any nonprimary key columns are dependent only on the whole primary key. It is also important to use intuitive, consistent, logical, full-word names when naming tables and columns, and then use full words in the database itself.

As a general rule, the data type tag prefixes should be used in naming fields in a database; however, this is not always practical or even possible. If the database already exists either because the new program is referencing an existing database or because the database structure has been created as part of the database design phase, then it is not practical to apply these tags to every column. Even for new tables in existing databases, it is poor design to deviate from the conventions already in use in that database.

Keep in mind that Web database construction crosses multiple languages and platforms. Some database engines do not support mixed case in data item names. For instance, a name like SBUYER_CODE is visually difficult to scan and it might be a better idea to omit the tag. Keep in mind, too, that some database formats allow only for very short names.

14.7 Visual Basic Project Design

Several considerations of sound Visual Basic project design can affect the success of the electronic commerce model. These standards include, but are not limited to, naming conventions, user-defined types, arrays, procedures, and application program interface

(API) declarations. Others include procedure length, commenting, and formatting code.

Naming Conventions

Standardization of naming conventions within the Visual Basic project design is the most visible and arguably the most important. Consistent names of variables, scope, and data types within the project will save time both during the design process and during the inevitable maintenance work of the Web site. Since variable names are used very frequently in code, a consistent naming convention for variables can minimize the amount of time spent searching the code for the exact spelling of a variable's name. In addition, encoding some information about the variable itself into the variable's name can increase the success of the model. It is easier to decipher the meaning of any statement in which variables with standardized names are used and easier to catch errors that would otherwise be very difficult to find.

Array names should be plurals. This will be especially helpful in the transition to collections in Microsoft's new .NET environment. Arrays should also be transitioned with both an upper and a lower bound. An example follows:

instead of

```
Dim mDogs(10) as TDog
```

use instead

```
Dim mDogs(0 To 10) as TDog
```

Arrays are usually easily recognizable by the subscripts after the array found in parentheses or by the range included within a function like UBound. As a general principle, create subscript ranges that allow for clean and simple processing in code.

Procedures should be named according to the following convention:

```
verb.noun
verb.noun.adjective
```

For instance:

```
FindBuyer
FindBuyerNext
UpdateBuyer
UpdateBuyerCurrent
```

Remember that event procedures cannot be renamed in Visual Basic and do not have scope prefixes; therefore, user procedures should include a scope prefix. Common modules should keep all procedures that are not callable from other modules private.

Because the Visual Basic code in the Web database design will reference database columns, the data type tag prefixes should be used in naming fields in a database. However, the reference must be consistent with the name used in the database.

The API is the specific method prescribed by a program by means of which a programmer writing an application program can make requests of the operating system or another application. All non-sharable code uses the standard API declarations. All common modules that will or may be shared across projects are banned from using the standard declarations. Instead, if one of these common modules needs to use an API, it must create an alias declaration for that API where the name is prefixed with a unique code, the same one used to prefix its global constants.

Procedure Length

Too often, programmers are taught that short procedures of no more than a page are the standard. However, actual research has shown that this is simply not true, and in fact, in several studies, just the opposite has been shown to be true. Empirical data suggest that error rates and development costs for routines decrease as the code size moves from small, or less than 32 lines, to larger routines, up to about 200 lines. Comprehensibility of code has been shown to be no better for code super-modularized to routines approximately 10 lines in length than for one with no routines at all. However, on the same code modularized to routines of around 25 lines, comprehension increases. Let the requirements of the process determine the length of the routine. Keep in mind that there is an upper limit beyond which it is almost impossible to comprehend a routine. A good rule of thumb is that a procedure should do one and only one task. In addition, ensure that each procedure has high cohesion and low coupling, the standard aims of good structured design.

Formatting Standards

The physical layout of code is very important in determining how readable and maintainable it is. The use of white space and indents aids in increasing the comprehension of the code. Indent three spaces at a time. Do not comment more than is necessary.

Summary

- **Discuss the factors that affect the success of electronic commerce.** Many factors affect the success of electronic commerce. As the size of the infrastructure increases, congestion and bandwidth have the potential to drag the pace of electronic commerce to a halt. Though greatly tightened in the last few years, security issues also remain a challenge to electronic commerce. Many cases of identity fraud or theft are associated with the nature of the Internet's open network; and, without a continued increase in comfort level with online purchasing, consumers may find reason to revert to more traditional means of trade. Electronic commerce also faces legal uncertainties such as re-interpretation of copyright laws and laws addressing intellectual property theft and taxation. However, as businesses and customers become more accustomed to the intricacies of the digital age and its new economy, electronic commerce will continue to transform the world of business and emerge as a viable model of a perfectly competitive market.

- **Discuss challenges to the efficiency and speed of the construction.** Though speed is an obvious element that can either enhance or detract from the Web site design, it may be the most abused. The single most important predictor of site success is the perspective from which the site has been designed. The site should be customer-centered—not designer-centered—and designed for those customers with the lowest capacity components. Be responsive to the typical Web user on a 56K modem. Even if it has been determined that the business' site is used primarily by high-end technology users, speed and download times must still be major design considerations.

- **Discuss Web layout issues.** Layout is another factor that affects the success of the electronic commerce design. Successful Web database constructions are well organized. The degree of hyperization, the number of levels within the site, must be balanced with page length to decrease the display and scrolling time required of the customer. A very effective way to increase stickiness at the Web site is to minimize scrolling. A business' Web site is said to be "sticky" if a customer tends to stay for a long time and to also make return visits. It is important that orphan pages be eliminated. These are pages that do not have a link to the business' home page and do not contain some indication of where they fit within the structure of the Web site. Because customers may access Web pages directly without entering through the home page, make sure that all pages have a clear indication of the Web site to which they belong. The inclusion of frames in the Web site design can also negatively affect the success of the electronic commerce model; use sparingly or offer alternatives.

- **Describe how change can be a mediating factor in the success of electronic commerce.** A constantly changing Web site can also affect the success of the electronic commerce model. Be consistent throughout the Web site. Similar concepts should be incorporated by utilizing identical terminology in the narrative of the Web site and in the choice of graphics. The layout should be uniform throughout the site as should the formatting and choice of type fonts. When change is necessary, minimize the discomfort customers may feel by increasing site interactivity. Dynamic sites engage the user and make the visit to the business more memorable. Maximize the use of the Web as an interactive hypermedia communication medium. Involve the customer and incorporate a sense of adventure and fun. Sites that do maximize interactivity get more hits and return visits. When this happens, the business can charge more for advertising space on its site.

- **Define searchability and discuss associated issues.** Searchability is a broad term used to describe the capability for searching and tracking within the site. Allow customers to search the business' Web site with search tools for Web servers. Be careful when incorporating search engines into your site that they do not take customers to other sites on the Web. A well-designed Web site will utilize myriad techniques to increase stickiness and keep customers within its own online business pages.

- **Discuss the importance of sound database structure to the electronic commerce model.** Sound structure of relational databases will lead to more successful electronic commerce designs. Normalization is the key to meeting this objective. Normalization is a refinement technique of database design that suggests certain criteria be used when constructing table columns and creating the key structure. Its purpose is to eliminate data redundancy of non-key data across tables. Normalization is usually referred to in terms of forms. In this book, only the first three are discussed, even though the more advanced forms, such as fourth, fifth, and Boyce-Codd, are more commonly used.

■ **Describe Visual Basic project design issues.** Several considerations of sound Visual Basic project design can affect the success of the electronic commerce model. These standards include, but are not limited to, naming conventions, user-defined types, arrays, procedures, and application program interface (API) declarations. Others include procedure length, commenting, and formatting code.

Chapter Key Terms

attribute	hits	searchability
automation	hyperization	Second Normal Form
bots	impressions	self-generating content
changing	invisible counter	speed
conjoint analysis	layout	stickiness
crawlers	local Spiders	Third Normal Form
field	normalization	transparent counter
First Normal Form	orphan pages	views
forms	primary key	Web spiders
frames		

Review Questions

1. List the factors negatively affecting the success of electronic commerce today. What can be done to mediate each of these factors?

2. List ways in which the speed of a Web site can be increased.

3. How can graphics and images be optimized for inclusion in a Web site?

4. Describe how poor HTML coding techniques can affect the success of the electronic commerce design.

5. What is hyperization?

6. What is stickiness? List three common approaches to "stick" customers to your Web site.

7. What is an orphan page? Why is it not a desirable component of a Web site?

8. Discuss three issues associated with change and how they can affect the success of the Web site.

9. What is searchability? How can it be increased?

10. What is a transparent counter? In what cases would it be more beneficial to the site to use a transparent counter rather than a visible counter?

11. What are spiders? Describe the difference between local spiders and Web spiders. Why should local spiders be used at the business' Web site?

12. Discuss issues relating to sound database design. Why is this important to the success of the electronic commerce design?

13. Why should standard naming conventions be used in the Visual Basic project design?

14. What are formatting standards? Discuss two that should be used in the Visual Basic project design.

Critical Thinking Using the Web

1. ASP can also be used to create a hit counter. Use your favorite search engine to surf the Web and find snippets of code to create an ASP hit counter. Bring two to class and be prepared to discuss how they could be incorporated into the Web database construction.

2. It is important to understand the global traffic coming into your site. You will want to know whether your visitors are repeat or first-time visitors. It will be important to analyze whether your referencing and marketing strategies are working. Use your favorite search engine and explore tools available on the Web that provide site traffic analysis. Using a table, compare and contrast five different tools. Quantify by price, statistics, user support, ease of use, and rapidity of information. You may also use your own metrics in addition to these. In a 200–400-word essay, discuss your findings. Be prepared to present your table and findings to the class.

3. Have you heard of Swing applets? Is your browser Swing-aware? Go to http://java.sun.com/products/jfc/tsc/articles/applets and test to determine whether the browser you are using has a native Java Virtual Machine (JVM) that works with Swing. If it does, it can run Swing applets without using a Java Plug-in. If it does not, Java Plug-in technology is available to write and distribute Swing applets that will run on any computer system using any browser. Also, use your favorite search engine to find out more about Swing and how it can be incorporated into the Web database design. Write a report on your test and search in a 200–400-word essay. Be prepared to discuss your findings in class.

Chapter Case Study

Albatross Records is a continuing case study in this book that illustrates the process of building electronic commerce with Web database constructions. In this last chapter, the factors that affect the success of the electronic commerce model will be assessed, and enhancement will be added to the design to increase its efficiency and effectiveness. In this chapter, you will complete the electronic commerce Web database construction for Albatross Records.

- Identify the challenges facing the business' electronic commerce design. Determine the browser compatibility, site readiness, site download time, dead links, and link popularity. Perform a thorough spell check and HTML check.

- Assess your database structure design and the Visual Basic code project design.

- Prepare a written assessment of your site from the two steps above. The assessment should also include strategies to improve any identified or inherent weaknesses. The assessment should be generated with a word-processor and should include appropriate spreadsheets, tables, and charts/graphs in a three-ring binder and presented to Cool and top management at Albatross Records.

- Finally, add a hit counter to your design to enable traffic analysis.

HTML Primer

Tag	Description	Example
<!-->	Comment	<!-- comment text -->
<	Escape Sequences	&amp &quot &emdash
<A>	Anchor	<A NAME="anchor-name"> <A HREF="#anchor-name">link-text</A> <A HREF="url">link-text</A> <A HREF="url#anchor-name">link-text </A>
<ABBREV>	Abbreviation	<ABBREV> text </ABBREV>
<ACRONYM>	Acronym	<ACRONYM> text </ACRONYM>
<ADDRESS>	Address	<ADDRESS> text </ADDRESS>
<APPLET>	Java Applet	<APPLET attributes> applet-content </APPLET>
<AREA>	Area	<AREA SHAPE="shape" ALT="text" CO-ORDS="co-ords" HREF="URL">
<AU>	Author	<AU> text </AU>
<AUTHOR>	Author	<AUTHOR> text </AUTHOR>
<B>	Bold	<B> text </B>
<BANNER>	Banner	<BANNER attributes </BANNER>
<BASE>	Base	<BASE HREF="base address"> <BASE TARGET="default target">
<BASEFONT>	Base Font	<BASEFONT SIZE=number>
<BGSOUND>	Background Sound	<BGSOUND SRC="URL"> <BGSOUND SRC="URL"LOOP=n>
<BIG>	Big Text	<BIG> text </BIG>
<BLINK>	Blink	<BLINK> text </BLINK>

Tag	Description	Example
<BLOCKQUOTE>	Block Quote	<BLOCKQUOTE> text </BLOCKQUOTE>
<BQ>	Block Quote	<BQ> text </BQ>
<BODY>	Body	<BODY> document-body </BODY>
 	Line Break	
<CAPTION>	Caption	<CAPTION> text </CAPTION>
<CENTER>	Center	<CENTER> text</CENTER>
<CITE>	Citation	<CITE> text </CITE>
<CODE>	Code	<CODE> text </CODE>
<COL>	Table Column	<COL> content </COL> <COL ALIGN=alignment> content </COL> <COL SPAN=number> content </COL>
<COLGROUP>	Table Column Group	<COLGROUP> column data </COLGROUP>
<CREDIT>	Credit	<CREDIT> text </CREDIT>
<DEL>	Deleted Text	<DEL> list entries </DEL>
<DFN>	Definition	<DFN> text </DFN>
<DIR>	Directory List	<DIR> list entries </DIR>
<DIV>	Division	<DIV ALIGN=align>
<DL>	Defined List	<DL> list entries </DL> <DL COMPACT> list entries </DL>
<DT>	Defined Term	<DT> term
<DD>	Definition	<DD> definition
<EM>	Emphasized	<EM> text </EM>
<EMBED>	Embed	<EMBED attributes> alternate HTML </EMBED>
<FIG>	Figure	<FIG attributes> figure-content </FIG>
<FN>	Footnote	<FN ID=anchor-name> text </FN>
<FONT>	Font	<FONT SIZE=number> <FONT COLOR="#RRGGBB"> <FONT COLOR="colorname"> <FONT FACE="facename1, facename2...">
<FORM>	Form	<FORM ACTION=action base> form tags </FORM> <FORM METHOD=method> form tags </FORM> <FORM ENCTYPE=media type> form tags </FORM>
<FRAME>	Frame	<FRAME attributes>

Tag	Description	Example
<FRAMESET>	Frame Set	<FRAMESET attributes> frame tags </FRAMESET>
<H1>	Heading 1	<H1> text </H1>
<H2>	Heading 2	<H2> text </H2>
<H3>	Heading 3	<H3> text </H3>
<H4>	Heading 4	<H4> text </H4>
<H5>	Heading 5	<H5> text </H5>
<H6>	Heading 6	<H6> text </H6>
<HEAD>	Head	<HEAD> head-section </HEAD>
<HR>	Horizontal Rule	<HR>
<HTML>	HTML	<HTML> entire-document </HTML>
<I>	Italic	<I> text </I>
<IFRAME>	Frame—Floating	<IFRAME attributes> frame data <IFRAME>
<IMG>	Inline Image	<IMG attributes>
<INPUT>	Form Input	<INPUT TYPE=CHECKBOX NAME=name VALUE=value> <INPUT TYPE=CHECKBOX NAME=name VALUE=value> <INPUT TYPE=CHECKBOX NAME=name VALUE=value CHECKED>
<INS>	Inserted Text	<INS> text </INS>
<ISINDEX>	Is Index	<ISINDEX> <ISINDEX HREF=URL> <ISINDEX PROMPT=prompt>
<KBD>	Keyboard	<KBD> text </KBD>
<LANG>	Language	<LANG> text </LANG>
<LH>	List Heading	<LH> text </LH>
<LI>	List Item	<LI> text </LI>
<LINK>	Link	<LINK REL=relationship HREF="URL"> <LINK REV=relationship HREF="URL"> <LINK REV=relationship HREF="URL" TITLE="title">
<LISTING>	Listing	<LISTING> text </LISTING>
<MAP>	Map	<MAP NAME="name"> area tags </MAP>
<MARQUEE>	Marquee	<MARQUEE> text </MARQUEE> <MARQUEE ALIGN="align"> text </MARQUEE> <MARQUEE BEHAVIOR="behavior"> text </MARQUEE>

Tag	Description	Example
<MARQUEE>	Marquee	<MARQUEE BGCOLOR="#rrggbb"> text </MARQUEE> <MARQUEE BGCOLOR="colorname"> text </MARQUEE> <MARQUEE DIRECTION="direction"> text </MARQUEE> <MARQUEE HEIGHT=n> text </MARQUEE> <MARQUEE HEIGHT=n%> text </MARQUEE> <MARQUEE HSPACE=n> text </MARQUEE> <MARQUEE LOOP=n> text </MARQUEE> <MARQUEE SCROLLAMOUNT=n> text </MARQUEE> <MARQUEE SCROLLDELAY=n> text </MARQUEE> <MARQUEE WIDTH=n> text </MARQUEE> <MARQUEE VSPACE=n> text </MARQUEE> <MARQUEE WIDTH=n%> text </MARQUEE>
<MATH>	Math	$math-content$
<MENU>	Menu List	<MENU> list entries </MENU>
<META>	Meta	<META HTTP-EQUIV="HTTP header field name" NAME="field name" CONTENT="field value"> HTTP-EQUIV="REFRESH"
<MULTICOL>	Multi Column Text	<MULTICOL attributes>
<NOBR>	No Break	<NOBR> text </NOBR>
<NOFRAMES>	No Frames	<NOFRAMES> alternate HTML </NOFRAMES>
<NOTE>	Note	<NOTE> text </NOTE> <NOTE CLASS=class> text </NOTE> <NOTE SRC=URL> text </NOTE>
<OBJECT>	Object	<OBJECT> object-content </OBJECT>
<OL>	Ordered List	<OL> list entries </OL>
<OVERLAY>	Overlay	<OVERLAY attributes>
<P>	Paragraph	<P> text <P> text </P>
<PARAM>	Parameters	<PARAM NAME="name" VALUE="value">
<PERSON>	Person	<PERSON> text </PERSON>
<PLAINTEXT>	Plain Text	<PLAINTEXT> text </PLAINTEXT>

Tag	Description	Example
<PRE>	Preformatted Text	<PRE> text </PRE> <PRE WIDTH=width> text </PRE>
<Q>	Quote	<Q> text </Q>
<RANGE>	Range	<RANGE FROM="from id" UNTIL="until id">
<SAMP>	Sample	<SAMP> text </SAMP>
<SCRIPT>	Script	<SCRIPT LANGUAGE="language"><!-- script statements --></SCRIPT>
<SELECT>	Form Select	<SELECT NAME=name> option entries </SELECT> <SELECT NAME=name MULTIPLE> option entries </SELECT> <SELECT NAME=name SIZE=size> option entries </SELECT>
<SMALL>	Small Text	<SMALL> text </SMALL>
<SPACER>	White Space	<SPACER attributes>
<SPOT>	Spot	<SPOT ID="id">
<STRIKE>	Strikethrough	<STRIKE> text </STRIKE>
<STRONG>	Strong	<STRONG> text </STRONG>
<SUB>	Subscript	_{text}
<SUP>	Superscript	^{text}
<TAB>	Horizontal Tab	<TAB INDENT=number> <TAB TO=tab id ALIGN=align> <TAB DP=character>
<TABLE>	Table	<TABLE attributes> table-content </TABLE>
<TBODY>	Table Body	<TBODY> table body </TBODY>
<TD>	Table Data	<TD attributes>
<TEXTAREA>	Form Text Area	<TEXTAREA NAME=name COLS=# columns ROWS=# rows> content </TEXTAREA> <TEXTAREA NAME=name COLS=# columns ROWS=# rows WRAP=type> content </TEXTAREA>
<TEXTFLOW>	Java Applet Textflow	<TEXTFLOW>
<TFOOT>	Table Footer	<TFOOT>
<TH>	Table Header	<TH attributes>
<THEAD>	Table Head	<THEAD>
<TITLE>	Title	<TITLE> title-text </TITLE>
<TR>	Table Row	<TR attributes>
<TT>	Teletype	<TT> text </TT>

Tag	Description	Example
<U>	Underlined	<U> text </U>
<UL>	Unordered List	<UL> list entries </UL> <UL COMPACT> list entries </UL>
<VAR>	Variable	<VAR> text </VAR>
<WBR>	Word Break	<WBR>
<XMP>	Example	<XMP> text </XMP>

FrontPage Primer

Microsoft's FrontPage 2000 and FrontPage XP version 2002 are popular electronic commerce Web database construction tools. FrontPage is more than an HTML editor. With FrontPage, electronic commerce developers can create dynamic Web site features such as search engines, sub-webs, or customer counters. An alternative to FrontPage is FrontPage Express, a free HTML editor with a graphical user interface that is based on the full-featured FrontPage Web authoring tool. FrontPage Express (formerly FrontPad) was first included in Microsoft Internet Explorer Suite version 4 and has not been updated in the version 5 or beta 6 releases of the browser suite.

FrontPage and FrontPage Express are WYSIWYG editors. This means electronic commerce developers see the Web page as it will appear in a customer's browser. These editors allow Web sites to be created without ever having to learn HTML code. They work much like word processors; however, the page is an HTML page rather than a Word document.

User Interface

As shown in Figure B.1, the FrontPage user interface is very similar to many Microsoft programs. Toolbars along the top of the application can be rearranged simply by dragging and dropping.

The primary freatures of FrontPage include the following:

- Form wizard
- Text layout tools
- Image tools

Figure B.1

The FrontPage Toolbar

- Linking tools
- Table creation tools
- Web publishing tools

Form Wizard

As shown in Figure B-2, the form wizard can be accessed by choosing New Page from the File menu. Template and style sheets can also be accessed from the New Page selection. These templates can be used to create a guestbook, user registration, or even a feedback form and add customer–business interactivity to the Web site.

Figure B-2

The Forms Wizard

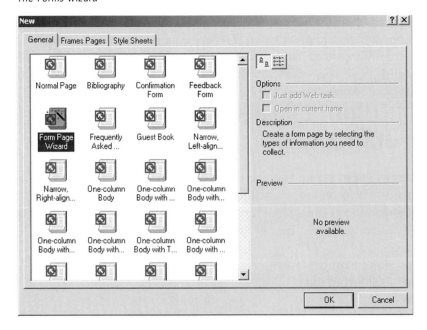

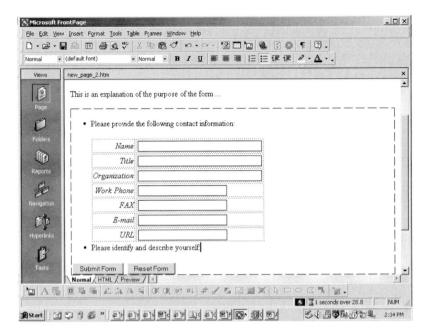

Figure B-3

A Dynamic HTML Form Created in FrontPage

The form wizard can aid the electronic commerce developer in creating dynamic Web pages to collect customer input. The choices made using the wizard can result in a Web page, customer CGI script, or text file for use on a Web server, as shown in Figure B-3.

Text Layout Tools

The FrontPage standard toolbar provides direct access to the file, and text format features of the application. Web pages can be created from existing documents or by typing in a new page. To convert an existing document into an HTML page, simply click on the Open button in the toolbar and then select the format desired. The text will be imported into FrontPage and can be saved as an HTML document.

Page formatting can be added either before text is entered or afterward just as with a word processor. To preselect, choose the formatting options and type. To format after typing, simply select the text to be formatted and apply the format changes.

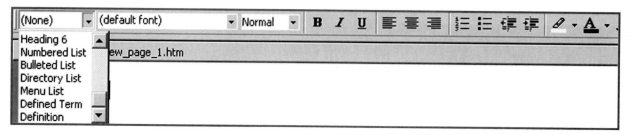

Figure B-4

The FrontPage Formatting Toolbar

Figure B-4 shows the FrontPage formatting toolbar. Various types of formatting styles are supported in FrontPage. Normal HTML text sizes are defined by a selection of tags that identify areas of text as paragraphs, headings, or lists. To use these in FrontPage, choose the format style from the drop-down menu list on the toolbar.

Next to the text size on the toolbar, a drop-down list allows font formatting. The drop-down list offers all the installed fonts. Multiple fonts can be used within a single HTML document. The fonts themselves are not included in the document, however, so care should be used in font selection. If a page is accessed by a customer who does not have the font, then the Web page will not look as the business intended on the customer site and may appear unattractive in the default font. Most Windows users will have Times New Roman, Arial, and Courier installed.

The formatting toolbar also contains tools for aligning text on the Web page and for creating bulleted lists.

Image Tools

Images and pictures make Web pages look more accessible and attractive. However, because picture files are often large in size, they will increase the download time for customers who access the page. One way to reduce the size of a picture is to limit the number of colors used. Also, the choice of picture file type is very important. If the image is a photograph, then .JPG files should be used. A .JPG (pronounced JAY-peg) is an acronym for Joint Photographic Experts Group and is a graphic image created by choosing a range of compression qualities from a suite of compression algorithms. Use .GIF, the de facto standard image form for the Web, for line art or simple graphics. The .GIF format uses the LZW compression algorithm, which is owned by Unisys; however, Unisys has not required users of .GIF images to obtain a license, even though their licensing statement indicates that it is a requirement. Additional software will be needed to edit images since no program within the Internet Explorer suite has this capability. Windows users can find paint and imaging programs from Accessories on the Start Programs menu to use for this task.

To add images, place the cursor where the picture should appear and click on the Insert Image icon in the FrontPage toolbar. The dialog box will ask you to insert an image. The image may be inserted from either a location on the Web or the local drives. It is important to note that pictures are not embedded into HTML pages, but are only linked. The link is made relative to the position of the saved HTML page. When the business' Web page is uploaded to the Internet, it is important to pay careful attention to the file and folder hierarchy.

Linking Tools

Hyperlinks can be created from text or graphics on an HTML page. Hyperlinks can also link to an e-mail address so when a customer clicks the link, an e-mail client, like Microsoft Outlook, will open with the e-mail address specified in the To: field.

To link text, select the text and click on the anchor icon on the FrontPage toolbar. In the dialog box, simply type in the address of a Web page to reference with the link. If the Web page is not stored locally, type in the full Web address including the http:// portion of the address.

Hyperlinks, as images, can also take a relative filename, which refers to Web pages relative to the position of the page on which the link is located.

Table Creation

The look of Web pages created in HTML will vary depending on the size of the customer's browser window. The layout will change dynamically as the window is resized. One way to remedy this is to restrict the layout by incorporating tables into the Web page design. Tables can be set to have zero borders so that customers to the site will never see them.

To insert a table into a Web page, click on the table icon on the FrontPage toolbar. When clicked, the table tool will display a grid from which the number of cells needed in the table can be defined. The Table Insert menu can also be used to create tables. Text or images can then be inserted directly into the cells of the table to restrict Web browser display variances.

Web Publishing

Once the HTML page has been created, the Web Publishing Wizard can be used to publish the page to the Web. The Web Publishing Wizard is another component available from the Microsoft Internet Explorer browser suite and is only installed with a full or custom installation. Upon installation, the wizard can be launched from Internet Tools in Accessories on the Start menu, and it is also integrated into the Save As dialog in FrontPage Express. In FrontPage, simply choose Web Publish from the File menu to display the dialog box shown in Figure B-5.

FrontPage will prompt the developer for information as needed as it steps through the Web publishing process. It will connect to the

Figure B-5

Publishing the Web Page

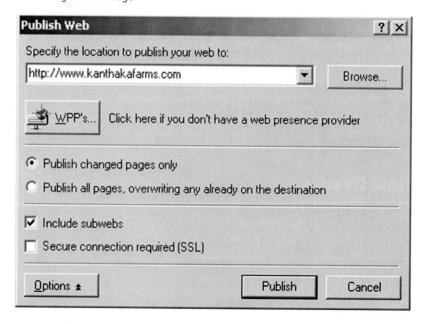

Internet, since until this point the Web page creation process was performed off-line. FrontPage will attempt to establish the method and location on the Web server in order to publish the page. If successful, it will prompt for username and password to authenticate with the Web server. Most of the time this process will be a File Transfer Process (FTP). When all the information has been accepted, the Web page will be uploaded, and a progress indicator like the Copy Files dialog under Windows will show the progress.

Other Tools Available in FrontPage

Both FrontPage and FrontPage Express have much more capability than simple HTML layout and creation. Both provide the added functionality of advanced Web features, such as inserting Java applets or ActiveX controls. Figure B-6 shows some of the developer resources available in FrontPage.

FrontPage also makes it easy to include Hit Counters, Hover Buttons, or Marquees into the electronic commerce design simply by choosing Components from the FrontPage Insert menu.

Figure B-6

FrontPage Developer Resources Available from the Insert Menu

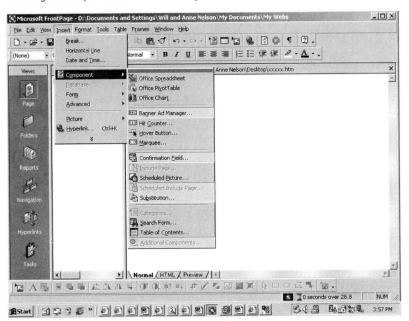

There are several Web bots included with FrontPage. A bot, short for robot, is a program that operates as an agent for a user or another program. The Search Form Web bot is a basic tool that allows the user to search for data according to its relevance on a page. The Text field and required buttons will be added to the Web page automatically and the dotted lines around the search function only indicate that it is a Web bot. They will not be visible in the browser. Include Pages is another Web bot feature available in FrontPage. This Web bot enables separate HTML documents to be included within an HTML file. This function is useful for adding a common page, or template, to several HTML pages and can greatly reduce the development time needed to alter Web pages.

Organization of Files and Description of Software on this Book's Companion Web Site

Web Site Hierarchy

The contents of the following folders should be copied to folders of the same name on C:\WebSite. If the folders do not exist on C:\WebSite, then they should be created before copying the files and folders from this book's companion Web site. These files and folders must be copied to the hard drive in order to benefit from the exercises in the book. Also, ensure that during the copy process, the read-only attribute is not turned on for any file or folder. To verify, from Windows Explorer, right-click on the file or folder in question and choose Properties. The attributes can be viewed from the General tab. If the Read-Only attribute is checked, click in the check box to deselect.

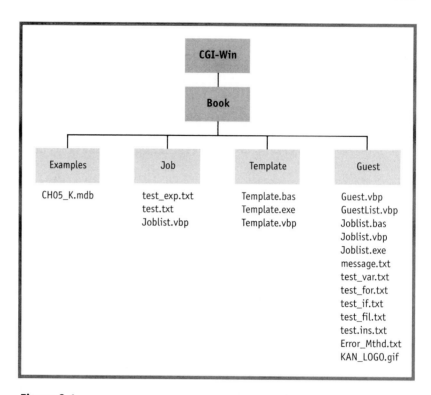

Figure C-1
C:\WebSite\CGI-Win folder

Figure C-2
C:\WebSite\cgi-src folder

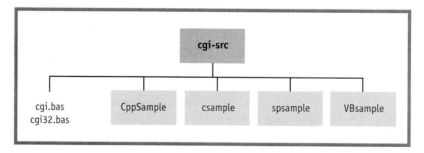

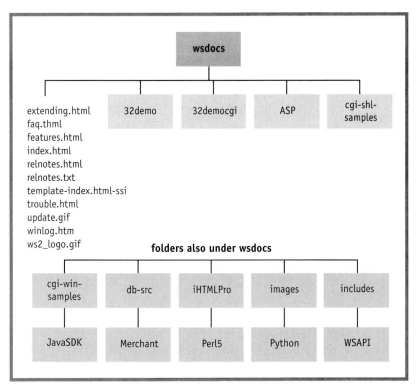

Figure C-3
C:\WebSite\ws-docs folder

Figure C-4
C:\WebSite\HTDOCS folder

Figure C-5
C:\WebSite\LIB

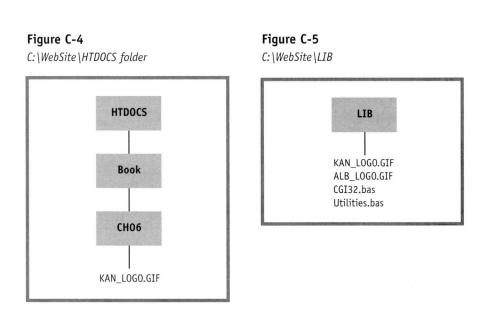

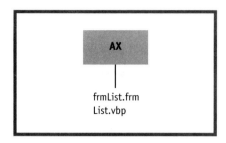

Figure C-6
C:\WebSite\AX

Software Available on the CD

First Page 2000 v2.0 Final HTML Editor The HTML editor is also available at http://www.evrsoft.com/shop as shareware. First Page 2000 is free and requires no license.

Amaya XHTML Editor The XHTML editor is also available as freeware at http://www.w3.org/Amaya/.

Deerfield WebSite Server Software The Web server software is a 120-day evaluation copy.

JRun Server 3.0 JRun Server 3.0 is a J2EE application server and integrated development environment for building and deploying server-side Java applications and is also available for evaluation at http://allaire11.allaire.com/download/.

Style Master 1.9 Cascading Style Sheets Editor The CSS editor is also available at http://www.westciv.com.au/style_master/ as shareware evaluation copy valid for 31 days.

Sun Chili!Soft ASP Chili!Soft ASP for Windows 2000/NT server-side scripting and runtime environment for the cross platform deployment of Active Server Pages (ASP or .asp) Web sites and Web applications can also be downloaded as a 30-day full-version trial at http://www.chilisoft.com/downloads/default.asp#asp.

XML Spy 3.5 XML Editor A demo copy of the XML editor is available at http://new.xmlspy.com/download.html and is good for 30 days.

Visual Basic Source Code

Source Code for Utilities Library Module

```
'Will and Anne Nelson / June 2001 / NMA, Inc.

Option Explicit

Const UTILITIES_MAX_RECORDSETS = 6
Global UTILITIES_rsarray(1 To UTILITIES_MAX_RECORDSETS) As
      Recordset
Const UTILITIES_DB_PATH = "\WEBSITE\LIB\ROOT.MDB"
Global UTILITIES_Error As Integer

Dim UTILITIES_db As Database

Sub UTILITIES_AddKeywordsToTempTable(rsSource As Recordset,
      KeywordDelimiters, rsDest As Recordset)
  Dim Ch As String
  Dim KeyWord As String
  Dim length As Long
  Dim Start As Long
  Dim i As Long
  Dim Description
  Dim Delimiters
  On Error Resume Next
  Delimiters = KeywordDelimiters & Chr(13) & Chr(10)
  Description = Trim(rsSource![KeywordField])
  length = Len(Description)
  If length = 0 Then Exit Sub
  Start = 1
  For i = 1 To length
    Ch = Mid(Description, i, 1)
    If InStr(Delimiters, Ch) > 0 Then
      KeyWord = Trim(Mid(Description, Start, i - Start))
      If KeyWord <> "" And Not IsNull(KeyWord) Then
        rsDest.AddNew
        rsDest![ID] = rsSource![ID]
```

```
            rsDest![KeyWord] = KeyWord
            rsDest.Update
          End If
          Start = i + 1
        End If
    End If
  Next
  If Start < i Then
    KeyWord = Trim(Mid(Description, Start, i - Start))
    If KeyWord <> "" And Not IsNull(KeyWord) Then
      rsDest.AddNew
      rsDest![ID] = rsSource![ID]
      rsDest![KeyWord] = KeyWord
      rsDest.Update
    End If
  End If
End Sub

Public Sub UTILITIES_IndexField(db As Database, rsSource As Recordset, KeywordsLinkTable,
      Delimiters)
  Dim TempKeywordTable
  Dim ErrValue As Integer
  Dim rsTemp As Recordset
  Dim i, SQL
  If rsSource.EOF Then Exit Sub
  Select Case rsSource![ID].Type
    Case dbText
      TempKeywordTable = "tblTMP_Keywords_Text"
    Case dbByte, dbInteger, dbLong
      TempKeywordTable = "tblTMP_Keywords_Numeric"
  End Select
  On Error Resume Next
  For i = 1 To 15000
    Set rsTemp = db.OpenRecordset(TempKeywordTable, dbOpenDynaset, dbDenyWrite)
    If Err = 0 Then Exit For
    DoEvents
  Next
  ErrValue = Err
  If ErrValue <> 0 Then
    On Error GoTo 0
    Error ErrValue
  End If
  Do Until rsTemp.EOF
    rsTemp.Delete
    DoEvents
    rsTemp.MoveNext
  Loop
  Do Until rsSource.EOF
    UTILITIES_AddKeywordsToTempTable rsSource, Delimiters, rsTemp
    DoEvents
    rsSource.MoveNext
  Loop
  rsTemp.Close
  On Error GoTo 0
  SQL = "INSERT INTO tblSYS_Keywords ( Keyword ) " & _
```

```
            "SELECT DISTINCT " & TempKeywordTable & ".Keyword" & _
            "FROM " & TempKeywordTable & " LEFT JOIN tblSYS_Keywords " & _
            "ON " & TempKeywordTable & ".Keyword = tblSYS_Keywords.Keyword " & _
            "WHERE (((tblSYS_Keywords.Keyword) Is Null));"
    db.Execute SQL, dbFailOnError
    SQL = "INSERT INTO " & KeywordsLinkTable & " ( ID, KeywordID ) " & _
            "SELECT DISTINCT " & TempKeywordTable & ".ID, " & _
            "tblSYS_Keywords.KeywordID FROM " & TempKeywordTable & _
            " LEFT JOIN tblSYS_Keywords ON " & TempKeywordTable & _
            ".Keyword = tblSYS_Keywords.Keyword;"
    db.Execute SQL
End Sub

Function UTILITIES_EmptyToNullField(FieldName As String) As Variant
    Dim value
    On Error Resume Next
    value = Trim(GetSmallField(FieldName))
    If value = "" Or Err <> 0 Then
        UTILITIES_EmptyToNullField = Null
    Else
        UTILITIES_EmptyToNullField = value
    End If
End Function

Function UTILITIES_GetParameter(ParameterString, ParameterNumber, Delimiter)
    Dim EndPos
    Dim Start
    Dim i
    If ParameterString = "" Then
        UTILITIES_GetParameter = Null
        Exit Function
    End If
    Start = 1
    For i = 2 To ParameterNumber
        Start = InStr(Start, ParameterString, Delimiter) + 1
        If Start = 1 Then
            Start = 0
            Exit For
        End If
    Next
    If Start = 0 Then
        UTILITIES_GetParameter = Null
        Exit Function
    End If
    EndPos = InStr(Start, ParameterString, Delimiter)
    If EndPos = 0 Then
        UTILITIES_GetParameter = Mid(ParameterString, Start)
    Else
        UTILITIES_GetParameter = Mid(ParameterString, Start, EndPos - Start)
    End If
End Function

Function UTILITIES_ConvertFromQueryString(StringValue As String)
    Dim ConvertedString As String
```

```
  ConvertedString = UTILITIES_ReplaceString(StringValue, "__", " ")
  ConvertedString = UTILITIES_ReplaceString(ConvertedString, "'", """")
  UTILITIES_ConvertFromQueryString = ConvertedString
End Function

Function UTILITIES_ConvertToQueryString(StringValue As String)
  Dim ConvertedString As String
  ConvertedString = UTILITIES_ReplaceString(StringValue, " ", "__")
  ConvertedString = UTILITIES_ReplaceString(ConvertedString, """", "'")
  UTILITIES_ConvertToQueryString = ConvertedString
End Function

Function UTILITIES_ReplaceString(SourceString, A, B)
  Dim i As Integer
  Dim NumCharsToReplace As Integer
  Dim NumCharsReplacedBy As Integer
  Dim Result As String
  Dim StringToReplace As String
  Dim Replacement As String
  Result = CStr(SourceString)
  StringToReplace = CStr(A)
  Replacement = CStr(B)
  NumCharsToReplace = Len(StringToReplace)
  NumCharsReplacedBy = Len(Replacement)
  i = InStr(1, Result, StringToReplace)
  Do While i <> 0
    Result = Mid(Result, 1, i - 1) & Replacement + Mid(Result, i + NumCharsToReplace)
    i = i + NumCharsReplacedBy
    i = InStr(i, Result, StringToReplace)
  Loop
  UTILITIES_ReplaceString = Result
End Function

Public Function UTILITIES_ProcessFile(ByVal InputFileNum As Integer) As Variant
  Const INPUT_PAST_EOF = 62
  Dim Char As String
  Dim TokenOutput As String
  Dim OutputChars As String
  Dim TokenChars As String
  Dim TokenResult As Variant
  Dim Result As String
  Dim NumCharsRead As Variant
  Dim ErrValue As Integer
  Dim ErrString As String
  Dim RecordsetNumber As Integer
  Dim MaxLoops As Variant
  Dim LoopCount As Variant
  On Error GoTo Err_UTILITIES_ProcessFile
  UTILITIES_Error = 0
  Result = ""
  Seek #InputFileNum, 1
  TokenChars = UTILITIES_InputUpto(InputFileNum, Chr(0), 0, Char, NumCharsRead)
  Result = Result + UTILITIES_ProcessString(TokenChars, "`")
```

```
Exit_UTILITIES_ProcessFile:
  On Error Resume Next
  If UTILITIES_Error <> 0 Then
    Result = Result & ErrString
  End If
  UTILITIES_ProcessFile = Result

Err_UTILITIES_ProcessFile:
  UTILITIES_Error = Err
  ErrString = "<!--UTILITIES_ProcessFile: " & Error$ & " -->"
  Resume Exit_UTILITIES_ProcessFile
End Function

Public Function UTILITIES_InputUpto(ByVal FileNum As Integer, Delimiters As String, MaxCharacters
      As Long, MatchedDelimiter As String, NumCharsRead As Variant) As Variant
  Dim Char As String
  Dim Done
  Dim Result As Variant
  NumCharsRead = 0
  Result = ""
  MatchedDelimiter = ""
  Done = EOF(FileNum)
  Do While Not Done
    Char = Input(1, #FileNum)
    NumCharsRead = NumCharsRead + 1
    If InStr(Delimiters, Char) > 0 Then
      MatchedDelimiter = Char
      Done = True
    Else
      Result = Result + Char
    End If
    If EOF(FileNum) Then Done = True
    If NumCharsRead = MaxCharacters Then Done = True
  Loop
  UTILITIES_InputUpto = Result
End Function

Public Function UTILITIES_Eval(TokenCharsToEval)
  Dim TokenChars, TokenLength
  Dim Start, i, BeginMatchPos, EndMatchPos
  Dim Variable, VariableType, RecordsetNumber
  Dim FieldName As String, FieldValue
  Dim rs As Recordset
  Dim QuoteChar As String
  Dim FieldType As Integer
  Dim SQL As String
  Dim qd As QueryDef
  On Error GoTo Err_UTILITIES_Eval
  TokenChars = Trim(TokenCharsToEval)
  TokenLength = Len(TokenChars)
  If TokenLength = 0 Then
    UTILITIES_Eval = ""
    Exit Function
  End If
```

```
    Start = 1
    Do While True
      QuoteChar = ""
      BeginMatchPos = InStr(Start, TokenChars, "[")
      If BeginMatchPos <> 0 Then
        EndMatchPos = InStr(BeginMatchPos, TokenChars, "]")
        If EndMatchPos = 0 Then EndMatchPos = TokenLength
        Variable = Mid(TokenChars, BeginMatchPos, EndMatchPos - BeginMatchPos + 1)
        VariableType = Mid(Variable, 2, 1)
        Select Case VariableType
          Case "R"   'e.g. R1:FieldName
            Eval_RecordsetField Variable, FieldValue, QuoteChar
          Case "F", "C", "Q", "V"   'e.g. F:FieldName, C:CGIVariableName, Q:ParameterNumber,
      V:FieldName
            Eval_VariableField VariableType, Variable, FieldValue, QuoteChar
          Case "I" 'e.g: I:FilePath
            Eval_IncludeFile Variable, FieldValue
            UTILITIES_Eval = FieldValue
            Exit Function
          Case Else
            UTILITIES_Eval = "Cannot handle variable: " & Variable
            Exit Function
        End Select
        If Variable = TokenChars Then
          UTILITIES_Eval = IIf(IsNull(FieldValue), "<!--Null-->", FieldValue)
          Exit Function
        End If
        If IsNull(FieldValue) Then
          FieldValue = "Null"
          QuoteChar = ""
        Else
          If QuoteChar = """" Then
            FieldValue = UTILITIES_ReplaceString(FieldValue, QuoteChar, QuoteChar + QuoteChar)
          End If
          FieldValue = QuoteChar & FieldValue & QuoteChar
        End If
        TokenChars = UTILITIES_ReplaceString(TokenChars, Variable, FieldValue)
        Start = BeginMatchPos
      Else
        'Go ahead and eval
        UTILITIES_OpenDatabase
        SQL = "SELECT " & TokenChars & " As Result FROM DummyTable;"
        Set rs = UTILITIES_db.OpenRecordset(SQL)
        UTILITIES_Eval = IIf(IsNull(rs!Result), "<!--NULL-->", rs!Result)
        rs.Close
        Exit Do
      End If
    Loop

Exit_UTILITIES_Eval:
    Exit Function


Err_UTILITIES_Eval:
    UTILITIES_Eval = "<!--" & Error$ & "-->"
```

```
    UTILITIES_Error = True
    Resume Exit_UTILITIES_Eval
End Function

Public Function UTILITIES_GetCGIVariable(VariableName)
    Select Case VariableName
      Case "ServerSoftware"
        UTILITIES_GetCGIVariable = CGI_ServerSoftware
      Case "ServerName"
        UTILITIES_GetCGIVariable = CGI_ServerName
      Case "ServerPort"
        UTILITIES_GetCGIVariable = CGI_ServerPort
      Case "RequestProtocol"
        UTILITIES_GetCGIVariable = CGI_RequestProtocol
      Case "ServerAdmin"
        UTILITIES_GetCGIVariable = CGI_ServerAdmin
      Case "Version"
        UTILITIES_GetCGIVariable = CGI_Version
      Case "RequestMethod"
        UTILITIES_GetCGIVariable = CGI_RequestMethod
      Case "RequestKeepAlive"
        UTILITIES_GetCGIVariable = CGI_RequestKeepAlive
      Case "LogicalPath"
        UTILITIES_GetCGIVariable = CGI_LogicalPath
      Case "PhysicalPath"
        UTILITIES_GetCGIVariable = CGI_PhysicalPath
      Case "ExecutablePath"
        UTILITIES_GetCGIVariable = CGI_ExecutablePath
      Case "QueryString"
        UTILITIES_GetCGIVariable = CGI_QueryString
      Case "RequestRange"
        UTILITIES_GetCGIVariable = CGI_RequestRange
      Case "Referer"
        UTILITIES_GetCGIVariable = CGI_Referer
      Case "From"
        UTILITIES_GetCGIVariable = CGI_From
      Case "UserAgent"
        UTILITIES_GetCGIVariable = CGI_UserAgent
      Case "RemoteHost"
        UTILITIES_GetCGIVariable = CGI_RemoteHost
      Case "RemoteAddr"
        UTILITIES_GetCGIVariable = CGI_RemoteAddr
      Case "AuthUser"
        UTILITIES_GetCGIVariable = CGI_AuthUser
      Case "AuthPass"
        UTILITIES_GetCGIVariable = CGI_AuthPass
      Case "AuthType"
        UTILITIES_GetCGIVariable = CGI_AuthType
      Case "AuthRealm"
        UTILITIES_GetCGIVariable = CGI_AuthRealm
      Case "ContentType"
        UTILITIES_GetCGIVariable = CGI_ContentType
      Case "ContentLength"
        UTILITIES_GetCGIVariable = CGI_ContentLength
```

```
      Case Else
        UTILITIES_GetCGIVariable = "<!-- Unknown CGI Variable Name: " & VariableName & " -->"
    End Select
End Function

Public Sub UTILITIES_OpenDatabase()
    Dim i
    On Error Resume Next
    i = UTILITIES_db.Name
    If Err <> 0 Then
        Set UTILITIES_db = Workspaces(0).OpenDatabase(Left(App.Path, 2) & UTILITIES_DB_PATH)
    End If
End Sub

Public Function UTILITIES_ProcessString(InputString As String, Delimiter As String)
    Dim StringToProcess As String
    Dim Char As String
    Dim ErrString As String
    Dim FirstChar As String
    Dim ErrValue As Integer
    Dim OutputChars As String
    Dim TokenChars As String
    Dim TokenResult As Variant
    Dim NumCharsRead As Variant
    Dim DelimiterChar As String
    Dim ProcessChars As String
    Dim Result As String
    On Error GoTo Err_UTILITIES_ProcessString
    Result = ""
    StringToProcess = InputString
    UTILITIES_Error = 0
    Do While StringToProcess <> ""
        Char = ""
        OutputChars = ""
        OutputChars = UTILITIES_ScanUpto(StringToProcess, Delimiter, 0, Char, NumCharsRead)
        StringToProcess = Mid(StringToProcess, NumCharsRead + 1)
        If StringToProcess <> "" Then
            FirstChar = Left(StringToProcess, 1)
            DelimiterChar = Mid(StringToProcess, 2, 1)
            ProcessChars = UTILITIES_ScanUpto(Mid(StringToProcess, 3), DelimiterChar, 0, Char,
            NumCharsRead)
            Select Case FirstChar
                Case Delimiter
                    OutputChars = OutputChars + Delimiter
                    StringToProcess = Mid(StringToProcess, 2)
                Case "."
                    StringToProcess = ""
                Case "A" '
                    ProcessString_Assign StringToProcess, NumCharsRead, Delimiter
                Case "?"
                    ProcessString_Condition StringToProcess, NumCharsRead, Delimiter, DelimiterChar
                Case "L"
                    ProcessString_LoopRecordset ProcessChars, StringToProcess, NumCharsRead, Delimiter
                Case "N"
```

```
              ProcessString_LoopIndex ProcessChars, StringToProcess, NumCharsRead, Delimiter
         Case Else
            TokenChars = UTILITIES_ScanUpto(StringToProcess, Delimiter, 0, Char, NumCharsRead)
            StringToProcess = Mid(StringToProcess, NumCharsRead + 1)
            TokenResult = UTILITIES_Eval(TokenChars)
            OutputChars = OutputChars & TokenResult
      End Select
    End If
    Result = Result + OutputChars
  Loop

Exit_UTILITIES_ProcessString:
  On Error Resume Next
  If ErrValue <> 0 Then
    Result = Result + OutputChars + " --" & ErrString & "-- " + "<PRE>" + StringToProcess +
      "</PRE>"
  End If

  UTILITIES_ProcessString = Result
  Exit Function

Err_UTILITIES_ProcessString:
  ErrValue = Err
  ErrString = Error$
  Resume Exit_UTILITIES_ProcessString
End Function

Private Sub ProcessString_LoopIndex(ProcessChars, StringToProcess, NumCharsRead, Delimiter)
  Dim MaxLoops As Variant
  Dim i As Variant
  Dim CharsRead As Long
  Dim TokenChars As String
  Dim FieldName As String
  Dim FieldNameMax As String
  Dim Char As String
  Dim PreviousMaxLoops As Variant
  TokenChars = ProcessChars
  FieldName = UTILITIES_ScanUpto(TokenChars, ",", 0, Char, CharsRead)
  TokenChars = Mid(TokenChars, CharsRead + 1)
  MaxLoops = UTILITIES_ScanUpto(TokenChars, ",", 0, Char, CharsRead)
  TokenChars = Mid(TokenChars, CharsRead + 1)
  FieldNameMax = FieldName & "_Max"
  i = UTILITIES_EmptyToNullField(FieldName)
  PreviousMaxLoops = UTILITIES_EmptyToNullField(FieldNameMax)
  If IsNull(PreviousMaxLoops) Then '
    MaxLoops = UTILITIES_Eval(MaxLoops)
    UTILITIES_AssignField FieldNameMax, MaxLoops
  Else
    MaxLoops = PreviousMaxLoops
  End If
  If IsNull(i) Then
    i = 1
  Else
    i = i + 1
```

```
    End If
    UTILITIES_AssignField FieldName, i
    MaxLoops = CLng(MaxLoops)
    If UTILITIES_Error = 0 And i <= MaxLoops Then
      StringToProcess = TokenChars & Delimiter & StringToProcess
    Else
      StringToProcess = Mid(StringToProcess, NumCharsRead + 3)
      UTILITIES_AssignField FieldName, ""
      UTILITIES_Error = 0
    End If
End Sub

Public Sub ProcessString_Condition(StringToProcess As String, NumCharsRead, Delimiter,
        DelimiterChar As String)
    Dim TokenChars As String
    Dim Condition As String
    Dim TrueExpression As String
    Dim FalseExpression As String
    Dim ConditionResult As String
    Dim Char As String
    Dim StoreError As Variant
    StringToProcess = Mid(StringToProcess, 3)
    Condition = UTILITIES_ScanUpto(StringToProcess, DelimiterChar, 0, Char, NumCharsRead)
    StringToProcess = Mid(StringToProcess, NumCharsRead + 1)
    TrueExpression = UTILITIES_ScanUpto(StringToProcess, DelimiterChar, 0, Char, NumCharsRead)
    StringToProcess = Mid(StringToProcess, NumCharsRead + 1)
    FalseExpression = UTILITIES_ScanUpto(StringToProcess, DelimiterChar, 0, Char, NumCharsRead)
    StringToProcess = Mid(StringToProcess, NumCharsRead + 1)
    StoreError = UTILITIES_Error
    UTILITIES_Error = 0
    ConditionResult = CStr(UTILITIES_Eval(Condition))
    If UTILITIES_Error <> 0 Then
      StringToProcess = ConditionResult & StringToProcess
    Else
      UTILITIES_Error = StoreError
      Select Case ConditionResult
        Case "<!--Null-->", "", "0", "False", "No"
          StringToProcess = FalseExpression & StringToProcess
        Case Else
          StringToProcess = TrueExpression & StringToProcess
      End Select
    End If
End Sub

Public Sub ProcessString_Assign(StringToProcess As String, NumCharsRead, Delimiter As String)
    Dim FieldName As String
    Dim Char As String
    Dim TokenChars As String
    Dim TokenResult As Variant
    TokenChars = UTILITIES_ScanUpto(StringToProcess, "=", 0, Char, NumCharsRead)
    FieldName = Mid(TokenChars, 3)
    StringToProcess = Mid(StringToProcess, NumCharsRead + 1)
    TokenChars = UTILITIES_ScanUpto(StringToProcess, Delimiter, 0, Char, NumCharsRead)
    StringToProcess = Mid(StringToProcess, NumCharsRead + 1)
```

```
      TokenResult = UTILITIES_Eval(TokenChars)
      UTILITIES_AssignField FieldName, TokenResult
End Sub

Public Function UTILITIES_GetKeyword(KeywordString, KeywordDelimiters, KeywordNumber)
    Dim Ch As String
    Dim KeyWord As String
    Dim length As Long
    Dim Start As Long
    Dim i As Long
    Dim Description
    Dim Delimiters
    Dim CurrentKeywordNumber
    CurrentKeywordNumber = 0
    UTILITIES_GetKeyword = Null
    Delimiters = KeywordDelimiters & Chr(13) & Chr(10)
    Description = Trim(KeywordString)
    length = Len(Description)
    If length = 0 Then Exit Function
    Start = 1
    For i = 1 To length
      Ch = Mid(Description, i, 1)
      If InStr(Delimiters, Ch) > 0 Then
        KeyWord = Trim(Mid(Description, Start, i - Start))
        If KeyWord <> "" And Not IsNull(KeyWord) Then
          CurrentKeywordNumber = CurrentKeywordNumber + 1
          If CurrentKeywordNumber = KeywordNumber Then
            UTILITIES_GetKeyword = KeyWord
            Exit Function
          End If
        End If
        Start = i + 1
      End If
    Next
    If Start < i Then
      KeyWord = Trim(Mid(Description, Start, i - Start))
      If KeyWord <> "" And Not IsNull(KeyWord) Then
          CurrentKeywordNumber = CurrentKeywordNumber + 1
          If CurrentKeywordNumber = KeywordNumber Then
            UTILITIES_GetKeyword = KeyWord
            Exit Function
          End If
      End If
    End If
  End If
End Function

Public Function UTILITIES_ScanUpto(InputString As String, Delimiters As String, MaxCharacters As
      Long, MatchedDelimiter As String, NumCharsRead As Variant)
    Dim Char As String
    Dim i, FoundPos
    NumCharsRead = 0
    MatchedDelimiter = ""
    For i = 1 To Len(Delimiters)
      Char = Mid(Delimiters, i, 1)
```

```
      FoundPos = InStr(InputString, Char)
      If FoundPos > 0 Then
        MatchedDelimiter = Char
        If MaxCharacters > 0 And FoundPos > MaxCharacters Then FoundPos = MaxCharacters + 1
        NumCharsRead = FoundPos
        UTILITIES_ScanUpto = Left$(InputString, FoundPos - 1)
        Exit Function
      End If
  Next
  MatchedDelimiter = ""
  FoundPos = Len(InputString)
  If MaxCharacters > 0 And FoundPos > MaxCharacters Then FoundPos = MaxCharacters
  NumCharsRead = FoundPos
  UTILITIES_ScanUpto = Left$(InputString, FoundPos)
End Function


Public Function UTILITIES_DLookup(db As Database, FieldExpression, RecordSource, Criteria,
      PickRecord)
  Dim SQL
  Dim rs As Recordset
  Dim CriteriaClause
  Dim RecordNumber, i
  UTILITIES_OpenDatabase
  CriteriaClause = ""
  If Criteria <> "" Then CriteriaClause = " WHERE " & Criteria
  SQL = "Select " & FieldExpression & " As LookupValue FROM " & RecordSource & CriteriaClause &
      ";"
  Set rs = db.OpenRecordset(SQL)
  If rs.EOF Then
    UTILITIES_DLookup = Null
  Else
    Select Case PickRecord
      Case "First"
      Case "Last"
        rs.MoveLast
      Case "Random"
        rs.MoveLast
        Randomize
        RecordNumber = Int(rs.RecordCount * Rnd)    ' Generate random value between 0 and
      RecordCount - 1.
        rs.MoveFirst
        For i = 1 To RecordNumber
          rs.MoveNext
        Next
    End Select
    UTILITIES_DLookup = rs!LookupValue
  End If
  rs.Close
End Function

Public Function UTILITIES_GetQueryParameter(ParameterNumber, Delimiter)
  UTILITIES_GetQueryParameter = UTILITIES_GetParameter(CGI_QueryString, ParameterNumber,
      Delimiter)
End Function
```

```
Public Sub UTILITIES_AddField(FieldName, FieldValue)
  CGI_FormTuples(CGI_NumFormTuples).Key = FieldName
  CGI_FormTuples(CGI_NumFormTuples).value = FieldValue
  CGI_NumFormTuples = CGI_NumFormTuples + 1
End Sub

Public Function UTILITIES_Min(Value1, Value2)
  If Value1 < Value2 Then
    UTILITIES_Min = Value1
  Else
    UTILITIES_Min = Value2
  End If
End Function

Public Function UTILITIES_Max(Value1, Value2)
  If Value1 > Value2 Then
    UTILITIES_Max = Value1
  Else
    UTILITIES_Max = Value2
  End If
End Function

Private Sub Eval_RecordsetField(Variable, FieldValue, QuoteChar)
  Dim FieldName As String
  Dim Operation
  Dim RecordsetNumber
  Dim CurrentBM As String
  Dim FieldType
  Dim FieldNumber As Integer
  RecordsetNumber = Mid(Variable, 3, 1)
  Operation = Mid(Variable, 4, 1)
  FieldName = Mid(Variable, 5, Len(Variable) - 5)
  Select Case Operation
    Case "."
      FieldValue = ""
      Select Case FieldName
        Case "Next"
          UTILITIES_rsarray(RecordsetNumber).MoveNext
        Case "Previous"
          UTILITIES_rsarray(RecordsetNumber).MovePrevious
        Case "First"
          UTILITIES_rsarray(RecordsetNumber).MoveFirst
        Case "Last"
          UTILITIES_rsarray(RecordsetNumber).MoveLast
        Case "Count"
          FieldValue = UTILITIES_rsarray(RecordsetNumber).RecordCount
          If FieldValue > 0 And Not UTILITIES_rsarray(RecordsetNumber).EOF Then
            CurrentBM = UTILITIES_rsarray(RecordsetNumber).Bookmark
            UTILITIES_rsarray(RecordsetNumber).MoveLast
            FieldValue = UTILITIES_rsarray(RecordsetNumber).RecordCount
            UTILITIES_rsarray(RecordsetNumber).Bookmark = CurrentBM
          End If
        Case "EOF"
          FieldValue = UTILITIES_rsarray(RecordsetNumber).EOF
```

```
                Case "BOF"
                    FieldValue = UTILITIES_rsarray(RecordsetNumber).BOF
            End Select
        Case Else
            If Operation = "/" Then
                FieldNumber = UTILITIES_EmptyToNullField(FieldName)
                FieldType = UTILITIES_rsarray(RecordsetNumber)(FieldNumber).Type
                FieldValue = UTILITIES_rsarray(RecordsetNumber)(FieldNumber)
            Else
                FieldType = UTILITIES_rsarray(RecordsetNumber)(FieldName).Type
                FieldValue = UTILITIES_rsarray(RecordsetNumber)(FieldName)
            End If
            Select Case FieldType
                Case dbDate
                    QuoteChar = "#"
                Case dbText, dbMemo
                    QuoteChar = """"
            End Select
        End Select
End Sub

Private Sub Eval_VariableField(VariableType, Variable, FieldValue, QuoteChar)
    Dim FieldName As String
    Dim Operation
    Dim RecordsetNumber
    Dim CurrentBM As String
    Dim FieldType
    FieldName = Mid(Variable, 4, Len(Variable) - 4)
    Select Case VariableType
        Case "F", "V"
            FieldValue = UTILITIES_EmptyToNullField(FieldName)
        Case "C"
            FieldValue = UTILITIES_GetCGIVariable(FieldName)
        Case "Q"
            FieldValue = UTILITIES_GetQueryParameter(Val(FieldName), "+")
    End Select
    If VariableType = "V" And IsNull(FieldValue) Then
        FieldValue = ""
    End If
    QuoteChar = """"
    If IsNumeric(FieldValue) Then
        QuoteChar = ""
    Else
        If IsDate(FieldValue) Then QuoteChar = "#"
    End If
End Sub

Private Sub Eval_IncludeFile(Variable, FieldValue)
    Dim FilePath As String
    Dim NumCharsRead
    Dim FN As Integer
    Dim MatchedDelimiter As String
    FilePath = Mid(Variable, 4, Len(Variable) - 4)
    FN = FreeFile
```

```
   Open FilePath For Input Access Read As #FN
   FieldValue = UTILITIES_InputUpto(FN, Chr(0), 0, MatchedDelimiter, NumCharsRead)
   Close #FN
End Sub

Public Function UTILITIES_AcquireField(FieldName As String, QueryParameterNumber)
   Dim FieldValue
   Dim CodedFieldValue
   CGI_RequestMethod = UCase$(CGI_RequestMethod)
   If CGI_RequestMethod = "POST" Then
     FieldValue = UTILITIES_EmptyToNullField(FieldName)
     If IsNull(FieldValue) Then
       UTILITIES_AssignField FieldName & "_Coded", ""
     Else
       UTILITIES_AssignField FieldName & "_Coded",
       UTILITIES_ConvertToQueryString(CStr(FieldValue))
     End If
   Else
     CodedFieldValue = UTILITIES_GetQueryParameter(QueryParameterNumber, "+")
     If Not IsNull(CodedFieldValue) Then
       FieldValue = UTILITIES_ConvertFromQueryString(CStr(CodedFieldValue))
       UTILITIES_AssignField FieldName, FieldValue
       UTILITIES_AssignField FieldName & "_Coded", CodedFieldValue
     Else
       UTILITIES_AssignField FieldName, ""
       UTILITIES_AssignField FieldName & "_Coded", ""
       FieldValue = Null
     End If
   End If
   UTILITIES_AcquireField = FieldValue
End Function

Public Sub UTILITIES_AssignField(FieldName, value)
    Dim i As Integer
    Dim FieldValue
    FieldValue = value
    If IsNull(FieldValue) Then FieldValue = ""
    For i = 0 To (CGI_NumFormTuples - 1)
        If CGI_FormTuples(i).Key = FieldName Then
          CGI_FormTuples(i).value = FieldValue
          Exit Sub
        End If
    Next i
    UTILITIES_AddField FieldName, FieldValue
End Sub

Public Function UTILITIES_GetShortFormField(FieldName As String) As Variant
    Dim i As Integer
    For i = 0 To (CGI_NumFormTuples - 1)
        If CGI_FormTuples(i).Key = FieldName Then
            UTILITIES_GetShortFormField = CGI_FormTuples(i).value
            Exit Function
        End If
    Next i
```

```
      UTILITIES_GetShortFormField = Null
End Function

Public Sub UTILITIES_LimitRecords(rs As Recordset, Start, Limit)
   Const DEFAULT_RECORD_LIMIT = 10
   Dim StartRecord As Long
   Dim RecordLimit As Long
   Dim EndRecord As Long
   Dim NextRecordLimit As Long
   If rs.RecordCount = 0 Then Exit Sub
   StartRecord = 1
   RecordLimit = DEFAULT_RECORD_LIMIT
   If Not IsNull(Start) Then StartRecord = Start
   If Not IsNull(Limit) Then RecordLimit = Limit
   rs.MoveLast
   EndRecord = UTILITIES_Min(StartRecord + RecordLimit - 1, rs.RecordCount)
   rs.MoveFirst
   rs.Move StartRecord - 1
   UTILITIES_AddField "UTILITIES_LR_Start", StartRecord
   UTILITIES_AddField "UTILITIES_LR_End", EndRecord
   UTILITIES_AddField "UTILITIES_LR_Limit", RecordLimit
   UTILITIES_AddField "UTILITIES_LR_CurrentLimit", EndRecord - StartRecord + 1
   UTILITIES_AddField "UTILITIES_LR_PreviousStart", UTILITIES_Min(StartRecord - RecordLimit, 0)
   UTILITIES_AddField "UTILITIES_LR_PreviousEnd", UTILITIES_Min(StartRecord - 1, 0)
   UTILITIES_AddField "UTILITIES_LR_PreviousLimit", UTILITIES_Min(StartRecord - 1, RecordLimit)
   UTILITIES_AddField "UTILITIES_LR_NextStart", UTILITIES_Min(EndRecord + 1, rs.RecordCount)
   UTILITIES_AddField "UTILITIES_LR_NextEnd", UTILITIES_Min(EndRecord + RecordLimit,
       rs.RecordCount)
   UTILITIES_AddField "UTILITIES_LR_NextLimit", UTILITIES_Min(rs.RecordCount - EndRecord,
       RecordLimit)
End Sub

Private Sub ProcessString_LoopRecordset(ProcessChars, StringToProcess, NumCharsRead, Delimiter)
   Dim RecordsetNumber As Variant
   Dim MaxLoops As Variant
   Dim i As Variant
   Dim Char As String
   Dim TokenChars As String
   Dim FieldName As String
   Dim FieldNameMax As String
   Dim CharsRead As Long
   TokenChars = ProcessChars
   RecordsetNumber = CInt(UTILITIES_ScanUpto(TokenChars, ",", 0, Char, CharsRead))
   TokenChars = Mid(TokenChars, CharsRead + 1)
   MaxLoops = UTILITIES_ScanUpto(TokenChars, ",", 0, Char, CharsRead)
   TokenChars = Mid(TokenChars, CharsRead + 1)
   FieldName = "Index_R" & RecordsetNumber
   FieldNameMax = FieldName & "_Max"
   i = UTILITIES_EmptyToNullField(FieldName)
   If IsNull(i) Then
      i = 1
      If MaxLoops = "EOF" Then
        MaxLoops = 2147483647
```

```
      Else
        MaxLoops = UTILITIES_Eval(MaxLoops)
      End If
      UTILITIES_AssignField FieldNameMax, MaxLoops
    Else
      i = i + 1
      UTILITIES_rsarray(RecordsetNumber).MoveNext
      MaxLoops = CLng(UTILITIES_EmptyToNullField(FieldNameMax))
    End If
    UTILITIES_AssignField FieldName, i
    If Not UTILITIES_rsarray(RecordsetNumber).EOF And i <= MaxLoops Then
      StringToProcess = TokenChars & Delimiter & StringToProcess
    Else
      StringToProcess = Mid(StringToProcess, NumCharsRead + 3)
      UTILITIES_AssignField FieldName, ""
    End If
End Sub
```

Source Code for CGI32.bas Library Module

```
'          *************
'          * CGI32.BAS *
'          *************
'
' VERSION: 1.8
'
' AUTHOR:   Robert B. Denny <rdenny@netcom.com>
'
' Common routines needed to establish a VB environment for
' Windows CGI programs that run behind the WebSite Server.
'
' INTRODUCTION
'
' The Common Gateway Interface (CGI) version 1.1 specifies a minimal
' set of data that is made available to the back-end application by
' an HTTP (Web) server. It also specifies the details for passing this
' information to the back-end. The latter part of the CGI spec is
' specific to Unix-like environments. The NCSA httpd for Windows does
' supply the data items (and more) specified by CGI/1.1, however it
' uses a different method for passing the data to the back-end.
'
' DEVELOPMENT
'
' WebSite requires any Windows back-end program to be an
' executable image. This means that you must convert your VB
' application into an executable (.EXE) before it can be tested
' with the server.
'
' ENVIRONMENT
'
' The WebSite server executes script requests by doing a
' CreateProcess with a command line in the following form:
```

```
'
'    prog-name cgi-profile
'
' THE CGI PROFILE FILE
'
' The Unix CGI passes data to the back end by defining environment
' variables which can be used by shell scripts. The WebSite
' server passes data to its back end via the profile file. The
' format of the profile is that of a Windows ".INI" file. The keyword
' names have been changed cosmetically.
'
' There are 7 sections in a CGI profile file, [CGI], [Accept],
' [System], [Extra Headers], and [Form Literal], [Form External],
' and [Form huge]. They are described below:
'
' [CGI]                    <== The standard CGI variables
' CGI Version=             The version of CGI spoken by the server
' Request Protocol=        The server's info protocol (e.g. HTTP/1.0)
' Request Method=          The method specified in the request (e.g., "GET")
' Request Keep-Alive=      If the client requested connection re-use (Yes/No)
' Executable Path=         Physical pathname of the back-end (this program)
' Logical Path=            Extra path info in logical space
' Physical Path=           Extra path info in local physical space
' Query String=            String following the "?" in the request URL
' Content Type=            MIME content type of info supplied with request
' Content Length=          Length, bytes, of info supplied with request
' Request Range=           Byte-range specfication received with request
' Server Software=         Version/revision of the info (HTTP) server
' Server Name=             Server's network hostname (or alias from config)
' Server Port=             Server's network port number
' Server Admin=            E-Mail address of server's admin. (config)
' Referer=                 URL of referring document
' From=                    E-Mail of client user (rarely seen)
' User Agent=              String describing client/browser software/version
' Remote Host=             Remote client's network hostname
' Remote Address=          Remote client's network address
' Authenticated Username=Username if present in request
' Authenticated Password=Password if present in request
' Authentication Method=Method used for authentication (e.g., "Basic")
' Authentication Realm=Name of realm for users/groups
'
' [Accept]                 <== What the client says it can take
' The MIME types found in the request header as
'     Accept: xxx/yyy; zzzz...
' are entered in this section as
'     xxx/yyy=zzzz...
' If only the MIME type appears, the form is
'     xxx/yyy=Yes
'
' [System]                 <== Windows interface specifics
' GMT Offset=              Offset of local timezone from GMT, seconds (LONG!)
' Output File=             Pathname of file to receive results
' Content File=            Pathname of file containing raw request content
' Debug Mode=              If server's CGI debug flag is set (Yes/No)
'
```

```
' [Extra Headers]
' Any "extra" headers found in the request that activated this
' program. They are listed in "key=value" form. Usually, you'll see
' at least the name of the browser here as "User-agent".
'
' [Form Literal]
' If the request was a POST from a Mosaic form (with content type of
' "application/x-www-form-urlencoded"), the server will decode the
' form data. Raw form input is of the form "key=value&key=value&...",
' with the value parts "URL-encoded". The server splits the key=value
' pairs at the '&', then spilts the key and value at the '=',
' URL-decodes the value string and puts the result into key=value
' (decoded) form in the [Form Literal] section of the INI.
'
' [Form External]
' If the decoded value string is more than 254 characters long,
' or if the decoded value string contains any control characters
' or quote marks the server puts the decoded value into an external
' tempfile and lists the field in this section as:
'     key=<pathname> <length>
' where <pathname> is the path and name of the tempfile containing
' the decoded value string, and <length> is the length in bytes
' of the decoded value string.
'
' NOTE: BE SURE TO OPEN THIS FILE IN BINARY MODE UNLESS YOU ARE
'       CERTAIN THAT THE FORM DATA IS TEXT!
'
' [Form File]
' If the form data contained any uploaded files, they are described in
' this section as:
'     key=[<pathname>] <length> <type> <encoding> [<name>]
' where <pathname> is the path and name of the tempfile contining the
' uploaded file, <length> is the length in bytes of the uploaded file,
' <type> is the content type of the uploaded file as sent by the browser,
' <encoding> is the content-transfer encoding of the uploaded file, and
' <name> is the original file name of the uploaded file.
'
' [Form Huge]
' If the raw value string is more than 65,536 bytes long, the server
' does no decoding. In this case, the server lists the field in this
' section as:
'     key=<offset> <length>
' where <offset> is the offset from the beginning of the Content File
' at which the raw value string for this key is located, and <length>
' is the length in bytes of the raw value string. You can use the
' <offset> to perform a "Seek" to the start of the raw value string,
' and use the length to know when you have read the entire raw string
' into your decoder. Note that VB has a limit of 64K for strings, so
'
' Examples:
'
'     [Form Literal]
'     smallfield=123 Main St. #122
'
'     [Form External]
```

```
'      field300chars=c:\website\cgi-tmp\1a7fws.000 300
'      fieldwithlinebreaks=c:\website\cgi-tmp\1a7fws.001 43
'
'      [Form Huge]
'      field230K=c:\website\cgi-tmp\1a7fws.002 276920
'
' =====
' USAGE
' =====
' Include CGI32.BAS in your Visual Basic project. Set the project options for
' "Sub Main" startup. The Main() procedure is in this module, and it
' handles all of the setup of the VB CGI environment, as described
' above. Once all of this is done, the Main() calls YOUR main procedure
' which must be called CGI_Main(). The output file is open, use Send()
' to write to it. The input file is NOT open, and "huge" form fields
' have not been decoded.
'
' NOTE: If your program is started without command-line args,
' the code assumes you want to run it interactively. This is useful
' for providing a setup screen, etc. Instead of calling CGI_Main(),
' it calls Inter_Main(). Your module must also implement this
' function. If you don't need an interactive mode, just create
' Inter_Main() and put a 1-line call to MsgBox alerting the
' user that the program is not meant to be run interactively.
' The samples furnished with the server do this.
'
' If a Visual Basic runtime error occurs, it will be trapped and result
' in an HTTP error response being sent to the client. Check out the
' Error Handler() sub. When your program finishes, be sure to RETURN
' TO MAIN(). Don't just do an "End".
'
' Have a look at the stuff below to see what's what.
'
'-------------------------------------------------------------------
Option Explicit
'
' ==================
' Manifest Constants
' ==================
'
Const MAX_CMDARGS = 8        ' Max # of command line args
Const ENUM_BUF_SIZE = 4096   ' Key enumeration buffer, see GetProfile()
' These are the limits in the server
Const MAX_XHDR = 100         ' Max # of "extra" request headers
Const MAX_ACCTYPE = 100      ' Max # of Accept: types in request
Const MAX_FORM_TUPLES = 100  ' Max # form key=value pairs
Const MAX_HUGE_TUPLES = 16   ' Max # "huge" form fields
Const MAX_FILE_TUPLES = 16   ' Max # of uploaded file tuples
'
'
' =====
' Types
' =====
'
```

```
Type Tuple                        ' Used for Accept: and "extra" headers
    key As String                 ' and for holding POST form key=value pairs
    value As String
End Type

Type FileTuple                    ' Used for form-based file uploads
    key As String                 ' Form field name
    file As String                ' Local tempfile containing uploaded file
    length As Long                ' Length in bytes of uploaded file
    type As String                ' Content type of uploaded file
    encoding As String            ' Content-transfer encoding of uploaded file
    Name As String                ' Original name of uploaded file
End Type

Type HugeTuple                    ' Used for "huge" form fields
    key As String                 ' Keyword (decoded)
    offset As Long                ' Byte offset into Content File of value
    length As Long                ' Length of value, bytes
End Type
'
'
' =================
' Global Constants
' =================
'
' -----------
' Error Codes
' -----------
'
Global Const ERR_ARGCOUNT = 32767
Global Const ERR_BAD_REQUEST = 32766            ' HTTP 400
Global Const ERR_UNAUTHORIZED = 32765           ' HTTP 401
Global Const ERR_PAYMENT_REQUIRED = 32764       ' HTTP 402
Global Const ERR_FORBIDDEN = 32763              ' HTTP 403
Global Const ERR_NOT_FOUND = 32762              ' HTTP 404
Global Const ERR_INTERNAL_ERROR = 32761         ' HTTP 500
Global Const ERR_NOT_IMPLEMENTED = 32760        ' HTTP 501
Global Const ERR_TOO_BUSY = 32758               ' HTTP 503 (experimental)
Global Const ERR_NO_FIELD = 32757               ' GetxxxField "no field"
Global Const CGI_ERR_START = 32757              ' Start of our errors


' =====================
' CGI Global Variables
' =====================
'
' ----------------------
' Standard CGI variables
' ----------------------
'
Global CGI_ServerSoftware As String
Global CGI_ServerName As String
Global CGI_ServerPort As Integer
Global CGI_RequestProtocol As String
Global CGI_ServerAdmin As String
```

```
Global CGI_Version As String
Global CGI_RequestMethod As String
Global CGI_RequestKeepAlive As Integer
Global CGI_LogicalPath As String
Global CGI_PhysicalPath As String
Global CGI_ExecutablePath As String
Global CGI_QueryString As String
Global CGI_RequestRange As String
Global CGI_Referer As String
Global CGI_From As String
Global CGI_UserAgent As String
Global CGI_RemoteHost As String
Global CGI_RemoteAddr As String
Global CGI_AuthUser As String
Global CGI_AuthPass As String
Global CGI_AuthType As String
Global CGI_AuthRealm As String
Global CGI_ContentType As String
Global CGI_ContentLength As Long
'
' ------------------
' HTTP Header Arrays
' ------------------
'
Global CGI_AcceptTypes(MAX_ACCTYPE) As Tuple       ' Accept: types
Global CGI_NumAcceptTypes As Integer               ' # of live entries in array
Global CGI_ExtraHeaders(MAX_XHDR) As Tuple         ' "Extra" headers
Global CGI_NumExtraHeaders As Integer              ' # of live entries in array
'
' --------------
' POST Form Data
' --------------
'
Global CGI_FormTuples(MAX_FORM_TUPLES) As Tuple ' POST form key=value pairs
Global CGI_NumFormTuples As Integer                ' # of live entries in array
Global CGI_HugeTuples(MAX_HUGE_TUPLES) As HugeTuple ' Form "huge tuples
Global CGI_NumHugeTuples As Integer                ' # of live entries in array
Global CGI_FileTuples(MAX_FILE_TUPLES) As FileTuple ' File upload tuples
Global CGI_NumFileTuples As Integer                ' # of live entries in array
'
' ----------------
' System Variables
' ----------------
'
Global CGI_GMTOffset As Variant            ' GMT offset (time serial)
Global CGI_ContentFile As String           ' Content/Input file pathname
Global CGI_OutputFile As String            ' Output file pathname
Global CGI_DebugMode As Integer            ' Script Tracing flag from server
'
'
' ==========================
' Windows API Declarations
' ==========================
'
```

```vb
' NOTE: Declaration of GetPrivateProfileString is specially done to
' permit enumeration of keys by passing NULL key value. See GetProfile().
' Both the 16-bit and 32-bit flavors are given below. We DO NOT
' recommend using 16-bit VB with WebSite!
'
#If Win32 Then
Declare Function GetPrivateProfileString Lib "kernel32" _
    Alias "GetPrivateProfileStringA" _
    (ByVal lpApplicationName As String, _
    ByVal lpKeyName As Any, _
    ByVal lpDefault As String, _
    ByVal lpReturnedString As String, _
    ByVal nSize As Long, _
    ByVal lpFileName As String) As Long
#Else
Declare Function GetPrivateProfileString Lib "Kernel" _
    (ByVal lpSection As String, _
    ByVal lpKeyName As Any, _
    ByVal lpDefault As String, _
    ByVal lpReturnedString As String, _
    ByVal nSize As Integer, _
    ByVal lpFileName As String) As Integer
#End If
'
'
' ===============
' Local Variables
' ===============
'
Dim CGI_ProfileFile As String             ' Profile file pathname
Dim CGI_OutputFN As Integer               ' Output file number
Dim ErrorString As String

'----------------------------------------------------------------------
'
' Return True/False depending on whether a form field is present.
' Typically used to detect if a checkbox in a form is checked or
' not. Unchecked checkboxes are omitted from the form content.
'
'----------------------------------------------------------------------
Function FieldPresent(key As String) As Integer
    Dim i As Integer

    FieldPresent = False            ' Assume failure

    For i = 0 To (CGI_NumFormTuples - 1)
        If CGI_FormTuples(i).key = key Then
            FieldPresent = True      ' Found it
            Exit Function            ' ** DONE **
        End If
    Next i
                                     ' Exit with FieldPresent still False
End Function
```

```
'----------------------------------------------------------------------------
'
'
'    ErrorHandler() - Global error handler
'
' If a VB runtime error occurs dusing execution of the program, this
' procedure generates an HTTP/1.0 HTML-formatted error message into
' the output file, then exits the program.
'
' This should be armed immediately on entry to the program's main()
' procedure. Any errors that occur in the program are caught, and
' an HTTP/1.0 error messsage is generated into the output file. The
' presence of the HTTP/1.0 on the first line of the output file causes
' NCSA httpd for WIndows to send the output file to the client with no
' interpretation or other header parsing.
'----------------------------------------------------------------------------
Sub ErrorHandler(code As Integer)

        Seek #CGI_OutputFN, 1      ' Rewind output file just in case
        Send ("HTTP/1.0 500 Internal Error")
        Send ("Server: " + CGI_ServerSoftware)
        Send ("Date: " + WebDate(Now))
        Send ("Content-type: text/html")
        Send ("")
        Send ("<HTML><HEAD>")
        Send ("<TITLE>Error in " + CGI_ExecutablePath + "</TITLE>")
        Send ("</HEAD><BODY>")
        Send ("<H1>Error in " + CGI_ExecutablePath + "</H1>")
        Send ("An internal Visual Basic error has occurred in " + CGI_ExecutablePath + ".")
        Send ("<PRE>" + ErrorString + "</PRE>")
        Send ("<I>Please</I> note what you were doing when this problem occurred.")
        Send ("so we can identify and correct it. Write down the Web page you were using,")
        Send ("any data you may have entered into a form or search box, and")
        Send ("anything else that may help us duplicate the problem. Then contact the")
        Send ("administrator of this service: ")
        Send ("<A HREF=""mailto:" & CGI_ServerAdmin & """>")
        Send ("<ADDRESS>&lt;" + CGI_ServerAdmin + "&gt;</ADDRESS>")
        Send ("</A></BODY></HTML>")

        Close #CGI_OutputFN

        '======
        End                     ' Terminate the program
        '======
End Sub


'----------------------------------------------------------------------------
'
'
'    GetAcceptTypes() - Create the array of accept type structs
'
' Enumerate the keys in the [Accept] section of the profile file,
' then get the value for each of the keys.
'----------------------------------------------------------------------------
Private Sub GetAcceptTypes()
    Dim sList As String
```

```
    Dim i As Integer, j As Integer, l As Integer, n As Integer

    sList = GetProfile("Accept", "") ' Get key list
    l = Len(sList)                              ' Length incl. trailing null
    i = 1                                       ' Start at 1st character
    n = 0                                       ' Index in array
    Do While ((i < l) And (n < MAX_ACCTYPE)) ' Safety stop here
        j = InStr(i, sList, Chr$(0))            ' J -> next null
        CGI_AcceptTypes(n).key = Mid$(sList, i, j - i) ' Get Key, then value
        CGI_AcceptTypes(n).value = GetProfile("Accept", CGI_AcceptTypes(n).key)
        i = j + 1                               ' Bump pointer
        n = n + 1                               ' Bump array index
    Loop
    CGI_NumAcceptTypes = n                      ' Fill in global count

End Sub

'- - - - - - - - - - - - - - - - - - - - - - - - - - - - - - - - - - - - - - -
'
'   GetArgs() - Parse the command line
'
' Chop up the command line, fill in the argument vector, return the
' argument count (similar to the Unix/C argc/argv handling)
'- - - - - - - - - - - - - - - - - - - - - - - - - - - - - - - - - - - - - - -
Private Function GetArgs(argv() As String) As Integer
    Dim buf As String
    Dim i As Integer, j As Integer, l As Integer, n As Integer

    buf = Trim$(Command$)                       ' Get command line

    l = Len(buf)                                ' Length of command line
    If l = 0 Then                               ' If empty
        GetArgs = 0                             ' Return argc = 0
        Exit Function
    End If

    i = 1                                       ' Start at 1st character
    n = 0                                       ' Index in argvec
    Do While ((i < l) And (n < MAX_CMDARGS)) ' Safety stop here
        j = InStr(i, buf, " ")                  ' J -> next space
        If j = 0 Then Exit Do                   ' Exit loop on last arg
        argv(n) = Trim$(Mid$(buf, i, j - i)) ' Get this token, trim it
        i = j + 1                               ' Skip that blank
        Do While Mid$(buf, i, 1) = " "          ' Skip any additional whitespace
            i = i + 1
        Loop
        n = n + 1                               ' Bump array index
    Loop

    argv(n) = Trim$(Mid$(buf, i, (l - i + 1))) ' Get last arg
    GetArgs = n + 1                             ' Return arg count

End Function
```

```
'-----------------------------------------------------------------
'
'    GetExtraHeaders() - Create the array of extra header structs
'
' Enumerate the keys in the [Extra Headers] section of the profile file,
' then get the value for each of the keys.
'-----------------------------------------------------------------
Private Sub GetExtraHeaders()
    Dim sList As String
    Dim i As Integer, j As Integer, l As Integer, n As Integer

    sList = GetProfile("Extra Headers", "") ' Get key list
    l = Len(sList)                          ' Length incl. trailing null
    i = 1                                   ' Start at 1st character
    n = 0                                   ' Index in array
    Do While ((i < l) And (n < MAX_XHDR))   ' Safety stop here
        j = InStr(i, sList, Chr$(0))        ' J -> next null
        CGI_ExtraHeaders(n).key = Mid$(sList, i, j - i) ' Get Key, then value
        CGI_ExtraHeaders(n).value = GetProfile("Extra Headers", CGI_ExtraHeaders(n).key)
        i = j + 1                           ' Bump pointer
        n = n + 1                           ' Bump array index
    Loop
    CGI_NumExtraHeaders = n                 ' Fill in global count

End Sub

'-----------------------------------------------------------------
'
'    GetFormTuples() - Create the array of POST form input key=value pairs
'
'-----------------------------------------------------------------
Private Sub GetFormTuples()
    Dim sList As String
    Dim i As Integer, j As Integer, k As Integer
    Dim l As Integer, m As Integer, n As Integer
    Dim s As Long
    Dim buf As String
    Dim extName As String
    Dim extFile As Integer
    Dim extlen As Long

    n = 0                                            ' Index in array

    '
    ' Do the easy one first: [Form Literal]
    '
    sList = GetProfile("Form Literal", "")  ' Get key list
    l = Len(sList)                                   ' Length incl. trailing null
    i = 1                                            ' Start at 1st character
    Do While ((i < l) And (n < MAX_FORM_TUPLES)) ' Safety stop here
        j = InStr(i, sList, Chr$(0))         ' J -> next null
        CGI_FormTuples(n).key = Mid$(sList, i, j - i) ' Get Key, then value
        CGI_FormTuples(n).value = GetProfile("Form Literal", CGI_FormTuples(n).key)
        i = j + 1                                    ' Bump pointer
```

```
        n = n + 1                               ' Bump array index
Loop
'
' Now do the external ones: [Form External]
'
sList = GetProfile("Form External", "") ' Get key list
l = Len(sList)                              ' Length incl. trailing null
i = 1                                       ' Start at 1st character
extFile = FreeFile
Do While ((i < l) And (n < MAX_FORM_TUPLES)) ' Safety stop here
    j = InStr(i, sList, Chr$(0))            ' J -> next null
    CGI_FormTuples(n).key = Mid$(sList, i, j - i) ' Get Key, then pathname
    buf = GetProfile("Form External", CGI_FormTuples(n).key)
    k = InStr(buf, " ")                     ' Split file & length
    extName = Mid$(buf, 1, k - 1)           ' Pathname
    k = k + 1
    extlen = CLng(Mid$(buf, k, Len(buf) - k + 1)) ' Length
    '
    ' Use feature of GET to read content in one call
    '
    Open extName For Binary Access Read As #extFile
    CGI_FormTuples(n).value = String$(extlen, " ") ' Breathe in...
    Get #extFile, , CGI_FormTuples(n).value 'GULP!
    Close #extFile
    i = j + 1                               ' Bump pointer
    n = n + 1                               ' Bump array index
Loop

CGI_NumFormTuples = n                       ' Number of fields decoded
n = 0                                       ' Reset counter
'
' Next, the [Form Huge] section. Will this ever get executed?
'
sList = GetProfile("Form Huge", "")         ' Get key list
l = Len(sList)                              ' Length incl. trailing null
i = 1                                       ' Start at 1st character
Do While ((i < l) And (n < MAX_FORM_TUPLES)) ' Safety stop here
    j = InStr(i, sList, Chr$(0))            ' J -> next null
    CGI_HugeTuples(n).key = Mid$(sList, i, j - i) ' Get Key
    buf = GetProfile("Form Huge", CGI_HugeTuples(n).key) ' "offset length"
    k = InStr(buf, " ")                     ' Delimiter
    CGI_HugeTuples(n).offset = CLng(Mid$(buf, 1, (k - 1)))
    CGI_HugeTuples(n).length = CLng(Mid$(buf, k, (Len(buf) - k + 1)))
    i = j + 1                               ' Bump pointer
    n = n + 1                               ' Bump array index
Loop

CGI_NumHugeTuples = n                       ' Fill in global count

n = 0                                       ' Reset counter
'
' Finally, the [Form File] section.
'
sList = GetProfile("Form File", "")         ' Get key list
```

```
        l = Len(sList)                        ' Length incl. trailing null
        i = 1                                 ' Start at 1st character
        Do While ((i < l) And (n < MAX_FILE_TUPLES)) ' Safety stop here
            j = InStr(i, sList, Chr$(0))          ' J -> next null
            CGI_FileTuples(n).key = Mid$(sList, i, j - i) ' Get Key
            buf = GetProfile("Form File", CGI_FileTuples(n).key)
            ParseFileValue buf, CGI_FileTuples(n)  ' Complicated, use Sub
            i = j + 1                             ' Bump pointer
            n = n + 1                             ' Bump array index
        Loop

        CGI_NumFileTuples = n                  ' Fill in global count

End Sub

'-------------------------------------------------------------------------
'
'   GetProfile() - Get a value or enumerate keys in CGI_Profile file
'
' Get a value given the section and key, or enumerate keys given the
' section name and "" for the key. If enumerating, the list of keys for
' the given section is returned as a null-separated string, with a
' double null at the end.
'
' VB handles this with flair! I couldn't believe my eyes when I tried this.
'-------------------------------------------------------------------------
Private Function GetProfile(sSection As String, sKey As String) As String
    Dim retLen As Long
    Dim buf As String * ENUM_BUF_SIZE

    If sKey <> "" Then
        retLen = GetPrivateProfileString(sSection, sKey, "", buf, ENUM_BUF_SIZE,
CGI_ProfileFile)
    Else
        retLen = GetPrivateProfileString(sSection, 0&, "", buf, ENUM_BUF_SIZE, CGI_ProfileFile)
    End If
    If retLen = 0 Then
        GetProfile = ""
    Else
        GetProfile = Left$(buf, retLen)
    End If

End Function

'-------------------------------------------------------------------------
'
' Get the value of a "small" form field given the key
'
' Signals an error if field does not exist
'
'-------------------------------------------------------------------------
Function GetSmallField(key As String) As String
    Dim i As Integer
```

```
        For i = 0 To (CGI_NumFormTuples - 1)
            If CGI_FormTuples(i).key = key Then
                GetSmallField = Trim$(CGI_FormTuples(i).value)
                Exit Function              ' ** DONE **
            End If
        Next i
        '
        ' Field does not exist
        '
        Error ERR_NO_FIELD
End Function

'-----------------------------------------------------------------------------
'
'   InitializeCGI() - Fill in all of the CGI variables, etc.
'
' Read the profile file name from the command line, then fill in
' the CGI globals, the Accept type list and the Extra headers list.
' Then open the input and output files.
'
' Returns True if OK, False if some sort of error. See ReturnError()
' for info on how errors are handled.
'
' NOTE: Assumes that the CGI error handler has been armed with On Error
'-----------------------------------------------------------------------------
Sub InitializeCGI()
        Dim sect As String
        Dim argc As Integer
        Static argv(MAX_CMDARGS) As String
        Dim buf As String

        CGI_DebugMode = True     ' Initialization errors are very bad

        '
        ' Parse the command line. We need the profile file name (duh!)
        ' and the output file name NOW, so we can return any errors we
        ' trap. The error handler writes to the output file.
        '
        argc = GetArgs(argv())
        CGI_ProfileFile = argv(0)

        sect = "CGI"
        CGI_ServerSoftware = GetProfile(sect, "Server Software")
        CGI_ServerName = GetProfile(sect, "Server Name")
        CGI_RequestProtocol = GetProfile(sect, "Request Protocol")
        CGI_ServerAdmin = GetProfile(sect, "Server Admin")
        CGI_Version = GetProfile(sect, "CGI Version")
        CGI_RequestMethod = GetProfile(sect, "Request Method")
        buf = GetProfile(sect, "Request Keep-Alive")     ' Y or N
        If (Left$(buf, 1) = "Y") Then                    ' Must start with Y
            CGI_RequestKeepAlive = True
        Else
            CGI_RequestKeepAlive = False
        End If
```

```
    CGI_LogicalPath = GetProfile(sect, "Logical Path")
    CGI_PhysicalPath = GetProfile(sect, "Physical Path")
    CGI_ExecutablePath = GetProfile(sect, "Executable Path")
    CGI_QueryString = GetProfile(sect, "Query String")
    CGI_RemoteHost = GetProfile(sect, "Remote Host")
    CGI_RemoteAddr = GetProfile(sect, "Remote Address")
    CGI_RequestRange = GetProfile(sect, "Request Range")
    CGI_Referer = GetProfile(sect, "Referer")
    CGI_From = GetProfile(sect, "From")
    CGI_UserAgent = GetProfile(sect, "User Agent")
    CGI_AuthUser = GetProfile(sect, "Authenticated Username")
    CGI_AuthPass = GetProfile(sect, "Authenticated Password")
    CGI_AuthRealm = GetProfile(sect, "Authentication Realm")
    CGI_AuthType = GetProfile(sect, "Authentication Method")
    CGI_ContentType = GetProfile(sect, "Content Type")
    buf = GetProfile(sect, "Content Length")
    If buf = "" Then
        CGI_ContentLength = 0
    Else
        CGI_ContentLength = CLng(buf)
    End If
    buf = GetProfile(sect, "Server Port")
    If buf = "" Then
        CGI_ServerPort = -1
    Else
        CGI_ServerPort = CInt(buf)
    End If

    sect = "System"
    CGI_ContentFile = GetProfile(sect, "Content File")
    CGI_OutputFile = GetProfile(sect, "Output File")
    CGI_OutputFN = FreeFile
    Open CGI_OutputFile For Output Access Write As #CGI_OutputFN
    buf = GetProfile(sect, "GMT Offset")
    If buf <> "" Then                              ' Protect against errors
        CGI_GMTOffset = CVDate(Val(buf) / 86400#) ' Timeserial GMT offset
    Else
        CGI_GMTOffset = 0
    End If
    buf = GetProfile(sect, "Debug Mode")    ' Y or N
    If (Left$(buf, 1) = "Y") Then                 ' Must start with Y
        CGI_DebugMode = True
    Else
        CGI_DebugMode = False
    End If

    GetAcceptTypes          ' Enumerate Accept: types into tuples
    GetExtraHeaders         ' Enumerate extra headers into tuples
    GetFormTuples           ' Decode any POST form input into tuples

End Sub
```

```
'------------------------------------------------------------------
'
'    main() - CGI script back-end main procedure
'
' This is the main() for the VB back end. Note carefully how the error
' handling is set up, and how program cleanup is done. If no command
' line args are present, call Inter_Main() and exit.
'------------------------------------------------------------------
Sub Main()
    On Error GoTo ErrorHandler

    If Trim$(Command$) = "" Then      ' Interactive start
        Inter_Main                    ' Call interactive main
        Exit Sub                      ' Exit the program
    End If

    InitializeCGI           ' Create the CGI environment

    '===========
    CGI_Main                ' Execute the actual "script"
    '===========

Cleanup:
    Close #CGI_OutputFN
    Exit Sub                              ' End the program
'------------
ErrorHandler:
    Select Case Err                   ' Decode our "user defined" errors
        Case ERR_NO_FIELD:
            ErrorString = "Unknown form field"
        Case Else:
            ErrorString = Error$     ' Must be VB error
    End Select

    ErrorString = ErrorString & " (error #" & Err & ")"
    On Error GoTo 0                   ' Prevent recursion
    ErrorHandler (Err)                ' Generate HTTP error result
    Resume Cleanup
'------------
End Sub


'------------------------------------------------------------------
'
'  Send() - Shortcut for writing to output file
'
'------------------------------------------------------------------
Sub Send(s As String)
    Print #CGI_OutputFN, s
End Sub
```

```
'-------------------------------------------------------------------
'
'   SendNoOp() - Tell browser to do nothing.
'
' Most browsers will do nothing. Netscape 1.0N leaves hourglass
' cursor until the mouse is waved around. Enhanced Mosaic 2.0
' oputs up an alert saying "URL leads nowhere". Your results may
' vary...
'
'-------------------------------------------------------------------
Sub SendNoOp()

    Send ("HTTP/1.0 204 No Response")
    Send ("Server: " + CGI_ServerSoftware)
    Send ("")

End Sub

'-------------------------------------------------------------------
'
'   WebDate - Return an HTTP/1.0 compliant date/time string
'
' Inputs:   t = Local time as VB Variant (e.g., returned by Now())
' Returns:  Properly formatted HTTP/1.0 date/time in GMT
'-------------------------------------------------------------------
Function WebDate(dt As Variant) As String
    Dim t As Variant

    t = CVDate(dt - CGI_GMTOffset)        ' Convert time to GMT
    WebDate = Format$(t, "ddd dd mmm yyyy hh:mm:ss") & " GMT"

End Function




'-------------------------------------------------------------------
'
' PlusToSpace() - Remove plus-delimiters from HTTP-encoded string
'
'-------------------------------------------------------------------
Public Sub PlusToSpace(s As String)
    Dim i As Integer

    i = 1
    Do While True
        i = InStr(i, s, "+")
        If i = 0 Then Exit Do
        Mid$(s, i) = " "
    Loop

End Sub
```

```
'----------------------------------------------------------------------
'
' Unescape() - Convert HTTP-escaped string to normal form
'
'----------------------------------------------------------------------
Public Function Unescape(s As String)
    Dim i As Integer, l As Integer
    Dim c As String

    If InStr(s, "%") = 0 Then                   ' Catch simple case
        Unescape = s
        Exit Function
    End If

    l = Len(s)
    Unescape = ""
    For i = 1 To l
        c = Mid$(s, i, 1)                       ' Next character
        If c = "%" Then
            If Mid$(s, i + 1, 1) = "%" Then
                c = "%"
                i = i + 1                       ' Loop increments too
            Else
                c = x2c(Mid$(s, i + 1, 2))
                i = i + 2                       ' Loop increments too
            End If
        End If
        Unescape = Unescape & c
    Next i

End Function

'----------------------------------------------------------------------
'
' x2c() - Convert hex-escaped character to ASCII
'
'----------------------------------------------------------------------
Private Function x2c(s As String) As String
    Dim t As String

    t = "&H" & s
    x2c = Chr$(CInt(t))

End Function


Private Sub ParseFileValue(buf As String, ByRef t As FileTuple)
    Dim i, j, k, l As Integer

    l = Len(buf)

    i = InStr(buf, " ")                         ' First delimiter
    t.file = Mid$(buf, 1, (i - 1))              ' [file]
    t.file = Mid$(t.file, 2, Len(t.file) - 2)   ' file
```

```
        j = InStr((i + 1), buf, " ")                  ' Next delimiter
        t.length = CLng(Mid$(buf, (i + 1), (j - i - 1)))
        i = j

        j = InStr((i + 1), buf, " ")                  ' Next delimiter
        t.type = Mid$(buf, (i + 1), (j - i - 1))
        i = j

        j = InStr((i + 1), buf, " ")                  ' Next delimiter
        t.encoding = Mid$(buf, (i + 1), (j - i - 1))
        i = j

        t.Name = Mid$(buf, (i + 1), (l - i - 1))  ' [name]
        t.Name = Mid$(t.Name, 2, Len(t.Name) - 1) ' name

End Sub

'-------------------------------------------------------------------------
'
'    FindExtraHeader() - Get the text from an "extra" header
'
' Given the extra header's name, return the stuff after the ":"
' or an empty string if not there.
'-------------------------------------------------------------------------
Public Function FindExtraHeader(key As String) As String
    Dim i As Integer

    For i = 0 To (CGI_NumExtraHeaders - 1)
        If CGI_ExtraHeaders(i).key = key Then
            FindExtraHeader = Trim$(CGI_ExtraHeaders(i).value)
            Exit Function                  ' ** DONE **
        End If
    Next i
    '
    ' Not present, return empty string
    '
    FindExtraHeader = ""
End Function
```

Case Studies for Building Electronic Commerce with Web Database Constructions

The real-world cases presented here provide an opportunity to practice using the tools and techniques needed to implement the electronic commerce theory discussed in the book. Six electronic commerce business scenarios present the framework for building relevant Web database constructions.

CASE 1
Common Centralized and Ordering Library (CCOL)

In 2001, a state-wide department of education has mandated the development of an electronic commerce model for their library database processing system. The state's 30 public libraries have back-office processes that include reviewing initial book-order lists as well as paying the publishers for inventory shipments. The CCOL back-office processing includes all tasks necessary for inventory to be placed on the library shelves for circulation. The first step in the process is reviewing advance publication lists from publishers, and the process ends with making the inventory available to the CCOL patron.

CCOL inventory includes books, magazines, CDs, tapes, videotapes, movies, education files, presentation materials, and art. All are listed in catalogs, and a set of catalog cards are physically housed in card catalogs sorted by International Standard Book Number (ISBN), a 10-digit multipart format that identifies language, publisher, book identifier within publisher, and a check digit. Each ISBN is a unique identifier for the inventory product and is assigned by the publisher, not CCOL.

The electronic commerce goal is to automate the back-office processes of CCOL and to integrate a user-friendly front-end Web interface. CCOL ascertained that Web database constructions were the best techniques to employ to meet the goal, and on the basis of their analysis of the current processes of CCOL, they decided an electronic commerce model would set a standard of consistency throughout the library's day-to-day functions. Web database constructions using CGI, ASP, JavaScript, ActiveX, and/or JSP in the CCOL Web site have been recommended to automate what has historically been a semimanual process.

After a careful analysis of the CCOL's strengths, weakness, opportunities, and threats (SWOT), the electronic commerce investigation committee released its findings:

Strengths

■ CCOL is ready for a change and the staff members express their anticipation of meeting the change requirements in a positive way.

■ The current system is outdated and ready for an upgrade that will serve the interests of the public.

Weaknesses

■ The majority of the branch employees have minimal computer training, and some have no computer training at all.

■ The current library inventory database was programmed on an old database system and contains many redundant data issues.

■ Each individual branch has been working independently and is not open to the idea of major change.

Opportunities

■ Since the current database has many redundant data issues, electronic commerce is seen as an opportunity to create a new and more powerful database system that will eliminate all data redundancy issues.

■ The current accounting system is in need of an upgrade.

■ Taking advantage of current technology, CCOL could introduce an electronic commerce Web site that will boost patron enthusiasm.

Threats

■ Some of the branches are expressing their unwillingness to change and make the time available for training and testing.

■ Incorporating security within the library system has become a negative topic of "conversation around the water-cooler," and the branches see it as an "extra hassle" rather than as an effective means of keeping patron and employee data safe.

Another goal of the CCOL project is to provide a streamlined information system that will reduce the time spent by the business manager on his current duties. The following functions were identified by the committee candidates for automation of current processes:

- Inventory control
- Reordering of new and used material
- Evaluating performance
- Patron satisfaction
- Overall cost reduction

The committee also identified the following benefits as ones that could be realized by the implementation of electronic commerce:

- A relational database for inventory control will provide additional reporting capabilities.
- Automation of the library card system will offer CCOL the opportunity to explore Electronic Data Interchange via the Internet.
- Adding an updated Accounting package will allow CCOL to have more accurate account processes for budgetary reports.

CASE 2
New Horizon Automotive

New Horizon Automotive is a new and used automobile dealership in a small market in northern California. There are a total of 14 employees, including the owner. The business sells, on average, four new cars and three used cars each week. Parts and service represent approximately half of the dealership's net profit. New Horizon Automotive has contracted with a local consulting company to have electronic commerce added to their business functions. It is assumed by New Horizon Automotive that the implementation of Web database construction will decrease the large amount of turnover in the business manager's position. This turnover has resulted in a great deal of confusion about and inefficiency in executing many business processes. New Horizon Automotive has decided it requires an information system that standardizes many of the daily processes of the business and that this will improve employee morale and efficiency.

The first step in the process is for the local consulting company to interview New Horizon Automotive's owner, Roy Schyster, senior management, and department directors, as well as everyday users among the staff. This process is necessary in order to conduct a needs assessment and gauge the current status of information technology at New Horizon. Every aspect of the company must be analyzed to facilitate the development of an electronic commerce system that meets the needs of the entire organization. It had been ascertained before the interview that New Horizon Automotive needs to develop relational databases to capture the vehicle sales, vehicle service, and parts inventory management processes.

The local consulting company must consider the following issues before the Web database construction is built:

- How receptive is New Horizon Automotive to electronic commerce? The Internet is a great way to increase revenue with low overhead. It would also increase customer satisfaction by making it possible to look at cars, schedule service appointments, and communicate with sales representatives online.
- Has New Horizon considered online banking? This is a very convenient and cost-effective means of conducting financial transactions.
- New Horizon Automotive's volume of business has remained stagnant over the last few years. What plans are under way to increase sales? If planning for an increase in sales, will the current information systems meet those needs?

New Horizon has determined that the scope of the electronic commerce project will encompass any function of the organization that deals with information and that may be improved as a result of access to information technology. This includes, but is not limited to, sales, service, parts, accounting, and payroll. As the project progresses and as information is gathered and aggregated, this section of the charter will be reviewed and its focus narrowed.

The plan of action for this project includes a 30-day information-gathering period during which the Project Managers will conduct interviews with senior management and staff to analyze the needs of the organization. At the request of the owner, the consulting company project managers will periodically update the management team regarding the progress of the analysis phase. If necessary, the analysis phase may be lengthened to accommodate the needs of the project managers and the organization.

Over the next 30 days, the project managers will design the new system, looking at all facets of the organization including networking, budget constraints, employee wishes, etc. At the end of this time period, the project managers will present their recommendations to the dealership's management team for discussion and approval.

After the analysis and design phases are complete, the project managers will assist with the implementation of the new system. This includes purchasing hardware and software, inputting data, and setting up the network. The actual implementation of the network will be contracted to an outside agency. The project managers will also oversee implementing system security and testing and will coordinate training sessions for the users. This phase will last approximately 60 days.

The critical success factors for New Horizon Automotive are the following: a sales system that ensures the customers' needs are met, a service system that functions efficiently, and a parts system that accurately maintains a lean but complete inventory. These factors are also critical for the new Web database construction system. Other functions, such as payroll, accounts payable, and accounts receivable, while important, are considered housekeeping functions. This project will focus on each aspect of the company including both critical success factors and housekeeping functions.

CASE 3
Computer Data-Processing Center Foundation (CDPCF)

The Computer Data-Processing Center Foundation (CDPCF) is a national not-for-profit organization made up of many local chapters. Chartered to advance the general understanding of data processing and to promote data-processing interests, the CDPCF has many services ranging from publications and functions to memberships. Members receive discounts on many CDPFC services.

The organizational hierarchy is one of elected officers and volunteer committee members, though the national headquarters is staffed by a small group of paid professionals. The headquarters is charged with maintaining membership records, processing membership renewals, collecting dues, organizing conferences and trade shows, and providing feedback and support for the membership.

At the most recent conference, the CDPCF determined that an electronic commerce model was needed to facilitate the communication between headquarters and members and among the membership. A Web database construction was recommended for dues collection, communicating membership information, answering frequently asked questions (FAQs), and disseminating other information such as the monthly newsletter.

The committee in charge looked at similar organizations' use of electronic commerce by navigating through the Web and viewing the Web database constructions of other not-for-profit organizations.

CASE 4
Dollar Dough Bakery

Though the name may imply a small company, Dollar Dough Bakery is a large corporation of 5000 employees, six baking plants, and 150 warehouses in six geographic regions. Dollar Dough is spread out over the continental United States, plus parts of Canada and Mexico. The term *unit* is used by Dollar Dough headquarters to define a bakery and its associated local warehouse. Each unit, or bakery/warehouse network, acts as an independent firm and makes the decisions about what the firm will produce and sell.

Ordering Methods

- Orders are placed in written or verbal form.
- Sometimes truck drivers accept and fill orders from their trucks.
- Retailers phone orders directly to warehouse sales staff.
- Daily, unit warehouse managers consolidate all orders from the sales staff and place a bulk order with the supplying bakery.

Products and Packaging

Location-to-location variations exist in package printing and in the product's taste, the latter of which is due to differences in flours, oils, and shortenings used. Though Dollar Dough is a large corporation, consolidated firm-wide data are not available. Even though each bakery keeps records on what products it produces and how those products are packaged, there is no firm-wide consolidated listing of all possible products and packaging designs and no consolidated list of salespersons or record of their individual performances. This makes bakery-to-bakery, warehouse-to-warehouse, and salesperson-to-salesperson comparisons almost impossible. Reporting is not available for individual products (units) produced or returned. All sales are reported as net dollars.

Rapid expansion has been at the root of many of Dollar Dough's challenges. Though Dollar Dough is now a national firm, one only has to look back at past sales to see the growth and expansion history of Dollar Dough. That growth rate is expected to continue—mainly because Dollar Dough is an old and established firm.

Dollar Dough has determined that an electronic commerce Web database construction will help lessen many of its current challenges. The new IS department will take advantage of both an intranet and the Internet. An intranet is a corporate network that uses the infrastructure and standards of the Internet and the World Wide Web. One of the greatest considerations of an intranet is security—making sure that sensitive company data accessible on intranets are protected from the outside world. This is accomplished through security software called firewalls. The firewall is a security program that connects the intranet to external networks, such as the Internet. It blocks unauthorized traffic from entering the intranet and can also prevent unauthorized employees from accessing the intranet.

The Internet is an international network connecting approximately 36,000 smaller networks that link computers of academic, scientific, and commercial institutions and making possible the sharing of all types of information and services for millions of people all around the world.

The electronic commerce construction must facilitate communication. It must focus first on Dollar Dough's internal network and bring unity and ownership throughout the Dollar Dough Corporation. Instead of having independent firms making decisions about their own operations, the new electronic commerce model must create an environment that encourages Dollar Dough "community." The corporation's goal is for the Web database construction to create a central origin for communications to all employees. Management also sees the construction as a way to share the changes that will be made to automate processes within the company and to monitor how those changes will impact the company.

The Web database will also improve customer service to internal customers of Dollar Dough. Employees will be able to order supplies centrally—this would eliminate variations in products and packaging. Employees will also be able to submit dollar-saving ideas. This is seen by management as an avenue with potential for increasing revenue, decreasing costs, and improving customer service. It should also be a place where production figures, sales, and returns can be tracked as well as a central place for maintaining policies and procedures. Eventually, it is assumed that the electronic commerce model will enable the analysis of consolidated firm-wide data and that it would contain forms for entering additional information such as new bakeries, new employees, warehouses, products, and/or packaging.

Management has articulated their vision for the electronic commerce project in the following needs assessment:

- Automate order/entry process via the Internet.
- Allow retailers to place their orders for products using the Internet to decrease costs.
- Eliminate lost or delayed orders.
- Reduce errors caused by verbal miscommunication.
- Fulfill orders in a shorter amount of time.
- Decrease costs by using less paper for forms.
- Minimize the time the warehouse manager spends consolidating orders from the sales staff.

Management recognizes that they must give retailers incentive to be online. To that end, they have agreed to pay 20 percent of online ISP or other connection fees for as long as the store agrees to order its baking goods from Dollar Dough. There will be a minimum set monthly order amount that must be maintained. In return, Dollar Dough will include the retail store on its Internet site, advertising the retailer's name and location.

E-mail is the first wave of electronic commerce benefits. Its ubiquity (presence everywhere or in many places simultaneously) simplifies access across all geographic boundaries and time zones. E-mail could be used by retailers to notify the warehouse of upcoming sales and is an excellent communication tool for customers to inform the company about products the company could sell.

CASE 5
Biggies Brokerage

Biggies Brokerage publishes their mission as: "To provide our customers with high-quality brokerage services at a reasonable price while giving our employees the best environment in which to be productive. Biggies Brokerage is committed to maintaining our reputation for fairness, quality, and dependability."

Management has recognized that there is an obvious need for an electronic commerce solution to many of their business inefficiencies. Management has determined that Biggies Brokerage stands to lose a considerable amount of new and existing business to other brokerage firms that can provide their customers with online services.

Biggies Brokerage wants to utilize the electronic commerce model to initiate a presence on the Internet and position the company to capitalize on the Internet's tremendous growth. The Web database construction will help Biggies Brokerage achieve its goal by giving its members access to real-time information, including stock quotes and research, portfolio management, online selling and trading, and financial news from the top news sources available on the Internet.

Management has determined that an electronic commerce on-line brokerage application, customized to fit the needs of Biggies Brokerage, must be developed. The implementation of the selling of financial products including mutual funds, commodities, retirement and annuity products, insurance products, and an investment newsletter should be included in the Web database design. The resulting electronic commerce application will provide Biggies Brokerage with a fast, accurate, and efficient on-line brokerage Web site with the following benefits:

- Increasing overall revenues 4 percent over a 6-month period
- Increasing the customer base by 12 percent over 12 months
- Increasing visitor traffic by 5,000 hits each quarter

The electronic commerce model should reduce the need for additional Biggies Brokerage customer service representatives while at the same time increasing total volume of business by 8 percent over 12 months.

CASE 6
The Bank of Everyone

The Bank of Everyone is a small, regional commercial bank with roots in North Carolina and southern Virginia. Its growth has come from acquiring other banks and merging their assets and customer bases with its own. Today, the Bank of Everyone has assets of over $4 billion with approximately 450,000 customers.

Though considered conservative in management philosophy, the top management has assessed the external environment and has noticed the proliferation of competition on the World Wide Web. Ethyl Nelson, the president, hired a research and consulting firm to determine how the bank might best enter the electronic commerce environment.

The following areas have been addressed for incorporation into the Web database construction:

- Offering product lines via the Web
- Expanding the automated teller machine (ATM) network
- Expanding into new product lines for financial and credit services
- Increasing accessibility to customers and offering greater customer service

The bank will offer several electronic commerce options to their customers. Each will help with detailed financial planning, as well as easy access to accounts. Customers may use the bank's free online banking product called We-the-Web or one of the popular financial software packages to access accounts, like Quicken or Money Manager. There will also be easy-to-access pages with answers to frequently asked questions (FAQ) and bank information.

Glossary

Note: The numbers in parentheses following each definition indicate the chapters in which these key terms are used.

@Transaction directive Must be on the first line of the ASP page and causes a transaction to run to competition unless an abort occurs. **(10)**

access logs Maintained by most Web servers. **(8)**

ACTION An HTML tag that denotes which URL of the HTTP server should process the form. **(6)**

ACTION attributes Identify what should happen to the data when the HTML form is submitted from the Web client to the Web server. **(6)**

action query Used to ask for additional operations on the data, such as insertion, updating, or deletion. **(5)**

Active Server Pages (ASP) Server-side technology developed by Microsoft that is designed to meet the need for dynamic interaction between customer and business in the electronic commerce model. Middleware that allows the necessary interaction between the Web front-end and the database back-end. **(2, 10)**

ActiveX Gives JSP applications compound document capability. **(13)**

ActiveX components Platform-specific, language-neutral snippets of code sent on demand from server to client that execute natively only in Microsoft's Web browser. **(3)**

ActiveX Data Objects (ADO) Object-oriented programming application program interface (API) from Microsoft that allows access to relational or nonrelational databases from both Microsoft and other database providers. **(10, 11)**

ActiveX documents Enable links to live documents on the Web. **(13)**

ActiveX installation package Contain the files that are necessary for the individual user to install an application. **(13)**

ActiveX Scripting The result of OLE Automation. **(13)**

ad hoc form A form that is "improvised" or created from the means at hand. **(4)**

aggregate functions Mathematical functions of count, sum, average, maximum, or minimum. **(5)**

alert One of three message boxes used by JavaScript. **(13)**

anchor A highlighted word or picture that can be selected by the user usually with a mouse click.

animated HTML See Dynamic HTML. **(6)**

API calls Allow data to be read from .INI files quickly and easily. **(7)**

applet A little program usually sent with a Web page to the Web client that can perform interactive tasks without having to send a Web client request back to the Web server. **(13)**

application Short for application program. An application is a program designed to perform a specific function for the user. **(1)**

application program interface (API) A set of routines, protocols, and tools for building software applications. The specific method prescribed by a computer operating system or by an application program by which a programmer writing an application program can make requests of the operating system or another application. **(10)**

application server A server program in a three-tier application that divides an application into front-end, middle-tier, and back-end. These programs allow dynamic interaction between the client and the server and can be integrated with a large number of current technologies. **(1, 3)**

arithmetic operators Mathematical operations performed by "+," "−," "*," or "/." **(5)**

ASP object model Formed from the Five Intrisics, together with their parent object, the ScriptingContext object. **(10)**

ASPs An alternative to CGI with which a script is embedded in a Web page and executed at the server before the page is sent. **(7)**

asynchronous Refers to objects or events that are not coordinated in time, or not real-time delivery, like e-mail. **(4)**

attribute An inherent characteristic of the object represented by an entire table. See field. **(5, 14)**

automation An aspect of Web site searchability. **(14)**

back-end The database, which must be updated, queried, and modified according to the interaction with the customer and the dynamic data needed by the front-end. **(2)**

backquote (`) The required beginning character for each embedded instruction in a template file. **(8)**

banner advertisements Used by businesses to advertise their products or services on other popular Web sites. **(4)**

base table The physical data table in a database the structure of which can be manipulated by using the DAO objects or data definition SQL statements. **(9)**

Beans Development Kit (BDK) A Java Beans development environment from Sun Microsystems. **(13)**

bgcolor Used to change background colors with JavaScript. **(13)**

binary executable file A compiled program file. **(8)**

body The main portion of the HTML document. **(7)**

bookmark A unique string assigned by the Jet Database Engine to every record in the Recordset. **(9)**

Boolean data Have a value of either true or false. **(8)**

bots Another term for local spider. **(14)**

brand-awareness A type of banner advertising designed to build positive awareness for the business. **(10)**

brand-centric An electronic commerce business model for selling a product. **(4)**

bridge program Links a database and OLE DB in the Universal Data Access strategy. **(10)**

BrowseCap object Lists the capabilities of a user's browser. **(10)**

built-in functions Functions for which code to perform actions is embedded in the template file. **(8)**

business-to-business electronic commerce (B2B) The relationship between two or more businesses using the Internet for the relationship channel. Most electronic commerce today is B2B. **(1)**

business-to-consumer (B2C) A popular form of e-commerce today, in which a business sells directly to a consumer. **(1)**

canonical Web activity The way in which Web clients and Web servers work together to deliver an HTML document that is not a dynamic form. **(6)**

cascading style sheets (CSS) Styles that define how to display HTML elements. These enable the separation of the content from the presentation layout. **(6)**

CERN Centre pour Européenne Recherche du Nucléaire, a European particle physics laboratory in Geneva, Switzerland. **(1)**

CGI application variables Can be listed using embedded instructions that instruct specific processing and functions to be performed on designated portions of the file. **(8)**

CGI executable Provides a consistent means for data to be passed from the Web client on request to the Web server and back-end of the electronic commerce construction. **(7)**

CGI mapping Allows the association of a URL to a specific type of script or other executable program. **(3)**

CGI output file This file contains the name and path of the file where the Web server will look for the Windows CGI application to write its result. **(7)**

CGI profile file The CGI primary input file. **(7)**

CGI.INI file Used to send input to the CGI application (also called a CGI initialization file). **(7)**

CGI_LogicalPath variable Holds all of the text entered after the actual URL. Logical or extra path information. **(8)**

CGI_Main procedure A portion of the CGI.bas program. It is the initial procedure in the VB code. **(7, 8)**

Cgi32.bas library module A program module that can be linked with other program modules to create a CGI executable program. **(7)**

changing Changing a site's design can lead to more efficiency by increasing interactivity. **(14)**

check boxes Used to allow the customer to select one or more options of a limited number of choices. **(4, 6)**

Chili!Soft ASP ASP technology with server-side, object-oriented components to provide an integrated Web development environment. **(10)**

classes Data that are assigned to categories in an object-oriented database. **(5)**

click-through A type of banner advertising in which banners are measured on a cost-per-click (CPC) basis. **(10)**

click-through rate (CTR) A measurement based on the number of customer Web responses, called clicks. **(10)**

client Provides an interface for the customer, and gathers and presents data, usually on the customer's computer. **(1)**

ClientCertificate collection Retrieves the certification fields from a request issued by the Web browser. **(10)**

client/server architecture An arrangement that involves client processes requesting service from server processes. **(1)**

client-server model A description of one computer, the client, requesting data from another computer, the server. The client/server idea can be used by programs within a single computer is most often found in a network. The client/server model is a foundation of network computing. **(7)**

Client-side scripts (CSS) An alternative to CGI. **(2)**

closing tag The end command inserted in a document that specifies how the document, or a portion of the document, should be formatted. Tags are used by all format specifications that store documents as text files. **(10)**

columns A way of categorizing or organizing data in a spreadsheet or database. **(5)**

COM+ Seen by the electronic commerce industry as Microsoft's answer to the Sun Microsystems-IBM-Oracle approach known as Enterprise JavaBeans (EJB). **(10)**

comment tag A JSP output tag that can be created using HTML and that may include only HTML or be combined with Java. **(13)**

commerce (P2P) A business model that refers to any transaction that transfers money from one individual to another.

committed A transaction that is applied to the database. **(11)**

Common Gateway Interface (CGI) An interface program to communicate with an external program or database. **(7)**

Common Object Request Broker Architecture (CORBA) A prominent distributed object technology. **(1)**

Common Warehouse Metamodel (CWM) Allows different data warehouse systems, databases, and other data repositories to exchange data automatically. **(12)**

Component Object Model (COM) Like Common Object Request Broker Architecture (CORBA), COM is a framework for the interoperation of distributed objects in a network. COM is Microsoft's framework for developing and supporting program component objects and provides the underlying services of client/server interface negotiation, determination of when an object can be removed from a system, and object event services. **(1, 10)**

components Re-useable applications or program building blocks that can be built with Java Beans. **(13)**

compound document capability Allows use by many applications or containers. **(13)**

compound documents Documents that incorporate more than one type of application in a single document, for example, a spreadsheet included in a word-processing document. **(13)**

conditional statements Allow a program to decide on a course of action on the basis of the result of a condition. **(8)**

confirm One of three message boxes used by JavaScript. **(13)**

connection string The database access layer used in ASP to pair the code to the database. **(11)**

Connection.BeginTrans This is a method executed to start the transaction. **(11)**

Connection.CommitTrans This is a method of the ADODB.Connection object that saves changes made within an open transaction on the connection and ends the transaction. **(11)**

Connection.Errors.Count This is a method of the ADODB.Connection object that allows access to the Errors collection of the wrapped ADODB.Connection object. **(11)**

Connection.RollbackTrans This is a method of the ADODB.Connection object that reverses any changes made within an open transaction and ends the transaction. **(11)**

Connection.State A property that indicates whether the connection to the database is open or not. **(11)**

connectionless Communication in which a connection is made and terminated for each message that is sent. **(2)**

connectivity Serving or tending to connect. **(1)**

consumer-to-business (C2B) A business model in which the consumer takes the initiative in the buying and selling relationship to contact the business. **(1)**

content file The .INP file created during the interaction between the Web server and the CGI application. **(1)**

content infrastructure The information framework of the Web database construction. **(4)**

content management Used to keep the infrastructure intact for the massive amounts of recycled, or "repurposed" data available today. **(4)**

content management software Designed to speed the delivery of Web content by pushing it closer to the customer and end-user. **(4)**

content mapping Used to allow appropriate display of a document. Directory icon mapping supports the special use of content types mapped to icons used in directory listings. **(3)**

Contents collection Contains all the items used in ActiveX script commands and adds them to the Web application. **(10)**

Contents objects Contain all the items used for script commands to be added to the Web session. **(10)**

Content-type Header fields that must be placed at the very top of the returned document and separated from the document body by a blank line. **(8)**

controls Form elements such as text fields, text area fields, drop-down menus, option buttons, and check boxes.

cookie property The means by which a cookie is associated with an HTML document and referenced. **(6)**

cookies Files stored as hidden fields on the Web server machine on the client side of a client/server communication that store customer preferences at a business's site as text strings. Briefly, information that the Web site puts on the customer's hard disk for later use. **(6,12)**

Cookies collection Contains a set of Web cookies, where each cookie contains a small amount of information about the Web user. **(10)**

cookies object collection Allows the retrieval of the values of the cookies sent in an HTTP request. **(12)**

cost per action (CPA) A method of charging for banner ads in which the advertiser only pays when a specific action, in this case the completion of a sale, occurs. **(10)**

cost per click (CPC) A method of charging for banner ads in which advertisers only pay when a customer actually clicks on the banner. **(10)**

cost per thousand (CPM, or cost per mille) A method of charging for banner ads in which businesses pay either a site or advertising network a set amount for the banners. **(10)**

crawlers Another term for local spider. **(14)**

CreateDynaset method Used to create a Dynaset-type Recordset by using the CreateDynaset method of the Database object. Creates an OraDynaset object from the specified SQL SELECT statement and options. **(9)**

crosstab query Presents a large amount of summary information in an easily understandable format, usually a spreadsheet, and makes comparisons and data analysis easy. **(5)**

custom tags Code located at the top of all content pages that is used to reference which template should be used for a particular Web client. **(12)**

customer relationship management (CRM) A complex, multifaceted undertaking in which businesses attempt to maintain intimate, one-to-one relationships with their customers. May include software and Internet capability. **(1, 8)**

customer-centric An electronic commerce business model for providing a service. **(4)**

data Text and values in the raw unprocessed form. **(6)**

Data Access Object (DAO) An application program interface available with Microsoft's Visual Basic that lets a programmer request access to a back-end Microsoft Access database and manipulate database objects. **(9, 10)**

database In business, generally used to automate business forms and to track shipping, inventory, and billing. **(5)**

database management system (DBMS) A program that allows one or more computer users to create and access data housed in a database. **(1)**

database object Used by the middleware to access and retrieve information about the connected database. **(9)**

Data Definition Language (DDL) The part of SQL that is used to create, change, or destroy the basic elements of a relational database such as tables, views, or schemas. **(11)**

datamining Also called data extraction. **(11)**

data modeling The process of identifying all the objects to be manipulated and their relations to one another. **(5)**

data objects The program code representations of the physical database, data tables, fields, and indexes. **(5, 9)**

dataset-oriented database systems Database systems in which operations are performed one set at a time, not one record at a time. **(9)**

Data Source Name (DSN) Allows all users of a particular machine to access the database through that data source. **(11)**

date object Represents a specific instant in time, with millisecond precision—a snapshot of an exact millisecond in time. It contains information on both date and time. **(13)**

DBEngine object The top level object in the Data Access Object (DAO) model. **(9)**

declaration Consists of a series of properties and their associated values, separated by semicolons. **(6)**

declaration tag A JSP tag used to declare a variable or method. **(13)**

delimiter A character that marks the beginning or end of a unit of data. **(8)**

DHTML See Dynamic HTML.

disintermediation A networked economy in which buyers can deal directly with sellers. **(1)**

distributed enterprise architecture The newest electronic commerce model, based on ORB technology and using shared, reusable business models on a business enterprise-wide scale. **(1)**

distributed Web constructions A framework within a three-tier application construction that has a Web front-end, middleware, and a database back-end. **(3)**

document mapping Allows a URL path to be mapped to a physical directory on the server. **(3)**

document object A document is an ordered collection of elements. An element is an object that contains all the content between the start and end tags of the element as objects, and any set of attributes that are defined for the element. The Document Object Model is the underlying structure. Objects are labeled containers. The Document Object is the container for all the objects defined in an HTML or XML document. **(13)**

Document Object Model (DOM) The W3C DHTML model in which each page division or section, such as heading, paragraph, image, or list, is viewed as an object. **(6)**

document type definition (DTD) A formal definition of the HTML syntax in terms of SGML. **(6)**

document.cookie A built-in JavaScript object that handles cookie interaction and stores all the valid cookies for the page on which the script is running. **(13)**

document.write A code that is a method of the document object. A method to write data. **(13)**

domain One of four optional attributes for a cookie in JavaScript. **(13)**

drill-down searches Use a hierarchical form of exploring to narrow down the search for the user. **(4)**

DSN-less connection The ODBC connection string that is set so that it utilizes a DSN or not. **(11)**

dynamic feedback form Used to identify the potential customers and their needs. **(4)**

dynamic HTML (DHTML) A combination of HTML 4.0, Style Sheets and JavaScript to allow documents to be animated. Makes HTML pages dynamic by using scripting to manipulate the style, layout and contents of the document, so that they can look and act like desktop applications or even multimedia productions. **(3, 6)**

Dynamic HTML Object Model Microsoft's DHTML model in which each page division or section, such as heading, paragraph, image, or list, is viewed as an object. **(6)**

dynamic-link library (DLL) A collection of small programs that are dynamically linked to larger programs as needed. **(11)**

ECMAScript Defined in the ECMA Standard as object-oriented programming language for performing computations and manipulating objects within a host environment. **(13)**

ECMA Standard Proposed by Netscape in 1996, JavaScript is the originating technology for this standard. **(13)**

e-CRM See electronic CRM.

electronic commerce Buying or selling goods or services of a business electronically, allowing businesses to exchange goods and services immediately while overcoming barriers of time or distance. **(1)**

electronic commerce business models A framework for allowing business and customer interaction. **(4)**

electronic CRM (e-CRM) Using the Internet to manage customer relationships. Rapidly becoming the business standard and embracing customer service and support features, data collection and analysis, and marketing campaign and sales applications. **(1, 8)**

electronic data interchange (EDI) Refers to the computer-to-computer transmission of business information from one business computer to another in standard data formats. **(1)**

Electrotechnical Commission Management Association (ECMA) An international industry association that was founded in 1961 and dedicated to the standardization of information and communication systems. **(13)**

elements Small pieces of data. **(5)**

embedded instruction A hard-coded instruction. **(8)**

encapsulate To include functions. **(10)**

ENCTYPE attribute Used to set or retrieve the MIME encoding for the form. **(6)**

Enterprise Resource Planning (ERP) An industry term used to describe the broad set of activities supported by the distributed enterprise architecture, aids management in overseeing and planning for the important parts of its business, including product planning, parts purchasing, maintaining inventories, interacting with suppliers, providing customer service, and tracking orders. **(1)**

environmental variables A method that the Web server uses to pass information to a CGI application. **(7)**

Err variable Used to store error code values for use by the currently active error-handling procedure. **(9)**

Error A Visual Basic built-in object that is a child object of the DBEngine and can be used to obtain additional details on the nature of the database errors that occur in a program. **(9)**

error handling Ensures that the CGI program will always terminate properly by passing control to the line labeled "ErrorHandler" when an error occurs. **(7)**

Execute method Used to perform an SQL action query. **(9)**

expires One of four optional attributes for a cookie in JavaScript. **(13)**

expression Anything within a template file that can be evaluated to get a single value. Contains a combination of fields, constants, and operators. **(5, 8)**

expression tag A JSP tag used to put data into an output buffer and can be used anywhere on a JSP page. **(13)**

Extensible Hypertext Markup Language (XHTML) A combination of HTML and XML (Extensible Markup Language) that lets you define your own markup language and data formats for new applications. **(6)**

extensible markup language (XML) Provides a way to access server-side Java components from the Web pages. **(2)**

external style sheets Enable both the appearance and layout of Web pages to be changed just by editing a single CSS document. **(6)**

FastCGI A server-side, language-independent program that manages multiple CGI requests within a single process, saving many program instructions for each request. **(7)**

fetched Retrieved from a Web server. **(6)**

fgcolor Used to change background colors with JavaScript. **(13)**

field The intersection of a column and row of a database table. **(5, 14)**

FieldName Refers to the name of the form field currently available to the CGI application. **(8)**

FieldValue Refers to the value of the form field to be created. **(8)**

file allocation table (FAT) A table located on the hard disk, maintained by the computer's operating system, that maps files to the cluster in which they are stored. **(3)**

File Name argument Used to point to a Universal Data Link (UDL) file. **(11)**

File Transfer Protocol (FTP) A standard Internet protocol that is the simplest way to exchange files in the electronic commerce model. **(1)**

FileSystem object Provides access to the server's file system. **(10)**

filter A set of criteria that describes the sequence of the records in a database. **(5)**

filter variable A new Recordset object and a new variable that holds the criteria for selecting records. **(9)**

Financial EDI Refers to Financial Electronic Data Interchange defined as the electronic transmission of funds and related data through the banking system, using standard formats. It is also called Electronic Funds Transfer, or EFT, by the Federal Reserve System. **(1)**

Find method Used to locate specific records in non-table objects. **(9)**

FindFirst A Find method that starts its search from the beginning of the file and works toward the end. **(9)**

FindLast A Find method that starts its search from the end of the file and works its way toward the beginning. **(9)**

FindNext A Find method used to continue a search that can return more than one recor, working from the beginning to the end of the file. **(9)**

FindPrevious A Find method used to continue a search that can return more than one record, working from the end to the beginning of the file. **(9)**

First Normal Form The "basic" level of normalization that generally refers to moving data into separate tables where the data in each table are of a similar type, or kind. **(14)**

Five Intrinsics A core set of objects provided by ASP. **(10)**

flag variables Indicate the location in the body of the procedure and then write logic in the error handler to take different actions on the basis of where the error occurred. **(8)**

Flash An example of plug-in. **(7)**

flat-file database Usually referred to as spreadsheets that use columns and rows to organize small pieces of data into a list. **(5)**

FORM An HTML tag that denotes a form. **(6)**

form data Name/value pairs separated by the ampersand (&) character. **(8)**

form elements Allow the customer to enter information into the form. **(6)**

forms Terms used to specify the degree of normalization of a database structure. **(14)**

forward tag A JSP tag used to transfer control to a different location on the server. **(13)**

frames An attempt to present multiple views of an information space of task domain. **(14)**

front-end The Web portion of an electronic commerce site that allows dynamic interchange between the customer and the business. **(2)**

fully qualified domain name (FQDN) Includes the hierarchical name of the computer and is written from the most specific to the least specific address. **(3)**

fully qualified host names (FQHN) Used interchangeably with fully qualified domain name (FQDN). **(3)**

gateways An external program. **(7)**

generic back-end database A database that can be copied to different Web server directories. **(9)**

GET method Used to submit an HTML form by appending data from the form controls as arguments to the action URL. **(6, 7)**

GET request method A standardized way to retrieve data from a server. **(8)**

global arrays Arrays that are accessible from every procedure of a CGI application. **(7)**

global variables Variables that are accessible from every procedure of your CGI application. **(7)**

graphical user interface (GUI) A graphical, rather than textual, interface between computer and user. **(1)**

guestbook An electronic commerce business model where the customer electronically sends the business information in a dynamic interaction. **(3, 4)**

hard-coded HTML Coded in place. Not changeable. **(8)**

header lines One or more lines of text separated from the body by a blank line. Used in processing template files. **(7, 8)**

hidden comment tag A comment that is included in the JSP code, but is not a part of the HTML returned from the container to the Web server. **(13)**

hidden controls Can be used to accomplish the same task as cookies. Using hidden controls, the form passes a user id value, in addition to the rest of the information. **(12)**

hidden form fields A field for which no field is presented to the customer, but the content of the field is sent with the submitted HTML form. A cookie is an example of a hidden field. **(6)**

HIDDEN VALUE Attribute that does not allow the value to be displayed to the user. **(6)**

hits A single file request for information that can be viewed in the Web server's access logs, serving as a meaningful measure of site traffic. **(4, 14)**

HomeSite An HTML editor for image map editing. **(3)**

host environment Location where the program resides. The host environment controls what, if any, external environmental objects may be addressed by language statements running in the host environment. **(13)**

HTML elements HTML tags. **(6)**

HTML form handler Used to start and stop each cgi-bin interface interaction. **(7)**

HTML forms A dynamic component of the front-end of the Web database construction that allows users to interact with the business' back-end database. **(6)**

HTML Object Model Netscape's DHTML model in which each page division or section, such as heading, paragraph, image, or list, is viewed as an object. **(6)**

HTML tags Codes that are used used to "mark up" the elements of a file for the client's browser. **(2)**

HTTP daemon (httpd) The generic name given to the many Web servers available. **(2)**

HTTP GET request method The fastest and simplest method for retrieving information specified in the URL absolute path request parameter. **(2)**

HTTP HEAD request method Most often used by the client to test the validity and availability of an information resource. **(2)**

HTTP POST request method Utilized by a client to interpret existing information resources that reside on a server or to supply supplemental data to a Web server. **(2)**

hybrid A database model that is a combination of the relational database model and the object-oriented model. **(5)**

hyperization The degree of hyperization refers to the number of levels within a Web site. **(14)**

hypermedia An extension of hypertext that includes graphics, audio, and other multimedia forms. Sometimes implies a higher level of user interactivity than the interactivity already implicit in hypertext. **(2, 6)**

hypertext The logical connectivity between computers and text, allowing a computer to interface with text through a system of cross-references to be followed in a nonlinear way. **(2, 6)**

hypertext links The associations of hypertext, also called links. **(6)**

Hypertext Markup Language (HTML) Communications software used by electronic commerce. **(1, 2)**

Hypertext Transfer Protocol (HTTP) Communications software used by electronic commerce. Sends the data from the software program on one computer through the network and reassembles it on another computer at the other end. **(1, 2)**

if (!a) Translated by the JavaScript program as if click Cancel. **(13)**

impressions Used to quantify the success of a Web site. Also called views. **(14)**

include tag A JSP tag used to allow the incorporation of JSP, HTML, or text into the JSP page. **(13)**

indexes Used to speed the process of locating records in data tables and to speed processing by allowing the databases to access the data in sorted order. **(9)**

infomediaries Needed to turn massive amounts of "dumb" data into usable information, offering aggregated services such as intelligent customer assistance, powerful technology-based buying aids, and even attractive, community-based buying environments. **(1)**

information servers See application servers. **(3)**

inheritance In object-oriented databases, data class subclasses share some or all of the main class characteristics to be defined. **(5)**

initial Catalog parameter Indicates the database to which the connection string will be associated. **(11)**

inner join A join where the records from two tables are only selected when the records have the same value in the common field that links the tables. **(5)**

INPUT An HTML tag that defines a visual interface element, such as the textbox or option button that allows dynamic Web interaction. **(6)**

Input fields Can be used to parse data to the back-end database to add more security to your site. **(6)**

instantiate Create a particular realization of an abstraction, such as a class of object or a computer process, by defining one particular variation of object within a class, giving it a name, and locating it in some physical place. **(10)**

InStr() Function A VBScript function used to check whether a field contains a character. **(12)**

Inter_Main() procedure A part of the CGI program used for calling the Inter_Main code. **(7)**

Internet Also called the Net, the Information Superhighway, or Cyberspace, the Internet is a network of computers that are connected to other computers for the purpose of resource and information sharing. **(1)**

Internet Information Server (IIS) A popular Web server program that comes packaged with the Windows NT server and Windows 2000 Server. **(1)**

Internet media type (IMEDIA) Formerly referred to as the Content Type MIME called text/thm. **(6)**

interpreted language A programming language that is transformed into machine language on the computer. **(13)**

invisible counter A stealth-tracking device that will keep the same statistics as the other counters. **(14)**

IP-less virtual servers Multiple virtual servers. **(3)**

IR AC IS An old IBM acronym pronounced *ear-ack-iss* and standing for Increase Revenue, Avoid Costs, Improve Service. **(1)**

Java A compiled language that must be transformed into machine language before it can communicate with a computer-compiled language. **(13)**

Java 2 Platform Enterprise Edition (J2EE) applications Applications developed by Sun Microsystems and based on the Java platform that are developed for the thin client n-tiered business environment. **(13)**

Java applet A client-side extending technology that is downloaded to the Web client from the server. The Web client then runs the program. Can be used to add interactive capabilities to the electronic commerce model. **(7, 13)**

Java Beans An object-oriented programming interface from Sun Microsystems. **(13)**

Java Plug-in software Plug-ins that enable Web browsers to use the JRE 2 to run applets and enterprise customers to direct applets or Java Beans on intranet Web pages to run instead of the Web browser's default virtual machine. **(13)**

Java Runtime (JRE) From Sun Microsystems and included with the Windows version of JRun. **(13)**

Java Server Pages (JSP) A dynamic scripting middleware that allows special tags to be embedded into the Web file. An alternative to ASP (which is costly to use and often ties up with the Windows platform) or CGI (which has portability issues and the disadvantages of non-object-oriented development). **(2)**

Java servlet A platform-independent Java server-side module that is incorporated into the electronic commerce model and can be used to extend the capabilities of a Web server with minimal overhead, maintenance, and support. A servlet is a small program that runs on the server, as opposed to an applet that runs on the client. **(2, 13)**

Java Virtual Machine (JVM) A key component of Java. A virtual computer, typically implemented in software on top of a "real" hardware platform and operating system, that runs compiled Java programs. **(3, 13)**

JavaScript An electronic commerce tool that is used in the Web database construction to create the dynamic interaction between the customer and the business. **(13)**

javascript: Can be typed into the Location box and the Enter key pressed before any JavaScript development. **(13)**

joins Allow you to work with the data from multiple tables. **(5)**

JRun Java application server A Java server from Allaire Corporation that provides a development and deployment platform for building and delivering Java 2 Platform Enterprise Edition (J2EE) applications. **(13)**

JRun Management Console (JMC) See JRun.

JRun Web Server (JWS) See JRun.

Jscript Microsoft's implementation of the ECMA Standard that is very similar to JavaScript, with only a few minor exceptions to maintain backwards compatibility. **(13)**

key-value pairs A set of printable ASCII pairs used in cookies that include the following: Expires, Domain, Path, and Secure. **(12)**

keyword search Uses pertinent words that appear in different fields to find information for the user in the back-end database. **(4)**

Language attribute An optional but recommended JavaScript attribute. **(13)**

layout A factor that affects the success of the electronic commerce design. **(14)**

left outer join A join that selects all records from the first, or left, table and only those records from the second table that have matching common field values. **(5)**

Len() Function A VBScript function used to check for empty fields. **(12)**

list An organizational framework used to maintain small pieces of data. **(5)**

list box Can be used by visitors to the Web site to answer questions, select options, or to limit user and data input error. **(4)**

literals Constants in Visual Basic that are similar to variables and can also be of any type. **(8)**

LiveScript The original form of JavaScript developed by Netscape. **(13)**

local area network (LAN) A group of computers and associated devices that share a common communications line. **(1)**

local spiders Can be used to read or search Web pages. Also known as crawlers or bots. **(14)**

Location headers Used in processing template files. **(8)**

Lock Used to ensure that multiple users do not try to alter a property simultaneously. **(10)**

loop A series of instructions that is repeated until a terminating condition is reached. **(8)**

loss-leader pricing Used to deliberately sell a product below its customary price to attract attention to it and the business. **(10)**

LTrim Function A VBScript function that returns a string without leading spaces. **(12)**

M-commerce See mobile electronic commerce. **(1)**

magic cookies UNIX objects, also called tokens, that are attached to a user or program and change depending on the areas entered by the user or program. **(12)**

Main() procedure For the CGI application, it is in the Cgi32.bas module and handles all of the setup of the Visual Basic CGI environment. **(7)**

marketspace A global electronic marketplace. **(1)**

message servers Provides methods for client applications to read, write, and request files and services from server programs. **(1)**

metadata A definition or description of data. **(5)**

metalanguage A definition or description of language. **(5)**

METHOD A programmed procedure that is defined as part of a class and included in any object of that class. A method can be re-used. **(2, 5, 6)**

Microsoft Data Access Components (MDAC) The key technologies that enable Universal Data Access. **(10)**

Microsoft Internet Server Application Programming Interface (ISAPI) A proprietary technology that eases the load on Web servers from server-side computing traffic. **(2)**

Microsoft Jet database engine A database engine used behind the scenes in Access. Short for Joint Engine Technology. It handles the I/O to the database and provides programmable objects representing the database. **(9)**

Microsoft Jet workspace The workspace object functions as a session for storing transactions between your front-end application and the back-end database. **(9)**

Microsoft.Jet.OLEDB.4.0 The OLE DB provider for Access. **(11)**

middle tier Added in the three-tier model between the client environment and the database management server environment. **(1)**

middleware The key link between the Web and the database. Used to describe the programming that glues the construction together. **(2)**

mobile electronic commerce A fast-emerging specialized class of electronic commerce that brings with it the promise of true comparison shopping whether in a store or listening to the car radio. **(1)**

modal A form that uses modality (provisions as to the mode of procedure) in its coding logic. **(13)**

modaless A form that does not use modality in its coding logic. **(13)**

Move methods A method to move the ADO pointer to another record. First, previous, next, and last are the four possible movements. **(9)**

MSDASQL Microsoft's OLE DB Provider for ODBC that is one of the oldest forms of connection and also known as ODBC. **(11)**

multiple-table queries A question used to search multiple database tables to retrieve useful information. **(5)**

multiprocessing The dynamic assignment of the software to one or more computers working in tandem. **(3)**

Multipurpose Internet Mail Extensions (MIME) Describes the transfer and format of the software files in order to maintain their format and integrity on the Web. **(2)**

multithreading The software's ability to manage multiple user requests, or threads, at one time. **(3)**

multitier architecture The three-tier commerce model developed to overcome the limitations of two-tier architecture. **(1)**

name The one required attribute for a cookie in JavaScript. Used to coordinate access to the stored state data. **(13)**

name=value pairs A sequence of characters excluding semi-colons, commas, and spaces that is a required attribute on the set-cookie header. **(6)**

Named Pipes The default network library. **(11)**

National Center for Supercomputing Applications (NCSA)/Centre pour Européenne Recherche du Nucléaire (CERN) format The oldest of the three formats of access logs for virtual servers. **(3)**

nested query A query that includes more than one type of operator. **(5)**

Netscape Server Application Programming Interface (NSAPI) A proprietary technology that eases the load on Web servers from server-side computing traffic. **(2)**

Network Library parameter Specifies the network library of choice. **(11)**

new economy A revolution in the rules of business in which huge value is being leveraged from the capture of employees' experience and knowledge. **(1)**

NoMatch method Used to get the results of the Seek operation. **(9)**

Normalization A refinement technique of database design that suggests certain criteria be used when constructing table columns and creating the key structure. **(14)**

NT file system (NTFS) The Windows NT equivalent to the FAT, which offers performance, extendability, and security improvements over FAT. **(3)**

object Each separate piece of data in an object-oriented database. **(5, 9)**

Object Data Management Group (ODMG) An industry group that is developing an object-oriented database interface standard. **(5)**

Object Linking and Embedding (OLE) controls Originally used for compound documents. **(13)**

object-oriented database management system (OODBMS) A database management system that supports the modeling and creation of data as objects and support for classes of objects, as well as the inheritance of class properties and methods by subclasses and their objects. **(5)**

Object-oriented programming (OOP) Programming that is organized around objects rather than actions and around data rather than logic. **(5)**

object-relational system A hybrid database that is a combination OF decision support systems. **(5)**

object request broker (ORB) The programming that acts as the mediary, or as a broker, between a client request for a service from a distributed object or component and server completion of that request. **(1)**

OCX An ActiveX OLE control that is the third version of OLE. (13)

ODBC driver Used to connect to a back-end database. (9)

ODBCDirect workspace An ODBC data source that is referenced directly through DAO. (9)

OLE Automation A COM-based macro programming technique used primarily for writing Visual Basic scripts that controlled Office applications. (13)

OLE DB Microsoft's strategic low-level API for access to different data sources. The underlying system service that a programmer using ADO is actually using. (3, 10, 11)

online job-listing services A Web database construction for pairing job applicants with businesses with job openings. (4)

online shopping cart A Web database construction that simulates an online virtual store with the capability of accepting orders and payments online. (4)

online surveys An electronic commerce business model where the customer submits preferences and user data to the business. (4)

"on the fly" Another term for ad hoc. (4)

OnTransactionAbort event This occurs with the ObjectContext object and explicitly aborts the transaction. (10)

OnTransaction-Commit event This occurs with the ObjectContext object when a transaction has been successfully completed. (10)

Open Database Connectivity (ODBC) A standard developed by Microsoft to enable any application to communicate with any database manager. (9, 11)

opening tag The first command inserted in a document that specifies how the document, or a portion of the document, should be formatted. Tags are used by all format specifications that store documents as text files. (10)

OpenRecordset method Used to create a dynaset Recordset object. (9)

open-source PHP A freely available script language used primarily on Linux servers. An alternative to Microsoft's ASP. (3)

option buttons Used to allow the customer to select one choice from among a limited number of choices. (4, 6)

orphan pages Web pages that do not have a link to the business' home page and do not contain some indication of where they fit within the structure of the Web site. (14)

outer joins Joins of the data from multiple tables. (5)

output files Used to pass data between the Web server and the CGI program. (7)

overhead Non-data contents. (5)

Parameter query Displays one or more predefined dialog boxes that prompt the user for the parameter value, or cri-teria. Often used when filtering records based on a criterion that varies in its condition values. (5, 9)

Partitioned Web technologies Share the processing duties between the server and the client. (3)

PASSWORD Attribute for adding security to the construction. (6)

path One of four optional attributes for a cookie in JavaScript. (13)

permanent cookies Cookies that are stored in a text file on the user's computer. See also persistent cookies. (6)

persistence One of the three elements of a state management system where data is "remembered" by the Web server. (6)

persistent cookies Cookies that are are stored in a text file on the user's computer. (6)

PHP Embeds server-side scripting in a pre-HTML page and ASP, which is Microsoft's version of a similar interface. (7)

PHP Hypertext Preprocessor A server-side, HTML-embedded scripting language created in 1994 by Rasmus Lerdorf. (3)

PHP4 Often shipped standard with Web servers, which support both of the most popular electronic commerce constructions: server-side and client-side technologies. See also PHP Hypertext Preprocessor. (3)

pieces of data Individual data units. (5)

plug-ins Code modules used to enhance the Web browser, allowing it to view specific file types. (7)

portability The degree to which a document can be used on many different types of computers without modification. (6)

portable document A document that can be used on many different types of computers without modification. (6)

POST method Used to submit HTML form information to Visual Basic script programs or JavaScript functions. (6, 7)

POST request method A standardized method to allow some block of data, such as the result of submitting a form, to be delivered to a data-handling process on the server. (8)

prefs.js file The JavaScript user's preference file and is located in the Netscape\Users directory. (13)

primary input file The CGI profile file used by the Web server to place data to be passed. (7)

primary key A unique identifier for a database table. (14)

prompt One of three message boxes used by JavaScript. (13)

proprietary plug-ins Server-side technologies, such as ASP, ISAPI or NSAPI, and Java servlets. (7)

pull technology The information that is available on the Web is downloaded on command, or "pulled," by the customer. (4)

push technology Analogous to a sales pitch in which the salesperson "pushes" the customer to buy. **(4)**

query languages Languages that are used to interact with databases. **(5)**

query string parameters Passed as command line parameters to the main program. **(8)**

query Used to search databases. **(5)**

Query_String CGI variable An environment variable used for appending file data. **(5)**

QueryDef objects The collection of SQL queries stored in the database that can also be used as replacements for the complete SQL statement. **(9)**

QueryString collection Contains a set of added URL arguments. **(10)**

QuickStats A tool for site traffic analysis. **(3)**

rapid application development (RAD) Example tools include Visual Basic and Delphi. **(7)**

record-oriented database systems Database systems in which operations are performed one record at a time. **(9)**

records General name given to rows of a database table. **(5)**

Recordset object The primary data object used in Visual Basic programs that holds the collection of data records used in the Web database construction. **(9)**

redirect mapping Allows the redirection of one URL to another URL, most often on a different server. **(3)**

Refresh method Used to refresh the Recordset by moving the record pointer using the arrow keys of the data control, or by using one of the Move methods. **(9)**

regedit Utility for updating the registry and registry keys. **(3)**

regedt32 Utility for updating the registry and registry keys. **(3)**

relational database A database model that takes advantage of uniformity to build completely new tables out of required information from existing tables. **(5)**

relational database management system (RDBMS) A program for creating, updating, and administering a relational database. **(1, 2)**

relations Two-dimensional tables that reduce data redundancy, duplication of entry effort, and storage space. **(5)**

Remote Automation (RA) Server A server that requires the addition of special files when the Package folder is created. **(13)**

Remote Data Objects (RDO) An earlier Microsoft data interface that works with Microsoft's ODBC to access relational databases, but not nonrelational databases. **(10)**

Remote Data Service (RDS) A component of the Microsoft Data Access Components (MDAC) that enables applications to access OLE DB providers, running on remote machines or in separate processes on the same machine. RDS provides services for distributed applications. **(11)**

Replace() Function A VBScript function that can be used to replace all the double and single quotes in the returned values with double double quotes (" ") and double single quotes (' '). **(12)**

"repurposed" data Recycled data. **(4)**

Request and Response objects Methods (two of the Five Intrinsics) that handle client requests. The request encapsulates data from the client. The response encapsulates the response to the client. The request object provides access to HTTP header data, such as any cookies found in the request and the HTTP method with which the request was made. The response object provides two ways of returning data to the user. **(10, 12)**

return on investment (ROI) A measure of the effectiveness of advertising, obtained in e-commerce by dividing the value of customer traffic at a site by the total cost of advertising. **(10)**

right outer join A join where all records from the second, or right, table, and only those records from the first table that have matching common field values are selected. **(5)**

rolled back A transaction that is undone from the database. **(11)**

rows The collection of data records. Also called records or tuples. **(5)**

RTrim Function A VBScript function that returns a string without trailing spaces. **(12)**

sandbox The protected memory space in which Java executes. **(3)**

scope of operation delimiters The boundary of a delimiter, or character, that identifies the beginning or the end of separate data items in a database or character strings within a program. **(5)**

script A small portion of a program; a set of instructions that take place automatically when a script is run. Macros, functions, and commands are other words for scripts. **(2)**

scripting language The ECMA Standard formalized the definition as a programming language used to manipulate, customize, and automate the facilities of an existing system. **(13)**

ScriptingContext object The parent object of the Five ASP Intrinsics or core set of objects of ASP. The primary object in the ASP programming model is the ScriptingContext object. Because it is always available to ASP applications, you don't need to explicitly create a reference to it. **(10)**

scriptlet tag The majority of the Java code in JSP is included in this type of tag. **(13)**

searchability A broad term used to describe the capability for searching and tracking within the site. **(14)**

Second Normal Form A state of database table normalization in which any column, or field, that does not determine the contents of another column is itself a function of the other columns in the table. Alternatively, a state of database table normalization in which each nonkey field is functionally dependent upon the primary key. **(14)**

security One of four optional attributes for a cookie in JavaScript. **(13)**

select query Used to simply retrieve data from the database. **(5)**

selector Usually used as the style name. **(6)**

self-generating content A benefit of dynamic Web sites. **(14)**

sell-through A type of banner advertising that results in immediate sales and that is used to generate revenue quickly. **(10)**

server A computer program that provides services to other computer programs in the same or other computers. Can also be the computer the server program resides in. **(1)**

server application programming interface (Server API) The method prescribed by the server software by which requests to the construction can be made by various operating systems or application software. **(2)**

server properties An administration utility program that is accessed by right-clicking on the server icon on the taskbar and choosing Server Properties. This program allows configuration of the WebSite server. **(3)**

Server-Side Includes (SSIs) A variable value that a server can include in an HTML file before it is sent to the front-end customer. SSIs are limited forms of CGI. SSIs are limited forms of CGI. **(2, 7, 8, 12)**

server-side scripting (SSS) One or more embedded scripts are executed at the server, and any output from the script is inserted into the HTML text stream of the Web page. **(2)**

server-side scripts A program, or sequence of instructions, that is interpreted or carried out by another program rather than by the computer processor. **(10)**

Server-side technologies Enhance HTML Web pages and are used to increase customer interactivity with the business. **(7)**

ServerVariables collection Contains a set of server environment variables. **(10)**

session cookies Cookies that are stored in memory and are deleted when the session with the Web browser is terminated. **(6)**

session objects One of the Five Intrinsics or core set of objects of ASP. A series of interactions between two communication end points that occur during the span of a single connection. The session begins when the connection is established at both ends and terminates when the connection is ended. **(10)**

SET SQL command Changes the value of a data field. **(9)**

SetAbort method A method used with the ObjectContext object. **(10)**

SetComplete method This is a method used with the ObjectContext object. **(10)**

Shockwave An example of a plug-in. **(7)**

snippets Small portions of code. **(9)**

SPAM Junk e-mail that is sent as a form of push technology. **(4)**

speed An element that can either enhance or detract from the Web site design. **(14)**

spreadsheets A computer application program in which data is arranged in rows and columns. **(5)**

SQL action query SQL statements that perform some action on the data table. **(9)**

SQLOLEDB Microsoft OLE DB Provider for SQL Server. **(11)**

SQL search Uses structured query language to find data by specifying valid SQL criteria. **(4)**

Standard CGI Differs from Windows CGI in that the input data are sent with environment labels and the standard input rather than temporary input/output files. **(7)**

Standard Generalized Markup Language (SGML) A standard for specifying the tag set and markup language of a particular document. **(2)**

standard output (stdOUT) Data that the httpd server expects a CGI program to produce. **(8)**

stateless Denotes that a computer or computer program has not stored previous interactions. **(2)**

state management system Maintains information about a customer's requests to session actions. **(6)**

StaticObjects collection Contains all the objects used in the HTML <Object> tag and adds them to the Web application. **(10)**

stickiness The degree to which a customer tends to stay at a Web site for a long time and to also make return visits. **(14)**

string expressions Required for sending any CGI output. **(8)**

structured query language (SQL) A standard interface and programming language for communication with a database. **(1)**

style A collection of information about displaying and positioning attributes that a Web author defines. **(6)**

sType A string that specifies or receives the format of the data being submitted by the form. **(6)**

subclass Classes within classes that inherit all or some of the characteristics of the class. **(5)**

submit button A click event used for electronically submitting front-end data to the back-end of the Web construction. **(4)**

Sun Microsystems The developer of Java. **(13)**

tab-delimited file A text file in which fields are delimited by commas and records are delimited by new line characters.

table The organization of small pieces of data into a list made up of columns and rows of related information. **(5)**

TARGET An attribute used to specify the destination for the media or file. **(6)**

TaskSelector variable A variable assigned to the task name specified in the CGI_LogicalPath variable. Leading forward slashes are removed from the logical path variable, and the remaining characters are converted to uppercase letters. **(8)**

template files Share a similar interface to provide a consistent customer experience throughout the business Web site. Built for output and require less hard-coded HTML. Make it easier to change the Web page. Contain standard unvarying parts to which dynamic parts are added. **(8, 12)**

temporary cookies stored in memory and are deleted when the session with the Web browser is terminated. See also session cookie. **(6)**

temporary input file Used to pass data between the Web server and the CGI program. **(7)**

text fields Used in an HTML form. **(6)**

TextIfFalse Text that is processed if the condition evaluates to a "false-type" value. **(8)**

TextIfTrue Text that is processed if the condition evaluates to a "true-type" value. **(8)**

thin clients Network devices that utilize older and less powerful client workstations, reducing hardware and software costs to the company. **(2)**

Third Normal Form A state of database table normalization in which each nonkey field is both functionally dependent upon the primary key *and* not functionally dependent upon any combination of the other nonkey fields. **(14)**

Tim Berners-Lee Credited with inventing the World Wide Web in late 1990 while working at the Centre pour Européenne Recherche du Nucléaire (CERN). **(1)**

total query Allow aggregate functions such as sum, average, count, or other totals on a set of records to be performed. **(5)**

TP heavy A condition when transaction processing is provided by third-party middleware vendors, because thousands of users can be serviced. **(1)**

TP lite When transaction processing is embedded in the database management system (DBMS) because the performance degrades when more than 100 clients are connected. **(1)**

traditional commerce Conducted using face-to-face interaction, printed and written documents, telephone communication, and postal mail. **(1)**

transaction A logical atomic unit of work that contains one or more SQL statements. **(11)**

transaction processing (TP) monitors A technology that involves a type of message queuing, transaction scheduling, and prioritization service where the client connects to the TP monitor of the middle tier instead of the database server. **(1)**

Transmission Control Protocol/Internet Protocol (TCP/IP) The standard protocol suite for Internet communication. **(2)**

transparent counter A counter that has a clear background and blends in with the site background color or image on the Web page. **(14)**

Trim() Function Returns a string without leading and trailing spaces. **(12)**

tuples See records. **(5)**

two-tier client/server model A model in which the user system interface is usually located in the user's desktop environment and the database management services are usually in a server that is a more powerful machine servicing many clients. **(1)**

Uniform Resource Locator (URL) The address of a Web page. **(1)**

Universal Data Access Microsoft's overall data access strategy. **(10)**

Universal Data Link (UDL) A file that can simply be created by creating an empty text file with a .udl extension and that is normally stored in a special folder located at Programs Files\Common Files\System\OLE DB\Data Links. **(11)**

Unlock methods Used to ensure that multiple users do not try to alter a property simultaneously. **(10)**

UPDATE SQL command SQL command that will update a table in the database. **(9)**

URL-encoding method Lists name=value string pairs delimited by the ampersand (&) character. **(8)**

User-defined variables Treated as special form fields that are not passed by a Web client but are created internally by the CGI application. **(8)**

value-added network (VAN) Offer reliability and security that was difficult to duplicate on business transactions on the public lines of the Internet in the early days of electronic commerce. **(1)**

var statement Used to declare a variable in JavaScript. **(13)**

variant Can be used for any of the supported data types. **(8)**

views Also called impressions and used to quantify the success of a Web site. **(14)**

virtual servers A server that is shared by multiple Web site owners. Each owner can use and administer the virtual server as if they had complete administrative control. **(3)**

virual marketing Advertising that propagates itself through an electronic commerce site. **(1)**

Web assessment tools Used to ensure sound front-ends and design techniques. **(2)**

Web client Another term for a Web browser. **(4)**

Web daemon A program that waits in attendance for Web client requests and forwards the requests as they come into other processes as appropriate. **(7)**

Web scripting language Defined by the ECMA Standard as a mechanism used to "enliven" Web pages in browsers and to perform Web server computation as part of the Web-based client–server architecture. **(13)**

Web server software Programs that use the client/server model and HTTP to serve files back and forth from the front-end to the back-end of the Web database construction. **(2)**

Web servers Computers that are connected to and make up the Internet. Also refers to the software these computers use to add functionality to a Web database construction in order to create electronic commerce. **(1)**

Web spiders Crawl through the site by following all the hypertext links in each page until all the pages have been read. **(14)**

Webcasting Users locate relevant sites and register their interest profiles. The business stores the data from these profiles, and the information server itself sends relevant information, at suitable times, to users without waiting for additional requests. **(4)**

WebSite Application Programming Interface (WSAPI) An application program interface through which a developer or user can make requests of the operating system or application. **(3)**

WebSite A popular Web server program. **(1, 3)**

WHERE SQL command Used to perform a logical comparison of field values. **(9)**

Windows CGI One type of middleware that defines how a Web server and the external program of the customer communicate with each other. Provides a common interface between business applications and Windows RAD tool technologies. **(7)**

Windows CGI libraries Available from the Internet, also provides support for programming environments, such as Borland Delphi and Microsoft Visual C++. **(7)**

Windows CGI test program usage A resource that can be accessed from the Start menu. **(7)**

Windows Common Gateway Interface See Windows CGI. **(2)**

wireless application protocol (WAP) The technology that allowed XTML to evolve. WAP telephones allow wireless access to information. **(6)**

World Wide Web One part of the Internet, usually just called the Web, that connects electronic documents, referred to as Web pages, containing information that may be in the form of basic text or intricate multimedia consisting of graphics, sound, video, or animation. **(1)**

write() method Used to output text in JavaScript. **(13)**

writeln() method Used to output text in JavaScript. **(13)**

wsauth A utility that lets you manage users and groups from a browser or the command line. **(3)**

Xanadu A software design project for a universal system of electronic information storage and access based on hypertext. **(6)**

List of Case Studies

Index